The Last Spike

The Last

"Late events have shown us that
we are made one people by that
road, that that iron link has
bound us together in such a way
that we stand superior to most
of the shafts of ill-fortune. . ."
– *Sir John A. Macdonald, June, 1885*

"All I can say is that the work
has been done well in every way."
– *W. C. Van Horne, at Craigellachie*

The Great Railway

1881-1885

Spike

By Pierre Berton

Anchor Canada

National Library of Canada Cataloguing in Publication Data

Berton, Pierre, 1920-
   The last spike : the great railway 1881–1885

Includes index.
ISBN 0-385-65841-9

1. Canadian Pacific Railway Company – History – 19th century. 2.
Canada – History – 1867-1914. 3. Railroads and state – Canada –
History – 19th century. 4. Railroads – Canada – History – 19th centu-
ry. I. Title.

HE2810.C2B482 2001   385'.0971   C2001-930605-9

Cover photo: William Cornelius Van Horne,
    courtesy National Archives of Canada (PA-171758)
Cover design: CS Richardson
Printed and bound in Canada

Published in Canada by
Anchor Canada, a division of
Random House of Canada Limited

Visit Random House of Canada Limited's website:
www.randomhouse.ca

FRI   10   9   8   7   6   5   4

Books by Pierre Berton

The Royal Family
The Mysterious North
Klondike
Just Add Water and Stir
Adventures of a Columnist
Fast Fast Fast Relief
The Big Sell
The Comfortable Pew
The Cool, Crazy, Committed
    World of the Sixties
The Smug Minority
The National Dream
The Last Spike
Drifting Home
Hollywood's Canada
My Country
The Dionne Years
The Wild Frontier
The Invasion of Canada
Flames Across the Border
Why We Act Like Canadians
The Promised Land
Vimy
Starting Out
The Arctic Grail
The Great Depression
Niagara: A History of the Falls
My Times: Living with History
1967, The Last Good Year

Picture Books
The New City (with Henri Rossier)
Remember Yesterday
The Great Railway
The Klondike Quest
Pierre Berton's Picture Book
    of Niagara Falls
Winter
The Great Lakes
Seacoasts
Pierre Berton's Canada

Anthologies
Great Canadians
Pierre and Janet Berton's
    Canadian Food Guide
Historic Headlines
Farewell to the Twentieth Century
Worth Repeating
Welcome to the Twenty-first
    Century

Fiction
Masquerade (pseudonym
    Lisa Kroniuk)

Books for Young Readers
The Golden Trail
The Secret World of Og
Adventures in Canadian History
    (22 volumes)

Contents

SIX

SEVEN

EIGHT

NINE

Maps

Drawn by Courtney C. J. Bond

Cast of Major Characters

The Politicians

Sir John A. Macdonald, Prime Minister of Canada, 1867–73, 1878–91.

Sir Charles Tupper, Minister of Railways, 1879–84; High Commissioner to London, 1884–96.

John Henry Pope, Minister of Agriculture, 1878–85; Minister of Railways and Canals, 1885–89. Tupper's deputy during his absence.

Senator Frank Smith, Minister without Portfolio, 1882–91. Wholesale grocer and railway executive.

Edward Blake, Leader of the Liberal opposition, 1880–87.

Edgar Dewdney, Indian Commissioner, Manitoba and North West Territories, 1879–88; Lieutenant-Governor of the North West Territories, 1881–88.

The CPR Syndicate

George Stephen, president of the CPR, 1881–88. Former president of the Bank of Montreal. He helped Donald Smith and James J. Hill organize the St. Paul, Minneapolis and Manitoba Railway in late 70's.

Duncan McIntyre, vice-president of the CPR, 1881–84. President of the Canada Central Railway.

James J. Hill, member of the executive committee of the CPR, 1881–83. Organized the Great Northern Railroad in the United States.

Richard Bladworth Angus, member of the executive committee of the CPR. Elected vice-president in 1883. Former general manager of the Bank of Montreal.

Donald A. Smith, Labrador fur trader who rose to become resident governor and Chief Commissioner of the Hudson's Bay Company in Canada. A major CPR stockholder and a director after 1883.

John S. Kennedy, New York banker allied with Hill, Stephen, and Smith in the St. Paul railway venture.

The Pathfinders

General Thomas Lafayette Rosser, chief engineer of the CPR, 1881–82; former chief engineer for the Northern Pacific Railroad.

ix

J. H. E. Secretan, locating engineer, head of a CPR survey party on the prairies.

Charles Aeneas Shaw, locating engineer, head of a CPR survey party on the prairies and later in the mountains.

Major A. B. Rogers, engineer in charge of the mountain division of the CPR. Formerly locating engineer for the Chicago, Milwaukee and St. Paul Railroad.

Tom Wilson, packer and guide, friend of Major Rogers.

Henry J. Cambie, former Canadian government engineer. Engineer for Andrew Onderdonk on Contract 60 in the Fraser Canyon area and later for the CPR between Kamloops and Eagle Pass.

Marcus Smith, the Canadian government's inspecting engineer on the Onderdonk contract between Port Moody and Emory in British Columbia.

Collingwood Schreiber, the government's engineer-in-chief, formerly chief engineer of the government-owned Intercolonial Railway.

The Builders

Alpheus B. Stickney, general superintendent of the CPR's western division, 1881; formerly superintendent of construction on the St. Paul, Minneapolis and Manitoba Railway.

William Cornelius Van Horne, general manager of the CPR, 1882; vice-president and general manager, 1884; president, 1888–99; chairman of the board, 1899–1910. Formerly general superintendent, Chicago, Milwaukee and St. Paul Railroad.

John Egan, superintendent of the CPR's western division after 1882. Formerly divisional superintendent, Chicago, Milwaukee and St. Paul Railroad.

Thomas Shaughnessy, general purchasing agent of the CPR, 1882–85; assistant general manager, 1885; vice-president and general manager, 1888; president, 1899–1917. Formerly general storekeeper, Chicago, Milwaukee and St. Paul Railroad.

Harry Abbott, in charge of the eastern section of the CPR's Lake Superior construction.

John Ross, in charge of the western section of the CPR's Lake Superior construction.

James Ross, in charge of construction for the CPR's mountain division. Built the Credit Valley Railway, 1878–79.

Andrew Onderdonk, contractor in charge of government construction between Port Moody and Savona's Ferry on Kamloops Lake, 1881–85.

Also built section of CPR line between Savona's Ferry and Craigellachie in Eagle Pass.

Michael J. Haney, superintendent of the CPR's Pembina Branch and Rat Portage divisions, 1882. General manager of the Onderdonk section, 1883–85.

The Native Peoples

Louis Riel, head of the Métis provisional government in Manitoba, 1869–70, and leader of the Red River uprising. Member of Parliament for Provencher, 1873–74. Leader of the Saskatchewan Rebellion of 1885.

Gabriel Dumont, Riel's adjutant general, "the Prince of the Plains," formed Métis government at St. Laurent, near Batoche on the South Saskatchewan, in 1873. Long-time chief of the Red River buffalo hunts.

Crowfoot, head chief of the Blackfoot tribes, a noted warrior, veteran of nineteen battles, wounded six times. Refused to join in the rebellion of 1885.

Poundmaker, a Cree chief, Crowfoot's adopted son, one of the leaders agitating for concessions from the government for Indians along the North Saskatchewan between 1881 and 1885. Captured and imprisoned for his role in the Saskatchewan Rebellion.

Big Bear, chief of the Plains Crees, organizer of first Indian council, 1884. His followers precipitated the massacre at Frog Lake during the Saskatchewan Rebellion. His capture on July 2, 1885, signalled the rebellion's end.

The Bystanders

Sir Henry Whatley Tyler, president of the Grand Trunk Railway, 1876–95; British Member of Parliament and engineer. Formerly inspector of railways in Great Britain.

Joseph Hickson, general manager of the Grand Trunk Railway, 1874–91.

Sir John Rose, former head of the British investment house of Morton, Rose and Company. John A. Macdonald's confidant and unofficial representative in London.

Sir Alexander Tilloch Galt, Canada's first high commissioner to London, 1880–83. One of the Fathers of Confederation. Canada's first minister of finance. A Conservative.

Charles John Brydges, land commissioner for the Hudson's Bay Company, 1882–83. Formerly managing director of the Grand Trunk Railway, 1861–74.

Arthur Wellington Ross, Winnipeg realtor and adviser on real estate matters to the CPR. Member of the Manitoba Legislature, 1879–82; Member of Parliament for Lisgar, Manitoba, 1882–96. A Conservative.

Michael Hagan, editor and publisher, Thunder Bay *Sentinel*, Port Arthur, 1874–79; editor and publisher, *Inland Sentinel*, at Emory, B.C., 1880, Yale, 1881–84, and Kamloops from 1884.

Nicholas Flood Davin, editor and publisher, the Regina *Leader*, 1883–1900. Formerly with the *Globe* and the *Mail*, Toronto, and leading British papers. Secretary to the Royal Commission on the CPR, 1880–82. Poet and author.

Father Albert Lacombe, O.M.I., roving missionary to the Indians of the western plains. Chaplain to railway navvies, Rat Portage, 1880–82.

Samuel Benfield Steele, in command of North West Mounted Police detachments along the line of CPR construction. Member of the original detachment of the NWMP. Acting adjutant of the Fort Qu'Appelle district.

John Macoun, naturalist. A member of Sandford Fleming's "ocean to ocean" party, 1872. Explored the prairies for the Canadian government. Appointed botanist to the Geological Survey of Canada in 1882.

The Last Spike

The Great Canadian Photograph

The men in the picture are like old friends, even though their names may not be familiar. There they stand in their dark and shapeless clothing, frozen for all time by the camera's shutter, the flat light of that wet November morning illuminating an obvious sense of occasion as they lean forward to watch a white-bearded old gentleman hammer home an iron railroad spike.

The setting is spectral. In the background the blurred forms of trees rise like wraiths out of a white limbo. The picture might have been taken anywhere, for there are no identifiable natural features. But, as every school child knows, the time is 1885 and the place is Craigellachie in the mountains of British Columbia.

It is not just the school children who know this picture; every Canadian knows it. Banks feature it on calendars; insurance companies reproduce it in advertisements; television documentaries copy it; school pageants re-enact it. But who remembers that just seven years before the photograph was taken, Sir John A. Macdonald called that same old gentleman the greatest liar he had ever known and tried to punch him in the nose? Probably very few; but then, the Prime Minister himself forgave and forgot. The old gentleman's name is Donald A. Smith and here, among the shrouded mountains in a damp clearing bearing a strange Gaelic name, he has managed once again to get himself into the foreground of the picture. That act will link him for all time with the great feat of railroad construction though, in truth, his has not been a major role.

George Stephen ought to be driving the final spike, but George Stephen is not even in the photograph. The CPR *president is eight thousand miles away, in London, resting briefly after his four-year battle to keep the struggling railway solvent.*

But Van Horne is there. The general manager stands directly behind Donald Smith, hands thrust deep in side pockets. John A. Macdonald once called him a sharp Yankee, but he has become more Canadian than any native. With his Homburg-style hat, his spade beard, and his heavy-lidded Germanic eyes, he looks remarkably like Bertie, the Prince of Wales, for whom he is occasionally mistaken. His poker face, so valuable in those legendary all-night card games, betrays no expression of triumph, jubilation, or sense of drama – only a slight impatience. "Get on with it," Van Horne seems to be saying. After all, the first transcontinental train in Canadian history is waiting to take him on to the Pacific.

1

Sandford Fleming stands to Van Horne's left. With his stovepipe hat and his vast beard, he almost dominates the photograph and perhaps that is as it should be; after all, it was he who made the first practical suggestion for a Pacific railroad nearly a quarter of a century before. Because of Fleming, the railroad engineer, the country runs on railroad time, so that now when it is noon in Toronto it is not 12.25 in Montreal.

Andrew Onderdonk is not in the picture. The man who brought the Chinese coolies to British Columbia to help build the railroad through the canyon of the Fraser is as elusive as ever. He has sent, in his place, his reckless Irish superintendent, Michael Haney, who can be seen craning his neck over Van Horne's great bulk, his handlebar moustache giving him the look of a Tammany politician. Not far away is another of Onderdonk's men, Henry Cambie, the engineer who hung by ropes to plot the railway's location along the walls of that same black canyon. He is standing a row or two behind the small boy, his long beard already whitening, a bowler tilted forward over his eyes. On his left, also bearded and bowlered, is one of the men chiefly responsible for the crazy-quilt pattern of Regina, John McTavish, the CPR's land commissioner; on McTavish's left, wearing a floppy hat, is the railway's western superintendent, John Egan, perhaps the only man ever to see Van Horne shed a tear.

Directly across from Donald Smith, hands plunged into the pockets of his short coat, eyes twinkling, is the stocky, black-bearded figure of James Ross, the man in charge of the CPR's mountain construction. He looks no different from the other roughly dressed labourers around him, but he will shortly become one of the richest and most powerful capitalists in Canada – a coal and steel baron, a utilities magnate, a financial wizard.

There are others present, though not all can be seen. Sam Steele of the Mounted Police, fresh from his pursuit of Big Bear, the rebellious Cree chieftain, is present but not in the picture. Young Tom Wilson, the packer who discovered Lake Louise, is just identifiable at the very rear in his broad-brimmed cowboy hat. And that most unconventional of all survey-ors, the peripatetic Major Rogers, holds the tie bar as Smith strikes the spike. In a less familiar photograph, taken a moment before, the Major can be seen quite clearly, white mutton chops, black string tie, gold watch-chain and all; but in most school books only his boot is showing. He does not need the immortality of this picture; his name is already enshrined on the long-sought pass in the Selkirks.

Do they realize, as the shutter closes, that this is destined to be the most famous photograph ever taken in Canada? Perhaps they do, for Canada, with their help, has just accomplished the impossible. In 1875, Alexander

2

Mackenzie, then Prime Minister, declared that such a task could not be completed in ten years "with all the power of men and all the money in the empire." Now it is 1885 and the job has been done with precious little help from the empire at all through a remarkable blend of financial acumen, stubborn perseverance, political lobbying, brilliant organization, reckless gambling, plain good fortune, and the hard toil of a legion of ordinary workmen.

It is these nameless navvies who really dominate the Great Canadian Photograph. Few of them have ever been identified and perhaps that is fitting. They have become symbolic figures, these unknown soldiers in Van Horne's army, standing as representatives for the thirty thousand sweating labourers – French and English, Scots and Irish, Italians and Slavs, Swedes and Yankees, Canadians and Chinese – who, in just four years and six months, managed to complete the great railway and join the nation from sea to sea.

Chapter One

1

The bitterest and longest parliamentary wrangle in the history of the young Canadian nation ended on February 15, 1881, when the contract to build the Canadian Pacific Railway finally received royal assent. The debate had occupied almost two months, consumed its major participants, and left the capital dazed and exhausted. It must have seemed to those who emerged bone weary but victorious, after those midnight sessions on the Hill, that the ten-year dream of a national highway tying the new Canada to the old had finally come true – that the in-fighting was at an end, along with the despairs, the heartaches, the scandals, and the rancours that had marked that first decade. Now it was simply a matter of driving the steel west to the Pacific; men of stature, means, and experience – most of them, thankfully, Canadians – had been found to do the job.

The ink was scarcely dry on the historic document when those same men met on February 17 in Montreal. The country knew them as "the Syndicate," a phrase that did not have the universally sinister connotations of a later century. Certainly to one segment of the nation (Liberal) they were seen as profiteers and exploiters; but to another (Conservative) they were financial geniuses and high-minded men of principle. Even their political opponents had a grudging admiration for them: they had all made a great deal of money in a very short time out of a bankrupt Minnesota railway. It was assumed they would bring the same acumen and drive to the Canadian venture.

If the members of the Syndicate could have foreseen the trials of the next four years, their understandable elation would certainly have been tempered with restraint, for the great debate in Parliament was not an end, as so many believed, but a beginning. The Canadian Pacific Railway Company was officially launched on that February afternoon; for the next generation and longer it would be the dominant force west of Ottawa. The initials – CPR – had already entered the national lexicon; soon they would be as familiar to most Canadians as their own. In the decades to follow they would come to symbolize many things to many people – repression, monopoly, daring, exploitation, imagination, government subsidy, high finance, patriotism, paternalism, and even life itself. There were few Canadians who were not in some manner affected by the presence of the CPR; no other private company, with the single exception of the Hudson's Bay, has had such an influence on the destinies of the nation. Nor has any other come so close to ruin and survived.

When the debate over the contract came to an end, Ottawa settled into a kind of doldrums. After two months of verbal pyrotechnics in the House everything else seemed to be anticlimactic. The glittering social season burned itself out, the session limped to its close, and the capital reverted to the status of a backwoods lumber village. When the Governor General arrived to prorogue Parliament on March 21, there was hardly anybody left in the House.

The rigours of the debate had wrecked the health of John A. Macdonald, Charles Tupper, and John Henry Pope, the three Conservative leaders most responsible for the railway contract. They had set off for England the previous summer to find the men and the money to build the railway. They had returned in triumph with the contract in their pockets to silence the shrill cries of "Failure!" in the Opposition press. They had steered the entire document through the House and preserved it *in toto* in the face of a cataract of oratory, a blizzard of pamphlets, a hastily conceived rival syndicate, and twenty-three hard-fought amendments. Now it seemed that their efforts had done them all in.

Macdonald, who had almost collapsed during his great speech in the Commons in January, seemed to be desperately – perhaps fatally – ill. The post-midnight sessions on which he himself had insisted (there were thirty of them) had sapped his strength so sorely that he could not be present when the Governor General finally approved the bill for which he had worked so hard. A few days before the session ended, he broke down completely: his pulse dropped to forty-nine and he was in an agony from bowel cramps. His physician was alarmed at his haggard appearance and his friends were aghast. With his fast-greying hair and his drawn features, he looked old before his time. He was dispatched to England in May with the unspoken fear that he was suffering from terminal cancer. It was expected that he would shortly resign. As for Tupper's condition, it was described by the press in February as "critical," while John Henry Pope, in Tupper's words, was "in a sad condition which promises little for the future."

Remarkably, all three of them recovered. Tupper's doctor told him that he had been "strained but not sprung." His condition was diagnosed in August as "catarrh of the liver" and Macdonald's not as cancer but as "catarrh of the stomach," phrases that doctors used when they could not explain an illness. "Sir John still suffers from languor and a sense of prostration," the Ottawa *Free Press* reported from London that summer. Obviously, the problem was exhaustion from overwork.

In contrast to the lassitude of the capital, Winnipeg, a thousand miles to the northwest, was all bustle and turmoil. The eyes of the country were focused on the new Canada beyond the Precambrian wilderness of the Shield. Tupper was preparing for an autumn visit to the country through

7

which the railroad would run. So was the Governor General, Lord Lorne, with a covey of foreign newspapermen. The great North West boom was about to begin.

Within a fortnight of its formation, the CPR company was established in Winnipeg in temporary headquarters pending the completion of the new Bank of Montreal building. A freight shed was under construction and fourteen new locomotives were on their way – all samples from various makers in the United States, sent up on trial for the company's inspection. "One of these machines is a regular giant, with driving wheels six feet in diameter and capable of making tremendous speeds," the Manitoba *Free Press* reported on March 10. Contracts had already been let for half a million railroad ties, six thousand telegraph poles, and fifty thousand feet of pilings. Mountains of timber were heaped in the yards waiting to be moved to the end of track. The great triple-decker construction cars were rolling westward. Workmen were pouring into town: three hundred from Montreal, another three hundred from Minneapolis. Five hundred teams of horses had been hired to move construction supplies. New settlers were beginning to trickle in, and Charles Drinkwater, who had once been John A. Macdonald's secretary and was now secretary to the CPR board, publicly predicted that the influx of immigrants that summer would be enormous.

There were other signs of the swiftly changing character of the old North West. The Ogilvie Milling Company had abandoned millstones and introduced steel rollers to cope with the hard northern wheat. The Manitoba Electric and Gas Light Company was planning to light the entire city by gas. ("It is now inevitable that gas is to be the light of the future – at least for some time to come.") There was talk of a street railway to run the whole length of Main. The Red River cart, held together by buffalo thongs, was all but obsolete; ingenious Winnipeg wheelwrights were working on new wagons with iron axles and iron tires to compete with the railway. And the herds of murmuring buffalo which, just ten years before, had blackened the plains, were no more. They seemed to have vanished the previous winter as suddenly as if the earth had opened and swallowed them – a phenomenon the Indians believed had actually occurred.

The railway builders estimated that they had close to two thousand miles of trunk-line to construct.* It could be divided into three sections:

In the East, some six hundred and fifty miles, between Callander on Lake Nipissing and Fort William at the head of Lake Superior, all heavy construction across the ridges of the Precambrian Shield.

---

* After the line was shortened, the figure was eighteen hundred miles.

On the prairies, some nine hundred miles from Winnipeg across the rolling grasslands to the Rocky Mountains.

In the West, some four hundred and fifty miles of heavy mountain construction.

In addition, the railway company was to be given, as a gift, some seven hundred miles of line built as a public work. There were three of these publicly built lines:

First, there was the sixty-five-mile branch line from Winnipeg to the Minnesota border known as the Pembina Branch, already completed. It connected with the St. Paul, Minneapolis and Manitoba Railway owned by members of the CPR Syndicate. Thus the CPR enjoyed a freight monopoly on goods and grain leaving Winnipeg for the East.

Secondly, there was the line between Fort William and Selkirk, near Winnipeg – 433 miles long – still under construction but slated for completion in the summer of 1882.

Thirdly, there was the 215-mile stretch that led from Savona's Ferry on Kamloops Lake through the Fraser Canyon to Port Moody on Pacific tidewater. Construction had begun on this line under the contractor Andrew Onderdonk in the spring of 1880, but very little had yet been built.

Construction would proceed in four major stages:

First, the surveyors would locate the actual line, laying out the curves and gradients and driving stakes along the centre line as a guide to navvies who followed.

Next, the road would be graded, ready to lay steel. This was the most important operation of all. A swath sixty-six feet wide would be chopped out of bushland and forest. Tunnels would be drilled through mountain barriers and galleries notched into the sides of cliffs. Bridges of various designs would be flung across coulees and river valleys. Cuts would be blasted out of rock and the broken debris thus obtained would be "borrowed" to fill in the intervening gorges and declines so that the grade might be as level as possible. Swamps and lakes would be diked or drained. On the plains, huge blades drawn by horses would scrape the sod into a ditched embankment four feet high and nine hundred miles long so that the trains could ride high above the winter snowdrifts.

The third operation was to lay the steel. Ties or "sleepers" would be placed at right angles across the grade at exact distances. Parallel rails would be laid on top of them and spiked to the ties. Fishplates would connect one rail to the next.

Finally, the line would be "ballasted," the space between the ties filled with crushed gravel so that the line would not shift when the trains roared over it.

In addition, all the varied paraphernalia of an operating line – stations, sidings, water towers, turntables – would have to be installed before the railway could be said to be complete. Later on, branch lines to serve neighbouring communities would connect with the main trunk so that the railroad would resemble an intricate tree more than twenty-five hundred miles long, coiling through all of western Canada.

Almost twenty years before, the perceptive Sandford Fleming had reckoned that such a trunk-line would cost about one hundred million dollars to construct. That rough estimate was probably in the minds of the Syndicate that contracted to build the CPR. From the government the company received a cash subsidy of twenty-five million dollars, to be paid out in stages as the railway advanced, and twenty-five million acres of prairie land, between the Red River and the Rockies, also to be awarded in stages as construction was completed. The Syndicate hoped to turn the land into ready cash as quickly as it was earned by mortgaging it, at the rate of one dollar an acre, through the issuance of "land grant bonds." It could also mortgage the main line at the rate of ten thousand dollars a mile, and issue capital stock up to twenty-five million dollars. Unlike other North American railway companies, the CPR shunned the idea of bonded indebtedness and heavy stock promotions. It expected – naïvely, as it developed – to build the railway with the subsidy, the proceeds of the land sales, the operating profits, and a minimum of borrowing. The first stock issue was fifty thousand shares at a par value of a hundred dollars a share; almost all of the five millions was subscribed on February 17, 1881, by the members of the original CPR Syndicate. By March 3, an additional $1,100,000 had been subscribed; that was the extent of the original stock sale.

The hustle in Winnipeg, that spring of 1881, was in sharp contrast to the vacillations of the previous year, when the railroad was being built as a public work. The government had originally planned the cheapest of colonization roads across the North West. It let the first hundred-mile contract in August, 1879, to John Ryan, who was unable to finish the job. The government took over his contract, and by the spring of 1880 the flimsy line had been completed for about seventy miles, as far as Portage la Prairie. A second hundred-mile section west of the Red River was let on May 3, 1880, to another contractor. An entire summer passed and nothing was done. That contract was also cancelled.

This section of the line, which the CPR, under the terms of the contract, purchased from the government, was virtually useless; the company determined to rebuild it entirely to better specifications and relocate most of it. A different mood had settled upon railway construction in Canada. For the first time in the long, tangled history of the Canadian Pacific, the rails were being laid under the supervision of the same men who would eventually operate the road; it would not profit them to cut corners.

On May 2, 1881, the company was ready to begin. At the end of track, the little community of Portage la Prairie – Manitoba's oldest town – clattered with activity. Strange men poured off the incoming coaches and elbowed each other in the mire of the streets, picking their way between the invading teams of snorting horses. Great heaps of construction materials transformed the railway yards into labyrinths. An army of ploughs and scrapers stood ready to rip into the unbroken prairie. Like soldiers poised on the start line, the navvies waited until the company's chief engineer, General Thomas Lafayette Rosser, ceremonially turned the first sod. Then the horses, the men, and the machines moved forward and began to fashion the great brown serpent that would creep steadily west, day after day, towards its rendezvous with the mountains.

2

Canada is deceptively vast. The map shows it as the second largest country in the world and probably the greatest in depth, extending through forty degrees of latitude from Ellesmere Island in the high Arctic to Pelee Island in Lake Erie, which is on the same parallel as Rome. It is almost twice as deep as the United States and considerably deeper than either China or the Soviet Union. If the tip of Canada were placed at Murmansk, the country would extend as far south as Cairo; if it were placed on the Manchurian border it would drop all the way down to Bangkok.

Yet all this is illusory. For practical purposes Canada is almost as slender as Chile. Traditionally half of its people have lived within a hundred miles of the United States border and ninety per cent within two hundred miles. It is a country shaped like a river – or a railway – and for the best of reasons: in the eastern half of the nation, the horizontal hiving of the population is due to the presence of the St. Lawrence, in the western half to that "sublime audacity," the Canadian Pacific.

The CPR was the natural extension of the traditional route used by the

How John Macoun altered the map

11

explorers and fur traders on their passage to the West. If that natural extension had been continued as was originally planned, Canada might today have a different dimension. But that was not to be. In the spring of 1881 a handful of men, gathered around a cluttered, circular table in an office in St. Paul, Minnesota, altered the shape and condition of the new country west of Winnipeg.

That decision affected the lives of tens of thousands of Canadians. It ensured the establishment of cities close to the border that otherwise might not have existed for another generation, if ever – Broadview, Regina, Moose Jaw, Swift Current, Medicine Hat, Banff, and Revelstoke. It doomed others – Carlton, Battleford, Eagle Hill, Bethlehem, Grenoble, Baldwin, Humboldt, Nazareth, Nut Hill, and Edmonton – to permanent or temporary eclipse. (Some, indeed, were never more than names on early railway maps.) It affected aspects of Canadian life as varied as the tourist trade and the wheat economy. In addition, it gave the railway company something very close to absolute control over the destinies of scores of embryo communities along the right of way.

This was not what the government had intended when the railway was conceived in 1871, or even in 1881, when the administration turned the task over to a private company. It had been conceded, since the days of the first explorers and surveyors, that any transcontinental line would have to cross the North West by way of the fertile, wooded valley of the North Saskatchewan, following more or less the route of the Carlton Trail, along whose rutted right of way the Red River carts had squeaked for the best part of a century. This route led north and west from Winnipeg, by way of Battleford, to Fort Edmonton and on to the Yellow Head Pass in the Rockies. From there the line was to continue in the fur traders' footsteps down the valleys of the Thompson and the Fraser to Burrard Inlet on the Pacific. It had taken a decade of bitter argument, vicious recrimination, political manœuvre, back-breaking exploration, and meticulous foot-by-foot location survey to settle upon that route. It had also cost many millions of dollars, the reputations of several public figures, and the lives of forty surveyors. The powerful little group of men in St. Paul threw it all away after about an hour's discussion.

There were three of them, all members of the four-man executive committee of the CPR – a remarkable trio: passionate, sometimes temperamental, strong-willed, and single-minded. Each had begun life in poverty with few prospects; each had known an astonishing personal success.

Of the three, George Stephen, the president of the new railway company, was the most sophisticated. The one-time draper's assistant, now impeccably turned out by his personal valet, moved easily in the financial

12

capitals of two continents. As president of the Bank of Montreal – a post he was about to resign – he had acquired a reputation as a financial wizard, respected for his integrity, admired for his audacity. Had he not transformed an expiring railroad, the St. Paul and Pacific, into the most profitable enterprise on the continent? He and his colleagues, Jim Hill and Donald Smith, had become multimillionaires as a result.

The second man, Richard Bladworth Angus, was Stephen's protégé – another dark, cool-eyed Scot, heavily moustached and side-whiskered, and just two years Stephen's junior. In an astonishing twelve-year period he had soared from an obscure post as a $600-a-year bank clerk to succeed E. H. King, "the Napoleon of Canadian Finance," as general manager of the Bank of Montreal, the most powerful financial institution in Canada. Known for his tact, his foresight, his amiability, and his modesty (he would eventually refuse a knighthood), he was called in business circles the Man of Peace. Stephen in 1879, while still the bank's president, had, in effect, stolen this shrewd, strict financier to manage the St. Paul railway. A year later, he seduced him into the great adventure of the Pacific road.

The third man was James Jerome Hill, a tougher and rougher specimen than his colleagues. With his single, burning eye, his short, lion's beard and long mane, he looked like a bit of a pirate, which, in truth, he was. Five years before, Hill, the ex-Canadian, had talked Stephen into the financial gamble of the St. Paul railway. It was said that he could talk the hardest-headed man into practically anything. In an age when most capitalists were prudently close-mouthed he was unexpectedly garrulous, enveloping adversaries and colleagues alike in a smoke-screen of words. In his business dealings he was often devious, in his ambitions, Napoleonic. A dangerous man to have as an enemy, he had, in his forty-three years, made a good many enemies. All the traditional adjectives used to describe nineteenth-century entrepreneurs apply to Hill: ruthless, dynamic, unscrupulous, hard-driving, and, above all, decisive. It was he who made the ultimate decision that day in St. Paul.

The three men, together with the CPR's new chief engineer, a one-time Confederate general named Thomas Lafayette Rosser, were seated around a table littered with maps of the Canadian North West and listening to an enthusiastic torrent of words from a Canadian naturalist and explorer, Professor John Macoun.

Macoun, a bright-eyed Irishman, almost entirely self-educated, had come to St. Paul at Hill's behest because he was familiar with so much of the southern prairie between Winnipeg and the Rockies. A decade before, Macoun, on a sudden whim, had accepted Sandford Fleming's invitation to cross half a continent with him from Lake Superior to the Pacific. As a result he had become enamoured of the North West. In 1879 and again in 1880, the Canadian government sent him out to the prairies to explore as far as the Bow River valley in the foothills of the Rockies. These investigations confirmed in his mind a belief that had been taking form since 1872 and had by this time become a kind of religion with him. He was convinced that the southern plains were not the desert that almost everybody thought them to be.

In spreading this dogma, Macoun was flying in the face of previous scientific reports. Both Captain John Palliser from Great Britain and Henry Youle Hind from Toronto had advised their respective governments that the southern plains were a continuation of the Great American Desert, an "arid belt" unfit for cultivation or settlement. It was Hind's enthusiastic espousal of the "fertile belt" along the North Saskatchewan that had influenced the original choice of a Pacific railway route.

Macoun resorted to the public platform as well as to the printed page to discredit both Palliser and Hind, and his infectious enthusiasm drew large crowds. He rarely gave the same speech twice. "I was so full of the question," he recalled, "that I could talk for a week without stopping." His estimates of arable prairie soil were far in excess of anyone else's and helped confirm John A. Macdonald's conviction that profits from the sale of prairie land could underwrite the cost of the railway subsidy. Since few Canadians wanted to pay higher taxes for the sake of a railway, this was a telling point with Parliament as well as public.

Both Macdonald and his minister of railways, Sir Charles Tupper, were a little wary of Macoun, and not without reason. He was a man with a fixed idea, which had come close to being an obsession. The evidence suggests that he was prejudiced in advance. Long before he actually visited the southern prairie he was making pronouncements about its riches. After he did see it, he tried to show that its fertility was even greater than that of the land to the north. So passionate an advocate was he that he once leaped up from the Visitors' Gallery of the House of Commons to berate Alexander Mackenzie, in opposition, for attacking the Government on the question of prairie soil. Mackenzie had Macoun's enthusiastic report of 1877 in his desk, and Macoun, at the risk of being ejected, was trying to get him to quote from it. Macoun did not visit the southern prairie, however, until 1879. Then he "fearlessly announced that the so-called arid country was one of unsurpassed fertility, and that it was literally the 'Garden of the whole country'. . . ."

How could one explorer have seen the plains as a lush paradise while another saw them as a desert? How was it that Macoun found thick grasses and sedges where Palliser reported cracked, dry ground? The answer lies in the unpredictability of the weather in what came to be called Palliser's Triangle. Frank Oliver, the pioneer Edmonton editor, once remarked that anyone who tried to forecast Alberta weather was either a newcomer or a fool. Palliser saw the land under normal to dry conditions; Macoun visited it during the wettest decade in more than a century. If the former was too pessimistic, the latter was too enthusiastic.

Macoun was brought to St. Paul to convince the CPR's executive committee (only Duncan McIntyre, the vice-president, was absent) that a more southerly route to the Rockies was practicable. Hill and the others were already partially convinced. Early in November, 1880, Angus wrote to Winnipeg inquiring about the possibilities of a more southerly route. His contact was that curious diplomatic jack-of-all-trades, the amiable American consul James Wickes Taylor, who had once been an agent for the Northern Pacific when that railway had hoped to seize control of the Canadian North West. Taylor, long an enthusiast about the southern prairies, had originally fired the botanist's imagination on the subject when Macoun visited Winnipeg with Sandford Fleming in 1872. At that time Taylor told Macoun that the area would become the wheat-producing country of the American continent. In his correspondence with Angus in 1880, Taylor (who was doing his best to get a retainer from the CPR) showed that his enthusiasm had not waned. He cited several Hudson's Bay Company reports to back up his belief that a southern route was feasible and he quoted John Macoun, who had told the press that "the roses were in such profusion that they scented the atmosphere" and that water could be found in any part of the Palliser Triangle by sinking shallow wells. Taylor had also talked to Walter Moberly, the surveyor who had long been a trenchant champion of a more southerly route through British Columbia; in his correspondence with Angus he made light of the problem of the three mountain ranges that barred the way to the Pacific.

Immediately the new company was formed, in February, 1881, Jim Hill hired an American railway surveyor, Major A. B. Rogers, and sent him off to the Rocky Mountains, which Rogers had never seen, with orders to examine the four most southerly passes, three of which – the Kicking Horse, Vermilion, and Kootenay – had been ignored by the government's survey teams. The fourth, Howse Pass (Walter Moberly's favourite), had been rejected by Sandford Fleming after a cursory examination. Rogers, a profane, tobacco-chewing, irritable Yankee, arrived in Kamloops late in April, prepared to start work. His presence raised the hackles of more than one Canadian nationalist. "We are not inclined to credit the Yankee employees of the Syndicate with all the prodigious engineering feats that

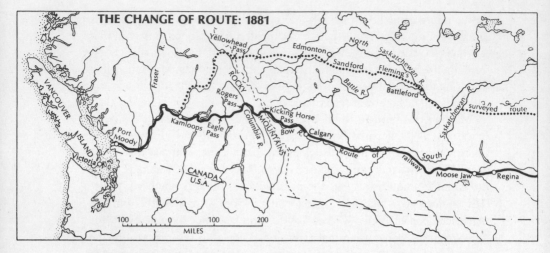

THE CHANGE OF ROUTE: 1881

they promised to perform," the Toronto *Globe* editorialized with some asperity on May 3. After all, the Canadians had spent ten years examining no fewer than seven passes in the Rockies before settling on the Yellow Head. Who were these American to suggest they were wrong?

But Hill and his colleagues were already leaning strongly towards a more southerly route. The only stumbling block was the historical belief that the land it would pass through was semi-desert. All they needed was Macoun to convince them that Palliser and Hind were wrong. It did not take the voluble naturalist long to effect their conversion. After he was finished, a brief discussion followed. Then Hill, according to Macoun's own account, raised both his hands and slammed them down on the table.

"Gentlemen," he said, "we will cross the prairie and go by the Bow Pass, [Kicking Horse] if we can get that way." With that statement, ten years of work was abandoned and the immediate future of the North West altered.

Why were they all so eager to push their railroad through unknown country? Why did they give up Fleming's careful location in favour of a hazardous route across two mountain ramparts whose passes had not yet been surveyed or even explored? If the Kicking Horse were chosen it would mean that every pound of freight carried across the mountains would have to be hoisted an additional sixteen hundred feet higher into the clouds. Even more disturbing was the appalling barrier of the Selkirk Mountains, which lay beyond the Rockies. No pass of any description had yet been found in that great island of ancient rock; the general opinion was that none existed. Yet the company was apparently prepared to drive steel straight through the Rockies and right to the foot of the Selkirks in the sublime hope that an undiscovered passage would miraculously appear.

The mystery of the change of route has never been convincingly un-

16

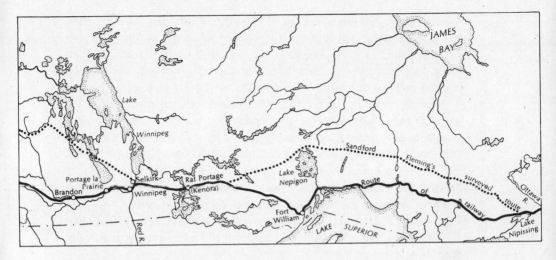

ravelled. A variety of theories has been advanced, some of them conflicting. Even the CPR's own records do not provide any additional clues
as to the real or overriding reasons for the decision that was made in May
of 1881.

The chief reason given by Sir Charles Tupper in Parliament a year later
was that it would shorten the line by seventy-nine miles and give it a greater
advantage over its American rivals. Certainly this would have appealed to
Jim Hill, with his knowledge of transportation, and to George Stephen,
whose mind moved in logical lines, straight from point A to point B. Yet
if no pass in the Selkirks could be found, then the railway would have to
circumvent those mountains by way of the hairpin-shaped Columbia
Valley and almost all the advantage over the northern route would be lost.
Moreover, as Edward Blake, the Opposition leader, pointed out, the company in changing the line of route along Lake Superior had actually
lengthened that section of the railway.

It is unlikely that the shortening of the line was the chief reason for
adopting a new route. Subsequent accounts have generally attributed the
move to fear of competition from American lines, which could send feed-
ers into the soft underbelly of the country if the Canadian Pacific trunk-
line ran too far north. Some historians, indeed, have suggested that the
change of route was inspired by the government for nationalistic reasons.
This is scarcely tenable, since it was the government that had authorized
and surveyed the northern route at great expense. It was the company and
not the government that pressed for the change, and the government, in
the person of John Henry Pope, Macdonald's minister of agriculture, that
seemed reluctant about the change. "They are trying the Howe [sic] Pass,"
he wrote to the Prime Minister on August 19, "... but I do not see how

17

we can accept that line as the charter says they must go by the other pass. . . . It seems to me without further legislation we cannot addopt How pass for maine line." The CPR might, in fact, have gone even farther south had the government allowed it; but the change was permitted only on condition that the railroad be located at least one hundred miles north of the border.

Stephen, certainly, was concerned about American encroachment in the shape of the Northern Pacific, a company that had been trying for more than a decade, under various managements, to seize control of the Canadian North West. It had reached no farther than North Dakota by 1881, but its new president, the brilliant if erratic journalist and financier Henry Villard, had already succeeded in buying control of a local Manitoba line, the Southwestern. Villard was planning to cross the Manitoba border at three points. If he did he would certainly siphon off much of the Canadian through trade and make the CPR line north of Lake Superior practically worthless.

On the other hand, Stephen had the controversial "Monopoly Clause" in the CPR contract to protect him. Under its provisions no competing federally chartered Canadian line could come within fifteen miles of the border; Macdonald was prepared to disallow provincial charters for similarly competing lines. No doubt Stephen felt that the more southerly route provided him with extra insurance against the Northern Pacific and against other United States railways (not to mention rival Canadian roads that might be built south of the CPR) when, in twenty years time, the Monopoly Clause would run out. Undoubtedly, this was a consideration in adopting the new route.

Was this the chief consideration? Perhaps. The hindsight of history has made it appear so. Yet Hill himself was already dreaming dreams of a transcontinental line of his own, springing out of the St. Paul, Minneapolis and Manitoba road. Stephen and the other major CPR stockholders all had a substantial interest in that American railway. If the frustration of United States competition was the reason for the decision of 1881, why was Hill the man who made the decision to move the route south?

Hill did give his reason for changing the route when he banged on the table and made the decision. Macoun, in his autobiography, quoted it:

"I am engaged in the forwarding business and I find that there is money in it for all those who realize its value. If we build this road across the prairie, we will carry every pound of supplies that the settlers want and we will carry every pound of produce that the settlers wish to sell, so that we will have freight both ways."

This was Hill's basic railroad philosophy – a philosophy he had expounded over and over again to Stephen in the days of the St. Paul adventure: a railroad through virgin territory creates its own business. It was for this reason that Hill was able to convince Stephen that the CPR should not attempt to make a large profit out of land sales but should, instead, try to attract as many settlers as possible to provide business for the railway. The philosophy, of course, would have applied to a considerable extent to the original Fleming line. On the other hand, that line ran through country where some settlement already existed and where real estate speculators – at Battleford and Prince Albert, for example – expected to make profits out of land adjacent to the right of way. It undoubtedly occurred to the railway company that it would be easier to control an area that had never known a settler and where there were no established business interests of any kind. Why should the road increase the value of other men's property? Why should the CPR become involved in internecine warfare between rival settlements? The unholy row between Selkirk and Winnipeg was still fresh in the minds of both Hill and Stephen. Winnipeg businessmen had forced a change in the original survey to bring the main line through their community. In striking comparison was the CPR's founding of the town of Brandon that spring of 1881. The company arbitrarily determined its location in the interests of real estate profit, and the company totally controlled it.

That was to be the pattern of future settlement along the line. In the case of Regina, Calgary, Revelstoke, and Vancouver, to mention the most spectacular instances, it was the company that dictated both the shape and the location of the cities of the new Canada – and woe to any speculator who tried to push the company around! The company could, and did, change the centre of gravity by the simple act of shifting the location of the railway station. For it was around the nucleus of the station that the towns and villages sprang up. The contract stipulated that if government land was available it would be provided free for the company's stations, station grounds, workshops, dock grounds, buildings, yards, "and other appurtenances." With a scratch of the pen the company could, and did, decide which communities would grow and which would stagnate; the placing of divisional points made all the difference. "It must not be forgotten," the *Globe* reminded its readers in 1882, "that the Syndicate has a say in the existence of almost every town or prospective town in the North-West. Individuals rarely have an opportunity of starting a town without their consent and co-operation." Since some eight hundred villages, towns, and cities were eventually fostered in the three prairie provinces by the CPR, the advantages of total control were inestimable.

19

There were other reasons given, after the fact, for the change of route. Perhaps these also helped convince the decision-makers in St. Paul, but no one knows for certain. There were, for instance, the coal-fields of southern Alberta, which the railroad could tap; Hill, one of the ranking coal experts on the continent, would certainly have been aware of them. And there was the undeniable fact that the new route would require far fewer bridges on the prairies than the original one, which crossed several deep valleys and innumerable coulees.

There were also problems, most of them unforeseen or unremarked. When General Rosser, the practical surveyor, bluntly asked Macoun where he thought they would get railway ties in that treeless waste, the professor airily replied that that was Rosser's problem. Apparently it did not unduly concern Hill and his colleagues.

Thus, for better or for worse, the die was cast, though an act of Parliament was required before the change could become official. Few single decisions by a private corporation have had such widespread public repercussions. As a result, and quite by accident, the most spectacular mountain scenery in North America was opened up in the early eighties; Canada gained a new image as a tourist attraction: Banff, Lake Louise, Glacier, and Yoho parks were all by-products of Jim Hill's table-pounding. So was a whole series of prairie communities strung out like beads on a string between Brandon and Calgary. So were the mines and farm lands of southern British Columbia, opened up by the trunk-line and its branches. So were the costly locomotives that had to be harnessed – as many as five at a time – to haul the trains over the Great Divide. So were the miles of snowsheds in the Selkirks and – after many deaths from avalanches and snowslides – the costly diversions of the spiral and Connaught tunnels. In later years it became railroad cant that the Canadian Pacific had the scenery but the Canadian National had the grades; from the company's point of view, it remains to this day a toss-up as to whether or not the change of route was really an economically sensible decision. There are too many imponderables to render a judgement. Who can say how important the mountain scenery was to a once-profitable passenger trade? Who can estimate whether or not the profits on townsites and the advantages of a shorter line cancelled out the increased construction costs and additional carrying charges over the mountain peaks?

From the point of view of the nation, a better guess can be hazarded. It is probable that the switch to the southern route was one factor in delaying the settlement of the North West for twenty years and thus partially frustrating John A. Macdonald's dream of filling up the empty plains. The settlers tended to take up land as close as possible to the railway; often enough they were driven off it by drought conditions.

Significantly, it was the CPR itself that implicitly debunked Macoun's enthusiastic reports of almost unlimited arable land by refusing to accept a great deal of the acreage that had been set aside for it in the forty-eight-mile belt along the route of the railway. The land subsidy in the CPR contract was unique. In effect, it allowed the railway to pick and choose the best available acreage anywhere on the prairies. The key phrase was the stipulation that the company could reject land that was "not fairly fit for settlement." Since the mountain and the Shield country was provincially owned (and could not be farmed anyway), the contract also provided that the land must lie between the Red River and the Rockies, ostensibly in alternate sections along the line of the railway in a belt forty-eight miles thick. The CPR held the government to the letter of that agreement. In 1882, the company's most generous estimate of "fit" land within the belt stood at six million acres; later that estimate was reduced to five million acres. Clearly, the CPR was saying that the land could *not* be settled. To keep its bargain with the railway, the government was forced to give it land elsewhere; much of this substitute acreage was found in the Fertile Belt, along the original line of route.

If the railway had followed the valley of the North Saskatchewan, it is probable that much more land would have been taken up because of the attractive combination of good soil and easy access by rail. The pattern of settlement would have been changed, larger cities would have sprung up in the north, and the far western plains might have filled up at an earlier date. Sooner or later, of course, branch lines or new transcontinental railways would also have brought settlers to the southern plains, but by then the pattern of the North West would have been set and that pattern would almost certainly have been a different one.

The CPR rejected tens of thousands of acres in the dry country west of Moose Jaw; and, in spite of the heavy immigration to the plains in the early 1880's, very few settlers were prepared to occupy land in that portion of Palliser's Triangle. By 1885, the year the railway was finished, only twenty-three homesteads had been taken up along more than four hundred miles of railway between Moose Jaw and Calgary.

The settlers, used to eastern Canadian conditions, were not prepared to cope with the special problems of prairie agriculture, especially in dry country. Indeed, it is doubtful if they were aware that the circumstances were radically different, since the government, in its settlement policy, neglected to make any distinction between the dry southwestern plains and

21

the more humid Red River valley. Regulations for taking up land were identical throughout the North West. The new arrivals were left to decide for themselves whether the soil was suitable for farming and to work out by a long process of trial and error the means of grappling with unfamiliar conditions.

The hard-baked sod required a heavier plough. The dry land demanded new methods of cultivation and cheap windpumps. Fuel, timber, and fencing had to be imported into the vast, treeless areas. There was also the necessary shift from fall to spring planting in a land where the winters were long and harsh and the growing season alarmingly brief. Some of these conditions would have existed no matter which route the railway followed. The choice of the southern route accentuated them.

The wet cycle, which had such an effect on Macoun in 1879 and 1880, continued through 1881 and 1882. These were years of very high water in the North West. The country north and south of the Qu'Appelle Valley, on both sides of the CPR line, was badly flooded, the ponds overflowing to the point where settlers were forced to make long detours. Then, in 1883 – the peak year for immigration – the dry cycle returned. Evaporation was so rapid that the ponds and marshes were swiftly drained. Reservoirs had to be built in the ravines or dug out of the prairie soil to hold back the run-off. By 1886 the land was so dry in many places that cracks a foot wide opened up in the parched soil. One trail, near Balgonie, just east of Regina, was so badly riven by fissures that it became too dangerous for wagon traffic. Immigration figures in the North West, which reached a record 133,624 in 1883, began to decline with three successive years of crop failures. It was twenty years before they again climbed above the hundred thousand mark. There was an equally spectacular drop in homestead entries: in 1884 they were halved. Thousands abandoned the embryo farms they had so eagerly taken up. By 1896, half of all contracts entered into with the railway by the various colonization companies had been cancelled; a total of 1,284,652 acres reverted to the CPR.

With the acceptance of the disc plough and more adaptable farming methods, the prairie country became, after the turn of the century, the granary of the world; Regina, which might not have existed had the northerly route been chosen, was found to be in the very heart of the richest grain-growing soil on the continent. In those portions of Palliser's Triangle where cereals would not grow, a healthy ranching economy developed. But the cycle of drought continued. The undue optimism of the seventies and early eighties was replaced in the decade from 1884 to 1894 by an extreme pessimism. So many farms were abandoned that the Canadian government began to entertain doubts about the future of the West. Once again, John Macoun was dispatched to the southern prairies to report on the seriousness of conditions and once again, just as he arrived on the scene, the rains came and Macoun was able to predict the end of the drought. The vast wave of immigration that filled up the prairies in the following years appeared to vindicate him. When he died in 1922, his friends triumphantly published his autobiography with a flattering foreword by Ernest Thompson Seton. It was not until the desperate years of the 1930's, when the rains ceased once more and the grasshoppers and the cutworms and the hot, dry winds returned, that there took place a rueful reassessment of his strange role in the shaping of the nation.

3

General Rosser's newly surveyed route led out of Portage la Prairie towards Grand Valley on the Assiniboine, and then through the Brandon Hills to Flat Creek (later known as Oak Lake). It was near the crossing of the Assiniboine that Brandon, the first of the CPR towns, sprang up. The method of its selection by the General provided an object lesson for the company in the value of establishing its own communities instead of building on existing ones.

The first of the CPR *towns*

Rosser was a Virginian gentleman of the old school – tall, handsome, swarthy, and popular. A West Point chum of General Custer, he had fought opposite him as a guerilla officer during the Civil War. After the war he had risen to become chief engineer of the Northern Pacific – his workmen, ironically, protected by Custer's troops – laying out the route along the Yellowstone River in Montana. Later, as a railway contractor, he had helped build part of Jim Hill's St. Paul, Minneapolis and Manitoba line. He was, according to the Winnipeg *Times*, "known as one of the most pushing men on the American continent." Hill, who hired all the key CPR personnel that year, was as partial to pushers as he was to Americans. (The *Globe* was already reporting "indignation against the Syndicate about employment of American instead of Canadian engineers and surveyors.")

Rosser was a man of precipitate action, as events were shortly to prove. During the Civil War he had risen from lieutenant to major general. He had refused to surrender with Lee at Appomattox, preferring instead to charge the Federal lines with two divisions of cavalry. When he was finally

23

captured, some time later, he was trying to reorganize the shattered remnants of the army of Northern Virginia for a final, dramatic stand. His subsequent civilian record was equally dashing. He had begun as an axeman and again worked his way up through the ranks from rodman to scout to chief surveyor. He was surrounded by an aura of legend – a record of hairbreadth escapes in war and peace. On one occasion, when surprised by Yankee cavalry and wounded above the knee by a bone-shattering bullet, he had ridden all night to safety with the broken limb swinging back and forth and the enemy hard on his tail. A decade later, near Bismarck, North Dakota, a party of Sioux had cut him off. One crept up behind a tree, used it as a shield, and began taking pot-shots at him. Rosser coolly waited until the Indian poked his head around the trunk to take aim, shot him squarely between the eyes, heaved his corpse onto a pony and again galloped safely away. In 1881, as chief engineer of the CPR, he brought the same dash and impulsiveness to the establishment of townsites.

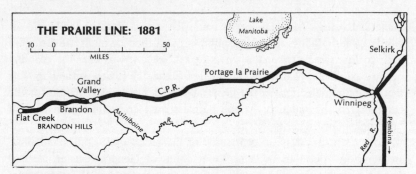

A fortnight before the first sod was turned, rumours of a great new city west of Winnipeg began to fly. Survey parties started to move out of Portage la Prairie in the last week of April, locating the new route. Everyone knew that the railway would require a divisional point about one hundred and thirty miles west of Winnipeg. That fitted almost to a mile the location of the little settlement of Grand Valley, clustered on the banks of the Assiniboine at the exact spot where the railway was to cross the river. Tents and shacks began to spring up in the vicinity as the surveyors drove in their stakes. There was a smell of big money in the air, and, as a correspondent reported to the *Free Press*, "many land grabbers and speculators." The excitement increased day by day. Two men from Perth, Ontario, arrived with fifteen tons of dry goods and groceries to set up a general store. Two more began to erect a sawmill. Another opened a "hotel" of canvas spread over wooden frames, the expanse of the sides

24

being used as an advertising medium. Dugald McVicar, the pioneer resident in the community, whose wife was the local postmistress, began making improvements to his home, doubling the size of his warehouse, and planning a new ferryboat to replace the one that he had been operating at the crossing. His brother John announced that he would also extend the size of his house so it would be equal to "the accommodation of the present influx of strangers."

"The boom in Grand Valley grows," the *Free Press* reported on April 30. "People are steering for that point from all directions. . . ." The real estate men steered themselves right to the McVicar homestead, for it was on this property that the new city would presumably be situated. The McVicar brothers were the first settlers in Grand Valley – humble, illiterate men who had come west in 1879 from Grenville, Quebec, to build the first sod dwelling in the region. The community might have borne their name had it not been for their innate modesty. They refused the offer of the chief dominion postal officer in Winnipeg to call it McVicar; since he had referred to the Assiniboine Valley as "grand," they suggested the alternate title. The little town grew around the site of their original homestead, and the McVicars expected to get rich from the Grand Valley boom.

In April, General Rosser paid a visit to John McVicar and made him an offer for his property as a future townsite for the CPR's divisional point. The accounts of exactly what took place are conflicting. One of the CPR's surveyors, J. H. E. Secretan, said that he, Rosser, and John McTavish, the CPR land commissioner, had settled on Grand Valley as the divisional point, offering McVicar fifty thousand dollars for his property. The farmer could scarcely believe that that much money existed. A discussion followed and some " 'wise guys' of neighbours and relations," as Secretan called them, were invited in. Around dawn, McVicar was persuaded by his friends to demand sixty thousand. Charles Aeneas Shaw, another of Rosser's locating engineers, gives a different version in his memoirs. Shaw wrote that Rosser empowered *him* to deal with McVicar and that he was given a maximum of thirty thousand dollars to buy the McVicar land for the CPR station and surrounding property. Shaw had dinner with McVicar but "some speculators had got hold of him, and he would not hear of anything less than eighty thousand dollars." Beecham Trotter, a Brandon pioneer who also related the story in his memoirs, reported that when Shaw and Rosser had offered McVicar twenty-five thousand, McVicar immediately demanded fifty thousand dollars down and a half interest in all future sales. Whereupon Rosser is said to have retorted: "I'll be damned if a town of any kind is ever built here."

Whatever the details of the legendary incident, one thing is clear: When McVicar, goaded by speculators, tried to bargain with the railway, the railway simply moved the site of its station two miles farther west. This would be the pattern in all future dealings when private individuals tried to hold up the company for speculative profits.

According to Trotter, General Rosser turned on his heel, ordered the horses saddled, crossed the Assiniboine, and made straight for the shack of D. H. Adamson, a squatter on the south bank of the river in the Brandon Hills. The site cost the CPR a fraction of the Grand Valley price, and its choice marked the end of Grand Valley as a viable community and the beginning of the town of Brandon.

What was not realized at the time was that Rosser and his immediate superior, Alpheus B. Stickney, the general superintendent of the western division of the CPR, were themselves speculating in real estate, using the inside knowledge that their positions provided them. This had, apparently, been one of the conditions of Rosser's appointment as laid down by Stickney, who had been Jim Hill's construction boss on the St. Paul railway; clearly, it had been the practice of himself and his colleagues in the various railway adventures in which he had been engaged. It is doubtful, however, from the course of later events that the directors of the CPR, with the possible exception of Jim Hill, were aware of it. Certainly it was not public knowledge at the time. When Charles Shaw's brother Duncan, who had homesteaded three miles south of the embryo community, learned from his brother of the impending development, he could easily have made himself wealthy from land speculation, but he refused to do so for fear of prejudicing Charles's position.

Another insider who could have made a fortune but refused to do so because of his calling was the Reverend George Roddick, who with his wife and seven children had left Pictou, Nova Scotia, in 1879 and come out across the prairie from Winnipeg in an ox cart loaded with all the family's possessions, including an organ and a grandfather clock. Like most pioneers in the days before the railway, the Roddicks had been forced to turn their cart into a scow, caulking the wagon box with mud, in order to cross the swollen Assiniboine. Shortly after that adventure they settled down in the Brandon Hills, their log home being the chief habitation between the river and the border and a favourite stopping place for travellers, who were assured of all the boiled potatoes and hot tea they could devour as long as they attended Sunday service. One Sunday evening in May, after service, two of the Roddick boys overheard a whispered conversation between two Winnipeg visitors and realized at once that the strangers had a clue to the new townsite. They asked their father for permission to go over at once and squat on the ground.

"No," Roddick replied, "it would not be honest. Besides, the Roddick family are in the country to live as farmers; and good neighbours are more valuable to us than land."

Others had fewer scruples. Charles Reay, a delegate of the Northwest Colonization Society of Montreal, reported in mid-May that the country between Grand Valley and the Brandon Hills was alive with land sharks:

"We met them at the place where the railway crosses the Assiniboine, they having squatted on every available location. Their operations were not confined to this locality, but wherever there was a prospect of a village these land sharks were to be found. Their movement was rapid. At first they put up tents and put men to guard them, and ploughed a furrow or two – and these are improvements! Time would not allow, however, for them to go to all this trouble, so frequently they dispensed with the formality of erecting the building (tent), and merely ran a furrow. I don't know how many sections were squatted on in this way, but if the Government recognizes their claim, a gross injustice will be perpetrated. They do not intend to settle. They have no intention of cultivating the land. They only desire to secure choice locations, sell out their improvements at from $20 to $30, and give up their pretended claims; or else to get up a 'city,' sell lots, and amass a small fortune out of its proceeds by auction sale at Winnipeg."

One of these squatters was D. H. Adamson, who had family banking connections in Winnipeg. It was to his hastily built shack on Section 23 that General Rosser proceeded in early May after his abortive attempts to buy up a station site at Grand Valley. Adamson, however, had little claim to the land. First, he had not registered title to it, and second, all odd-numbered sections were closed to homesteaders anyway; they could be purchased but they could not be homesteaded. Late in April, the most astute real estate man in the North West, Arthur Wellington Ross, arrived on the scene apparently on the railway's behalf, or at least with the knowledge of its Winnipeg officials, and proceeded to wangle the land away from Adamson. It is doubtful if Adamson had inside knowledge of the railway route; Ross certainly did. Ross was to become one of the most powerful figures in the approaching land boom; he would make and lose an immense fortune in the space of two years. On April 27 he made an agreement with Adamson whereby he would secure title to the land and Adamson would retain a one-seventh interest. Ross secured the title on May 9 and sold the property, which was to become the centre of the city of

Brandon, on May 30 to A. B. Stickney, acting for the CPR. The price was $2,560; Adamson got $350. On the same day, Ross's firm was advertising lots for sale in the new community.

One of the squatters mentioned in the press was Joseph Woodworth, a hearty man with black side whiskers and a flowing moustache, "a great mixer and free spender" and an influential Nova Scotia Conservative. Woodworth and his brother D. B., a former Nova Scotia M.P.P., took the even-numbered section, Number 24, adjoining Adamson's and were careful to secure title to it in March and April. It was one of more than twenty properties that they had taken a chance on. Woodworth, whom Charles Reay referred to as "a discredited politician" and the Liberal *Free Press* called "a Conservative adventurer," went personally to Ottawa in May to have his homestead confirmed. As the *Free Press* predicted, his "grab game" was endorsed by the government (". . . what could commend a man more to Sir Charles Tupper than utter unscrupulousness and confirmed shamelessness?"), possibly because of his political connections but also, no doubt, because he had been careful to plough and seed thirty acres in conformity with the homestead act. In July, Woodworth divided the property into lots and sold several to General Rosser for twenty thousand dollars. Rosser, it is said, turned them over at a profit of ten thousand. Woodworth eventually made two hundred thousand dollars from his property and "cheerfully confessed his wealth." In his expensive sealskin coat he swiftly became a familiar and popular figure in the town. He ran for mayor and was defeated but went on to oust J. W. Sifton, the Liberal railway contractor, in the forthcoming Manitoba provincial election.

Woodworth was prescient enough to give away free land for schools, churches, and public buildings. Beecham Trotter, who knew him well, recalled that "he had his own ideas of how to give a dollar so as to get three. It was that sentiment, rather than a passion for incorruptible justice, which led him to give a free site for the court house. . . . He believed the court house would attract the lawyers to its neighbourhood as their residential district. Where lawyers flocked, he thought, other rich men would flow, and the price of lots would rise." The lawyers would include the two sons of his political rival Sifton, who set up a law office in the new town and laid the base for two outstanding political careers.

Brandon's beginnings can be traced to May 9, 1881, the day on which Arthur Wellington Ross officially secured title to Section 23 and on which J. W. Vaughan, a Winnipeg surveyor, arrived to subdivide it into avenues, streets, blocks, and lots. The main street was named after General Rosser, who decreed that the lots should be small, since more money could be made from the land in that way. The survey took until mid-August but the lots went on sale long before it was completed. Once the location of the new town was known, people began to appear and tents to blossom all along the high bank of the Assiniboine.

After the realtors, the first businessman on the scene, not unnaturally, was a lumber merchant: Charles Whitehead, the son of Joseph Whitehead, the railway contractor who had beggared himself building Section Fifteen of the government line in the muskegs that lay along the Ontario-Manitoba border. Whitehead, whose descendants would own the Brandon *Sun*, purchased the first parcel of land sold by the CPR.

On Whitehead's heels, in late May, came a doctor, a grocer, and a hotelman. The grocery store was the one that had been erected the previous month at Grand Valley, but when it became clear that the original settlement was dying, the proprietors moved it in sections by barge to the new townsite. The McVicar brothers were stubbornly trying to sell lots on the old site in the wistful hope that the CPR might locate a station on their land, but their neighbours were less sanguine. By June, two more stores and a billiard hall had been moved to Brandon.

The CPR's clear intention was to destroy Grand Valley as a community. Lots on both townsites were advertised in mid-May and went on sale at the end of the month. A brief advertising war took place in the columns of the Winnipeg papers, with "McVicar's Landing" proclaiming that it was the CPR crossing and Ross advertising the as yet unnamed city of Brandon as "the site of the next great city on the CPR." The name of the new town first appeared on May 30. The Brandon lots sold swiftly at prices that ranged from $63 to $355. Grand Valley lots went badly and sold for an average price of $33. The original community was clearly doomed by the decision to move the station two miles west.

The first newcomers had great difficulty finding Brandon at all. James Canning, who had trudged across the prairie from the end of track looking for work, arrived at the corner of Tenth and Rosser and asked a man who was helping to erect a new building where the town was.

"Right here," came the reply.

Canning climbed up on the windowsill of the half-completed structure and looked around him. There was only one other building in sight, a house on First Street being put up by Joseph Woodworth.

"I don't see any town," Canning said, as he climbed down.

"Well it is only a paper town yet," his acquaintance replied.

The paper town blossomed swiftly into a tent community. The first post office was nothing more than a soap box with a slit in it placed outside the tent of L. M. Fortier and his new bride. The first restaurant was a plank laid across two barrels on the trail that was to become Pacific Avenue. The proprietor was an eccentric, white-bearded cockney named Tom Spence whose entire stock consisted of a keg of cider, a bottle of lime juice, a couple of pails of water, and two drinking glasses. To attract trade, Spence had chained a live badger to a nearby post, "just far enough from the counter to be unable to bite the customers."

The first church service was held out of doors in a driving rainstorm in June by the Reverend Thomas Lawson, a Methodist. The local harness-maker held an umbrella over the minister's head while the congregation, composed entirely of young men, sang lustily, oblivious of the downpour. Lawson was able to move his service indoors thanks to the hospitality of a Mrs. Douglas, "a motherly lady of no mean proportions," who operated one of the two tent hotels. The beds of this "pretentious hostelry" were built double-decker fashion along one side of the tent, screened by Pullman-style curtains. A lean-to at one end served as a kitchen. The rest of the tent did duty as dining room and lobby and, on Sundays, as a church. An early Brandon settler, J. A. Smart, who was a regular attendant, remembered noticing with some amusement the ample landlady accompanied by her daughter emerging silently from a corner of the tent, "dressed in her most stately attire, not omitting bonnet, coat and gloves," creeping out the back flap through the kitchen, manœuvring round to the front, entering through the front flap, and marching up before the congregation "in high reverential style" to a front seat a few feet from the curtained bunks from which they had just emerged.

In that golden summer of 1881, the pattern of the new Canada began to take hesitant shape along the line of the railway. Brandon was the beginning – the first of the scores of raw communities which would erupt from the naked prairie. Its birth pangs would be repeated over and over again as the rails moved west. There was a kind of electric feeling in the atmosphere – a sense of being in on the start of a great adventure – which those who arrived in Brandon that summer would never forget. In future years, when recollections of later events became blurred, they would still retain unclouded the memory of those first months when the sharp, spring air was pungent with the incense of fresh lumber and ringing with the clamour of construction; when lasting friendships were forged among the soiled tents on the river bank; when every man was young and strong and in love with life; and when the distant prairie, unmarked by shovel or plough, was still a mysterious realm waiting to be claimed. Some forty years later, J. A. Smart, who had stood out in the rain during that first church service, wrote about those days "when the world, full of opportunity and hope," lay before him. "No small town in Canada or elsewhere," he wrote, "could possibly have contained a happier army of young men than did Brandon in its earliest years."

For the newcomer who planned to stay and grow with the community, the opportunities were almost unlimited. Of the first seven lawyers who arrived, four became ministers of the Crown, and one the Leader of the Opposition in the Manitoba legislature. The first organist in Thomas Lawson's new frame church (the seats were two-by-ten planks without backs) became mayor of the city four times running. Douglas Cameron, from grading the bumps out of Sixth Street, rose to be lieutenant-governor of his province. And a jovial young Irish ploughboy from Kirkfield, Ontario, named Pat Burns, who broke sod on J. W. Sifton's farm at six dollars an acre, went on to become the meat-packing king of the Canadian West. Sifton's own sons, Arthur and Clifford, became, respectively, Premier of Alberta and Minister of the Interior in the federal government.

By the time the survey of Section 23 was completed in August, 1881, the town had acquired a dozen frame buildings including two hotels named, in the tradition of the age, the Royal and the Queen's. By October 11, when the first official passenger train pulled into the new station, bearing Sir Charles Tupper, a boom of epic proportions was in full swing. The coming of the railway was already transforming the West and the changes were spectacular enough to set the continent buzzing.

In April, J. H. E. Secretan's tent had been the only habitation on the site. The surveyor was loading horse-feed onto a wagon, preparing to head farther into the unknown, when he encountered a young Englishman who wanted to be a farmer. Three months later when Secretan returned he found a Brandon seething with activity – hundreds of tents, billowing in the prairie wind, lined geometrically along what would some day be streets and avenues, places of business rising "as if by magic," sternwheel steamboats unloading passengers and merchandise, and storekeepers hawking their wares. He ran into his English acquaintance, who was bemoaning the fact that he had sold his homestead to a land shark for a piebald pony, a second-hand meerschaum pipe, a broken German silver watch, and $7.25 in cash.

Since no transfer papers had been executed, the surveyor was able to get the tenderfoot's homestead back for him. He did not return to Brandon again until Christmas, by which time the rails had passed through "and a real live town was in full swing." Alas, the young homesteader had grown homesick and had again sold out, this time for three pairs of navy-blue socks, a second-hand concertina, six packages of cigarettes, eighteen dollars in cash, and steerage passage to Liverpool. Shortly afterwards, Secretan discovered, that little piece of land was purchased for eighty thousand dollars.

As for Grand Valley, which might have been the new metropolis, it lapsed into decay. The McVicar brothers, still trying to peddle lots, offered Robert Adamson, the Winnipeg banker, a half interest in the site if he could persuade the CPR to build a station on their property. That was September. Adamson was unsuccessful. In January, the McVicars and their neighbours tried again: they offered eight hundred acres of their land free to two lumber merchants if they could persuade the CPR to put in a station by May, 1882. But the trains went roaring through without stopping and the McVicars eventually sold out their townsite for fifteen hundred dollars. When Beecham Trotter passed through, early in 1882, "Grand Valley was a living corpse. The few buildings were forlorn. The business that was still being done . . . made a noise like a death rattle. The c.p.r. had refused to stop trains there." Some years later, Charles Aeneas Shaw happened upon John McVicar ploughing in the vicinity with a team of mules. The farmer ran out onto the road. "Oh, Mr. Shaw, I was a damn fool. If I had only taken your advice, I would have been well off now!"

For future speculators in townsites, the fate of the little community on the Assiniboine was an object lesson in how not to deal with the great railway.

4

The "paid ink- slingers" Sir Henry Whatley Tyler was the kind of man who, on his visits to the United States, enjoyed riding conspicuously on the cowcatchers of loco- motives. He had been, variously, a captain in the Royal Engineers, a British railway inspector, and a Member of Parliament. Since 1876 he had been president of the Grand Trunk Railway of Canada, an enterprise that was directed from England. He might also have been president of the Canadian Pacific, but he could not stomach the idea of an all-Canadian route over the barren desert of the Canadian Shield. Like most Britons and many Canadians, including perhaps half of Sir John A. Macdonald's cabinet and several directors of the CPR, he believed it an act of incredible

32

folly to build seven hundred miles of line across country incapable of settlement. His own road ran south of the Great Lakes on its route from Sarnia to Chicago. That, clearly, was the sensible route to take. Macdonald was one of the few public figures who believed otherwise. Even George Stephen, in the early months, was unconvinced.

A handsome and debonair man with a military bearing, Tyler was noted for the brilliance of his conversation and his effectiveness at repartee. Shareholders' meetings held no terrors for him; he apparently enjoyed being baited. His sense of humour was infectious and his wit often ironic. He could hold his own in any verbal battle. Behind the sophisticated façade there was a will of steel. With the help of his shrewd general manager Joseph Hickson, he had beaten the Vanderbilt interests and pushed his railway into Chicago, consolidated several lines in the New England states, and made the Grand Trunk one of the great railway systems of North America. But was it a Canadian system? Its ownership and its direction were largely British. Its main purpose seemed to be to link the American midwest with the U.S. Atlantic coast, using the St. Lawrence lowlands of Canada as a convenient route between Chicago and Portland. Its directors clearly did not grasp the significance of the Canadian North West.

Tyler had never thought of the CPR as a competitor. Indeed, until the contract was signed in 1880, he considered the entire transcontinental railway scheme an elaborate political pipe dream, designed to get votes. Even if it was built it would never threaten the Grand Trunk. It would start at Lake Nipissing in the wilds of Ontario and terminate at Port Moody in the wilds of British Columbia. It did not, apparently, occur to Sir Henry that a railway of that length, built at enormous cost, would have to continue on into the settled East. If the CPR had stopped at Callander it would, of course, have become a valuable feeder for the Grand Trunk. But it is clear from the CPR charter that the Syndicate intended from the very outset to establish a complete transcontinental system.

In the midsummer of 1881, Tyler woke up to the fact that the Canadian Pacific was to be a major competitor. The first CPR shareholders' meeting, held in London on May 31, had approved the amalgamation of the new company with the government-subsidized Canada Central whose president, Duncan McIntyre, was also vice-president of the CPR. The Canada Central linked Lake Nipissing with Ottawa. On July 20, the CPR moved to extend its operations further into Grand Trunk territory. Stephen and McIntyre were elected directors of the Ontario and Quebec Railway, a company that held a charter to build from Montreal to Toronto. It shortly became apparent that the CPR intended to swallow this line. The CPR,

33

through Stephen, also had an interest in the Credit Valley Railway, which connected Toronto with Georgian Bay. In addition it had announced a branch line to Sault Ste Marie to connect with another line on the United States side being taken over by Jim Hill. The new company was not yet six months old and already it was posing a serious threat to the older railway.

Thus was the scene set for a battle between the two roads – a battle that was to run unchecked for the whole of the construction period and for many years after. The Grand Trunk's strategy was to discredit the CPR in public while crippling it financially behind the scenes in London and New York. In his campaign of attrition, Tyler had some powerful allies. Two great financial houses, Baring Brothers and Glyn, Mills, were on his side; they had originally financed the Grand Trunk. So were a large number of newspapers on both sides of the water, including most of the financial press, many of them enjoying the largesse of Grand Trunk advertising. Sir Alexander Galt, who had made a fortune out of Grand Trunk contracts, had been appointed Canada's first high commissioner to London in 1880; he might not be an advocate of the railway, on whose board he had once sat, but he certainly would not be an enemy. Joseph Hickson, Tyler's general manager in Canada, was on friendly terms with Sir John A. Macdonald – the two were pen pals; and the Grand Trunk could always be depended upon to deliver the vote of its employees to the Conservatives in federal elections. These links with the Canadian government were not decisive ones, but they might serve as a brake on the ambitious plans of George Stephen.

The Grand Trunk's English shareholders had some cause for righteous discontent. The railway's stock had not been the profitable investment they had hoped for. For the best part of thirty years, the company had teetered on the edge of financial disaster. Now, under sounder and bolder management, its prospects seemed much brighter. Suddenly the new railway came along to dampen that future. No wonder the overseas investing public looked with jaundice on the CPR: The Canadians, having asked the Englishmen to pump millions into one faltering railway, were now asking them to pour more millions into its chief competitor! The Grand Trunk propaganda to discredit the CPR in the British market found fertile ground.

All that summer and fall, the Canadian Pacific Railway and the Canadian North West were subjected to a torrent of abuse in the press of Canada, the United States, and Great Britain, some of it inspired by the Grand Trunk, some of it by the Liberal opposition, some of it by United States railway and immigration interests, and some of it by honest doubts as to the practicality of a scheme as wild as this one seemed to be. After all, Canada was attempting a far more ambitious project than the United States had tried when the United States had almost ten times the population.

The American attitude was summed up in a brief interview in the New York *Herald* with the taciturn Jay Gould, the American railroad financier, shortly after the CPR was formed:

REPORTER: There is a great project underway up in Canada?

GOULD: The Canadian Pacific Railroad?

REPORTER: Yes; what do you think of it?

GOULD: Visionary.

REPORTER: No dividends?

GOULD: Perhaps in one hundred years. It will be a good excursion line for English tourists and Canadian statesmen when Parliament adjourns.

REPORTER: But they say there are great possibilities.

How about the great agricultural resources . . .?

GOULD: One, the chief one, of the successful agricultural conditions is not there.

REPORTER: Which is?

GOULD: Population.

A large section of the British press, led by *The Times* of London, had convinced would-be immigrants that Australia was a far better prospect than the forbidding Canadian plains. The Governor General, Lord Lorne, the handsome and poetic son-in-law of the Queen, determined to remedy this impression by a personal tour of the railway's route to the Rockies. He invited four British journalists, including a man from *The Times*, to accompany him at his personal expense. Single-handedly, the young marquis had decided to change the minds of his countrymen about the new Canada.

It was a colourful excursion, though the start could not have been prepossessing. The viceregal retinue set off from Port Arthur at the head of Lake Superior on the still-unfinished government line that led towards Winnipeg. The rails stopped at Lake Wabigoon where the passengers were forced to forsake the carpets and sofas of their specially accoutred caboose and, after a brief steamer trip, to endure the ordeal of a nine-mile portage. It was an exhausting tramp, rendered more uncomfortable by a forest fire which had destroyed the half-way house prepared for the party's refreshment. The smoke-grimed travellers arrived, more than a little breathless, at the shanties and workshops of Eagle Lake to be greeted by the sound of bagpipes and the spectacle of a fleet of canoes, gaudily painted and decked with flags for the occasion. Crews of voyageurs and Indians hustled them across the water to a vast barge groaning with iced wines and elaborate dishes served up on spotless linen.

The remainder of the journey was marked by similar contrasts – stretches of bleak rockland, awkward portages, handsome private coaches, interspersed with triumphal arches and uniformed guards of honour. On the outskirts of Winnipeg, Donald A. Smith, one of the largest shareholders of the CPR, entertained His Excellency at his home, Silver Heights, whose façade had been temporarily transformed into a replica of Inveraray Castle, the viceroy's ancestral seat. At Rapid City, a town of real estate speculators struggling for recognition west of Winnipeg, a retired British colonel, flawlessly attired in formal afternoon dress, read an official welcome; the Governor General was more relaxed in flannel shirt and riding breeches. At the end of track, thirty-five miles beyond Portage la Prairie, the marquis laid a rail: "Considering the limited experience he has had in laying rails, it is said he accomplished the feat tolerably well," the Manitoba *Free Press* reported guardedly.

From the end of steel, the party set off across the "limitless, marvellous green meadows" to the foothills of the Rockies in a horse-drawn cavalcade of barouches and Red River carts, accompanied by forty white-helmeted Mounted Policemen. It was an exciting and romantic journey. No British writer could resist the ceremony of a Blackfoot powwow, nor could he fail to be impressed by the unbroken ocean of grass or by Lorne's own enthusiastic speeches along the way. ("You have a country whose value it would be insanity to question. . . . It must support a vast population," he told the Manitoba Club.) The coverage was good, and *The Times* changed its editorial line and ceased to thunder against Canada.

But the gibes from other British newspapers and journals continued. The most memorable, titled "The Canadian Dominion Bubble," was published in *Truth* on September 1, 1881. The author was Henry Labouchère, a piquant journalist and financial critic whose uncle and namesake had been Colonial Secretary in 1857 when Captain John Palliser made his gloomy report on conditions in the Canadian North West.

Labouchère said flatly that the floating of a Canadian government bond issue in England and ten million dollars worth of CPR land grant bonds in New York and Montreal that fall was a fraud. New York investors, he declared, would never be such fools "as to put their money into this mad project. I would as soon credit them with a willingness to subscribe hard cash in support of a scheme for the utilization of icebergs." As for the Canadians, they were "not such idiots as to part with one dollar of their own if they can borrow their neighbours'. The Canadians spend money and we provide it."

"The Canadian Pacific Railway will run, if it is ever finished, through a country frost bound for seven or eight months in the year, and will connect with the eastern part of the Dominion a province which embraces about as forbidding a country as any on the face of the earth." British Columbia was "a barren, cold, mountain country that is not worth keeping." It would never have been inhabited at all had it not been for the mining boom: "Ever since that fever died down the place has been going from bad to worse. Fifty railroads would not galvanize it into prosperity."

Manitoba was equally formidable: "Men and cattle are frozen to death in numbers that would startle the intending settler if he knew; and those who are not killed outright, are often maimed for life by frostbites."

Canada was "one of the most over-rated colonies we have . . . poor and crushed with debt." In the end, the editorial said, the country would have to go into liquidation, and when the load got too heavy Ontario would quit and join the United States. As for the railway, it was "never likely to pay a red cent of interest on the money that may be sunk into it."

This broadside and others that followed had their effect on the British money market. They were accompanied that fall by the first of the anti-CPR pamphlets, said to have been written by the Grand Trunk's "paid ink-slingers," as Stephen called them. One pamphlet, entitled *The Canadian Pacific Railway and the Schemes of the Syndicate*, by "Diogenes," warned investors not to risk their money in what was represented as a reckless enterprise. Another, entitled *Financial Notes*, by "Ishmael," denied the fertility of the twenty-five million acres of land that the CPR was to receive from the government. Ishmael accused *The Times*'s correspondent with the Lorne party of having been bought up by Stephen to pretend that the Great Lone Land was flowing with milk and honey.

At about the same time the *Money Market Review*, a respected British financial journal, devoted four issues to a series of articles warning British investors against putting money into CPR bonds. In reply, Alexander Begg, a journalist and CPR employee, charged in a pamphlet of his own that the periodical had lent its columns for the purpose of enabling the Grand Trunk "to make a violent attack upon a new corporation, the Canadian Pacific, which it insists upon regarding as its deadly enemy, and dangerous rival."

There was no doubt in George Stephen's mind about who was behind the press attack. "The G.T.R. is bound to do all the harm they can," he wrote to Macdonald. "They are now a through line to Chicago and inter-

37

ested in drawing the traffic of the North West to that city and will do all they can to that end. . . ." Stephen was seriously contemplating going to England himself to educate English investors regarding the land grant bonds: "I mean to make 'John Bull' buy these bonds by sending orders to this side for them at a *premium*."

Stephen, as his letters to the Prime Minister reveal, was a far more complicated man than his outward appearance suggested. To the world he presented the picture of suave good manners – a flawlessly tailored executive, courtly in bearing and rather solemn. But he was also an emotional man, and temperamental to boot; those who were not passionately devoted to the cause of the railway were seen to be enemies, traitors, blackguards, and cowards. Such terms cropped up constantly in his astonishingly garrulous correspondence with Macdonald, almost all of it scrawled in Stephen's own sloping hand.

Galt, the High Commissioner, who had been angling unsuccessfully that spring for a post with the railway, was in the enemy's camp as far as Stephen was concerned. "The Diogenes pamphlet has evidently scared him," the CPR president advised Macdonald that winter. "We have had it here in these two weeks and no one cares a cent for it and Galt's simulated anxiety lest we should find ourselves short is wasted. The disreputable method adopted by the subsidized Grand Trunk scribblers to discredit the country, the Governor General and the CPR company, will end in nothing but mischief to the GTR. Galt having done his friends, Barings [and] Glyn, a service and placed himself under obligation to them and the GTR, it is not to be expected he would be mildly agitated if we get into trouble. As to his judgment in our financial arrangements . . . it is simply an impertinence for him to write to you and say that *he* forsooth, *thinks* we are *mistaken* if we do not need to come to London for money. What does he know about it? . . . It makes me mad to have a fellow pretending to advise us for our good who would gladly see us both busted."

Stephen urged Macdonald to write to the High Commissioner to tell him that "we have seen all that has been written by the tools of his G.T.R. friends, and have not thought it worth while noticing any of the attacks that have been made . . . and that so far as you can learn, we are confident of our ability to carry out the contract of the Government in half the stipulated time, without asking London for a cent. . . ."

Macdonald, who did not care greatly for Galt, felt it necessary to defend him from these attacks. Stephen, however, would have none of it. "I agree with you in what you say about Galt," he replied, "but in regard to us, individually, he is controlled by an other element of his character . . . envy.

38

. . . He would like to see the C.P.R. a success for the sake of the venture he has embarked in." Stephen was referring to Galt's attempt to raise money to exploit the coal-fields which his son had helped discover in the foothills of the Rockies near the site of the future city of Lethbridge.

Galt was, however, a minor worry. Stephen saw himself beset on all sides by more formidable forces intent on crushing the CPR. One of these was the Northern Pacific, whose dynamic new president, Henry Villard, seemed determined to thrust his rapidly expanding railway into the Canadian North West. Villard was one of those phenomenal business successes thrown up by the yeasty society of nineteenth-century America. A Bavarian immigrant, he had arrived in New York at the age of eighteen and eked out a living working as a reporter for German-American newspapers. He had shot up swiftly in both the journalistic and the financial fields. As a reporter for leading United States dailies, he had covered the Lincoln-Douglas debates, the Pike's Peak gold rush, and the Civil War. Beginning as an agent for German bondholders, he moved into railway finance and helped reorganize an Oregon railroad and steamship line. By 1881, at the age of forty-six, he owned the *Nation* and the New York *Evening Post* and controlled the Northern Pacific, whose construction he was pushing westward with a reckless enthusiasm that took little account of rising costs.

In Manitoba two private railways were being built towards the United States border. The Northern Pacific had bought control of one and was ready to buy control of the other, believing, in Stephen's words, that "they can force a connection at the boundary and so strangle the Canadian Pacific; which they are determined to do if they can." With both Macdonald and Tupper absent from Ottawa, Stephen feared the government might yield to pressure from the prairie province and allow the two lines to connect at the border with a spur from the Northern Pacific's through line. Stephen urged Macdonald to instruct Ottawa at once to hold matters over until he returned; he cabled him that a decision in favour of the Manitoba lines "must effectually destroy Pacific as National through line, rendering Eastern section useless. . . ."

All that fall of 1881, Stephen kept up continual pressure on the Prime Minister to disallow by federal decree any provincially chartered lines that came within fifteen miles of the border. Again and again he made the point that a "Yankee line" into Manitoba would make it impossible to operate or even to build the Lake Superior section of the CPR. With such American competition no one could prevent the products of the North West being drawn through the United States to Chicago, whose attraction as a market for wheat was almost irresistible. Stephen used every argument in his power to convince Macdonald to disallow the Manitoba charters: it would, he told him, mean the disgrace not only of the railway but also of the Conservative government itself, since the country would not stand for the enormous expense of the Lake Superior line if it turned out to be worthless. "It would be a miserable affair to find that the benefit of all our efforts to develop the North West had by our own acts, fallen into Yankee hands."

Many of Macdonald's followers, especially those in Manitoba, were eager to subvert the spirit of the contract which protected the railway through its Monopoly Clause. Because of the British North America Act the clause did not prevent the provinces from chartering lines to the border in competition with the transcontinental railway. This was Stephen's fear. The Liberal press was already crying "Monopoly!" Stephen wanted the Prime Minister to counter this opposition by exerting pressure on friendly newspapers: "Don't you think it would be well for you to take some steps to prevent the friendly portion of the Press being led astray by the cry of Monopoly? . . . I think it would be well for you to instruct the Mail and Gazette on these points, and expose the 'Monopoly humbug.' " Stephen also hoped to bring pressure on the Liberal *Free Press* in Winnipeg through the company's land commissioner, John McTavish, who did considerable advertising, and through Donald A. Smith, who held a mortgage on the *Free Press* property and was believed to own shares in the paper as well.

Stephen even felt it necessary to bolster Macdonald with some of his own arguments, pointing out that disallowance was simply another aspect of the protectionist platform that had won the Conservative Party its smashing victory in 1878. "The policy of the Government in disallowing all extensions into Manitoba of Yankee lines is nothing more or less than the N.P. [National Policy] in Railways, and is defensible on precisely the same grounds."

There is no doubt that Macdonald intended to back Stephen up but there is also no doubt that the Monopoly Clause was already causing him grave political uneasiness. To ride roughshod over the legitimate desire of Manitoba settlers for more railways to service their communities was to alienate politically an entire province. From the beginning he had seen the railway as a device to unite the nation – to tie the settled East to the new country beyond the Shield. Now in the very first year of its construction the railway had become a divisive force, antagonizing the very people it was supposed to link together. The Prime Minister gave vent to his view in the presence of some of Stephen's colleagues on the subject of the "cussed" Manitoba charters and Stephen wrote to him in alarm that "they have all come back more or less full of misgivings and fears lest in some way the 15 mile Yankee barrier will not be maintained."

There was another threat on the horizon. The ubiquitous Northern Pacific was about to purchase the railway owned by the Quebec government – or so the Premier, J. A. Chapleau, kept insisting. This was the Quebec, Montreal, Ottawa and Occidental and its eastern section, familiarly termed "the North Shore Line." Quebec had been trying to unload this white elephant – it had eaten up fourteen million dollars and was steadily losing money – ever since the days of Sir George Etienne Cartier, who had promised to make it part of the CPR. The previous winter, Chapleau had made the purchase of the partially completed railway a condition of French-Canadian support for the CPR contract.

Macdonald had managed to evade such an out-and-out promise. But now he was again facing the same kind of political blackmail. If the aggressive Henry Villard came to the rescue of Quebec by buying up the railway, it would give him a threefold advantage in his drive to tap Canada for the Northern Pacific's profit. With one stroke he would occupy a key position between the government-owned Intercolonial on the east and the Canadian Pacific on the west. Secondly, it was clear that he meant to link the Quebec line with the Northern Pacific at Sault Ste Marie; thus the country faced the possibility of a Yankee transcontinental railway mainly on Canadian soil. But there was more: By taking the faltering railway off the hands of the Quebec government, Villard would be buying considerable political leverage in that province and, consequently, in Ottawa. Macdonald feared that he would use this new political strength to persuade the Quebec members to vote in a bloc against federal disallowance of the Manitoba railways. If Villard's gambit succeeded, he would have a through line from Quebec City to Winnipeg by way of Sault Ste Marie and Duluth; and Macdonald's dream of an all-Canadian route would be shattered, perhaps forever.

The Prime Minister confessed to Stephen that he was "very uneasy." If the rumours were true, "it means danger ahead." A Quebec election was coming up. The president of one of the Manitoba lines, the Manitoba and Southwestern, had taken a house in Ottawa and was tactlessly predicting that the Northern Pacific would be a factor in that election. No doubt Chapleau, in his election speeches, would magnify the Villard offer, but if Stephen was to act at all, Macdonald urged, then he must act at once. The CPR president had been reluctant to buy the Quebec railway, but now he changed his mind and decided he must make an offer for the section

41

running west to Ottawa from Montreal in order to head off the American attempt to control Canada's transcontinental transportation system.

Stephen, who had once thought the idea of building the line north of Lake Superior "great folly," was becoming an enthusiastic champion of an all-Canadian route. When the contract was signed in 1880, he and, indeed, all the CPR directors had been cool to Macdonald's plan to build it across the Shield. But in late August, 1881, Stephen confessed to the Prime Minister that "all misgivings I had last year . . . have disappeared with a better knowledge of the position of the whole country. I am now satisfied that the C.P.R. without the control of a line to the *Atlantic* seaboard would be a *mistake*. If for instance, it terminated like the Northern Pacific, at Lake Superior it never could become the property it is certain to be having its own rails running from sea to sea. I am sure you will be glad to hear this from me because I do not think but for your *own* tenacity on that point, would the line North of the Lake *ever* have been built, events have shown you were right and all the rest wrong."

Some of this was flattery and some of it was close to being blackmail. Stephen had been aware, from the outset, of Macdonald's obsession with an all-Canadian railway. He used his knowledge to good advantage – to bargain toughly for the insertion of the Monopoly Clause in the contract. The Prime Minister was made to understand that he could not have one thing without the other. If the CPR was to pay through the nose for an unprofitable line through an uninhabitable wilderness, it must receive compensation. Stephen might argue that this was merely an extension of the Conservative Party's National Policy of protection, but that protection was paying big dividends for the proprietors of the CPR and of the St. Paul, Minneapolis and Manitoba Railway whose directorates interlocked. The contract gave them a monopoly of all traffic out of Winnipeg into the United States and they made the most of it.

At the time he wrote that letter, Stephen had an additional reason for his enthusiasm. He had just returned from Winnipeg, where he discovered that the white elephant might not be as unprofitable as he and his colleagues had believed. Lumber from Ottawa could be laid down in the Manitoba capital at ten dollars a thousand less than the city was paying elsewhere. He confided to the Governor General that the company would not give up the controversial portion of the line "even if the Government wished us."

The safety of the railway and of the country – the two were often identical in Stephen's mind – could, he now felt, be guaranteed only by keeping the traffic of the North West on the Canadian side of Lake

Superior. (He did not, apparently, count the branch out of Sault Ste Marie, which circumvented the lake by connecting with Jim Hill's road.) For that reason, the line from Lake Nipissing west must be "in all respects a first class road, capable of easy operation at high speed." Stephen was eager to complete it in the shortest possible time: indeed, he was talking about driving steel from Portage la Prairie all the way to the foot of the Rockies by the late fall of 1882 – a forthright policy that would bring additional financial pressures to bear on the new company. Stephen was aware of the danger, but determined to press ahead: "This new and urgent necessity . . . is going to tax us to the full extent of our capacity, but I mean we shall do it. . . ."

Again, as in the case of the prairie and mountain sections, Stephen and his colleagues had rejected Sandford Fleming's surveys. The Fleming line took the easiest route, well to the north of Lake Nipigon, but Stephen wanted to adopt a new location that would hug the granite-ribbed shores of Superior. "The line north of Nipigon would be easy of construction and operation too, but it *never* can support settlers, there is absolutely no *land*, nothing but bare rocks and pools of water." Moreover, by building close to the lake the contractors could be supplied by water transport. Stephen argued that because of this, construction time would be cut, perhaps in half. "Do not forget," he told Macdonald, "that its adoption means the completion of the road in 5 years." The Prime Minister, by mid-November, 1881, had become a convert.

Though he thought the new route along the lake ought to be most acceptable to Ontario, Stephen had no illusions about the attitude of the *Globe*, which he believed was "conspiring with the Northern Pacific to strangle Canada's national road." The *Globe* could be depended upon to blackball the idea and "perhaps declare that we do not mean to build the Lake Superior section at all."

It was "simply disgusting" to have to swallow the "lying charges" of such newspapers. The best answer was "to take care to avoid anything that even looks like a breach, or even an evasion, of the terms of the contract. It will be the duty as well as the interest of the Company to ask nothing of the Government savoring of a favoritism not provided for in the contract, and you may be sure, that so far as I know, I will be guided by this principle. Acting in this way and pushing our work with the utmost energy and especially that part of the contract which the *Globe still insists we mean to shirk*."

Few railroad executives in North America had ever talked this way before, but then Stephen was not cast in the traditional mould of the railway entrepreneur. Among his own colleagues he was unique. Certainly Jim Hill had no intention of blasting a railroad out of the black scarps that frowned down on the slate waters of the great lake. Hill pinned his hopes on the branch line that Stephen had announced would be built to Sault Ste Marie to link up with Hill's road from St. Paul. Like Villard of the Northern Pacific, Hill saw Canadian freight being diverted south of the lake and up through the underbelly of Manitoba. One of his chief reasons for joining the CPR Syndicate was that his St. Paul road would get all the construction traffic for the line being built west of Winnipeg. The line across the Shield, he was convinced, "would be of no use to anybody and would be the source of heavy loss to whoever operated it."

In the fall of 1881, Hill picked the best railwayman he could find to look over the Precambrian country to the north and west of Lake Superior. According to William Pearce of the Dominion land department – a man privy to a good deal of CPR gossip – Hill's plan was to have the visitor damn the all-Canadian route as impractical. He chose for this task the dynamic young general manager of the Chicago, Milwaukee and St. Paul Railroad; though no one yet realized it, his influence on the future of the young nation was to be enormous. His name was William Cornelius Van Horne.

5

Enter
Van Horne

The new man was being considered for something more permanent than a mere report on the Lake Superior route. The CPR badly needed a new general manager. Stickney had managed to build only one hundred and thirty miles of railway that season; moreover, he was under a cloud because of his land speculations. At the end of August, the *Globe*, always ready to report dissension in the ranks of the company, published a rumour of "serious trouble between the Syndicate and Superintendent Stickney on account of the latter having obtained the title to lands including the town plot of Brandon, ostensibly for the Syndicate but really on his private account." The *Globe* added: "It is said the Syndicate make the condition that the lands and proceeds of sales be given up to them or Mr. Stickney is to quit their service. . . . There are also reports that General Rosser has largely improved the chances, which the early knowledge of the location of the line gave him, in speculation." The friendlier Manitoba

Free Press denied the story flatly, but it was about this time that the company began looking for a general manager.

As usual George Stephen turned to Hill, who had done the major share of the hiring for the top echelons of the company that year and whose preference for American railroad men and engineers (they were, after all, the only ones he knew from experience) had already caused rumblings in the Canadian press. Hill recommended Van Horne. Of all the men he knew, Van Horne was the best equipped mentally for the job, and in every other way as well. A pioneer was needed, Hill told Stephen, "and the more of a pioneer, the better."

"You need a man of great mental and physical power to carry this line through," Hill said. "Van Horne can do it." He added a word of caution: "But he will take all the authority he gets and more, so define how much you want him to have."

Stephen undoubtedly recognized the type; he had seen it once before in his career when he, Donald Smith, and Jim Hill were fighting to turn a bankrupt, half-finished railway into a profitable business. Hill in those days had been the pioneer – a man of seemingly inexhaustible mental and physical power – cozening politicians, figuring out balance sheets far into the night, and even taking a hand with a snow shovel to raise the morale of a track gang. Now Stephen was being offered a second Jim Hill. It was small wonder that he was prepared to pay Van Horne the largest salary ever dangled before a railroad man in the West – a princely fifteen thousand dollars a year.

In the two-volume authorized biography of James Jerome Hill there is not, in all of 957 pages, a single reference to his remarkable protégé. Physically and temperamentally, Hill and Van Horne were very much alike; that similarity may help to explain the unyielding antagonism that developed between them over the rival interests of the Great Northern and the Canadian Pacific – two parallel transcontinental lines that fought for business. They were both powerful men with big chests and huge heads sunk on massive shoulders. Their strong faces were half hidden by short beards, which tended to mask the expression of their mouths. The eyes differed: Hill's single eye was like a smouldering coal; Van Horne's, impassive and ice-blue, were the product of his Dutch-German ancestry. If you removed Van Horne's beard, cropped his hair, and gave him a Bismarck moustache he could have been mistaken for a Junker general. Indeed, it was often remarked that the CPR's gain was the military's loss. After all, like Hill, he was used to controlling armies of men – "the ablest railroad general in the world, all that Grant was to the U.S.A.," in the admiring phrase of a fellow railroader, Jason C. Easton, president of the Chicago, Milwaukee and St. Paul.

Van Horne's speech was military in its decisiveness – blunt, direct, and simple. So was Hill's; the ex-Canadian hated adjectives, preferred short, pungent words, and often spoke of *Pilgrim's Progress* as a model of style. Both men had the ruthlessness of great generals and great statesmen. Both were single-minded to the point of obsession in any cause they served. Both knew how to seize and hold power. Hill, the Canadian-turned-American, and Van Horne, the American-turned-Canadian, would both push their railroads through to the Pacific. It was inevitable that when their interests clashed they would find themselves locked in battle. It was also understandable that, given their temperaments, they would be hard to reconcile. The sophisticated Stephen remained Hill's mentor for all of his life and was called on more than once to act as arbiter between the two strong men who were both his closest friends and business associates.

On October 7, Hill brought Van Horne into Winnipeg to look over the CPR's prairie construction and also the government line still being built between the Red River and Fort William. The town was then locked in the throes of a great real estate boom, which had been touched off by the railway and which was to astonish the nation and cause a ferment in the North West for more than a year. Winnipeg was a city of contrasts – buildings springing up everywhere; "the streets full of garbage, egg shells, rinds of lemons and other forms of refuse cast out in broad daylight"; stray horses prowling around the suburbs where they "mangle shade trees, stamp around at nights and make a nuisance of themselves generally"; tents blossoming so thickly in St. Boniface along the Assiniboine that the police tried to burn them out; workmen and settlers jamming the broad, muddy avenues. Arthur Rowe Miller, a young music student from England on his way to join a survey party, noted in his diary that the town was "just old enough to be dirty, and smells dreadfully."

Nonetheless it was beginning to acquire a patina of culture. The Nathal Opera Troupe performed at the city hall on the very day Hill and Van Horne arrived. "Miss Louise Lester . . . was particularly effective, her performance in the wine drinking scene being most artistic in every respect." The wine drinking was not confined to the stage: "This city," the *Free Press* had complained the previous month, "is suffering from drunken Indians. They are to be met on almost every street at almost every hour. They seem to have no difficulty in procuring whiskey."

The white population was as addicted to drink as the Indians. The opening that August of Winnipeg's pride, the Louisa Railway Bridge, had been accompanied by an "incarnal orgy . . . a great, hilarious, illimitable guzzle," in which small boys quaffed glass after glass of free champagne and beer, provided by the city, "with the easy nonchalance of veterans," and the crowd, on learning that the liquor was cut off, "acted generally more like wild beasts than rational creatures," tearing down the ceremonial tent, appropriating the forbidden stock of spirits, and indulging in a "debauch . . . the largest and most varied the city has seen for many a day."

There were other problems, all reflected in the letters column of the local newspapers. One man wrote of "Winnipeg's brazen shame": prostitutes who promenaded the streets by the dozen every afternoon. Another deplored "the disgraceful state of that leading thoroughfare, Portage Avenue. . . ."

Hill, Van Horne, and Hill's two sons, who had come along for the excursion, stayed overnight in Winnipeg and then went west – through Portage la Prairie ("for its size . . . perhaps one of the hardest for drink in the Dominion"), through the booming community of Brandon, and on to the end of track. The trip impressed Van Horne: the quality of the grain in the fields was good, the vegetables unusually large, the crops abundant. Van Horne, who knew a great deal about soils, gardens, and crops, took it all in. The following day, the party headed east along the line to Thunder Bay, which the government had begun in 1875 and was still in the process of completing before turning it over to the CPR.

It must have been a stimulating two days. Both Van Horne and Hill were insatiably curious. Hobbies with them became obsessions. Hill had made himself one of the continent's leading experts on coal. Van Horne was an amateur geologist who constantly chipped away at rock cuts in his search for new fossils, nine of which carry to this day the descriptive suffix "Van Hornei." Once, in Alton, Illinois, he had been tantalized for several weeks by the spectacle of a fine trilobite embedded in a slab sidewalk until, unable to resist the impulse, he had smashed at the pavement with his hammer and borne the trophy away.

Of the two, Van Horne was the broader in his interests. Hill usually made his curiosity work for him in a business sense; transportation, fuel, forwarding attracted him. But Van Horne indulged his varied fancies for the sheer love of it. He was a first-rate gardener (roses were his specialty); he was a caricaturist; he was a conjuror; he was a mind reader; he was a violinist; he was a practical joker; he was a gourmet; he was a marathon poker player.

He was also the more sybaritic of the two. Both Hill and Van Horne were furious smokers but the latter's long Havana cigars were to become such a trademark that a brand was named after him, his likeness on every band. All his appetites appeared to be gargantuan. He ate prodigiously and was known as a man who fed his workmen generously. He could sit up all night winning at poker and go to work the following morning without showing a trace of fatigue. He liked his cognac, his whiskey, and his fine French vintages, but he did not tolerate drunkenness in himself or others. Inebriates were fired out of hand. So were slackers, dunces, cravens, cowards, slowpokes, and labour organizers. Van Horne did not suffer laziness, stupidity, inefficiency, or revolt.

He was probably appalled by what he found between Winnipeg and Thunder Bay. The vast muskegs were bad enough; they had swallowed thousands of tons of gravel, miles of track, and even, on occasion, entire locomotives. But the black ridges of the Canadian Shield, rolling on for mile after mile through a land as desolate as the moon, were worse. Later Van Horne was to describe a section of this desert east of Fort William, as "200 miles of engineering impossibilities."

It may be that, at this juncture, he shared Hill's belief that it would be madness to try to push a railroad across the Shield, when the country south of the lake was easy of access and more arable. Did he actually damn the Lake Superior route, as Hill wanted him to? William Pearce, the land commissioner, believed that he did. "I have no doubt he carried out what he was asked to do," he wrote in a memoir years later. But Van Horne at the time was not a committed officer of the company, nor had he yet fallen under the spell of George Stephen.

Events, however, were moving rapidly. The pressure was on him to leave his job in Milwaukee and take over the Canadian railway. It was an enormous risk. His prospects south of the border were as bright as those of any rising young railway executive in the country. He could, almost certainly, have had the pick of half a dozen sinecures; yet he chose the CPR. Certainly the salary that Hill was dangling before him was attractive, but it was not really the money that turned William Cornelius Van Horne into a Canadian. The Canadian Pacific Railway company was launched on a breath-taking gamble. The line had been diverted south of the Yellow Head Pass. The steel was creeping across the prairie like an arrow pointed at the successive bulwarks of the Rockies and the Selkirks. At that moment, no one knew exactly how the rails were to penetrate those two mountain series or, indeed, if they could get through the Selkirks at all. The railway's future depended on that eccentric little wisp of a surveyor,

Major Rogers, who, all that summer, had been clambering over the naked peaks looking for a notch in the rampart. Few Canadian engineers believed he would find what he was seeking, but Van Horne, the poker player, had talked to Rogers. The gamble, the challenge, the adventure, the desire "to make things grow and put new places on the map" were too much for a man of his temperament to resist.

Just twelve days after Van Horne returned to St. Paul with Hill, the first rumours appeared in the press announcing his imminent departure from the Milwaukee road. A day later a second rumour in Winnipeg named him the new general manager of the CPR. The following day, October 25, Alpheus Stickney announced he would retire from the post of general superintendent at the end of the year. He had, he insisted, only consented to hold the position temporarily until the company could find someone else to fill it; as it was, he had remained longer than he intended.

Van Horne's appointment was confirmed on November 1. He paid a second visit to Winnipeg on November 11 and arrived to stay on New Year's Eve, 1881. He began work on January 2, 1882, in the CPR offices in the new Bank of Montreal building. By that time the astonishing real estate boom, which swept across all of western Canada from the Red River to Fort Edmonton and electrified most of the continent, was at its height. On the very day that Van Horne arrived to take up residence, the *Free Press* carried a description of Winnipeg as seen through the eyes of a Dr. Gouinlock of Seaforth, Ontario:

"The bustle and stir can only compare to Wall St., New York. The sidewalks are thronged from morning to night by shrewd anxious looking men, hurrying hither and thither, and intent only on their own business and speculations while the streets are crowded with vehicles of every description."

The smell of money was in the air. Expensive sea otter coats "for New Year's calls" were being advertised along with costly oil paintings "from the brush of Canada's greatest painter, W. L. Jodson." Stickney's employees had little trouble raising a thousand dollars among themselves to pay for a handsome silver service as a departing gift for the retiring superintendent. For the past several months, ever since the founding of Brandon, the people of Manitoba had seemed to be going stark, raving mad over real estate. When Van Horne arrived the insanity had reached a kind of crescendo. It would continued unabated until the snows melted and it was snuffed out by the angry floods of spring.

49

Chapter Two

1

The great Winnipeg boom

2

Fool's paradise

3

"Towns cannot live of themselves"

4

The bubble bursts

1

Van Horne's first official act, on assuming office, was to place a small advertisement in the Winnipeg newspapers cautioning the public against buying lots at prospective stations along the line until he had officially announced their locations. All but five sites, he pointed out, were still temporary. Future townsites would be chosen by the company and by the company alone, "without regard to any private interest whatever."

This clear warning to real estate speculators that they could expect no aid or comfort from the CPR fell largely on deaf ears. The little ad was almost lost in an ocean of screaming type, trumpeting unbelievable bargains in lots on townsites many of which were non-existent and in "cities" that could scarcely be found by the most diligent explorer. Such ads had fattened Winnipeg's three dailies, the *Free Press*, *Times*, and *Sun*, for all of the latter half of 1881; they would continue to dominate the press for most of the first half of 1882. "MAKE MONEY!" the advertising shrieked. "GET WEALTHY!" "GOLDEN CHANCES! GOLDEN SPECULATIONS!" "MILLIONS IN IT!"

The boom had been launched the previous June with the opening sale of lots in Brandon. By January, the value of those lots had tripled, the town had been sold seven or eight times over, and the price was said to be rising at a rate of one hundred dollars per lot per week. In March, lots on Brandon's main street were selling at $140 a front foot. In Portage la Prairie the price was $230 a front foot. In Winnipeg, on Main Street the price rose as high as two thousand dollars a front foot for choice locations. This meant that real estate in Winnipeg was more expensive than it was in Chicago. An idea of the inflated values of that spring may be gained from a study of modern real estate prices in the same city. By 1970, real estate at the corner of Portage and Main was again worth two thousand dollars a front foot; but in 1882 the dollar value was worth at least four or five times its 1970 value. In short, the cost of land in Winnipeg was never higher than when the city was in its infancy.

The town was said to have been surveyed into city lots for ten miles – enough real estate to support a population of half a million. In St. Boniface, across the river, the value of land had quadrupled in three months. In three years, farm land in the vicinity had soared from twelve to one hundred dollars an acre. By April, when the boom began to decline, it was estimated that fifteen million acres of land had changed hands. To eastern ears this was little short of miraculous. In all of southwestern Ontario, which had a population seventeen times that of Manitoba, there were only eleven million acres of land.

Winnipeg, with a population of some sixteen thousand, supported no fewer than three hundred real estate dealers. Its population had doubled in a year, its assessment had tripled. Buildings were popping up like toadstools; the air was thick with sawdust; along Main Street, half-finished buildings echoed to the sound of mallet and chisel. Accommodation was at such a premium that the smallest building – a storey-and-a-half structure, thirty feet by thirty – could rent for five thousand dollars a year before it was completed. A new courthouse, a new government house, and a new legislative building were all being erected. In 1881, more than two millions had been poured into building improvements. In 1882, the figure was expected to exceed five millions.

"Winnipeg . . . looks as if it had been laid out by a man in delirium tremens," the *Globe*'s reporter on the scene told his Ontario readers. "The result is that the business portion of the city must be along the line of the old Indian trail now known as Main Street . . . the frontage on Main Street will be as valuable as that of King Street. . . . Winnipeg will have half the population of Toronto in five years. . . ."

The news from Winnipeg caught the imagination of the continent. On March 7, the New York *Graphic* devoted two full pages to "the wondrous city of northwestern Canada." "Think of $1000 a front foot!" exclaimed the Fargo *Argus*. "If you haven't a lot in Manitoba you had better buy one at once," cried the London, Ont., *Herald*. "If you find yourself among a group of four or five citizens you will discover that you are quite 'out of form' unless you have something to relate about your speculation." The Thunder Bay *Sentinel* editorialized that in Winnipeg there was "more money to the square inch than in any other city on the continent double or quadruple the size."

The Toronto papers were crammed with advertisements from Winnipeg real estate men who had come east offering lots. "The woods are full of them," the *World* reported. "You can't turn a corner without seeing a Manitoba man with a tin case full of maps, St. James, St. John's, St. Boniface and the everlasting Kildonan, anything from the heart of Winnipeg to its outer skin. There were five land brokers at the Queen's and three at the Rossin yesterday." The *Globe*, noting that auction rooms dealing exclusively in Manitoba lots were springing up in towns and cities all over Ontario, warned its readers of "the necessity of receiving with very heavy discount the rose-coloured descriptions and prognostications of interested agents."

53

The eastern press covered the Manitoba boom as if it were a war, sending correspondents into the front lines. Some stayed to speculate themselves. "I have yet to hear of any one who has not made money," the reporter for the St. Catharines *Journal* enthused to readers at the end of January. "The 'race for wealth is a neck and neck one.' Every one dips in. Some of the more godly wrestle with the Lord with the left hand and gamble in land with the other. I suppose they don't let the left know what the right hand doeth."

"Unsophisticated people from Ontario, when they land in Winnipeg go through several stages," another correspondent reported. "First they deem you all, well, crazy. You all have lots and big figures on the brain. Presently they come a little to themselves. . . . They gradually begin to think there is something in it. You are not all quite demented. . . . [Then] they go the whole hog, and talk 'lots' at breakfast, dinner and supper, and all intervening times during weekdays, and on Sunday, doubtless meditate on what their 'lot' will be in the next world. The boom strikes them sooner or later."

Stories of fortunes made and lost excited the nation. There was, for instance, the tale of one elderly man who owned a parcel of fifty-four acres of land on the outskirts of the city. In 1880 he had tried, unsuccessfully, to sell it for seven hundred dollars. He moved to Toronto and tried to sell it there, again without success. In 1881 he returned to Winnipeg, intending to pack up and leave the country. Soon after his arrival two strangers knocked on his door and asked if he wanted to sell his land. The old man was afraid to ask for seven hundred dollars for fear of driving them away. Seeing him hesitate the visitors jumped in with an offer of forty thousand dollars. The old man, concluding that he was in the presence of lunatics, shooed them off his property and then went to his lawyer with tears in his eyes and told him that a couple of scamps had been poking fun at him. It was some time before he could be convinced that the offer was genuine. By the time he had been persuaded to sell, the price had risen by another five thousand dollars.

A newspaperman from St. Catharines purchased several lots on Portage Avenue well before the boom. In September, 1881, a friend dropped in and offered him twenty-five hundred dollars for one lot. When the reporter hesitated the friend increased the offer to three thousand. The news of the available property travelled swiftly. The following morning, as the St. Catharines man walked down the street he was besieged with offers that seemed to increase block by block. An acquaintance rushed up to him and offered to buy all his lots at three thousand apiece. A few hundred yards farther along, a man popped his head out of the window and raised the price to thirty-five hundred. Another few hundred yards and he was stopped by a stranger who offered four thousand dollars per lot. He had scarcely moved another block before the figure had reached six thousand.

Harry Armstrong, who had helped survey the government line between Thunder Bay and Red River and who was working in the CPR's engineering department in Winnipeg early in 1882, managed to buy a lot on Portage Avenue for fifteen hundred dollars before the boom began. He sold it late in 1881 for ten thousand dollars. A short time later it was resold for forty thousand.

Such tales crowded the world news out of the papers. Even the exploits of Billy the Kid and the revelations of Robert Ford, the man who killed Jesse James, were overshadowed by more piquant items:

"W. J. Ovens used to sell nails for a cent in a hardware store in Yorkville four years ago but he can draw his check for $100,000 to-day."

"A man who worked on the street here last spring, wore a curly dog-skin coat this spring, smokes 25 cent cigars and talks with contempt about thousands."

"Mr. Wm. J. Twigg, of Thompson, Twigg & Co., Real Estate, has retired from business after making one hundred thousand dollars. . . ."

It puts matters in perspective to realize that twelve hundred dollars a year was considered, in 1882, to be a very good income. A hundred-thousand-dollar profit then could keep a man and his family in luxury for life. No wonder John A. McDougall, the pioneer Edmonton trader, wrote to his brother from Manitoba that he intended to invest every dollar he could spare in land: "Any person with experience, good judgment and a few thousand dollars can make his fortune. . . ."

But many of these fortunes were paper ones. George Ham, one of the great raconteurs of the West, who later went to work for the CPR, was staying that winter in the Queen's Hotel along with La Touche Tupper, a government employee who was deeply involved in land speculation. "He was a fairly good barometer of the daily land values," Ham recalled. "Some days when he claimed to have made $10,000 or $15,000 everything was lovely. The next day, when he could only credit himself with $3,000 or $4,000 to the good, things were not as well, and when the profits dropped, and some days they did, to a paltry $500 or $600, the country was going to the dogs. We faithfully kept count of La Touche's earnings, and in the spring he had accumulated nearly a million in his mind."

The Reverend James Boydell, who was appointed Church of England missionary to Brandon in 1882, recalled that "nothing but lots was talked about day in and out. I was perhaps an almost solitary exception, not because I was a parson, but because my pocket was empty." In mid-February, one minister preaching a sermon about Lot's wife had to make it clear to his congregation that it was not his intention to talk about real estate. A performer at a skating carnival that same week costumed himself as a coffin on which was inscribed: "Talked to death by a real estate agent. Lots for sale." In Brandon, the first wedding was provoked by an offer from the municipal council of a free lot to the first bride and groom. A man named Robbins immediately proposed to a woman popularly known as English Nell. One old timer recalled that "no questions were asked whether it was a love match but most folks were satisfied it was principally to get the city lot." The nuptials were celebrated at the city hall and then the entire congregation, singing "One More River to Cross," followed the newly-weds across the Assiniboine, where the city fathers delivered up to them the certificate and title.

Children and teenagers were caught up in the speculative fever. "Little girls gamble in lots for doll-houses," the astonished representative of *The Times* of London reported, "and when two youthful partners begin whispering earnestly in the intervals of a dance, the chances are that their theme is not love, but land." In Selkirk, in February, an old resident, Major Bowles, was so bucked up by a local real estate boom touched off by rumours of additional railroad facilities that he was inspired to christen his infant son "Selkirk Boom Bowles" in honour of the event.

Everybody from the lowest tradesman to the leading citizens of the province was involved in land speculation. General Rosser was not the only highly placed official who used inside information to turn a profit. The chief commissioner of the Hudson's Bay Company, James A. Grahame, and his land commissioner, Charles Brydges, together with the company solicitor, all of whom had inside knowledge, bought fifty-six of their company's lots at Fort Garry for $280,000 and within eleven days sold eleven of them for $275,000. The company's surveyors speculated in land as did ordinary clerks, all of them privy to information regarding Hudson's Bay property that had not yet been advertised to the public. The inspector of Indian agencies, Lawrence Herchmer (a future commissioner of the NWMP), Alexander Galt's son Elliott, Macdonald's old law partner Alexander Campbell, the Senate leader, and Edgar Dewdney, the Lieutenant-Governor of the North West Territories, were all involved in buying and speculating in lands from the Hudson's Bay Company reserve; all undoubtedly had inside information from the company's officials.

So all-pervasive was the talk about real estate that it did not occur to the average citizen that there could be any other topic. In January, a stranger seeking a church service inquired of "a respectable elderly gentleman" where the town hall might be, since it did double service as the Presbyterian meeting place. The Winnipegger jumped to the obvious conclusion that the stranger wanted to buy the property and informed him that it had already been sold at eight hundred dollars a front foot. He "was unable to realize the possibility of any one coming to Winnipeg for any other purpose than to learn how real estate was going."

Certainly, the dividing line between God and Mammon was blurred that hectic winter. Early in February, the trustees of Knox Presbyterian Church succumbed to the craze. The church occupied a valuable corner lot at the junction of Fort and Portage; it had cost twenty-two thousand dollars to build; the land had been secured for a few hundred. The trustees announced that the building would be auctioned off on February 18, 1882, to the highest bidder. Not surprisingly, the crowd that attended in the basement formed the largest congregation the church had ever known. An eyewitness described the scene:

"At the hour announced for opening the sale the basement was filled to its utmost capacity with what undoubtedly constituted the wealthiest, as well as the most intelligent, audience that ever gathered in any similar building in Canada. The auctioneer occupied the platform from which thoroughly orthodox Calvinistic doctrines had been so frequently and acceptably preached. The trustees occupied seats behind him. The crowded audience was decidedly given to the worship of the 'God of Mammon.' Not a hat removed. The puffing cigars held in several hundred mouths soon rendered the atmosphere of the sacred edifice disagreeable in the extreme...."

The trustees had reckoned on realizing between seventy-five and a hundred thousand dollars from the sale. But the first bid was $110,000 and his was rapidly increased until the property was knocked down for $126,-000 to a syndicate headed by two men from Chatham, Ontario. (The minister was immediately voted a bonus of two thousand dollars by his exultant parishioners.) A man in the audience instantly offered to lease the building as it stood, without any alteration, for five years for an annual rental of $17,500 and taxes. The syndicate turned the offer down and resold the church, realizing a cash profit of fifty thousand dollars. The first tenants included the Bank of Montreal and the Canadian Pacific Railway.

The Anglicans were not far behind the Calvinists. (The Methodists were already renting out their Wesley Hall as a theatre, of all things, on week nights.) On February 26, the congregation of Holy Trinity learned from their rector that a meeting was being planned "for the purpose of considering whether it was advisable to sell the church." That was too much for one aggrieved parishioner. "To what are we tending?" he cried, and then he quoted St. Paul's familiar dictum about the love of money being the root of all evil – an admonition which for all that winter had been ignored by Christian and heathen alike. Few paid him any attention.

2

Fool's paradise "If there ever was a fool's paradise," wrote George Ham, "it sure was located in Winnipeg. Men made fortunes – mostly on paper – and life was one continuous joy-ride."

The joy-ride lasted from June, 1881, until mid-April, 1882. For all of those eleven months, the business section of the city resembled nothing so much as a giant carnival, which seemed to run day and night. Almost every visitor remarked on the immense crowds jostling each other on the streets, on the general air of wealth, on the feeling of hustle and energy, and on the smell of money. J. C. McLagan, in a contemporary essay, wrote that all was "bustle and excitement." He talked of cabmen and bus drivers "plying their vocation with lusty lungs," of immense piles of baggage blocking every available space, of conveyances of all descriptions clogging the winding streets, "magnificent turnouts with coachmen and footmen fully equipped," ox sleds laden with lumber and produce, dog trains of great length yapping their way through the throngs, farmers, newly rich, driving spanking teams. "Men, old and young, hurry along with anxious looks – eagerly intent on business – and, as a rule, a roll of plans under the arm or a notebook in the hand. . . ."

Two-thirds of those on the streets were men. "I doubt if to-day any other city on the continent, according to its population, can boast of so many wealthy, young and middle-aged men," one eyewitness wrote in March. "In physique and general appearance no place can produce their equal. This is the general theme of conversation indulged in by all newcomers, who stand in utter amazement admiring the busy throng as they pass by. Eagerness and determination are depicted on every countenance." It was a cosmopolitan crowd. McLagan noted that the "vast congregation" in the churches on Sunday, which were as crowded as the hotels, was composed of "the very bone and sinew of other lands."

Samuel Benfield Steele, one of the original detachment of North West

58

Mounted Police that went west in 1874, saw Winnipeg in its salad days and recalled it in his memoirs. "People were ready to buy anything," he remembered. "The hotels did a roaring trade and the bars made profits of hundreds of dollars a day. . . . In the forenoon the speculators were at their writing tables going through their correspondence; the city was quiet, though crowded with men. At noon there was the usual hearty luncheon; at 3 p.m. the fun began, and was kept up until a late hour. Those who had made money were ready to re-invest it, and the real estate offices were crowded with men ready to buy or sell lots."

The most unlikely people became real estate entrepreneurs. The Winnipeg dailies were full of stories of long-time employees being presented with gold watches or silver tea services because they were leaving their jobs in the post office, the Hudson's Bay Company, the government service, or even the press itself to go into the land business.

The "king of the land," in the Winnipeg *Sun*'s phrase, was 36-year-old Arthur Wellington Ross, M.P., the agent who had been first on the scene at the founding of Brandon. A small, thin man with a dark spade beard, Ross was reputed to be worth half a million dollars at the height of the boom, owning for a period almost all of the Fort Rouge subdivision where he was constructing one of the most palatial residences in the West. Ross was an opportunist. He had begun life as a school teacher and was later a school inspector in Ontario but had gone back to school himself to study law. After he moved to Winnipeg he became a solicitor for the Mackenzie administration, but in 1882 he switched his allegiance to the party in power and ran successfully as a Conservative, first for the Manitoba legislature and then, in 1882, for the federal seat of Lisgar. He was a man who clearly made it a practice to be in with the right people. He also had a shrewd eye for land. As early as 1878 he was buying lots in St. Boniface for three hundred dollars an acre; within three years their value had increased eightfold. He always seemed to know where opportunity lay; wherever the CPR went, there was Arthur Wellington Ross, quietly moving ahead of it, buying up property, always unobtrusively. He was, the *Sun* declared, known for his tact. He was also known for his Calvinist principles: "While others played, he worked. While others were enjoying themselves in social festivities, he was thinking and working and he has only himself to thank for his present success."

Ross's real estate advertisements overshadowed the slender columns of news on the front pages of the Winnipeg papers from the very first day of the boom, when his firm put the CPR's original Brandon subdivision on the market. Shortly thereafter two other names became household words in

Manitoba – those of the two colourful real estate auctioneers, Jim Coolican and Joseph Wolf. Wolf, "portly and indefatigable," sold half a million dollars worth of real estate in the first six months of the land fever. He was known as the Golden Auctioneer because he operated from the Golden Hotel and Real Estate Exchange. When the CPR decided to place a second Brandon section on the market in February, it was Wolf who was chosen to handle the bidding. The crowds were so huge that no auction room in the city was able to accommodate them and so the city hall itself was transformed into a real estate office. Wolf worked for three nights in a row and sold $133,000 worth of North Brandon lots. His personal fortune was estimated at two hundred thousand dollars, but his exertions were so great that he suffered a collapse in the late spring and was ordered east by his doctor for a five-week rest.

Coolican, "the Real Estate King," was perhaps the most ebullient and resourceful real estate man in Winnipeg, a rotund and florid Irishman with a huge black moustache, his plump fingers and silk tie glittering with "real diamonds," in the phrase of the day. (The *Sun* invariably referred to him as "the jewelry king.") At work he wore a snappy black velvet jacket; on the streets he sported the status symbol of the city – a five-thousand-dollar sealskin coat with matching cap. He, too, was building what was described as a "palatial residence" on the Assiniboine to which he was conveyed in a magnificent carriage known as an English state coach, the first of its kind ever brought into the North West.

Coolican's advertisements for the paper towns he auctioned off – often a half or a full page in size – were masterpieces of hyperbole, studded with exclamation marks and superlatives rendered in heavy black type. In a single fortnight in February he spent four thousand dollars on newspaper advertising. It was worth it; in the same period he auctioned off almost a million dollars worth of property. He did his business at the very hub of the city, in the Exchange at the corner of Portage and Main which he was forever enlarging to handle the crowds, "a transformation more wonderful than anything experienced in the Arabian nights." The Exchange had begun as a hardware store, with a frontage of sixty feet. Coolican, who paid a hundred thousand dollars for it, turned it into a combined auction room, hotel, restaurant, and billiard parlour.

He was an expansive and popular figure about town. One night when lots were selling particularly well, he bought out the entire stock of a passing apple vendor and scattered the fruit "promiscuously amongst the audience." The next night he gave away seven hundred cigars to his customers. This was in mid-February, when Coolican had placed the entire "city" of Cartwright on the market. "Cartwright Leads Them All," his ads screamed. "Unquestionably the Best Situated Rising Town in the Province." Coolican's silver tongue moved Cartwright lots at the rate of twenty thousand dollars a night. The town itself, as the investors discovered, consisted of a single building, a general store that also did duty as a post office. Everything else – the advertised shops, mills, schools, and churches – were, as one investor ruefully put it, "the merest castles in the air."

For every two hundred permanent residents in Winnipeg that winter there was a liquor store or a saloon. Champagne replaced whiskey as the class beverage. On the same day that Coolican auctioned off the Cartwright lots an entire carload of champagne arrived in town in specially heated cars. "It was nothing unusual to see a lucky speculator throwing away $100 a week, if not oftener, on champagne suppers," one reporter recalled after the boom subsided. So great was the run on champagne that on one occasion the city's entire supply gave out and a fashionable wedding had to be celebrated without it – a disaster grave enough to be reported as news. One man actually bathed in champagne. He was Captain Vivian, a monocled English aristocrat who had arrived in the summer of 1881 with a thousand pounds in his pocket. Vivian sank the entire sum into a quarter section homestead in the Brandon district, which he proceeded to sell at inflated prices. By February he was said to be worth four hundred thousand dollars. Unable to drink up all the champagne he had purchased, he filled a bathtub with it and invited his friends to watch him splash about. The affair cost him seven hundred and fifty dollars.

The scene is no more unreal than Winnipeg itself was that winter and spring. It seemed as if all belief had been temporarily suspended, all rational conjecture swept aside. A young lawyer from Hamilton named William White who moved through the town early in 1882 wrote that money meant nothing: "Everything was 'jake' to use a Western expression denoting perfect satisfaction with life generally."

Coolican and Ross were not the only *nouveaux riches* who indulged themselves with mansions and carriages. One easterner wrote home that "women, who a few years ago were cooking and washing in a dirty little back kitchen, now ride about in carriages and pairs, with eccentric looking individuals for coachmen sitting in the back seat driving, the mistress looking as if the world were barely extensive enough for her to spread herself in." But it was not easy to secure such servants. *The Times* of London reported that "you find that your hackney coachman is a landowner, and cease to feel surprised at this when he declines to drive you five miles for less than $4 or to drive you at all at any but his own pace."

61

It was a winter of conspicuous extravagance. Diamonds became baubles on scores of fingers; Coolican's sealskin coat was widely copied. "Twenty gold pieces were just nothing." Next to the advertisements for lots were others for crystal ware, mantle ornaments, music boxes, choice gas fixtures, fine Etruscan jewellery, India and China tea, Weber pianos, cornice poles, and "beautiful dado hand painted shades." The Palace Hotel advertised quail on toast, and no luncheon could be considered complete without the customary dozen oysters on the half-shell. Woltz, "the princely Toronto jeweler," set up shop in March. "Even if you buy nothing," the *Sun* told its readers, "the rich splendor of his wares will feast you with the artistic and educate you in the beautiful." Woltz was identified as a member of "one of the most extensive and most trusted firms in Toronto . . . [who] offers nothing snide. From the tiny house-fly worked on a locket up to a watch worth hundreds, his wares are the choicest and the best."

Woltz pressed a gold watch as a gift upon the reporter who wrote that embroidered prose. It tells something about the times, and about the state of the press, that he not only accepted it with alacrity but also boasted about his good fortune in print. In Winnipeg that year, the accumulation of sudden and unexpected wealth was looked upon with favour and greeted with applause. Speculators were heroes, profiteers were the new nobility. Businessmen, normally reticent, boasted openly about their killings and gave interviews to newspapers detailing their worth. The *Sun*, revealing some of the largest of the new fortunes, reported that the mayor himself led the list with an accumulation estimated at three hundred thousand dollars. Cabinet ministers, back-benchers in both parties, and the Queen's representative were all speculating in real estate in the most open manner possible.

"Yesterday," the *Globe* reported on February 23, "the Hon. M. Cauchon, Lieut-Gov. of Manitoba, who is at present in Ottawa, received a telegram from his agent at Winnipeg in effect that he had sold 470 acres of his land at St. Boniface, opposite Pt. Douglas, for the handsome sum of $283,000. This is but one of a number of good speculations made by Mr. Cauchon, and he is still the holder of many other parcels of land which are daily increasing in value. It is said that he has cleared a million dollars so far out of his knowledge of Northwest speculations."

Clearly, it was a mark of considerable status to have made a fast dollar. M. C. Cameron, one of the powers in the Liberal Party, made a seventy-five-thousand-dollar killing in Winnipeg real estate and cheerfully gave the details to the newspapers. The property was quickly resold for one hundred thousand, but Cameron announced that he was perfectly satisfied with the lower figure, "having got the price he asked." The point was implicit: no one had put anything over on M. C. Cameron. Shrewdness was more highly prized than virtue during the boom.

The *Globe*'s man in Winnipeg, himself caught up in the land craze, ventured to admit that "the moral aspect of this real estate fever is a cause for considerable anxiety, more especially in the Eastern Provinces." He hastened to reassure his Ontario readers that nothing could be further from the truth: "No doubt to many the whole movement appears to be evil in the extreme. . . . To us, however, who are living on the ground . . . the matter appears in a different light. The transactions are largely for speculative purposes, it is true, but we claim that there is a perfectly solid basis on which it rests. . . . There is no reckless enthusiasm in Winnipeg. Every man studies the matter calmly and carefully, and if he has any spare funds puts it into what he knows is a sure investment. . . . I would be very sorry to countenance gambling in any way, but I look on speculation here, when legitimately conducted, as perfectly safe and proper. If one can grasp the magnitude of this North-West and believe in its rapid development he can invest his money in city or farm property without any anxiety or chidings of conscience."

Everybody in Winnipeg, it seemed, was affluent – or believed himself to be. Visitors remarked on the absence of beggars in the streets and the total lack of copper coins. J. C. McLagan remarked on "the almost entire absence of pauperism, or anything approaching to squalor." The Winnipeg city council, in 1881, had not found it necessary to distribute so much as one hundred and fifty dollars for charity.

The signs of prosperity were everywhere. By March, one hundred and eighty of Alexander Graham Bell's newly developed telephones were in operation. Gas lighting, hailed the year before, was already becoming obsolete. On June 13, three sample electric lights were installed on the grounds of the CPR station at the head of Main Street, which was "illuminated as if by sunlight. . . . Books and newspapers could be read with ease." In April, a syndicate which included Arthur Wellington Ross, Mayor Alexander Logan, and A. G. Bannantyne, a former Liberal Member of Parliament – all heavy land speculators – was formed to sell shares in a floating bath complex to be moored on the river at the foot of Post Office Street.

"It almost seems too good to be true that anyone in this prosperous dollar-worshipping city should have had the leisure even to entertain the idea," one citizen wrote wryly to the *Times*. ". . . who will not gladly lend a helping hand to procure this public boon, especially where the glitter of the eternal dollar need not be lost sight for a moment even when we plunge beneath the waters, but when we may in possession of shares not only wash and be clean, but wash and be richer. Many waters cannot quench love, and it appears that they cannot avail to drown the dollar. Oh, Red River, who would have thought to have found both health and wealth in thy waters."

Long before the winter snows swelled those waters to flood heights, thousands of adventurers were preparing to set out from the cities and towns of eastern Canada for "the New Eldorado," as the Winnipeg *Times* dubbed the North West. In March, the Brantford *Telegram* reported that every day the "Manitoba fever" was strengthening, "and scores of young and old are only waiting for spring to open to start for the land overflowing with milk and honey." The same week, the Ottawa *Free Press* wrote that "the 10 p.m. train of the C.P.R. was crowded last evening with victims of Manitoba fever, and it is expected that the evening trains for some time will have full fares for Manitoba." The irreverent *Sun* insisted that Phineas T. Barnum, then at the peak of his fame, was advertising in Ontario for a man who was *not* going to Manitoba to travel with his show as a companion curiosity to the Most Beautiful Woman in the World. The paper solemnly added that the showman had not been able to find such an oddity.

By early April, every train from St. Paul was bringing in hundreds of immigrants from eastern Canada and from every part of the world. One traveller taking an immigrant train from Toronto to Winnipeg described the scene: the men, women, and children crowding aboard at every stop with their kits and baggage and all their household goods, "their faces beaming with satisfaction at being at last on the way to Manitoba." During the journey, "nothing was talked of but Manitoba and the North-West...."

Everybody who was anybody, it seemed, was heading for Winnipeg and beyond – from Peter Redpath, "the sugar king," to Captain Boycott, the Irishman whose name had gone into the language. Some of them pushed on to the very shadow of the Rockies. Mr. Brassey, "the celebrated contractor of London" (his firm had built the Grand Trunk), was one; he bought three hundred square miles of ranchland in the Bow River valley as soon as the Kicking Horse Pass route was chosen. Senator Matthew Henry Cochrane of Quebec was another; he acquired one hundred square miles near by. "It is stated that several Englishmen intend to follow these illustrious examples," the Manitoba *Free Press* reported. It went on to

64

complain that "at this rate Canada will soon be landless and our magnificent heritage a cattle ranch."

The influx of newcomers created an unprecedented demand for space to which the overcrowded community was unequal. Since the previous May when, in the words of the *Free Press*, "a shake-down is a luxury that is not always obtainable," Winnipeg's hotels had been scandalously overtaxed. By the spring of 1882 they were so crowded that every available space was used for sleeping accommodation, including parlours, corridors, and lobbies. Beecham Trotter, who lived in Winnipeg during the boom, had trouble getting so much as a corner in a public room. Finally he put up at a "miserable hotel" on Main Street, where he paid two dollars to spend a night in a chair. Even a chair was a rarity that winter and spring, and the same was true in the outlying towns. Rev. James Boydell, who arrived in Brandon in January to take up his mission, felt himself lucky to get a room in a boarding house on Rosser Avenue; by nightfall, men and women were lying in their furs in the passageways. A fellow clergyman and his wife were turned away in thirty below zero weather but returned, unable to find any space in town. The proprietor took pity on them and found them each a space on the crowded floor.

One mathematically inclined newcomer to Winnipeg figured out that in the house where he was boarding each occupant had exactly twenty-eight square feet of floor space for his own use, compared to an average of between two hundred and fifty and three hundred square feet in Ontario. Meal times, by all accounts, were savage: ". . . long ere the dining room doors are thrown open, a crowd gathers, eager to charge the tables and anxious to satisfy the cravings of the inner man. Frequently weak men are seriously injured in these jams. The tables have to be cleared and re-set several times ere the guests are all dined." At one of the leading hotels the crush was so great that one diner suffered a broken arm.

Several "mammoth hostelries" were being planned for the city, including one to be built by a syndicate headed by the owner of Toronto's famous Queen's. It would be "the most complete hotel building in the West outside of Chicago," but this was cold comfort to those who tumbled off the cramped trains into the snow without a hope of accommodation. During one fearful blizzard in early March, when the wind reached hurricane force and it was impossible to see half a dozen yards in any direction, several immigrant parties had to be lodged temporarily in the CPR's passenger depot. During that month the National Manufacturing Company of Ottawa rushed fifteen hundred heavy cotton tents to Winnipeg. On the outskirts of town giant tent boarding houses began to rise in rows. These gargantuan marquees were large enough to accommodate within their folds a cluster of smaller tents, each capable of sleeping eight men. By May, the ever-alert Arthur Wellington Ross was importing portable houses from an eastern manufacturer. Space was at such a premium that he was able to rent them all before they arrived.

That social phenomenon, the Winnipeg boarding house, had its birth that year. It was unique – "a style to be found nowhere else in the Dominion," in the words of a man who endured one. Architecturally it was a hybrid – half tent, half ramshackle frame. Entirely unpartitioned, it served as a combined dormitory, dining room, scullery, and smoker.

"You open the door and immediately there is a rush of tobacco smoke and steam mingled with indescribable results which makes you want to get outside and get a gulp of fresh air. You go to the counter and get tickets from the man behind the desk for supper, bed and breakfast. There are no women about and no children. Nor are there any elderly people – they are all young men. You have no time to study them for through the mist of smoke in the great room there breaks the jangling call of a bell and a terrible panic seizes the crowd. It is not an alarm or fire nor is there any danger of the building caving in, neither is it a fight nor a murder – it is only supper."

Supper consisted of a plate of odorous hash, flanked by a mug of tea and a slab of black bread, served up by a number of "ghastly, greasy and bearded waiters with their arms bare to their elbows and their shirt bosoms open displaying considerably hairy breast." The meal was devoured in total silence, the only sound being "a prodigious noise of fast-moving jaws, knives, forks and spoons."

The boarders themselves were a motley lot: "Men who were at one time high up in society, depraved lawyers, and decayed clergymen brought down by misconduct and debauchery, but still bearing about them an air of refinement . . . carpenters smelling strongly of shavings, mill hands smelling of sawdust and oil, teamsters smelling of horse, plasterers fragrant with lime, roofers odorous with tar, railway laborers smelling of whiskey, in short all sorts and conditions of men."

At night, when the tables were cleared and the occasional drunk subdued with a club, a man at the end of the building picked up a ladder, planted it against the wall, and told the inmates to clamber into their bunks among the grey horse-blankets that served as bedding.

For such accommodation, new arrivals were happy to pay double the rates at better-appointed eastern hotels. "The cost of living is something incredible," the *Globe* informed its readers. "Housekeeping here must be done with the most rigid economy or it is ruinous." Wages were the highest in the land. Day labourers got as much as three dollars a day, triple the Ontario rate. Carpenters were paid up to four dollars a day, plasterers seven dollars, masons eight dollars. As one immigrant wrote back home, however, since there was such a shortage of accommodation "mechanics are spending what they earn in trying to live." A single cramped room cost as much as twenty-five dollars a month. (The Toronto price was five dollars.) Frozen potatoes were two dollars a bushel, eggs forty-five cents a dozen, beefsteak thirty-five cents a pound, and milk – sold in the winter in frozen blocks – ten cents a quart.

Still the immigrants poured in. Often their enthusiasm was dampened when they reached the city. One carpenter, arriving in March, found he could get no work because his employer had no shop. Moreover, the station platform was covered with tool boxes and he realized that his fellow artisans, arriving by the score, would make his services a drug on the market. In St. Paul that same week, an unnamed Canadian uttered one of the few murmurs of gloom voiced about the prospects in Manitoba. "When the tumble comes in Winnipeg it's going to be something awful," he said. But among the swirling crowds in the auction rooms of Main Street, bidding higher and higher for lots in towns and "cities" like Emerson, Shoal Lake, West Lynne, and Minnedosa, there was still no hint of the reckoning to come.

3

The Winnipeg land boom can be divided into two parts. The boom of 1881 was followed by a lull in late January and February before the spring boom of 1882 began. The weather in mid-February was as fickle as the market, being warm and sunny one day, chill and gusty the next. On February 16, the city fell under the lash of one of the worst storms it had yet known, a truly blinding blizzard, which cut through the thickest clothing and brought all movement to a stop. Speculators who had come into town from outlying points found themselves imprisoned by the cold. Even the CPR trains were unable to travel west to Portage la Prairie and Brandon; although the track had been built high and ditched carefully to prevent just such a calamity, the roadbed was effectively blocked by a wall of packed snow.

February, it was said, would test the stability of the boom. At first, the storm seemed to act as a depressant; the demand for city property ebbed.

"Towns cannot live of themselves"

67

Undismayed, the entrepreneurs began to boost other Manitoba "cities" to the point where those who held property on Winnipeg's outskirts tried to sell out in order to take advantage of more attractive bargains. In most cases they found they could not sell. The boom had moved on to Mountain City, Selkirk, and a score of unfamiliar communities where, it was whispered, new railroads would soon be built.

As a result, extraordinary efforts had to be made to sell outlying lots in the immediate Winnipeg area. Curiously, the prices of these lots did not go down; rather they rose. Properties many miles from the centre of town, which could have been purchased the previous fall for fifty dollars an acre, carried, in late February, price tags ranging from two hundred and fifty to one thousand dollars.

The asking prices were so high, in fact, that it was doubtful whether any purchaser would be able to make more than the downpayment. This, apparently, did not matter. Real estate speculation in Winnipeg that spring resembled very much the dime chain-letter crazes and the pyramid clubs of a later era. Everybody reasoned that the real profits would be made by those who moved in early and got out swiftly; every man expected that somebody would eventually be left holding the bag; but no one was so pessimistic as to believe that he would be caught with worthless property.

The sellers had so little confidence that the prices would be maintained that they tried to get the largest possible downpayment and the shortest terms. The new purchasers, in turn, arranged at once with a broker to have their interest transferred to a syndicate at a handsome advance on first purchase consideration. The syndicates, in their turn, hired groups of smart young men to extoll the virtues of the property as "the best thing on the market."

Because it was difficult to move properties that could not be shown on the latest map of Winnipeg and its environs, the land sharks resorted to subterfuge. Maps were cut and pasted so that outer properties seemed to be much closer to town than they really were. In late February, lots 25 by 110 feet in size more than three miles southwest of the Assiniboine, far out on the bald prairie, were selling for fifty dollars each. It was several decades before the city extended that far.

On Main Street, Winnipeg's lung, where Red River carts in staggered line had once squeaked through the mud twelve abreast (thus ensuring that it would become the widest street in Canada), the prices continued to climb. At the corner of Main and Thistle, a lot with a frontage of eighteen feet on which the Cable Hotel was situated sold for thirty-five thousand dollars or $1,944 a front foot. But the real action was taking place in the smaller communities of Manitoba.

The safest investments were to be found at Brandon and Portage la Prairie, for these were established centres on the main line of the CPR. The boom in Brandon had not abated since the summer of 1881. "Nobody who saw Brandon in its infancy ever forgot the spectacle," Beecham Trotter wrote. Trotter nostalgically recalled a variety of sights and sounds: the hillside littered with tents, the symphony of scraping violins playing "Home, Sweet Home" and "The Girl I Left Behind Me," the cries of the auctioneers: "All wool from Paisley; and who the hell would go naked?" Brandon lots were still rising in price. Early in January a syndicate which included Alexander Morris, a prominent Conservative and a former lieutenant-governor of Manitoba, had been formed especially for the purpose of buying the remainder of the townsite from the CPR; the price was a quarter of a million dollars. (The railway promised, in return, to locate its workshops in Brandon.) The demand for these lots when they went on the market in Winnipeg was acute enough to force the Queen's Real Estate Exchange to close its doors after seven in the evening to all save those who wanted to deal in Brandon property. So all-embracing was the real estate fever in Brandon that when the town was laid out no provision was made for a cemetery. The dead had to be brought to Winnipeg for burial.

Portage la Prairie, advertised in March as the "Greatest Bargain of this Spring Boom!" was in a perfect frenzy of speculation. "A craze seemed to have come over the mass of the people," an early chronicler recounted. "Legitimate business in many cases was thrown aside, and buying and selling lots became the one aim and object of life. . . . Carpenters, painters, tailors, and tradesmen of all kinds threw their tools aside to open real estate offices, loaf around the hotels, drink whiskey and smoke cigars. Boys with down on their lips not as long as their teeth would talk glibly of lots fronting here and there, worth from $1,000 to $1,500 per lot."

The Portage, at that time, had a population well below four thousand. Of the 148 business institutions, forty-one were real estate offices, operated by every kind of human specimen from former cowboys to ex-priests; three more were banks loaning money to speculators, five others were loan and investment companies backed by eastern capital, and another nine were jobbing houses acting as agents for private capitalists.

"Men who were never worth a dollar in their lives before, nor never have been since, would unite together, and, on the strength of some lots, on which they had made a small deposit, endorse each other's paper, and draw from the banks sums which they had never seen before, only in visions of the night."

69

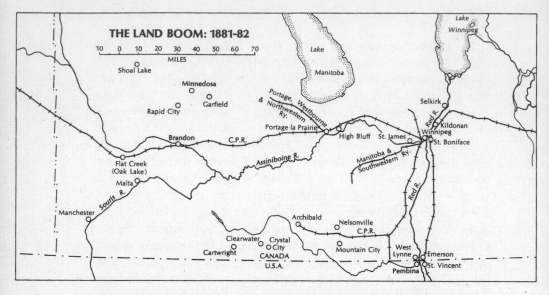

THE LAND BOOM: 1881-82

The Portage boom was at least understandable, since the town was a prominent station on the main line of the railway. The Rapid City boom was more mysterious. It may have been, as some suggested, that the very name of the community caught the imagination of the speculators. Certainly it remained a favourite for months, at times running a close race with Winnipeg itself. It was surely one of the most remarkable paper communities in the province: although its population was well under four hundred, the city was laid out with intersecting streets for eight square miles.

The fever persisted in the face of the obvious fact that the CPR had passed Rapid City by. In 1879, when it had been established by a private syndicate, Sandford Fleming's survey gave every indication that the CPR would pass that way. The decision to move the line south through Brandon ought to have destroyed its hopes but, such was the optimism of those times, the belief persisted that Rapid City would shortly become a great railway centre. "The flow of immigration into and through this town is unprecedented in the history of the settlement of this country," one resident informed the Winnipeg *Times* in early April. The road between Brandon and Rapid City was lined with wagons loaded with speculators, settlers' merchandise and effects, and with horses, cattle and sheep. Every hotel and every stable in town was overcrowded. Vacant land was being snatched up so swiftly that two or three men would sometimes arrive at the land office within minutes of one another, each intent upon grabbing the same section.

As late as May 30, a Rapid City doctor reported that "Rapid Cityites are not at all despondent over the change of route of the CPR but con-

70

fidently expect having a railway connection with some place or other before twelve months – even if the people have to build the line themselves." Advertisements in the Winnipeg papers actually boasted that *six* railways would soon run through the community.

In that demented winter people no longer asked, What will the land produce, only, What will it sell for? "People seem to have forgotten," the Edmonton *Bulletin* wrote, "that towns cannot live of themselves." In Winnipeg scarcely a week passed that did not see a new community extolled in print. Towns that did not exist, such as Garfield, were given non-existent suburbs such as North Garfield. "It stands," Coolican's huge advertisement disclosed, "Upon An Eminence, From Which The Land Slopes Gradualy [*sic*] Down To Garfield Itself." One series of lots purporting to be in the West Lynn subdivision (on the banks of the Red River just opposite Emerson near the border) sold for ten thousand dollars. Actually the property was two miles away, far out on the empty prairie.

For the moment at least the railway was king; it seemed to bring the Midas touch to the smallest shack-towns. Like a golden highway, the CPR had brought prosperity to Manitoba beyond the wildest dreams of the most optimistic pioneers. The very whisper of a railway – *any* railway, real or imagined – drove people to greater and greater financial excesses. Local councils offered fat bonuses for CPR branch lines to their communities; rumours of newly formed railway ventures were greeted with the greatest enthusiasm and a resultant rise in real estate prices. As George Grant, the principal of Queen's, commented: "Gray-haired men seemed to lose not only their old-fashioned honesty, but their senses. They talked as if half a million or a million people could be poured into a country by one road in a year or five or six months, and a wilderness of stubborn glebe turned into the garden of the Lord by affixing names to townsites and locating railway stations." The day would come when the people of Manitoba, in their grief and disappointment, would turn against the railway; but in the early months of 1882, the CPR could do no wrong.

Emerson, the customs point on the Pembina Branch of the CPR, confidently expected that it would be *the* great railway centre of the North West, the largest metropolis in western Canada, easily outdistancing Winnipeg, since it had been for some time the only point of entry into Manitoba. It had two newspapers and a population of fourteen hundred; it appeared to be the logical gateway to the rich farm lands of southwestern Manitoba, "the great country whose fame is now the theme of almost every tongue," as one eastern visitor described it. "Nothing is to be heard but 'boom,' 'boom,' 'boom,' in every hamlet you pass; 'boom' in every person's mouth. In fact the excitement is fully as great as if a mountain of gold had been discovered near Toronto."

That was in the first week of January, 1882. Three weeks later it was Selkirk's turn. "The 'boom' so long looked for by the people of Selkirk at last struck that pretty little town early this week," a correspondent recorded on the twenty-third. The excitement stemmed from a new by-law guaranteeing a bonus of seventy-five thousand dollars to the CPR to construct a branch line into the community. In addition, a bridge was planned across the river so that the rails would connect the town directly with Portage la Prairie and the trunk route west. The news instantly raised real estate prices in Selkirk and reporters on the scene could hardly contain themselves: "In the carrying out of this the owners of lots in Selkirk see a great city rising to rival, and possibly eclipse, Winnipeg."

In the same week, lots in "Manitoba City" began to boom with the news that the terminus of the Pembina Mountain branch line of the CPR had been settled upon. A syndicate had already purchased the townsite and was busily advertising lots in the new and still unpopulated community, while decrying the neighbouring settlement of Archibald, three miles away, which now found itself bypassed and which would shortly become a ghost town.

Minnedosa, "the railway centre of the North West," had also been bypassed but it was booming anyway. In mid-February it experienced a new flurry of excitement on the strength of a report that it would be the seat of a judicial district. "Thank fortune, the 'boom' has also struck Minnedosa!" the *Times*'s resident correspondent burbled. "Happy name! High flown and sweet sounding. A place with such a name and such a vicinage, and, shall I say it? such people, could not but boom. Again, I say, the boom has struck Minnedosa...."

Though Manitoba's population, in 1882, was only sixty-six thousand, a casual newspaper reader in a foreign country, perusing the advertisements, might have believed it to be the crossroads of the continent, teaming with people and jammed with great cities. There was Crystal City, "the featured great city of Manitoba"; Mountain City, "the embryo city"; Dobbyn City, "the future great manufacturing city of the Souris district"; St. Vincent, "one of the leading cities of the Great North West . . . booming beyond imagination"; Manchester, "the future great manufacturing town of the North West"; Clearwater, "the Brandon of Southwestern Manitoba"; Nelsonville, "the largest town in Southwestern Manitoba"; Kildonan, "the Yorkville of Winnipeg"; Rapid City, "the Minneapolis of the North West"; Malta, "situated in the garden of the North

West"; Cartwright, "unquestionably the best situated and rising town in the province"; Pembina Crossing, "the most prosperous town in Southwestern Manitoba"; and High Bluff, "the best chance of the season."

As the frenzy continued, unabated, the advertisements became larger and shriller, the methods used to peddle property wilder and more unscrupulous, and the paper communities more ephemeral. William White, in his brief stay in Winnipeg, recalled walking into one auction room and being attracted by the sale of lots in "Minnedosa the Beautiful." An immense map of the community covered an entire wall. "It had to be large in order that the river flowing through the town, called the Little Saskatchewan, should be properly displayed." Majestic steamers were shown sailing down the river or moored at handsome landing docks. White decided to visit Minnedosa the Beautiful and was glad that he had done so before speculating in lots there. The Little Saskatchewan was so little that in midsummer a man could jump across it. There were no steamers to be seen and the only landing docks were the ones painted on the map. The town itself was a hamlet.

The land sharks used patently transparent devices to victimize the newcomers. Two men from Barrie, Ontario, were persuaded to buy, sight unseen, for sixty thousand dollars, a piece of swamp five miles from Winnipeg. The sellers played upon their greed: As the easterners were mulling over the deal, a third man came up and, pretending to believe the transaction was closed, offered them eighty thousand dollars for the property. It did not occur to the two that the offer was bogus and that the new buyer was operating as a shill. They handed over the money cheerfully and ended up in possession of a piece of useless land.

Such tales filtering back east helped to drive a wedge between settled Canada and the new North West. "At this moment Winnipeg is filled with thousands of the vilest villains," the Bobcaygeon *Independent* declared in an editorial in late March, "and it is possible that never before on this continent was there assembled together so large a congregation of scoundrelism. Leadville may, perhaps, in its early days, have approached Winnipeg in the number and intensity of its rascality, but it never quite equalled that which now exists in Winnipeg. It is a saddening spectacle to observe the universality of this disgusting degradation. It is confined to no class. You read on the walls notices of pastors selling off to go to Manitoba, just as you hear of Tom, Dick and Harry starting off for the same purposes of fraud and swindling. . . . It is an outbreak of the worst passions of human nature. . . . The business of men's lives in Winnipeg . . . is the gratification of that vile lust of gold which completely overpowers the moral sense, extinguishes reason, annihilates the sense of responsibility, renders crime no longer repulsive, and unfits the miserable and wretched beings for any other companionship than that of themselves and the devil."

To this Victorian invective, the Winnipeg *Times* made a scoffing reply: "Listen to the sage of Bobcaygeon," it sneered, "– and laugh." One of its own editorial writers, C. R. Tuttle, had himself become a leading Winnipeg speculator.

The *Globe*, which carried a good deal of Manitoba real estate advertising, uttered several gingerly warnings ("Beware Of Paper Town Site Frauds!") while generally approving of the boom: "The man who does an honest business in the transfer of properties is rendering a service. . . . The evil arising from untruthful representations addressed to inordinate cupidity is one against which people cannot be too earnestly warned, but it is one which is unfortunately inseparable from the circumstances. Wherever there is room for fraud there will always be found defrauders in abundance. . . ."

The *Globe*'s man in Winnipeg described his own experience with land sharks. An old Ontario friend had approached him about "a big thing" in the wind: "There's a thousand for every dollar you put up." When the reporter showed his interest he was introduced to the organizer of a new syndicate, who pulled from his pocket a preliminary agreement in the form of a half-sheet of foolscap, "dirty as a stage document," purporting to be a legal instrument whereby the owner of a certain half section agreed to transfer his rights for $2,880. The *Globe* reporter wrote that "the extraordinary resources of the average curbstone organizer may be inferred from the fact that instead of purchasing . . . the broker in question proposed a Syndicate of no less than 90 shares at $32 each." The 320 acres were to be chopped up into 32,000 lots to be peddled in Ontario at $20 a lot. An attractive name had already been settled upon, surveys were to be undertaken immediately, and "brilliantly illuminated plans were to be constructed." Great store would be set on the news that a railway would run through the property, "but the other fact that the railway in question had been abandoned in favour of a shorter cut, through better country, was to be studiously concealed."

In spite of all this, the *Globe*'s man admitted that he had actually bought a share in the syndicate. But by this time it was early April; there was a feeling of let-down in Winnipeg; the share was clearly worthless. "Our eyes have been open," he wrote, "and we have seen silly fish ready to jump at every fly, and the fish have been tempted and landed on

74

the banks. We now perceive that the pool is nearly empty, and we have returned to legitimate business."

4

The bubble bursts

Two events, one man-made and the other natural, following hard upon each other in mid-April, killed the great North West boom. The first was the sale of Edmonton lots beginning April 12, which soured the most optimistic speculators. The second was the three-week rampage of the Red River which began a week later, causing the most serious flood in memory, drowning the railway line, and cutting off the city from the outside world.

Fort Edmonton lay on the very rim of the unknown. Perhaps for that reason it caught the fancy of the Winnipeg land buyers. As soon as rumours began to fly about an impending sale of lots almost a thousand miles to the North West, they began to hoard their funds for a new investment. The word was that the Hudson's Bay Company had surveyed the environs of the old trading post into town lots and was about to throw them onto the market. On April 12, the news was made public in gigantic advertisements by Arthur Wellington Ross. "EDMONTON! EDMONTON!" the ads screamed, "EDMONTON AT LAST!" The settlement – it contained scarcely five hundred souls – was referred to in the press as "the future Golden City of the Dominion" and was described in block letters as the country of "Gold, Coal, Timber, Minerals and Wheat . . . Bounded on the South by the grazing land of the Bow River District, on the North by the Peace River and on the West at a distance of seventy miles by an uninterrupted forest of timber."

The lots went on sale immediately and Ross's office was jammed with purchasers. The previous fall, lots in Edmonton had been sold for an average of twenty-five dollars; now three hundred went in a single night at prices ranging between two and four hundred. Yet Edmonton could scarcely be said to be booming. In the interval only five buildings had been constructed on the three thousand acres of its townsite. John A. McDougall, the Edmonton trader, who was in Winnipeg at the time, gazed in astonishment upon the huge painted maps of his town showing subdivisions on land he knew to be dense bush. McDougall put his knowledge to good use. He had taken an option on a group of lots for ten

75

thousand dollars, putting five hundred dollars down and promising to pay the remainder within a month. He turned them over in Winnipeg within hours for twenty thousand dollars, paid off his debt, and pocketed the rest.

McDougall was one of the very few who profited from the brief Edmonton land boom. A strange thing happened that week. On April 13, scores of speculators poured into Arthur Wellington Ross's office, waving marked cheques for thousands of dollars, intent on picking up Edmonton lots. The following day, almost all of them tried to sell the lots at a profit, but there were no buyers. The boom was collapsing, though nobody would yet admit it.

Coolican, the auctioneer, tried to resuscitate the good times. On April 14, the day of the Edmonton collapse, he engaged a private train for himself and a group of Winnipeg businessmen and steamed off to St. Paul to sell Manitoba lots. It was a gala excursion, a kind of last gasp by Winnipeg's leading speculators. Coolican's car, "Selkirk," was "laden with the good things of this life. McCaffrey of the Hub had such a selection as ought to please the most fastidious epicure." Dan Rogers, also of the Hub, was on hand with the wine. "If the eagle eye of the custom officer at St. Vincent can only be escaped the members of the party will have a jolly time," the *Times* predicted. Since Coolican was promising to turn St. Vincent into a great "International City," straddling the border and including within its limits all of Pembina, Emerson, and West Lynne, it can be assumed the customs officers were not too vigilant.

The mayor himself appeared at the station to wish the party Godspeed. He was supposed to go along to St. Paul but his time was fully occupied trying to establish a real estate bank in the city, "one not restricted in its dealings to purely commercial transactions, but which should entertain applications for discount on bona fide real estate paper or other good security" – a bank, in short, that would continue to underwrite the boom.

Coolican and his friends took St. Paul by storm. "There is a smack of enterprise, push and dash in the Winnipeg boomers who are now visiting St. Paul which commands admiration," a local editor wrote. It was strange to see such phrases applied by Yankees to Canadians; for years it had been the other way around.

"It is true that they are speculators," the St. Paul journalist admitted, "but as one of their speakers remarked Saturday night, it is speculation which opens the country and builds towns and cities. It is speculators who build the railroads out upon the prairies in advance of population in order

76

to bring their property into market and build up business."

The Winnipeg press covered the expedition with its own men on the scene. The Coolican party was reported to be having "a high old time." The boomers had left "an excellent impression, not only as businessmen but socially as well." In Sherman's Hall, St. Paul, Coolican sold one hundred thousand dollars worth of Canadian border lots.

There was only one problem: the boomers could not get back to Winnipeg. The Red River was on the rise. Bridges were being ripped away before the onslaught of mountains of water. Entire communities listed the previous week as attractive buys were half submerged. Many of the lots sold in St. Paul had turned to lakes, and the CPR line between Minnesota and Winnipeg was washed out.

It began with the mud – the terrible, tenacious, glutinous mud of Winnipeg, to which every traveller for a decade and more made spirited reference. The unseasonably hot sun of April had caused a sudden thaw, sending torrents coursing down the hills and turning the streets of the city into a quagmire. The crossroads and thoroughfares were afloat with what one Torontonian described as "a black, shining fluid that looks not unlike stove-pipe varnish." Everybody sought out metaphors to describe Winnipeg mud. To Sandford Fleming, the surveyor, it was exactly as if you were walking on treacle. To Alex Stavely Hill, a visiting British Member of Parliament, it was a mixture of putty and birdlime. To a former British Army trooper, John Donkin, it resembled cement. Donkin had served at Constantinople and thought he had seen the worst mud in the world until he came to Winnipeg. For "fixity of tenure" there was nothing to beat it. Another Englishman, a retired army officer, wrote that the mud was "so tenacious that it will take the hair off a horse's legs in attempting to brush it off." That was the special quality of the gumbo that clogged Winnipeg's streets that April. To step into it was like stepping into a pot of glue. When a horse became mired in it, twenty men on ropes were sometimes required to pull the beast free. The mud dried in a few hours and was of such a consistency that it did not convert to dust but packed solid as wax on footwear and clothing. It was said that you could enter a private home caked with Winnipeg mud without fear of leaving a trace on carpet or furniture.

The mud was only the prelude to greater disaster. As the mass of snow vanished with terrifying suddenness, the Red began to rise at a rate of two feet a day. For the so-called International City, the result was catastrophic. The bridge at Emerson was swept away on April 16. By April 19,

West Lynne had almost disappeared beneath the waves. Across the river, Emerson's citizens were forced to live for weeks on their second floors. The steamer *Cheyenne*, pushing a barge-load of lumber, steamed right up the main street and unloaded its cargo at the steps of the Presbyterian church.

The crest hit Winnipeg on April 19. The water had been rising steadily all night, and when a field of ice, acting as a dam, broke away it rose another three feet. Shortly after one o'clock that afternoon, the Broadway Bridge, nine hundred feet long, began to surge and sway until it plunged down the river on the breast of a six-mile current, its piers toppled by tumbling ice floes. Hundreds thronged the banks to watch the dazzling spectacle of a river out of control – a seething mass of ice, boiling, twisting and writhing, the bright sunshine glistening on the huge blocks "with all the prismatic hues of the diamond."

The bridge collapse seemed to confirm Sandford Fleming's original selection of Selkirk as the crossing point for the CPR. Fleming had always maintained that the past history of floods on the Red made Winnipeg a poor choice, but he had been overruled for political reasons. Now he was seen as a Cassandra.

By April 23, train service to and from St. Paul was suspended because of washouts along the line. Thousands were thwarted in their desire to reach the boom town. Two thousand people were stranded between St. Paul and the border. Another fifteen hundred immigrants were held that day in the Minnesota capital. The same afternoon five more coaches arrived in St. Paul, all packed with immigrants vainly trying to reach Winnipeg. Four more arrived at midnight; another fifteen were being loaded in New York with Europeans fresh off the Cunard steamer *Bavaria*.

Winnipeg was like a morgue. Mail failed to arrive. Freight was at a standstill. Some immigrants managed to reach the city by barge and boat, but since no food was carried, shortages began to drive the prices higher and higher. Bread went up to fifty cents a loaf – half a day's pay for a Toronto working man. Beef rose to fifty cents a pound. Building operations came to a standstill. Half-constructed homes, offices, boarding houses, and hotels stood silent; there were neither nails nor lumber available. Trade fell off because the merchants had no spring goods to sell. People were wary of placing orders for fear they would not be filled until late summer. Mechanics arriving by boat, expecting to work at high wages, found there was no work for them at any price. On May 4, the river crept to within eighteen inches of the Assiniboine Bridge. That same day, one of the two newspapers in Emerson, the *International*, was forced to suspend publication.

By the time the floods subsided, the boom was finished. The railway blockade lasted for three weeks and did irreparable harm to Winnipeg's business community. The gigantic advertisements vanished from the newspapers as swiftly as the snows. The *Free Press* was forced to reduce its size. The *Sun* on April 28 dropped the title of its lively column "The Big Boom" and ran such information as there was under the heading of "Real Estate Transactions." On some days such news did not occupy more than two paragraphs.

By this time the CPR had moved against the speculators by changing its regulations for the sale of prairie lands. The nominal price was raised from $1.25 to $5.00 an acre, a quarter of which had to be paid at the time of sale and the balance in five years without interest. But the rebate for land placed under cultivation was also raised to three-quarters of the original five dollars. Thus bona fide settlers who were prepared to work the land actually got it for $1.25 an acre. Those who bought land in the hope of a quick turnover paid four times as much.

Coolican, who finally managed to get back to Winnipeg by boat on April 28, took one last advertisement on the front pages headed: "COOLICAN'S RETURN! and the Boom Returns Also!" But the boom did not return. When Coolican tried to auction off lots in Prince Albert a month later, there were no takers. In vain real estate dealers announced: "No paper cities! No humbug! A new boom in a new quarter!" The public was not buying. Coolican was reduced to auctioning off carpets and tapestries.

Arthur Wellington Ross also tried again, offering lots at Port Moody, British Columbia, the terminus of the CPR. Ross, too, was at the end of his financial rope. When real estate values plunged, he lost most of his huge fortune. He was forced to give up his land holdings – he owned hundreds of acres in the northern and western portions of the city – for taxes. It is said that seven thousand dollars would have cleared the property, but once the boom was over, seven thousand became an impossible figure. Ross did not have it and his credit was exhausted.

Of those who speculated in land in Manitoba in 1881 and 1882, it was estimated that only about five per cent made any money at all. The lucky ones broke even. The less fortunate ended their days in destitution – like Harry Armstrong's Toronto friend, Helliwell, "who cleaned up sixty thousand dollars, put it in his pocket, went broke and walked the streets till he died," or a Brockville man named Sheppard, whose obituary appeared in the dying days of the boom: "The rumour current Sunday evening was that he had lost $30,000 in speculating and hanged himself in consequence."

As a result of the bubble's sudden collapse, Winnipeg and, to a lesser degree, Manitoba entered into a period of recession which had far-reaching effects. Confidence in the North West was badly shaken. The international financial world began to look askance at any venture in the new Canada; the CPR would feel the pinch especially. The breach between West and East widened; the depression left by the boom – psychological as well as financial – prepared the climate for the farm agitation that followed, with all its attendant bitterness. People who had once extolled the railway as a bearer of gifts now looked on it darkly as the source of their misfortunes.

The immediate effects were devastating. It was estimated that seventy-five per cent of the business institutions in the province wilted away. A good example was the meat market built in Portage la Prairie during the flush of optimism in 1882. The city already had a perfectly satisfactory meat market; still, nothing would do but that another larger and more ambitious establishment be erected. When the boom collapsed the scheme fell through. The meat market was converted into a biscuit factory. That failed. The biscuit factory became a manufacturing establishment. That failed, too, and the building was finally converted to a hard-tack shop.

Such insecurity was reflected in small business tragedies all over the province. Robert Hill, Manitoba's pioneer historian, wrote eight years later that men "once deemed honest and good for any amount, were turned out of house and home, their goods and chattels liened on and sold by the sheriff, in many cases not bringing the latter's fees." The wide-open credit system, which saw properties sold for small downpayments, was the real culprit. People had been speculating with money they did not have. Buggies, buckboards, and wagons were shipped to Manitoba in wholesale lots by Ontario manufacturers and sold to anyone who would buy them on time. So extravagant was the spirit of optimism engendered by the coming of the railway that any newcomer who claimed to have taken up a farm or who said he had come to stay was granted almost instant credit as a safe risk; indeed, it was considered well-nigh an insult to turn him down. As a result of this reckless policy, scores of farms and, indeed, entire townships fell eventually into the hands of the loan companies. Worse, bona fide settlers, hacking away at the tough prairie sod, found they could get no further loans for stock, farm equipment, or seed. The boom collapsed just as the first great wave of immigration reached the prairies. The newcomers ran squarely into a wall of pessimism. The financial hangover that followed was one of the reasons why so many were forced to leave their new-found homes and retreat to the East and why the immigrant tide, which seemed to be unending during that roseate spring, eventually slowed to a halt for another generation.

In the years that followed, the pioneers of Manitoba looked back upon those bizarre months and wondered how they could have been so foolish. There was the case of J. A. Little, a blacksmith from Portage la Prairie who threw up his job in 1881 to sell real estate – so successfully that he soon became an acknowledged authority on the value of property. Little made one hundred thousand dollars during the boom. He was so flushed with success that he resolved to build a residence elaborate enough to eclipse any similar structure in the North West. He had completed the stable and the cellar when the end came. All the remaining years of his life were spent trying to earn enough money to pay back his crushing debts. He did not quite succeed. Shortly before he died in 1890 the stable was sold to a livery company and the great cellar, the last remaining testament to his folly, was filled in.

There was also the tale of Roderick McLeod, who owned a river lot of two hundred and forty acres. He sold it for fifty thousand dollars of which fifteen thousand was the down payment. When the boom burst, the purchaser, unable to pay the balance, offered to return the land. Such was McLeod's avarice that he refused and the case went to court. In the soberer climate of a later period, the judge saw that the land had been overvalued. McLeod did not receive a nickel more for his inflated property; worse, the legal expenses gobbled up all of his original fifteen thousand and his homestead as well. Perhaps he contemplated, ruefully, the irony of his stand. Stretching off from that disputed parcel of real estate, in every direction, were millions of acres of prime farmland, available for homestead or pre-emption, all free for the asking.

The boom had a sobering effect on Winnipeg. All during the decade of the seventies it had been a lusty infant of a village. In one incredible winter it had reached its adolescence and sowed its wild oats. By the fall of 1882, it had matured to become a sadder and wiser city. As men recall their lost youth, old timers recalled wistfully those halcyon days before the bubble broke. One of these was George Ham, who wrote in 1921 that "since the boom of 1882, the soul of Winnipeg has never been what it was before."

"The later Winnipeg may be a better city," Ham admitted, but he regretted the good old days. "It was a short life from '71 to '82, but while it lasted, it was a life with a 'tang' to it – a 'tang' born of conditions that cannot be repeated and therefore cannot be reproduced."

Chapter Three

1
The new broom

2
Five hundred miles of steel

3
End of Track

4
Edgar Dewdney's new capital

5
The Grand Trunk declares war

1

Van Horne arrived in Winnipeg that January with a considerable reputation among railwaymen. The previous year, the *Railway Journal* had called him "a man of wonderful power and shrewdness." He was known, too, as a railway iconoclast, "an idol-smashing heathen" who had no respect for the rigid dogmas of a tradition-ridden business. It was said that he could make eight hundred freight cars do the work of a thousand by his ingenious methods of loading. In Chicago he had astonished his contemporaries by the amount of trackage he had managed to work into a limited area in the yards. He used locomotives to their fullest capacity over the protests of engineers who wanted to treat them like horses and let them rest quietly in the shops. He had a reputation for doctoring sick railroads until they were made to pay. He was also known as a fighter: he had fought the grasshoppers, he had fought the labour unions, he had fought the encroachment of other railroads, and always he had won.

He seemed to know a terrifying amount about railroading. He knew all about yards and repair shops. He understood the mysteries of accounting. He could work out a complicated system of scheduling in his head while others sweated laboriously with pins and charts. He could comprehend the chatter of the fastest telegraph key. He could operate any locomotive built. He had even redesigned, with considerable grace and taste, that ugliest example of nineteenth-century American architecture, the railroad station.

He was a true Renaissance man, the most engaging and versatile immigrant that Canada ever enticed across its borders and one of the few larger-than-life figures in the Canadian story. It is interesting to speculate on what he might have been in another era: a prince of the Church in the Middle Ages? the ruler of a dukedom in the sixteenth century? a Roman conqueror? In any age Van Horne would have fitted his times exactly. In a century when railways were venerated above all else – when a private railway car had equal status with a yacht, when entire magazines were devoted to news and opinions about railways, when railway financiers were numbered among the real rulers of the land – it was ordained that Van Horne would become a railway man. He was probably the greatest that the continent ever produced.

There are a great many adjectives that apply to him: buoyant, capable, ingenious, temperamental, blunt, forceful, boyish, self-reliant, imaginative, hard-working, puckish, courageous; but the word that best sums him up, and the one that his contemporaries used more than once, is "positive." He exuded confidence. J. H. E. Secretan, who worked for him as a surveyor, recorded that "the word 'cannot' did not exist in his dictionary." Was he ever bedevilled by doubts of his own or haunted by fears of private failure? If he was he hid his emotions well behind the grave mask of his face and those unrevealing eyes of penetrating blue. Even when the mask slipped a little to reveal the sensitive man behind it, the approach was characteristically blunt. Once, in Milwaukee, when he had been given a job that seemed to be far beyond his years, he sensed hostility all around him. He went straight to one of the clerks and asked him, point-blank: "Why are you prejudiced against me?" Startled, the man replied that he was not prejudiced, "and, now that I come to think of it, I have no reason to be against you at all."

Van Horne believed in coming to the point swiftly, with an economy of words. It was the same with railway lines. The best-run railways were the ones that achieved their destinations with an economy of mileage. One of Van Horne's first tasks was to ensure that the CPR would reach Pacific tidewater by the shortest possible route.

He had not yet met George Stephen, but he had encountered Major A. B. Rogers, "the Railway Pathfinder," a gnarled little whipper-snapper of a man, notorious for the length of his white Dundreary whiskers, the astonishing profanity of his speech, and his apparent ability to exist for days on little more than hard-tack. After a summer in the mountains, Rogers (though he harboured some secret doubts) had decided to announce that the Kicking Horse Pass in the Rockies was feasible. In the second week in January, 1882, he and Van Horne went to Montreal to meet Stephen, McIntyre, and Angus to discuss the matter.

The meeting took place on January 13 and resulted in two major decisions. The first was communicated to the press by Van Horne himself, with characteristic bluntness.

"We have changed the point," he said, "at which the road will enter the Rockies." The Kicking Horse Pass, still unsurveyed, had officially been chosen, confirming the tentative decision of the previous year. Although, as the *Globe* pointed out, only the Dominion government could "change the point," it had in fact been changed almost without that authority. "There is nothing surprising in the General Manager's assurance," the *Globe* declared, "for the House that ratified the monstrous bargain at the bidding of a Government dictated to by the Syndicate is not likely to refuse new concessions demanded by the same Ministry under the same dictation."

The second decision was that there would be a change of route between Lake Nipissing, the official start of the railway, and Fort William, to allow the line to hug the shore of Lake Superior, something Stephen had suggested to Macdonald months before. In addition, a branch line contemplated from Lake Nipissing to Sault Ste Marie would be greatly shortened, placing the Sault virtually on the main line, a change that caused some lengthening of the road.

This announcement was a significant one for it underlined the company's intention of proceeding with the Lake Superior section. Up to that point, several of the directors – certainly James J. Hill and his friend John S. Kennedy, the New York banker – had not contemplated building the line across the Precambrian Shield. Their plan was to divert it from Callander Junction, on Lake Nipissing, by way of the Sault, to join up with a branch of Hill's road, the St. Paul, Minneapolis and Manitoba, in which Stephen, Donald Smith, Angus, and Kennedy were all leading shareholders.

From a business point of view, the plan made great sense. Had it been adopted, it is conceivable that the CPR might have become part of the railway empire that the ambitious Hill was constructing – a Canadian feeder line for the Great Northern, which was to grow out of the original St. Paul railway.

It is probable that Stephen himself felt originally that the Sault branch would for many years carry Canadian passengers and freight south of the Shield through American territory into Manitoba and thence west before any all-Canadian line could be successfully undertaken. By 1881, Stephen, who wanted the Monopoly Clause tied down tightly, had changed his mind. He now had an ally in Van Horne, who helped to swing the issue in Montreal. The new general manager became that year the most trenchant advocate the Lake Superior line had. His railway sense rebelled against a connection with another railroad. He wanted a through line, independent of local traffic; and there is little doubt that he saw more clearly than the others the consequences to the CPR of linking up with Hill's road. The railway would become Hill's railway and there was no room, in one company, for two practical railwaymen as ambitious and as strong-minded as Jim Hill and W. C. Van Horne. It was the start of a memorable antagonism. When Hill heard of Van Horne's opposition to his plan he burst out that he would get even with him "if I have to go to hell for it and shovel coal."

No doubt Hill ruefully recalled his advice to Stephen that Van Horne would take all the authority he could. The new general manager was a man of towering ambition whose love of power had its roots in his childhood and youth. At the age of eighteen, he had breathlessly watched the arrival of the general superintendent of the Michigan Central – an awesome figure to a young telegraph operator – coming forward to meet his assistants with, as he later put it, "that bearing of dignity and importance which consciously or unconsciously attends the great majority of men who have long been accustomed to command." When the "mighty man," as Van Horne called him, moved away, the youth walked around the official car and gazed on it with awe. He found himself wondering if he might not some day attain the same rank and travel about in a private car of his own. "The glories of it, the pride of it, the salary pertaining to it, all that moved me deeply," he told his grandson many years later, "and I made up my mind then and there that I would reach it." He did, in just ten years; at the age of twenty-eight he became the youngest railway superintendent in the world.

To achieve that end he had "avoided every path however attractive that did not lead in its direction." Now, with a new railway in his grasp – the longest in the world and potentially one of the mightiest – he had no intention of sharing his power with any man.

He could get along quite easily with George Stephen, for Stephen was a financier, not a railroad man. Stephen had been persuaded to head the CPR on the condition that he was to have nothing to do with the actual building of the line. That "was to be done at St. Paul by Hill and Angus, and I to hear nothing about it." But with the advent of Van Horne, Hill's influence began to fade. Van Horne would build the road; Stephen would look after the money.

The two men hit it off from the beginning, though their backgrounds were dissimilar. The slender Stephen was a Highland Scot with a mathematician's brain, single-minded in his interests, passionate in his loyalties and hatreds. The stocky Van Horne was a mixture of Dutch, French, and German; in his drive and hustle he was the epitome of the American businessman – Macdonald's "sharp Yankee" – so despised by Canadian merchants and politicians. He had already rubbed his subordinates in Winnipeg the wrong way. On the very day he arrived in Montreal, the *Globe* published a rumour that he did not like his new position and that the Chicago, Milwaukee and St. Paul was holding his old post open for him. His cronies, hearing of the chill in Winnipeg, urged him to leave his crusty colleagues to "build their own road and come back here to your friends."

But Van Horne was not a man to quit something he had scarcely tackled. There was a quality of enthusiasm about him that Stephen must have admired, for Stephen had it too. When Stephen threw himself into a project he went all the way; so did Van Horne. Once he became general manager of the CPR, he was a Canadian railwayman through and through. The difference was that Stephen, in his own phrase, was "born utterly without the faculty of doing more than one thing at a time." His only passion outside of the CPR was the very Scottish pastime of salmon fishing. Van Horne, on the other hand, seemed able to switch from one pursuit to another and make himself master of all of them.

He threw himself into half a dozen hobbies. As a gardener he thought nothing of travelling for miles to seek out and dig his own leaf-mould for roses. He studied fertilizers and soil mixes and bred new varieties – a triple trumpet flower, for example, and a perfect hyacinth. As an amateur geologist he was not content to pore over the works of Louis Agassiz; he must meet the great man himself and correspond with him; he must discover and name new trilobites and brachiopods. Old railwaymen working in quarries along any line of road with which Van Horne was connected knew that he was a sure market for fossils; the slightest hint of a discovery would send him speeding towards the source with his geologist's hammer and his sample box. He carried his rock collection about with him as other men carried a dispatch case.

Like Stephen, Van Horne had been raised in poverty, born literally in an Illinois log cabin. Like Stephen, he revered his mother, "a noble woman, courageous and resourceful," he called her. (Stephen's was "one of the best mothers that ever lived.") His father had died when he was eleven; at fourteen he had been forced to forsake his education to support his family. Again like Stephen, who had risen from draper's clerk to bank president in a remarkably short period, he had worked hard all his life to achieve his ambitions. In his ten-year drive to the top he had never known a holiday or even an evening or a Sunday off. When others sought respite, the young Van Horne cheerfully assumed the burden of their tasks; that was how he learned so much about railways, haunting the repair shops, mastering the use of every tool, watching the engineers building bridges, learning line repairs from roadmen and section hands, studying accounting and figures.

As a train dispatcher in Alton, Van Horne's official work day was twelve hours, but when it was over he did not go home; instead, he lurked about the yards, shops, and offices, soaking up the railway business. He was convinced that "an object can usually be attained through persistence and steadiness of aim" and in all his activities – from track-laying to poker – he held fast to that credo.

Van Horne had been in office only one month and was still in Montreal when he fired General Rosser, the courtly and popular chief engineer of the western division of the company. Long before he came to Canada, the new general manager had cultivated the reputation of being able to smoke out incompetence, dissent, and dishonesty in an almost supernatural fashion. A good deal of this sprang from the fact that he could read a telegraph key and thus listen in to the gossip and sometimes disgruntled small talk that clattered over the wires and into the railway offices through which he wandered. On one occasion he discovered by eavesdropping on a key that a group of trainmen had appropriated the cushions from a first-class passenger car and were making themselves comfortable in the baggage car playing poker. When Van Horne reached a station farther down the line, he shot off a message that the cushions were to be returned and that poker playing was not allowed on CPR time (he clearly did not include himself and his cronies). For all of their lives the men thus caught in the act were mystified as to how the general manager found them out.

But it required no such prescience to learn that Rosser was using inside knowledge of future railway locations to speculate in real estate. The *Globe* had published the fact the previous fall and Rosser himself apparently did not go to any great lengths to keep it a secret; he appeared to regard it as part of the compensation for the job.

In January, Van Horne came across a letter in which the General had revealed to a railway contractor, John Stewart, the exact location of the terminus of the CPR's Pembina Mountain branch. This was valuable and privileged information. On February 1, Van Horne wired to Rosser that he had seen the letter and on account of his "unwarranted and unauthorized action on this and other matters" he was notifying him that his services were no longer required. (About the same time, Stewart, having acquired the townsite land, sold it to a syndicate which included several government officials.)

Rosser was not an easy man to dismiss. The wire had come at an extremely awkward time. He was about to leave for the western foothills on an ambitious twelve-hundred-mile reconnaissance, which had already received considerable publicity. In making this "difficult and hazardous journey," Rosser told the newspapers, he and his assistant would be provided with Arctic outfits, such as rabbit-skin robes and Eskimo suits, "prepared to resist any eccentricity of the season and the high latitude." They planned to cover forty-five miles a day, using husky dogs "with wolf blood in their veins" hitched Eskimo-fashion eight to a sled, each team pulling eight hundred pounds. The party intended to fight its way through the blizzards as far as Fort Walsh, the North West Mounted Police outpost near the Cypress Hills, and, en route, determine a satisfactory crossing of the Saskatchewan River.

This romantic odyssey, which would have provided the chief engineer with priceless information about the future location of western townsites, was quashed by Van Horne's blunt telegram. Rosser was forced to postpone his journey. He rushed to St. Paul where he planned to intercept Van Horne who was returning from Montreal. Meanwhile he denied the inevitable rumours. "There is no foundation for the report of my resignation," he told the St. Paul *Pioneer Press* on February 9. "I have not resigned nor formally tendered my desire to do so. The fact is there has been a little misunderstanding, such as is liable to occur in business matters, and of such a character as to be hardly explainable or interesting to the general public." The misunderstanding, Rosser said, had grown out of "land department matters." He expected everything to be adjusted satisfactorily. Meanwhile his assistant had gone on with the dog teams; the General expected to catch up with him at Fort Qu'Appelle.

But matters could not be adjusted. In Van Horne, Rosser was up against an unyielding obstacle. The two met on February 10; Rosser asked the general manager to reconsider; Van Horne gave him a blunt No. He added that he was not disposed to do anything that would unnecessarily injure the reputation of the old cavalryman. On reaching Winnipeg, Rosser would be allowed to resign. Rosser did so on February 13, declaring that he did not care to conform to certain rules with regard to speculation laid down by the directors. He wanted his resignation to take effect on March 10. Again, Van Horne was blunt: he wanted him out immediately, with his desk cleared, that very day. Indeed, he had already replaced him temporarily with his wife's cousin, Samuel B. Reed of Joliet, Illinois.

Rosser's dismissal was followed shortly afterward by that of his entire engineering staff. On March 13, a fire destroyed the new Bank of Montreal building, in which the CPR had its offices. During the transfer of some of the engineering department's documents to temporary quarters in the Knox Church it was discovered that some were missing. These included plans and profiles of the contemplated route of the railway west. Van Horne told Reed to find the leak, and if he could not, to fire the whole staff on the spot. At the same time, Reed laid an information against his predecessor, charging that Rosser, "by falsely pretending that he was acting for the C.P.R.," had fraudulently obtained the profiles of the line extending all the way to Calgary.

In the end, the CPR dropped the case. When it came to court on June 1, the company's solicitors declined to appear and Rosser was immediately acquitted. That might have been the end of matters had Rosser not accidentally encountered Van Horne on a hot July evening in the Manitoba Club. Van Horne was no man to back away from any encounter – as a child in Joliet he had taken on every boy in school. In the *Sun's* spirited account of the affair, "their slumbering anger broke out in words, and the words would have ended in more than blows had it not been for the interference of a couple of peacemakers." Winnipeg, in fact, almost witnessed its only Western-style gunfight. Rosser and Van Horne both drew pistols. and a serious battle was averted only when "the better counsels of cooler heads prevailed, and the belligerents were separated before their passions were cooled in gore."

It was probably this encounter that caused Rosser to sue the CPR on August 9 for one hundred thousand dollars. He was awarded, in October, twenty-six hundred dollars on the ground of malicious prosecution. The court held that the railway company, had it chosen to, could have abandoned the case well before it came to trial. The CPR had to pay up, but it took Rosser's defection seriously enough to change slightly the route of the railway west, especially in the vicinity of the site of the new capital of the North West Territories, which would be called Regina.

Harry Armstrong, who was one of the engineers fired (and subsequently rehired) by the company, did not believe that Rosser was really at fault, since he had been told by Stickney that he might speculate in real estate. (The *Globe* estimated that Stickney and Rosser between them had made a total of $130,000 in speculation.) The real villain "who had been outwitting the company," Armstrong insisted in his memoirs, was that most persistent of land sharks, Arthur Wellington Ross.

2

When Van Horne met the CPR directors in Montreal, he was able to convince them that he could lay five hundred miles of track during the 1882 season. That was what Stephen wanted to hear: he had already told Macdonald that the company was planning to finish the railway in half the ten-year period allowed by the contract. It was, indeed, essential that the through line get into operation as swiftly as possible, since there would for many years be very little local traffic. The CPR would stand or fall on its transcontinental trade – cargoes such as silk, for example, that de-

Five hundred miles of steel

manded speedy dispatch. The Canadian road was far shorter than any United States transcontinental route – the company expected to have an enormous advantage in this area – but it could not turn a dollar of profit on its through line until the last spike was driven.

Van Horne's announcement was greeted with considerable scepticism. It was, as Charles Drinkwater announced, a "feat unparalleled in Railway history." During the previous season Stickney had been able to lay only one hundred and thirty miles of track. Van Horne seemed to be promising the impossible.

Back in Winnipeg in mid-February, 1882, with the Rosser nuisance disposed of, he gave no hint that he was embarked on anything remarkable. He told Secretan, who had surveyed four hundred miles of preliminary line as far as Moose Jaw Bone Creek, that he wanted "the shortest commercial line" between Winnipeg and the Pacific coast. He added that he would not only lay five hundred miles of track that summer but would also have trains running over it by fall. Secretan, a great, bulky Englishman with a waxed moustache took a rather lofty view towards his fellow humans. He ventured a modicum of doubt, whereupon Van Horne declared that nothing was impossible; all he wanted his engineers to do was to show him the road; if Secretan could not do that, then he would have his scalp.

The general manager did not care much for engineers, most of whom were inclined to be temperamental, jealous, and often overbearing. He resented, as Secretan noted, their professional interference; it clashed with his own dictatorship. "If I could only teach a section man to run a transit," he once remarked, "I wouldn't have a single damned engineer on the road." Secretan himself (as his memoirs reveal) was as snobbish an engineer as ever took a level; but he admired Van Horne, "the most versatile man I have ever encountered."

Secretan noticed that as Van Horne talked he had a habit of making sketches on blotting pads, "well worth framing," which he tore up as fast as he drew them. All his life, since he had been old enough to handle a slate, the artist in Van Horne had struggled to be released; indeed, in another age and another climate – the Renaissance, perhaps – the artist might have won out over the hard-headed man of action. As a small boy, unable to afford paper, he had covered the whitewashed walls of his house with drawings. One of the most telling incidents in his biography is the story of how he fell so much in love with Hitchcock's *Elementary Geology* that he determined to use his copyist's skill to make it his own. Night after night by candlelight the determined child copied the book in ink onto sheets of foolscap – copied every page, every note, and every picture right down to the index. It did great things for him, as he later admitted: "It taught me how much could be accomplished by application; it improved my handwriting; it taught me the construction of English sentences; and it helped my drawing materially. And I never had to refer to the book again."

In later life, Van Horne the amateur painter attacked great canvases as he attacked the building of the railway – with huge brushes and considerable spontaneity; he believed that work was best done when it was done as rapidly as possible.

Not surprisingly, his art was meticulously literal. His drawings were so real that they could be, and sometimes were, mistaken for actual engravings by other artists. Once he managed to purloin a copy of *Harper's Weekly* before it reached his mother. With great care, Van Horne transformed a series of portraits of American authors into bandits – and did his work so well that they did not appear to have been altered. His mother complained to the mystified editor about his apparent policy of desecrating the images of great Americans. The baffled illustrator, Wyatt Eaton, when shown the same copy some years later was equally indignant. The issue became a collector's item.

This was the puckish side of Van Horne's nature. He could not resist a practical joke. Van Horne the artist left one school as a consequence of caricaturing the principal. Van Horne the young telegrapher lost his first job when he set up a ground plate that gave a mild shock to any man who stepped upon it, including the railway superintendent, who fired him. Van Horne the gardener could not resist planting skunk cabbage along the lot line of his neighbour, a clergyman.

He was thirty-one years old when he tampered so expertly with his mother's copy of *Harper's*. A colleague described him at the time (he was about to become president of the Southern Minnesota Railroad) as grave and thoughtful: "His constant manner was that of a person preoccupied with great affairs." But behind that poker face – so useful to him in his swift climb to the top and in those all-night card games along the line of the CPR – lurked the curiosity, the high spirits, and the ingenuousness of a small boy. Thomas Shaughnessy in his valedictory of Van Horne said truly that "he possessed the splendid simplicity of grown up boyhood to the end."

Secretan had reason to like and admire the general manager, for Van Horne saved him from a Spartan existence on the prairies that year. Secretan was a man who loved his food; indeed, he often supplemented the standard CPR fare with game shot in the field. Before setting off on his western location survey he prepared what he considered to be a reasonably modest list of supplies. But the company's new chief purchasing officer, a former American army man named Burdick, cut the requirements in half.

Secretan made sure Van Horne heard about the change. The general manager was indignant. Van Horne worshipped food as only a man can who has known what it is to go hungry; as a boy in a family left destitute by the father's sudden death from cholera he had had bread but seldom butter and sometimes only hominy for three meals a day. In his American railroading days it was understood by all that he would tolerate no eating house along the line unless the food was the very best available. He often tested the quality personally. It was his habit, when travelling, to wire ahead for roast chicken dinners to be set out for two. When he arrived he would eat both of them himself. Once, when asked to sketch his personal coat of arms, he produced a drawing of "A Dinner Horn, Pendant, upon a Kitchen Door."

Van Horne called Burdick into his office and tore into him: "Are you the God-forsaken idiot who buys the provisions? If so, I'll just give you till six o'clock to-night to ship a car-load of the very best stuff you can find up to Secretan, the engineer at the front; and see here, you can come back at six o'clock and tell me you have shipped it, you understand, but if you have not, you need not come back at all, but just go back to wherever you came from."

All that summer small luxuries continued to arrive at Secretan's camp. The climax came when Burdick himself turned up personally with the latest English illustrated papers, two boxes of the best cigars, and a bottle of Hudson's Bay rum. He told the surveyor that Van Horne had given him "the gol darndest settin' out I ever had in my life."

In Winnipeg, Van Horne faced greater problems than the matter of his commissariat. One was the general chilliness of his staff, and, indeed, of Winnipeg itself, a city preoccupied with making a fast dollar. Another was the spring floods that threatened to disrupt the goal he had so recklessly and publicly set for himself.

His reputation as a Yankee go-getter had a reverse side to it. It was generally held, and not without considerable evidence, that he was favouring Americans over Canadians when new employees were hired for the railway. This was especially true in the key jobs. The *Globe*, which led the newspaper pack in listing every American appointment, commented as early as January 25 that "a notice, 'No Canadians need apply,' should be posted at all CPR offices, and appended to all their advertisements. . . .

94

Thus the managers of the Company would be saved from the trouble of refusing Canadian applications." The paper pointed out that the general manager, chief engineer, and superintendent were all Americans and "so are a host of well-paid minor employees."

The situation grew more acute as Canadians were fired and replaced by Americans or "sour mash," as they were called. In April, the *Sun* revealed that five Canadian conductors had been fired and two more suspended, while of eleven new conductors, six were Americans. The paper listed eight other minor Canadian executives – yard masters, dispatchers, a construction superintendent – who had been replaced by Americans. The list was widely reprinted and the subject raised in the House of Commons by George Ross, the Liberal member for Middlesex, who quoted a Winnipeg correspondent who charged that "other Canadians, who cannot be got rid of for just reasons, are having their berths made so warm for them that they will have to leave if they want to live in peace."

The *Sun*, which was generally friendly to the railway, felt it necessary to admit editorially that a feeling prevailed among Canadians in the company's employ that their jobs were not secure and that there was a determination to weed them out on any pretext. These remarks had little effect upon Van Horne. On June 10, the *Globe*'s correspondent reported that "there are very few Canadians left. The new appointments, so far as I can discover, are every one of them 'sour mash.' Not a single Canadian has been made a conductor, though 57 Minnesota men have been put in charge of trains. . . . Quite a number of new drivers have been appointed but every one of them is an American, and the Govt. drivers who were promised engines are still waiting for orders."

It was not in Van Horne's nature to take notice of such criticism. He was, in fact, doing his best to lure another American into the fold, a Milwaukee Irishman named Thomas Shaughnessy, who had once been on his staff in the United States. Van Horne needed Shaughnessy to act as quartermaster-general for the vast army he intended to throw into the West once the floods subsided that spring. Shaughnessy required some persuading and did not arrive until late in the year, "a fashionably-dressed, alert young man, sporting a cane and giving general evidence of being what we call a live wire," in the words of Van Horne's private telegrapher, E. A. James.

It is an irony that from the very beginning the CPR – that most nationalistic of all Canadian enterprises – was to a very large extent managed and built by Americans. The government section in British Columbia, from Kamloops Lake to Port Moody, was contracted to an American engineer,

Andrew Onderdonk, backed by a syndicate of American financiers. On the prairies another American company, Langdon and Shepard, held the prime contract. The remainder of the railway, involving the most difficult work of all – the mountain section and the section north of Lake Superior – was given to a third American concern, the North American Railway Contracting Company of New Jersey. This firm was to be paid partly in cash and partly in CPR stock; in November, 1883, after the shares tumbled on the New York exchange, the company backed out and the CPR took over construction in the mountains and across the Shield. On both these sections most of the subcontractors were Canadians, several of whom went on to become internationally famous entrepreneurs.

But in the eighties, most of the experienced railway talent was American. No major trunk-line had been built in Canada since the Grand Trunk, almost thirty years before. It was natural that Van Horne, like Jim Hill before him, should employ men he knew something about and felt he could depend upon. Many of these came from the Milwaukee and St. Paul railroad – executives like his old colleague John Egan, who became general superintendent of the CPR's western division, or his home-town in-law from Joliet, S. B. Reed. Neither was popular with Canadians. By July, 1884, the Prime Minister himself was complaining to George Stephen about Egan's reputation for dismissing Canadians and hiring Americans. A friend, "on whose calmness of judgment I can rely," had called the western superintendent "a low down blasphemous Yankee Fenian." Macdonald reported to the president that Egan's policies in Winnipeg had, rightly or wrongly, "made the CPR so unpopular that the feeling amounts to hatred." Egan also fought with John Ross, the Canadian who was in charge of CPR construction on the western section of the Lake Superior line, but Van Horne stuck by his friend.

The presence of so many Americans at every level in the CPR's hierarchy was the subject of bitter complaint for all of the construction period; but there was another side to the coin. The brain-drain to the United States, about which Canadians had complained for more than a decade, was being partially reversed by the great project of the railroad. Many of the "sour mash" became dedicated Canadians; as someone remarked, the building of the CPR would make a Canadian out of the German Kaiser. It certainly made Canadians out of Van Horne, Shaughnessy, and Isaac Gouverneur Ogden, the company's western auditor, who, after he became vice-president, was known as the Finance King of the CPR. (Secretan called him "an ambidextrous marvel [who] could write with both hands at the same time, I believe, and could also add up a couple of columns of figures simultaneously.") These men, and many lesser executives, turned their backs on their native land forever when they joined the railway. Business dictated that they must, since their chief rivals were the transcontinental Yankee lines. Shaughnessy, the policeman's son who became a baron, was an Imperialist's Imperialist, a staunch supporter of Monarch, Empire, and Nation – so British in outlook that he was offered a cabinet post (which he declined) in the Asquith government. As for Van Horne, he was more Canadian than any Canadian. "I am a Chinese-wall protectionist," he told Augustus Bridle before his death. "I don't mean merely in trade. I mean – everything. I'd keep the American idea out of this country."

But in the late spring of 1882, Van Horne was more concerned over floods than he was with "sour mash." The high water had already thrown his careful schedule off balance by postponing construction for nearly a month. The *Globe*, which seized every opportunity to knock the Syndicate in general and Van Horne in particular, ignored the unseasonable weather and laid the blame at the feet of the general manager. On June 23, it reported that "Van Horne's men have not laid one solitary rail upon the grading done under his regime." The paper dug up "a well known tracklayer who has been in the business out west for 20 years" who was quoted as saying that "the idea of Van Horne talking about laying 500 miles of track this year, after the way time has been frittered away, is preposterous."

"Never mind who is doing the work, sir," the anonymous tracklayer told the *Globe*'s reporter; "figures will tell you who the men are that know their business. Give Van Horne a trial, but you'll find, as we all know, that there is more construction in Stickney's little finger than in Van Horne's body. He's alright in his place, and that's in his office, scheming to cut down wages on an old road."

Nonetheless, the general manager was making his presence felt. He was positively indefatigable, an iron man who never knew a moment's sickness and did not seem to require any sleep. Years later, when asked to reveal the secret of his stamina, he summed it all up with characteristic candour: "Oh," said he, "I eat all I can; I drink all I can; I smoke all I can and I don't give a damn for anything."

"Why do you want to go to bed?" he once asked Secretan. "It's a waste of time; besides, you don't know what's going on." He could sit up all night in a poker game and then, when seven o'clock came, rub his eyes, head for the office, and do a full day's work. He loved poker and he played it expertly. It was not a game, he would say, but an education. He enjoyed all card games and he was good at them all. James Mavor, the Toronto professor who knew him well in later years, thought this was his secret – his ability to "turn rapidly from one form of activity to another and to avoid over-anxiety about any one of his enterprises."

Many colleagues were to remark upon this characteristic in Van Horne. When he had done his work he was free to play games, to eat a good supper, to smoke one of his gigantic cigars, to pore over his collection of Japanese porcelains, to work with his rock specimens, or to best a colleague at billiards or chess. Chess intrigued him; he kept a set of chessmen in his private car and would challenge anyone – private secretary or merchant prince – to a game.

He loved to play and he loved to win. He was reluctant to leave any poker table when he was losing. He liked to dare his associates to duplicate the feats of memory with which he astonished acquaintances and utter strangers. His memory for obscure detail was quite remarkable and he revelled in it. Armstrong, the engineer, had one experience of it that remained with him all his life. Early in 1882 Van Horne told him to substitute nine-inch discharge pipes for the seven-inch on a water tank in order to save six minutes' time. Armstrong did not receive any nine-inch pipe before he and his fellow workers were dismissed. Two years later, when he was once again working for the CPR, he received a note from Van Horne, naming the date on which the order had gone out. "I told you to have those goosenecks made 9 inches," Van Horne wrote. "Why wasn't it done?"

By June, Van Horne had become the terror of the railway, a kind of superman who had an uncanny habit of always turning up just when things went wrong. The *Sun*'s uninhibited columnist, R. K. Kernighan, who signed himself "The Dervish Khan, the Screamer of Qu'Appelle," had been dispatched to Flat Creek – or Flat Krick, as he invariably called it – the transitory community at the end of the track. There he watched, with a mixture of awe and amusement, the descent of Van Horne upon the unsuspecting settlement.

"The trains run in a kind of go-as-you please style that is anything but refreshing to the general manager. But when Manager Van Horne strikes the town there is a shaking up of old bones. He cometh in like a blizzard and he goeth out like a lantern. He is the terror of Flat Krick. He shakes them up like an earthquake, and they are as frightened of him as if he were the old Nick himself. Yet Van Horne is calm and harmless looking. So is a she mule, and so is a buzz saw. You don't know their true inwardness till you go up and feel of them. To see Van Horne get out of the car and go softly up the platform, you would think he was an evangelist on his way west to preach temperance to the Mounted Police. But you are soon undeceived. If you are within hearing distance you will have more fun than you ever had in your life before. He cuffs the first official he comes to just to get his hand in and leads the next one out by the ear, and pointing eastward informs him the walking is good as far as St. Paul. To see the rest hunt their holes and commence scribbling for dear life is a terror. Van Horne wants to know. He is that kind of a man. He wants to know why this was not done and why this was done. If the answers are not satisfactory there is a dark and bloody tragedy enacted right there. During each act all the characters are killed off and in the last scene the heavy villain is filled with dynamite, struck with a hammer, and by the time he has knocked a hole plumb through the sky, and the smoke has cleared away, Van Horne has discharged all the officials and hired them over again at lower figures."

As Van Horne's admirer, the Wisconsin banker and railway president Jason Easton, remarked, "Van Horne was one of the most considerate and even-tempered of men, but when an explosion came it was magnificent." Yet he rather enjoyed it when somebody stood up to him. In June he finally managed to secure the services of the flamboyant Irish construction boss, Michael J. Haney, as superintendent of both the Pembina Branch and the Rat Portage divisions, both of them originally built under government contract. Haney, one of the most resourceful railway men in the country, had managed to pull Section Fifteen of the government line into shape after the original contractor, Joseph Whitehead, had been forced to abandon it for lack of funds. A hard-muscled Galwayman with a flowing moustache, he was as lucky as he was tough; he had survived a whole series of accidents any of which ought to have put him in his grave. He was also impetuous and derisive of red tape. It was inevitable that, sooner or later, he and Van Horne would clash.

Haney had already tangled with Van Horne's western superintendent, John Egan, and won. Egan, on an inspection tour, discovered what he considered to be a shortage of railroad ties; since Haney was in charge of the delivery of construction supplies, he sent him a memorandum telling him to ship every tie available and in the future to attend to his work more closely. The irate Haney went straight to Winnipeg, gathered up every unemployed man he could find around town, and shipped them out along the line on flat cars. At every point where spare ties were available, Haney and his crew loaded them onto the cars and moved forward. In two days, Haney had loaded one hundred and forty cars and blocked every siding between Rat Portage and the end of track. A heated wire arrived:

"What in hell are you doing?" Back came Haney's laconic answer: "Filling orders, send more flat cars and will double quantity in 24 hours." It was the last time the chastened Egan sent Haney any kind of a blanket instruction.

Haney was in the Winnipeg freight yard one day when his secretary came hustling down the track to warn him that Van Horne was on the warpath.

"He's hot enough to melt the rails," Haney was told. "If you've got any friends or relatives at home who are fond of you I'd advise you to hunt a cyclone cellar."

As Haney recalled it, many years later, he was feeling pretty hot himself at the time. Everything seemed to have gone wrong that day. Jobs had been held up by a shortage of materials. He was, as he put it, in a humour to look for somebody with trouble. Instead of getting out of Van Horne's way he stalked resolutely down the yards to meet him.

Van Horne began an exhaustive recitation of the system's defects, punctuating his remarks with a colourful selection of profanity that turned the air blue. The pugnacious Haney waited until the general manager stopped for breath.

"Mr. Van Horne," he said, finally, "everything you say is true and if you claimed it was twice as bad as you have, it would still be true. I'm ready to agree with you there but I'd like to say this: Of all the spavined, one-horse, rottenly equipped, bad managed, badly run, headless and heedless thing for people to call a railroad, this is the worst. You can't get anyone who knows anything about anything. You can't get materials and if you could it wouldn't do you any good because you couldn't get them where you wanted them."

Haney followed up this outburst with a list of counter-complaints far more complete than Van Horne's, since he was in closer touch with the work. His tirade made Van Horne's explosion "sound like a drawing room conversation." The general manager waited patiently as Haney unleashed his torrent of grievances; by the time Haney had finished he was grinning.

"That's all right, Haney, I guess we understand one another," he said. "Let's get to work."

3

The contract to build the prairie section of the Canadian Pacific Railway *End of*
was probably the largest of its kind ever undertaken. Tenders were called *Track*
for in the third week of January, 1882, and the prize was awarded the
following month to the partnership of General R. B. Langdon of Minneapolis, a one-time stonemason of Scottish heritage, and D. C. Shepard of
St. Paul, a former engineer who had helped build the Chicago, Milwaukee
and St. Paul Railroad. The firm undertook to build six hundred and
seventy-five miles of railroad across the plains from the end of track at
Flat Creek to Fort Calgary on the Bow River. This was a formidable task
– just fifteen miles short of the entire length of the Central Pacific. In
spite of the *Globe*'s remarks about sour mashers, it is probable that no
Canadian company existed that could tackle a job of such magnitude.

Shepard, an extremely shrewd contractor and an old friend of James J.
Hill's, was well aware of this. He did not believe that there was another
firm on the continent that had the resources, the experience, or the personal following of subcontractors reliable enough to carry out the job
with the speed the CPR required. Hill knew this just as well as Shepard,
but he also felt that Shepard, operating from a position of strength, had set
his bid unreasonably high.

Shepard had a habit of dropping in on his friend in St. Paul almost
daily. A day or so after he and his partner had submitted their bid he
called, according to habit, at Hill's office. Lying face down on the desk,
where he could not fail to notice it, was a telegraph form. Ostensibly
it contained a lower bid from a large firm of contractors in the Middle
West. Hill made an excuse to leave his office. When he returned a few
minutes later, Shepard, apparently unconcerned, was seated in the same
position. There was some small talk and then Shepard took his leave.
But the next day he and Langdon submitted a revised bid which was somewhat lower than the one in the telegram – a telegram that Hill, of course,
had invented. The new terms suited Hill, who accepted them on behalf of
the CPR. In later years he used to joke about the incident with Shepard
who never betrayed by so much as a lifted eyebrow that he knew what
Hill was talking about.

On the day after the contract was signed, Langdon and Shepard advertised for three thousand men and four thousand horses. The job they
faced was staggering: it would require no fewer than three hundred subcontractors. Between Flat Creek and Fort Calgary the partners would

101

have to move ten million cubic yards of earth. They would have to haul every stick of timber, every rail, fishplate, and spike, all the pilings used for bridge-work, and all the food and provisions for 7,600 men and 1,700 teams of horses across the naked prairie for hundreds of miles. To feed the horses alone it would be necessary to distribute four thousand bushels of oats every day along one hundred and fifty miles of track. It was no wonder that Van Horne's boast about building five hundred miles in a single season was openly derided.

Winnipeg was transformed that spring of 1882 into a gigantic supply depot. Stone began to pour in from every available quarry, railroad ties from the Lake of the Woods country to the east, lumber from Minnesota, and rails from England and from the Krupp works in Germany. Since the St. Lawrence would still be frozen well into the construction season, Van Horne had the steel shipped to New York and New Orleans and dispatched to Manitoba by way of St. Paul. Whole trainloads of material destined for the Canadian North West were constantly passing through American cities where hundreds of checkers reported on them daily so that the exact moment of their arrival could be plotted. As fast as the supplies arrived they were hauled away to the end of track. Long trains loaded with rails, ties, fishplates, and provisions rattled westward to Flat Creek, dumped their loads, and returned empty. No newly completed line of steel had ever known such activity in the first year of its construction.

The floods of April put a halt to all this activity, causing a formidable log-jam of supplies in Winnipeg and another in St. Paul. The valley of the Red was inundated – as were the Portage plains. Beecham Trotter, travelling out towards Portage la Prairie in one of the last freight trains to get through, recalled that "it seemed as though we were traversing the ocean." The Assiniboine near Brandon spilled over its banks and covered the entire valley. The CPR bridge would have been swept away had it not been held down by flat cars, loaded with steel rails. Settlers streaming west had to move on foot and swim their cattle and horses across the swollen rivers. Even oxen were mired. On the cart trail leading towards Qu'Appelle, a carpenter named William Oliver happened upon the strange spectacle of three wagons and six oxen all lying half buried in an ocean of gumbo, while their owners, six mud-caked Englishmen, sat helplessly by, making the best of things by downing a breakfast of bread and ale. Oliver, who later became mayor of Lethbridge, Alberta, hauled them out with the help of two hundred feet of rope.

The floods forced almost all work on the railway to come to a standstill. Trotter, who was employed west of Flat Creek digging five-foot

102

postholes for the telegraph line that followed directly behind the rails, wrote that "every thrust with the bar brought a splash of mud to the face." Flat Creek itself, which seemed to be "the repository of more railway material than the whole world contained," was a quagmire. Tents of every shape and size, some brand new, some filthy and tattered, stretched out in all directions on a gloomy expanse of swamp.

Save for the prostitutes, the population was almost entirely male – freighters, farm labourers, bull-whackers, railroad navvies, muleteers, railway officials, and, of course, whiskey peddlers. "Terribly hard and depraved faces could be seen on every side," along with camp followers – "lewd women, the lowest of the low." For any but the strongest, the community could be a death trap. There was no place to sleep and the food was of the very worst and sometimes non-existent. Men were "herded together like rats in a hole, [and] . . . given food which a well kept dog wouldn't eat." Perhaps fortunately, Flat Creek had a brief life. When the railroad blockade ended and the tracks began to creep west once more to the newer community of Broadview, the town virtually disappeared. Even the name was changed to the pleasanter one of Oak Lake.

By the time the floods ended, scores of would-be homesteaders were disheartened and ready to quit the North West. In Brandon, building was at a standstill because the CPR was rushing all available construction materials to the front; even before the floods began, hundreds of men were idle. The railway yards "looked like a great country fair." Trunks were piled along the grade like cordwood, as high as men could throw them, but many of the owners were already trying to sell their outfits and leave.

In late May an unexpected blizzard struck, destroying scores of tents and causing great suffering. Fuel was at such a premium that men resorted to stealing lumber, stick by stick. Charles Alfred Peyton, who lived in a small tent on the river bank at Brandon, remembered crawling one night on his stomach towards a pile of dry poles his neighbour had collected. Just as he seized a stick a bullet whizzed through the wood, no more than a foot away. Such nightly fusillades, he recalled, were not uncommon. People began to tell each other that it would be better to leave the land to the Indians. " 'Why should we take such a country away from them?' was heard on all sides." The first passenger train to leave Brandon for Winnipeg after the flood pulled three coaches loaded to the doors with men and women quitting the North West, never to return.

At last, with the waters subsiding and blizzards ended, the sun came out and warmed the frigid plains. The prairie evenings grew mellower and soon the sweet incense of the wolfwillow drifted in from the ponds and sloughs to mingle with the more familiar odours of salt pork, tamarack ties, wood smoke and human sweat. The early spring blossoms – wild pansies, strawberries, and purple pasqueflower – began to poke their tiny faces between the brittle grasses. Then, as a flush of new green spread over the land, the ox carts started west again until they were strung out by the hundreds ahead of the advancing line of steel.

As soon as the waters ebbed, a mountain of supplies descended upon Winnipeg. On a single day, May 15, eighteen thousand dollars worth of freight poured into the city, the largest amount since the Pembina Branch had been opened. The following day eighty freight cars arrived from St. Paul. The day after that fifty thousand bushels of oats and eleven carloads of mules were checked into the yards. With the freight came people. By June, three thousand immigrants were under canvas in Winnipeg, all buoyed up by the expectation of an entirely new life on the Canadian prairies: "Hope furnishes dessert for the frugal meal, expectation sweetens their daily life."

Though few people believed it would be possible for the CPR to achieve its season's goal or anything close to it after the delays, Van Horne was immovable. Langdon and Shepard had signed a contract promising to drive five hundred miles of steel that year; five hundred miles it would have to be. The general manager made it clear that he would cancel the contract if they did not live up to its obligations.

The prime contractors responded by increasing their army of men and horses, by adding an extra shift to the track-laying, and by lengthening the total work day from eleven hours to fifteen. "The iron now is going down just as fast as it can be pulled from the cars," Shepard announced. "We shall show a record at track-laying which has never been surpassed on this continent."

There followed a whirlwind of construction that was, in the words of the *Quarterly Review*, "absolutely without parallel in railway annals." The grade, winding snakelike across the plains, moved so swiftly that Secretan and his surveyors were hard put to stay ahead. Sometimes, indeed, they were awakened at night by the rumble of giant scrapers being dragged past their tents. "We had never seen the like in Canada before," Secretan wrote.

The prairie section of the CPR was built telescopically from a single base – a feat that a leading London journal, commenting on a projected British road in the Sudan, declared to be impossible. Winnipeg was the anchor point: from there the steel would stretch for a thousand miles into the mountains; there would be no supply line for the railway builders other than the rails themselves.

104

The previous year's operations had seen small knots of men, working in twos and threes with loaded handcars, pushing the track forward at about three-quarters of a mile a day. Van Horne determined to move at five times that speed. This would necessitate the kind of timing that divisional commanders require of troops in the field when an assault is launched. Van Horne's army worked that summer with a military precision that astonished all who witnessed it. "Clockwork" was the term used over and over again to describe the track-laying technique.

The pulse of the operation was at "End of Track," that unique, mobile community that never stayed in one place for more than a few hours at a time. Turner Bone, who worked in the engineering office of Herbert Holt, one of the subcontractors, described End of Track as "a real live community, a hive of industry, in which teamsters, track layers, blacksmiths, carpenters, executive officers and other trades and professions all had a part." At the end of each day's work the town-on-wheels had moved three or four miles west of where it had been that morning.

The nerve centre of End of Track was the line of boarding cars – eight or nine of them each three storeys high – that housed the track-laying crews. The ground floors of these cars served as offices, dining rooms, kitchens, and berths for the contractors and company officials; the two storeys above were dormitories. Sometimes there were even tents pitched on the roofs. These huge cars formed part of a long train which contained smaller office cars for executives, a cooking car, freight cars loaded with track materials, shops on wheels and, on occasion, the private car of the general manager himself. Van Horne was continually to be found at End of Track, spinning yarns with the workmen, sketching buffalo skulls, organizing foot races and target-shooting at night, and bumping over the prairie in a buckboard inspecting the grade. Every day some sixty-five carloads of railroad supplies, each carload weighing eighteen tons, were dumped at End of Track. Most of these supplies had been carried an average of a thousand miles before reaching their destination.

To a casual visitor the scene, at first glance, was chaotic: cars constantly being coupled and uncoupled, locomotives shunting back and forth pushing and pulling loads of various lengths, little handcars rattling up and down the half-completed track at the front, teams of horses and mules dragging loaded wagons forward on each side of the main line – and tents constantly rising like puffballs and vanishing again as the whole unwieldy apparatus rolled steadily towards the Rockies.

The apparent anarchy was illusory for the organization was meticulous, down to the last railway spike. Each morning two construction trains set out from the supply yards, far in the rear, for End of Track. Each was loaded with the exact number of rails, ties, spikes, fishplates, and telegraph poles required for half a mile of railway. One train was held in reserve on a siding about six miles to the rear; the other moved directly to the front where the track-laying gang of three hundred men and seventy horses was waiting for it.

The tracklayers worked like a drill team. "It was beautiful to watch them gradually coming near," one observer wrote, ". . . each man in his place knowing exactly his work and doing it at the right time and in the right way. Onward they come, pass on, and leave the wondering spectator slowly behind whilst he is still engrossed with the wonderful sight."

The ties were unloaded first, on either side of the track, to be picked up by the waiting wagons and mule teams – thirty ties to a wagon – hauled forward and dropped all the way along the graded embankment for exactly half a mile. Two men with marked rods were standing by, and as the ties were thrown out they laid them across the grade, exactly two feet apart from centre to centre. Right behind the teams came a hand-truck hauled by two horses, one on each side of the grade, and loaded with rails, fishplates, and spikes. Six men marched on each side of the truck, and when they reached the far end of the last pair of newly laid rails, each crew seized a rail among them and threw it into exact position. Two more men gauged these two rails to make sure they were correctly aligned. Four men followed with spikes, placing one in each of the four ends of the rails. Four others screwed in the fishplates and another four followed with crowbars to raise the ties while the spikes were being hammered in. All worked in a kind of rhythm, each man directly opposite his partner on each separate rail. More men followed with hammers and spikes to make the rails secure, but by this time the hand-truck had already moved forward, passing over the newly laid rails before the job was complete. W. Henry Barneby, an Englishman who watched this operation when it had reached a peak of sophistication, noted that "all the men must keep in their places and move on ahead, otherwise they will be caught up by those behind them."

As each construction train dumped its half-mile of supplies at End of Track, it moved back to the nearest siding to be replaced by the reserve train. There was no time lost. As the track unfolded the boarding cars were nudged ahead constantly by the construction train locomotive so that no energy would be wasted by the navvies in reaching their moving mess halls and dormitories.

The operation was strung out for hundreds of miles across the open

106

prairie. Up ahead were the survey camps, followed by the grading gangs and the bridge-makers. Far to the rear were other thousands – saddlers and carpenters, cooks and tailors, shoemakers, blacksmiths, doctors, and provisioners. Vast material yards were established at hundred-mile intervals between Winnipeg and End of Track. The supply trains moved west on schedule, unloading thousands of tons of goods at the yards; here the material was sorted daily into train lots and dispatched – as many as eight trains a day – to the front.

The organization left nothing to chance. In case track-laying should proceed faster than expected, reserves of supplies were held on the sidings and in the yards themselves. There were always rails available for three hundred miles and fastenings for five hundred, all within one hundred miles of End of Track. When the steel moved past the hundred-mile point the yards moved, too. An entire community of office workers, sorters, dispatchers, trainmen, labourers, and often their families as well, could be transported a hundred miles in a single night without the loss of an hour's work, because the houses were all portable and could be fitted easily on flat cars. "Flat Creek has folded its tents and gone *en masse* to Broadview," is the way the *Sun* laconically reported the first of such moves on July 28.

Right behind the track-laying gang came the telegraph teams. The telegraphers camped in tents and moved their gear forward every afternoon on handcars. The construction trains that brought half a mile of track supplies also brought half a mile of poles, wires, and insulators to the front. One hour after the day's track was laid, End of Track was in telegraphic communication with the outside world.

Far out on the barren plains, miles to the west of End of Track, were the bridging teams, grading units, and surveyors, all driven forward by the knowledge that the tracklayers were pressing hard behind them. Although the work was broken down into subcontracts, the organization was so arranged that no weak link could hold up construction. The head contractor had a flying wing of his own men standing by, prepared to complete immediately any work that seemed unlikely to be ready in time for the "ironing" of the track. This work was, of course, charged against the subcontractors; it served to force the pace. When the flying wing was not needed for this purpose, it was employed in completing the ballasting of the line, which was laid so swiftly that it was necessary to go over it again with great care. In addition, the flying wing built the sidings which were required at six-mile intervals across the prairies.

The grading was accomplished by immense scrapers pulled by teams of horses. Their task was to build an embankment for the railway four feet above the prairie and to ditch it for twenty yards on either side. This was more than the original contract had called for; but Van Horne, who always looked ahead, knew that in the long run a solidly built line – the standards here exceeded those of the Union Pacific – would pay off. At that height the rails would be protected from the blizzards of winter and costly delays from snow blockage would be avoided.

The bridgers worked in two gangs, one by day and one by night. Every sliver of bridging had to be brought from Rat Portage, one hundred and forty miles east of Winnipeg, or from Minnesota; for this reason the bridge-builders were seldom more than ten miles ahead of the advancing steel. The timbers were unloaded as close to End of Track as possible and generally at night so as not to interfere with other work. "Sometimes," one eyewitness reported, "not a stick of timber nor any preparation for work could be seen one day, the next would show two or three spans of a nicely finished bridge. Twenty-four hours afterwards the rails would be laid, and trains working. . . ."

"The history of the world offers no such evidence of push as the work of this year has done," R. B. Conkey, Langdon and Shepard's general manager declared at Winnipeg in August. "Sherman's march to the sea was nothing to it. When the road is completed there will be nothing in history to compare with it."

The nation was electrified by the speed with which the railroad was being forced across the plains. One man on the scene noted that it seemed to move as fast as the ox carts of the settlers who were following along beside the tracks. Alex Stavely Hill, the British Member of Parliament, going in for lunch on one of the boarding cars around eleven one morning, noted, on emerging at two that afternoon, that a wagon that had been parked beside the car was already two miles to the rear. William White, homesteading near Pile o' Bones Creek, left his camp one morning to bring in wood from a copse six miles away. When he left there was no sign of construction for two miles to the east. When he returned, he and his companions had to cross a newly completed track.

The North West of Canada, once so haunting and so mysterious, was being transformed by the onslaught of the rails. A single incident illuminates that change: a young homesteader and his sweetheart eloped successfully in the face of parental obduracy by commandeering a handcar and speeding towards Winnipeg along the line of steel, thus throwing off their pursuers.

One railway employee, A. C. Forster Boulton, who came from a notable Toronto family, wrote that the progress of construction was so swift that antelope and other game migrating north were cut off on their return that fall by the lines of rails and telegraph posts, "and terrified by the sight . . . gathered in hundreds on the north side, afraid to cross it." It was probably the last summer in which herds of buffalo and antelope freely roamed the prairie.

Father Albert Lacombe, the voyageur priest who had served his time as chaplain to the railroad navvies of Rat Portage and was now back among his beloved Blackfoot nation, watched the approach of the rails with both sadness and resignation:

"I would look in silence at that road coming on – like a band of wild geese in the sky – cutting its way through the prairies; opening up the great country we thought would be ours for years. Like a vision I could see it driving my poor Indians before it, and spreading out behind it the farms, the towns and cities. . . . No one who has not lived in the west since the Old-Times can realize what is due to that road – that c.p.r. It was Magic – like the mirage on the prairies, changing the face of the whole country."

The Indians watched in silence as the steel cut through their hunting-grounds. They would arrive suddenly, as if from nowhere, squat on their haunches in double rows, and take in the scene with only the occasional surprised grunt. To them the engines were "fire wagons." They were a little puzzled by the lack of white squaws and papooses. Why would men want to work in a wilderness without women and children? But if they realized that their wild, free existence was at an end they gave no sign.

Onward the track moved, cutting the plains in two. It moved through a land of geese, snipe, and wild ducks, whose eggs were prized by those navvies who took the trouble to search them out. It moved through a land fragrant in the soft evenings with the scent of willow and balsam. It cut across acres of yellow daisies, tiger lilies, purple sage, and briar rose. It bisected pastures of waist-high buffalo grass and skirted green hay meadows which, in the spring, were shallow ponds. As it travelled westward it pushed through a country of memories and old bones – furrowed trails fashioned decades before by thousands of bison moving in single file towards the water, vast fields of grey and withered herbage, dead lakes rimmed with tell-tale crusts of alkali. Day by day it crept towards the horizon where, against the gold of the sunset, flocks of fluttering wildfowl, disturbed by the clamour of the invaders, could be seen in silhouette; or where, sometimes, a single Indian, galloping at full speed in the distance, became no more than a speck crawling along the rim of the

109

prairie. This had been the Great Lone Land, unfenced and unbridged, which explorers like Palliser, Butler, and Grant had discovered and described as if it were on the dark side of the moon. The line of steel made Butler's phrase obsolete, for the land would never again be lonely. All that summer it reverberated with the clang of sledge and anvil, the snorting of horses and mules, the hoarse puffing of great engines, the bellowing of section bosses, the curses of thousands of sweating men, and the universal song of the railroad navvies: "Drill, ye tarriers, drill."

History was being made, but few had time to note that fact. Trotter was to write, a little sheepishly, that "few, if any of us were historically minded enough to think of the interest that might attach to a running diary of what was seen, and said, and done, from day to day. We talked a good deal about what would follow in our wake – the towns that would appear, and the sort of population that would spread over the illimitable plain . . . [but] we enjoyed the life, as you would expect men busy in physical labour to enjoy the wonderful atmosphere; the open space; the zest with which the whole scheme of advance was prosecuted; the barbarian who came to behold us putting the enemy of uncommercial distance under our feet." Nor did William Oliver in his ox cart heading west, almost always in sight of the railway grade, watching idly the straining mules and men, consider the significance of what he saw: "It never came to my mind in watching the building of the railway . . . that in the next fifty years it would play so important a part in the commerce of the country and in fact of the world. . . . We were more interested in our own affairs and the prospects of a future home. . . ."

At the same time the spectacle of the steel-laying gangs remained in Oliver's memory all his life. They were "a sight never to be forgotten. . . . Ties to the Irish and Swede giants were like toothpicks, steel rails like crowbars. They were soon gone and out of sight."

They were a mixed lot, these railroad navvies. Charles Alfred Peyton, walking down the track and looking for work, came upon a gang of Italians who "looked like guys who would cut your throat for a dime." A few miles farther on, however, he joined a team of young Englishmen, "a very nice bunch of lads," and went to work for $1.25 a day. Stavely Hill, who was a barrister, encountered a man ploughing, "throwing almost as much strength from himself into his work as he was getting out of his horses." It developed that he was a former doctor. That night, the man who cooked his dinner in the boarding car turned out to be the same solicitor's clerk who had once visited his London chambers with briefs.

R. K. Kernighan was introduced to one track-laying gang by a section boss who identified some of them: "Do you see that person yonder, that man can read and write Greek and is one of the most profound scholars on the continent; that man next him was once one of the foremost surgeons in Montreal, and that man next him was at one time the beloved pastor of one of the largest congregations in Chicago."

The general run of railroad navvies was far rougher. One eastern reporter found them "ill-bred and offensive in their manners, applying the most obscene epithets to every passerby, jostling with their heavy teams every traveller they meet upon the trail, and in all respects making themselves as disagreeable as they know how to be. In their personal habits they are much more uncleanly than the poorest and most degraded of Indians, and in all respects they fairly represent the class from which they were drawn, that is, the scum and offscourings of the filthiest slums of Chicago and other western cities."

They were paid between $2.00 and $2.50 a day, which were good wages for the era, and often enough after they had made a little money they quit. Of the twenty-eight men who left Winnipeg in the spring in Beecham Trotter's telegraph gang, only half a dozen remained by autumn. Swedes who had learned how to lay track in the old country were highly prized. One Broadview pioneer claimed that "if they were given enough liquor they could lay two or three miles of tracks a day." Liquor, being prohibited by law in the North West, was hard but not impossible to get; it existed in private caches all along the line. "If I were not a total abstinence man," the Khan wrote in his *Sun* column, "I could get more whiskey in Flat Creek this blessed minute than would float this pork barrel on which I pen these immortal lines from here to Hong Kong." No law, the Khan believed, would succeed in driving the whiskey peddlers away. Not even the threat of execution or torture with red-hot irons would do it. "Inside of ten hours a daredevil would be selling budge on the sly." The liquor itself was described as "a mixture of blue ruin, chain lightning, strychnine, the curse of God and old rye."

The *Sun* recorded one raid in which Major J. M. Walsh, the Mounted Policeman who had literally kicked Sitting Bull in the pants, descended on Flat Creek with a posse of recruits and smashed forty gallon casks of whiskey and eighty bottles of cognac:

"While all this was going on in Reid's tent a perfect panic took possession of the town. The other whiskey sellers could be seen running in every direction with kegs of whiskey under their arms, throwing them into wells, ditches and holes on the prairie, men cursed and swore, women shrieked, and to make the panic worse rifles and revolvers were discharged into the air."

As autumn approached, the pace of the railway quickened still more.

At the end of August one of the superbly drilled crews of Donald Grant, the seven-foot-tall track boss, managed to lay four and a half miles of steel in a single day. Next day they beat their own record and laid five miles. It was all horribly expensive, as a worried Stephen reported to Macdonald in September: "This so called prairie section is not a prairie at all in the sense that the Red River valley is a prairie. The country west of Portage la Prairie is broken rolling country, and the amount of work on our road bed is more than double what it would have been had it run along the valley. In short the road . . . is costing us a great deal more than the subsidy and a great deal more than we expected. We are just about even with the world at the moment, but to reach this position, we have had to find 5 million dollars from our resources. *To enable me to make up my quota I had to sell my Montreal Bank stock.*"

There were those who thought that Van Horne "seemed to spend money like a whole navy of drunken sailors." Actually he counted every dollar. In the interests of both speed and economy he allowed steep grades and tight curves, which he planned to eliminate once the line was operating. In the rolling country to which Stephen referred, the road, in places, was like a switchback; it remained that way until the end of the century.

The contractors did not reach Van Horne's goal of five hundred miles; the spring floods had frustrated his ambition. By the end of the season, however, they had laid four hundred and seventeen miles of completed railroad, built twenty-eight miles of siding, and graded another eighteen miles for the start of the following season. In addition, Van Horne had pushed the Southwestern branch line of the CPR in Manitoba a hundred miles and so could say that, in one way or another, he had achieved the aggregate he sought.

As far as the general public was concerned, he had wrought a miracle. Only the waspish *Globe* refused to be impressed. The paper, which had earlier attacked the company for the lethargy of its progress, now hit out at it for the opposite reason:

"The public has nothing to gain by this breakneck speed. . . . If . . . a southerly pass had been found across the Rocky Mountains, there might be some object in making haste across the plains. But from present appearances, the entire Prairie section will be crossed long before it is positively known whether or not there is a better crossing than the Yellowhead Pass. . . . We are satisfied that the public good would have been better served if the Company had built about 200 miles only of its plains line every year, and had put some of its superfluous energy upon the Eastern Section. . . ."

112

There was a modicum of truth in the *Globe*'s carping. In the heart of the Rocky Mountains that summer, Major A. B. Rogers was still plagued with doubts about the feasibility of the Kicking Horse Pass as a railway route. Equally serious was the whole question of the barrier of the Selkirks. The plain truth was that Van Horne and his men had been driving steel all summer at record speed, straight at that double wall of mountains, without really being sure of how they were going to breach it.

4

*Edgar
Dewdney's new
capital*

The Honourable Edgar Dewdney, Lieutenant-Governor of the North West Territories and Indian Commissioner to boot, was a handsome giant of a man. With his fringed buckskin jacket and his flaring mutton chop whiskers (which won for him the Indian name of "Whitebeard"), he made an imposing figure as he stalked about accompanied by his two gigantic Newfoundland dogs, the gift of the Marquis of Lorne. It was not difficult to spot Dewdney at a distance – he stood "like Saul, head and shoulders above most men." In the late spring of 1882 there were a good many who wanted to keep him in view: The Lieutenant-Governor had been charged with staking out the site for the new capital of the Territories. No more profitable parcel of real estate could be imagined.

Battleford had been the original capital, but Battleford was no longer on the route of the CPR. The location of the railway would determine the site of Battleford's successor – clearly the most important city between the Red River and the Bow. The owners of the railway would have the final word in its selection. Though Dewdney had what amounted to Macdonald's carte blanche to choose the site, it would be the CPR's directors who would have to confirm it.

For all of the winter of 1881–82, Winnipeg speculators, knowing that the seat of government was about to be changed, had been dispatching platoons of men to squat on every promising location. It is fairly clear that General Rosser himself had his eye on land profits in the vicinity of the new capital; that was one reason why the preliminary survey of the line in Saskatchewan was altered and the location moved about six miles to the south.

A likely townsite along that preliminary survey had been at the crossing of the Wascana or Pile o' Bones Creek. Wascana is a corruption of a Cree word, "Oskana," meaning "bones." Along its banks, the bleached bones of thousands of buffalo lay in heaps. The remains of an old

113

"pound," or corral, lay on one side of the stream; it was into this enclosure that the Indians had driven the bison to be slaughtered. For years, on the opposite side, there had been a heap of bones six feet high and forty feet across, laid out with considerable artistry and used, apparently, as a signal station for a native sentry to announce the approach of the herd. Captain John Palliser in 1857 mentioned the presence of these bones, though he did not think much of the surrounding country. There appeared to be little water and there was no fuel at all.

Because water was so scarce, the river bank seemed a probable site not only to the first surveyors but also to the squatters who followed in their wake or even, on occasion, preceded them. There was a well-wooded area at one point, not far from the pile of buffalo bones; it was here that the speculators squatted and it was here that the original line crossed the creek. When the railway location was moved half a dozen miles to the south, across an absolutely treeless plain, the land sharks were left out in the cold.

When the relocation took place on May 13, 1882, there were only three settlers at the spot where the line crossed Pile o' Bones Creek. One of these, Thomas Sinclair Gore, was himself a former Dominion land surveyor. He had come out from Ontario earlier in the spring and, perhaps because of his calling, had not waited for good weather before striking west. He trekked two hundred miles from the end of steel, reaching Pile o' Bones Creek on April 27. Gore's practised eye told him exactly where the new survey might be expected to cross: there was an awkward loop in the northern location that added considerable distance with no observable gain. The new site was "by far the best I have seen in the North West."

Most speculators and settlers, however – and indeed most Canadians familiar with the country – felt that the only possible site for a capital city of the plains lay a few miles to the northeast near Fort Qu'Appelle in the broad, wooded valley of the Qu'Appelle River, perhaps the loveliest spot on all that sere steppe. Here were the necessary requirements for a townsite: an established community, sweet water and plenty of it, sheltering hills, good drainage, and timber for fuel, lumber, and shade.

The railway, however, was designed to skirt Fort Qu'Appelle. The reason given was that the steep banks of the valley would make construction difficult and costly. An equally strong motive was undoubtedly the company's policy of bypassing established communities in the interests of greater land profits. After all, if the capital had been established in the valley, it would not have been difficult to run a sixteen-mile spur into the

114

community. But the environs of Fort Qu'Appelle were crawling with squatters.

There was a second factor to be considered, although it was mere rumour at the time. Governor Dewdney had an interest in the land surrounding Pile o' Bones crossing. He and several friends, most of them leading politicians and public officials, had formed at least two syndicates earlier that year and in great secrecy purchased some twenty-eight sections of Hudson's Bay Company lands – the only land for sale at the time – along the future route of the CPR. One of the syndicates, in which Dewdney had a one-eleventh interest, owned four hundred and eighty acres on the very spot that Dewdney selected as the site of the future capital.

Dewdney was a prime mover in much of this land speculation. Something of the atmosphere of the times is revealed, unwittingly, in a letter he wrote to the Prime Minister explaining how one of the Hudson's Bay land sales was made. He knew of a Hudson's Bay section "he was sure would be valuable" but, rather than go himself to see Charles Brydges, the Company's land commissioner, about buying the acreage, sent a friend named Eden, a newly arrived merchant from England who was looking for speculative properties. As he told Eden, "if I go to Mr. Brydges to get them [the properties] he will think I have some good reason in securing them & I shall have to take in all his friends but if you go he will probably let you have them without a word. . . ."

Dewdney of course did have good reason, since he was in a position to know and to chart the future course of the North West. In the case of the property on Pile o' Bones Creek he did have to let in some of Brydges's associates, including his son Frederick and John Balsillie, long a high official of the Hudson's Bay Company's land department. Again the property was bought in the name of a trustee, with the ever-present Arthur Wellington Ross, the Winnipeg politician and realtor, handling the details and taking a share. It was to the advantage of the members to have their names kept secret, for most were well-known and several could have been accused of a conflict of interest. Frederick White, the comptroller of the Mounted Police, was one; the NWMP barracks would likely be built very close to the property in question. Alexander Galt's son Elliott, who worked under Dewdney as an Indian commissioner, was another. There were, altogether, five politicians and a future Manitoba judge, J. F. Bain, involved. (Another of Dewdney's syndicates included Alexander Campbell, the Prime Minister's former law partner and leader of the Senate.)

115

Dewdney was himself a surveyor, a Devonshire Englishman who had come out to the Crown Colony of British Columbia in 1859 as a young man of twenty-four. He had helped to survey the town of New Westminster and to lay out the trails and roads between the sparsely settled communities of the early gold-fields. He was also a loyal Conservative who, as a Member of Parliament, had supported Sir John A. Macdonald during and after the Pacific Scandal. In his new post he was reaping the rewards of that loyalty.

He was suffering from rheumatism that May, hobbling about on a stick as he examined the banks of Pile o' Bones Creek. By the middle of the month, he was certain enough of the site to reveal it to Tom Gore. "Well, Gore, you have hit it off pretty nicely," were his first words to his fellow-surveyor. "It is just about here that the capital of the North West Territories is likely to be located."

William White arrived a few days later. He had learned from a knowledgeable friend in Winnipeg that the CPR had fired Rosser for speculating in land and had, as a result, changed the location of the line at the creek crossing. White and five others immediately decided to make a dash for the new townsite. They bought a complete farming outfit, a yoke of oxen, tents, wagons, bob-sleighs, and provisions, took the train as far as Brandon and, in mid-April, pushed off into the snows, which were then two feet deep on the trails. The going was so bad that it required six oxen to haul their outfit over one hill near Fort Ellice. The ruts on the Carlton Trail were so deep, the ponds and sloughs so treacherous, that they rarely covered more than a dozen miles in a day. One day it took them seven hours to move two miles. When they reached Pile o' Bones Creek, they almost drowned when the overloaded ferry sank in midstream; White was saved only when a friend applied artificial respiration. On May 17 they were caught by a shrieking blizzard that imprisoned them for three nights, doubled up in their buffalo robes to keep from freezing. But, like so many who would follow, they persevered and on May 20 reached their mecca.

White immediately occupied a 160-acre homestead near the banks of the river where the survey line crossed it. This was to be the exact site of the business section of Regina, but to White it looked so desolate that he could not believe anyone would be foolish enough to locate a capital city on that naked plain. He relinquished his homestead and took up another two miles away, thereby depriving himself of one of the most valuable parcels of real estate on the prairies.

116

By this time rumours were flying in the Qu'Appelle Valley about the choice of a new capital. More tents were rising. At the Fort, the speculators were keeping a careful watch on Dewdney's movements. It was not expected that he would leave the community during the Dominion Day festivities; a considerable celebration had been arranged at which, it was felt, the Lieutenant-Governor would have to be present. Dewdney took advantage of this conviction to slip quietly away. Late in the afternoon of June 30 he posted a notice near Thomas Gore's tent reserving for the government all the land in the vicinity. The syndicate property, in which he had an interest, adjoined the government reserve directly to the north.

Thus was the city of Regina, as yet unnamed, quietly established. At Fort Qu'Appelle, when the news came, there was anger, frustration, disappointment, and frenzy. Most of the settlers hitched up their teams and moved themselves and all their worldly goods to the bank of Pile o' Bones Creek.

Though it would require the sanction of the CPR, it was almost a foregone conclusion that this was the site of the new capital. Squatters, "advancing, like an army with banners," began to pour towards the embryo city. Few of them were bona fide homesteaders. Dewdney reported to the Prime Minister, four days after the site was chosen, that most of them were paid monthly wages by Winnipeg speculators to squat on land and hold it "until it is found out where the valuable points are likely to be. . . ." By fall, the squatters, mainly young professional men – lawyers, engineers, clerks, and surveyors – held most of the available homestead land in the area of both Pile o' Bones and Moose Jaw Bone creeks. Their "improvements" under the homestead law consisted of putting up a small tent or a log framework four or five feet high which was called a house. As Dewdney described it, "when a settler comes along looking for a homestead he is met by these ruffians who claim it. . . ." Genuine settlers, who were supposed to get homesteads for nothing, found themselves paying up to five hundred dollars for them. The speculators used a variety of devices to swindle the newcomers. One method was to use a bogus lawyer to confuse settlers about their pre-emption rights to quarter sections adjacent to their homesteads. If that failed, Dewdney noted in an interview that fall, "a revolver is produced."

The matter of the capital was settled on August 12, though it was not so designated officially until the following March. Stephen arrived in Winnipeg, met Dewdney, and informed the Prime Minister by wire that he had agreed to the site of the new capital and had fixed on Assiniboia

117

as the appropriate name. Macdonald demurred; Assiniboia was already the name of the provincial district, established during the previous session. He suggested that the Governor General be consulted. For a while it seemed that the city would be named Leopold after the Queen's youngest son, but this too was rejected. Lord Lorne left the matter to his wife, Princess Louise, and she chose Regina in honour of her mother.

The new name produced an instant, adverse reaction. Princess Louise was not the most popular chatelaine that Rideau Hall had known; her boredom with the capital was the subject of public comment. Nor was the Governor General immune from the political mudslinging that enlivened the period. The comment of the Manitoba *Free Press*, which was typical, might easily have been characterized as lese-majesty in a later and more reverent era:

". . . the Governor-General . . . after harassing his massive intellect for a few days, evolved the word Regina from the chaos of his thoughts, and now the aforesaid capital will go down to posterity under the aegis of that formidable cognomen. From the foregoing fact we infer that His Excellency is not a success at christening cities. . . . Regina . . . is enough to blight the new city before it gets out of its swaddling clothes. If we have to put up with such outrageous nomenclature, it would have been better to stick by the old stand-by, Pile of Bones."

The *Sun* queried a number of leading Winnipeggers on the subject of the name a few days after it was made public in late August. "Regina!" cried Joseph Wolf, the portly auctioneer, "well, that's a fool of a name. Some old Indian name, musical to hear and pleasant to read of, conveying some poetical allusion to the spot, would have been just the thing." Another leading citizen, Fred Scoble, referred bluntly to the new title as "a double-barrelled forty-horse-power fool of a name." A third, John Peter Grant, insisted on calling the city "Re-join-her!" "Pooh," he declared. "No name at all. Too effeminate altogether. The Marquis must have been thinking of the Princess' frequent absences when he thought of that name. A city must be of the masculine persuasion to be of any use on general principles."

The choice of the site provoked even greater controversy than that of the name. The press indulged in what the Edmonton *Bulletin* described as a "terrible onslaught" against the new capital. Some of this resulted from a Canadian Press Association visit to the townsite in August. The eastern reporters, used to the verdant Ontario countryside, were dismayed to find nothing more than a cluster of tattered tents, huddled together on a bald and apparently arid plain. They were also influenced by Major J. M.

118

Walsh, in charge of the Mounted Police detachment at Qu'Appelle, who did not like the choice of the new site and made no secret of it. Walsh greeted the newspapermen and their families in spectacular fashion, concealing a strong force of Mounted Police in the woods near Qu'Appelle and breaking cover just as the train puffed up the grade. To the shrieks of the engine and the cheers of the passengers the Major and his troop galloped alongside the track and escorted the entourage towards the new settlement on the Wascana, which Walsh then proceeded to condemn to the reporters. Walsh's motives appeared to be as suspect as Dewdney's since he had land interests at Qu'Appelle and, according to the Lieutenant-Governor, had "attended more to his land speculations . . . than to his Police duties. . . ."

Dewdney was convinced that Walsh was one of the chief reasons why the press turned almost en masse against Regina. The London *Advertiser* called it a "huge swindle." The Brandon *Sun* said it should have been named Golgotha because of its barren setting. The Toronto *World* declared that "no one has a good word for Regina."

Early visitors were astonished that such a bleak plain should have been preferred over the neighbouring valley. Beecham Trotter, the telegraph construction man, stringing copper wire across it early in July, thought of it as a lifeless land: ". . . there was not a bush on which a bird could take a rest. . . . Water was invisible for mile after mile." One of Trotter's companions remarked that a touring rabbit would have to carry all his lunch with him. "If anybody had told us that the middle of this billiard-tabled, gumboed plain was the site of the capital of a territory as big as France, Italy and Germany, we would have thought him daft." Stavely Hill, the itinerant British politician, recorded that the site, as he encountered it in 1882, "was as little fitted for a capital city as any place could well be conceived to be." Marie Macaulay Hamilton, who arrived as a child, remembered the embryo capital as "a grim and dismal place"; to Peter McAra, who later became its mayor, Regina was "just about as unlovely a site as one could well imagine." Even George Stephen, who had picked the location sight unseen, was dubious after he visited it. "I hope Dewdney is right about Regina," he wrote to Macdonald in September, "but, I 'hae my doots.' "* Stephen would have preferred Moose Jaw.

* When Sinclair Lewis, the American novelist, visited Regina he was taken for a drive through the Qu'Appelle Valley and, impressed by its beauty, asked why the capital had not been placed there instead of on an arid plain. "Political skulduggery, likely," Lewis commented.

Dewdney stuck to his stated conviction that he had chosen the best possible location. He publicly declared that the site had been selected because "it was by all odds the most favorable location for a city on the main line of the Canada Pacific . . . it was surrounded by the best soil, it has the best drainage, and the best and greatest volume of water, of any place between the Assiniboine and Swift Current Creek." He told Macdonald, quite accurately as it turned out, that the new capital was in the very heart of the best wheat district in the country.

In the light of Dewdney's personal interest in Regina real estate (at 1882 prices, he and his partners stood to make a million and a half dollars from their property if they could sell it) these statements were greeted with jeers, especially in the Opposition newspapers, which smelled another Conservative scheme to enrich the Government's supporters through the building of the railway.

"It is intolerable that the high official whose prerogative it is to locate a capital city should have the privilege of first buying up the site in order to speculate in corner lots," the *Globe* cried. Dewdney, of course, was only one of many public officials in both parties who were speculating in western lands, often with inside knowledge. "Suppose he did speculate in land or what not!" said the Fort Macleod *Gazette* of Dewdney. "Is not everyone from the highest to the lowest doing the same?"

The rest of the press was not so lenient. Dewdney protested to John A. Macdonald that his interest in the Regina syndicate was a small one and that he had a much larger share in land at the Bell Farm, Indian Head, a site he had rejected as a capital. Even the friendly Winnipeg *Times* could not stomach the obvious conflict of interest. Dewdney might say that he held the land not as lieutenant-governor but as plain Mr. Dewdney, but "it is impossible, however, to distinguish between the two entities more especially as Lieutenant Governor Dewdney and Mr. Dewdney have a common pocket."

Dewdney's Regina interests inevitably led to a clash with the CPR. The railway was already hard pressed for funds. Its main asset was the land it owned on the sites of new towns. It did not intend to share these real estate profits with outsiders.

In Regina, the railway's interests were identical with those of the government, which was also in the land business. Under the terms of the contract, the CPR had title to the odd-numbered sections along the right of way, save for those originally ceded to the Hudson's Bay Company. In Regina and in several other important prairie towns, the government and the CPR pooled their land interests, placed them under joint management, and agreed to share the profits equally. That summer the railway, in order to raise funds, agreed to sell an immense slice of its land – five million acres – to a British-Canadian syndicate, the Canada North-West Land Company, for $13,500,000. The syndicate's job was to manage townsite sales in forty-seven major communities, including Moose Jaw, Calgary, Regina, Swift Current, and Medicine Hat. The railway was to receive half of the net proceeds of these townsite sales. Thus, in Regina, one quarter of the land profits went to the railway, one quarter to the land company, and one half to the government.

The townsite property was held in trust by four men, Donald A. Smith and Richard Angus for the CPR and Edmund B. Osler, the Toronto financier, and William Scarth for the land company. Scarth was a loyal Tory and close friend of the Prime Minister ("your devoted follower from my boyhood"). Since he was resident in Regina, it was he who managed the townsite; and since, in Stephen's phrase, the land company was "practically a branch of the Land Department of the C.P.R.," the railway controlled all of the Regina land save for that held by the Dewdney syndicate.

A struggle now ensued between Scarth and John McTavish, the CPR's land commissioner, on one side and Dewdney on the other over the exact location of Regina's public buildings. The former wanted the nucleus of the new capital on the railway- and government-owned sections; Dewdney wanted it on his property. Both sides, in their many submissions on the subject, pretended that they had the future interest of the community at heart. ("McTavish . . . is trying to induce me to build in a locality most undesirable in order to bring the town in the direction he wants," Dewdney complained to Macdonald in August.) But Regina was the product not of careful town planning but of commercial profiteering.

In the real estate contest that followed the railway held most of the cards. Its trump was the arbitrary location of the station two miles east of the Dewdney river property in a small and muddy depression far from any natural source of water. Dewdney was beside himself: ". . . in the spring it will be a mud hole," he complained to Macdonald. It was "imperatively necessary in the interest of the City" that a change be made. But the CPR had no intention of making a change; although Regina began, at first, to grow up on two locations, the magnet of the station was too much for the settlers, whose tents started to rise in clusters on the swampy triangle known as The Gore in front of the makeshift terminus.

In October, the survey of the new capital was completed and lots put up for sale. The survey included everything but the Dewdney syndicate's property on Section 26, Township 17, Range 20. Nonetheless, the owners

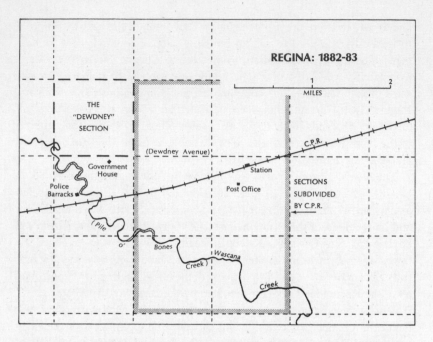

REGINA: 1882-83

THE "DEWDNEY" SECTION

(Dewdney Avenue)

Government House

Police Barracks

C.P.R.

Station

Post Office

SECTIONS SUBDIVIDED BY C.P.R.

Pile O' Bones Creek

Wascana Creek

MILES

of Section 26 subdivided their land and put it up for sale as well. The struggle between Dewdney and Scarth moved to Winnipeg, where the rival properties were "boomed," as the phrase of the day had it, in huge competing advertisements.

On October 26, Scarth announced a sale of Regina lots near the station set for October 31. Two days later, his rivals announced that their lots would be sold on October 29. Scarth moved his sale ahead and warned prospective buyers: "Do not be led astray by advertisements of lots falsely represented to be in the new Capital . . . at least two miles from the permanent Railway Station." The Dewdney syndicate replied with sales figures designed to show that theirs was the more popular subdivision. The lack of water was a strong factor against the railway land and Scarth was forced to promise that "a large reservoir is now being constructed . . . which eminent engineers are satisfied will supply a great city. . . ."

The railway won. Scarth sold some half-million dollars worth of Regina real estate that winter; the rival sales were negligible. A further struggle, however, developed over the location of government buildings. Dewdney wanted them on the river, where, as he pointed out, the drainage was good (and also where they would be next door to his syndicate's land); Stephen and Scarth wanted them near the station where, they contended, the government as well as the railway would profit. In the compromise that followed Macdonald tried to placate all his Conservative friends by scattering the locations of the public buildings. The police barracks and the Lieutenant-Governor's residence were on the river. Dewdney had made these selections himself and it was probably no coincidence that they were right next to the property in which he had an interest. Certainly his fellow syndicate member Frederick White, the Mounted Police comptroller, went to great lengths to try to hide the compromising fact that the site was chosen by Dewdney himself and not by Irvine, the commissioner. Irvine pointedly denied that he had anything to do with it.

The customs office, land office and, eventually, the post office were placed in the station area some two miles away, partly as a result of George Stephen's complaint to the Prime Minister that Dewdney had an interest in the Hudson's Bay section and was trying to place all the public buildings adjacent to it. As a kind of compromise between the two warring factions, the offices of the Indian Commissioner and North West Council were placed half-way between the station and the river. Later, when the registry office went up, it was on a block of its own. The queer community straggled for two and a half miles across the prairies, the various clusters of official buildings standing like islands in the prairie sea. Regina was a city without a centre.

In all the wheeling and dealing over land profits no public or corporate leader ever bothered to consider the interests of the people who would build the Queen City of the Plains and make it their home. Ottawa ignored the settlers who pleaded that the public buildings be concentrated in one area. The CPR and the land company were equally culpable; together they had contrived to split the community in two. The settlers had an awkward town plan imposed upon them by men from eastern Canada, few of whom had any intention of making Regina their home.

Traditionally, squatters in the North West had been protected on any land where they settled. Even when they were found to have squatted on lands reserved for the Hudson's Bay Company, their rights were generally respected, the Company accepting equivalent land elsewhere. But after 1880, the government, in effect, did away with squatters' rights where railway lands were concerned.

Bona fide settlers who had arrived on the scene early, taken up land. and built homes found that they were given no special consideration. Arbitrary prices were placed on such parcels by the land officials not only in Regina but also elsewhere. This led to bitter recriminations against "the East," the echoes of which lingered for decades. "It makes a fellow's blood fairly boil with rage to know of the treatment squatters are subject to in this country by a rotten Dominion Govt.," one newcomer, Edwin Brooks, wrote home to his wife from Indian Head. "Conservatives here are just as bitter as they can be, and denounce their actions in more forcible than polite language."

It was typical of eastern indifference to local North West interests (an indifference that would have bloody results in 1885) that when the first train arrived on August 23 with a carload of officials to christen the town, the settlers themselves were given no part in the ceremony. They had trekked across the prairie by ox cart, buckboard, horseback, and construction train; one, at least, had walked all the way from Rapid City, two hundred miles to the east. But no one thought to ask any of them to participate in the official beginning of the new town; in fact, when Regina's lots went on sale, these first settlers were forced to pay exactly the same rate as everybody else for the property they had vainly tried to appropriate as their own. W. H. Duncan, who was present and who, like many others, watched the scene from behind a tent flap, wrote half a century later that since most of them had been living under canvas for two or three months, "our work clothes were not considered in good enough condition to appear among the well-dressed people from the East."

The ceremony took place in Van Horne's private car. The assemblage was a glittering one, representative of the most powerful interests in the Dominion. Van Horne, Donald Smith, Duncan McIntyre, and John McTavish of the CPR were all present along with the company's solicitor, J. J. C. Abbott, a future prime minister. (Stephen, who had come as far as Winnipeg, had returned to Montreal.) Both the Hudson's Bay Company and the Bank of Montreal were represented on the highest level. Judge Francis Johnson of Quebec, a former territorial official, proposed the toast to Mr. and Mrs. Dewdney and "Success to Regina, the Queen City of the Plains."

It makes, in retrospect, an ironic little scene: there are the eastern dignitaries in their dark suits, wing collars, and striped trousers, lounging on the rear platform of the private car with their well-bustled wives; and there are the first families of Regina in their shapeless clothing, peering curiously out from behind the protection of the canvas flaps. Among the onlookers that day were at least three future mayors and one future chief justice; in the years that followed they and their fellows would help to shape the destinies of Saskatchewan and perhaps to nurture the seeds of dissidence sown in those formative months. But none of this occurred to the gentlemen on the train, sipping their French champagne and squinting across

124

the parched prairie, flat as a deal board, where the little tents stretched off in ragged clusters to the distant river.

5

From his vantage point at Winnipeg, George Stephen must have contemplated the astonishing progress of the railway with mixed feelings. Certainly his strategy, and Van Horne's, was working; but the company itself was in a desperate cash position.

The Grand Trunk declares war

The strategy had been to get the prairie section of the CPR operating as swiftly as possible. In that way a great chunk of the subsidy, which was paid to the company on the completion of each twenty-mile section, could be gained. Equally important, the paying portion of the line could go into operation and begin to show a profit at once.

Critics might carp that the company was building the easy part of the railway first, but Stephen's strategy was dictated as much by necessity as by guile. The mountains could not be tackled until there was a line of steel to bring supplies to the passes. As for the Lake Superior section, there were new surveys to be completed before the roadbed could be graded. The Opposition press – and some government newspapers, too – charged the company with dragging its feet on the section between Callander and Fort William. The Prime Minister, pushed by some of his cabinet colleagues, was uneasy about the lack of progress in the East for political reasons. After all, he had staked his career on an all-Canadian route. He urged that an immediate start be made that summer of 1882 at Thunder Bay. Later that fall, he wanted to hold back payments unless the company complied. John Henry Pope balked at this. He had already "talked very sharp" to Stephen and his colleagues and believed they were doing all they could. Pope felt strongly enough about the matter to offer his resignation. He knew the CPR's precarious financial position and urged the Prime Minister not to delay payments. "It really would amount to destroying their summers work to throw this Bomb Shell into their camp in the middle of the working season their expenses are now enormous. Men scattered over hundreds of miles. I really do not see how this can be done without breaking everything down."

Macdonald wrote Stephen a mollifying letter: "All I want is to be able to brag a little next Session as to the progress of the Eastern Section." Obviously, a start would have to be made by 1883; the Opposition had predicted all along that the Lake Superior section would never be built. Neither Macdonald nor Stephen could afford to allow Blake to cry: "I told you so!" Any lingering hopes by Syndicate members that the project could be postponed until the CPR began to make money were dashed. Somehow the money would have to be found.

All that year the climate in the money markets of London and New York had been bad for railway stocks and bonds in general and Canadian Pacific bonds in particular. As far as English investors were concerned, Canadian railways were the most disappointing foreign investment of all; they earned only a quarter as much, on an average, as other overseas investments. Since the British had already sunk two hundred million dollars into various Canadian railroad schemes, the arrival of the Canadian Pacific on the financial scene was not propitious. That was one reason why Stephen made no effort to place CPR securities on the London market, though he hoped to intrigue British investors into ordering land grant bonds from Montreal and New York.

There was a kind of lassitude in England as far as Canada was concerned – an indifference that maddened a man like Stephen who, in February, 1882, noted with disgust that P. T. Barnum's most recent acquisition, the huge elephant Jumbo, was "a matter of ten times more interest to London than twenty colonies." The emigrants might be flocking towards the new land but this did not make those at home feel any happier: ". . . the genuine insular Britisher hates all emigration efforts and would rather have people remain to struggle and sometimes starve than emigrate."

The market was so bad that when the CPR was driven to issue the remainder of its authorized stock in May, 1882 – about 190,000 shares with a par value of $19 million – the best price it could get was twenty-five cents on the dollar. Stephen was loath to issue any stock at all; from the outset he had tried to desist from the normal practice of floating large issues of shares and bonds, a technique employed over and over again – usually with lamentable results – by North American railways, ostensibly to raise money for construction. As often as not the proceeds were siphoned off into the pockets of promoters through such devices as dummy construction companies. Stephen was no longer a promoter. He had already made an immense fortune out of watered stock on the St. Paul railway. In Canada he was not as interested in personal profit as he was in the adventure of actually building a transcontinental line and making it run.

126

He had promised Macdonald that there would be "no financial fire works." Before issuing stock to the public he wanted to prove, by land sales and by earnings, that the CPR was a paying proposition. For that reason the company had issued only sixty-one thousand shares of its stock at par value in 1881 – almost all of it to members of the original syndicate. But in 1882 Stephen was faced with an unexpected expenditure: he had to find $4,300,000 to buy up the western section of the Quebec government railroad (the Quebec, Montreal, Ottawa and Occidental) and its branch lines in order to give the CPR access to Montreal. To raise the money he was forced to sell four times as much stock as he originally reckoned on.

He received a second financial blow that May of 1882: he had fully expected to lay his hands on an additional million dollars in cash to help with the work that Van Horne was planning for the season. The million was deposited with the government as security for the construction of the road. Stephen had believed that he could replace the deposit with gilt-edged securities and release the cash; it did not occur to him that the government would balk, but the government did. He did not get his million until December and only when he put up his personal property – debentures of the Credit Valley Railway, a company he had bailed out of a financial muddle in 1880.

There were other problems on which no one had reckoned in those first intoxicating days. There were the extra costs brought about by the unexpected influx of settlers: more rolling stock to buy and grain elevators to erect. Further, there was the expensive decision to build the road to better specifications than called for (a policy that quickly had to be abandoned). In doing this, Stephen and Van Horne were looking far into the future; but in the summer of 1882 cash was very short. In July Stephen went down to Macdonald's summer home at Rivière du Loup to warn him that the CPR's cash requirements had exceeded all calculations. The cost of the prairie section was "enormously in excess of our estimate." On the other hand, "we cannot afford to build a cheap road" – the Canadian climate conspired against it.

One of the unforeseen problems lay in the manner in which the twin subsidies – cash and land – were paid by the government to the railway. The money was advanced in equal instalments after each twenty-mile section was completed and approved by government engineers. This worked very well on the prairie section, where the track was advancing at the rate of twenty miles a week. But Stephen realized that he would shortly be faced with the two mountain barriers and the Canadian Shield. Here,

127

men would have to struggle for months to complete twenty miles of track. Cash from the subsidy would not be available to the company until long after the actual outlay. The CPR had already spent more than the subsidy on the prairie section. Where would it get the money to pay for labour and materials on the more difficult stretches of the road?

The matter of the land subsidy was even more complicated. On paper it all sounded so simple. Every time the railroad moved twenty miles it was to be given a proportionate number of acres from the land grant of twenty-five million. The only Crown land available was situated on the prairies between Winnipeg and the Rockies, but even if every alternate section in the forty-eight-mile belt across the plains had been fit for settlement, it would have been impossible to locate all of the twenty-five million acres in that strip. Some of it, for instance, had already been sold, some of it belonged to the Hudson's Bay Company, and, in addition, the CPR rejected a great deal of it. Clearly, additional land must be found elsewhere.

Stephen's dilemma, then, was this: since the land that the railway was earning did not exist in large enough quantities along the right of way, the government must be persuaded as quickly as possible to set aside extra tracts in the North West. In point of fact, four-fifths of the grant would have to be located outside the original limits and, being far from the right of way, would be harder to sell. (Nothing, as Stephen told Macdonald, could ever compensate the company for that loss.) Nonetheless it could stand as security for the land grant bonds that the company was issuing as fast as the land was located. The trouble with governments, as Stephen was discovering, is that they do not move very swiftly.

As the fall of 1882 wore on, Stephen's letters became increasingly importunate. By the end of the season, he realized, the company would have earned ten million acres of land; but there were only three million available along the completed right of way. Where would the rest come from? The government itself was selling land as fast as it could in the North West. It began to look as if there would not be enough left for the CPR. "We cannot build and equip the C.P. Railway without money," Stephen complained, "and money can only come from the resources we have at command . . . we shall need every acre of the grant to enable us to find the money . . . delay will be fatal to us – we cannot wait. . . ."

But, of course, he had to wait. A hint of panic crept into the letters that arrived, sometimes daily, on the Prime Minister's desk: "It is a matter of the utmost importance to the Company that it gets its lands as fast as they are earned, and it is of still greater importance that there should be no question about getting the full grant according to the terms of the con-

128

tract. . . ." "I . . . cannot move till I have the patents for the lands earned, up to this time." ". . . The demand on us for money is something appalling. *$400,000* went to Winnipeg last week and one million more to be there on the 10th. Those demands are quite enough to scare timid folks. But I have no fear so long as you stand by and trust us."

Macdonald, however, was not to be pushed. Politically he was in an unenviable position. If, as Stephen insisted, there were only five million out of a total of twenty-five million acres along the prairie belt, then the government was in a dilemma. Stephen was asking for six and a half million acres of good land south of the railway and another twelve and a half million to the north, along the fertile belt and at the foot of the Rockies. To convey large tracts of this land to a private company would cause an unholy row. On the other hand, to give the railway the even-numbered sections along the line in addition to the odd-numbered ones would intensify the spreading cry of monopoly.

In late October, Old Tomorrow wrote a soothing letter to Stephen: "Let us go by degrees in what we do. The Orders in Council for lands will be passed by next Monday. We are endeavouring to discover some plan for the issue of the patents speedily, but I fear that will need legislation."

Stephen, who was always impatient with the circumlocutions of politics, was almost beside himself. For most of his life, in the laissez-faire atmosphere of Victorian business enterprise, he had operated on his own, coming to grips with problems speedily, making his swift and often daring decisions with an economy of purpose, his logical mind unfettered by outside interest or political vacillation. That was how he had made his name in the textile business, seizing a sudden opportunity without recourse to his superiors; that was how he had met and solved the problem of the creaky St. Paul railroad. Now, for the first time in his life, he found himself in a kind of political straitjacket, and he was irritated. He did not care about the actual patents; he could deal with the land for some time without them. All he wanted the government to do was to pick out the land that was legitimately owed to the railway and certify it. He began to underline words for emphasis with great slashes of his pen: "It is most *essential* it should be settled *where* we are to get these lands." The CPR's account at the Bank of Montreal was badly overdrawn. Without the land it had no hope of raising further cash. "Our pinch is *now*," he wrote in frustration at the end of November. Bit by bit the Canadian Pacific Railway got its land, but it was another twenty-two years before the last acre was finally set aside for the company.

Even the acreage the company received at the time did not produce the hoped-for revenue; the land grant bonds were not selling. The only other possible source of ready cash was stock. In December, 1882, the company increased its authorized capital stock from twenty-five million dollars to one hundred million. Stephen, in New York, persuaded a number of leading American financial houses (including that of his friend and fellow director, John S. Kennedy) to form a syndicate to take a potential thirty millions in three equal instalments over a nine-month period. To get cash Stephen had to offer a substantial discount: he sold the stock at slightly better than half price. (The average was $52.50.) Moreover, the purchase of the second two instalments was conditional on the successful sale to the public of the first. Stephen set off immediately for London to attempt the impossible: to find buyers for the new issue in a market which, as Macdonald's confidant, the British financier Sir John Rose, wired, was "practically shut against Canada Pacific."

Stephen succeeded. He convinced financial houses in London, Amsterdam, and Paris that they should purchase blocks of the stock from the Americans (CPR shares were listed on the New York exchange but not in London). It was a considerable piece of financial legerdemain, given the business climate, "almost entirely due," Rose told the Prime Minister, "to the untiring efforts of our friend Stephen, whose zeal, energy, confidence in himself and the enterprise seemed to inspire everybody else with like confidence." The first instalment of ten million shares was paid on February 1, 1883, netting the company five millions in cash – a payment that arrived almost at the eleventh hour. The Canadian Pacific Railway was now, on paper at least, in the hands of Americans; as of October 28, 1883, when the final instalment was taken up, 50.3 per cent of all CPR shares were held in the United States.

This did not mean, however, that Americans controlled the Canadian Pacific Railway. The American-held stock was spread among 320 investors. Another thirty per cent was held in Britain and Europe by 157 shareholders. The remainder – just under twenty per cent – was controlled by a tight group of forty-two Canadians. All but a few thousand of these Canadian-held shares was in the hands of four men – Stephen, Angus, McIntyre, and Donald Smith – or their friends.

This Canadian control of the CPR was even more pronounced at stockholders' meetings. At the general meeting of March 3, 1884, sixteen Canadians by their presence or by proxies voted 96,141 shares. By contrast, the forty-two Americans voting could muster only 90,212 shares. There were ten shareholders represented from continental Europe, voting 17,437 shares, and eighteen from Great Britain voting 51,795 shares. Many of the latter were Stephen's friends and supporters: his son-in-law Harry Northcote, for example, his Scottish friend Lord Elphinstone, and, more important, Sir John Rose's old firm, Morton, Rose and Company, which voted 36,832 shares.

This tight ownership of a substantial slice of the company by a Canadian group was one of the reasons for the continuity of management that continued well into the following century. For almost thirty years, the CPR was run by members of the original Stephen-Angus-Van Horne-Shaughnessy combination which built it. The dynasty was continued when Baron Shaughnessy stepped down in 1918. His successor, Edward Beatty, was the son of Henry Beatty, a charter member of the original syndicate of 1880 who was placed in charge of the company's lake transportation division in 1882. When Beatty's son took over as president, fourteen of the CPR's seventeen directors were Canadians as were thirty-one of its thirty-four executive officers.

But even in 1883 it would have taken a major proxy battle to have ousted the Canadians from control of their own railway. Such a move was unthinkable; the shareholders had every confidence in Stephen – and with good reason. His efforts in London that January attested to his abilities. The work, as Rose told Macdonald, had been uphill, "greatly aggravated by the gross misrepresentation and unfriendliness of those whose interest in Canada should have led them to maintain silence even if they did not help." By this he meant the Grand Trunk Railway and, to a lesser but still significant extent, Charles Brydges and Sir Alexander Galt.

Stephen, whose assessment of people was generally black or white depending on how they viewed the Canadian Pacific Railway, was virtually refusing to speak to Galt. During a trip west in the summer of 1882, the High Commissioner had made some disparaging remarks about the quality of the land west of Moose Jaw Bone Creek. Stephen called him a "sorehead" and wanted Macdonald to get rid of him. He was equally disaffected towards Brydges, a former Grand Trunk general manager, who, as Hudson's Bay land commissioner, had made some slighting references to the Canada North-West Land Company.

Some of the antipathy undoubtedly grew out of the Regina situation. Galt had an interest in the rival Dewdney syndicate through his son Elliott; Brydges had an interest through his son Frederick; other Hudson's Bay Company officials were also involved. Donald A. Smith (the major Hudson's Bay stockholder), who was in England with Stephen, believed that Brydges was personally profiting from sales in Hudson's Bay lands as a result of inside knowledge; an investigating committee eventually

131

corroborated this suspicion, declaring that Brydges had "erred on the side of prodigality." His antipathy to the CPR's land company could scarcely be described as disinterested.

Stephen was up in arms over Brydges's remarks. "How can he expect us to be friends with him stabbing us in the back that way?" he asked Macdonald. "I get mad when I think of the meanness of the man's character. . . ." He added, ominously, that "his time is coming" and so it was. Later that year, Donald Smith made a sudden move that shocked his colleagues; by voting his vast block of stock he was able, single-handed, to overturn the entire Hudson's Bay board of directors and replace it with his own candidates. Both Brydges and the resident commissioner, James A. Grahame, who had made a killing in Winnipeg real estate through inside knowledge, were forced to resign.

Stephen's personal antipathies and strong passions disturbed the suave and conciliatory Rose, who had been trying to get the fur-trading company and the railway to combine on land sales in the North West. Though he conceded that Galt was "the reverse of friendly" to the CPR and Brydges indiscreet and nepotistic, his own sense of the diplomatic proprieties was offended by Stephen's public passions. Stephen had "become very imperious, & intolerant of opposition." Rose was afraid he would make enemies by the bluntness of his attitude. ". . . conciliation would be more politic," he advised Macdonald. "His earnestness and force of character are invaluable qualities, considering the gigantic work he has on hand, but it is no easy matter to hold an even balance between *his* views and those of *more cautious men*."

Rose could not have it both ways. It was Stephen's very earnestness and force of character, his passionate devotion to and belief in the Canadian Pacific Railway and the Canadian North West that finally persuaded the businessmen of four capitals to take up his new stock issue. "I have never had misgivings about eventual success in spite of all opposition," Stephen declared, "but sometimes it has taken some courage to keep weak-kneed associates from wilting."

By "opposition," Stephen meant the Grand Trunk, which was continuing to fight the railway on several new fronts – political, journalistic, and financial. The GTR's forceful general manager, Joseph Hickson, was no minor adversary. He was a Northumberland man who had been involved with railways since boyhood, working his way up from apprentice clerk to chief accountant and finally to the very top, "a straightforward and fair-dealing man," a contemporary biographer called him, punctual as a conductor's watch and tough as a rail-spike. He was known as a shrewd negotiator, patient and tenacious. One American railway president is said to have remarked that when he put his feet under the table with Hickson he always took off his boots. His brain moved like quicksilver: he had a habit of sizing up a situation almost instantly, recognizing its potentialities, and acting with dispatch. He had the kind of supple mind that grasps the significance of statistics and turns them to account. He could, said one admirer, make pounds, shillings and pence, traffic miles and ton miles, dance in sarabands. In Canada he was a power in both the political and the financial worlds. Married to a member of the Dow brewing family, he was a long-time crony and supporter of Sir John A. Macdonald.

During his tenure of office, Hickson had been creating a route for the Grand Trunk through Ontario and into the American midwest. After saving the railway from bankruptcy in the seventies, he had, in a "masterstroke of railway tact, ability and diplomacy," managed to dump the unprofitable section of his road onto the Canadian government's lap and use the proceeds of the sale to seize control of a direct line into Chicago. He did not intend to stand idly by and watch a new railway destroy his creation. As long as the CPR stayed in the northwest of Canada, Hickson and his president, Sir Henry Tyler, had no quarrel with it; but now it had invaded Grand Trunk territory, buying up a link with Montreal and controlling the Ontario and Quebec Railway out of Toronto. Van Horne considered this move essential. Had the CPR stopped at Lake Nipissing, it "would have existed only as a sickly appendage of the Grand Trunk." It would be like "a body without arms . . . dependent . . . upon the charity of a neighbor whose interest would be to starve it." Over the next several years, the two rival general managers, both men of stubborn courage and determination, would be at loggerheads.

In the election of 1882, Macdonald found himself caught between the Canadian Pacific and the Grand Trunk. He confidently expected that his railway policy would win him the election; the dream of a Pacific railway had been a Conservative project from the start and now that the dream was coming true in such spectacular fashion, it could be seen as a political asset. On the other hand, Macdonald needed Grand Trunk support, especially in Ontario where he faced a hard fight. The older railway's political muscle in that province was considerable. Among other things it told its employees exactly how they must vote, and, according to Stephen, Hickson's control of the provincial government of Oliver Mowat amounted to a scandal. Stephen tended to see sinister plots everywhere where the CPR was concerned, but Macdonald agreed with him. "Mowat has sold himself to the GTR and passes everything they ask," he told Stephen. "That must be put down – and we *must* defeat Mowat & Co. . . ." It was the first of a series of continuing hints, at first gentle and then progressively blunter, that the CPR must become politically involved, as the Grand Trunk was.

With Hickson, the Prime Minister did not hedge. He openly solicited his political assistance. "I have, as you know, uniformly backed the GTR since 1854 and won't change my course now," he reassured him in February, 1882, as the campaign started to warm up. In May he was writing to ask him to "put your shoulder to the wheel and help us . . . in the elections." Four days later he was naming specific candidates he wanted the Grand Trunk to back: "All your people must vote for Robert Hay. He is *my* candidate and will be elected. He will follow my lead and do as I ask him." Hay, a furniture manufacturer running for Toronto Centre, was, among other things, a director of the Credit Valley Railway, which the CPR controlled.

Hickson appeared happy to comply: he put a private car at Macdonald's disposal for four weeks of the campaign; but he was determined to exact a price for his support. On the very eve of the election he sent a letter to Macdonald by special messenger and asked for a reply by telegraph. In it he asked the Prime Minister to put a stop to the CPR's invasion of Grand Trunk territory in Ontario: "Mr. Stephen and his friends . . . strong in the conviction that they are more powerful than the government or the Grand Trunk Company, continue to pursue a course of irritation and injury." Specifically, Hickson was talking about the Ontario-Quebec line. The government, he was convinced, "have the power to put an end to these wanton attacks on British investments and could do so if they wished. . . . Now is the time to call a halt if the foolish course being pursued is to be abandoned."

Hickson was careful to add: "I believe you have never had cause to complain of any action of mine in political matters. I do not intend you have so as long as I remain in my present position."

Here was a delicate matter for a party leader to face on election eve. Macdonald, who liked to seek refuge in delay, wired Hickson that he could not reply by telegraph but would write by the next mail – "meanwhile you may depend on my exertions to conciliate matters." In a later wire he was a little more specific: "Government not committed to any adverse line you may depend upon what I can possibly do personally to meet your views." With that fuzzy promise Hickson had to be content. Later Macdonald told him that he was overrating the government's influence with the CPR;

"they are quite independent of us." Hickson scarcely believed that convenient remark. Macdonald, he declared, had created a power which believed itself to be stronger than either the government or the rival railway. "The result will be serious trouble in a good many quarters in the near future." The Grand Trunk was moving into the Liberal camp.

Meanwhile, Hickson was attacking on a second front. The Grand Trunk's chief rival in southwestern Ontario was the Great Western, which operated a network of lines between Toronto, London, Hamilton, and Windsor. Hickson, by aggressive competitive tactics, brought the Great Western to its knees and forced an amalgamation in August, 1882, outbidding the CPR which also wanted to acquire the line. Hickson now controlled every rail approach to the United States. If he linked up with the Northern Pacific at Duluth he would shortly be part of a transcontinental through line that could undercut the Canadian Pacific.

Hickson struck again in Quebec. The CPR now owned half of the Quebec, Montreal, Ottawa and Occidental Railway – the section between Montreal and Ottawa. Hickson, in a swift coup, bought the other half – the "North Shore Line" – to prevent the CPR from getting into Quebec City. The story at the time was that the Canadian Pacific, which was negotiating for the line with Louis-Adélard Sénécal, the railway's superintendent, had tried to force down the asking price by getting the bank to call a demand note for a quarter of a million dollars on a day's notice. The angry Sénécal sold out to the Grand Trunk.

In London, William Abbott, a Grand Trunk shareholder and its former secretary who had helped negotiate the merger with the Great Western, kept up a propaganda barrage aimed directly at the CPR. "The attacks here on the country as a place for settlers to go are abominable," Stephen reported to Macdonald in January, 1883, "and everything that the G.T.R. people in Canada can find in any wretched sheet against the country, is sent over here for republication by Abbott the notorious. The worst feature for us in Canada is that there is hardly a newspaper in the whole country which is in a position to say a word against the G.T.R. no matter what it may say or do against the country – without losing Hickson's advertising. . . . I will yet pay off Hickson and his road for the unfair weapons they have used against me."

The insidious Abbott, according to Stephen, was saying aloud that Hickson had such complete control of the press and of the Canadian parliament that he could do anything he liked. (In Canada, Hickson was doing his best to damage the CPR by making the same charges against Stephen.) The "enemy," as Stephen was now calling them – "because no other word expresses their opposition" – was producing a stream of pamphlets declaring that the Canadian Pacific could never pay its investors but must inevitably lose money. The pamphlets harped on the foolhardiness of crossing the country north of Lake Superior. It was "a perfect blank, even on the maps of Canada. All that is known of the region is that it would be impossible to construct this one section for the whole cash subsidy provided by the Canadian Government for the entire scheme." A letter planted in the *Money Market Review* and signed "Experience," declared that "no more hopeless project than that line, or a more baseless speculation than its land grant . . . was ever started to enveigle the British public." Stephen decided to fight back with a weekly paper of his own, "avowedly devoted to Canadian interests"; and thus the *Canada Gazette* was born. Its editor was Thomas Skinner, chairman of the Canada North-West Land Company.

Before the new paper was published, the Grand Trunk held its semi-annual meeting in London and here its president, Sir Henry Tyler, made what Stephen called "an official declaration of war against all Canadian Pacific interests." ("My policy of contemptuous silence has bothered them very much," Stephen proudly confided to the Prime Minister.) Tyler attacked the CPR for invading Grand Trunk territory and entering "upon schemes of aggression." Abbott, the pamphleteer, charged that the railway was shirking its commitments north of Lake Superior. There were threats about the purse-strings of England being closed to the Canadian Pacific.

Stephen, "our somewhat impulsive friend," as Rose called him, was temperamentally incapable of taking this lying down; he abandoned his policy of contemptuous silence and fired off a circular letter to Grand Trunk shareholders replying to Tyler's charges and declaring he and his colleagues had done "all in their power to discredit and damage the C.P.R. Company in the eyes of the British public."

Sir John Rose attempted, and almost achieved, a conciliation between the two antagonistic presidents. On April 6, 1883, Tyler and Stephen were persuaded to sit down together and hammer out an agreement which, in effect, reserved all traffic to the Pacific for the CPR but gave the Grand Trunk Ontario. The purpose was "to avoid competition and work together in all respects for mutual benefit." Both men came reluctantly to the bargaining table. Rose's velvet glove hid an iron hand, which he revealed to Stephen when he told him that "he had got to the limit of financial support." His own firm, Morton, Rose and Company, had reached the limit of the load it would assume, and Stephen could not expect any more aid on the continent or in New York. As for Tyler, he, too, was "completely under stock exchange influences, and they saw what a serious blow these new arrangements could be if promoted in a hostile spirit."

The rapprochement did not last long. In Montreal the CPR's directors could not stomach what they conceived to be surrender in eastern Canada. Van Horne was one who thought it sheer madness to abandon the projected line between Toronto and Montreal. The board vetoed the arrangement. "I consider the course of Mr. Stephen and his friends as extremely foolish," Hickson remarked, "for the simple reason that they have gone out of their way to bring about a collision with the Grand Trunk and those interested in it."

The GTR stepped up its propaganda campaign while the Canadian Pacific moved to acquire more lines in Ontario and Quebec. Van Horne said bluntly that he would match Hickson foot for foot if necessary.

But in the matter of passenger and freight rates, business was still business and profits were still profits. Much of Van Horne's invective against Hickson in the years that followed was confined to charges that Grand Trunk personnel were breaking rate-fixing agreements which the two companies, in spite of their public enmity, had secretly entered into in eastern Canada. Such rate cuts, in Van Horne's words, were "simply idiotic." He gave orders that any CPR agent who dropped rates below those established by the two companies should be subject to instant dismissal – and he wanted the same understanding from his rival.

Had the newspapers and general public, who watched the battle of the two giants like spectators at a prize fight, been privy to some of the general manager's private correspondence with his adversary, they might have viewed the contest with more cynicism.

"I fully agree with what you say about the desirability of friendly and frank intercourse between the officers of the two companies," Van Horne wrote to Hickson on one occasion. ". . . we are earnestly in favor of the maintenance of all rates and agreements and nothing that will secure them will be left undone on our part. . . . I have again instructed our traffic officers not to fail on any occasion to meet those of your company in the most friendly spirit and to join in any movement calculated to secure net earnings rather than gross tonnage."

And again: ". . . I will be very glad to see the Passenger Agents of the two Roads following the practice of the Freight Agents and meeting at regular intervals for the purpose of discussing and adjusting their differences and I have indicated to the officers of our Passenger Department my wish that they should do so. I do not think there ought to be any difficulty in absolutely maintaining rates between the two Companies. . . ."

In areas where direct revenue was not concerned, Van Horne continued to do battle with Hickson. When the Grand Trunk played down the CPR's route on its own folders, Van Horne instructed Alexander Begg, the company's general emigration agent, to strike back with a map of his own. He told Begg to show the GTR's Toronto-Montreal road as a faint line and to drop out their Toronto-Chicago line entirely. In the matter of cartography, the general manager was quite prepared to smite his rivals; but free enterprise in the nineteenth century did not extend to the costly competition of a rate war.

Chapter Four

1

"Hell's Bells Rogers"

2

On the Great Divide

3

The Major finds his pass

4

The Prairie Gopher

5

"The loneliness of savage mountains"

1

One of Jim Hill's several executive strengths was an ability – it verged at times on the uncanny – to settle upon the right man for the right job at the right moment. His choices, however, were not always obvious ones. Certainly his decision to employ a former Indian fighter to find a practicable railway route through the Rockies and Selkirks must have seemed, at the time, to be totally outrageous. For one thing, Major A. B. Rogers had never seen a mountain; he was a prairie surveyor, used to the rolling plains of the American midwest. Yet here was Hill, sending him off to British Columbia to explore the most awesome peaks in the cordilleran spine of the continent and expecting him to succeed where dozens of more experienced engineers had failed! For another thing, Rogers was perhaps the most heartily disliked man in his profession. Few were prepared to work under him for more than one season and many quit his service in disgust or fury before the season's end. He fed his workmen wretchedly, drove them mercilessly, and insulted them continually. There were some who considered him an out-and-out sadist; all agreed that he was, to put it mildly, eccentric. Admittedly, he was honest; he would have scorned to engage in the kind of real estate profiteering that had intrigued General Rosser. He pared corporate expenses with a fealty that almost amounted to fanaticism. He was also ambitious, not for money but for fame; and it was this quality that clearly attracted Hill when he called him into his office in February, 1881, and proceeded, with great shrewdness, to dangle before him a chance at immortality.

Hill liked to study men thoroughly, in the same way he studied transportation, fuel, or the works of Gibbon. Undoubtedly he knew a good deal about Rogers's background – that he had gone to sea as a youth, that he had begun his adult life as an apprentice to a ship's carpenter, that he had studied engineering at Brown University and then entered Yale as an instructor. Though Rogers was a Yale graduate, with a bachelor's degree in engineering, it is quite impossible to think of him as a "Yale man," with everything that phrase connotes. In a profession remarkable for its individualists, he was unique. He was short and he was sharp – "snappy" was an adjective often used to describe him – and he was a master of picturesque profanity. Blasphemy of the most ingenious variety sprang to his lips as easily as prayer to a priest's. Because of this he was saddled with a variety of nicknames, such as "the Bishop" and "Hell's Bells Rogers." The young surveyors who suffered under him generally referred

140

to him as "the old man." He was fifty-two when he set off into the mountains, but he must have seemed more ancient than time – a crotchety old party, seemingly indestructible and more than a little frightening. Small he may have been, but his mien was forbidding: he possessed a pair of piercing eyes, blue as glacial ice, and a set of white side whiskers that were just short of being unbelievable; they sprouted from his sunken cheeks like broadswords, each coming to the sharpest of points almost a foot from his face.

He had won his military title by displaying a quick mastery of bushfighting in the Sioux uprising of 1861 and gained his professional reputation as "the Railway Pathfinder" while acting as a locating engineer for the Chicago, Milwaukee and St. Paul Railroad. In the field he carried a compass, an aneroid barometer slung around his neck, and very little more. Generally he was to be seen in a pair of patched overalls with two pockets behind, in one of which he kept a half-chewed plug of tobacco and in the other a sea biscuit. That, it was said, was his idea of a year's provisions.

The tobacco he chewed constantly. Secretan, who did not care at all for Rogers, paid tribute to him as "an artist in expectoration." There were many who believed that he was able to exist almost entirely on the nutritive properties of chewing tobacco. "Give Rogers six plugs and five bacon rinds and he will travel for two weeks," someone once said of him. Everyone who worked for him or with him complained about his attitude towards food; he was firmly convinced that any great variety – or even a large quantity of it – was not conducive to mental or physical activity.

His own diet was supremely Spartan: Harry Hardy of Chatham, who worked with him in 1883, recalled that "he was stingy with the Company's money, but generous to a fault with his own. . . . I have heard it said that he carried raisins to eat with him on his trips. There were no raisins in the country. It was beans – just ordinary beans – that he carried. He used to eat them raw." A. E. Tregent, who was with him that first year in the mountains, agreed: "His idea of a fully equipped camp was to have a lot of beans. He would take a handkerchief, fill it with beans, put a piece of bacon on top, tie the four corners and then start off." John F. Stevens, who worked for him as an assistant engineer, described Rogers as "a monomaniac on the subject of food." The Major once complimented Stevens on the quality of his work but then proceeded to qualify his remarks by complaining that he "made a god of his stomach." Stevens had dared to protest about the steady diet of bacon and beans which, he said, were the camp's *pièce de résistance* three times a day. His demands

141

for more varied fare marked him in Rogers's eyes as an "effeminate gourmet."

Van Horne tried constantly, and with only intermittent success, to get Rogers to provide more appetizing food in larger quantities for his men. On one occasion, while visiting his camp, he challenged the Major on the subject.

"Look here, Major, I hear your men won't stay with you, they say you starve them."

"'T ain't so, Van."

"Well, I'm told you feed 'em on soup made out of hot water flavoured with old ham canvas covers."

"'T ain't so, Van. I didn't never have *no hams!*"

Van Horne, so the story has it, moved hurriedly on to James Ross's mountain camp where plenty of ham was available. It is small wonder Rogers had trouble keeping men working for him.

Outwardly he was a hard man – hard on himself and hard on those who worked for him. Only a very few, who grew to know him well, came to realize that much of that hardness was only an armour that concealed a more sensitive spirit. "Rogers was a queer man," A. E. Tregent remembered, "lots of bluff and bluster." It was a shrewd assessment. The profane little creature with the chilly eyes and the rasping voice was inwardly tormented by intense emotions, plagued by gnawing doubts, and driven by an almost ungovernable ambition. "Very few men ever learned to understand him," his friend Tom Wilson wrote of him. Wilson, a packer and later a Rocky Mountain guide, was one of those few. Rogers, he said, "had a generous heart and a real affection for many. He cultivated a gruff manner to conceal the emotions that he seemed ashamed to let anyone sense – of that I am certain. His driving ambition was to have his name handed down in history; for that he faced unknown dangers and suffered privations."

James Jerome Hill understood those ambitions when he offered to put Rogers in charge of the mountain division of the CPR. Rogers's main task would be to locate the shortest practicable route between Moose Jaw Bone Creek, west of Regina, and Savona's Ferry in British Columbia, where Andrew Onderdonk's government contract began. That meant finding feasible passes through the southern Rockies and also through the mysterious Selkirks. There were several known and partially explored passes in the Rockies, including the Vermilion, Kootenay, Kicking Horse, and Howse, but no one had yet been able to find an opening in the Selkirk barrier. Hill made Rogers an offer he knew he could not refuse: If the Major could find that pass and save the railroad a possible hundred and fifty miles, he promised, the CPR would give him a cheque for five thousand dollars and name the pass after him.

Rogers did not care about the cash bonus. But to have one's name on the map! That was the goal of every surveyor. He accepted Hill's offer on the spot and, from that moment on, in Tom Wilson's words, "to have the key-pass of the Selkirks bear his name was the ambition he fought to realize."

Rogers's first move was to read everything that was available about the mountain country, including the journals of Walter Moberly, a man who knew more about the Selkirk mountains than anyone alive. In 1865 and 1866, and again in the winter of 1871–72, this tough, dedicated, and often difficult engineer had sought a pass in the Selkirks without success. He had come to believe that none existed, but there was one possibility that he had not fully pursued. That was the east fork of the Illecillewaet River, a foaming tributary of the Columbia whose smoke-blue waters tore down the western wall of the Selkirks through jungles of spruce and cedar to join the mother river at the site of what is now Revelstoke, British Columbia.

An entry in Moberly's journal of 1866, published by the British Columbia colonial government, caught Rogers's eye:

"*Friday, July 13th* – Rained hard most of the day. Perry returned from his trip up the east fork of the Ille-cille-waut River. He did not reach the divide, but reported a low, wide valley as far as he went. His exploration has not settled the point whether it would be possible to get through the mountains by this valley but I fear not. He ought to have got on the divide, and his failure is a great disappointment to me. He reports a most difficult country to travel through, owing to fallen timber and underbrush of very thick growth. . . ."

Perry was Albert Perry, known as the Mountaineer. Rogers was not able to interview him for he had died under rather gaudy circumstances. A man who hated Indians, he had often predicted that one would eventually murder him. One night, while Perry slept in his blankets under a tree near Burrard Inlet, an Indian made good that prophecy.

It is possible that Rogers did go up to Winnipeg, a day's journey from St. Paul, to talk to Moberly, though it is doubtful he learned much more since Moberly had clearly rejected the Illecillewaet as a feasible route for the railway. Five years after Perry's abortive foray, Moberly returned to the mountains on the Canadian Pacific Survey; he crossed the Selkirks on foot in midwinter but did not bother to explore the neglected valley, which

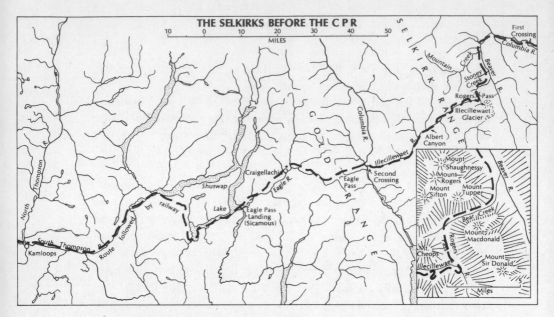

THE SELKIRKS BEFORE THE CPR

his earlier journal entries had suggested would bear further scrutiny. Indeed, he reported to the chief engineer, Sandford Fleming, that there was no practicable pass in that mountain rampart.

Nonetheless, Rogers determined to complete Perry's exploration. With his favourite nephew, Albert, he set off at the beginning of April for Kamloops, the settlement closest to the Selkirks, which lay one hundred and fifty miles to the east beyond the intervening Gold Range. It took him twenty-two days to reach the town, for he had to travel by train to San Francisco, by boat to Victoria and New Westminster, and by stage-coach the rest of the way. When he arrived, he engaged ten "strapping young Indians" through a remarkable contract made with their leader, Chief Louie. Its terms rendered them up to Rogers as his virtual slaves, to work "without grumbling" until they were discharged. If any of them came back without a letter of good report, his wages were to be forfeited and the chief agreed to lay one hundred lashes on his bare back. The Indians were all converted Christians, but the local priest did not complain about this barbarism; rather he was a party to it, for he was the man to whom the letters of good report were to be addressed, and his church was to be the beneficiary of the forfeited wages. It is perhaps unnecessary to add that, in spite of the hardships the party encountered, no murmur of complaint ever escaped the Indians' lips.

Rogers, who knew about three hundred words of Chinook jargon, the traders' pidgin tongue, did not have a very high opinion of Indians, possibly because they ate too much – a fatal weakness in his eyes. "Every Indian," he once declared, "is pious and hungry. Their teachings and their stomachs keep them peaceably inclined. Any one of them can out-eat

144

two white men, and any white man can out-work two Indians." The Major spent eight days in Kamloops trying to find out how far an Indian could travel in a day with a hundred-pound pack on his back and no trail to follow, and how little food would be required to keep him alive under such conditions. He concluded – wrongly, as it turned out – that the expedition's slim commissariat could be augmented by game shot along the way and so set off with a minimum of supplies. He was to regret that parsimony.

The twelve members of the party left Kamloops on April 29. It took them fourteen days of hard travel to cross the rounded peaks of the Gold Range (or Monashees as they were later called). They proceeded down the Columbia by raft, with the unfortunate Indians swimming alongside, until, about May 21, they reached the mouth of the Illecillewaet. Here Rogers found himself standing on the exact spot from which Moberly's assistant, Perry, had plunged into the unknown, fifteen years before.

It must have been a memorable moment. The little group, clustered on the high bank of the Columbia, was dwarfed by the most spectacular mountain scenery on the continent. Behind them the rustling river cut an olive path through its broad evergreen valley. Above them towered the Selkirks, forming a vast island of forest, rock, ice, and snow – three hundred miles long – cut off from the rest of British Columbia's alpine world by two great rivers, the Kootenay and the Columbia. These two watercourses, rising within a mile and a quarter of each other, together described a gargantuan ellipse which virtually encircled the mountain chain. The Selkirks, as Rogers probably knew, were of a different geological age and structure than the neighbouring Rockies; their distinctive shapes helped to tell that story – massive, cloud-plumed pyramids bulking against the sky. Once they had formed the crest of the continent's spine, rising high above the prehistoric ocean, eons before the Rockies were born. It was only after the earth's crust cooled and inner convulsions shifted the position of the continental divide that the Selkirks were subordinated to the younger peaks.

Now began a terrible ordeal. Each man balancing a hundred-pound pack on the back of his neck struggled upward, picking his way over mud-falls, scaling perpendicular rock points, wading through beaver swamps dense with underbrush and the "villainous devil's clubs," whose nettles were almost inescapable. Albert Rogers later wrote that without the fear of his uncle's dreadful penalty, all the Indians would have fled. Recalling the journey two years later, Rogers remarked that "many a time I wished myself dead," and added that "the Indians were sicker than we, a good deal."

145

In the gloomy box canyon of the Illecillewaet (later named for Albert Rogers) the snow was still several feet deep. Above them, they could see the paths of the avalanches – the timber crushed to matchwood in swaths hundreds of feet wide. Sometimes, unable to move farther on one side of the river, they were forced to crawl gingerly over immense snow bridges suspended one hundred and fifty feet above the frothing watercourse. At this point, the toiling men, bent double under the weight of their packs, were too concerned with the problems of terrain to marvel greatly at the beauty around them; that luxury would have to await the coming of the railway. But there was a touch of fairyland in those shadowed peaks. The music of running water was everywhere, for the torrents of spring were in full throat. Above them they could catch glimpses of an incredible wedge-shaped glacier, hanging like a jewel from the mountain pinnacles. Before many years passed the Illecillewaet Glacier would become one of the CPR's prime tourist attractions.

The Indians could no longer carry packs weighing a hundred pounds. When the fish and game the Major had expected to garner along the way proved to be nonexistent, the party was forced to go on short rations. They were seldom dry. The heavy rains and wet underbrush, the continual wading in glacial waters and soft snow – some of the drifts were ten feet deep – the lack of proper bedding at chill altitudes (half a pair of blankets per man was all that Rogers allowed) – all these privations began to take their toll.

They held cautiously to the lee of an obelisk-shaped peak, which would later be named Mount Sir Donald, after Donald A. Smith. Here, in the cool shadows, there was still a crust on the snow which allowed them to walk without floundering. At four one afternoon they came upon a large level expanse that seemed to them to be the summit. They camped there, on the edge of timber, out of range of the terrible snowslides. When the sun's rays vanished and the crust began to re-form they made a hurried trip across the snow-field. At the far end they heard the sound of gurgling water and to their satisfaction saw that it separated, some of it running westward, some to the east. They had reached the divide; was this the route the railway would take?

Mountains towered above them in every direction. A smear of timber extended half-way up one slope between the scars of two snowslides and they determined to make their ascent at this point. Each man cut himself a stick of dry fir and started the long climb. "Being gaunt as greyhounds, with lungs and muscles of the best, we soon reached the timber-line," Albert Rogers recounted.

Here the going became very difficult. The party crept around ledges of volcanic rock, seeking a toehold here, a fingerhold there, staying in the shade as much as possible and kicking steps in the crust. Several feet above the timber line, the route followed a narrow ledge around a promontory exposed to the sun. Four of the Indians tied pack-straps to each other's belts and then the leader crept over the mushy snow in an attempt to reach the ledge. He fell back with such force that he lost his footing and all four men plunged thirty feet straight down the dizzy incline, tangled in their pack-straps, tumbling one over another until they disappeared from sight. The others scrambled down after them; miraculously, none was injured.

It was late in the day when the twelve men reached the mountain top, but for Albert Rogers, at least, it was worth the ordeal:

"Such a view! Never to be forgotten. Our eyesight caromed from one bold peak to another for miles in all directions. The wind blew fiercely across the ridge and scuddy clouds were whirled in eddies behind great towering peaks of bare rocks. Everything was covered with a shroud of white, giving the whole landscape the appearance of snow-clad desolation. Far beneath us was the timber line and in the valleys below, the dense timber seemed but a narrow shadow which marked their course."

The Major was less poetic, though he read a great deal of poetry and loved it. On occasions such as this it was his habit to doff his hat, ruffle his long hair, and say, reverently: "Hell's bells, now ain't that thar a pretty sight!"

The party had neither wood for a fire nor boughs for beds. They were all soaked with perspiration and were wolfing great handfuls of snow to quench the thirst brought on by their climb. "But the grandeur of the view, sublime beyond conception, crushed out all thoughts of our discomfort."

They were in a precarious position, perched on a narrow ridge where a single false move could lead to their deaths. They crawled along the razorback on all fours until they encountered a little ledge in the shadow of a great rock, which protected them from the wind. Here they would have to wait until the crust formed again and the morning light allowed them to travel.

It was a long night. Wrapped in blankets, nibbling on dried meat and stamping their feet continually in the snow to keep their toes from freezing, they took turns flagellating each other with pack-straps to keep up the circulation. At two o'clock, the first glimmer of dawn appeared. They crept back to the ridge and worked their way down the great peak to the upper south fork of the river. It seemed to Rogers that this fork paralleled the valley on the opposite side of the dividing range through which, he concluded, the waters of the Beaver River emptied into the Columbia on the eastern flanks of the mountain barrier. If that was true, then a pass of sorts existed.

Unfortunately, he could not be sure. There were eighteen unexplored miles left, but by this time the party was almost out of food. Rogers's notorious frugality had destroyed all chances of finding a pass in the season of 1881; he did not have supplies enough to allow him to press forward and so was forced to order his men to turn their backs on that tantalizing divide and head west again. He must have been bitterly disappointed. It would be at least another year before he would be able to say for certain whether a practical route for a railway led from the Beaver to the Illecillewaet. By that time the rails would be approaching the valley of the Bow, and he still had not explored the Kicking Horse Pass in the Rockies, which had scarcely been glimpsed since the day when James Hector, Palliser's geologist, first saw it in 1858.

Rogers sent all but two of his Indians back to Kamloops. The others guided him down the Columbia and across the international border to Fort Colville in Washington Territory. There he hired a packtrain and saddle horses and made his way by a circuitous route back into the Kootenay country to the mining camp at Wild Horse Creek.

The Major had a long trek ahead of him. He had that spring dispatched the main body of his survey party from the East to the State of Montana with directions to enter Canada from the south and proceed towards the eastern slopes of the Rockies by way of the Bow Valley. He planned to join them by crossing the Kootenay River, hiking over the Brisco Range, and then working his way down the Spray to the point where it joined the Bow. It was wild, untravelled country, barren of human habitation, unmarked by trails or guideposts; but short of going back to San Francisco and across the American West by train, it was the best route available to Rogers if he was to link up with his men on the far side of the mountains.

He did not take his nephew with him. It was late June by this time and it was imperative that somebody explore the Kicking Horse Pass from its western approach. Rogers decided that Albert must take the packtrain to the mouth of the Kicking Horse River and from that point make his way to the summit of the continental divide. Only one white man had ever come that way before – James Hector; but he had descended from the summit. Even the Indians shunned the Kicking Horse; they preferred to follow the Ottertail and go over the high pass (known as the MacArthur

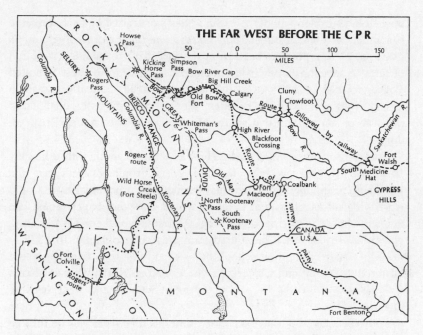

THE FAR WEST BEFORE THE C P R

Pass) and then descend to the divide. The terrible valley of the Kicking Horse was considered too difficult for horses. On his first trip into the Rockies, young Albert, aged twenty-one – "that little cuss" as the Major fondly called him – was being asked to attempt a feat that no human being had yet accomplished.

2

Major Rogers and his men were advancing on the Rockies from three directions that spring of 1881. While Albert worked his way towards the unknown slopes of the Kicking Horse and his uncle guided his packhorses over the Brisco Range, the main body of surveyors, most of them Americans, were heading westward from St. Paul towards Fort Benton, Montana, the jumping-off point for the eastern slopes of the Canadian Rockies. Waiting impatiently for them at the steamboat landing was a 22-year-old stripling from Ontario. His name was Tom Wilson and he was positively lusting for adventure.

For many an eastern Canadian farmboy in the 1870's, the lure of the North West was impossible to resist; it got into their blood and it remained in their blood all of their lives. They were raised on such romantic best sellers as William Butler's *The Great Lone Land* and George Grant's *Ocean to Ocean*. Soldiers back from the Red River expedition were full of tales of adventure in the wide open spaces. The North West Mounted Police, formed in 1873, were already forging an authentic Canadian legend in the shadow of the Rockies. To any lusty youngster, confined to the drab prison of farm and village life, the great lone land spelled freedom.

Tom Wilson was one of these. He was a rangy youth with a homely Irish face. His long jaw, high cheekbones, and prominent teeth gave him something of a horsy look, and this was perhaps prophetic for he would work with horses all his life. Later he would grow the shaggy moustache that was almost a trademark with Rocky Mountain packers. He was easygoing, industrious, good humoured, and incurably romantic. In 1875 at the age of sixteen, he quit school, bade good-bye to his family, and set off through Detroit and Chicago for the Canadian North West. At Sioux City he was overcome by a bout of homesickness and went back to Ontario.

Four years later he tried once more, and this time there was no turning back. He joined the North West Mounted Police and was stationed at Fort Walsh, not far from the present town of Maple Creek, Saskatchewan. There was adventure in the air. The Sioux, who had moved into Canada under Sitting Bull following the Custer massacre, posed a constant threat. The Blackfoot bands and their traditional enemies, the Crees, were held in uneasy check. Those curious geological formations known as the Cypress Hills, a spur of authentic desert complete with cacti and rattlesnakes, lay just to the south – the scene of a notorious massacre of Indians by Yankee traders. Most important of all, it seemed likely that a railroad would soon be pushed across the parched coulees directly into the heart of the mountains.

In April of 1881, when it became clear that a private company was actually embarked on the CPR's construction, Wilson could stand it no longer. He had to be part of the action, and so he wangled a discharge, made his way south with a freight outfit, and reached Fort Benton, Montana, one week before Major Rogers's survey crew – a hundred men in all – disembarked from the steamer. He was the youngest man to be hired by Rogers's deputy, a stickler of a civil engineer named Hyndman.

The surveyors, whose task it was to find a route through the southern mountain chains, had come by way of the United States because that was the only existing route leading to the Canadian foothills. The traffic moved

150

north and south between Fort Benton and Fort Calgary as it would until the coming of the railway confirmed the lateral shape of the new Canada. The only evidence of an international border was a small cairn of stones placed along the wagon trail. The customs office was at Fort Benton, and the customs officer had only one question for travellers moving into British territory: "Got any T&B tobacco?" He was not interested in collecting duty – the distinction between Canadian and American territory was too hazy for such formalities; it just happened to be his favourite brand and it was hard to come by.

It took three weeks for the I. G. Baker Company, the pioneer border freighters, to shepherd the survey party to the site of Old Bow Fort in the shadow of the Rockies. There were nine prairie schooners drawn by twenty-four teams of horses together with eighty pack animals strung out across the coulee-riven prairie. Most of the men walked the entire distance.

It was unsettled country, populated largely by roving bands of Indians – Blackfoot, Piegans, and Bloods – and the occasional trader, priest, and Mounted Policeman. The wagon train wound through Coalbank, the site of the future town of Lethbridge, and crossed over the Oldman River, then in turbulent flood. Nick Sheron, a white pioneer who dug the coal from the banks in his spare time and shipped it south, ferried the men and supplies across. The wagons had to be converted into boats, the canvas lashed around the boxes, the running gear secured by strong ropes. The horses and ponies swam beside the wagons.

At Fort Macleod, the Mounted Police post, the party encountered Dr. George M. Dawson, the hunchbacked assistant director of the government's Geological Survey, whose name would later be given to the most famous of the Klondike mining camps. The next settlement, High River, consisted of a single log trading post. Fort Calgary was slightly more pretentious: here were four log buildings – police barracks, mission, Hudson's Bay post, and I. G. Baker store – and here "all went merry until midnight."

Hyndman, the engineer in charge, was a puritan and a disciplinarian. He had, before leaving Fort Benton, drawn the attention of the party to a list of strict rules that were promptly dubbed "Hyndman's Commandments." Three aroused the special ire of the men:

*Not a tap of work to be done on Sunday.

*Men caught swearing aloud to be instantly discharged.

*Men caught eating, except at the regular camp meal, to be instantly discharged.

When the party left Fort Calgary and camped at Big Hill Creek (the present site of the town of Cochrane), Hyndman's rule against eating between meals was broken by two surveyors who caught and cooked a mess of fresh trout. Hyndman fired both of them, thus precipitating the first strike in Alberta. The party refused to move until the men were reinstated, and the resultant deadlock lasted two days until the transport boss suggested the matter be settled by the higher authority of Major Rogers, who was to meet them at Bow Gap.

Guided by the pioneer Methodist missionary John McDougall, who happened upon the surveyors and offered his services, the wagon train moved forward again. The hills became so steep that sixteen horses were needed to move one wagon and forty men to hold it back on the down grades. "Just as soon as the snow begins to fall I am, as sure as Christ, getting out of this God-forsaken country," one of the men blurted (thereby again breaking a Hyndman commandment). McDougall cannily seized upon the phrase "as sure as Christ" for the sermon he preached that Sunday.

When the Baker Company's freighters turned back at the end of their contract point, Old Bow Fort, McDougall's brother Dave, a pioneer trader, moved the freight forward to the Bow River Gap where Hyndman and his men were to rendezvous with their chief. Although the party was several days late, there was no sign of Rogers.

About a week later – the date was July 15 – Tom Wilson was sitting on a narrow Indian trail west of the camp, smoking his pipe, when a mottled roan cayuse appeared around a curve carrying a man wearing an old white helmet and a brown canvas suit. The rider, accompanied by two Shuswap Indians, was more than trail-worn. "His condition – dirty doesn't begin to describe it," Wilson remembered. "His voluminous side-burns waved like flags in a breeze; his piercing eyes seemed to look and see through everything at once. . . . Every few moments a stream of tobacco juice erupted from between his side-burns; I'll bet there were not many trees alongside the trail that had escaped that deadly tobacco juice aim."

Wilson realized at once that the tattered creature on the scarecrow horse must be the notorious Major Rogers.

"This Hyndman's camp?" the Major asked in his jerky manner.

Wilson nodded and guided Rogers to Hyndman's tent. Hyndman stepped out, but there was no word of greeting from his chief.

"What's your altitude?" he shot at Hyndman. The engineer stammered that he did not know.

"Blue Jesus!* Been here several days and don't know the altitude yet. You ——!" There followed what Wilson described as "a wonderful exhibition of scientific cussing [which] busted wide all of Hyndman's 'Holy Commandments' and inspired delighted snickers and chuckles of admiration from the men who had quickly gathered around." No further word was heard about either the strike or the commandments.

Rogers told the men that the utmost speed was essential if the survey was to keep up to schedule since the season was late and the work well behind. One party left the following morning for the Kananaskis summit of the Bow; the others worked their way westward, widening the Indian trail as they moved.

Three days later Rogers announced that he intended to set off on his own to do some exploring, but when he asked for a volunteer to accompany him, the request was greeted by absolute silence.

There was good reason for it. As Wilson put it, "every man present had learned, in three days, to hate the Major with real hatred. He had no mercy on horses or men – he had none on himself. The labourers hated him for the way he drove them and the packers for that and the way he abused the horses – never gave their needs a thought."

In spite of himself Wilson thought he might as well take a chance, and follow Rogers.

"You were the only man who would go with the old geyser," A. E. Tregent reminded him in a nostalgic letter, forty-eight years later. "Nobody else had the pluck to run the chance of being starved to death or lost in the woods."

The parties began to peel off from the main force on their various assignments, Rogers and Wilson accompanying one up towards the head of the Bow Valley. The Major was clearly worried about the fate of his nephew, whose task it was to come directly across the mountains by the Kicking Horse and Bow rivers.

"Has that damned little cuss Al got here yet?" was his first question on riding into camp one afternoon after an exploration. It was some time before Wilson came to understand that Rogers's manner of speaking about his nephew was part of his armour – a shield to conceal his inner distress.

* Tom Wilson's memoirs, written in the straight-laced thirties, reproduce the Major's favourite bit of profanity as "Blue ——!" Since it is doubtful that he would have censored so mild a word as "blazes" (and equally doubtful that the Major himself would have lapsed into such a euphemism), I have filled in the blank with the most obvious expletive.

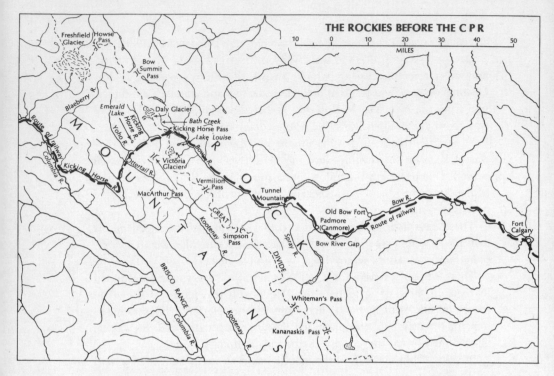

When Rogers learned that there was no sign of Albert, he began to prance around and shout.

"Where has that damn little cuss got to?" he kept asking, over and over again. "If anything happens to that damn little cuss I'll never show my face in St. Paul again." He was beside himself. The fact that he had given a 21-year-old youth a task that the Indians themselves would not tackle did not seem to have occurred to him; obviously, he expected the impossible.

Rogers decided to search for his nephew in the mountains south of the Bow, and shortly, he and Wilson turned their horses down the great valley.

It was a searing day in late July – a day in which the melting glaciers had turned the gentle streams to torrents. They reached an unnamed creek pouring out of the ice-field on Mount Daly and found it terribly swollen, the current tearing at top speed around enormous boulders. Wilson knew that all glacial streams begin to rise in the afternoon after the sun melts the ice in the mountains. He suggested they halt for the night and cross over when the water had subsided in the cool of the morning. Rogers swore a blue oath.

"Afraid of it are you? Want the old man to show you how to ford it?"

He spurred his horse, forged into the current, and was immediately caught by the racing stream. The horse rolled over and the Major dis-

154

appeared beneath the foaming, silt-laden water. Wilson seized a long pole, managed to push it towards the spot where the struggling form had disappeared, was rewarded by an answering tug, and proceeded to pull his bedraggled chief to the safety of the bank. Rogers gave him a funny look.

"Blue Jesus! Light a fire and then get that damned horse. Blue Jesus, it's cold!"

In such a fashion did Bath Creek get its name. The story was soon all over the mountains. In the flood season, when the creek pours its silty waters into the larger river, the normally pristine Bow is discoloured for miles, and for years when that happened old surveyors would mutter sardonically that the old man was taking another bath.

A further day of searching failed to locate the missing Albert. When Rogers and Wilson returned to the summit, hoping for word of him, there was only silence. The Major grew more and more excitable. He tried to rout the men out to search in the black night, but they sensibly refused. "How the Major put in that night I do not know," Wilson confessed, "but I do know that at daybreak next morning he was on the warpath cursing about late risers." The members of the summit party were dispatched in all directions to fire revolvers and light signal fires if the lost should be found. Somewhere down below, on the tangled western slope of the Rockies, wrinkled by canyons and criss-crossed by deadfalls, was the missing man – dead or alive, no one could say.

Down that western slope Tom Wilson and a companion made their way through timber so thick they could not see a yard ahead and over carpets of deceptive mosses, which masked dangerous crevices and deep holes. Finally they reached the mouth of a glacial stream later to be called the Yoho. There they made camp, tentless, cooking their tea, bannock, and sowbelly all in the same tin pail. They had scarcely finished their meal when a shot cracked out in the distance. They sprang to their feet and began clambering down the stream bed, shouting as they went; rounding a curve, they came upon the missing man. Albert Rogers was starving and on the point of mental and physical exhaustion. His rations had long since been used up and for two days he had had nothing to eat but a small porcupine. He had picked it clean, right down to the quills.

The ascent back up the Kicking Horse, which the trio made the following day with Albert Rogers's two Indians, was so terrible that half a century later Wilson insisted that it could not be described. Nearing the summit, they fired a fusillade of revolver shots and a moment later the little major came tearing down the trail to meet them. He stopped, motionless, squinting intently at his nephew; and then Wilson was permitted, for a moment, to glimpse the human being concealed behind that callous armour of profanity.

"He plainly choked with emotion, then, as his face hardened again he took an extra-vicious tobacco-juice-shot at the nearest tree and almost snarled . . . 'Well, you did get here, did you, you damn little cuss?' There followed a second juice eruption and then, as he swung on his heel, the Major shot back over his shoulder: 'You're alright, are you, you damn little cuss?' "

Al Rogers grinned. He understood his uncle. "He also knew that, during the rest of the walk to camp, the furious activity of his uncle's jaws and the double-speed juice shots aimed at the vegetation indicated our leader's almost uncontrollable emotions."

There was an eerie kind of undercurrent drifting about the Rogers camp that evening. As twilight fell, purpling the valleys and making spectres of the glacial summits, the men began to gather around the fire, sucking on their pipes and gazing off across the unknown ocean of mountains. Albert Rogers, still shaky from his ordeal, was present; so was Tom Wilson, together with eighteen others – axemen, chainmen, packers, transit men, and cook. Only the Major, toiling in his tent, was absent.

They were perched on the lip of the Great Divide – the spine of the continent – and they were conscious of both the significance and the loneliness of their situation. The feeling of isolation that descends on men who find themselves dwarfed by nature in an empty land was upon each of them. In all of that vast alpine domain there was scarcely, so far as they knew, another human soul. The country was virtually unexplored; much of it had never known a white man's moccasins. They themselves had trudged through forests, crossed gorges, and crept up slopes that no man, white or native, had ever seen. What nameless horrors did these peaks and ridges hold? For all they knew (as Wilson was to write), ferocious animals of unknown species or fearful savages of barbaric habit lurked somewhere beneath them in those shrouded hollows. To many it was inconceivable that the mountains would ever be conquered or the chasms bridged.

One declared emphatically that no railroad would ever get through such a God-forsaken land and several grunted agreement. Others argued that the success of the project depended on Rogers's ability to discover a pass in the Selkirks.

"Wonder where we will all be this time next year," someone said.

"Not here! No more of this for me!" another responded. He wanted to go where there was decent grub and "not seven days work a week, wet or dry." A chorus of approval greeted this remark. For weeks they had all existed on dried salt pork, boiled beans, and tea. They had seen no butter, eggs, vegetables or fruit; and there was no time to hunt for the game that abounded. The monotonous diet and the need to be one's own boot-maker, tailor, barber, and laundryman was beginning to tell. "Let me get back to the settlements and this damn country won't see me again," one man declared.

Again, they discussed the railroad and again, when one of the party remarked that no line of steel could get through the Kicking Horse – that if a railway ever reached the west coast it would be by way of Fort Edmonton and the Yellow Head Pass – a majority of heads nodded in agreement.

There followed a strange and moving scene. The fire crackled. The peaks above stood out like ghostly shadows against the night sky. The men pulled on their pipes and stared into the flames. Nobody spoke for some time. At length, one man broke the silence:

"Let's make a deal," he said. "Let's promise to keep in touch with each other at least once a year after we get out of here."

The twenty men got to their feet and, without further prompting, took part in a solemn ritual. Each one raised an arm to the sky, and all gravely vowed to keep the Pledge of the Twenty, as it came to be called. In the years that followed, almost all were faithful to it.*

As a result of Albert Rogers's ordeal, the Kicking Horse Pass had been explored, after a fashion. The next task was to survey a preliminary line from the summit to the base. Wilson resumed his job as personal attendant to Major Rogers, visiting all the survey parties in the vicinity save for the one working along the Kananaskis. Rogers, who was a creature of whim and hunch, apparently had no faith in that route. He had pinned his hopes on the Kicking Horse, with the Bow Summit as his second choice. In this stubborn espousal of a single route, Rogers resembled most of the other leading railway surveyors. Each had a fixed idea in his mind from which he could not be budged. In a remarkable number of cases, they fell in love with the country they first explored. With Walter Moberly, it was the Howse Pass; with Sandford Fleming, the Yellow Head; with Charles

* After forty-five years only two of the originals were left alive. The last letter linking the men of the Great Divide was scribbled in pencil by Al Rogers in Waterville, Washington, on two report sheets of the Seattle Grain Company. It reached Tom Wilson in Banff late in February, 1924. "Dear Old Tom," Rogers had written, "you are a loyal soul as ever lived and I love you for it. . . ." Three months later Rogers, too, had gone, leaving Tom Wilson as the sole survivor of the group that sat around the campfire and talked about the great railway on that haunting night in the mountains.

Horetzky, the Pine Pass; with Marcus Smith, Bute Inlet. Each of these unyielding and temperamental men jealously embraced the cause of a piece of real estate almost as if he were married to it.

On their last joint trip of the year, Rogers and Wilson all but came to blows. They had been travelling all day; the horses were worn out; Rogers had refused to halt for lunch; and Wilson was hungry, tired, and boiling mad. Since the indefatigable Major gave no sign that he intended to make camp, Wilson took matters into his own hands, bringing the packhorses to a stop in a small meadow where there was plenty of feed. Rogers continued stubbornly on and soon disappeared into the trees. Wilson attended to the animals, pitched the tent, and made supper. Looking up from his work he saw that the Major had returned and was sitting on his horse, staring at him strangely. The two ate their evening meal in silence. When they were finished Rogers finally exploded.

"Hobbled or picketed those horses?" he snarled.

"Neither," Wilson growled back.

"Blue Jesus! You'll walk to Padmore* in the morning," Rogers fairly screamed.

Wilson yelled back at him: "In that case you'll go with me and I'll have the poor consolation of damned poor company."

Wilson broke the silence that followed with a question:

"What am I here for?"

"To look after me and tend the horses."

"Haven't I done that? Haven't the horses always been ready when you wanted them?"

"Blue Jesus. Yes."

"Then stop your damn growling and kick when they are not – kick when you've got a reason to."

They did not speak again until the following morning at breakfast, when Rogers turned to Wilson and calmly said: "That's a good idea letting the horses feed loose. They get more food that way and we can travel further and get more out of them next day."

It was the nearest he ever came to an apology, but as a result the air was cleared and, as they set out once more, there sprang up between them for the first time a true intimacy that never faded.

At this point Rogers played a hunch that was to cause him a good deal of mental anguish during the months that followed. The two men were not far from the survey gang working at the headwaters of the Bow

* Now Canmore.

River, trying to find whether a possible railway route led from that point over the Howse Pass. Rogers abruptly decided not to proceed further with the survey. Though he knew nothing about the Howse Pass, he had come to the sudden conclusion that it was not a feasible route and was not worth bothering with. As Wilson noted, "Always the Kicking Horse ruled his mind, and although at times he had doubts regarding it being the best route, yet those fears never lasted long." But his sudden decision that morning caused him many misgivings the following summer, long after the Kicking Horse Pass had been officially chosen by the CPR's board of directors and agreed to by Parliament.

Wilson, also on a hunch, quit Rogers at this juncture. By doing so he saved himself a good deal of hardship. The survey crews lingered too long in the mountains. They did not emerge until late October, and by the time they reached High River they were frozen in. Crowfoot, the sagacious Blackfoot chief, chose this moment to enter their camp. He was in an ugly mood because the Governor General on his trip west that summer had promised him a buggy and a piano, which had not arrived. Crowfoot called upon the stranded surveyors to produce the gifts; when they could not, the Indians robbed them of their food and some of their clothing. Half starved and freezing, the party managed to trudge to Blackfoot Crossing, where they were given some assistance. Then they began the long, sub-zero trek across the prairies, through the snowstorms and blizzards, to the end of steel near Flat Creek, Manitoba.

J. H. E. Secretan encountered the party, starving and in rags, on the high bank of the South Saskatchewan. The sight of them – and of Rogers in particular – offended the sensibilities of the fastidious Englishman who believed, above all else, in cleanliness, good order, and discipline (he even had gunny sacks sewn together to carpet the floors of his tents). Rogers he later described as "the worst looking, long-haired ruffian of them all."

An avid sportsman, Secretan had been living all summer on ducks, prairie chickens, geese, cranes, and other game, which he shot himself. Rogers was as horrified by such Lucullan fare as Secretan was horrified by Rogers's appearance. The two did not get along, but Rogers had his revenge – or thought he did. When he reached Winnipeg he informed General Rosser, who was then in command, that Secretan "was living like the Czar of Russia [with] tents carpeted with Brussels carpet [and] living upon roast turkeys and geese and other expensive luxuries unheard of in the cuisine of a poor, unsophisticated engineer."

"Thus," wrote Secretan, "did the Major bite the hand that fed him."

159

3

By the time Rogers reached Winnipeg, late in 1881, Van Horne's appointment had been announced. The new general manager took Rogers with him to Montreal in January, 1882, to convince the CPR directors – the Syndicate, as the press and public still called them – that the Kicking Horse route was practicable with grades of 2.2 per cent and that there appeared to be a feasible pass through the Selkirks.

Rogers had not fully convinced himself, though his pronouncements to the board exuded confidence. Others were sceptical. The *Inland Sentinel* at Yale, in the heart of Andrew Onderdonk's construction empire, reported with some asperity Rogers's abortive attempt to cross the mountains, pointing out correctly that he had not taken enough supplies and had neglected also to bring along snowshoes. "Now Mr. Rogers reports that he has found a practicable route through the Selkirk Range with a grade of 80 ft. to the mile; if he has, he has done better than any engineer who preceded him."

In truth, Rogers had discovered half a pass only. To confirm his findings he would have to scale the eastern wall of the Selkirks and make sure that the gap he thought he saw from the Illecillewaet actually pierced the mountain barrier.

Tom Wilson had sworn that he would never return to the mountains. Rogers thought he knew otherwise: "You may think you're not coming back but you'll be here next year and I'll be looking for you," he told him when they parted. Wilson rode off, muttering to himself that Rogers would have to look a long time. He spent the winter hunting and trapping in the Little Snowy Mountains of Montana, but as the snow began to melt, "longings for the unexplored solitudes of the far-away Canadian Rockies assailed me, nor could they be cast out." The first of May, 1882, found him once again at Fort Benton impatiently awaiting the arrival of the survey parties from the East.

M. F. Hurd, the new engineer in charge (under Rogers), was one of the most experienced men on the continent. He had helped to build the Union Pacific across the American Rockies and had been prominent in surveys and explorations for the Denver & Rio Grande. Van Horne had hired him personally. He was a small, dynamic man – the antithesis of his predecessor, Hyndman – a solitary creature who shunned company. Like Rogers, he was a prodigious tobacco-chewer. In Wilson's words, "tobacco chewing played a great part in the building of the Canadian Pacific Railway."

Two of the routes explored the previous year – the Kananaskis route and the Simpson Pass route – had proved to be unsuitable. Rogers, on a whim, had also rejected the Bow Summit–Howse Pass route. That left only the Kicking Horse. The entire party immediately pushed full speed for the summit to try to locate a line of railway through the Rockies.

In the meantime, Major Rogers once again was attacking the Selkirks. He left St. Paul at the end of March, bought supplies in San Francisco and Walla Walla, Washington, and reached the Columbia Valley on May 20. One of his engineers, Donald McMillan, and nine men had spent the winter camped at the mouth of the Kicking Horse, shuttling supplies down the frozen Columbia towards the Beaver Valley, at the base of the hoped-for pass. On May 22 Rogers decided to try to reach the summit of the Selkirks and complete his exploration of the previous year. No detailed account of that abortive journey remains but it was clearly an ordeal. Swollen torrents, coursing down from the snow-fields above, heavy timber, and a dense undergrowth of vine-like alders, nettles, and devil's clubs frustrated their movement. Once again Rogers had failed to bring along enough supplies. He put his grumbling men on half rations, relenting only on his birthday when he allowed them a little sugar to sweeten their tea in celebration. Only the discovery of an old canoe, which brought them swiftly back to camp, prevented the entire party from starving to death.

On July 17 Rogers tried again, taking two white men and three Indians with him and setting off from the point where the Beaver flows into the Columbia. Here, before the railway builders helped destroy it, was some of the loveliest scenery to be found in the mountains. There was a softness about it all – the river, pale milky green, winding through the golden marshland, the shining ponds winking through the dark spruces, the cataracts traced like tinsel strands on the crags above. Farther up the trail, the river knifed through the shaggy forest, boiling and frothing over shale steps and winding through carpets of ferns and thick tangles of saskatoons and raspberries. The timber was stupendous: the cedars were often ten feet or more in diameter; sometimes they rose two hundred feet above the matted forest floor.

Through this unknown country Rogers and his party climbed for hour after hour along a spectacular route that millions would one day traverse in comfort. They followed the Beaver through its canyon and then cut up a smaller tributary, the Bear, turning off again on a smaller stream that branched away to the south. The brush was so dense that they could make little more than two miles a day. Rogers suffered severely from blackflies and mosquitoes. His forehead swelled and his ears puffed up so badly that

161

they swayed as he walked and he remarked that they felt like pieces of liver. "Not one engineer in a hundred," his friend George Grant later remarked, "would have risked, again and again, health and life as he did."

Above them loomed glaciers fifty feet thick and mountains that would one day bear the names of famous Canadians – Shaughnessy, Sifton, Tupper, Macdonald – and of Rogers himself. The lower mountain slopes were flawed, each forested flank scarred by the paths of snowslides, the trees snapped off dozens of feet from the base. These mountains – conical, pyramidal, serrated – looked familiar to Rogers, for he had seen them all the previous year from the opposite side. There, before them, was the very peak on which he had stood in the summer of 1881 and there was the same broad meadow that he had spied from his vantage point. He and his party had reached an altitude of forty-five hundred feet and were standing in a valley that seemed completely enclosed by mountains. Ragged black precipices (later named for Macdonald and Tupper) stood guard at the entrance, apparently forming an impassable wall between them. To the north and west the black smudge of timber rose up to blend with sloping meadows, the soft grasses flecked with wild flowers. Beyond these spangled pastures were glacial fields of glistening white, tilting upwards to curved ridges which, in turn, led the eye higher to frosted peaks. A sharp-cut pyramid (it would later, appropriately, be named "Cheops") was silhouetted against the sky. To the southwest more mountains stretched off into a haze of misty blue. Somewhere in the distance a brook gurgled above the sound of the wind in the swaying spruces. Here the waters flowed in opposite directions, spilling down both sides of the Selkirks. Now the Major knew he had found at last the long-sought passage through the barrier. In the face of considerable hardship – and some foolhardiness – he had succeeded where others had failed and done what his detractors had said was impossible. There was a way through the Selkirks after all, and its discovery would make him immortal. Almost from this moment, this smiling, mountain-ringed meadow would bear the name of Rogers's Pass. The date was July 24, 1882, and Rogers, after searching vainly for an alternate pass, lost no time in retracing his steps so that he might let the world have the news of his discovery.

Tom Wilson, meanwhile, was engaged in packing supplies from Padmore in the foothills to the summit of the Kicking Horse in the Rockies. One day in August he ran into a small band of Stony Indians and asked them about the roar of avalanches which was clearly audible in the distance. One of the band, a man known as Gold-seeker, told him that these slides occurred on "snow mountain," which Wilson later identified as

Victoria Glacier. This mountain of snow, the Indian told him, lay high above "the lake of the little fishes," whose source it was.

Something about the Indian's description intrigued Wilson and he asked him to guide him to the lake. It was not a difficult passage on horseback and it was well worth the trip. The two men burst out upon a small, emerald gem, framed by a backdrop of dark evergreens, a dazzling white glacier, and a curtain of blue mountains.

"As God is my judge, I never in all my explorations saw such a matchless scene," Wilson recalled. He sat down, pulled out his pipe and, as he smoked, gazed for a long time on that mirror of blue-green water, soon to become one of the most famous tourist attractions on the continent. It was noon, and the sun, directly above him, shone down upon the pool around which mountains and glacier formed an almost perfect horseshoe. Forests that had never known an axe seemed to grow directly out of the shining surface. A mile and a half beyond, the backdrop of the scene was divided into three distinct bands of colour – white, opal, and brown – where the glacier merged with the water. Wilson decided to name it Emerald Lake, and so it appeared on the first geological map of the Canadian Rockies. But even as the map was published the name was changed to Lake Louise in honour of the Governor General's lady. (Wilson that same season discovered a second gem of a lake, which he also named Emerald Lake; this time the name stuck. So did that of the Yoho Valley, which he also discovered and which was to become a national park.)

Later that afternoon – the date was August 21 – Wilson arrived at one of the survey camps and ran into Major Rogers.

"Blue Jesus!" roared the Major. "I knew you'd be back. I knew you'd be back. You'll never leave these mountains again as long as you live. They've got you now." As it turned out, Rogers was absolutely right.

Rogers confided to Wilson that he still had doubts about his choice of the Kicking Horse Pass. Perhaps the Howse Pass, after all, was an easier grade. Both passes led to adjacent points on the Columbia; both were about the same length. What if, after the road was built, Rogers should be proved wrong?

Very little was known about the Howse Pass. Years before it had been used by Hudson's Bay packers moving to and from the Columbia. James Hector had climbed the eastern slope in the days of the Palliser expedition more than fifteen years before. Walter Moberly and his men had ascended the western side and made a preliminary survey down from the summit to the Columbia in 1871. Moberly had been convinced at the time that the pass was the best possible route for the railway to follow; his persistent and often foolhardy espousal of it had, in the end, forced his retirement from the Canadian Pacific Survey. What if Moberly should be proved right after the fact? He was not the sort of man who would ever let Rogers forget it.

"Tom," the Major said as the two men sat outside his tent that evening, "I mustn't make any mistakes and I am not quite easy in my mind about the Howse Pass. It might be an easier one than this and I must be sure about it. I'd like to take a trip over it and I'd like you to go with me."

Wilson agreed, and the two set off with packhorses the following morning, struggling through muskegs and over fallen timber and chopping their way through trails rendered impassable by deadfalls. After the second day they found they had travelled only half the distance they had planned. Rogers began to fret. He still had the Selkirks to worry about. He had assigned a team of natives to cut a pathway to the summit. "I wonder how those damn Indians are getting along with that trail," he kept muttering. Finally at supper he let flow a stream of profanity.

"Blue Jesus! We won't get through here to the Columbia in two weeks at this rate. A man carrying a pack on his back, could travel twice as fast as we are doing. I'll give you a fifty dollar bonus if you'll go through alone on foot. . . . You ought to do it in ten days easy."

Rogers promised to meet Wilson in ten days' time on the far side of the Rockies where the Blaeberry, flowing down from the Howse Pass, empties into the Columbia. Then he went off with the horses leaving Tom Wilson to face the most terrible ordeal of his career.

There was no trail. He groped his way through a forest of eternal night – the trees and underbrush packed so tightly that he could get his bearings only by glimpsing the tips of the mountains above. Bear Creek (another Bear Creek), its banks walled in by an impenetrable mass of tangled willows, was in flood and he used it as a guide. It proved to be a fickle ally. At one point he broke out of the gloomy labyrinth of the evergreens only to find his way blocked by an immense wall of ice – the Freshfield Glacier. He had taken the wrong fork and lost a day.

He kept plugging along like a blind man, following the racing waters, which led him ever upward. This was virgin country; there was no sign that any human being, white or native, had passed this way before. Then, when he seemed to have penetrated to the very core of the wilderness, he saw on the trunk of a tree a scar that could only have been made with an axe; it was grey with age and he realized that this must be a surveyor's blaze, left by one of Moberly's men a decade before. He had reached the summit of Howse Pass.

The descent from the pass was even more difficult than the descent from the Kicking Horse. Nature, jealous of invasion, appeared to have devised a series of obstacles to frustrate all human passage. Wilson's account of his odyssey is reminiscent of those medieval tales in which an invisible wizard bestrews the hero's path with frightening examples of his sorcery. Wilson faced mile upon mile of deadfalls – great trees torn up and tossed helter-skelter, as if by an unseen hand, forming an apparently unending series of eight-foot barriers over which he had to scramble. There were other pitfalls. A canyon barred his way at one point; he was forced to scale a mountain wall to circumvent it. Later he faced a vast slide – an unstable desert of shattered rock. There was no way around, and so he was forced to strike out directly across it, like a man on shifting ice, knowing that a single slip or even the displacement of a loose piece of shale could send the whole mass roaring into the depths below.

There were more canyons and more delays, and, because of the delays, the greatest obstacle of all came to be hunger. After twelve days of exhausting travel – he could sometimes cover no more than a mile in an hour – Wilson was down to a half a bannock. Every mile began to count, but every mile was criss-crossed with uprooted tree trunks. His pace grew slower and slower and for the first time he began to grow alarmed. Would he die in this maze of fallen timber? He decided, at last, on a desperate gamble. After a night's sleep he cast aside every scrap of equipment except for his axe and made for the Columbia as swiftly as he could. Late the following day, as fatigue dragged his movements to a crawl, he ran into Major Rogers.

"Blue Jesus! What kept you so long?" was Rogers's only greeting. Then he snorted, turned on his heel, and uttered no further word until Wilson had been fed. The others in the camp later told the packer that the old man had paced up and down for hours like a caged lion, crying over and over again: "If that boy don't show up what in hell will I do? No-one but a fool would send a lad on such a trip alone, and no-one but a fool would try to make it alone." Wilson's journey served to confirm his original hunch that the Kicking Horse provided a better route for the railway than the Howse.

By early fall Rogers was ready to leave the mountains. He wanted to carry the news personally to Montreal. Wilson, who had departed earlier, encountered him on the prairies one Sunday morning in a democrat drawn by four horses, galloping towards the end of steel, "feeling jubilant, for his ambitions were promising realization."

At Blackfoot Crossing, Rogers met the saintly Father Lacombe and, in the presence of the Oblate missionary, made a herculean effort to avoid any blasphemy.

"Blue ——," he began, and checked himself as he paid off I. G. Baker's men for provisions. He stared at the bills remaining in his hand and then turned to the priest, who had just finished conducting Mass.

"You've got a mission here, haven't you?" he began, speaking slowly and carefully, watching every word.

He handed the priest the rest of the money: "This is no use to me until I get to the end of steel where I can get lots more. Here, take it – you've got some sort of school, haven't you?"

Lacombe, who had become used to profanity serving as chaplain to the railroad navvies out of Rat Portage, appeared to hesitate. Wilson, who was present, was certain that the priest was trying to make Rogers lose control of his tongue. The Major became embarrassed and "with what looked like a do-or-die attempt," pushed the money into Lacombe's hands.

"Here, take it," he burst out. "If you can't use it that way then buy yourself some cigars. Blue Jesus, what in hell's the use of me toting it across these damnation prairies."

Lacombe, Wilson noted, uttered a guffaw that could be heard at Fort Calgary.

Some time later, George Stephen, faultless in white tie and tails, was entertaining guests in his home in Montreal. His butler was taken aback to discover on the doorstep a wiry little man, roughly dressed and sporting a set of the largest Dundreary whiskers he had ever seen. The butler protested that Stephen could not be disturbed, but the little man was adamant. The CPR president reluctantly came to the door and instantly recognized the Major. He ordered the butler to array him in suitable style and then bring him down to dinner. There he heard at first hand the tale of the discovery of the pass through the Selkirks.

True to Jim Hill's promise, the railway presented Rogers with a cheque for five thousand dollars. To the frustration of the CPR's accounting department, he refused to cash it. A year later Van Horne tried to remonstrate with him on the matter.

"What! Cash that cheque?" Rogers cried. "I would not take a hundred thousand dollars for it. It is framed and hangs in my brother's house in Waterville, Minnesota, where my nephews and nieces can see it."

"I'm not here for money!" the Major added. It was an unnecessary comment – but one which must have given considerable satisfaction to James J. Hill, the man who originally made that puzzling decision to send a prairie surveyor into the unknown Selkirks.

166

4

Rogers's discovery of a feasible pass through the Selkirks intensified the Canadian-American rivalry, which was a feature of railway location and construction in the West. How could a Yankee engineer, with no mountain experience, succeed where seasoned Canadians had been forced to admit defeat? Sandford Fleming's official survey report had published in 1872 the entry for December 22, 1871, from Walter Moberly's journal: "I found there was not any practicable pass through the Selkirk range." Two years later, the man in charge of the Canadian Pacific Survey in British Columbia, Marcus Smith, wrote that "there is little probability of a pass being found across the Selkirk range between the upper and lower arms of the Columbia river." That was one of the reasons why a southern route had been ignored for all of the seventies.

The Opposition press was sceptical of Rogers's report. ". . . on the face of it, the story appeared highly improbable," the Edmonton *Bulletin* wrote in February, 1883. It published a rumour that the route was a failure and that Rogers was to be dismissed, a tale for which the newspaper offered an intriguing explanation: "There is very little doubt that these favorable reports of Major Rodgers have been a put up job from the first. . . . The question may very naturally be asked, what object would the syndicate have in so misleading people. The answer is plain. When they took the contract for building the C.P.R., it was with the full intention of gobbling up the entire North West. . . . The failure to find a pass through the Selkirks will form a sufficient excuse for building another line on the prairie, and receiving another grant of good land, before the heavy work in the mountains is commenced. . . ."

The *Bulletin*, of course, had a vested interest in the failure of the southern route, which had doomed Edmonton to the status of village for the foreseeable future. The fact was, however, that although Rogers had found a pass there was not much hard evidence that it was a practicable one. He had measured it with his eye alone. No one had put a surveyor's chain on a foot of the Selkirk Mountains. No human being, white man or Indian, had succeeded in making a continuous passage from west to east along the route that he was recommending. One thing was fairly clear: the pass was a steep one – so steep that it might not be diplomatic to call it a pass at all. "I want to tell you positively. that there is no pass in the Selkirk Range," the company's western superintendent, John Egan, told

The
Prairie
Gopher

167

the press that year. "It has to be crossed in the same manner as any other mountain. The track must go up one side and down the other." Nonetheless, the decision had been made. The Governor General himself was worried about the heavy mountain grades but, as he told the Prime Minister, "it wd be better to have them than further delay, with the N. Pacific gaining Traffic."

Stephen was himself concerned about Rogers's credibility. Could that strange, tobacco-chewing little man really be trusted? The president decided that a disinterested party of proven ability and integrity must be engaged to check up on him. The choice fell, obviously, on the former engineer-in-chief Sandford Fleming, who had left the government service in 1880 and had since been living in England.

Van Horne also had some reservations about Rogers and was planning a second expedition to check up on him. He quite liked Rogers and respected his ability ("While the Major is somewhat eccentric and given to 'burning brimstone,' he is a very good man . . . honest and fair dealing"), but he was not happy about the location survey over the Kicking Horse, he was not certain about the practicability of the Selkirk pass, and he was greatly concerned about Rogers's penchant for economizing on food and pay.

"We must take no chances on this season's work," he told the Major early in 1883, "because any failure to reach the desired results and have the line ready to put under contract will be serious if not disastrous. I think it important that you should take an extra engineer, who is fully competent, to take charge of a party in case of sickness or failure of any of your regular men.

"It is also exceedingly important that an ample supply of food be provided and that the quantity be beyond a possibility of a doubt.

"Very serious reports have been made to the Government and in other quarters about the inadequacy of the supplies provided last year and a good many other reports have been made tending to discredit our work. The officials at Ottawa, as a consequence, look upon our reports with a good deal of suspicion. . . .

"We cannot expect to get good men for that work at as low or lower rates than are paid further East and we must feed the men properly in order to get good service. It will be cheaper for the Company to pay for twice the amount of supplies actually necessary than to lose a day's work for lack of any."

But to a New York businessman, one of those who reported rumours "tending to discredit our work," Van Horne defended Rogers:

168

"There has been a good deal of feeling among some of the Canadian Engineers particularly those who have been accustomed to the Government Service against Major Rogers, partly from natural jealousy of one who is looked upon as an outsider, partly from his *lively* treatment of those whom he looks upon as shirkers or 'tender feet' and partly from his somewhat peculiar methods of securing economy, but more than all perhaps from his having succeeded, as is supposed, in doing what was unsuccessfully attempted by the Government Engineers, namely, in getting through the Rocky and Selkirk Mountains by a direct line.

"I believe him to be capable and I know him to be thoroughly honest. He is something of an enthusiast and is disposed to undertake himself and put upon his men more severe duties than most engineers are accustomed to and I have reason to believe that in his anxiety to economize in every possible way he has gone too far in some cases and that a good deal of unnecessary discomfort, although no suffering, has resulted from it."

Van Horne admitted that most of the men under Rogers were "utterly useless" but pointed out that the shortage of good engineers was so great he had to take chances in his hiring. He also admitted that "it may be that his work in the Selkirks will not turn out as well as his reports would lead us to believe." He planned to send "two competent and disinterested engineers" over the work in the early spring to make sure of it. Van Horne revealed that he had considerable correspondence in his file on the subject of Rogers and that he believed there was something more than the mere dissatisfaction of subordinates behind it – "it may be that our friends of the Grand Trunk have something to do with it."

The two "competent and disinterested engineers" were Charles Aeneas Shaw, who had spent more than half his thirty years working at his profession, and James Hogg, a cousin of James Ross, the man in charge of mountain construction. Competent they were; "disinterested" they were not. No surveyor was disinterested in those days. They were ambitious, often blindly stubborn and jealous of their fellows, brave to the point of being foolhardy, and sometimes temperamental; but they were never disinterested. The petty hatreds and suspicions within the engineering division of the Department of Public Works in the early days of the Canadian Pacific Survey were legendary. Walter Moberly and Sandford Fleming, who had once been staunch friends and drinking companions, were practically at each other's throats at one point; Charles Horetzky tried to blackmail his chief; Marcus Smith, while acting as Fleming's deputy, connived against him; James Rowan refused to speak to Marcus Smith or answer his letters. Such passions did not cool when the railway passed into

169

private hands. Shaw could not stand Secretan, whom he called "selfish" and "disagreeable." The snobbish Secretan took every opportunity to denigrate Shaw. Shaw despised Hogg, who was to be his companion in the mountains. And all three men had very little use for Rogers.

The conditions of the surveyors' existence make much of this understandable. They were thrust into one another's company far from civilization for months and sometimes years. The food was often bad and at times non-existent. Living conditions were generally uncomfortable if not subnormal. The work was exhausting and the hours were long. Perhaps most important, they were, for a great portion of their lives, without the company of women. They were also a garrulous bunch, much more so than the contractors, many of whom – Ross, Holt, Mackenzie, Mann, and Sifton – went on to public fame and private fortune without leaving behind a scrap of memoir. If the contractors were consumed by petty jealousies, they kept it a secret, but the surveyors told all. They were used to spinning yarns around the campfire and so developed a flare for anecdote, both witty and malicious. Moreover, it was part of their job to keep a journal. In the diaries and memoirs they left behind, full of conflicting evidence, each writer tends to play the hero, fighting off his villainous colleagues. They were an egotistical lot, as their memoirs show, craving public notice far more than money, as Jim Hill guessed when he made Rogers his original proposition. Rogers was equally well aware of this trait in his colleagues. On his second attempt to scale the Selkirks, he was able to persuade a reluctant transit man to climb a distant peak, even though the party was down to its last bannock, by offering to name the mountain after him. The starving surveyor eagerly leaped to his feet and headed for the crags.

Charles Shaw first tangled with Rogers, by his own account, in Winnipeg early in March of 1883. James Ross, then in charge of all engineering on the railroad's western division, outlined the plans for the coming season and then asked Shaw to look over the profile of Rogers's final location line between Calgary and Bow Gap – a distance of some sixty miles: "It's a nightmare to me and I'm afraid it will hold us back a year."

Shaw examined the plan and announced at once that he could get a far better line. A stranger working near by sprang to his feet and cried out: "That's the best line that can be got through the country. Who in hell are you, anyway?" It was Rogers. Shaw told Ross that he was prepared to relocate the Major's line and "if I don't save at least half a million dollars over the estimated cost of construction of this line, I won't ask any pay for my season's work."

A fight threatened to break out between Shaw and Rogers. Ross calmed both men down but, at a later meeting, asked Shaw to go ahead.

Van Horne in the meantime was examining Rogers's profiles and plans out of Fort Calgary and was not happy. He called in Secretan and there took place a memorable encounter, which became part of the Van Horne legend.

"Look at that," the general manager exclaimed. "Some infernal idiot has put a tunnel in there. I want you to go up and take it out."

"But this is on the Bow River – a rather difficult section. There may be no other way."

"Make another way."

Secretan hesitated, whereupon Van Horne hurled a question.

"This is a mud tunnel, isn't it?" Secretan nodded. Engineers shunned mud tunnels; it was impossible to keep the track in line as the bank tended to move constantly.

"How long would it take us to build it?"

"A year or eighteen months."

Van Horne swore and banged his fist on the desk.

"What are they thinking about? Are we going to hold up this railway for a year and a half while they build their damned tunnel? Take it out!"

Secretan picked up the profile and studied it as he headed for the door. He turned back for a moment:

"Mr. Van Horne," he said in his sardonic way, "those mountains are in the way, and the rivers don't all run right for us. While we are at it we might as well fix them, too."

But Van Horne insisted that Secretan personally "take that damned tunnel out. Don't send anybody else." The engineer was spared the trip, however, when Shaw found a route around the offending hill by way of a small creek valley, which actually shortened the main line by a mile and a half.

By the end of June, when Shaw had finished his task of relocation, James Ross had arrived. He told Shaw that the new line would save the company an estimated $1,350,000 in construction costs and assigned him to relocate the rest of the line to the summit of the Rockies. At a mountain near the future site of Banff, Shaw eliminated another tunnel by routing the road through a valley to the east. It was a simple matter to go around the mountain rather than through it, and Shaw could not understand why the engineers following the switchback trail had missed the valley route. "Rogers' location here was the most extraordinary blunder I have ever known in the way of engineering," he wrote in his memoirs. The mountain without the tunnel is still known as Tunnel Mountain.

At the summit, Shaw was met by James Hogg, who had arrived with instructions from Van Horne: he and Shaw were to examine and report on the pass through the Selkirks because, in Shaw's words, "Rogers's reports were very unsatisfactory and inconclusive." They set off down the difficult incline of the Kicking Horse on the zigzag pathway, which the survey crews had already christened "the Golden Stairs" because it was the most terrifying single stretch of trail on the entire route of the railway. Actually it was little more than a narrow ledge, less than two feet wide, cut into the cliffs several hundred feet above the foaming river. It was so frightening that some men used to hang on to the tails of their packhorses and keep their eyes tightly shut until they had passed the most dangerous places. Shaw had one horrible moment when his horse ran into a nest of hornets and another when he met two men with a packhorse coming from the opposite direction. Since it was impossible for anybody to turn around, they simply cut the lashings off one of the horses and pushed the wretched animal over the cliff.

At the base of the Golden Stairs, on the banks of the Columbia, they ran into Rogers. Shaw noticed that the seat of his pants was patched with a piece of buffalo hide that still had the hair on it. Apparently the Major did not recognize his antagonist of the previous spring.

"Who the hell are you, and where the hell do you think you're going?" was Rogers's greeting.

"It's none of your damned business to either question," Shaw retorted. "Who the hell are you, anyway?"

"I am Major Rogers."

"My name is Shaw. I've been sent by Van Horne to examine and report on the pass through the Selkirks."

Shaw recalled that Rogers practically frothed at the mouth when he heard the name.

"You're the —— Prairie Gopher that has come into the mountains and ruined my reputation as an Engineer." A stream of profanity followed.

Shaw, a big man with a high, intelligent forehead and an all-encompassing black beard, was not inclined to take this sort of abuse. His Scottish ancestors were all notorious fighters – chiefs of the Clan Chatten in the Inverness country. His grandfather had fought at Waterloo, and his father in the Papineau rebellion and the Fenian raids. Since the age of fourteen Charles Shaw had been doing a man's work, first as a farmhand and later as a surveyor. He was as hard as nails and would live to his eighty-ninth

172

year. Before Rogers was finished Shaw had leaped from his horse and seized him by the throat; in his own words, he "shook him till his teeth rattled."

"Another word out of you," said the infuriated Shaw, "and I'll throw you in the river and drown you."

Rogers immediately apologized for losing his temper and said that the engineers in charge of the relocated section had let him down badly. He offered to guide Shaw to the pass in the Selkirks.

"That will be all right," Shaw told him, "as long as you keep a civil tongue in your head."

The trip to the mouth of the Beaver could not have been very pleasant, since Shaw kept up a continual barrage of criticism regarding the line that Rogers had located along the east bank of the Columbia. Shaw kept insisting that it was on the wrong side of the river and, as a result, "relations between us were strained for the rest of the day." In this instance, however, Shaw's advice was ignored by the CPR and the railway followed Rogers's location.

Shaw's version of the scene at the pass along with the "prairie gopher" incident, which clearly rankled, were told and retold by him in his old age, half a century later. He recounted it in letters to various editors, in newspaper interviews, in an article in the CPR's staff publication, and in his memoirs, which were set down in 1936 but not published until 1970, twenty-eight years after his death.

According to Shaw, Rogers, "in his usual pompous manner," after gazing up at the great Illecillewaet Glacier, turned to him and remarked: "Shaw, I was the first white man ever to set eyes on this pass and this panorama."

Shaw walked over to a small spring to get a drink and there, he related, he found the remains of a fire, some partly rotted poles, evidently used for a tent, and a couple of badly rusted tins. He called Rogers's attention to these.

Rogers's reaction, as quoted by Shaw, was astonishment: "How strange! I never noticed those things before. I wonder who could have camped here."

"These things were left here years ago by Moberly when he found this pass!" Shaw claimed he replied.

It was the repetition of this story that helped convince Canadian engineers and journalists that Major Rogers was a fake and that the credit for discovering the pass rightfully belonged to Walter Moberly. Even Moberly began to believe it in his declining years, as his imperfect reminiscences

173

reveal, though he was generous enough at the time. In 1885 he wrote: "I cannot . . . but pay a high tribute to the dauntless energy and untiring zeal that has characterised and, I am glad to say, crowned with success the unwearying struggles of my successor in the mountain surveys, Major A. B. Rogers." Thirty years later he was insisting that Rogers had not seen the pass named after him until the railway had gone through it, and that it should have been named the Perry Pass after his assistant who, Moberly came to believe, actually *had* seen the pass. The memoirs of aging surveyors are not very good evidence when set against words actually written on the spot at the time. Moberly's journal of 1866 makes it clear that the campfire Shaw said he found did not belong to his party.

Then who left those relics? Certainly, they could not have been as old as Shaw thought they were. The snow on the top of the Rogers Pass reaches a depth of fifty feet or more in the winter; it is scarcely credible that the remains of a small fire could have survived for seventeen years. It is more likely that (assuming that Shaw was not indulging in a pipe dream) the camp was left by Rogers himself the previous season or by his men, who had hacked a road to the summit and were working on the western slopes of the pass at that very time.

5

"The loneliness of savage mountains" On their way back to the summit of the Rockies, on the Kicking Horse Trail, Shaw and Hogg ran into the second party dispatched by the CPR to check up on Major Rogers: Sandford Fleming, at the invitation of George Stephen, was also heading for the Selkirks, accompanied by his son Frank and his old comrade George Grant, the Presbyterian minister who had been with him on the memorable trip from ocean to ocean in 1872.

Shaw informed Fleming that he and Hogg had gone as far as it was possible to go – a short distance down the west side of the Selkirks – that there was no path or track of any description beyond the point they had reached, and that no one had been through to the western slope of the mountains. This was the second such report that Fleming had received from Canadian surveyors. Earlier, two other men had told him that Rogers had not been able to pass over to the far side of the mountains and that "it was questionable, if it were possible to find a route which could be followed." Fleming took it all with a grain of salt: "I had some very serious reflections on what I heard from these gentlemen."

Nonetheless, the Selkirks remained a mysterious, unknown land for some time. Morley Roberts, the British adventurer and novelist who worked on the railway the following year, wrote: "I could find no one who had been on the journey, and the reports about it were so contradictory that in the Kicking Horse Pass it was impossible to find out how far it was across the Selkirk Range, whether it was 60 or 120 miles or even more. There was a halo of romance thrown over the whole place west of us, and when we passed in imagination the Columbia for the second time all beyond was as truly conjectural as El Dorado or Lyonesse." James Ross himself, who kept sending Indian couriers out to the Selkirks, had only the vaguest idea of what lay ahead.

Fleming and Grant were far more concerned about the terrible descent down the Golden Stairs of the Kicking Horse. It was almost a dozen years since these two companions had set out, in the prime of life, to breast the continent. Now the years were beginning to tell. Fleming, though a superb physical specimen, was fifty-six. For the past three years he had been leading an intriguing but sedentary life in England with side visits to various European capitals, attempting, without much success, to interest the Royal Society in his proposals for standard time and engaging in such mild adventures as a gondola ride in Venice and a trip in a hot-air balloon. Grant, who was forty-seven and inclined to a paunch, had quit his ministry in Halifax for the principal's chair at Queen's. Now these middle-aged explorers were forced to negotiate a trail that terrified the most experienced mountaineers.

Fleming dared not look down. To do so "gives one an uncontrollable dizziness, to make the head swim and the view unsteady, even with men of tried nerve. I do not think that I can ever forget that terrible walk; it was the greatest trial I ever experienced."

At that point the members of the party found themselves teetering on a ledge between ten and fifteen inches wide, eight hundred feet above the river. There was nothing to hold on to – not a branch or even a twig. Grant, who had lost his right hand in childhood, was especially vulnerable: "It seemed as if a false step would have hurled us to the base, to certain death." The sun, emerging from behind a cloud, beat down upon them until they were soaked with a perspiration that was accentuated by their own state of tension. "I, myself, felt as if I had been dragged through a brook, for I was without a dry shred on me," Fleming admitted. It was an exhausted party that finally arrived that evening at Rogers's camp on the Columbia.

Rogers's men were highly amused at the idea of the hard-swearing

"Bishop" entertaining a man of the cloth. They warned Grant of the Major's roughness of speech and attitude: "He can blow, he can swar, and he can spit tobacco as well as any man in the United States."

Because Grant was addressed as "Doctor," Rogers at first believed him to be a medical man. When, on the following morning – a Sunday – Fleming proposed that his companion hold a service, Rogers thought the idea was a practical joke. He indulged in a good deal of jubilant profanity and bustled about, drumming up his men for the event, until the truth dawned upon him.

Grant was no mean preacher. In his Halifax parish, before he moved to Queen's, confirmed sinners used to rush to their favourite pew to hear themselves scourged in masterly fashion. One Irish saloonkeeper, attacked unmercifully from the pulpit for his public vices, emerged from St. Matthew's, his face beaming, and insisted on congratulating the baffled clergyman.

"A grand sermon, Mr. Grant. A grand sermon; it did me good to listen to it." ,

Grant was taken aback. "To tell the truth," he ventured, "I rather thought that some parts of it hit you rather hard."

The publican laid an affectionate hand on the minister's shoulder: "My dear fellow," said he, "it's a poor sermon that doesn't hit me somewhere."

On the banks of the Columbia, Grant used subtler tactics. As always when he had a captive and willing audience (a sermon was, after all, a diversion from common toil), he preached at great length. Slowly he brought the subject around to profanity and, being careful not to single anyone out, pointed out that it was a useless device and one not generally heard any longer in the conversation of gentlemen. Grant was a shrewd judge of character. He had grasped an essential aspect of Rogers's motivation: above all, the little engineer wanted to be thought of as a gentleman. Then and there Rogers resolved to abstain from swearing. He was not always successful; at one point, when something went wrong with the canoes and Rogers made herculean efforts to suppress his normal vocabulary, Grant took pity upon him. The Major was standing with his mouth open, struggling to force the words back. The minister laid a hand on his arm: "Major, hadn't you better go behind a tree and say it?"

In spite of such lapses, Rogers stuck to his resolve. Van Horne encountered him the following fall and was baffled by him.

"What's the matter with you, Rogers?" he asked. "You haven't cursed once."

Rogers told his tale briefly and succinctly: "Fleming passed through the camp last summer, and he had with him a parson named Grant. Thought he was a sawbones at first, but he was a parson. He gave us a sermon on swearing, and he made out it wasn't gentlemanly. So I quit."

That Sunday evening, Grant and Fleming climbed to the benchland five hundred feet above Rogers's camp to ponder the "noble landscape" and to soliloquize on the future of the virgin country that stretched off below them.

The scene was like a painted backdrop – the great river winding its slow way through the forested valley; the evergreen slopes of the foothills rising directly from the water; a line of blue mountains, sharp as sword blades, limned behind the dark hills; and behind them another line of peaks, stark white, chiselled into the blue of the evening sky.

"I asked myself," Fleming wrote, "if this solitude would be unchanged, or whether civilization in some form of its complex requirements would ever penetrate this region? . . . Will the din of the loom and the whirl of the spindle yet be heard in this unbroken domain of nature? It cannot be that this immense valley will remain the haunt of a few wild animals. Will the future bring some industrial development: a future which is now dawning upon us? How soon will a busy crowd of workmen take possession of these solitudes, and the steam whistle echo and re-echo where now all is silent? In the ages to come how many trains will run to and from sea to sea with millions of passengers?"

All these thoughts crowded in on Fleming as the sun dipped down behind the white plumes of the Selkirks: "I do not think that I can ever forget the sight as I then gazed upon it."

The following day he and his son with George Grant, Albert Rogers, and the Major set off up the valley of the Beaver for the pass. Grant thought that it "was like riding through a deserted garden." The trail was bordered with half a dozen varieties of ripe fruits and berries, which the travellers could pick and eat without dismounting. The gooseberries were as large as grapes and the red clusters that hung suspended from the mountain ash along the trail formed bright splashes of colour against the dark wall of evergreens. Asters, bluebells, and fireweed spangled the forest floor. Refreshed by such luxuriance, the travellers emerged from the forest and into the saucer-shaped meadow where Rogers had planted a yew stake to mark the actual summit.

Fleming had had the foresight to bring along a box of cigars and these were smoked as the group sat down on natural seats of moss-covered rock and listened to the Major tell the story of how he discovered the pass. The whole company was in high spirits. Fleming proposed that a

Canadian alpine club be organized on the spot. This was done, with Fleming named interim president, Grant secretary, and Frank Fleming treasurer. A toast was drunk in the ice-cold waters of Summit Creek. Then the entire party set about picking and eating wild fruit; it was a treat after the Spartan fare of Rogers's camp. To show that they were still young and unaffected by the journey, Fleming proposed a game of leap-frog, "an act of Olympic worship to the deities in the heart of the Selkirks!"

The following day the Major returned to the Columbia while the others, with Albert Rogers as their guide, set off down the western slope. Twenty-four miles from the summit, the freshly cut trail came to an end, and from this point on the party bade farewell to all civilization. It was to be Grant's last journey. After it was over he vowed that he would never attempt to pioneer through a wilderness again. "In all my previous journeyings," he later wrote, "other men had been before me and left some memorial of their work, a railway, a Macadamized or gravel road, a lane, a trail, or at least, blazed trees to indicate the direction to be taken. Now we learned what it was to be without benefit of other men's work. Here, there was nothing even to guide, save an occasional glimpse of the sun, and the slate-coloured, churned-up torrent . . . hemmed in by cañons, from which we turned aside only to get mired in beaver dams or alder swamps, or lost in labyrinths of steep ravines, or to stumble over slides of moss-covered rocks that had fallen from overhanging mountains."

They were now in the true Pacific coast rain forest. "It rained almost every day. Every night the thunder rattled over the hills with terrific reverberations, and fierce flashes lit up wierdly [sic] tall trees covered with wreaths of moss, and the forms of tired men sleeping by smouldering camp fires."

For five days, in which they managed to travel only seventeen miles, they struggled on, in Grant's description, "through acres of densest underbrush where you cannot see a yard ahead, wading through swamps and beaver dams, getting scratched from eyes to ankles with prickly thorns, scaling precipices, falling over moss-covered rocks into pitfalls, your packs almost strangling you, losing the rest of the party while you halt to feel all over whether any bones are broken, and then experiencing in your inmost soul the unutterable loneliness of savage mountains."

Fleming, with his scientist's eye, noted that the undergrowth was formed of "the genuine flora of the Pacific slope" including *echinopanax horridus* and *Symplocarpus foetidus* – devil's club, "perpetually wounding us with their spikes," and skunk cabbage "in acres of stinking perfection." The nettles of the devil's club were so bad that long after reaching civilization again, at Kamloops, the travellers felt the effects of them; their hands had to be wrapped in oatmeal poultices and even then the pain was so severe that one member of the party was unable to sleep.

All this time James Ross had been worrying about the suitability of the Kicking Horse Pass. Like Rogers before him, he began to wonder whether every other method of crossing the Rockies had been considered. The terrible descent from the Great Divide by way of the Kicking Horse River bothered almost everybody: if grades of 2.2 per cent were to be maintained, as the contract stipulated, construction costs would be very heavy. But if steeper grades were agreed upon, maintenance and running costs would be vastly increased and the government would probably not pay a subsidy on any part of the line that did not adhere to the contract.

Ross asked Shaw to explore the headwaters of the Bow and the Howse Pass – the very region which Tom Wilson, the packer, had reported on to Rogers the year before. If Shaw found a better pass, Ross was prepared to move swiftly. Shaw was instructed to run an immediate trial line from the summit without waiting for further orders while Ross stood ready to rush a survey crew to the spot. There was not a day to be lost; the rails had moved across the prairies at record speed and were now inching into the mountains.

Ross, meanwhile, decided to move over the summit, down the Kicking Horse, and then down the Columbia to the spot where the Blaeberry River flows to join it from the Howse Pass. He took James Hogg with him; en route he picked up Major Rogers and Tom Wilson.

Rogers was desperately worried when he learned that another attempt was being made on the Howse. Would "his" pass be rejected after all? Was Wilson's report of the previous year accurate? He stoutly defended it, but he was reminded that "Wilson is not an engineer so what does he know about grades?" Ross was inclined to agree with Wilson and abandoned his idea of climbing to the top of the Howse Pass to rendezvous with Shaw. Hogg, however, was determined, in Wilson's words, "to prove that my report was wrong." He insisted on heading up the mountainside with only a day's rations in his pack. It was almost the end of him. Shaw found him, quite by accident, crouched over a dying fire, insensible from exhaustion and frostbite, with most of his clothing burned away.

It was late October by this time; already the snow was falling thickly. Rogers left the mountains without knowing the results of Shaw's explorations. By now Tom Wilson had become his friend and confidant and he revealed to him something of his feelings. He was in a state approaching despondency. All his work, he felt, had been for nothing: the contractors wanted to circumvent his pass in the Selkirks by taking the long way round, using the hairpin valley of the Columbia, "and if they did that he would be robbed of his ambition." The Kicking Horse was also in doubt. If it were rejected, too, there would be nothing in the mountains to mark his passing. "Are you sure you're right about the Howse Pass, Tom?" he asked time and time again.

In Calgary, to his great relief, the Major learned that Shaw and Ross had rejected the rival pass. The gradient was easier but the summit was one thousand feet higher than that of the Kicking Horse, and its employment would lengthen the railway by thirty miles. For better or for worse, the route which he had so enthusiastically and so profanely endorsed would become the main line of the CPR, and the name of Rogers would go down in history.

Chapter Five

1

Almost every leading figure connected with the building of the great railway – with one notable exception – achieved the immortality of a place name. The map of western Canada is, indeed, a kind of coded history of the construction period. The stations along the way (some of them now abandoned) tell the story of the times: Langevin, Tilley, Chapleau and Cartier, Stephen and Donald, Langdon and Shepard, Secretan, Moberly, Schreiber, Crowfoot, Fleming, and Lacombe. Lord Dunmore, who tried and failed to secure the original contract, has his name so enshrined along with Lord Revelstoke, who came to the company's rescue by underwriting a bond issue. Harry Abbott, the general superintendent, has a street named after him in Vancouver, along with Henry Cambie, the surveyor, and Lauchlan Hamilton, who laid out most of the CPR towns; Thomas Shaughnessy has an entire subdivision. Macoun, Sifton, and even Baron Pascoe du P. Grenfell, one of the more obscure – and reluctant – members of the original syndicate, are recognized in stations along the main line. Rosser and Dewdney are immortalized in the names of the main streets in the towns they founded. Most of the leading figures in the railway's story had mountain peaks named after them; Van Horne, indeed, had an entire range. But the connoisseur of place names will search in vain on mountain, village, park, avenue, subdivision, plaque, or swamp for any reference to the man who built the railway between Eagle Pass and Port Moody through some of the most difficult country in the world. There is not so much as an alleyway named for Andrew Onderdonk.

Perhaps he would have wanted it that way, for he was a remarkably reticent man. He did not inspire the kind of anecdote that became part of the legends of Van Horne, Rogers, and Hill. No biographer appeared before or after his death to chronicle his accomplishments, which included the San Francisco sea-wall, parts of the Trent Valley Canal, and the first subway tunnels under New York's East River. In the personal memoirs of the day he remains an aloof and shadowy figure, respected but not really known. Rogers, Hill, and Van Horne were each referred to by their underlings, with a mixture of awe, respect, and terror, as "the old man." Onderdonk was known to everybody, from the most obscure navvy to the top engineers and section bosses, by the more austere title of "A.O."

If those initials had a Wall Street ring, it was perhaps because Onderdonk looked and acted more like a broker than a contractor. In muddy Yale, which he made his headquarters while his crews were blasting their way through the diamond-hard rock of the Fraser Canyon, he dressed exactly as he would have on the streets of his native New York. He took considerable care about his personal appearance. His full moustache was neatly trimmed and his beard, when he grew one, was carefully parted in the middle, as was his curly brown hair. He was tall, strapping, and handsome, with a straight nose, a high forehead, and clear eyes – an impeccable man with an impeccable reputation. "Onderdonk," recalled Bill Evans, a pioneer CPR engineer, "was a gentleman, always neat, well dressed and courteous." When he passed down the line, the white workers along the way – Onderdonk's lambs, they were called – were moved to touch their caps. A woman in Victoria who knew him socially described him as very steady and clear headed, but added that he did not have much polish. In that English colonial environment, where tea at four was as much a ritual as an Anglican communion, few Americans were thought to be polished. But to the men sweating along the black canyon of the Fraser, Andrew Onderdonk must have seemed very polished indeed. Henry Cambie, the former government engineer who went to work for him, described him, as many did, as "a very unassuming man" and added that he was both clever and a good organizer and was "possessed of a great deal of tact." In short, Onderdonk had no observable eccentricities unless one counts the monumental reticence that made him a kingdom unto himself and gave him an air of mystery, even among those who were closest to him.

But no one was really close to him. If any knew his inner feelings, they left no record of it. If he suffered moments of despair – and it is clear that he did – he forbore to parade them before the world or even before his cronies. It was not that he shunned company; the big, two-storey, cedar home, with its gabled roof and broad verandahs, which he built in Yale to house his wife and four children, was a kind of social centre – almost an institution, which, indeed, it later became. Onderdonk was forever entertaining and clearly liked to play the host. "We lived as if we were in New York," Daniel McNeil Parker, Sir Charles Tupper's doctor and friend, wrote of his visit there with the minister in 1881. The contractor and his wife were described by a friend as "a happy-go-lucky couple . . . fond of enjoying themselves." Cambie, in his diaries, notes time and again that he dined at the Onderdonks'. But Cambie, who had a good sense of anecdote, never seems to have penetrated that wall of reserve.

Onderdonk's modesty was matched by that of his wife Delia, a short, plump and pretty blonde, who was "the most modestly dressed woman in Yale," a frontier town where all the engineers' wives, having precious little else to occupy them, vied with each other in the ostentation of their frocks and gowns. "A nice, unaffected American lady," Dr. Parker wrote of her.

If Onderdonk presented a cool face to the world, it was partly because he did not need to prove himself over and over again. He had been raised in security; in his daughter's words, "his family on both sides were gentle people of education." Onderdonk differed from most of the contractors of his time and from all the other major figures in the story of the railway. Each one of them – Donald A. Smith, Duncan McIntyre, John S. Kennedy, Norman Kittson, James J. Hill, George Stephen, Sandford Fleming, and William Van Horne, right on down to Michael Haney and A. B. Rogers – had been a poor boy who made it to the top on his own. Most were either immigrants or the sons of immigrants; but Onderdonk came from an old New York family that had been in America for more than two centuries. He was a direct descendant of Adrian van der Donk, a Dutchman who sailed up the Hudson in 1672. His mother was pure English – a Trask from Boston. Fourteen members of his immediate family had degrees from Columbia. His ancestral background was studded with bishops, doctors, and diplomats. Onderdonk himself was a man of education with an engineering degree from the Troy Institute of Technology. He did not need to swear loudly, smoke oversize cigars, act flamboyantly, or throw his weight around. It was not in his nature to show off; he was secure within himself, a quiet aristocrat, "very popular in local society circles," as the Victoria *British Colonist* put it.

Onderdonk's sense of security was also sustained by the knowledge that he had almost unlimited funds behind him. He was front man for a syndicate that included H. B. Laidlaw, the New York banker, Levi P. Morton of Morton, Bliss and Company, a prominent eastern banking house, S. G. Reed, the immensely powerful vice-president of the Oregon Railway and Navigation Company, and last, but by no means least, Darius O. Mills, the legendary San Francisco banker.

Mills handled the financial end of the Onderdonk syndicate. He was everything that Onderdonk was not, having clawed his way to his position as one of the boldest and most astute financiers in America by striking it rich in California in 1849 – not by finding gold but by chartering a sailing vessel, loading it with all the commodities likely to be in short supply in the California camps, and sailing it successfully around the Horn. Mills sold out his stock to the eager miners at fabulous prices and went on swiftly to fame and fortune, becoming the first president of the Bank of California and marrying off his daughter to Whitelaw Reid, proprietor of the New York *Tribune*.

184

In 1880, when he and Onderdonk were securing their first contracts in British Columbia from the Canadian government, everybody was talking about Mills's palatial office building being planned on Broad Street, New York (the finest in the world, it was said: thirteen structures had to be demolished to accommodate it), and his even more palatial private home opposite St. Patrick's Cathedral, "a mansion of which a Shah of Persia might be proud," for which, it was reported, he had paid the highest frontage price in history. The carved woodwork, painted ceilings, inlaid walls and floors cost him an additional four hundred and fifty thousand dollars. As for his office building, it was garish with Corinthian pillars, red Kentucky marble, and Italian terracotta. No wonder the Canadian government was intrigued when it learned who was bankrolling Andrew Onderdonk.

Charles Tupper, the Minister of Railways, had had his fill of under-financed contractors, some of whom had been forced to give up on the Thunder Bay–Red River line, to the embarrassment of the government. Although Onderdonk's tenders for the four British Columbia contracts were by no means the lowest, he managed with Tupper's help to buy them all up from the successful low bidders. It was agreed that one firm could do the job much cheaper than four: there would be no competition for labour; materials could be purchased in quantity; and, perhaps most important, the line could be built in an orderly and progressive manner so that the newly laid rails could be used to transport materials to the unfinished portion.

At thirty-seven, Onderdonk was known as a seasoned contractor with a reputation for promptness, efficiency, and organization. He had just completed the massive sea-wall and ferry slips in San Francisco on time, in spite of serious troubles with the incendiary labour chieftain, Dennis Kearney, a one-time sailor who rose to power as a coolie-hater and was prominent in the riots of 1877. Onderdonk made it clear to the government that he would have the entire 127 miles between Emory's Bar, at the start of the Fraser Canyon, and Savona's Ferry, near Kamloops – or he would pull out. He got what he asked for.

Some time later, when the government let the rest of the British Columbia line from Emory's Bar to Port Moody on the coast, Onderdonk was again awarded the contract, though again he was not the lowest bidder. Certainly in this instance, if not before, the government made use of some fancy sleight-of-hand to ensure that he was successful. Under the terms of tendering, each firm bidding was required to put up substantial security to prove it could undertake the work. The lowest bidder,

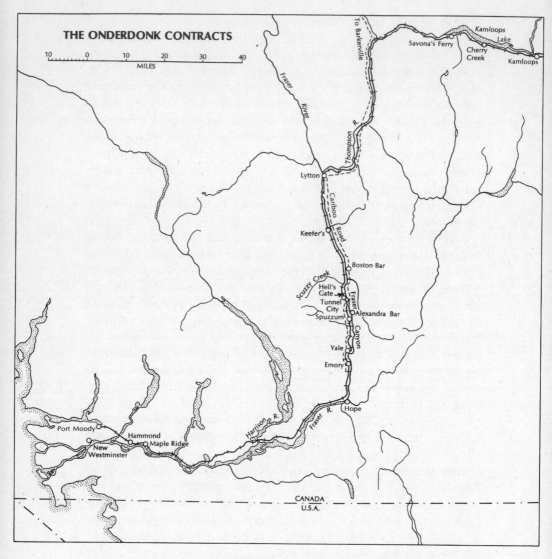

THE ONDERDONK CONTRACTS

MILES

Duncan, McDonald and Charlebois, deposited a cheque, which was certified for a specified period. Tupper waited until this period had expired; then he awarded the contract by default to Onderdonk, whose bid was $264,000 higher. This was barefaced favouritism. There was a howl from the Opposition and its newspapers ("a gross fraud," cried the *Globe*), but Tupper made it stick. There was another suspicious aspect to the case. For the first time the contract was let as a lump sum, without being broken down into component parts. This method, as the *Globe* pointed out, "is essentially a corrupt method, and is so considered by contractors." For one thing, it made it difficult to check up on extras. Normally, the government's practice was to supply its own estimates of quantities to the competing firms. In this case it declined to do so, thereby putting an enormous financial burden on each company tendering. Clearly, the government wanted Onderdonk to have the job, which was, admittedly, as difficult a one as had ever faced a contracting firm in the Dominion. As Henry Cambie wrote: "No such mountain work had ever been attempted in Canada before."

The first four Onderdonk contracts were signed in 1880, before the Canadian Pacific Railway Company came into being. The CPR, under the terms of its agreement with the government, would inherit the stretch between Port Moody and Savona's Ferry on Kamloops Lake. Onderdonk then, unlike Van Horne, was building a railway that he would never have to manage himself once it was completed. It was a considerable distinction and the basis of a long and bitter dispute between the CPR and the government in the years that followed the driving of the last spike.

By the time the CPR turned its first prairie sod in May, 1881, Onderdonk had been at work for a year, but he had not laid a mile of track. For all of those twelve months, the people of Yale had grown accustomed to the ceaseless reverberations caused by rock being blown to bits twenty-four hours a day. There were, within a mile and a half of the town, four tunnels to be drilled; it took Onderdonk eighteen months to blast them out of the rock of the canyon – a compact granite, striped with extremely hard veins of quartz. Mountains of this granite – the toughest rock in the world – border both sides of the river, rising as high as eight thousand feet. In the first seventeen miles upriver from Yale there were no fewer than thirteen tunnels; between Kamloops and Port Moody there was a total of twenty-seven. The sixty-mile stretch of road between Emory and the Thompson River was considered to be the most difficult and expensive on the continent. The blasting was painfully slow; even when the big Ingersoll compressed air drills were used, it was not possible to move more than six feet a day. The flanks of the mountains were grooved by deep canyons; as a result, some six hundred trestles and bridges were required above Yale. One hundred of these were needed in a single thirty-mile section. To build them Onderdonk would need to order forty million board feet of lumber.

The approaches to many of the tunnels had to be galleried. Gallery work was only slightly less demanding than tunnelling. The trains were destined to travel on the very lip of the precipice into which a kind of notch had been blasted, the roof consisting of solid rock which was usually several hundred feet thick and sometimes several thousand. One such gallery ran for one hundred feet; at its rim was a perfectly perpendicular wall of rock, two hundred feet high.

At Hell's Gate on the Fraser, a traveller could stand and watch the agony of construction taking place directly across the foaming waters. It seemed impossible that a road could be carved out of those dripping black cliffs. Here men could be seen suspended at dizzy heights against the rock walls, let down the cliffs on ladders secured by ropes attached to trees on the summit so that they could drill blasting holes into the face of the escarpment. Each time a shot was fired, the men had to clamber up the ladders as swiftly as possible to escape the effect of the explosion. Engineers made their measurements and took their cross-sections suspended for hours and sometimes days "like Mahomet's coffin between heaven and earth." They worked often in their bare feet, which they believed ensured them a better footing. A break or a slip in the rope, a rock toppling from above, or a premature blast meant certain death.

All along the right of way, a traveller on the far side of the river could see the gaping mouths of the tunnels, ragged as a shattered windowpane, and hear the continual crump of the blasting. Splintered trees toppled into the Fraser's muddy gorge, huge rocks catapulted into the sky, vast chunks of mountainside slid into the river.

High above the grade and sometimes below it, running along the same cliff face was the old corduroy road to the Cariboo mines, which Sir James Douglas, Governor of British Columbia, had caused to be built in the 1860's. It was jammed with traffic. Twelve-mule teams thudded by. Ungainly prairie schooners, pulled by sixteen oxen with six spares plodding behind, rattled past, loaded with everything from rice for the coolie labour to portable sawmills for the construction camps. The road itself had been an engineering miracle in its day – a crazy, unbelievable highway cut into the cliffs, the only link between the coast and the interior plateau of British Columbia. In some spots in the Fraser Canyon the road had to be carried around the precipice on trestle-work, like the balcony of a house, so that passengers on the Cariboo stage were travelling directly over the boiling waters three hundred feet below.

Onderdonk was pledged to keep the road open; without it the economy of the Cariboo would be throttled. Besides, he needed it himself to bring supplies to his construction camps. The difficulty of achieving this, while the blasting and the building was going on all around – above it, below it, and right beside it – was indescribable. Great chunks of the road sometimes slid into the Fraser. Sometimes the railway itself required the right of way; when that happened, construction had to be halted until a new section of road was built.

The traffic on the Cariboo road presented a constant problem. Two covered wagons linked in tandem and hauled by nine yoke of oxen made a cavalcade well over a hundred feet long. It was bad enough getting around the tight curves, but added to this was the loose rock blown from tunnel openings or cuts, which often held up the stages or caused accidents. Henry Cambie liked to tell the story of the time Steve Tingley, the most famous whip on the road, was waved through a pile of debris by the foreman, Dave McBeth. The stage struck a hidden rock, which McBeth had overlooked, with disastrous results. Inside the coach was Judge John Foster McCreight, the first premier of the province – "a nervous, fidgetty, queer tempered man," the Lieutenant-Governor had called him. The infuriated McCreight warned McBeth that if he was ever brought before him he would have no compunction in condemning him to be hanged for his carelessness in allowing such an accident to happen.

By June of 1882, when Van Horne launched his record-breaking push across the prairies, Onderdonk had driven scarcely twenty miles of steel. (It had taken eighteen months working day and night to build the first two miles out of Yale.) An explosives factory was turning out four thousand pounds of nitro-glycerine a day. Ten vessels containing six thousand Chinese coolies were on their way from the Orient to swell his labour force, strung out all along the right of way from Port Moody on Burrard Inlet to the arid banks of the Thompson. Expenses were mounting alarmingly. The average cost of a mile of railroad on the Onderdonk contract was eighty thousand dollars, but there were many places where the price was three times that amount.

The freight rates on the old Cariboo corduroy road were strangling Onderdonk. He was paying as much as ten dollars a ton for a few miles' haulage. As a result he decided, in the spring of 1882, to attempt a task that almost everyone else considered impossible: he proposed to build a steamer that could actually negotiate the most treacherous section of the Fraser Canyon, known as Hell's Gate. Veteran rivermen all believed Hell's Gate to be impassable. Here the river reached a peak of fury, hurling itself at ten knots over a ledge of black basalt and squeezing between twin ramparts only eighty feet apart. It was Onderdonk's plan to force a steamboat through this chute and put her into service between Lytton and Boston Bar.

189

The sturdy little craft that he ordered was to be built at Spuzzum near Tunnel City (named for the Big Tunnel, sixteen hundred feet long, being drilled twenty miles upriver from Yale). It would be a 250-ton craft, 127 feet long with a beam of 24 feet and with 20 bulkhead compartments to keep it buoyant. It was to be called *Skuzzy*, after a mountain stream "that comes dancing and falling through the opening in the rocks at times causing attractive falls and finally uniting its clear stream with the less pleasant waters of the Fraser." The little ship was launched on May 4 by Mrs. Onderdonk, modestly dressed, as always, in a long skirt and a plain whaleboned blouse.

It was easier to construct such a craft than it was to persuade a crew to man it. Old river hands pleaded with Onderdonk to abandon the scheme. One pioneer skipper said that to take a steamboat up the torrent of Hell's Gate would be the same as announcing one's intention of jumping from a tall building and expecting to live to tell about it. Onderdonk's first choice as captain was Nat Lane, Jr., a man whose ability with steamboats was known from the Stikine to the Fraser; but Lane would have no part of the venture. By this time the river was in spring flow, rising rapidly day after day, spilling over its banks and endangering small settlements. At the last moment a skipper, Asbury Insley, was found to attempt the feat. He set off on May 17, using every river trick he had learned to pit the *Skuzzy* against the furious waters. Time after time he was beaten back until, at length, he turned the boat about and returned to Spuzzum with defeat written on his features.

It was generally agreed that the *Skuzzy* would be dismantled and scrapped or else taken overland to Boston Bar and reassembled. Then, to the astonishment of all, Onderdonk announced that another attempt would be made to force the boat through the canyon. He had gone all the way to the upper Columbia to find three expert boatmen foolhardy enough to make the attempt. These were Captain S. R. Smith of Lewiston, Idaho, his brother David, and J. W. Burse, who was to act as engineer. Smith had taken the steamer *Shoshone* one thousand miles down the Snake River to the Blue Mountains and then safely over the falls at Willamette, Oregon – the only boat in history to make such a perilous passage. If anyone could battle through Hell's Gate, Smith and his colleagues were the men to do it.

On September 7, Onderdonk brought five flat cars loaded with guests from Yale to witness the ordeal. They rattled over the newly laid track, the train swaying around the sharp curves and plunging into the recently driven tunnels where from the jagged roofs of black rock water dripped

190

steadily. They crowded the high bank of the Fraser, laying wagers of gold, timber, and other merchandise on the outcome – the odds running as high as a hundred to one against the boat's getting through.

The crowds could not stay to witness the full struggle. After four days only a few miles of headway had been made. After ten it became apparent that the *Skuzzy* was losing the battle. At this point Andrew Onderdonk took command. He ordered ring-bolts driven into the rock walls of the canyon and he placed one hundred and fifty Chinese labourers at intervals along the banks passing heavy ropes through the bolts. These ropes were attached to the ship's capstan. Finally on September 28, with the aid of the engines, the steam winch, fifteen men on the capstan, and the mass of coolies tugging and straining along the bank (to cling to the ropes and pull was imperative, for to lose one's grip and fall meant certain death), the boat finally got through, and a public holiday was declared in Yale.

It took the *Skuzzy* another seven hours to fight her way upstream to Lytton before she went into freighting service. The current was so swift that it took only an hour to make the run back to Boston Bar, and on her first voyage she was badly damaged, with a gaping hole in her hull and her sides, it was said, scraped almost to the point of transparency. She limped into berth, had her wounds repaired, and for the next year worked the river, emerging splintered and battered after every journey.

All this time men were being mangled or killed by falling rock, by slides, by runaway horses, and above all by the incessant blasting that went on day and night. The temporary names along the way give a clue to the working conditions: "Jaws of Death Arch," for example, and "Indictment Hole," so named because, it was said, anyone who tried to put a right of way through the spot ought to be indicted.

Men grew careless with blasting powder and nitro-glycerine. At the ferry crossing at Spuzzum, tons of black powder were hauled to the edge of the bank by wagon and hurled down a chute into a waiting boat, the only cushion against the shock being a bale of hay. Some men whose hands were covered with blasting powder suffered severe burns when they recklessly tried to light their pipes. Others, returning prematurely to a half-finished tunnel following a blast, were met by a second, which blew them to pieces. One Chinese near Yale hid behind a tree two hundred feet from a tunnel about to be blasted and thought himself perfectly safe; a flying splinter sheared off his nose. Often, huge rocks came hurtling out of the mouths of tunnels like cannon-balls. One sank a boat, causing a man to drown. Another knocked down a bridge. The larger blasts touched off avalanches and mud slides. Almost every time heavy shots were fired

191

inside a tunnel, great boulders were ripped free from the mountainside by the reverberations. One of these tore through the roof of the engine house at Number One Tunnel, "somewhat injuring a couple of men," in the casual report of the Yale *Inland Sentinel*. One slide came down from such a height that it carried part of an oak forest and an entire Indian burying ground into the river, allowing the oaks to continue to grow "and the dead men's bones to rest without being in the least disturbed – fences, roots, images and all." (The natives were more concerned about the "arbitrary and illegal removal of Indian dead" when the right of way happened to coincide with one of their cemeteries, but the railway builders paid little heed to such obstacles.)

Another rock slide actually blocked the Thompson River, forming a dam half a mile long and a hundred and fifty feet wide, raising the water two hundred feet and flooding several farms while leaving the channel below almost dry. The Chinese and Indians working in the vicinity dropped their tools and rushed to the river-bed to collect the hundreds of fish wriggling and gasping in the mud and also to recover the gold, which was still plentiful and, with the water down, easy to pan. Some made two hundred dollars a day in this manner until the river, working its way round the barrier of rock, formed a new channel. Another slide in November, 1882, blocked the track east of the Big Tunnel to a depth of sixty feet; it was mid-April before the debris could all be cleared away. An unexpected slide near Keefers station was struck by a train with such impact that the locomotive became detached. It hurtled over a 250-foot embankment, did a full somersault, and landed upright at the river's edge. The fireman and engineer climbed out, unhurt.

There was a curious accident at Cherry Creek caused by the near desert conditions of the Interior Plateau of British Columbia. To one teamster hauling blasting powder by wagon, the rocks on the roadbed beneath suddenly seemed to take fire. The sight caused the horses to plunge forward, breaking loose from the wagon and pulling the driver, who held fast to the reins, right off his seat and away from the vehicle, which blew up with a roar. Later the mystery was unravelled: the dry weather had shrunk the staves of the powder barrels so that every seam leaked explosive. Thus both the floor of the wagon and the road beneath it were covered with loose powder, which was finally ignited by sparks made by the horses' shoes striking the rocks.

There were other odd mishaps caused by the treacherous terrain. It was not even safe to get drunk. One veteran railroader who did staggered to the top of a bluff not far from the Big Tunnel one January day and toppled to his death. Even as careful and experienced an engineer as Henry Cambie was not immune. His horses bolted on the Cariboo Road – a fairly common occurrence – his carriage struck a new stump, and he, his wife, and his child were thrown out. The child escaped unhurt but both parents were injured, Mrs. Cambie suffering a severe concussion.

The danger was so great that it became difficult to get men who were willing to be suspended by ropes to drill holes in the chasm walls for explosives. The Indians were the most fearless; fortunately, they turned out to be first-class rock workers. Their task was to go down first and blast out the footholds in which other men could stand and work. But the Indians had a habit of working until payday and then quitting to spend their earnings.

Six months after Onderdonk began his contract the hospital at Yale had to be enlarged to take care of the accident victims. Mrs. Onderdonk, capable and unpretentious, acted as superintendent. Most of the injured arrived in bad shape because of the difficulty of conveying them back to Yale over the impossible terrain. Deaths occurred almost weekly, as a study of the *Inland Sentinel* reveals:

May 18, 1881 – Flying rock from a blast in a cut sprays eight men, killing one.

June 2, 1881 – The white boss of a Chinese work gang ignores a warning that all the charges have not yet gone off, walks forward, and is killed instantly when a blast hurls a rock straight into his face.

June 9, 1881 – Two workmen die when rock is dislodged from the ceiling of a tunnel in which they are working.

"Our attention has been called to the neglected condition of the cemetery here, of late," the *Sentinel* wrote that June. "The fact that it is rapidly filled up with victims and strangers from the railway works . . . should not cause less interest than has heretofore been displayed upon 'the city of the dead.' " The same issue reported "many unnecessary sacrifices of life along the railway construction line." That day a local man, the proprietor of the Romano House, had a narrow escape when a dynamite blast showered his carriage with pieces of rock.

By August the paper was becoming alarmed at the accident rate: "Life is held too cheap, generally, in this country, and it will evidently require severe punishment to teach parties that they cannot trifle with other people's lives even if they are careless of their own existence." Exactly one week after those words were written, two more men working in Number Seven Tunnel were killed by falling boulders.

193

2

When Andrew Onderdonk arrived in British Columbia there were perhaps thirty-five thousand white citizens in the province. Since he would need at least ten thousand able-bodied men to build his part of the railway – and actually many more, because of the turnover – it was clear that he would have to look elsewhere for much of his labour force. From the very outset there was a kind of terror that he would solve the problem by importing and employing Chinese.

The *British Colonist*, which since the days of its eccentric founder Amor de Cosmos had stoutly opposed all Oriental immigration, showed this feeling early in January, 1880, after the Seattle *Post* had warned the British Columbians that they might as well "resign themselves to all the evils of Chinese competition for but little short of a miracle will prevent the San Francisco contractors from employing Chinamen on their work." The *Colonist* voiced the fear that Onderdonk would exclude "white free labor . . . and by the employment of Chinese slave labour conspire to send beyond the seas the eight or ten millions of Canadian money required to be spent on the work of construction." However, the paper reassured its readers, "we have reason to know that in assenting to the transfer of the contract the Can. Govt. asked for the employment of the surplus *white* labour of the Province and of Canada."

The difficulty was that there was very little surplus white labour because of the railroad boom in the western United States and in Canada. Onderdonk, when he arrived in Victoria in April, 1880, was met by a deputation from the Anti-Chinese Association. He was not evasive in his reply to their demand for assurances that he would not employ Orientals, but he was careful to avoid committing himself. It was his intention, he informed the delegation, to give white labour the preference in all cases. When the white labour of the province was exhausted he would, if necessity compelled him, fall back on the French Canadians of eastern Canada. Should that not be sufficient, he would with reluctance engage Indians and Chinese.

The first Chinese had come to British Columbia from California in 1858, attracted by the gold of the Fraser and Cariboo. Anti-Chinese feeling had been rising steadily since the early 1860's and had reached a peak in 1878 when the Legislature passed a resolution banning their employment in the public works of the province. At that time there were some three thousand Chinese in British Columbia, all of them prepared to work for lower wages than any white labourer; that was the chief cause of the discontent. The *British Colonist*, which wanted Chinese immigration restricted, exclaimed in 1878 that "the Chinese ulcer is eating into the prosperity of the country and sooner or later must be cut out." That same year the provincial government imposed a head-tax of ten dollars on all Chinese, an act that met with the most stubborn resistance. Stores in Victoria's Chinatown closed their doors; Chinese merchants refused to sell goods to whites; laundrymen abandoned their daily operations; vegetable peddlers ceased to call; cooks, housemaids, and houseboys deserted their posts in restaurants and private homes. The impasse was resolved after a fortnight or so when the British Columbia Supreme Court ruled that the tax was unconstitutional; but the bitterness remained. There was no politician in the province who could have been elected had he advocated, even in the most tentative terms, the continued admittance of any Chinese to Canada. Indeed, it was considered to be political suicide to take any stand but one that was anti-Chinese.

The feeling elsewhere in Canada, though less intense, was generally against the Chinese. The Trades and Labour Council of Toronto wanted them banned outright from Canada. Almost all newspapers were editorially opposed to Oriental immigration. The general theme was that the "Chinamen" (they were rarely referred to in any other way) were filthy, stupid, insensitive, immoral heathens. "A Chinaman does not know the meaning of filial love," the Port Moody *Gazette* wrote of a race obsessed with ancestor worship. There was, the paper said, no affinity between the white and the yellow races, "nor ever can be, in spite of all that is preached about the universal brotherhood of man." In Winnipeg, where Chinese were all but unknown, the *Times* published a fairly typical series of opinions about "the beardless and immoral children of China," as it called them; they possessed "no sense whatever of any principle of morality"; their brains were "vacant of all thoughts which lift up and ennoble humanity"; and "it is an established fact that dealings with the Chinese are attended with evil results." But then other races did not fare much better in Canadian newspapers. Negroes, who were invariably referred to as "darkies" or "niggers," were generally presented as shiftless, lazy, dirty, immoral, sexually depraved, and dangerous. Jews were caricatured unmercifully by cartoonists, referred to as "sheenies," and depicted as grasping, cheating, and conniving.

The Prime Minister himself agreed that the Chinese were "an alien race in every sense that would not and could not be expected to assimilate with our Arian population," but he was far too pragmatic to exclude

195

Orientals from Canada until the railway was built. He put it bluntly to Parliament in 1882: "It is simply a question of alternatives: either you must have this labour or you can't have the railway."

The vanguard of Onderdonk's white labour force came from San Francisco, then the only real source of supply. Some of these men, sent up by employment agents, "had never done a hard day's work before." To quote Henry Cambie, they were for the most part clerks out of employment, "broken-down bar-keepers, or men of that class," men who had never handled a shovel before and who often appeared on the scene attired in fashionable garments in a rather tattered state. Some of these new labourers actually went into the cuttings wearing patent leather shoes with trousers sprung over the foot. W. H. Holmes, who worked under Onderdonk in the Fraser Canyon, described the early labour force as "roughnecks from San Francisco and the Barbary Coast as well as good men." The bad, however, tended to drive out the good. "The few good men declined to associate, or herd at bed and board, with 'Sand-lot hoodlums' from San Francisco," the *Globe* reported. "The residue also sought their former haunts across the line, so that even to keep up a modicum of white labour was a work of no little difficulty. . . ."

In the early days of the contract there were wild scenes at Emory and Yale. The streets of both communities were jammed with men, some arriving for work, some idling about, some departing. The saloons did a roaring business; fights were a daily occurrence. Steamboats arriving daily with freight found there was no place to stack it. Every available teamster had been hired, but there were not half enough teams to haul the goods away. Boatloads of grain poured in, along with tools, lumber, and blasting powder. Men of all kinds had to be sorted out – stewards, cooks, flunkeys, drillers, carpenters, teamsters, stable men, and blacksmiths. Manpower was vital, for there was no machinery to speak of. Later on Onderdonk brought in drills that were worked by steam and compressed air, but in the first hectic months everything was done by hand.

Onderdonk was operating on a tight budget. He had been forced to accept four contracts at bids which were more than a million and a half dollars lower than his own tendered price. He had paid out an additional two hundred and fifteen thousand dollars to purchase the contracts of the successful bidders. In short, he had almost two million dollars less to work with than he had contemplated when he undertook to tender on the Fraser River section of the CPR.

Moreover, he was asking men to come all the way to the wilds of British Columbia for wages that were lower than those the Northern Pacific was

196

offering through more settled country. Onderdonk paid his labourers between $1.50 and $1.75 a day; the American railway was offering between $1.75 and $2.00 a day. For skilled labour, the gap was even greater: Onderdonk's bridge carpenters, for example, were paid between $2.00 and $2.50 a day; the same tradesmen working on Northern Pacific bridges received a dollar a day more.

Chinese coolies, on the other hand, could be employed for one dollar a day. The contracts, furthermore, stipulated that they must buy their provisions at the company stores, where the prices were inflated; if they took their custom elsewhere they were to be paid only eighty cents. In addition, the white workers required all the paraphernalia of a first-class camp, including cooks, flunkeys, and a wide variety of supplies. The coolie was prepared to take care of himself: he could move about in the wilderness, set up his own camp, and pack all his belongings, provisions, and camp equipment on his back. Michael Haney, who went to work for Onderdonk in 1883, discovered that it was possible to move two thousand Chinese a distance of twenty-five miles and have them at work all within twenty-four hours. The same task could not be performed with a similar number of white workmen in less than a week. It is small wonder, then, that almost from the outset Andrew Onderdonk began hiring Chinese in spite of a volley of protests.

The United States transcontinental railway system had already established the efficiency of coolie labour. The first Chinese to work on any railway were imported by that colourful and gargantuan innovator Charles Crocker, the ex-peddler, ex-miner, and ex-trader who built the Central Pacific. Crocker, realizing that Irish-Americans were not in sufficient supply to complete the railroad, had first tried to arrange the mass immigration of Mexican peons. When this plan was aborted he turned, in desperation, to the Chinese, who were at the time working the old California placer claims, growing vegetables in market gardens, operating laundries, or serving as houseboys. Few believed that these small, frail people were tough enough to stand the back-breaking labour that would be required in the high Sierras, but Crocker reasoned that any race that could construct the Great Wall of China could also build a railroad. He decided to experiment with fifty coolies, whom he hauled to the end of track. To his astonishment and delight, they quickly put together a clean and efficient camp, cooked a rice supper, and dropped off to sleep as if they had lived all of their lives in the mountains. They were up with the sun, picks in hand, and by sunset Crocker was wiring Sacramento for more. By 1866 six thousand of them were at work on the Central Pacific.

197

Crocker paid them thirty-one dollars a month, out of which they supplied their own keep. His white labourers received thirty dollars a month and their board.

Some of these men were undoubtedly numbered among the first Chinese to go to work for Andrew Onderdonk. The first consignment came from the Northern Pacific Railroad in Oregon in 1880, the second from the Southern Pacific in California in 1881. These early arrivals – there were fifteen hundred of them – were fairly green, possibly because the non-Chinese foremen were themselves inexperienced. Cambie, after walking along the right of way on June 7, 1880, confided to his diary that the work force was "so large in many places, the Chinamen seem to be in each other's way." At this point there were no animals on the line moving earth and rock; the Chinese were themselves employed as beasts of burden. At one point, to his horror, the thrifty Cambie found forty Chinese moving ten small wagons a distance of four miles, "a waste of money – for four mules could do the same work much more quickly." Later arrivals, however, included "some trained gangs of rock men as good as I ever saw." In the Report of the Royal Commission on Chinese Immigration in 1885, J. A. Chapleau wrote that "as a railway navvy, the Chinaman has no superior."

Almost every Chinese who immigrated to North America came from South China, a fact that explains why almost all of the so-called Chinese cuisine eaten by westerners is a corruption of Cantonese cooking. Specifically, the coolies came from eight districts of Kwang Tung province whose capital, Canton, was the only port in the country through which foreign trade was permitted. Kwang Tung was China's window on the West – Hong Kong was only a few miles away – and this situation, together with the extreme poverty and crowded conditions of the coolies (who were hived together, 241 to the square mile), made the prospect of emigration attractive. Each Chinese farmer yearned for financial independence, and all it took to buy financial independence in Kwang Tung (where the average wage was seven cents a day) was three hundred American dollars. It was the ambition of almost every immigrant to save that much money and then return to his homeland after perhaps five years of work on the railroad or in the mining camps, a situation which helps explain the British Columbians' continuing complaints about money leaving the province.

The Chinese were not hired individually but in large groups of as many as a thousand through agents representing the Six Companies of Kwang Tung. These companies were rather like commercial guilds. Colonel F. A. Bee, who acted as Chinese consul in San Francisco, described them as benevolent associations, comparable to the Masons or Oddfellows; indeed, it was said that they had patterned themselves after similar western institutions when they were first formed in the early days of the California gold-rush. The companies handled the shipment of Chinese to North America as well as their contracts with their employers and their eventual return to China. Each Chinese paid a fee of 2½ per cent of his wages to the company, together with his passage money – about forty dollars. The company, in its turn, was pledged to look after each man's welfare in North America, protecting him, for instance, if he got into legal difficulties.

This was certainly not "slave" labour, as many British Columbia politicians and newspapers called it, or even indentured labour. Undoubtedly the companies were a good deal more than mere benevolent associations: those who operated them made a good profit and, through an arrangement with the steamship companies, made it impossible for any Chinese to return home before he had paid his debts. On the other hand, from the point of view of the individual coolie, who could speak no word of English and who was totally uninformed about North American customs and society, the Six Companies represented the only real method of getting to the promised land.

In the winter of 1881–82, Onderdonk, having employed all the labour he could get at his prices – white, Chinese, and Indian – chartered two sailing ships to bring one thousand coolies each from Hong Kong. They arrived after a long, rough winter passage – "the men below decks slept in closed hatches with bad ventilation," Cambie recalled – but in good physical condition. In New Westminster they were "penned in the wharf overnight like so many cattle" and then packed aboard the little stern-wheeler *William Irving* – as many as 642 to a boatload – transferred to flat cars at Emory, and sent directly out along the line.

Altogether in 1882, Onderdonk brought in ten shiploads of Chinese, a total of about six thousand. The figures were greatly exaggerated by the press. The *Globe* of Toronto and the *British Colonist* of Victoria announced that Onderdonk intended to import twenty-four thousand, almost enough to outnumber the whites. The New Westminster *British Columbian* found this too much to swallow: "We yield to none in a sincere desire to see this yellow wave swept back," the paper said, "but surely success is not to be obtained by indulging in such palpable misrepresentation." The new arrivals, according to the *Globe*'s British Columbia correspondent "Senex," were "not free from the direful and contagious disease, leprosy." Senex added a doleful coda to his dispatch: "We are now fully in the grip," he said, "of Americans and Chinamen."

199

Michael Haney declared that in his entire experience of dealing with the Chinese companies and with the individual coolies, he could not recall one case of dishonesty. They lived up to their contracts, and if there was a dispute with a sub-contractor, "it only needed the presence of a representative of the contractor to assure them that their grievances would be considered, to send them cheerfully to work again." Nor did Haney know of a single instance of disagreement between the individual worker and the Chinese company that paid the wages. The experience of the contractors with the Chinese on the job was in marked contrast to the general feeling against them in Victoria. Everybody who dealt with them as labourers, from Andrew Onderdonk down, praised them. George Munro, who had charge of a construction gang from Yale east to Sicamous, echoed the general attitude when he said they "were easy to handle if they were properly dealt with." But woe to any white boss who dealt with them improperly! If they thought their rights were being trampled on, they ceased to be docile. After all, in the days of Imperial China, Kwang Tung had a persistent reputation for disaffection; most of the active leaders of the subsequent revolution, including Sun Yat-sen himself, were Cantonese. Munro ruefully recalled his first payday when, through an error in the payroll department, the Chinese workers received one cent less per hour than had been agreed upon. ". . . there was a little war declared right there. They stormed the Company's stores like madmen, and it didn't take the men at fault long to discover their mistake. The Chinamen were paid their cent and peace reigned once more."

Such incidents were not uncommon. The coolies were divided by the company that provided them into gangs of thirty labourers plus a cook, an assistant cook, and a bookman, whose task it was to keep count of the payments to be made to each individual. In charge of each work gang was a white boss or "herder," who dealt directly with the bookman. Any foreman who did not get along well with his Oriental labourers could expect trouble. Once when a white boss refused to allow his coolies to build a fire along the grade to heat their big teapots, they quit en masse and headed for Yale. On several occasions, white foremen were physically assaulted. One foreman who tried to fire two Chinese over the head of the gang's bookkeeper precipitated a riot near Lytton. He and the white bridge superintendent, the timekeeper, and a teamster were attacked by the entire gang, which seriously mangled one man with a shovel. The following night a party of armed whites attacked the Chinese camp, burned their bunkhouses, and beat several coolies so severely that one died.

200

In such instances feeling ran high against the coolies. The Chief Justice of the province, Matthew Baillie Begbie, was horrified by "the terrible outrages against Chinamen" in the neighbourhood of Lytton. One case, he said, "in its wholesale unconcealed atrocity equalled anything which I have read of agrarian outrage in Ireland." Begbie was aghast that in all cases "the perpetrators have escaped scot free." In one instance the ring-leaders were positively identified by four of the surviving victims but were acquitted by the jury "upon evidence of an *alibi* which the prosecutors might well deem perjured."

The Chinese could also escape detection; since all coolies looked alike to whites, it was difficult and sometimes impossible to swear out warrants for their arrests. The *Sentinel* reported in August, 1882, that "the Chinese workers below Emory went this week for another boss and he had to make tracks for Yale. An effort has been made to get out 8 warrants in the names of the Chinamen, but they could not be had, consequently the effort failed."

Two Chinese who attacked a foreman near Maple Ridge in February, 1883, were summonsed but later released "by a howling mob of Chinamen holding in their hands . . . axes, picks, shovels . . . [who] declared that unless the prisoners were released they would tear the houses to pieces and rescue them." The prisoners were let go but were later recaptured, fined sixteen dollars each, and returned to camp without further trouble.

Many of these incidents occurred because of accidents along the line, for which the Chinese blamed the white foremen. On one such occasion, at Hammond, after a big slide killed several coolies, the foreman had to hold their angry co-workers at bay with a levelled revolver. Another time, about ten miles below Hope, a foreman named Miller failed to give his gang proper warning of a coming explosion; a piece of rock thrown up by the subsequent blast blew one coolie's head right off. His comrades took off after Miller, who plunged into the river to save himself. Several Chinese dived in after him while others on the bank pelted him with stones. Miller was saved by one of the tunnel contractors who rowed a boat through the hail of missiles and hauled him in, but not before one of the Chinese had got off two shots from a pistol. Miller and his rescuer rowed desperately upstream, followed for two miles by an angry mob, before they made good their escape. Commented the *Sentinel*: "Not even Chinamen should be unnecessarily exposed to injury or loss of life."

Deaths appeared to be more frequent among the Chinese labourers than in the white group. A single month in the late summer of Onderdonk's first season, culled from Henry Cambie's diary, gives an idea of their frequency:

August 13 [1880] – A Chinese drilling on the ledge of a bluff near Alexandra Bar is killed when a stone falls from above and knocks him off.

August 19 – A log rolls over an embankment and crushes a Chinese to death at the foot of a slope.

September 4 – A Chinese killed by a rock slide.

September 7 – A boat upsets in the Fraser and a Chinese is drowned.

September 11 – A Chinese is smothered to death in an earth cave-in.

Yet, in that last week – on September 9 – the *Sentinel* proudly announced that "there have been no deaths since the 15th of June." Clearly, it did not count Chinese.

The coolies were generally fatalistic about death. Haney, calling one day at a tent where a sick Chinese lay, asked the bookman: "Will he die to-day?" The bookman shook his head. "No, to-morrow, thlee o'clock." Haney claimed that at three, to the minute, the man expired.

Several memoirs of the era suggest that when one of their fellows sickened the Chinese lost interest in him. Cambie recounted that "as soon as a man was stricken with scurvy the others would not wait upon him or even give him a drink, and the government agent at Yale had great difficulty in getting them buried when they died." He added that many of the corpses were so lightly covered – often with little more than a few rocks – that "one became unpleasantly aware of the fact while walking along the line." Haney believed that when it became obvious that a coolie could not get better he was actually helped into the next world by his friends. W. H. Holmes remembered streams of Chinese pouring up the Cariboo Road all day long, each with so much rice and his belongings on the end of a stick. Those who took sick, he said, or fell back from fatigue, were given a bowl of rice by their companions, who appropriated the victims' packs and moved on. "We picked up some who would have died if they had not been helped." Mrs. George Keefer, wife of one of the divisional engineers, had a curious experience as a result of tending to one of these deserted coolies, whom she picked up by the side of the road and nursed back to health in her own home. When she took him back to camp, his former comrades thought he was a ghost and fled from the scene. It was some time before they came to believe that he was actually alive.

The Chinese would not work in the presence of death, which they considered bad luck. When a man died on the job, the gang that worked with him usually had to be moved to another section of the line. Haney once came upon two thousand Chinese all sitting idle; one of their number had fallen off the bank and his corpse lay far below, spread-eagled on the rocks. In vain the walking boss argued and swore. He pointed out that it was impossible to reach the body. The bank was a sheer precipice, and no boat could approach it through the boiling waters.

"Well," said Haney, "what do you propose to do? Can't have these Chinamen standing around until that Chinaboy disintegrates."

The walking boss scratched his head. "There's an Indian who promises to move that body for ten dollars. I've tried to make a deal with him but he won't budge on that price and it's too much."

"Never mind how much it is," Haney retorted. "Pay it and get those men back to work."

He moved off down the line. During the evening a sharp explosion was heard in the canyon. When Haney returned, the Chinese were back at work and the body had vanished. The Indian had stolen some dynamite and caps, lowered them with a smouldering fuse down the canyon wall, and blown the cadaver to bits.

The Chinese subsisted mainly on a diet of rice and stale ground salmon, scorning the white man's fresh meat and vegetables. As a result they died by the score from scurvy, and no real attempt was made to succour them. Two hundred who came over from China died during their first year in Canada, causing a panic among the citizens of Yale, who believed the newcomers were suffering from smallpox. The deaths continued into 1883. "Here in British Columbia along the line of the railway, the China workmen are fast disappearing under the ground," the *Sentinel* reported in February of that year. "Within a week no less than 6 have died out of a gang of 28 employed a few miles below Emory." Two more died suddenly the following week and a fortnight later the paper reported further deaths. As in other deaths of Chinese from accident or illness, there was no coroner's inquest and no medical attention supplied by either the government or the contractor, a fact that aroused the *Sentinel*, which was far more solicitous of the welfare of the Chinese than any other British Columbia newspaper.

"Why no more interest is felt for the semi-slaves of China is somewhat surprising," it wrote; and again, "No medical attention is furnished nor apparently much interest felt for these poor creatures. We understand Mr. Onderdonk declines interfering, while the Lee Chuck Co, that brought the Chinamen from their native land, refuses, through their agent Lee Soon, who is running the Chinese gang at Emory, to become responsible for doctors and medicine. . . . Surely some action should be taken by the locals," the paper urged, ". . . if not for the sake of the unfortunate China-men themselves but for the protection of the white population. . . ."

The cold winters caused the Chinese great hardship. Most found it impossible to work after mid-November. Cambie, on November 22, noted: "Chinamen who are still at work (only a few gangs) appear to suffer dreadfully from cold. They work in overcoats and wrap their heads up in mufflers." In the winter of 1883–84, when Onderdonk's work force was diminished, the suffering was very great. When the contractors had no more need of them, the Chinese were discharged and left to scrabble for pickings in the worked-out bars of the Fraser or to exist in near destitution in the dying towns along the completed track.

In January, 1884, the *Sentinel* reported that "a number of railway Chinamen are in old buildings along Douglas Street (the Chinese quarter of Yale), some of them in very poor circumstances." The paper reported that when somebody in a store on Front Street threw out some frozen potatoes one "poor old Chinaman" was seen to stand out in the cold picking out those few that were not decayed. "Persons that witnessed the scene thought the sight a pretty hard one."

Not all of the Chinese who came to Canada with the hope of securing financial independence achieved their dream. The sudden completion of the Onderdonk contract made return to Asia impossible for thousands who had not been able to raise the price of passage home or the minor fortune of three hundred dollars that they had expected to amass. Although a Chinese labourer was paid about twenty-five dollars a month on the railway, it was difficult for him to save much more than forty dollars in any one year. First of all, he was not paid for the three months of winter when work was at a near standstill. Then there were expenses: for clothes, $130; for room rent, $24; for tools and fares, $10; for revenue and road taxes, $5; for religious fees, $5; for doctors and drugs, $3; for oil, light, water, and tobacco, $5. These typical expenses (given to a Royal Commission by an informed Chinese witness) left the average coolie with exactly forty-three dollars after a full year of toil on the railway. That scarcely covered his debt to the steamboat company.

At the peak of Onderdonk's operation he had an estimated seven thousand Chinese in his employ. There must have been a considerable turnover. Between 1881 and 1884, a total of 10,387 coolies arrived from China together with an additional 4,313 from Pacific coast ports. (Not all, of course, were employed on the railway.) Most of the immigrants from American ports were probably able to return to the United States.

But the census figures of 1891 indicate that some five thousand coolies were unable to go back to Asia in the years following the completion of the Onderdonk contract.

Because the Chinese left home expecting to return in a few years, they made no attempt to learn the language or alter their mode of life. They clung to the simple coolie jacket, loose trousers, cloth slippers, and pigtail. They kept to their own ways, for they had no intention of losing their character in what they believed would be a temporary abode. Thus they were forever strangers in a foreign land and their continued presence gave to British Columbia a legacy of racial tension that was to endure for the best part of a century.

An incredible preamble to the province's Chinese Regulation Act, enacted in 1884, conveys the mounting feeling against the coolies as the Onderdonk contracts neared completion. The Chinese, it says, "are not disposed to be governed by our laws; are dissimilar in habits and occupation from our people, evade the payment of taxes justly due to the Government; are governed by pestilential habits; are useless in instances of emergency; habitually desecrate graveyards by the removal of bodies therefrom and . . . are inclined to habits subversive of the comfort and well being of the community. . . ."

The act was declared *ultra vires* the following year but other discriminatory laws followed until, by 1904, the head tax imposed on incoming Chinese had risen to a prohibitive five hundred dollars.

The railway workers who remained left few descendants (since they brought no women with them) and few, if any, memories. Some, however, returned to Kwang Tung and then came back to Canada with their families to settle permanently in British Columbia. One of whom there is some slight record was a farmer from Toyshan named Pon Git Cheng. One of his sons became a houseboy for Benjamin Tingley Rogers, the Vancouver sugar magnate. And one of *his* sons, Dr. George Pon of Toronto, was in 1971 a leading scientist in the employ of Atomic Energy of Canada. Dr. Pon was told something of his family background and was able to return to China to visit his grandfather's village in Toyshan. But he never discovered exactly what it was his grandfather did on the railway – how he was hired, where he worked, or what he felt about the strange, raw land which was to become his home. Such details were not set down and so are lost forever – lost and forgotten, like the crumbling bones that lie in unmarked graves beneath the rock and the rubble high above the Fraser's angry torrent.

205

3

Cheap Oriental labour undoubtedly saved Onderdonk from bankruptcy. Without the Chinese it is probable that he could not have completed his contract. He would have had enormous difficulty in finding enough man-power to do the job, and the competitive market would certainly have forced up the cost of white labour. Between 1880 and 1884, at their lower rate of pay, the coolies saved him between three and five million dollars. Their presence also acted as a damper on wage demands. During the mosquito season, whites and Indians fled the line, but the Chinese continued doggedly to work away. In 1884, when workmen near Port Moody struck and demanded a raise from $1.75 to $2.00 a day, they were instantly replaced by a gang of Chinese rushed down from Yale. ("Some of those most active in the anti-Chinese movement found them-selves under the disagreeable necessity of 'bossing' these Mongolians," the Port Moody *Gazette* reported.)

The Governor General believed that the presence of the Chinese was keeping costs down by at least twenty-five per cent, but even with this advantage Onderdonk's operation was a marginal one. "I can't imagine how Mr. Onderdonk has got anything out of his contract as yet," His Excellency wrote to the Prime Minister in the fall of 1882. By 1883 Onderdonk was clearly in financial trouble. Marcus Smith, the govern-ment engineer who acted as Ottawa's watchdog on the line, reported that winter that "it was painfully apparent to myself and even to outsiders that the men were not working to advantage nor were they being well directed. . . ." Smith had his staff estimate the amount of work being done per man and found – on the basis of cubic yards of earth moved – that the averages were very low. Unless some drastic changes were made, he felt, Onderdonk could not pull through without heavy loss.

By March, 1883, when Onderdonk in desperation hired Michael Haney, he was showing a book loss of two and a half million dollars on the work completed. Haney, who had made his reputation as a cost-cutter on Joseph Whitehead's contract on the line out of Thunder Bay, was given the management of the entire Onderdonk contract from Port Moody to Kamloops.

The crusty Marcus Smith was of two minds about Haney. "He seems to fully realize the gravity of your position and is anxious to improve it," he told Onderdonk, but he also warned that if Haney thought he could save the situation by evading or curtailing essential portions of the works, "he is bordering on dreamland."

"I hope Mr. Haney has not caught the disease of the American mind to do something rapid or astounding," Smith wrote. Haney, after all, was known as an impulsive Irishman, given to bold escapades that had left him with the reputation of being accident-prone. He did, however, know a good deal about saving money. Many of Onderdonk's problems, he quickly discovered, had come about through slack organization, slow handling of materials, and delays in transportation. He immediately tightened up discipline and speeded deliveries. He introduced his invention, the wing plough, which unloaded gravel from a line of open cars at bewildering speed. He developed a large nitro-glycerine factory at Yale, and when it blew up, breaking every window in town, he rebuilt it. He travelled the line on horseback, using relays of steeds so that he could inspect as much as a hundred miles of track a day. In this way all of the work in progress came under his personal inspection twice each month.

One of the chief reasons for the delays, Haney discovered, was the inordinate amount of trestle bridging required. Timbers had to be shaped and cut at each bridging point, always at enormous cost. Haney streamlined the operation by building a mill capable of producing one hundred and fifty thousand board feet of lumber a day – every stick marked and numbered for its exact position on the bridge for which it was destined. By this method, the great trestles, prefabricated in advance, were sent forward ready for immediate erection. At the scene, an ingenious foreman named Dan McGillivray had worked out a method of sending each marked timber to its destination by means of a cable and pulley system stretched across the trestle.

Haney was a man who did everything with flair, a characteristic that helps explain why he was viewed as a kind of walking accident. On the Thunder Bay line he had survived at least four brushes with death. When the new governor general, Lord Lansdowne, came out to inspect the line shortly before its completion, Haney insisted on taking him on a wild ride to the coast. The viceregal train rattled along at seventy miles an hour, careering around the tight curves which the government had insisted upon in the interests of cutting costs. Lansdowne, a quiet man, scarcely uttered a word as Haney enthusiastically pointed out to him how well the track was laid. Finally, when they stopped at a small station to take on water, His Excellency spoke up:

"How far is it to Port Moody?"

Haney replied that it was another forty-eight miles.

"Will we be running as fast the balance of the way?"

Haney responded that he thought he could better the pace.

"I have a wife and family in Ottawa and I am rather anxious to see them again," the Governor General replied, "so if you are continuing that rate of travel, I think I will just stay here." A chastened Haney brought the train crawling into Port Moody.

It was inevitable that Marcus Smith, the most irritable engineer in the service, would tangle with Haney, who was doing his best to cut corners in order to get the track-laying completed and so reduce the staggering costs of freight to the contracts on the upper river. Smith poured out his feelings in a letter to Onderdonk, charging Haney with using "supercilious language irritating to the engineers, and stating that the specifications & contract are mere matters of form without vital importance. That his *vast* experience and *high* standing are a sufficient guarantee that he will make a good railway in his own way. . . . It is evident that your chief superintendent has quite mistaken his position which is to carry out the works to the best of his ability under the *directions of the engineers*, and I shall take care that you are not asked to spend one dollar unnecessarily. . . ."

In spite of Smith's watchfulness, Haney's cost-cutting, and cheap coolie labour, Onderdonk's financial problems continued. In the fall of 1883 he set off for Ottawa to lobby for a further subsidy for the unfinished line. In Victoria he ran into James Hartney, who had been cutting timber for him and who had not yet been paid. It says something for the state of Onderdonk's finances that the railway builder, who had a continent-wide reputation for prompt payment, kept putting Hartney off. He was preparing to leave for San Francisco with his family on a Sunday evening, but just before the ship sailed, Hartney served him with a writ. Thus was the island community treated to the strange spectacle of the province's biggest employer of labour being pulled from his bunk at two in the morning, hauled back to shore, and lodged in jail where he languished for two hours before his friends bailed him out.

4

The Sentinel
of Yale

The optimism of frontier communities along the line of the railway in the 1880's knew no bounds. The transitory aspect of railway building did not seem to impress itself on those who settled in the small towns, which boomed briefly and just as quickly faded. When it became clear that the Pacific railway was finally to be built and the details of the Onderdonk contract were made public, the price of lots rose swiftly in Emory, the steamboat landing at the head of the navigable section of the Fraser – a town that had seen an earlier period of prosperity flare and fade during the gold rush of 1858.

Emory, the real estate ads announced, "cannot fail to become one of the most important and prosperous Cities on the Pacific slope." Even before Andrew Onderdonk set foot on the Fraser's banks, lots were auctioned off for as much as five hundred and fifty dollars apiece, demonstrating, according to the *British Colonist*, "a confidence in the future of Emory that is thoroughly justifiable." The newspaper added that "it would be no matter of surprise to learn within the course of a few months that any one of the lucky speculators yesterday had bought himself suddenly rich." The speculators included the pioneer merchant David Oppenheimer, who would one day be mayor of Vancouver, and the *Colonist*'s former editor, John Robson, proprietor of the New Westminster *Dominion Pacific Herald* (later renamed the *British Columbian*) and a future premier of the province. It was Robson and Oppenheimer who with the offer of a free lot induced a black Irishman named Michael Hagan to start a newspaper at Emory. "We expect by the time Emory is a city, to have an enlarged daily, issued by steam," Hagan confidently announced in the first issue of the *Inland Sentinel*. But Emory was not destined to be a city. It soon became clear that the real centre of the Onderdonk operations would be at Yale. "Next summer will be a boom for Emory sure," Hagan wrote wistfully in January, 1881. But in May the *Sentinel* itself moved its offices to Yale – a roaring, wide-open community which for the next three years was to be the railway centre of British Columbia. Then it too would fade as merchants, workers, and major institutions – once again including the *Sentinel* – packed up and moved to Kamloops.

Hagan belonged to that vanishing breed, the itinerant journeyman newspaper jack-of-all-trades. His memories went back to the journalistic days of the martyred Thomas D'Arcy McGee, who had once been his associate – though to the meticulous Hagan it was an unsatisfactory partnership, because McGee had a habit of putting subscription and advertising payments in his pocket and, in all innocence, forgetting about them.

When Hagan arrived at Emory in the spring of 1880, there was not much about a newspaper office that he had not mastered. He was prepared to write every word himself, set it all in type, buck the hand-press, and trudge up and down the line between Emory and Yale, a stout staff in his hand, drumming up business.

He had something of the look of a patriarch about him, as befitted a

209

man who was to be the voice of three communities along the Onderdonk contract. His shoulders were stooped and his long hair and scanty beard were flecked with grey. A benevolent smile generally illuminated his otherwise lugubrious features for, like all small-town editors, he was a professional optimist; it was part of his job to be an unrelenting local booster. Apparently he was attracted by railway construction towns. Six years before he had launched another *Sentinel* at Thunder Bay, in the days when Prince Arthur's Landing was fighting with Fort William to secure the CPR terminus. There he had been a firebrand, driving rivals to the wall and ferreting out corruption. A kind of restlessness had caused him to trek across half a continent and start a new paper in the heart of British Columbia.

Hagan got his type second-hand from the *British Colonist* in Victoria. His hand-press was also an ancient second-hand affair, soon replaced by an even more antique machine of French origin, brought to British Columbia, it was said, by a nobleman who had fled his native land after the Napoleonic *coup* of 1851. It had seen service at Victoria and then at Barkerville during the Cariboo gold-rush. The little paper – four pages in size and five columns wide – was published from a storey-and-a-half structure of rough frame on the hillside just above the Cariboo wagon road, immediately opposite the hard, shelving beach, unadorned by wharf or pier, that served as the main steamboat landing for Onderdonk's supplies.

Looking out from his office at Emory, Hagan could see the sleek steamboats of the rival Irving and Moore lines unloading thousands of tons of steel rails and other railway materials. The rivalry did not last long. Following a memorable race with Captain Billy Moore in the summer of 1880, John Irving had the river to himself. The most colourful steamboater in British Columbia, Irving wagered that his new sternwheeler, the *William Irving*, could outpace Moore's powerful *Western Slope* on the upriver run from New Westminster. Irving, who had a habit of hiring bands to play on the upper deck and dispensing free beer and whiskey on inaugural trips, won easily, setting a new record and creating a legend. Moore cut rates recklessly in order to beat his rival but succeeded only in bankrupting himself. Irving bought his boat for a song and built another one, the *Rithet*, the queen of the river, complete with electric lights, gilt and plush public rooms, and bunks that were advertised as having real bed springs.

This floating splendour was a symbol of the general ebullience felt by those who flocked to Emory and Yale in the early months of the Onderdonk operation. Yale, in Henry Cambie's description, became "a curiosity in the matter of vice flaunting itself before the public along the main

210

streets." The *Sentinel* proudly boasted that it had "more saloons to the acre than any place in the world," a fact not to be wondered at, since there were three thousand railroad workers in the vicinity – Swedes, Hindus, Irishmen, French Canadians, and Chinese – "and it requires considerable lubrication to keep them in trim." A timekeeper with the railway wrote that "everything at Yale ran wide open; the town was the scene of many a riotous night, and not a few men found death or injury as a consequence." Hagan's assistant, George Kennedy, always remembered his first sight of Yale. The paper was still being published at Emory when he and Hagan, with the latest edition strapped to their backs, poled and paddled a canoe through the ripples of the canyon the four miles to the neighbouring community.

"The town of Yale was *en fête* that day in a 'wild and woolly' sense, and the one long main 'business' street fronting the river, presented a scene and sounds, at once animated and grotesque – bizarre and risque. The shell like shacks of saloons, whereof every third building, nearly, was one, fairly buzzed and bulged like Brobdignagian [*sic*] wasps' nests, whose inmates, in a continual state of flux, ever and anon hurled in and out, in two's and three's or tangled wrangling masses. Painted and bedizened women lent a garish color to the scene. On the hot and dusty road-side, or around timbers, rails, and other construction debris, men in advanced stages of intoxication rolled and fought or snored in bestial oblivion. One drunken duel assumed a gory and tragic guise, when one of the sweating, swearing gladiators started sawing at his antagonist's neck with a jack knife. A tardy conservor of the peace, at this stage, separated the bloody belligerents, while a handy medicine man did a timely mending job on the lacerated connecting-piece of the chief victim."

It was a brilliant scene that greeted the newcomers who poured into Yale on John Irving's steamboats. Every shape of face and every kind of costume was observable along the main street. Long-haired Indians shuffled by carrying freshly speared salmon over their shoulders. Englishmen in bowlers and leather leggings rubbed shoulders with teamsters in broad hats; drillers, known as "cousin Joes," axemen, tall Swedes, wiry Italians, turbaned Hindus, chattering coolies, and painted women in Paris fashions picked their way between bucking cayuses, mule teams, and yokes of oxen. The saloons, with names like the Rat Trap, Stiff's Rest, and the Railroader's Retreat, were packed with gamblers playing faro, poker, chuck-a-luck, and dice. Three-card monte, the confidence man's game, was to be found everywhere. Against the incessant hammering of drills and the periodic crump of blasting powder, there was a cacophony of

211

foreground noises – saw, mallet, and hammer, mouthorgan, fiddle, and concertina, blending with the harsher music of rattling wheels. The air reeked with the mingled pungencies of fresh salmon, sawdust, black powder, and tobacco smoke. Yale, in short, was very like any raw frontier town in Wyoming, Montana, or Arizona save for one thing: all the saloons were shut tight on Sunday.

The Irish were everywhere. There were five local characters named Kelly, all unrelated. Big Mouth Kelly had the contract for burying dead Chinese. Kelly the Rake was a professional gambler who seemed to have been sent out by a casting office: he dressed totally in black from his wide sombrero and knotted silk tie to his leather leggings and narrow boots. Silent Kelly was so called because he played solitaire day after day. Molly Kelly ran a bawdy house. Long Kelly worked for her.

The Toronto *Mail* dispatched a man to examine the phenomenal community. He observed that "people don't walk in Yale, they rush. Yale is no place for a gentleman of leisure. From 'peep o' day' til long into the night the movement of men, horses and wagons along the one business street goes on scarcely with intermission. As we gaze at the hurrying throngs we wonder how on earth they all find beds or even space in which to lie down when they at last seek repose. It seems that the sides of the buildings might burst from a plethora of inmates."

The *Mail*'s reporter had arrived on a payday and was able to report that "the 'boys' with the month's wages burning holes in their pockets are making matters lively, keeping the constable's hands full of business and giving the honorary J.P. (Mr. Deighton) no opportunity to attend to his legitimate calling." Although prices were double and triple those in San Francisco, nobody seemed to grudge spending a dollar. Hagan continually warned his readers – one suspects in vain – of the dire consequences of spending all their wages the day they received them: "Those with robust constitutions may stand it for a time, but such abuse will undermine health and leave disease and want in train. Once the money is squandered very little care need be expected and . . . a premature death is the result. . . . Let those unfortunately addicted to strong drink take heed. . . ."

In spite of his pride in the quantity of Yale saloons, Hagan was enough of a newspaperman to understand the value of a crusade for prudence and morality. He called, equally vainly, for stricter liquor laws: "Public houses will, in the end, suffer by administering to depraved appetites. The law of the land should be upheld and common decency respected. Unless this is done the strong hand of authority must step forward and check natural depravity."

212

A Mr. N. Shakespeare of the Independent Order of Templars came to town and delivered "a very interesting and instructive lecture on the question of total abstinence," but since he was speaking to the converted in the Methodist Church this had little effect on the sporting fraternity. Liquor convictions were rare and explanations ingenious. A Mrs. Conklin, one of the busiest bootleggers in town, argued that she did not know she was breaking the law by serving liquor without a licence – she had been told, she said, that she could charge twenty-five cents for a cigar and throw in a free drink. Out along the line, the coolies were busily making and selling a concoction known as "Chinese gin," while white vendors were peddling more familiar brands with little fear of apprehension.

"It is thought that far too many of those who should be zealous to keep order along the line have 'a weakness for the cup' and wink at selling to others while they themselves receive free drinks," Hagan wrote. Later, the paper revealed that a series of camps along the line between fourteen and eighteen miles from Yale "had continuous scenes of drunkenness and riots." At one camp, a bootlegger was able to operate within a hundred yards of the company boarding house, "where the men spent the last cent of their money for liquor, which was often carried in bottles into the . . . tents." At Tunnel City, an enterprising Chinese operated a bootlegging establishment *inside* the company boarding house; he had rented a room next to the dining room and was dispensing liquor during mealtimes from a secret supply.

Hagan took an equally high moral attitude to the practice of working on the Lord's Day. When the railway officials announced that there were "no Sundays in railway building times," Hagan declared that nine-tenths of the railway work was unnecessary. The "violation of the laws of God and man" had wrecked the good name of the community, he insisted; travellers had formed "a low estimate of our people"; the practice of Sabbath desecration was having "a very demoralizing effect upon the Indian population," not to mention the heathen Chinese. The editorial aroused the church-going members of the community to action: they mounted a public meeting demanding that all work cease on Sundays. To their protestations Onderdonk made one of his oblique replies: he would, he said, be very glad to co-operate in reducing work on the Lord's Day, but unfortunately the steamboat schedule on the river made that impossible. Hagan, who knew a good campaign when he saw one, did not give up. In the summer of 1883 he was still hammering away: ". . . the Sunday work system places an effectual bar to all religious influences. It debars every class from the worship of God, it starves the soul, hardens

213

the heart and destroys every germ of life in the whole being."

It was a strange and rather artificial world the people of Yale inhabited. Almost all of them must have known in their hearts that it was a temporary existence, but no one voiced that feeling. Hagan wrote optimistically about the town's great future from vague mining properties once the railroad had passed by; perhaps he actually believed it, for he was an enthusiastic amateur mineralogist who had amassed, from all over Canada, an impressive collection of specimens of which he was very proud. In his editorial columns there was a growing peevishness towards the Onderdonk company as the railway out of Yale neared completion. The feeling of optimism gave way to a kind of carping against established forces. On May 3, 1883, following a rumour that the roundhouse and machine shops were to be moved, Hagan called a meeting to discuss "this desertion of the town." But a year later, he too was forced to desert.

The impermanence of the community was underlined by the shifting population and by the terrible fires that ravaged the business section, so that Yale in 1881 presented an entirely different appearance from the Yale of 1880, while the Yale of 1882 bore no physical resemblance to the Yale of 1881. Seen from the steamer, the chief characteristic of the community was its newness. The buildings were always new; so were the fences, the sidewalks, and the people. Yale had no opportunity to grow old.

In its brief, three-year joy-ride, Yale suffered two disastrous fires, both started by drunks. On July 27, 1880, a third of the town was burned to the ground, only a month after Hagan had warned the townspeople of the dangers of just such a conflagration: "Frame buildings . . . burn rapidly when fairly started. Yale is at present very much exposed; a spark has laid the principal parts of larger towns in ashes. Why not meet at once and organize, at least, a hose and bucket company . . . ?"

Yale was no different from scores of similar frame settlements on the edges of civilization, from Fernie to Dawson; but ebullient communities rarely look to the future, being concerned with the pleasures and profits of the moment. Hagan was a Cassandra whom everyone ignored. It took a second fire in August of 1881, which reduced half the town to ashes in three hours, before there was any serious talk about gathering funds to buy a steam pumper. A grand ball was held, supposedly to symbolize the phoenix-like spirit of the community; unfortunately the weather turned cold and wet and only a handful of merrymakers turned up.

The newly acquired fire engine was of little use in the summer of 1883 in keeping a bush fire away from Michael Haney's powder works, a mile and a half from town. The entire building blew up in a series of explosions so powerful that nearby houses were flattened and one woman was blown right out of the window of a neighbouring shack.

The news of such disasters took some time to leak to the outside world for, in spite of the human traffic, Yale existed in a kind of vacuum. There was no telegraph or telephone service; as a result, almost every item carried in the weekly *Sentinel* was a local one. Mail from the East came by way of San Francisco and took weeks to arrive. Much of the news from Europe was two months old. A simple journey from Victoria could be an exhausting undertaking, as Michael Hagan discovered in the fall of 1883.

Normally, one took a ship to New Westminster, transferred to a river boat, and transferred again to a smaller steamboat at Harrison. But when Hagan made the trip, the water in the Fraser was so low and full of ice that the passengers were forced to walk from Harrison River three miles to the head of steel at Farr's Bluff, where they boarded the train.

An engine had backed down with a tender full of wood, pulling an open flat car normally used for carrying ballast for the roadbed, with the usual iron rail down the centre to keep the gravel plough in place. It was an unprepossessing conveyance encased in a rime of dirt, snow, and ice. The passengers piled aboard by the light of the conductor's lantern. Most had fur coats, "but not so ye editor who left home in good weather and depended upon his waterproof."

The night was cold and stormy. The train, which had jumped the track four times en route, crept hesitantly east. "Passing around Seabird Bluff, where the storm had a sweep at the unfortunates, Dana's narrative of going round Cape Horn was uppermost in our minds." Finally, a snow-drift blocking the right of way brought the train to a stop.

The passengers helped to get it moving again. As they entered the first tunnel above Hope, huge icicles were sheared from the roof by the loco-motive, the glass on the cab was smashed, the fireman cut about the face and head, and one passenger injured when a jagged chunk of ice crushed his leg.

There was a second delay above Emory when the train ploughed into another snowbank, came to a halt on the very lip of the canyon, backed away, and gathered steam to make a rush at the blockade. "As one gazed to the left and beheld the steep embankment, with boulders below, and, looking up the right, hanging trees and threatening rocks were not pleasant to behold while the storm raged. But the 'sensation' was experienced when with increased speed the engineer was trying to get good headway to get through the snowdrift and a wheel got off the track and jumped and jarred over half a dozen ties before the track was again taken. In an instant the

215

conductor sprang to his feet and a few of the passengers were agitated. Not a word was uttered by any person; our stretched along position caused us to feel the shock acutely and our hand grasped as if by instinct the iron rail placed upon the centre of the car. Finally the passengers reached Yale at 1 o'clock in the morning, cold, tired, but hopeful that they will never experience another such ride."

After the town burned down for the second time, it began to take on a more sober and less flamboyant appearance. Concerts, recitals, lectures, and minstrel shows (with "comic Chinese skits" as well as the mandatory "comic Negro skits") began to vie with the saloons for patronage. An entertainment institute was formed, for whose first recital Mrs. Onderdonk kindly lent her piano. "Applause was liberally indulged in and enthusiastic encores followed some of the pieces. . . . Prof. Pichelo, the violinist, especially, met with marked approval." The Chinese opened their own Freemason's Lodge with an ornamental flagstaff, as well as a joss-house – institutions which, in the *Sentinel*'s rosy phraseology, demonstrated "that our Chinese population have faith in the future of Yale." Grand balls were held, in which people danced all night – and even longer – to the music of scraping violins. "A ball out here means business," wrote Dr. Daniel Parker, Charles Tupper's travelling companion. "The last one . . . commenced at 12 o'clock on Monday morning and lasted continuously day and night until 12 o'clock the next Saturday."

On the great fête-days the community, bound by a growing feeling of cohesion, turned out en masse. The Queen's Birthday on May 24 was an occasion for a half-holiday for whites and Indians. Chinese New Year, celebrated by the coolies early in February, ran for an entire week and "favourably impressed the white people of Yale." The biggest event of all was the Fourth of July, since Yale was very much an American town; indeed, Hagan declared in his newspaper that the large number of Americans working on the railway "have caused the B. Columbians to worry about the possibility of the Americans forcing the province into American hands."

Nonetheless, everyone turned out to honour the day that, again in Hagan's words, "gave birth to free America – the home of the oppressed of all nations." Half the population of New Westminster chugged up the river for the occasion on the *William Irving*, decked with greenery and flying pennants, a band playing on her upper deck. Cannons roared. Locomotives pulled flat cars crammed with excursionists from neighbouring Emory. Indians climbed greased poles. "The Star-Spangled Banner" was enthusiastically rendered outside of the Onderdonk home. Couples tripped

216

"the light fantastic toe," in the phrase of the day, on a special platform erected on the main street. There were horse races, canoe races, caber-tossing, and hurdles. "It was conceded on all hands that the day was a gala one. . . ." By comparison, July 1, celebrating a Confederation that was less than a generation old, passed almost unnoticed. British Columbia was part British and part American; it would require the completion of the railway to make her part of the new dominion.

Far off beyond the mountains – beyond the rounded bulks of the Gold Range, beyond the pointed peaks of the mysterious Selkirks – the rails were inching west; but as far as Onderdonk's navvies were concerned, that land was almost as distant as China. ". . . we really knew very little about what they were doing on that side," Henry Cambie recalled. Any letters, if such had been written, would have had to travel down the muddy Fraser by boat, on to Victoria and thence to San Francisco, across the United States to St. Paul, north into Winnipeg, and then west again until they reached End of Track. The distance involved was more than five thousand miles, and yet, in 1883, End of Track was only a few hundred miles away.

217

Chapter Six

1

By the spring of 1883, Canada was a country with half a transcontinental railroad. Between Port Moody and Ottawa, the track lay in pieces like a child's train set – long stretches of finished road separated by formidable gaps. The easiest part of the CPR was complete: a continuous line of steel ran west for 937 miles from Fort William at the head of Lake Superior to the tent community of Swift Current in the heart of Palliser's Triangle. To the west, between Swift Current and the half-completed Onderdonk section in British Columbia, was a gap of 750 miles on parts of which not even a surveyor had set foot. The section closest to civilization was graded, waiting for the rails to be laid. The remainder was a mélange of tote roads, forest slashings, skeletons of bridges, and engineers' stakes. An equally awesome gap, of more than six hundred miles, extended east from End of Track near Fort William to the terminus of the newly completed Canada Central Railway on Lake Nipissing. Again, this was little more than a network of mired roads chopped out of the stunted timber and, here and there, some partially blasted tunnels and rock cuts.

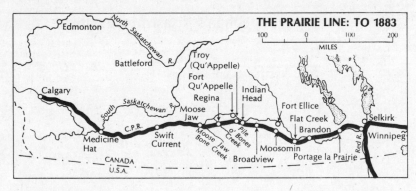

By the time the snows melted almost the entire right of way for twenty-five hundred miles, from the rim of the Shield to tidewater, was abuzz with human activity. In the East, the timber cutters and rock men who had endured the desolation of Superior's shore the previous winter were ripping a right of way out of the Precambrian wilderness. In the Far West, more thousands were invading the land of the Blackfoot tribes and clambering up the mountains. Little steel shoots were sprouting south, west, and east of the main trunk-line in Manitoba. And wherever the steel went, the settlers followed with their tents and their tools, their cattle and their kittens, their furniture and their fences.

220

From the famine-ridden bog country of Ireland, the bleak crofts of the Scottish hills, and the smoky hives of industrial England, the immigrants were pouring in. They clogged the docks at Liverpool – three thousand in a single record day, half of them bound for Manitoba – kerchiefed women with squalling infants, nervous young husbands, chalky with the pallor of the cities, and the occasional grandmother, all clutching in a last embrace those friends and relatives whom they never expected to see again. They endured the nausea of the long sea journey, emerged from the dank holds of Sir Hugh Allan's steamships at Halifax and Montreal, and swarmed aboard the flimsy immigrant cars that chugged off to the North West – the "land of milk and honey," as the posters proclaimed it. Occasionally some sardonic newcomer would scribble the qualification, "if you keep cows and bees," beneath that confident slogan; but most of the arrivals cheerfully believed it, enduring the kennels of the colonist cars in the sure knowledge that a mecca of sorts awaited them.

The land moved past them like a series of painted scenes on flashcards – a confused impression of station platforms and very little more, because the windows in the wooden cars were too high and too small to afford much of a view of the new world. They sat crowded together on hard seats that ran lengthwise and they cooked their own food on a wood stove placed in the centre of the car. They were patient people, full of hope, blessed by good cheer. In the spring and summer of 1883, some 133,000 of them arrived in Canada. Of that number, two-thirds sped directly to the North West.

No one, apparently, had expected such an onslaught. The demand for Atlantic passage was unprecedented. The CPR found it had insufficient rolling stock to handle the invading army and was obliged to use its dwindling reserves of cash to buy additional colonist cars second-hand. In Toronto, the immigrant sheds were overflowing; in May alone ten thousand meals were served there – as many as had been prepared in the entire season of 1882. The young Canadian postal service was overtaxed with twelve thousand letters destined for the North West. The number had quadrupled in just two years.

In Winnipeg, the *Globe* reported, the scene at the station was "as good as a show . . . it reminds one of exhibition times in Toronto." The settlers from the Old World – some had come from places as remote as Iceland – had been joined by farmers from the back concessions of Ontario. Hundreds of Winnipeggers poured down to meet friends from the East or to see them off for the new land; "the amount of indiscriminate kissing done in a day would have shocked the Ettrick shepherd." Already the rough democracy of the frontier was making itself felt. It was "noth-

221

ing unusual to see a man who would scorn to carry a small parcel on the street in the east rushing for the train with a tent rolled over his shoulder and a camp stove under his arm. Pioneer life plays havoc with false pride and northwest mud is no respecter of persons."

Off to the west the trains puffed, every car crammed – some people, indeed, clinging to the steps and all singing the song that became the theme of the pioneers: "One More River to Cross." The CPR by April was able to take them as far as the tent community of Moose Jaw, four hundred miles to the west, and, on occasion, a hundred and fifty miles farther to Swift Current. As many as twenty-five hundred settlers left Winnipeg every week, "not to wander over the prairie as was the case last spring, but to locate on land already picked out for and entered for by themselves or their friends." Under such conditions it was not always easy to tell blue blood from peasant. The man on the next homestead or the waiter serving in a tent restaurant might be of noble birth; the son of Alfred, Lord Tennyson, the poet laureate, was breaking sod on a homestead that spring. Nicholas Flood Davin, the journalist, on his first day in Regina was struck by the gentlemanly bearing of the waiter in the tent where he breakfasted. He turned out to be a nephew of the Duke of Rutland, engaged in managing a hastily erected hotel for the nephew of Earl Granville, who had opened a similar establishment in Brandon.

The most singular settlement of all was Cannington Manor, founded forty miles south of Moosomin and named for a village in Somerset. Here a group of former English public school boys, led by a British officer, Captain E. M. Pierce, attempted to re-create the folkways of the aristocracy on the bald prairie. In its hey-day Cannington Manor boasted a twenty-two-room mansion, a private race track (complete with imported steeplechase jockeys), and a hunt club replete with authentic foxhounds and thoroughbred horses. The residents played cricket, rugger, and tennis, engaged in amateur theatricals, raised game chickens, and established a stock farm, a pork packing plant, two cheese factories, and a variety of village trades. But when the CPR branch line, which all had hoped for, was built ten miles to the south, Cannington Manor became a ghost town.

Few settlers arrived in the North West with the advantages of the residents of the Manor. Many were almost destitute. There exists a touching description of a scene at a wayside "refreshment station" where a man was seen to order lunch for himself and his small boy. He was given a chicken leg, three cakes, and a cup of weak tea, most of which he gave to his son. A three-course roast beef dinner could be had that year for a quarter at McConkey's, Toronto's finest restaurant, but the price of that

222

prairie snack came to fifty cents. It was all the immigrant had left and he was still two hundred miles from his destination.

The immigrants brought everything to the prairies from pet kittens to canaries. One enterprising arrival from Ontario, sensing the loneliness of the settler's life, brought in a crate full of cats. They were snapped up at three dollars apiece. An early pioneer, Esther Goldsmith, always remembered the wild scene at the Brandon station when a birdcage was sucked from a woman's hand in the scramble for the train. Another recalled her first real view of the prairie driving eighty-five miles north from Broadview with a canary in a cage on her lap. A typical menagerie was that brought to Moosomin in April 1883 by the Hislop family. It included two horses, four cows, three sheep, a little white sow, a dog, a cat, eleven hens, and a rooster.

"Freedom?" wrote William Oliver sardonically. "There never was such a thing; every acre was won by hard toil and the sweat of man." The breaking up of the prairie sod was gruelling work. Oliver noted that the land was dotted with small rosebushes, whose interwoven roots added to the toughness of the turf. A man with a good team of oxen was lucky if he could till three-quarters of an acre in a day. It was a harsher life than many would-be pioneers had bargained for. Oliver, who was a carpenter, was asked by one well-to-do young Englishman to build him a home not far from Regina on two sections of land. It was a substantial house for those parts, complete with carpeting, window drapery, and furniture imported from England. When the job was finished, the settler's wife arrived with two maids and a manservant and stared at the results with something approaching horror. "I cannot describe her arrival," Oliver wrote. "It was pathetic in the extreme." She lasted exactly six months and then left her husband who, having wasted a fortune, could not face returning to England and instead took a job with the Indian Department.

Few homes were as palatial as his. Most settlers counted themselves fortunate that first year if they could construct a hovel out of the hard-packed sod of the plains. A typical one, built near Regina in 1884, consisted of a big cellar dug out of the side of a hill over which were laid poles in the shape of a gable roof, the ends resting on the ground. On top of these was placed hay to the depth of a foot, and over the hay, huge squares of sod chinked with dried earth. At the ends of the gables were small poles, plastered together with a mortar of yellow clay and straw. A tiny window was cut in one end, a door in the other. The floor was a mixture of clay and straw and water, about six inches thick, tamped tightly to the ground. The inside walls and ceiling were plastered with

223

mud and then whitewashed. In such cave-like dwellings entire families existed winter after winter.

The central piece of furniture and the sole source of heat in all pioneer homes was the cookstove. Few settlers saw the inside of a general store more than once or twice a year. For most, a shopping trip meant an exhausting journey, fifty or a hundred miles by ox cart. Pork was the staple meat, when meat was available at all. Molasses did duty for sugar. Coffee was often synthetic, made from roasted barley, rye, or wheat – or even toast crumbs. Many a settler lived almost entirely on potatoes, bread, treacle, porridge, and rabbit stew. Under blizzard conditions more than one family went hungry. John Wilson of Saltcoats always remembered the winter of 1883 when, as a boy of seven, he and the other members of his family were reduced to a single slice of bread each three times a day. The snow was so deep they could not reach their nearest neighbour, six miles distant.

One of those who set down her memories of those times was Mrs. Hartford Davis, born May Clark, who at the age of nine arrived in Regina from England with her family on a soaking wet day in May, 1883. The Clarks had expected to find a "town" in the old country sense; they discovered, instead, a ragged cluster of tents rising from the muddy prairie, and when they were sent to a hotel, they found it was a tent too, with nothing between their bedroom and the next but a partition of stretched blankets.

Regina that spring was largely a city of women and children; most of the men were off on the prairie prospecting for homestead land. After several days, Septimus Clark located a suitable quarter section some thirteen miles to the northeast. The family – there were six of them at the time – packed all its belongings, including pigs and chickens and a bowie knife to ward off wild Indians, into a prairie schooner and set off across the hummocky plain behind two oxen, with a milk cow bringing up the rear.

They seemed totally unfitted for pioneer life. Mrs. Clark was sickly and frail; her husband, thin-faced and pale, had never driven a team before. The family, used to the gentle beauty of the English midlands, was appalled by the sweeping loneliness of the prairie. The homestead, when they finally located it (they camped at first, in ignorance, on the wrong piece of property), seemed as remote as a desert island. The far horizons enveloped them and in all that immense circle there was no sign of human kind. Off to the north was a vague smudge, which the children were told was a copse of trees. In three other directions the prairie rolled off to its

224

distant rendezvous with the sky, a green and tenantless carpet glistening with small ponds and sloughs.

The Clarks spent most of their first summer tilling a few acres of soil and trying to build a log house. It was a time of troubles. Septimus Clark overstrained himself putting up the log walls and was confined to his bed. When he recovered he found he did not know how to build the roof, doors, or windows. There was never quite enough to eat. The children were sometimes so hungry they tried to fill their stomachs with wild leaves and berries. Polly, the cow, refused to give milk. On one memorable night, both parents became lost on the open prairie and the children spent a terrifying twelve hours alone in the tent wondering if they would ever see them again.

Yet, in spite of it all, the family survived and thrived, improving in both health and spirits, the hard work, fresh air, and open life acting as a tonic on parents and children alike. They were driven back to the city that winter, but they returned again to prosper. Mrs. Davis's memoirs are remarkably sunny, illuminated by sensuous little scenes that stayed with her for more than seventy years – the flash of sunlight on prairie ponds, for instance, and the sensation of awakening in the bright mornings and feeling "the delightful newness and strangeness of everything" – the spectacle of acres of tiger flowers spangling the plains in midsummer, the taste of wild strawberries and prairie plums and, perhaps above all, the feeling of being present at the beginning of a new life. That life may have been harsh but it was clearly invigorating: when Mrs. Davis published her memoirs at the age of eighty-one, four of the five Clark children were still alive to share them.

Government land, such as the Clarks', was free up to a limit of a quarter section; the homesteader who worked it for three years was given title to it and could, in addition, pre-empt an adjoining quarter section; that is, he could take an option to purchase it in the future and thus prevent himself from being hemmed in. Those immigrants who bought CPR land in the forty-eight-mile belt along the railway paid five dollars an acre but were rebated all but $1.25 if they cropped three-quarters of it within four years; if they put up buildings as well, they did not need to crop more than a half.

"I do not expect each immigrant to cultivate at first anything like the whole of his allotment," George Stephen wrote the editor of the London *Spectator* in the spring of 1883. "But it is easy for any man to till enough land of his own to supply his family with food, and then in the great amount of spare time he will have on his hands, to earn handsome wages, either as a railway labourer, or by hiring himself out to work on some of the large wheat farms which are springing up with incredible rapidity throughout the Northwest Territory."

Stephen was far more interested in filling up the land and providing future traffic for the railway than he was in making money from land sales outside the townsites. In London, his general emigration agent, Alexander Begg, had launched an advertising campaign worthy of a Barnum to boom the Canadian North West. He had folders advertising "free homes for all," together with maps and pamphlets, translated into German, French, Dutch, Finnish, Danish, Swedish, Norwegian, Welsh, and Gaelic, which he distributed through thousands of agencies in Great Britain and more than two hundred centres in northern Europe. In six months he managed to circulate one million pieces of literature. The CPR, in addition, took extensive advertising in 167 British journals and 147 continental papers. In London, would-be emigrants were treated to ambitious displays of prairie products and soil samples in the company's offices. Begg's men moved about the British Isles, especially Scotland, nailing posters to the walls of railroad stations, hotels, and other public places and giving lectures illustrated by that new-fangled toy, the magic lantern.

By the autumn of 1883, Begg, surely one of the earliest public relations men in Canada, had worked out a way of distributing carefully selected news items to the British and Irish press; he compiled them himself from clippings sent over from the Montreal office. Five hundred journals received free service, all of it designed to paint the North West in the most glowing colours. In addition Begg's staff kept a complete record of all publications in England, checking every item detrimental to Canada and counteracting it immediately. Begg published a small newsletter entitled *Along the Line*, dealing with news from western Canada; this he sent to all leading hotels and reading rooms. And he never failed to enter a stand of Canadian produce in the major exhibitions and agricultural fairs – thirty in all. He even gave away samples of Canadian grain.

In the North West, as the rails pushed steadily towards the mountains, new communities began to take shape. "These towns along the line west of Brandon are all the same," the Fort Macleod *Gazette* reported. "See one, see all. There are some board houses, but most of them are board frames (rough) with a canvas roof." Both Moose Jaw, with its "bare, freckled and sunburnt buildings" and Medicine Hat, another canvas town in a coulee of that name, were in this category. The former, in spite of its youth, already had three newspapers by 1883. The latter, by July,

226

boasted six hotels, though most of them were mere tents sheltering half a dozen bunks.

This was Sam Steele's territory. The remarkable Mounted Policeman had been named acting adjutant of the Fort Qu'Appelle district the previous year and placed in command of detachments along the line of CPR construction. As the rails made their way from the coulees of Saskatchewan to the final spike at Craigellachie, Steele would always be on hand to keep the peace. A huge man with a deep chest and a bristling moustache, Steele's background was solidly military: one ancestor had fought with Wolfe at Quebec, another with Nelson at Trafalgar, a third with Wellington at Waterloo. At seventeen, Steele had joined the militia, serving against the Fenians in 1866 and taking part in General Garnet Wolseley's Red River Expedition against Riel in 1870 (when he managed to hoist three-hundred-pound barrels of flour onto his massive shoulders to negotiate the portages of the Precambrian Shield). Steele was a perennial volunteer. When the first permanent force unit was formed in 1871, he rushed to the colours. When the North West Mounted Police were organized in 1873, he joined them immediately, becoming the force's first sergeant-major. He had a habit of being present when history was being made: he took part in the thousand-mile march to the Rockies in 1874; he bargained with Sitting Bull after the Custer affair; now he was presiding at the building of the first transcontinental railway; he would go on to become "the Lion of the Yukon" during the Klondike gold-rush. Steele was the prototype Mountie, one of several who gave the force its traditions and turned it into an international symbol of the Canadian frontier. Even his name had a ring of romance to it: "Steele of the Mounted." James Oliver Curwood, the American novelist, borrowed the phrase for one of his books about the North.

Steele, in his capacity as police magistrate, worked without rest under primitive conditions. In Regina his courtroom had been a marquee, sixteen by fourteen feet. It was so cold that winter that the water froze in the bathtubs and the clerks had to keep their ink-bottles on the tops of stoves. Between Moose Jaw and Medicine Hat Steele had no courtroom at all. At Swift Current he tried cases while seated on a Red River cart, with planks stretched across it for a bench and the evidence taken down on the flap of his dispatch bag. As he worked he counted the trains roaring by to End of Track, loaded with ties, rails, and spikes. He could tell by the number how many miles were being laid that day.

By July, the organization had been perfected to the point where ninety-seven miles of track were laid instead of the monthly average of fifty-eight.

227

As Langdon and Shepard approached the end of their contract, the track-laying guides were seized by a kind of frenzy; on July 28, about two weeks out of Calgary, they set a record that has never been surpassed for manual labour on a railroad: 6.38 miles of finished railway – earthworks, grading, track-laying and ballasting – were completed in a single day.

It was, of course, a stunt, theatrically produced by an organization that had reason to feel cocky. Special men were brought in for the job: the tireless Ryan brothers, world champion spikers, who could drive a spike home with two blows, and Big Jack, a Herculean Swede who was said to be able to hoist a thirty-foot rail weighing 560 pounds and heave it onto a flat car without assistance.

The statistics of that day have been preserved. Sixteen thousand ties and more than two thousand rails (totalling 604 tons) were used. The ties were unloaded by a precision team of thirty-two men and hauled forward by thirty-three teams of horses. On the track a team of eight men unloaded and distributed the ties and a second team of four men spaced them out. Two men following behind spaced and distanced the joint ties while two more were detailed to arrange and adjust the misplaced ties in front of the leading spikers. Twelve men unloaded the rails, twelve more loaded them onto the four iron trolleys which hauled them to the front. Here a team of ten men, five on each side of the track, swung the rails onto the ties. Behind these came a platoon of bolters, fifteen in all, each putting in an average of 565 bolts, followed by thirty-two spikers, who drove a total of sixty-three thousand spikes handed to them by four peddlers. The lead and gauge spikers each drove 2,120 spikes, averaging four blows to a spike, which meant that in fourteen hours they each delivered an average of eighty-four hundred blows with a sledge hammer. The first two miles of material were hauled ten miles across the prairies and the remainder came up from a two-thousand-foot siding three miles away, which was itself installed that same day by the regular side-track gang. Such was the organization that the contractors had perfected in fewer than eighteen months.

The city of Calgary was not yet born but some of its future citizens were at work along the line of track, oblivious of the fact that they would help to build the foothills community. Turner Bone, the engineer, recalled in his memoirs how many men he bumped into who later became prominent Calgarians. When he arrived in Moose Jaw late one night, the CPR's watchman guided him, with the aid of a sputtering lantern, to a large marquee, pretentiously named Royal Hotel. The man's name was

Thomas Burns; he later became assessor and city treasurer of Calgary. In a Medicine Hat office there was a small messenger and chore boy, about twelve years old, who answered to the name of George. Years later in Calgary, Bone met him again, when George Webster was mayor. In the company boarding house, Bone encountered a former supply officer who had opened a law office in Medicine Hat but continued to eat with the engineers from force of habit. This was James Lougheed, soon to become the most noted lawyer in the West, Conservative leader in the Senate, cabinet minister in the Borden government, and a Knight Commander of St. Michael and St. George.

As the railway towns began to prosper, the parochial jealousies that were a feature of Canadian life from Vancouver Island to the Maritimes blossomed out on the prairies. A bitter three-cornered battle, fought largely in the newspapers, took place all that year and the next between Winnipeg, Moose Jaw, and Regina. The argument, ostensibly, was over the choice of Regina as capital, but it was really over real estate. The Winnipeg *Times* charged that the new capital was nothing but a few tents and shacks, that the water was anything but pure and wholesome, and that the accommodations were terrible. The *Sun* said the capital should be moved – why, the CPR was so ashamed of it, the trains went through only in the dark of night! The Moose Jaw *News* declared that Regina was "dead beyond the hope of resurrection."

Fortunately Regina had acquired a champion in the person of Nicholas Flood Davin, one of the most distinguished journalists in Canada. Davin had come to Regina the previous fall for a visit at the invitation of W. B. Scarth of the North-West Land Company, who had brought a private carload of prominent Canadians to look over the new city, no doubt in an attempt to nullify the bad press publicity. (Dr. John Rae, the famous Arctic explorer who had discovered the first clues to the fate of the lost Franklin expedition, was one of the guests.) In Regina, Davin met a delegation of leading citizens who pleaded with him to start a newspaper in their city. He told them that he could not afford to start "a paltry concern." It might be a small paper, but it would have to contain the latest news "and would I hoped be something of a power." To launch such a journal, Davin said, would certainly entail an initial loss of five thousand dollars.

"We'll give you a bonus of $5,000," somebody exclaimed.

Davin, looking about him at the huddle of tents and timber houses, only laughed. Nonetheless, he agreed to meet them that evening at a dinner in the Royal Hotel. There, to his astonishment, they voted him the

229

five thousand he asked for, subscribing $2,700 in cash on the spot and promising the remainder within a few days. Davin, cane in hand, took a long walk out onto the prairie to think about it. He was a creature of impulse, a romantic who lived for the day; his contempt for money – he spent it as swiftly as he made it and existed for most of his life on the cliff-edge of penury – was equalled by his love of good food, fine wine, comely women, and high adventure. He had been wounded at the siege of Montmorency while covering the Franco-Prussian war and injured so badly while riding to hounds in England that he had come to Canada in 1872 on sick leave, never to return home. His life appeared to be a series of accidental encounters. Here he was, a barrister, politician, and international journalist used to the sophistication of London and Paris, suddenly transported to the rawest of frontiers, trudging about on the open plains on a chill November night, pondering a journalistic future in a one-horse prairie town. He could not resist it; he succumbed. Regina had its champion.

A Limerick Irishman, Davin was a commanding presence, almost six feet tall with a massive head, entirely bald save for a sandy fringe about the ears. At forty, he was a bachelor with a long record of romances and flirtations. His dress, like his personal life, was unconventional, but his professional reputation in a variety of fields was enviable. As a journalist he had worked for the London *Standard*, the Irish *Times*, and the *Pall Mall Gazette*; he had been literary critic for the *Globe* of Toronto and editorial writer for the *Mail*. He had read law at the Middle Temple and had been called to the bar in both London and Ontario. His defence of the murderer of George Brown, the *Globe*'s publisher, had increased his reputation ("one of the most masterly appeals for human life that has ever been heard in a Toronto courtroom"), even though his client was later hanged. He was an author of note (*The Irishman in Canada*), a poet of distinction, an unsuccessful candidate for office, a friend of Sir John A. Macdonald, a master of six languages, and one of the best impromptu orators in the country. Regina had got him cheap. So great was the enthusiasm over the catch that, as a sweetener, Scarth and some others threw in an additional five thousand dollars worth of choice lots.*

Several names were suggested for Davin's newspaper – the *Shaganappi*, the *Blizzard*, the *Scalper*, the *Buffalo*. He chose to call it the *Leader*, for he intended to make it the leading publication in the North West and in

---

*Davin did not realize much from this gift; shortly after he received the lots the real estate bubble broke and he could not sell them. As a result he was forced to mortgage his newspaper.

this ambition he was eminently successful. With his bonus money he set out to purchase the best possible equipment and was able to boast in the first issue that "in truth, so much money was never before sunk in a newspaper enterprise in a place the size of Regina. Nor ever before were such complete fonts of type and so able a staff combined to furnish a paper for a town six months old."

Once established in the editor's chair, Davin struck back at Regina's critics. He charged the CPR with intentionally trying to boom Moose Jaw ("Loose Jaw," he called it), and he engaged in a running statistical battle with that city's press over their respective populations. "To give Moose Jaw a lift at the expense of Regina, has been the fondest hope of poor God-forsaken, bankrupt Winnipeg," he wrote; and he put the blame where it properly belonged, on the shoulders of Arthur Wellington Ross, the real estate "shark" who had been behind the abortive sales of the Dewdney syndicate's land. "The commercial interests of Winnipeg and this gentleman were in one tangle," Davin wrote, "and Mr. Ross got left in his speculations regarding his surveyed sections near Regina. Nobody bought them. Ross was badly bitten and he howled. His howls found echo in the throats of his worthy 'hangers-on.' "

When he ran out of prose, Davin turned to poetry to hit at Regina's detractors. Then, in the fall of 1883, he invaded Winnipeg itself and sent back sarcastic reports of the post-boom atmosphere:

"Things are in such a condition here now that millionaires have had to leave their stately dwellings and go into lodgings . . . the owners of splendid mansions – the drivers of fast horses and swell rigs with footmen having rosettes in their hats . . . have shrunk to three rooms in the Cauchon Block. . . . What a revolution in one brief twelve months! Mr. A. W. Ross, M.P., has got into his house. But he is paying $60,000 interest. A few days ago one of the papers published a list of Winnipeg's wealthy citizens. Many of those published there as worth a half a million could not get a $500 note discounted. . . . Could you know the anxiety, the calculations, the sleepless nights spent by some of Winnipeg's reputed millionaires, you would bid your fellow-citizens of the Pile of Bones to congratulate themselves that Regina has not boomed, but is a subject of steady, quiet progress."

Five thousand dollars was a handsome sum in the 1880's; it was enough to keep a man and his family in luxury for four years. But, reading that sweet invective, the embattled Regina citizens who had subscribed to Davin's bonus must have reckoned that they had already been given their money's worth.

2

The whole country marvelled, that spring and summer of 1883, over
the feat of building the railway across the prairies in just fifteen months
– everybody, that is, except the people it was displacing. To the Indians,
the railway symbolized the end of a golden age – an age in which the
native peoples, liberated by the white man's horses and the white man's
weapons, had galloped at will across their untrammelled domain, where
the game seemed unlimited and the zest of the hunt gave life a tang and
a purpose. This truly idyllic existence came to an end with the suddenness
of a thunderclap just as the railway, like a glittering spear, was thrust
through the ancient hunting grounds of the Blackfoot and the Cree.
Within six years, the image of the Plains Indian underwent a total transformation. From a proud and fearless nomad, rich in culture and tradition,
he became a pathetic, half starved creature, confined to the semi-prisons
of the new reserves and totally dependent on government relief for his
existence.

The buffalo, on which the entire Indian economy and culture depended,
were actually gone before the coming of the railway; but the order of their
passing is immaterial. They could not have existed in a land bisected by
steel and criss-crossed by barbed wire. The passing of the great herds
was disastrous, for without the buffalo, which had supplied them with
food, shelter, clothing, tools, and ornaments, the Indians were helpless.
By 1880, after the three most terrible years they had ever known, the
emaciated natives were forced to eat their dogs and their horses, to scrabble
for gophers and mice, and even to consume the carcasses of animals found
rotting on the prairie.

On top of this the Indians were faced with the sudden onslaught of a
totally foreign agrarian culture. Because of the railway, the impact was
almost instantaneous. In eastern Canada, the influence of the white
strangers had been felt gradually over a period of generations. In the North
West it happened in the space of a few years. It did not matter that the
various treaties guaranteed that the old, free life would continue and that
the natives would not be forced to adopt white ways. With the buffalo
gone and the grasslands tilled and fenced, such promises were hollow.

The government's policy, born of expediency, was a two-stage one. The
starving Indians would be fed at public expense for a period which, it was
hoped, would be temporary. Over a longer period, the Indian Department
would attempt to bring about a sociological change that normally occupied

232

centuries. It would try to turn a race of hunters into a community of peasants. It would settle the Indians on reserves, provide them with tools and seed, and attempt to persuade them to give up the old life and become self-sufficient as farmers and husbandmen. The reserves would be situated on land considered best suited for agriculture, all of it north of the line of the railway, far from the hunting grounds. Thus the CPR became the visible symbol of the Indians' tragedy.

It was a tall order. Only the terrible privations of the late seventies and early eighties could have caused thousands of once-independent people to abandon so meekly an entire way of life. The famine of 1879–80 forced thousands of reluctant Indians onto the new reserves. Others, led by such free spirits as Big Bear and Piapot (both Cree chieftains), continued to defy the authorities and follow the will-o'-the-wisp of the buffalo through the Cypress Hills and into the United States. It was not the buffalo they were chasing but the shadows of the past; the great herds were always over the next hill. By the winter of 1882–83, five thousand disillusioned Indians were starving in the neighbourhood of Fort Walsh. In the end, all the tribes moved north to the reserves. To the south lay the line of the railway: a steel fence barring them from their past.

Some of the chiefs accepted the coming of steel with a certain amount of fatalism; Poundmaker, for one, urged his Cree followers to prepare for it. Poundmaker had negotiated a treaty with the Canadian government in 1879 and settled on a reserve on the Battle River. In the spring of 1881, after a fruitless search for game on the prairie, he realized that the buffalo were gone and the old nomadic life was ended. At the New Year he gathered his followers and told them to work hard, sow grain, and take care of their cattle: "Next summer, or at latest next fall, the railway will be close to us, the whites will fill the country, and they will dictate to us as they please. It is useless to dream that we can frighten them; that time is past; our only resource is our work, our industry, and our farms. Send your children to school . . . if you want them to prosper and be happy."

It was sensible advice, given the inevitability of settlement, but not every chieftain took it, not even Poundmaker himself. His fellow Cree leader, Piapot, ran afoul of Secretan's survey crews in 1882, pulling up forty miles of the surveyors' stakes on the line west of Moose Jaw. Secretan, who had little patience with or understanding of the Indians, threatened to shoot on sight any "wretched ill-conditioned lying sons of aborigines" if they pulled up more stakes – a statement that caused consternation in Ottawa. That year Piapot was further disillusioned by what he considered government betrayal. In May, he ordered the railway workmen to advance no farther into his hunting grounds. When they ignored him, he ordered his followers to camp directly upon the right of way. The railway, he said, was the cause of all his troubles.

There followed one of those gaudy little incidents that helped to build the growing legend of the North West Mounted Police – a scene that was to become the subject of one major painting and a good many romantic illustrations:

The two young men from the Maple Creek detachment ride up on their jet-black horses. There squats Piapot in front of his tepee, quietly smoking his pipe, directly in the line of the railroad. Around him the young braves wheel their horses, shouting war cries and firing their rifles into the air, egged on by the usual rabble of shrieking squaws. The prairie, speckled with spring wildflowers, stretches off to the low horizon. From somewhere in the distance comes the ominous sound of hammers striking on steel.

The sergeant tells the chief that he must make way for the railway. The brown old man refuses to budge. The sergeant takes out his watch. "I will give you just fifteen minutes," he says. "If by the end of that time you haven't begun to comply with the order, we shall make you."

The braves jostle the policemen, trying to provoke them into a fight. The two young men in the pillbox hats and scarlet tunics quietly sit their horses. The minutes tick by. Birds wheel in the sky. The chief remains impassive. The young Crees gallop about. Finally, the sergeant speaks again. "Time's up!" he says and, throwing his reins to the constable, he springs from his steed, strides to the tepee, and kicks down the tentpoles. The painted buffalo skin collapses. Other tepees topple under the kicks of his polished boot. "Now git!" says the sergeant and, astonishingly, the Indians obey. Piapot has been stripped of his dignity.

This incident, told and retold in most of the books about the early days of the North West Mounted, helped to bolster the tradition of the redcoats as fearless upholders of the law. Yet, in the light of the Indians' tragedy, it is inexpressibly sad; and the day was swiftly approaching when no Mounted Policeman would again dare to act in such a fashion. The Indians, already beginning to feel that they had nothing to lose, were growing bolder.

Many of the native peoples greeted the oncoming rails with scepticism and the stories of the snorting locomotives with disbelief. They watched the construction in silence. The squaws pulled their shawls over their heads in terror of the whistle and refused to cross streams on the new trestles, preferring to wade up to their armpits. Some of the younger braves, their faces painted brilliant scarlet, would try to race the train on their swift ponies. Few would actually touch the cars. Piapot believed that the smoke of the locomotive was an evil medicine that would ruin his people; again, his fears were not groundless, but his personal appeal to Dewdney, who was Indian Commissioner as well as Lieutenant-Governor, was, of course, fruitless. Secretan, as usual, was scornful of Dewdney's handling of the Indians, which he believed to be far too lenient. The Lieutenant-Governor's only experience with Indians, Secretan said, was derived from the calm contemplation of a wooden image outside of Roos's Cigar Store on Sparks Street, Ottawa. This opinion was not quite fair; Dewdney was far more aware of the Indians' plight than his political masters in the East.

Not far from Calgary, the railway builders encountered the most remarkable Indian leader of all, the sagacious Crowfoot, chief of the Blackfoot nation – a slender, intelligent man with the classic Roman nose, who carried himself with great dignity and was renowned for his many feats of bravery. He had fought in nineteen battles, had been wounded six times, and had once rescued a child from the jaws of a grizzly bear, dispatching the animal with a spear while the whole camp watched. Crowfoot had many good qualities – eloquence, political skill, charity, and, above all, foresight. Long before his fellows he saw what was coming: the end of the buffalo, the settlement of the West, the spread of the white man's style of living across the plains. Crowfoot pinned his hopes on the government and signed a treaty in 1877.

Thus, when the tents of the construction workers went up on the borders of the Blackfoot reserve, there was anger and bitterness among Crowfoot's followers. The tribe was in a ferment: the white man was invading the land of the Blackfoot. The chief sent envoys to warn the foremen that no further construction work would be permitted and that seven hundred armed braves stood ready to attack.

At this point, Albert Lacombe, the Oblate missionary to the Blackfoot bands, stepped into the picture. For some time Lacombe had been concerned about the creeping advance of civilization, which would change his own way of life as surely as that of the natives. "Now that the railway gangs are coming nearer to our poor Indians," he confided to his diary in May, 1883, "we can expect all kinds of moral disorders." When Lacombe learned of the trouble at the Blackfoot reserve, he rode immediately to the construction camp – a homely priest in a tattered cassock, bumping over the prairie, his silver curls streaming out from beneath his black hat.

235

At Cluny Station, where the steel ended, Lacombe met with a brusque rebuff when he tried to alert the foreman to the danger. The Indians, he was told, could go to the devil; the rails would continue to advance. Lacombe decided he would have to make his appeals to higher authority. He had met Van Horne during his period as chaplain to the railway workers on the Thunder Bay Branch. The general manager had been impressed.

"Near the Lake of the Woods at sunrise one morning in 1882," Van Horne wrote some years later, "I saw a priest standing on a flat rock, his crucifix in his right hand and his broad hat in the other, silhouetted against the rising sun, which made a golden halo about him, talking to a group of Indians – men, women and pappooses – who were listening with reverent attention. It was a scene never to be forgotten, and the noble and saintly countenance of the priest brought it to me that this must be Father Lacombe of whom I had heard so much. . . ."

Lacombe dispatched telegrams to Van Horne, Donald A. Smith, and Edgar Dewdney. The answers were not long in coming; nobody wanted another Custer-style massacre. The orders went straight to End of Track: cease all work until the Indians are placated. Lacombe was asked to appease them any way he could.

The priest had known Crowfoot for years. They had met first under dramatic circumstances near Rocky Mountain House on a snowy December night in 1865, after a band of Crees had attacked a Blackfoot camp where Lacombe was sleeping. After ten hours of bloody fighting, in which Lacombe himself had been temporarily felled by a spent bullet, the outnumbered Blackfoot warriors had been saved by a strong relief force under Crowfoot. The incident, besides launching a lifelong friendship between the two men, also helped foster the legend of Lacombe's invincibility – he appeared to have risen from the dead. This legend was strengthened in the years that followed. In 1867, Lacombe led a party of starving Crees for twenty-two days through a blizzard to apparently miraculous safety. On another occasion, when an entire Blackfoot camp was succumbing to scarlet fever, Lacombe worked tirelessly among the stricken for twenty days before he himself contracted the disease; he recovered. Again, in 1870, when smallpox ravaged the North West, Lacombe exhausted himself in succouring the victims, his only protection against the disease being a piece of camphor held in his mouth. Fellow priests died and so did three thousand Indians, but Lacombe kept working, scraping out mass graves with knives, axes, or his own hands, comforting the sick, solacing the dying. Hundreds of Indians were so moved that they became Christians in tribute to his selflessness.

At the CPR's behest the priest set out to placate his old friend. He arrived at Crowfoot's camp bearing gifts: two hundred pounds of sugar and a like amount of tobacco, tea, and flour. At Lacombe's suggestion, the chief called a grand council where the priest, standing before the squatting braves, spoke:

"Now my mouth is open; you people listen to my words. If one of you can say that for the fifteen years I have lived among you, I have given you bad advice, let him rise and speak. . . ."

No one budged. It was a dangerous, electric situation. Lacombe kept on:

"Well, my friends, I have some advice to give you today. Let the white people pass through your lands and let them build their roads. They are not here to rob you of your lands. These white men obey their chiefs, and it is with the chiefs that the matter must be settled. I have already told these chiefs that you were not pleased with the way in which the work is being pushed through your lands. The Governor himself will come to meet you. He will listen to your griefs; he will propose a remedy. And if the compromise does not suit you, that will be the time to order the builders out of your reserve."

Lacombe sat down and Crowfoot stood up. "The advice of the Chief of Prayer is good. We shall do what he asks." He had already consulted with Lieut.-Colonel A. G. Irvine, the Commissioner of the North West Mounted Police, and asked him if he thought he, Crowfoot, could stop the railway. Irvine replied by asking Crowfoot if all the men in the world could stop the Bow River running. The sagacious chief resigned himself to the inevitable. He did not believe in foolhardy gestures. Not long afterward, Dewdney arrived and agreed to give the Indians extra land in return for the railway's right of way.

3

In a curiously roundabout way, the presence of the Indians in the North West had aided the railway in its swift progress across the plains. Without the Indians it is doubtful whether prohibition would have existed; without prohibition it would have been impossible to drive steel so efficiently. The entire North West Territories were dry by law – a law that had its roots in the scandalous days of the whiskey forts and the trek across the Great Lone Land by Lieut. William F. Butler, who wrote in his

Prohibition

report to Ottawa that he felt "convinced that if proper means are taken the suppression of the liquor traffic of the West can be easily accomplished." Long before the railway was commenced, the liquor traffic west of Manitoba had been driven underground.

A. C. Forster Boulton, a CPR land examiner, gave in his memoirs a remarkable picture of a bone-dry Medicine Hat, as he first came upon it in 1883.

"It was a rough place then. . . . Miners, cowboys, trappers, prospectors gathered in the saloons to drink soft drinks and play cards. I remember I thought at the time what a fine thing it was that no spirits could be bought for love or money. If whisky had been allowed, then life, with the men gathered in these saloons, would have been cheap." It makes an incongruous and somehow typically Canadian spectacle – the rough frontier town full of men in outlandish dress crowding into the saloons to purchase mugs of sarsaparilla.

Lively they certainly were, and never entirely dry, but the prairie railway camps, in contrast to those south of the border, were relatively tame. The contractors, American and Canadian, were grateful. "When a man breaks the law here," one American boss told George Grant, "justice is dealt to him a heap quicker and in larger chunks than he has been accustomed to in the States. I tell you there is a way to do it, and they *are* doing it here, right from scratch." What he was praising, of course, was the Canadian passion for order imposed from above – a British colonial heritage – as against the American concept of localized grass-roots democracy. There were no gun-toting town marshals keeping the peace in the Canadian West; instead there was a federally appointed, quasi-military constabulary. The Mounties did not have to stand for election, they were relatively incorruptible, and they were fair; that was one of the reasons why the Canadian West lacked some of the so-called colour of its American counterpart. Many an American felt some of his basic freedoms curtailed when he crossed the border. He could not buy a drink in a saloon, he could not carry a gun on his hip, and he could not help select the men who enforced the law. On the other hand he was safe on the streets and in the bars from hoodlums and bandits, and on the lonely plains from painted savages. If he did overstep the mark he could be sure that no hastily organized mob of vigilantes would string him up to the nearest tree.

Though the prohibition laws had been made originally to protect the natives, they were enforced as strictly as possible for the railroad workers – sometimes too strictly to suit the local residents. There were some intriguing arrests. In Maple Creek a man was charged because a chemist

238

without his knowledge put six bottles of vanilla in a case of chemicals he was carrying. He was clapped into jail overnight and fined one hundred dollars. Another was haled before a magistrate for having a small bottle of peppermint in his possession. It may be that both were not as innocent as was supposed, since explanations tended to be ingenious. One man in Medicine Hat, arraigned as a drunk, pleaded that he had got high from drinking Worcestershire sauce.

For all of the railway construction period, the Mounted Police were locked in a battle of wits with the whiskey peddlers. Every device that human guile could invent was used to smuggle liquor into the North West and to keep it hidden from official eyes. Egg-shells were blown of their contents and alcohol substituted. Imitation Bibles, made of tin, were filled with intoxicants and peddled aboard CPR passenger cars; metal kegs of alcohol were concealed in the centre of barrels of kerosene; mincemeat soaked in brandy and peaches marinated in Scotch were also common. At Silver City, not far from Calgary, the police seized nineteen tins of corn, peas, and tomatoes which, on inspection, were revealed to contain alcohol, not vegetables – all shipped by an Ontario distiller. Eleven barrels supposedly filled with pork, imported into Calgary, were found to contain 1,584 bottles of liquor, which, at five dollars a bottle – the regulation price in those days – would have realized almost eight thousand dollars, a tidy profit at a time when whiskey sold for something like fifty cents a gallon in eastern Canada.

On the treeless prairie where concealment was difficult, the ingenuity of the bootleggers met its greatest test. One favourite hiding place was the boiler of a disabled or wrecked locomotive laid up on a siding. Another was one of the many carcasses of pack horses that lay strewn along the route of the line. It was said that hundreds of these dead animals were used to conceal bottles of liquor. The "dives," as they were called, were always close at hand – innocent-appearing log huts unmarked by any sign and totally empty of whiskey. A thirsty man knocking on the door might be met by a rough-looking proprietor, who, on being asked for a drink, would crawl out to the apparently empty prairie, poke around for a loose sod, lift it, and produce a small bottle, or – in more elaborate cases – actually pump the liquor from the bowels of the earth with a pocket instrument.

"The low cunning . . . used by these serpents . . . is marvellous," one eyewitness declared. "Nothing but the able assistance of his satanic majesty himself could enable these men to conceive of half their truly unique schemes." One good-looking man in a plug hat, white tie, and black coat shipped an organ to End of Track, ostensibly for the use of the navvies during divine service. It was actually a hollow shell lined with tin, loaded with spirits. Another walked the line carrying the familiar knapsack which apparently contained nitro-glycerine canisters; he bore a red flag in his hand, which kept the Mounties away – as well as everybody else. As the *Globe* remarked dryly, there was not much deceit in that: "The whiskey will kill almost as quick as dynamite." Known variously as Chain Lightning, Tangle Foot, Death on Wires, and Injin Killer, it was generally a fearsome concoction made by mixing a gallon of good liquor with nine gallons of water into which was sunk a quantity of blue-stone and oil of smoke and later, for colouring, a little black tea. The price, in the dives, was twenty-five cents a glass.

Perhaps the most ingenious of the whiskey peddlers on the prairies was a Mrs. Hobourg of Regina, "a woman of daring and originality" who used to arrive back in town from a trip to the wet cities of Winnipeg and Brandon looking more than pregnant from a circular rubber bag she wore around her waist. Another of her devices was to dress up a keg of liquor to resemble one of her offspring asleep on the seat beside her or to disguise it as a pillow on which she might rest her head while the police rummaged vainly through her old-fashioned bag. Mrs. Hobourg boasted that she "could down all the police in the Northwest," but she was finally caught one June day and fined two hundred dollars and costs for importing two barrels of "beef and beans."

Under the prohibition laws the Mounted Police in the North West Territories could legally enter and search any premises at any hour of the day or night. This "detestable duty," as Sam Steele called it, did not add to the popularity of the force. The constables themselves indulged, on occasion, in some private bootlegging. When John Donkin, the former British Army trooper, first went out to Regina to join the Mounties, he noticed that his escort had purchased in Winnipeg "a cargo of whiskey," which he stored in his baggage to distribute to his fellow policemen. "Each member of the force," Donkin wrote, "is expected by his comrades when entering the territory to bring a libation of 'old rye' or 'bourbon' with him, from the more favoured regions. This is a pretty commentary upon the prohibition law."

Donkin's gloomy description of Regina's sporting life explains the fervour with which the occasional furtive bottle, no matter how villainous, was welcomed:

"The solemnity which perennially reigns in a North-West hotel is beyond words. Long-faced men sit silent around the stove, only varying the grim monotony by an occasional expectoration of tobacco juice. Sometimes they may break out, and engage in the congenial pastime of 'swapping lies.' The bar dedicated to teetotalism (cider is sold and hop beer) makes a ghastly attempt at conviviality and jocoseness, by having an array of bottles of colored water and cold tea marshalled upon a series of shelves and labelled 'Old Tom,' 'Fine Old Rye,' Hennessy's 'Silver Star,' or 'Best Jamaica.' With what hideous humour do these tantalizing legends taunt the thirsty tenderfoot from 'down East.' "

In sharp contrast to this morose spectacle were the occasional orgies of drinking that broke out in the North West, especially when a party of surveyors or traders was leaving civilization for an extended period for "the purity of the uncontaminated prairie," as the *Globe* called it.

"It is generally night. As the men feel the affects [*sic*] of the treacherous mixture the noise becomes dreadful. Indians, Half-breeds, camp followers, and navvies join in the hideous orgy.

"Men have been known to be torn from their beds, dragged to the spot, and forced to drink. Yells, curses, howlings, ribald songs fill the air and if a pile of ties can be fired it adds hugely to the effect. This lasts all night but morning finds them strewn everywhere in a drunken stupor or deadly sick. Men have died after one of these terrible orgies. . . ."

Brandon, on the edge of Manitoba, was the farthest western point at which liquor could be sold. That, no doubt, explained why a visitor from Fort Macleod remarked on the number of men "staggering about the streets considerably under the influence of the juice of Bacchus." The first station west of Brandon was Moosomin, and here the train was supposed to be searched for whiskey but, according to Donkin, "a constable or corporal merely promenades with clanking spurs down the aisles of the cars."

Sometimes, however, the search was more intensive, as Nicholas Flood Davin discovered. Davin had been attacking the Mounted Police vigorously in the *Leader*, especially Superintendent W. M. Herchmer. He had the ill luck to be on the same train as Herchmer on August 4, 1884, when a constable came through on a routine liquor check at Moosomin. Davin had a small flask of whiskey lying on the seat behind him. The constable pounced. Normally, the practice was to order the offender to pour the liquor out and leave it at that, but Davin got special treatment. He was charged and haled into court in Regina, where the magistrate was none other than Herchmer himself.

Davin the journalist gave way to Davin the lawyer. Appearing in his own defence, he charged that Herchmer was interpreting the liquor act in

241

a narrow and capricious manner for personal reasons. In an impassioned address, he declared that he had never imported liquor into the Territories, that he never carried it, and that he was being trapped "into appearing as to be a lawbreaker." His eloquence was of no avail; he was fined $50.00 and $15.50 costs.

The following day in the *Leader*, Davin struck back at "the tyranny of Colonel Herchmer," attacking "the alarming powers temporarily placed in his hands." Herchmer had "caused the law to be strained in order to gratify what everybody knows, was a desire to avenge fancied wrongs suffered by himself . . . because of comments imposed on us from time to time as public journalists, by the conduct of this or that member of the N.W.M.P." In this, Davin was supported by most of the North West and Manitoba newspapers, many of which had been attacking him on the subject of Regina as a capital city.

The Prime Minister, to whom Davin wrote a "half crazy letter" on the matter, felt, however, that the editor could only hurt himself by keeping up the battle. "His continual attacks on Herchmer . . . will be considered as an evidence of spite against a public official for doing his duty. This will destroy his prestige and that of his paper." The Prime Minister suggested Davin would have been better advised to pay the fine without fuss and pass the whole matter off with a laugh.

Davin was probably more embarrassed at being publicly found with liquor than he was by being arrested, since, in his newspaper, he had been a strong temperance advocate. Most frontier editors were hard drinkers, but because temperance was as popular a cause in the eighties as pollution was ninety years later, the majority publicly embraced it. Everybody, indeed, seemed to pay lip-service to the principle, including the worst topers. Davin himself thrived on whiskey. Before preparing a speech it was his habit to lock himself in his room with a shelf of books and a full bottle. The more the wine flowed, the greater became his powers of improvisation. At one well-lubricated banquet in eastern Canada, he was called upon to speak every half-hour or so, as the glasses were filled and refilled, and did so, in several languages, until four o'clock in the morning. Though he paid public homage to prohibition, he did not go so far as to approve the spilling of confiscated liquor on the ground, an accepted practice which must have caused many an inward shudder. Davin suggested editorially that it ought to be sold and the proceeds given to the editors of North West newspapers. The Moose Jaw *News* took this facetious remark seriously and piously declared that "we hereby give notice that we do not want whiskey money and will not take it. Our mind is made up."

242

There was only one way in which the settlers, railwaymen, and temperance advocates of the North West could legally purchase alcohol and that was on the time-hallowed grounds of health. "Now that the Governor is here," Davin wrote on Queen Victoria's birthday in 1883, "he will be pestered for permits by vigorous pioneers who want a gallon or two of whiskey, to be used for 'medicinial' purposes. Even five and ten gallons, we believe, have been asked for on medicinal grounds."

Prohibition or no, a good deal of liquor was consumed along the CPR right of way during the construction period. Edwin Brooks, migrating with his brother from Quebec in 1883, was stopped by a Mounted Policeman on the treeless alkali desert between Brandon and Qu'Appelle and asked if they had any liquor. The brothers replied that they were temperance men, whereupon the constable remarked acidly that nearly everybody on the road was a temperance man but a great deal of whiskey was getting through in spite of that. Sam Steele, who resented the strict laws and the nuisance of enforcing them, went so far as to claim that "the prohibitory law made more drunkards than if there had been an open bar and free drinks at every street corner." That is scarcely credible. When Brooks reached Regina in August he was able to write to his wife Nellie: "I can tell you they (the police) look after these whiskey dealers awfully sharp. One never sees a drunken man in this N.W.T. or if ever very seldom. . . ." The truth was that because of prohibition the CPR was able to keep its men on the job and, in spite of occasional sprees, stabilize a work force whose training and precision made it possible to drive almost nine hundred miles of steel in fifteen months. When it was all over and the trains were running from Winnipeg to the base of the Rockies, the Moose Jaw *News* summed it up:

"The order and quiet which have prevailed during the construction of the Canadian Pacific, where thousands of men, proverbially not of the tractable kind, have been employed far in advance of civilization and settlement, have been unexampled in the history of any similar enterprise."

4

Langdon and Shepard completed their contract in mid-August, 1883, when the rails reached Calgary. (The last two stations on their contract were named after the partners.) Until that moment, the old Hudson's Bay fort and its cluster of adjacent log buildings – Roman Catholic and Methodist missions, freighters' cabins, I. G. Baker store and two hotels – had been more closely linked with the United States than with Canada.

The magical influence

The chief mode of travel to Fort Benton, Montana, was by bull train – an American transportation device – rather than by Red River cart, and all the mail carried United States stamps because it was posted south of the border.

To a newcomer from the East, such as William Murdoch, the harness-maker who put up the first commercial sign on the site in May, the embryo town seemed like a distant planet. "I was dreaming about home almost all last night," Murdoch wrote in his diary on a bitter, windy June day. "How I long to see my wife, mother and little ones. My heart craves for them all today more than usual." Murdoch, who would become Calgary's first mayor, could not get so much as a sliver of dressed lumber, for there were no sawmills in the foothills. All that was available were rough planks, whip-sawed vertically by hand. Fresh fruit was so rare that when half a box of apples arrived they were sold at fifty cents each (the equivalent of more than two dollars in modern terms); they were the first that had been seen in that part of the North West.

The railway was to change all that. It was even to change the location of the town, as it had in the cases of Brandon and Regina.

Until the railway arrived, Fort Calgary was situated on the east bank of the Elbow River near its confluence with the Bow. As usual, there were squatters living in rough shanties, hired by Winnipeg land speculators to occupy the most likely ground until the townsite was subdivided.

The settlement watched the railroad approach with a mixture of apprehension and anticipation. Where would the station be located? Under the terms of its contract, the CPR had title to the odd-numbered sections along the right of way. The fort and surrounding log structures, together with all the squatters' shacks, were situated on an even-numbered section – Number Fourteen. The adjacent section, Fifteen, on the opposite bank of the Elbow, had been reserved by Order in Council as pasturage for the police horses. Surely then, everyone reasoned, the town would have to be put on the east bank, where the fort was located.

The scrapers, clearing the right of way, lumbered through on June 21, followed by an army of graders. The tension began to mount. The bridge across the Bow was completed on August 10; two days later a construction train puffed in. On August 15, a train carrying a temporary station arrived, and the community held its breath. Where would it stop? To everyone's surprise and dismay it shunted directly through the settlement, across the new bridge and was established, together with a siding, on Section Fifteen on the far side of the Elbow.

A state of uncertainty existed at this point on the banks of the Elbow.

244

Nobody quite knew what to do. No survey had been taken. The owner-ship of Section Fifteen was in dispute. The town was growing rapidly on the east bank, but because everyone wanted to wait for the decision about the townsite, no one wanted to go to the expense of erecting any-thing permanent; and so for all of 1883 Calgary was a tent city.

On August 20, two young men arrived from the East, erected a tent, and prepared to publish a newspaper, the *Herald*. The paper announced in its first edition, dated August 31, that it would always have the courage of its convictions and would not be afraid to speak its mind freely when wrongs were to be redressed or "manifest abuses to be remedied." It started out with the usual trenchant editorial against the demon rum: "The *Herald* will always lend its influence against the introduction of intoxi-cating liquors as a beverage in the N.W.T., believing that the liquor traffic engenders vice, immorality and crime."

The first edition also announced the arrival, on August 27, of the leading directors of the CPR, aboard Van Horne's private car. Stephen, Angus, Donald A. Smith, and Van Horne had all come to Calgary together with their guests, Baron Pascoe du P. Grenfell, one of the European backers, and His Royal Highness, Prince Hohenlohe of Germany, who was looking over the country with a view to recommending it to prospec-tive German emigrants. The trip had been made from Winnipeg over the new track at an average rate of more than thirty-five miles an hour, and at some points the locomotives, fed from recently discovered coal deposits near Medicine Hat, had pulled the cars at a clip of sixty miles an hour.

The directors invited Father Lacombe, who had saved them so much grief, to be their guest at luncheon. On a motion by Angus, Lacombe was made president of the CPR for one hour. Taking the chair, the priest immediately voted himself two passes on the railroad for life and, in addi-tion, free transportation of all freight and baggage necessary to the Oblate missions together with free use for himself for life of the CPR's telegraph system.

The directors were only too happy to grant Lacombe what he asked. He was the one man who had the full confidence of the Indians. All the promises made that day were honoured by the railway. Moreover, La-combe's rather cavalier use of the passes, which he lent out indiscrimin-ately (as he did most of his belongings), was regularly tolerated. On one occasion the two passes, which became familiar along the line, were pre-sented by two nuns, newly arrived in the west. "May I ask," the conductor politely inquired, "which one of you is Father Lacombe?" He let the blushing sisters go on their way.

Van Horne, who described Lacombe as "a great friend of the Company and of our people," always made sure the donations to Lacombe's mission were shipped free of charge from Montreal to Calgary. When Lacombe was in Montreal, he visited Van Horne who so amused him one Saturday night with conjuring tricks that the priest, who was staying at a nearby religious home, was forced to creep back in the early hours of the Lord's Day. From then on he was accompanied on such visits by a stern-faced ecclesiastical watchdog who got him back before midnight.

Van Horne also sent personal gifts to Lacombe. An art connoisseur, he was prowling around a private gallery in New York one day when he came upon a religious picture he thought would appeal to the priest. He dispatched it to Montreal with his other purchases, with instructions to have it framed and sent on to the mission. When he received no acknowledgement from Lacombe he made some inquiries and found to his horror that there had been a mix-up. Instead of the religious painting, the shippers had substituted a Dégas study of a scantily clad and leggy ballet dancer, pirouetting on a stage before footlights. Van Horne wired an abject apology to the priest, who made a tactful reply. He had, he said, been surprised on receiving the picture but had treated it with the respect due to the generosity of the giver; some of his colleagues, however, had insisted that he put it out of sight, so he had been keeping it under his bed.

After honouring the priest, the distinguished visitors departed Calgary without leaving the questing settlers one whit the wiser about the future over which they themselves quite clearly had no control. The state of indecision continued all that fall, with half the community swearing that it would not budge an inch to accommodate the railway. "There are some people here who have a mind of their own and do not propose to follow the meanderings of the CPR," the Fort Macleod *Gazette* declared. The *Herald* continued to demand, in vain, that the matter be settled one way or the other. "The people in Calgary have by this time the elements of suspense and patience reduced to a science," it wrote in November. The following month it reported that "we have much pleasure in announcing that our friends east of the Elbow have definitely decided upon the permanent location of the city in that quarter. Already the surveyors are hard at work upon the sub-division of the Denny Estate, and our next issue will contain the date of the sale of this beautiful spot so well adapted for the future capital of Alberta."

But the CPR itself and nobody else – editor, banker, merchant, or real estate man – would make the decision as to where Calgary was to be; and in January, when the Order in Council regarding the NWMP pasturage was finally rescinded, the CPR spoke. The city would be on the west side of the Elbow River and not on its original location on the east side. To underline that point, the government, which stood to profit equally with the railway, moved the post office across the river to the west.

In vain the Denny subdivision on the east side advertised that it was "the centre of Calgary City." As soon as the post office crossed the river, James Bannerman followed with his flour and feed store. All the solemn pledges about staying put and refusing to follow the meanderings of the railway were forgotten and a kind of wild scramble ensued as butcher shop, jeweller, churches, billiard parlour, and hotels packed up like gypsies and located on the favoured site. The *Herald* reported that buildings were suddenly springing up "as though some magical influence were being exerted" and that what had been barren prairie just three weeks before "is now rapidly growing into the shape of a respectable town."

Once again the railway, in truth a "magical influence," had dictated the lineaments of the new North West.

5

When George Stephen returned from the North West on October 1, 1883, the company's financial situation was even darker than before. Van Horne had spent the thirty million dollars raised the previous year. Hill had left the company and was selling out most of his stock. One of his reasons, and probably the major one,* for this abrupt and unexpected departure was the CPR's announced intention of taking the route north of Lake Superior, together with Van Horne's decision to order three lake steamers to compete with American railways south of the border and to carry

George Stephen's disastrous gamble

---

*Hill's biographer, Pyle, does not give this as a reason, citing only Hill's preoccupation with his own railroad, but both John Murray Gibbon, in the CPR's quasi-official history, *Steel of Empire* (Gibbon was public relations officer for the company at the time), and Vaughan, Van Horne's biographer, specifically state that Hill left because of the Lake Superior decision. Though a final judgement must await the opening of Hill's papers in 1981, his departure was unexpected enough to surprise Stephen. It is reasonably clear from his action that, although more than half the voting stock of the CPR was held by American investors, the control of the railway was in Canadian hands. It would have been in the American interest to have abandoned or postponed the Lake Superior line.

railway materials across the lakes to the men building the line. Hill, who expected to get all the freight to the North West for his St. Paul road, had never contemplated such a turn of events. Both Donald A. Smith and George Stephen resigned simultaneously from the board of the St. Paul, Minneapolis and Manitoba Railway – Hill's line – though they retained their stock and their friendship with the ex-Canadian. (Smith's share in Hill's railroad was always larger than his share in the Canadian Pacific.) Smith replaced Hill as a director of the CPR. J. S. Kennedy's subsequent resignation from the CPR board – it was inevitable that the New York banker would follow Hill – made a bad impression in financial circles, since Kennedy's firm had made its reputation in railroad securities. Moreover, the country was entering a depression. CPR stock began to drop. On June 25, 1883, when the international syndicate formed the previous year by Stephen to raise funds had picked up its last option for another ten millions, the stock had reached a peak of 65½ on the New York stock exchange. Following that, it began to slide to the point where brokers were advertising it as a bargain – "The foundations of many fortunes will be laid with the profit accruing to men who buy this stock whilst it is low." There were few takers. By October 31, it had dived to 49⅜.

That same fall, the North West, still reeling from the collapse of the real estate bubble, was struck a second blow. An early frost wiped out the wheat crop. In the United States, the Northern Pacific was teetering on the edge of insolvency. By December, its president, Henry Villard, who had risen in a few years from obscurity to commanding financial leadership, would be deposed – his health wrecked, his worldly goods abandoned to his creditors. On October 26, the *Globe* used the word "depression" to describe the economic crisis. A "demoralization in railway stocks occurred" (to quote Charles Tupper); if the CPR were to throw any more of its outstanding common stock on the market it would be sacrificed. Stephen was as concerned about the shareholders as he was about the company. He was afraid that many of them, egged on by speculators, would rush to dump their stock on the market at great personal loss – and to their later regret. He decided upon a bold gamble.

He arrived in Ottawa on October 24 and saw the Prime Minister the following day. Macdonald, as he told Tupper a month later, was seriously concerned over his friend's appearance. It was the first time he had seen him so depressed. But the plan the CPR president unfolded was a tribute to "his enormous pluck," as Macdonald called it.

Stephen had forty-five million dollars worth of authorized stock as yet unissued. At the moment no one would buy it, except at a price so low the company could not benefit. Stephen wanted to force the stock up and

248

make a market for it; only in that way could he secure adequate funds to finish the railway. He had decided upon a plan he thought would work: with the government's help, the CPR was prepared to guarantee a five per cent dividend for the next ten years on all issued and unissued stock.

Stephen wanted the government to guarantee three per cent; the remainder he felt, could be paid out of the company's resources. Because the government had had a disastrous experience with previous railway guarantees, Stephen was prepared to pay in advance for the privilege; he was in effect buying a government annuity. He had reckoned the cost as an insurance company reckons a policy: the price tag came to twenty-five millions. He was prepared to pay fifteen million dollars down, an additional five millions the following February, and the rest in securities and assets, including postal subsidies. All this would be deposited with the government, which would be acting merely as trustee for the fund.

This was exactly the kind of daring gambit that had won for Stephen a reputation for financial wizardry in international banking circles. But it *was* a gamble. If the gamble succeeded, then Stephen could sell the rest of the company's stock at something close to par and get enough money – he calculated that he needed about thirty millions – to finish the railway. But if he lost, he would be tying up a huge block of cash at a time when the railway was desperately short of money. The situation out along the line was already serious. At Brandon, eighty men on the staff of the freight office had not been paid for three months; at the end of that period the company was able to give them only one month's back wages. Brandon's storekeepers had no other choice but to carry them. As one put it: "We've got to carry them. If the CPR goes bust, we will all have to pack up and go back to Bruce County, Ontario."

In theory, Stephen's plan was workable. He was proclaiming to the financial world that CPR shares were gilt-edged and that the Canadian government had confidence in them. All during the construction period the company had never passed a dividend. With three per cent guaranteed and only two per cent for the company to raise from current revenue, the investing public would look favourably on the proposition.

Macdonald liked the idea and the Cabinet passed it. The Prime Minister felt that the guarantee would boom the CPR's stock to seventy or more. He turned to other matters, specifically, the Grand Trunk's persistent campaign against the railway, which looked very much like a campaign against Canada. In Macdonald's view the Grand Trunk had become an American line running between Chicago and Portland: its Canadian business had been made secondary to its foreign through traffic.

249

That being the case, he intended to "throw out a hint next session that would make Hickson tremble to his boots." If Charles Tupper, now High Commissioner in England, could, perhaps with the help of John Rose, gather reliable evidence that the GTR was behind the attacks on the Canadian Pacific, then he, the Prime Minister, was prepared to threaten the older railway with a powerful weapon. Technically, the Grand Trunk still owed the government $15,500,000, with thirty years' accumulated interest; the amount had been considered waived long ago, but it was still on the books. If necessary, Macdonald was prepared to use it as a lever to "bring those people to their bearings."

The Prime Minister's rosy predictions did not come true. Canadian Pacific stock shot up briefly to a little over sixty-three dollars. It hovered at that price for a few days and then began to drop back again, fluctuating day by day but slipping slowly until, by the end of 1883, it was down to fifty-two.

Long before that point was reached, Stephen was forced to revise his plan. He would guarantee a dividend, not on one hundred million dollars worth of stock but only on sixty-five millions. That meant that, since fifty-five millions were already issued, he had only ten million dollars worth of unissued stock available to him. He dared not put that up for sale at the reduced price but was able to use it as security to get a loan of five million dollars in New York through J. S. Kennedy's firm.

The gamble had been disastrous. To raise five million dollars, George Stephen had put up nine millions in cash and pledged another seven millions in securities. The railway was worse off than it had been before he took the plunge. And in December it was hit by another blow: the Canada North-West Land Company was in difficulties. The CPR, to keep it alive, was obliged to take back about half of the land grant bonds that it had sold to the company on time, and an equivalent amount of land, to bail it out.

The CPR's situation was critical. The *New York Times*, in predicting that the stock would drop out of sight, had remarked darkly that "Canada politics and Wall-street stock jobbery seem equally mixed up in the affair" and declared that the Canadian people "may expect to see Canadian securities, stocks, bonds, and all go down in a heap together." Stephen realized that the railway had scarcely a friend left in the international financial capitals: "Things in New York are simply disgusting, every fellow there and in London too is ready to cut our throats if he could be sure of robbing us." He tried to keep his spirits up: "I am not discouraged and confident that in some way we shall triumph over all obstacles and disappoint all our *enemies* and pretended *friends*." But

250

Macdonald, to whom he poured out his feelings, knew that he was close to despondency. The incurable Stephen optimism was beginning to wear thin in banking circles, as Rose confided to the Prime Minister in his oblique way: "Most strictly between us, our friend Stephen's assurances are rather regarded now with less trust than I like to see." Stephen's reputation for financial legerdemain had suffered a bad blow as a result of the gambit that failed. Rose wanted to know about CPR securities. Many of his friends were "foolishly sacrificing" their shares as a result of adverse reports. Would he be warranted in advising them to hang on? Even a hint from Macdonald would help.

Macdonald had already, though with great reluctance, made his decision: the government would have to come to the company's aid and find some way of forcing a new loan down the throat of Parliament. It had taken considerable persuasion to budge the Prime Minister. One evening late in November a powerful CPR delegation visited Macdonald at his private residence, Earnscliffe. Stephen, Angus, McIntyre, Van Horne, and Abbott, the lawyer, were all present to make the case, but Macdonald could not be moved. Van Horne later described the scene and its aftermath to O. D. Skelton, the historian.

"Gentlemen, I need not detain you long," the Prime Minister told the group. "You might as well ask for the planet Jupiter. I would not give you the millions you ask, and if I did the Cabinet would not agree. Now, gentlemen, I did not have much sleep last night, and should like to go to bed. I am sorry but there is no use discussing the question further."

Stephen and the others tried to argue; Macdonald refused to listen to any further entreaties. The five men went dolefully back to the city to wait for the four o'clock morning train to Montreal. It must have seemed to them that their careers were at an end.

They stopped in at the old Bank of Montreal cottage to spend the intervening hours. There they encountered John Henry Pope, the acting Minister of Railways, stretched out on a couch reading, a strong habitant cigar between his teeth and a glass of whiskey at his side.

"Well, what's up?" Van Horne remembered Pope saying.

While McIntyre danced nervously about, Stephen gave him the bad news.

Pope rose slowly, lit a new cigar, heaved his gaunt frame into his shaggy coat, clapped his old otter cap on his head, and called for a carriage.

"Wait till I get back," was all Pope would say. It was now past one o'clock.

He returned an hour and a half later, poker-faced, kicked off his rubbers without a word, doffed his cap and coat, poured out another pony of whiskey, lit, with maddening deliberation, a fresh cigar, and finally broke the tension: "Well, boys, he'll do it. Stay over until tomorrow."

Pope, who had got the Prime Minister out of bed, had used the one argument that could convince his chieftain that the CPR must get its loan: "The day the Canadian Pacific busts the Conservative party busts the day after," he told him.

The following day Stephen and his colleagues appeared before the Council to find the Prime Minister out of sorts, Alexander Campbell totally opposed to further help, and Leonard Tilley, the finance minister, openly advocating that the government take over the railway. Macdonald desperately needed Tupper at his side. Sir Charles, though still a Member of Parliament, had been dispatched to London to replace Galt as High Commissioner. Now that most pugnacious of political in-fighters, "the most fearless combatant that ever sat in the Parliament of Canada," was required in Ottawa. Tupper, said his political opponent George Ross, "wrestled with his subject as a strong man would wrestle in the amphitheatre with an antagonist." Since his original memorandum in the spring of 1880, he had been the Canadian Pacific's greatest defender within the Cabinet. On December 1 Macdonald sent him a curt cable: "Pacific in trouble. You should be here." The new high commissioner was handed the message just as he was rising to speak at a dinner in his honour, but he was not long in dispatching a reply: "Sailing on Thursday." When he arrived in Ottawa, he "found everybody in despair."

Stephen was frantic: "Something must be done at *once*," he told the Prime Minister, otherwise he must give up and let the government take over the railway. He needed $3,850,000 cash by January 1, 1884, to pay immediate debts. By January 8, he needed an additional $3,812,240 to pay off a short-term loan in New York. Another payment was due the government – $2,853,750 – by February 1. The company's total debt was fifteen millions, the remainder of the money owing being on a longer-term basis.

Stephen, flitting between New York and Montreal trying to stave off disaster, apologized to the Prime Minister for the heavy stream of correspondence. "I am doing my best to keep the Bank [of Montreal] quiet," he told him two days before Christmas, ". . . but our wants are great and constant and not very easily supplied. Smithers [the president] knows very well that I would not allow the bank to lose a cent by the CPR so long as I could pay the money myself, and that feeling helps us not a little just now."

252

A bank crisis was not inconceivable. Stephen himself feared that if the heavy advances to the railroad, made without adequate security, became known to the public, there would be a run on the Bank of Montreal. The bank's chief executive officers were in a state of terror. Tupper privately told them that they must advance the railway the money it needed; the government stood right behind the company and would guarantee payment. That was not good enough for the bankers. Confidence in the CPR had reached such a low point that they demanded a secret memorandum, which they insisted be signed not only by Tupper but also by Tilley, the Minister of Finance, and by the Prime Minister himself. They had to be satisfied with a paper, signed by Tupper alone; in a close vote they agreed to extend the loan. It was, as Stephen knew, "a narrow squeak." Several of the directors were determined to refuse the application and "smash the whole thing up." Stephen was convinced that they were under Hickson's control and also motivated by "envy, hatred and malice."

This short-term aid did not solve the railway's long-term problems. There could, in fact, be only one solution – a government loan. Stephen, who needed fifteen millions to pay off the company's debts, figured he could complete the road with an additional twenty-seven millions, of which he had twelve millions coming in unpaid government subsidies. In short, he needed a loan of thirty million dollars.

He formalized the request in mid-January, asking for a loan of $22,-500,000, repayable May 1, 1891, and further relief in the form of a five-year postponement on the second instalment of more than seven millions that he had so recklessly promised in order to guarantee the dividend. This was an enormous sum for any company to raise in 1884; it represented almost a whole year's revenue of the federal government. In addition, Stephen asked that both the remainder of the subsidy and the extra money provided by the loan be paid out to the CPR, not on a mileage basis but on the basis of actual work done. In return, he promised to finish the job in exactly half the time stipulated in the original contract. To get the necessary working capital, Stephen was forced to mortgage the railway. As security, he put up "everything they had in the world" (in Van Horne's words) – the main trunk-line, all the rolling stock, and everything else connected with the railway, including outstanding stock and land grant bonds. With this loan, the CPR had exhausted all further means of raising capital.

This was the medicine that Macdonald and Tupper must force their reluctant followers to swallow. It would not be easy. A platoon of powerful forces was arrayed against the railway: the Opposition under Edward

Blake, the most eloquent man in the House; half the newspapers in the country; the great international press associations – Reuters and AP – which seemed to be spokesmen for the Grand Trunk; the large financial houses; and a good many of Macdonald's own followers, including several Maritimers (who had no interest in a western railroad), most of the Quebec *bleus* (who wanted an equal share in any largesse the government intended to dispense), and the Manitobans, who represented a growing popular antagonism to the CPR.

The building of the railway had laid a bundle of annoying problems at the Prime Minister's door that Christmas season of 1883–84. Andrew Onderdonk was haunting the lobbies trying to get a further subsidy for his section of the road. He had arrived at a singularly unpropitious moment. A few days before Christmas, disgruntled Manitoba farmers had organized themselves into a pressure group, the Manitoba and North-West Farmers' Union. Its formation marked the beginning of a vexing and perennial Canadian problem: the disaffection of the agrarian West with the industrial East. The symbol of that disaffection was the CPR.

There were a good many reasons for western discontent in 1883 and not all of them were the fault of the railway. The collapse of the Manitoba real estate boom, followed in September, 1883, by a killing frost, had left a legacy of despair and disillusionment. Economic conditions, which had been steadily improving since 1878, took another downturn throughout the continent. The pioneer settlers along the North Saskatchewan were bitterly disappointed over the CPR's unaccountable change of route: they had expected to make a killing out of land speculation. The government's land policy was also in contention; its treatment of squatters along the railway line suggested an indifference to the interests of western Canadians. In Manitoba, the farmers wanted to run their own show – to establish their own land policies and build their own railways. The tug of war between provincial and national interests was beginning.

Overriding these specific dissatisfactions there was a more serious and subtle grievance – a feeling on the part of the western farmers that the new Canada was being exploited purely for the material advantage of the wicked and grasping East. There was considerable historical evidence for this belief. A generation before, when the good land ran out in Ontario, Toronto expansionists began to envision the North West as a kind of suburb. Montreal interests, of course, had been mining it of furs for two centuries. Macdonald himself had seen the Pacific railway project in the context of his National Policy. The CPR would haul away the prairie's great natural resource – grain – to eastern Canada and, in turn, deliver the

254

protected manufactured goods of Ontario and Quebec to the prairie consumers. As the farmers saw it, they were paying through the nose in two ways. First, they felt the prices on manufactured goods – especially agricultural implements – to be exorbitant because of the protective tariffs. Secondly, they felt the freight rates to be equally excessive because of the CPR's monopoly.

The railway, then, was seen mainly as an arm of the eastern industrialists – a tool to crush the farmer. The time would come when the CPR would be blamed for almost every catastrophe on the plains. The story about the settler whose crop was flattened by hail and then devoured by grasshoppers, shaking his fist at Heaven and crying, "God damn the CPR!" was not too far-fetched.

More than anything else, it was the Monopoly Clause in the original contract that enraged the westerners. If they were suspicious of the CPR's motives in the matter of freight rates, they had cause to be, for the CPR Syndicate was the lineal descendant of the hated Kittson Line, whose steamboats had enjoyed a monopoly of Red River traffic in the seventies. The Kittson Line, which, as everybody knew, was controlled by Jim Hill and Donald A. Smith, had charged outrageous rates. Its successor was the Pembina Branch of the CPR and its corporate cousin south of the border, the St. Paul, Minneapolis and Manitoba Railway. Since no competing line was allowed, the two connecting railways linking Winnipeg with St. Paul could and did charge what the traffic would bear. John Henry Pope, a good friend of the CPR, was one who thought the rates were "exorbitant." Van Horne's letters indicate that a rate-fixing agreement between the two companies existed. In July of 1883, for example, he wrote a letter to the general manager of the St. Paul road, chiding him for selling any second-class tickets at all to eastern Canadian points. "It looks to me like an unnecessary loss of revenue," he said.

The Winnipeg Board of Trade, in a bitter complaint to Van Horne in the spring of 1883, pointed out that Canadian Pacific freight charges between St. Vincent on the border through Winnipeg to Regina were an average of 65 per cent higher for all classes than comparable Grand Trunk rates in eastern Canada. Moreover, the Grand Trunk carried certain goods such as grain, flour, butter, cheese, and potatoes at substantially lower rates. The CPR rates for these commodities were 133 per cent higher in the North West. The CPR replied that the cost of operating in the North West was much higher than in eastern Canada, and the government backed it up.

But the farmers believed – and with some reason – that it was the

255

monopoly clause that kept rates high. In addition, of course, it frustrated the building of rival lines. The building of a railway meant a period of dazzling prosperity, however brief. But in 1883, Macdonald, at Stephen's prompting, had disallowed the provincial charters of three Manitoba railways because they came too close to the international border. Apart from speculative considerations, the small communities of Manitoba needed more railways. Van Horne was plagued with letters from various towns asking for branch lines. The general manager, who firmly believed that Grand Trunk agents were behind the farmers' attacks on the CPR, replied that the railway could not afford any further construction: stories of the agitation had been blown up in the British press, he said, making it impossible for the railway to raise additional funds in Europe. There was some truth in this. J. G. Colmer, Tupper's deputy in London, informed the Prime Minister by cable that telegrams from Ottawa in all the London papers reported that the farmers' agitation was assuming "gigantic proportions" and that if the grievances were not redressed, it was being said that Manitoba would have to look to Washington. "Such telegrams very harmful here," Colmer cabled.

"It is very extraordinary," Van Horne told John Egan, his western superintendent, "that people with common sense should, while demanding the construction of branch lines, with the same breath attempt to destroy the credit of the Company and render it powerless to build them."

But the general manager's characteristic bluntness with his correspondents did nothing to alleviate the problem. The *Globe* accused him of addressing the people of the North West in a tone which was that "of an autocrat to serfs whose murmurings and grumblings annoyed him. . . . In his eagerness to apply the lash to the discontented he more than once inflicts severe blows on his associates."

The farmers also believed that the W. W. Ogilvie Company had conspired with the CPR to get a monopoly on all grain elevators in the province, arranging for special rates from the railway. That was not true, but, as Stephen told Macdonald, "W. W. O. is an awful fool both in speech and action, and no saying what he might not do or say to create an impression in the minds of other buyers that it was useless to try and compete with him in wheat buying in the North West."

The farm agitation did not die down. In March, 1884, the farmers' union held a second convention greater than the December demonstration – "the most momentous gathering of men ever held in the northwest," according to the Brandon *Sun*. It meant either emancipation or open rebellion, the paper said. "There can be no middle course now."

In addition to the disaffected Manitobans, Macdonald had the Quebeckers to contend with. If the CPR was to get a loan, then how about French Canada? The province intended to use the situation as a lever to get further federal assistance.

Stephen, meanwhile, was struggling to keep the company afloat. On January 22, 1884, he scribbled a note to Macdonald that he was going back to Montreal to try to "keep things moving . . . until relief arrives." There was a note of despair and resignation in this letter: ". . . you must not blame me if I fail. I do not, at the moment, see how we are going to get the money to keep the work going. . . . If I find we cannot go on I suppose the only thing to do will be to put in a Receiver. If that *has* to be done the quicker it is done the better."

It was the first time that the possibility of bankruptcy had been mentioned, and Stephen sounded almost comforted at the prospect: "I am getting so wearied and worn out with this business that almost any change will be a relief to me."

When the CPR president reached Montreal, he picked up a copy of the *Star* in which, to his fury, he read an editorial which insinuated that he, Smith, McIntyre, Angus, and the others had been robbing the company for their own personal benefit. Since all of them had pledged their own stock in the St. Paul railway – the basis of their personal fortunes – against the CPR's bank loan, the words cut deep. The fact that he had recently completed, at a cost of some three million dollars, a mansion on Drummond Street "fitted up and furnished with regal magnificence," did not help the company's image.

There was also the matter of the guaranteed dividend. The CPR's critics were not slow to point out that, in guaranteeing an annual five per cent on the par value of the issued stock, the members of the Syndicate were ensuring a cosy income for themselves since all of them owned large blocks of shares. As Blake put it, later, in the House: "They invest money with one hand for the purpose of taking it out with the other."

The real interest rate, of course, was far higher than five per cent, since all but the fifty thousand shares had sold at a heavy discount. One block of 200,000 shares had sold for twenty-five cents on the dollar, much of it to insiders. Stephen got most of his stock at that price – about 23,000 shares out of his total of 31,000 odd. A study of his stock holdings during this period indicates that he was enjoying an average return on all of his CPR shares of almost twelve per cent – an enormous rate of interest for that or any time.

Stephen's annual income from his CPR stock came to about one hundred and fifty thousand dollars, all of it guaranteed and none of it taxable. In 1971 that would represent a *net* income of close to three-quarters of a million, something that few men are able to achieve in the 1970's. No wonder then that the "scribblers," as Stephen contemptuously called them, were carping. That winter the CPR president, at the Prime Minister's suggestion, apparently made an attempt through Donald A. Smith to silence the *Globe*, the railway's most persistent critic. Macdonald suggested that the paper was in financial difficulty and thought that Smith could "come to a business arrangement" with George Brown's widow and thus influence it. The Prime Minister thought the paper should be allowed to keep its character and position as a Liberal journal but should change its attitude to the railway – a situation that already existed with two other Opposition organs, the Montreal *Herald* and the Manitoba *Free Press* (the latter for some years under Smith's financial influence). Smith did make an attempt to buy the *Globe*, but nothing came of it and the paper continued to attack the railway.

Stephen had to put up with the scribblers as he had to put up with the politicians. Macdonald warned him in mid-January that it would take another six weeks to get the loan through Parliament. Stephen was aghast. Six weeks, when every day counted! "Had I supposed it would take to 1st March before help could reach us I would not have made the attempt to carry on."

In Montreal, he learned the magnitude of the railroad's financial dilemma. Every cent coming in from the government subsidy had to go directly to the Bank of Montreal to cover the loan of three and a half millions. Nothing could be diverted to pay wages or meet the bills for supplies that were piling up in Thomas Shaughnessy's office. He must have an advance of at least three and a half millions by February 8 in order to pay off the bank. "If this cannot be obtained," he told Tupper, "it is not a bit of use of my trying to carry on any longer."

But he had to carry on as he had been carrying on all that year, putting off creditors, trimming costs, postponing expenses. In spite of further threats to Ottawa, cries of despair, and attacks of fatigue and nerves, he would continue to carry on. It was not in his nature to give up.

There was trouble north of Lake Superior. On December 15, 1883, John Egan had been forced to cut off the cost-of-living bonuses that Van Horne had instituted in that unprepossessing environment. The men were bluntly asked to sign a new contract agreeing to the reduction or to leave their jobs. Some thirty-five hundred refused, and the work on the line was suspended. In the end, however, most of the men were forced to return to work because at that season of the year it was hard to get employment. *The* CPR *goes political*

In his brusque interviews with the press, the general manager exuded confidence. In Chicago the previous August, he had announced that the CPR was employing twenty-five thousand men and spending one hundred thousand dollars a day.

"How much will it cost per mile through the Rockies?" a reporter asked him.

"We don't know," Van Horne replied.

"Have you not estimated the amount beforehand?"

"The Canadian Pacific Railway," declared Van Horne, "has never estimated the cost of any work; it hasn't time for that; it's got a big job on hand, and it's going to put it through."

"Well, but if you haven't estimated the cost of the construction through the mountains how do you know that you have sufficient funds to push the road as you are currently reported to have?"

"Well," replied Van Horne, airily, "if we haven't got enough we will get more, that's all about it."

The reporter retired, "forcibly impressed with the resolute frankness of character displayed by the man who is the administrative head of this great Canadian enterprise."

Van Horne was not being frank. He, too, was scrambling for cash and pinching every penny possible. There scarcely seemed to be an expenditure in 1883 that did not come under his personal scrutiny as a constant stream of letters to his staff showed:

"I think this is the second lot of revolvers that has been purchased for the use of the Paymaster. What became of the others? Why were silver mounted revolvers permitted to be purchased when others just as good could be had for half the money? P.S. Referring to item about cab hire at Portage la Prairie. I do not understand why a bill for such an amount was passed without enquiry."

"I understand that the stock of stationery at Winnipeg amounts to about $40,000. This is about four times the largest stock ever carried on the C.M. & St.P. Please look into the matter at once and put on the brakes firmly. I find also that five men are employed where one man and a boy should be amply sufficient. There is something radically wrong in the manner in which the business is carried on if such an office is necessary."

"Aside from putting the Thunder Bay Line in order, we must cut our improvement account down to the lowest possible notch leaving any work that may be safely postponed until money is more plenty."

Van Horne watched every item, large or small. He could berate a man for sending a telegram "containing 35 words and costing this Coy about $2.00 and which could have just as well have been sent by mail," and he could also give orders for mammoth savings north of Superior, where construction had just got underway. His general superintendent there was another Ross – John, no relation to the James Ross in charge of mountain work. When John Ross asked for sixteen steamshovels in addition to the two he had working, Van Horne turned him down. They cost ten thousand dollars each and the company could not afford to tie up that amount of money. The general manager suggested the number could be reduced by putting in permanent trestles of round timber. The trestles would last for seven or eight years. This would mean that large earthworks – filling in and replacing the temporary bridging – would not immediately be required. Steel trestles, at that point, were out of the question.

Van Horne's idea was to get a workable line through – one that would stand up for at least six years – make it pay, and then begin improving it. "We have a long way to go before completing our contract," he explained to John Ross, ". . . and we must therefore cheapen our earlier work as much as we safely can in order to make sure that our money will hold out. . . . We must in every other way possible reduce the first cost of the road wherever it can be done, but not at the expense of gradients or curvature."

Masonry could certainly wait. Van Horne gave orders that all rock quarrying, dressing of stone, and installation of masonry should cease except in those places where an iron bridge was absolutely essential. The CPR could not afford that kind of luxury. And when John Egan wanted an extra telephone wire installed between Winnipeg and the lakehead, Van Horne turned him down: ". . . I think you will be able to get along without difficulty as two wires properly worked under a strict censorship

260

as to unnecessary telegrams and telegrams of unnecessary length can do an enormous amount of work. . . . We must not spend one dollar where it can possibly be helped."

Van Horne was in the House of Commons Visitors' Gallery on February 1, with Stephen and Donald A. Smith, when Tupper rose to propose the new Canadian Pacific Railway resolutions. The *Globe* was quick to note Smith's presence; it was less than six years since, in that same setting, both Tupper and Macdonald had called him a liar and a coward and had tried to assault him physically as the House was about to prorogue. Now Smith could lean down "and hear the man who in 1878 denounced him in the most infamous manner in the same chamber labouring hard to show the company of which Mr. Smith is a leading member is composed of men of great wealth, enterprise, unblemished honour and undoubted integrity. Time certainly brings its revenge."

It was time, Stephen realized, for a reconciliation between his colleague and the Prime Minister, to whom the name of Smith had been anathema since that dark night in 1873 when the old fur trader had turned against his leader on the issue of the Pacific Scandal. Stephen felt he owed it to his cousin; Smith was not greatly interested in railways, did not know much about them, and took little part in the CPR's affairs; but in desperate times he was like a rock. When extra money was needed, Smith raised it. When he was asked to put up his personal fortune to back a loan, he signed it away without so much as raising one of his tangled eyebrows. And yet, beneath that hard shell, tempered in the service of the great fur company and in the hurly-burly of politics, there was an uncommon, child-like sensitivity. When Stephen prudently kept Smith's name off the original CPR board, Smith became petulant. He wanted the honour and glory of publicly participating in great national deeds. The disaffection of the Prime Minister clearly irked him; he wanted to make up. Now his grateful cousin handed him that prize. Macdonald's reception was kind and cordial and Stephen thanked him for it; the two, it was said, settled their differences over a bottle of good Scotch whiskey. Smith did not mention the particulars to Stephen; that was not his way, but "I know he *felt* a good deal and I know – without his saying it – that he is today a much happier man."

That was the only gleam of light in an otherwise gloomy month. The debate on the railway resolutions turned into a bitter and lengthy parliamentary wrangle, sparked by a daily diet of rumour, speculation, and minor sensation fed to the country through the Opposition press. Why were the CPR's directors haunting the lobbies of Parliament if they believed in the justice of their case? It was said they had a special room near the Commons chamber "where the speeches of the Government supporters are probably manufactured to order." Charles Brydges, who had once managed the Grand Trunk, was in Ottawa supposedly to feed information to the Liberals. So was Hickson, Brydges's successor, who protested officially on the GTR's behalf the expenditure of public funds "for competition against private 'enterprise.' " On February 12, Hickson published all of the correspondence between the Grand Trunk and the Government respecting advances to the CPR. According to the *Globe*, it "fell like a bomb-shell in the Ministerial ranks." There was a rumour that the Government was seeking a way to abandon the loan. The Quebec *bleus* were in open revolt. All these stories, opinions, and bits of gossip filtered through the crowded capital and out across the country.

One thing was clear: the CPR was in deep trouble. As the *Globe* had not failed to point out, the people of Canada at the time of the signing of the contract had been told that "this Company possessed vast resources; that its credit was unlimited; that they would never, never ask for any further aid from the country; that the people should rejoice because the amount of their burdens and obligations on account of this road were absolutely and immutably fixed." The news from Ottawa made the declarations of 1881 sound hollow indeed. "The thirty millions once gone will be gone for ever," mourned the *Globe*.

The tension grew. On February 15, *Les Canadiens*, regarded as the special organ of Sir Hector Langevin, Macdonald's Quebec lieutenant, virtually declared war on the Government. The position of the three Quebec cabinet ministers, it said, was critical in view of the railway's unjustifiable demands; they could save themselves only by conforming to the public sentiment in their province. As for Macdonald, he was in decline; he would probably be gone within a year along with Tupper and Tilley. There was a hint of a union between Blake and Langevin himself. On February 17, a mass meeting was held in Quebec City to protest the Government's railway policy.

On February 19 it was noted that not a single minister of the Crown was in his place; there was trouble within the Cabinet. Nobody quite knew what it was the Quebeckers wanted except that they wanted money – some favoured Ottawa's taking over the provincial debt; some wanted an increased federal subsidy on railway mileage within the province; some demanded a bonus for Quebec railways already constructed.

The Grand Trunk continued to work on its friends in the House. Stephen believed the company was trying to force the Government "to impose conditions in making the proposed loan, the effect of which would be to prevent investors ever interesting themselves in the property." He added: ". . . it is clear that we have nothing to look for from the G.T.R. but the bitterest and meanest kind of hostility. . . ." In London, John Rose underlined the obvious: the campaign was terrifying the British investors and even intimidating the banks.

By February 20, the excitement in the House was intense. Only two French Conservatives were present; there were rumours of Cabinet resignations; the Quebeckers were locked in a heated caucus. Forty-two of them, it was whispered, had bolted the party; only one of them had yet spoken in the debate. The Prime Minister himself looked drawn and pale, but determined. When a vote was finally taken at two-thirty the following morning on an Opposition amendment, the Quebec members surprised the Opposition by falling faithfully, if sullenly, into line. Macdonald had given in to the French and promised a retroactive subsidy to Quebec on the somewhat dubious premise that the line between Montreal and Ottawa, now owned by the CPR, was a work of national importance.

It was by no means over, however. It was noticed that Sir Charles Tupper was purposely absenting himself at every division, rising from his seat and retiring to the galleries. As the divisions on the Opposition amendments continued, Tupper's repeated retirements began to provoke jeers. Why this inexplicable conduct? The answer was that Tupper was serving in two roles; he was both Minister of Railways and High Commissioner to Great Britain – a dual position that prompted the *Globe* to call him "a sneak." The climax came when a writ was served on Tupper, claiming five thousand dollars for infringement of the Independence of Parliament Act, a law that barred any Member from holding another salaried job with the government. That was cleared up the following month by an amendment, which allowed Tupper to hold both positions with the provision that he be paid for only one of them. The Opposition immediately dubbed it "the Tupper Whitewashing Bill."

To a casual newspaper reader, it must have seemed as if the debate was tearing the country apart. Such was the level of acrimony within Parliament that the Speaker was forced, on February 23, to call a Minister of the Crown to order: it was John Henry Pope, the faithful friend of the railway, embroiled in a squabble with Blake and Mackenzie.

The following Tuesday the *Globe*, which never let up, summed up the state of the nation in an editorial that was only too accurate:

"To what a sad condition Sir John Macdonald and his colleagues have reduced the country! Quebec, separating herself from the other Provinces, compels the Government to yield to her demands. Manitoba talks secession, and is certainly discontented. The other Provinces, including Ontario, are dissatisfied, and the Indians – ill-treated, cheated and half-starved by the partisans whom Sir John tries to satisfy at their expense – threaten hostilities. Perhaps it is sufficient offset to all this that the Grand Old Schemer maintains his serenity, that Lieut. Governor Dewdney has received an increase of salary, that Sir C. Tupper is content, and that the C.P.R. Syndicate are satisfied." Only British Columbia, once "the spoilt child of Confederation," appeared to be at peace.

It was the first time, really, that Canadians had become aware of the new kind of nation they were tying together through the construction of the railway – an unwieldy pastiche of disparate communities, authored under varying circumstances, tugged this way and that by a variety of conflicting environmental and historical strains, and all now stirred into a ferment by the changes wrought through the coming of steel. Macdonald had been used to governing a tight, familiar community from the federal capital. Until the coming of the railway he had known most of it intimately – the people, the places, the problems. Suddenly he was faced with an entirely different political situation. Far out along the half-completed line of track, new political leaders whom he had never heard of in communities he had never visited were demanding a say in matters which he only partially understood. It is significant – and tragic – that, though the Prime Minister was also Superintendent General of Indian Affairs, he himself had never been to the North West or entered a Cree or Blackfoot tepee.

He had not taken much part in the loan debate; the public argument he left to Tupper. His own labours took place behind the scenes and in the party caucus. To the French Canadians he had offered conciliation: the terminus would be extended to Quebec City and there would be a subsidy for the provincial railways. To the remainder of his irresolute followers he offered a familiar threat: if they did not support him, Parliament would be dissolved and they would face the prospect of going to the country on the heels of a Government defeat in the House. Meanwhile, he told Stephen, "the CPR *must* become political and secure as much Parliamentary support as possible." The Grand Trunk was now in opposition to the Government and would use its considerable political influence to fight Macdonald. All railway appointments in Ontario and Quebec henceforth must be made on a political basis: "There are plenty of good men to be found in the ranks."

This was something that both Stephen and Van Horne had fought against – the almost universally accepted Canadian business practice of hiring a man on the basis of his party affiliation (not to mention his religion). Stephen considered himself above politics. As for Van Horne, he placed ability before any other consideration. Now, however, they were both forced to bow to the inevitable. "It has always been a matter of principle with me never to enquire into a man's politics in transacting business," the general manager wrote ruefully to the Hon. Peter Mitchell that spring, "but I must say that our past winter's experience at Ottawa has somewhat staggered me. . . ." Before the debate was over Macdonald was able to write to a political friend that Stephen had informed him that Van Horne "is fully aware now of the necessity of not appointing anybody along the line who has not been 'fully circumcized' – to use his own phrase."

Van Horne's conversion to politics is fascinating. At first he pretended to have nothing to do with it. Late in 1886 he wrote to Nicholas Flood Davin that "I think it is for the interest of all parties and for the whole country, that the Canadian Pacific railway should not become a political machine." He would not allow any employee to take part in elections, he said, under penalty of dismissal. Indeed, when Macdonald tried to persuade Stephen to let the popular Harry Abbott run federally as a Conservative in Algoma, Van Horne resisted it. Nonetheless, he could not escape politics. Just three months after his declaration to Davin he was secretly aiding the political cause of Arthur Wellington Ross, who had so strongly supported the CPR in the loan debate of 1884. Van Horne wrote to William Whyte, Egan's successor in Winnipeg, that "while of course we cannot afford to act openly in his case . . . we must neglect nothing to secure his election and vindication." He then went on to make some specific suggestions:

"If, on election day, the special trains which you will probably run do not fit in just as Mr. Ross would like, it will be necessary to run trains to suit him, letting it be understood that he has hired them and paid for them. Make regular bills for the service at a good round rate and send them to Ogden and I will attend to the matter when they get here. Make the rate at least one dollar per mile for the round trip. You had better say to such of the officers as you can fully trust in the matter, that it is a question to vindicate Mr. Ross in the course he took in favor of the Company at a time when it was a question of the salvation or the destruction of the whole enterprise but caution them to work with the greatest discression [*sic*] and if any man should divulge the fact that he has been spoken to on this subject by anyone connected with the Company he should be bounced without much ceremony."

From this point on, Van Horne appeared to plunge into politics, apparently throwing caution to the winds as far as discretion was concerned. His letters to the Prime Minister tell the story:

February 21, 1887: ". . . Our men are solid with very few exceptions and these can't be spared from duty [to vote]. . . . We will have sixty men at Brockville to vote for Woods and everyone who would vote otherwise will be far away."

February 26, 1887: "We are doing everything possible for Dawson. . . . I told the Goderich people they would be pretty certain not to get a branch of the C.P.R. if they sent M. C. Cameron back. . . ."

January 3, 1888: "I have given our people in the North West instructions to do everything possible to secure Macarthur's defeat. . . ."

February 28, 1891: "Our canvass is nearly complete and the CPR vote will be practically unanimous – not one in 100 even doubtful."

The CPR also secretly backed some newspapers, especially in Winnipeg, where opposition to the railway was the most vocal. Both the Winnipeg *Call* and the Manitoba *Free Press* were subsidized by the company though Van Horne went to great lengths to conceal that fact. "I feel sure we will be able to keep the 'Free Press' in hand," he wrote to Macdonald in January, 1889, "but that of course should be a profound secret as should our past dealings with the 'Call.' I wouldn't have that known for the world – it is something I am very ashamed of."

The CPR not only persuaded its men to vote for Conservative candidates (and made sure that the Liberal-minded employees did not get to the polls) but it also pumped large sums of money into Conservative election funds. In 1890, Stephen somewhat ruefully reminded the Prime Minister of that fact. Since 1882, he said, he had "personally and otherwise, through Pope *alone* spent over one million dollars" and added that in the previous election, at the moment when the Grand Trunk was being promised a subsidy for a line between Toronto and Ottawa, he was wiring J. H. Pope a remittance of two hundred thousand dollars to save the day. Macdonald's advice, given in the heat of the critical loan debate of 1884, that the CPR "*must* become political," certainly bore fruit.

For George Stephen, watching that debate from the galleries one day and hurrying back to Montreal to stave off creditors the next, the political arguments dragged on interminably. The president wanted another extension on his Bank of Montreal loan but, in spite of Tupper's intercession, the bank refused. On February 27, 1884, the CPR president wrote another desperate note to the Prime Minister:

"McIntyre goes down to N.Y. tonight to raise by way of a loan for a few days $300,000 which we think will keep us out of the sheriff's hands till Tuesday or Wednesday. I hope he will manage this, though he may not be able. In that case I do not know what we shall do. . . ."

The following day, the CPR relief bill passed the House. How soon could Macdonald get it through the Senate? Again Stephen implored the Prime Minister to move swiftly. It would have to be made law by Wednesday, when McIntyre's short-term loan (negotiated successfully in New York) fell due; and on Wednesday, dramatically, it was done. At the very last moment the company had been saved from ruin. That final denouement was reminiscent of one of the cheap, yellow-backed thrillers that Macdonald liked to read to clear his mind from the cares of the day.

Those cares were very real ones. The Prime Minister was in his seventieth year and was complaining more and more of being tired every night. When he had driven the original CPR contract through Parliament in 1881 he had believed his main worries to be at an end, at least as far as the railroad was concerned. Stephen, he thought, would take the responsibility off his back. But the railroad, which was wearing Stephen down too, was pressing upon Macdonald's stooped shoulders like a great weight, as it had a dozen years before in the days of Sir Hugh Allan and the first, abortive Canada Pacific Company. "He is the slave to the C.P.R. Syndicate, and dare not do anything they dislike," the *Globe* was declaring. This was not true, but he *was* a slave to the railway idea; until the last spike was driven, there would be no relief. Once again the papers were hinting that he would retire and accept for himself the job of high commissioner in London – he was suffering once again from an old nervous disease, inflammation of the stomach; but he could not retire while the railway remained unfinished. "It is only because I want to be *in* at the completion of the CPR that I remain where I am," he had told Stephen the previous November. ". . . I may say I groan for rest."

By the summer of 1884, Macdonald was worried that Stephen himself might give in. "I would leave the Govt tomorrow," he admitted to Tupper in July, "if it were not that I really think George Stephen would throw up the sponge if I did. He was so worried & sleepless that his wife became alarmed." The Prime Minister insisted that Stephen go off to the seaside for a vacation. A few days later, he himself came down to visit him, and for three days the two men on whom so much depended basked in the sun and talked about the railroad and the future of the country. Macdonald thought Stephen had "chirped up a good deal" as a result of his rest. He would need to, to survive the trials that lay ahead.

Chapter Seven

1

The price of building the line north of Lake Superior was appalling. One ninety-mile section ate up ten million dollars, and one single, memorable mile of track was laid through solid rock at a cost of seven hundred thousand. By the summer of 1884, John Ross had close to fifteen thousand men and four thousand horses working between Lake Nipissing and Thunder Bay; every month the company sent a pay car out along the line with $1,100,000 in wages. The awesome quantities of food consumed by the workmen flabbergasted old-time traders. Gilbert Spence, a squaw man working for the Hudson's Bay Company near Peninsula Harbour, "seemed somewhat upset" when Harry Armstrong, the engineer, told him that the navvies in the vicinity were consuming twelve tons of food a day and using four tons of tobacco a month. At that point the country was so primitive that Spence's wife had never seen a horse or cow or even heard of a telegraph line. But all this was about to change. As the Thunder Bay *Sentinel* (Michael Hagan's old paper) put it in June: "That which has been hitherto a howling wilderness untrodden by the foot of man, will in the course of a few months resound with the rush and bustle of railway life." The amount of explosives required to blast through the Precambrian cliffs was staggering. To save money and time, Van Horne had three dynamite factories built in the Caldwell-Jackfish area, each capable of turning out a ton a day. The bill for dynamite, nitro-glycerine, and black powder came to seven and a half million dollars.

The line hugged the armoured shores of Lake Superior, where construction was heavy but supply relatively easy. Van Horne had ordered three big lake boats built in Scotland, each with a burden of two thousand tons and a speed of fifteen knots. Two were delivered in 1883 but the third capsized in the middle of the Clyde during the launching ceremonies, drowning one hundred workmen. The others, on arrival at Montreal, were cut in two and reassembled on the upper lakes in time to do duty between Algoma Mills and Thunder Bay in the early summer of 1884. In this way freight could be shipped by water from Montreal to Port Arthur and by rail from Port Arthur to Winnipeg – a distance of 1,320 miles – in sixty-six hours. This was the start of the Canadian Pacific Steamship service, under Henry Beatty, whose son was to become president of the CPR at a time when it was able to advertise itself as "The World's Greatest Travel System."

The company, through its control of the Toronto, Grey and Bruce Railway, also had a port at Owen Sound on Georgian Bay. From there, supplies were shipped forward and distributed at points one hundred miles apart along the north shore of Superior. Rough portage roads had to be blasted between each delivery point to bring provisions to the tracklayers. Much of this transportation was done in winter when the lakes were frozen and the snow packed hard as concrete. It required three hundred dog teams, working incessantly, to keep the railroad supplied.

To Stephen, watching every penny in Montreal, the whole operation must have been disturbing. This was the section that almost everybody, Stephen included, had once said should not be built. This was the section that had caused Hill's disaffection – and Kennedy's. Now it was devouring the millions that the company had managed to pry loose from Ottawa. In May, John Ross was brought to a meeting in Montreal to see if the vast army of men, crawling over the sombre rock of the Shield, could be cut back. It was not really possible. To get his loan Stephen had promised that the job would be completed in five years instead of ten; they had to press on with it.

There was no thought of stopping for winter. Track must be laid in all seasons, in snow five feet deep and in temperatures that dropped to forty and fifty degrees below zero. Sometimes the drifts were so high that in the absence of an embankment it was impossible to locate the centre line of the roadbed, the markers themselves being hidden. At first the contractors sent gangs of men ahead with shovels to try to locate the route, but this wasted too much time and held up construction. In the end, the ties and rails were laid directly on top of the snow, the centre being determined by the perimeter of the clearing. Sometimes, when spring came, it was found that the rails had not been laid on the grade at all.

All sorts of short cuts were attempted. There was one rock cutting seven hundred feet long and thirty feet deep, about ten miles east of White River, on which the contractors were well behind. A delay of a month or more seemed inevitable until it was decided to lay the track directly on top of the rocky escarpment, to one side of the half-finished cut. It was not easy to get a locomotive over this barrier. The first that attempted to reach the top slipped back. The rails were sanded and the track smoothed out a little until finally a single car was pulled over safely. When the engine crews grew used to the hazard they were able to cross it easily with two cars. By the time the cut was finished, track had moved on thirty miles.

In the interests of greater speed, Van Horne imported a track-laying machine. This was really a train loaded with rails, ties, and track fasten-

271

ings. Shallow, open-top chutes, with rollers spaced along the bottom, were hung on either side, and the ties and rails were rolled along by manpower to the front of the device, where they were manhandled onto the grade. Joint bars and bolts accompanied the rails, which moved along on one side of the machine, while the track spikes, in long narrow boxes, together with the ties, were rolled along on the other side. (In later years the rollers were powered by machinery.)

The usual method of cut and fill was abandoned in the interests of saving money. It would have cost more than two dollars a cubic yard to cut through the hills and fill up the hollows with teams hauling the rock and gravel thus removed. Van Horne had decided at the outset to carry the line high, building timber trestles over the intervening valleys, gullies, and clefts, and filling them in later with materials brought in by rail rather than by the more expensive teams. The cost of these trestles was about one-tenth the cost of the filling operation.

To Alan Brown, a pioneer in Ontario railway development, "the rock cuttings were wonderful." Brown, who travelled the line shortly after it was completed, said he felt weak in his powers of description: "It is impossible to imagine any grander construction. . . . Everything is synonymous with strength. . . . The bridges, the tunnels, the rock cuttings almost make you aghast, and after seeing the tunnel work I was not surprised to think that the Hon. Alexander McKenzie at one time spoke of them as 'impassable barriers'. . . . What has been done in that part of the line proves that nothing is impassable or impossible in engineering and construction."

The blasting of the Shield was done, as always, at a considerable cost in men's lives. A stabler invention, dynamite, had largely replaced the more dangerous nitro-glycerine that had caused so many deaths on the Thunder Bay–Red River line. But even dynamite, carelessly handled, can bring tragedy. One man tried to pack a dynamite cartridge tighter by tamping it down with an iron crowbar; he was blown to pieces. A hotel proprietor from Port Arthur on a fishing expedition reached into the water and encountered a live discarded dynamite cap among the rocks; it blew his hand off. In another instance a man asleep in a cabin near McKay's Harbour was killed when a rock from a blast tore through the roof and crushed him.

Harry Armstrong, making camp in the summer of 1884, pulled a heap of green boughs over his fire to keep it going and discovered, to his horror, that they had concealed a half box of explosives, the side of which was already ablaze. His first impulse was to flee, but fearing that he would not get far enough before the box exploded, he picked it up, raced to the lake, flung it in, and escaped. John Macoun had a similar close call that same year while walking the line near Rossport with his son. He arrived at one cutting to discover that the men were heading for a shelter because of the impending blast. Macoun's fleeter-footed boy gained cover, but the botanist was caught on a plank crossing a stream and deluged by a shower of stones.

Macoun wrote that his journey down the unfinished line of the railway that year was "indescribable, as we were tormented by flies, and our path was not strewn with roses." Yet there was a kind of perverse grandeur about the country through which the steel was being driven. The dark, contorted rocks – riven at times as if by a giant cleaver and tinted each summer with the bright accents of lily, rose, and buttercup – and the sullen little lakes wearing their yellow garlands of spatterdock had a beauty that was peculiarly Canadian; it existed nowhere else in the world. Superintendent John Egan found himsef waxing poetical about it to the press: "The scenery is sublime in its very wildness; it is magnificently grand; God's own handiwork stands out boldly every furlong you proceed. The ravines and streams are numerous and all is picturesqueness itself. As to the character of the work, it will remain an everlasting monument to the builders."

To the men on the job – throats choked with the dust of shattered rocks, ears ringing with dynamite blasts, arms aching from swinging sledges or toting rails, skin smarting and itching from a hundred insect bites, nostrils assailed by a dozen stenches from horse manure to human sweat – the scenery was only a nuisance to be moved when it got in the way. The summers were bad enough but the winters were especially hard; in the flat light of December, the whole world took on a dun colour, and the cold wind blowing off the great frozen inland sea sliced through the thickest garments.

Even festive days had an air of gloom about them. One navvy described Christmas Day, 1883, at End of Track out of Port Arthur:

"Somehow Christmas Day fell flat. Here and there a group were playing cards for ten cent points. Some few melancholy-looking Englishmen were writing letters. I was smoking and cursing my stars for not being at home in the family group. I wondered how many men were in the same mood. Instead of having a good time, that Christmas afternoon was gloomy. Some of us turned it into Sunday and began darning socks and mitts. By and by a fair-haired boy from the old sod approached with a sigh: 'Where were you, old fellow, this time last year?'

" 'Never mind,' I answered, 'Where were you?' "

The boy replied that he was driving his girl behind a spanking team to see his family. Then he blurted out the rest of the story: "It was an old tale. Someone drew a herring across his track, a fit of jealousy, etc., etc., which ended in his leaving home, and now he was sitting in the gloom beside a rough coon like me dressed only as a bushman or a railroader can dress and pouring into my ears a long love story."

There was an interruption. A Finn tried to hang his shirt and socks on the navvy's peg by the stove. A bitter argument followed, and the Finn withdrew.

"The evening was as melancholy as the afternoon. Our room was almost deserted. . . . A few of us . . . lingered around the stove, and Ned, who had no heart to ramble, finished his love story. No friendly whiskey peddler came around that night. . . . We brewed some punch out of hot water, sugar and pain-killer, but still we were a gloomy party, and all was stale, flat and unprofitable.

"At last, Ned, just as we were going to bed, rummaged in his box and brought forth a small packet of photographs, mostly of the opposite sex. One was remarkably good looking – at least we thought so then, for many of us had not seen a woman for months. As the photograph went round, it fell at last into the hands of a grim old railroader. He had not seen a petticoat for ages, he said. We watched his face as he eyed the fair damsel, and it was a picture. We ceased talking and awaited his comment, which was long in coming. 'Here,' he said, handing back the photograph at arm's length and spitting a quid of pent-up tobacco to the other end of the room. 'Here, take it back.' He straightened himself and with an expression I shall not soon forget he said to himself, 'My God – but women are fine things.'

"I thought I heard the old sinner sigh as he went off to his bunk.

"Christmas Day was over and many of us lay awake later than usual that night and were not sorry to be at work on the dump the next day."

Because of the isolation, conditions in the camps north of Lake Superior were undoubtedly the worst of any along the line of the railway. The track-laying gangs on the prairies enjoyed the relative comfort of the boarding cars. Together with the mountain crews, they were supplied directly by rail from Winnipeg. But the navvies who drove steel across the Shield lived like men on another planet in gloomy and airless bunkhouses, which were little better than log dungeons.

The traditional Canadian bunkhouse was a low-walled building, sixty feet long and thirty feet wide, built of spruce logs chinked with moss and plastered with clay or lime. Into these hastily constructed, temporary structures, often badly situated and inadequately drained, between sixty and eighty men were crammed. They slept in verminous blankets on beds of hay in double-decker bunks that extended around three sides of the building. The atmosphere was oppressive and the ventilation meagre. The faint light that entered from two small windows at either gable was rarely sufficient for reading or writing. The nights were fetid with steam from the wet clothes that habitually hung over the central stove. In the summer, the air was rancid with smoke from burning straw and rags set afire to drive off the maddening hordes of mosquitoes and black flies. The board floor was generally filthy and the roof often leaked. Baths and plumbing were unknown; men washed and laundered or not as they wished. Medical attention was minimal.

Although Van Horne believed in feeding his men well, the conditions north of Superior, especially in the winter, made for a monotonous and unhealthy menu. The only real delicacy was freshly baked bread; otherwise the staples were salt pork, corned beef, molasses, beans, potatoes, oatmeal, and tea, varied by the occasional carcass of frozen beef. There was little if any fresh or green food to lighten this excessively coarse and heavy diet which, when it did not lead to actual scurvy, produced in most men a feeling of sluggishness and lassitude.

In spite of these circumstances it was not usually difficult to get cheap labour. Economic conditions were such that, in the summer of 1883, ordinary shovel men were being paid $1.50 for a ten-hour day along Lake Superior and in some instances as little as $1.00 a day, which was the going rate in the eastern cities. ("Mr. Ross is trying to reach the $1 without a strike," Van Horne informed John Egan in June. "It may take him some weeks to do it.") Any attempt at labour organization brought instant dismissal; Van Horne had a reputation as a union buster. In the rare instances when strikes did occur, they were quickly broken.

When Van Horne was told that James Ross had posted notices at Duluth offering two dollars a day for ordinary labour in the Rockies, he dispatched a crisp note pointing out that the offer had "caused great demoralization among John Ross's men on the Lake Superior section." Van Horne felt that labour was so plentiful the mountain superintendent ought to be able to keep the rate down to $1.75: the difference would mean a saving of between one and two million dollars for the CPR.

As the winter of 1883–84 approached, however, the company discovered that, in spite of considerable unemployment, prospective navvies were not keen to be locked up for an entire season on the Lake Superior line. Wages rose again to $1.75 a day for shovel men and $2.00 for rock

275

men. Board, however, was increased to four dollars a week; as Van Horne put it, "the difference in wages . . . will not amount to much on account of the difference in board but it looks much better to the men."

The cost of board was only one of several factors that made the pay seem better than it was. Men were paid only for the days on which they worked; if the weather, sickness, or construction delays kept them in the bunkhouses, they received no wages. Eight wet days a month – a not uncommon situation – could reduce a navvy's net pay, after board was deducted, to four dollars a week. In addition he had the cost of his clothing and gear, much of it purchased at company stores at inflated prices, and sometimes his meals and transportation en route to the site.

The company held him in thrall because the company controlled both the shelter and the transport. If he complained, he could be fired out of hand. If he wanted to quit, he had to continue to pay board until the company was ready to transport him to civilization; then he had to pay his fare out as well. Under such a system it was difficult for a man to accumulate much money.

Yet the conditions of the wage earners were far superior to those of the men who worked for themselves on small subcontracts, grading short strips of right of way with shovel and wheelbarrow, or clearing the line of brush and stumps for fixed prices, arrived at by hard bargaining. Such work might involve two men working as partners, or a group of a dozen or more. These subcontracts had one apparent advantage: the men were their own bosses. They could work or not as they wanted. The advantage was generally illusory; most of the self-employed men worked much longer hours under worse conditions than the wage earners, yet made no more money. The real beneficiaries were the larger contractors, who got the job done at minimal cost.

Living arrangements for those employed on small subcontracts were especially squalid. Harry Armstrong came upon one such camp of French Canadians that he thought was the worst he had ever seen. It was a log cabin without windows or floor. The only light was supplied by a sort of candle made from a tin cup filled with grease with a rag as a wick. The men ate at a long, hewn plank table. In one corner stood a cookstove. In another was a straw mattress occupied by an injured man waiting for a doctor. There was nothing in the way of a floor except black mud, kept thawed by the heat of the stove. To bridge the mud there were several scattered poles across which the men were supposed to pick their way; if they slipped off the poles they sank into the mud to their ankles. Armstrong had dropped in looking for something to eat. Dinner was

276

over, "but I was welcome to best they had, all the refuse from table had been scraped off after each meal which didn't improve the mud."

Many of the French Canadians lived this way, in traditional shanties built by themselves without chimneys – merely a hole in the roof from which the smoke of the "camboose" fire was supposed to escape. No wonder that a reporter, moving up the line, noted that "the men look badly smoke dried."

The camps of the Italian immigrants – who suffered badly from scurvy – were even worse. One group, which took a contract clearing the line, lived during the winter in a kind of root cellar, dome-shaped and without windows. To enter, they crawled through an opening in the bottom, and there they lay most of the time, playing cards, but going out into the snow when the sun shone to do a little work. Once a week they bought a sack of flour and a little tea on credit. By spring they had managed to clear half an acre; the proceeds may or may not have paid for the winter's provisions.

These hovels were in sharp contrast to the quarters of the major contractors, who lived in relative luxury. One of them, James Winston, in the Nepigon area, had a home complete with Brussels carpet and a grand piano. Another, one Erickson, near Port Caldwell, had his own cow and was able to dispense milk punches to his guests on festive occasions. The contractors and the senior engineers enjoyed another privilege: they had their wives and children with them and so escaped the aching loneliness that settled like a pall over the men in the bunkhouses.

Under such conditions the navvies turned inevitably to alcohol. By special act, the government had banned the sale of liquor along the line of the railway as far as the Manitoba border. Here as everywhere else in Canada, government agents fought a running battle with whiskey peddlers. In May, 1881, the Thunder Bay *Sentinel* estimated that no fewer than eight hundred gallons of spirits were sold every month to the twenty-five hundred people living between Whitemouth River and Lake Wabigoon. The price was fifteen dollars a gallon. (In Toronto a gallon of whiskey sold for as little as fifty cents.) The methods used to deceive the police were as ingenious as those employed on the prairies and led to much greater lawlessness.

"If the slightest laxity should be shown in the enforcement of the law, there would be no possibility of living among these men," a CPR official declared in May, 1884. The North West Mounted Police did not patrol the Ontario section of the line; the job was left to the local constabulary, some of whom were plainly corrupt. A regular count made by the com-

277

pany revealed that there were five thousand revolvers and three hundred shotguns and rifles, together with the same number of dirks and bowie knives, in the possession of railroad workers on the Lake Superior line. "With so many men of such a class and so generally armed, it is impossible to say what crimes would be committed if the whiskey peddlers were not rigidly repressed. . . ."

The peddlers tried every possible scheme to stay in business, even going to the length of getting railway foremen drunk and bribing them with cheap liquor to act as salesmen. Another method derived from the American frontier tradition of seizing control of the local police force and thus controlling the town through a "vigilante committee." Both Peninsula Harbour (described by one visitor as "the worst place in the world") and Michipicoten were for several months under the control of gangs of desperadoes who terrorized the citizens and held a tight rein on the whiskey trade, keeping out all competition and running the community for their own personal profit.

In Michipicoten, the vigilante gang that ran the town was actually headed by the former police chief, Charles E. Wallace, one of whose henchmen, Harry Cleland, was an escaped convict from Jackson, Michigan. In October, 1884, the gang attempted to shoot the local magistrate, whose life had been frequently threatened. He took refuge in the construction office, ducking bullets that were fired directly through the walls. A force of Toronto police was called to the scene to restore order. They arrived on October 23 and were met at the docks by a rowdy crowd that would give them no information as to the identity of the culprits. Some persons among the throng on the dock were members of the gang; the others were too terrified to talk, believing that the police would fail in their mission and that on their departure informants would be punished.

The police made their headquarters in a local boarding house, and, after the mandatory four o'clock tea, set out to apprehend the instigators of the attack on the magistrate. By nightfall they had seven prisoners in custody. As a result, the boarding house became the target of hidden riflemen who pumped a fusillade of bullets into it, grazing the arm of the cook and narrowly missing one of the boarders. When the police emerged from the building, revolvers drawn, the unseen attackers departed. It was said that forty men armed with repeating rifles were on their way to rescue the prisoners. The police maintained an all-night vigil but there was no further trouble.

Meanwhile, about thirty prostitutes, driven out of Peninsula Harbour by Magistrate Frank Moberly, the redoubtable brother of Walter Moberly,

278

the British Columbia surveyor, had descended on Michipicoten, seeking refuge. They had no sooner debarked from the steamer than they learned that the police were in control. The gaudy assembly wheeled about and re-embarked for another destination.

The police destroyed one hundred and twenty gallons of rye whiskey, captured and dismantled a sailboat used in the illicit trade, and laid plans to capture the four ringleaders of the terrorist gang, including the ex-police chief, Charles Wallace. After some careful undercover work they descended upon a nearby Indian village where the culprits were supposed to be hiding. The police flushed out the wanted men, but Wallace and his friends were too fast for them. A chase ensued in which the hoodlums, apparently aided by both the Indians and the townspeople, easily evaded their pursuers.

No sooner had the big city constabulary departed the following day with their prisoners than Wallace and his three henchmen emerged from the woods and instituted a new reign of terror. Wallace, "in true bandit style," was carrying four heavy revolvers and a bowie knife in his belt and a Winchester repeating rifle on his shoulder. The four finally boarded the steamer *Steinhoff* and proceeded to pump bullets into the crowd on the dock before departing for Sault Ste Marie. Their target was actually the CPR ticket office and, more specifically, the railway's agent, Alec Macdonald, who had taken refuge within it. Before the steamer departed Wallace and his friends had managed to riddle the building with a hundred bullets without, fortunately, scratching their quarry.

Frank Moberly arrived shortly afterwards with a posse and cleaned up the town, but Wallace himself and his partners were not captured until the following February, after a gunfight in the snow in which one of the arresting constables was severely wounded. Wallace was sentenced to eighteen months in prison. By the time he was released, the railway was completed and the days of the whiskey peddlers were over forever.

2

Between Thunder Bay and Lake Nipissing there was no single continuous line of track. The contractors, supplied by boat, were strung out in sections of varying length, depending on the terrain; indeed, some contracts covered country so difficult that only a mile was let at a time. For administrative purposes, the Lake Superior line was divided into two sections: the difficult section led east from Fort William to meet the easier section,

Treasure in the rocks

which ran west from Lake Nipissing, the point at which the Canada Central, out of Ottawa, joined the CPR proper.

In the summer of 1882, a young Scot of eighteen named John McIntyre Ferguson arrived on Nipissing's shore. Ferguson was the nephew of Duncan McIntyre, president of the Canada Central and vice-president of the Canadian Pacific – an uncle who knew exactly where the future railway was going to be located. The prescient nephew purchased 288 acres of land at a dollar an acre and laid out a townsite in the unbroken forest. He also built the first house in the region and, in ordering nails, asked the supplier to ship them to "the north bay of Lake Nipissing." Thus did the settlement unwittingly acquire a name. By 1884, when the CPR established its "company row," North Bay had become a thriving community. Ferguson went on to become the wealthiest man in town and, after North Bay was incorporated, its mayor for four successive terms.

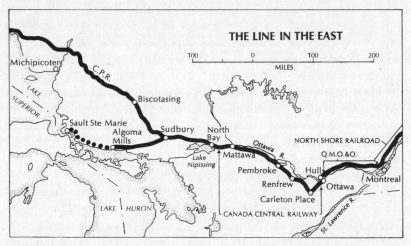

North Bay was totally the creation of the railway. Before its first buildings were erected, the main institutions were located in railway cars shunted onto sidings. The early church services were held in these cars and the custom continued for some time until the first church was constructed in 1884. The preacher, an imperturbable giant of a man named Silas Huntington (whose son Stewart founded the town's first newspaper), used an empty barrel, up-ended, as a pulpit and brooked no opposition from the rougher elements in his congregation. When two muscular navvies took exception to one of his sermons, Huntington quit his makeshift pulpit and started down towards them, preaching as he went. As he drew opposite the intruders he took one in each hand and dropped them

280

out the door without pausing for breath or halting the flow of his sermon.

Such *savoir-faire* was a Huntington trademark. There was another occasion during a service when his box-car church was parked on a siding on a hillside. Someone accidentally let the brake off and as Huntington was in the middle of his sermon, the car gave a jerk and began slowly, and then with gathering speed, to roll downhill. The car ran down to the main line and off to the edge of the new town while Huntington, without so much as a raised eyebrow, continued to preach. When he had finished, the congregation sang the doxology and walked back without comment.

The land between North Bay and Lake Superior was generally considered to be worthless wilderness. For years, the politicians who opposed an all-Canadian railway had pointed to the bleak rocks and stunted trees of the Shield country and asked why any sane man would want to run a line of steel through such a sullen land. The rails moving westward from North Bay cut through a barren realm, denuded by forest fires and devoid of all colour save the occasional sombre russet and ochre, which stained the rocks and glinted up through the roots of the dried grasses on the hillsides. These were the oxides of nickel and copper and the sulfides of copper and iron, but it needed a trained eye to detect the signs of mineral treasure that lay concealed beneath the charred forest floor.

By the end of 1882, the rails of the Canada Central, following the old voyageurs' route up the Ottawa and Mattawa rivers from Pembroke, had crossed the height of land and reached Lake Nipissing. By the end of 1883 the first hundred miles of the connecting CPR were completed. Early that year the crudest of tote roads, all stumps and mud, had reached the spot where Sudbury stands today. Here, as much by accident as by design, a temporary construction camp was established. It was entirely a company town: every boarding house, home, and store was built, owned, and operated by the CPR in order to keep the whiskey peddlers at bay. Even the post office was on company land and the company's storekeeper, Stephen Fournier (who was to become Sudbury's first mayor), acted as postmaster. Outside the town, private merchants hovered about, hawking their goods from packs on their backs. It was not until 1884 that the most enterprising of them, a firm-jawed peddler named John Frawley, discovered that the CPR did not own all the land after all; the Jesuit fathers had been on the spot for more than a decade and held title to adjacent property. Frawley leased a lot from the religious order for three dollars a month, opened a gents' furnishing store in a tent, and broke the company's monopoly. By then a mining rush was in full swing and Sudbury was on its way to becoming a permanent community.

The first men to examine the yellow-bronze rocks in the hills around the community made little or nothing from their discoveries. The earliest to take heed of the mineral deposits was probably Tom Flanagan, a CPR blacksmith, who picked up a piece of ore along the right of way about three miles out of town and thought (wrongly) that he had found gold. He did not realize that he was standing not only on a copper mine but also on the largest nickel deposit in the world. Flanagan did not pursue his interest, but John Loughrin, who had a contract for cutting railroad ties, was intrigued by the formations and brought in three friends, Thomas and William Murray and Harry Abbott. In February, 1884, they staked the land on what became the future Murray Mine of the International Nickel Company. It subsequently produced ore worth millions, but not for the original discoverers.

Other company employees became millionaires. One was a gaunt Hertfordshire man named Charles Francis Crean. Crean, who had been working on boats along the upper Ottawa carrying provisions to the construction camps, arrived on the first work train into Sudbury in November, 1883. At that time the settlement straggling along the tote road had yet to be surveyed; buildings were being thrown together and laid out with no thought for the future. The first hospital, built of logs by the CPR construction crews, turned out to be in the middle of what was later the junction of Lorne and Elm streets. The mud was so bad that a boy actually drowned in a hole in the road opposite the American Hotel. Crean, on his arrival, walked into the company store and noticed a huge yellow nugget being used as a paperweight by the clerk behind the counter. The clerk said the ore was probably iron pyrites – fool's gold – but he let Crean have a piece of it. Crean sent it to a chemist friend in Toronto who told him it was an excellent sample of copper. In May, 1884, Crean applied for a mining claim and staked what was to become famous as the Elsie Mine.

A month later, the observant Crean spotted some copper ore in the ballast along the tracks of the Sault Ste Marie branch of the railroad. He checked back carefully to find where the material had come from and was able to stake the property on which another rich mine – the Worthington – was established. Later he discovered three other valuable properties, all of them steady producers for years.

A week after Crean staked his first claim, a timber prospector named Rinaldo McConnell staked some further property which was to become the nucleus of the Canadian Copper Company's Sudbury operation – the forerunner of the International Nickel Company. (It was copper, of

282

course, that attracted the mining interests; nickel had few uses at the time.) Another prospective millionaire that year was a railway construction timekeeper named Thomas Frood, a one-time druggist and schoolteacher from southwestern Ontario who acted on a trapper's hunch and discovered the property that became the Frood Mine, perhaps the most famous of all.

For every fortune made at Sudbury there were a dozen lost. Well before the staking rush – in the fall of 1883 – Andrew McNaughton, the first magistrate of the new settlement, arrived with the CPR construction crew to maintain the law and keep the camp free of liquor. McNaughton went for a stroll in the hills and became lost in a heavy fog. The search party that found him also picked up some copper-stained rocks. The newly arrived physician, Dr. William H. Howey, sent some of those rocks to Alfred Selwyn, the director of the Geological Survey of Canada and perhaps the ranking expert in the nation on the subject of mineral deposits. Selwyn pronounced the samples worthless and Howey threw them away. Later it developed that McNaughton had been standing on the site of the Murray Mine when his searchers found him. From then on, Howey had an understandable contempt for geological experts.

But then the story of northern Ontario mining is the story of happenstance, accident, and sheer blind luck. Sudbury itself was an accident. The line was supposed to be located south of Lost Lake, but the locating engineer, William Allen Ramsay, took it upon himself to run it north, an act which caused his boss, James Worthington, to rename the body of water Lake Ramsay (later spelled "Ramsey"). Worthington himself named the town Sudbury Junction after his wife's birthplace in England. He had not intended to use such an unimportant spot on the map to honour his spouse – for Sudbury at the time was seen as a transitory community. However, the station up the line that was expected to be the real centre of the area had been named for Magistrate McNaughton, and Worthington had to settle for the lesser community. He was not the only man to underestimate the resources of the Canadian Shield. Long before, when John A. Macdonald had talked of running a line of steel through those ebony scarps, Alexander Mackenzie, the Leader of the Opposition, had cried out that that was "one of the most foolish things that could be imagined." Edward Blake had seconded the comment, almost in the same words. Right up until the moment of Sudbury's founding, some members of Macdonald's cabinet, not to mention a couple of the CPR's own directors, were opposed to such madness. It was only when the land began to yield up its treasure that the fuss about the all-Canadian line was stilled.

3

In the Rockies, that summer of 1884, the weather was wet and miserable. The naked peaks were masked by dismal clouds and the numbing rain that poured down ceaselessly turned the milky Kicking Horse into a torrent that spread itself across the Columbia flats, cutting the tote road so badly that it was almost – but not quite – impossible for the teams to struggle through. Severe frosts persisted until late June. Snow swept the upper slopes of the mountains. In the shacks that did duty as offices near the summit, roaring fires had to be maintained well into the early summer.

The rails had sped out of Calgary the previous fall along the easy incline of the Bow Valley at the same rapid rate that had taken them across the plains. Indeed, another record had been set. The CPR gangs set out to better the achievement of the Northern Pacific, one of whose track-laying teams had captured the short-distance record by laying six hundred feet of track in six and a half minutes. Not far from Bow Gap, where the roadbed headed for the Kicking Horse Pass, the Canadians managed to lay six hundred feet in four minutes and forty-five seconds. It was a considerable feat, since the Northern Pacific had achieved its result by sponsoring a race between two gangs working against each other. On the Canadian line, as one onlooker noted, "it was accomplished in cold blood and without the least preparation except putting more than the ordinary quantity of rails on the car."

Once the pass was entered and the incline grew steeper, the speed of track-laying slowed down. The rails crept to within a few miles of the summit and came to a halt. The track crews were laid off and thousands of men quit the mountains, leaving behind a skeleton force of five hundred whose job was to cut timber for the coming season. They produced half a million railroad ties and twenty thousand cords of fuel for the locomotives, coal being far too expensive to haul to such heights.

For all of the summer of 1884, the construction headquarters of the Mountain Division of the CPR remained near the summit where the end of track stood the previous fall. The community that sprang up was at first known as Holt City, after Tim Holt, a veteran of the Zulu wars who ran the company store, and whose brother, Herbert, was one of the major contractors on the division. Later on it acquired the name of Laggan; today it is known as Lake Louise station.

Holt City, surrounded by acres of lodgepole pine, sat on the banks of the Bow – the beautiful Bow, "swift and blue, and heavenly and crystal, born of the mountains and fresh from snowfield and glacier." It was to

284

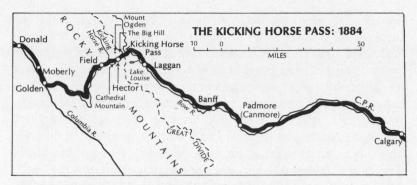

THE KICKING HORSE PASS: 1884

this little camp, raucous with the pandemonium of squeaking fiddles, that the pay car came on its monthly rounds; and it was here that men crowded in on payday to squander their earnings at the three hotels, or at the poker, faro, and three-card monte tables, or at the surreptitious little cabins along the route that did duty as blind pigs.

James Ross had announced that he would need twelve thousand men in the mountains in the summer of 1884. By June they were pouring in. Every train brought several carloads of navvies who had come across the plains from Winnipeg. Turner Bone, who worked for Herbert Holt that summer, recalled that the scene "might well have been compared to a gathering of the clans in response to the call of the fiery cross; all keyed up and ready to go." They tumbled off the cars and trudged up the right of way to the construction camps, in a land hitherto seen by only a handful of men, singing the song of the construction men in the mountains:

> *For some of us are bums, for whom work has no charms,*
> *And some of us are farmers, a-working for our farms,*
> *But all are jolly fellows, who come from near and far,*
> *To work up in the Rockies on the* C.P.R.

One of them, a young labourer named George Van Buskirk, wrote to his mother in the East, shortly after his arrival on June 17, that "the scenery out here for wildness & grandeur is well worth what I have gone through." It was a considerable tribute to the future tourist attractions of the mountains, for Van Buskirk had gone through a good many trials in the previous weeks. He had arrived in Calgary absolutely penniless, "in a foreign land, 4,000 miles away from home and no money and not a chance to get any." By pawning his baggage and selling his bridle and saddle he finally managed to reach Holt City with four dollars in his pocket. It was not hard to find work. "A rough looking labour man" instantly offered him a job; he was about to accept when a second man appeared and said he

285

wanted some men to shovel. Van Buskirk liked his looks better and accepted. He was told to throw his baggage onto a cart and follow behind it. He hiked ten miles "over the hardest road it was ever my luck to see – nothing but rocks and mud up to my knees" and, about one o'clock that afternoon, "pretty well fagged out," was put to work erecting tents and chopping down foot-thick trees for shanties. In spite of the scenery, young Van Buskirk was pretty discouraged by evening: "Taking it all and all the North West is not what it is cracked up to be," he informed his mother. "Some of these chaps who write in the papers ought to be shot, for the country although a fine one is terribly overrated & the reports one sees mislead entirely." A fortnight later he had cheered up considerably: "I am very well with the exception that my blood is very coarse from eating strong food. Too much beans."

The British novelist Morley Roberts, who arrived that summer, watched the tenderfeet from the cities heading off up the line to the various camps – a miscellaneous throng of about a hundred, loaded down with blankets and valises – and noted that many had never worked in the open air at all. Some indeed had not done a hard day's work in their lives:

"It was quite pitiful to see some little fellow, hardly more than a boy, who had hitherto had his lines cast in pleasant places, bearing the burden of two valises or portmanteaus, doubtless filled with good store of clothes made by his mother and sisters, while the sweat rolled off him as he tramped along bent nearly double. Perhaps next to him there would be some huge, raw-boned labourer whose belongings were tied up in a red handkerchief and suspended from a stick."

Behind the labourers came the first tourists, some of them travelling all the way from Winnipeg to gaze upon the wonders of the mountain scenery, which the construction of the railway had suddenly disclosed. "Every week now sees excursions, walks, horseback rides, picnics, mountains scaled, scenery explored, and a dance or two." The government's engineer-in-chief, Collingwood Schreiber, was ecstatic, as all were, about the scenery: it "far surpasses the scenery upon the other transcontinental lines, if I mistake not it will be a great resort for tourists and madmen who like climbing mountains at the risk of breaking their necks."

Some of that scenery was fast disappearing under the human onslaught. "Round me," wrote Morley Roberts, "I saw the primæval forest torn down, cut and hewed and hacked, pine and cedar and hemlock. Here and there lay piles of ties, and near them, closely stacked, thousands of rails. The brute power of man's organised civilisation had fought with Nature and had for the time vanquished her. Here lay the trophies of the battle."

The mountainsides that year were ablaze with forest fires started by the construction workers. At times the entire pass, from the summit to the Columbia and westward, seemed to be aflame. "The mountainsides bear testimony to the destructive tendencies of irregenerate [*sic*] man," the Grand Trunk's Sir Henry Tyler wrote to his wife from End of Track the following year. Tyler, making a careful inspection of the rival line, was horrified to learn that some of the fires had been purposely ignited in his honour. "Several railway men had argued that it would be right to celebrate our visit by means of a presidential blaze!"

The most distinguished tourists that summer were the members of the British Association for the Advancement of Science, who held their annual meeting in Canada in 1884. The association, including the future Lord Kelvin, then plain William Thompson, went to End of Track and beyond, where they almost lost Alfred Selwyn, the distinguished geologist. Selwyn was crossing a temporary wooden scaffold over a ravine when an avalanche thundered down, tearing the bridge apart. The geologist was carried a considerable distance, caught in a mass of broken and dislocated timbers, but emerged unhurt.

Avalanches were frequent in the Rockies that season, many of them set in motion by the continual blasting that went on along the line. Everyone who witnessed a Rocky Mountain avalanche was awestruck. "They resembled exactly a large mow taken down with a scythe in the fields," Alexander Mackenzie wrote to his daughter. (The former Liberal Prime Minister was on a tour of the North West as a guest of the railway and, as a result, was to change his mind about the barrenness of prairie land.) "If one of these avalanches should descend on the road, no protection man could find would prevent a complete wreck of road, bridge or train." Sam Steele wrote that "glaciers, which had never left their rocky beds . . . broke away and came crashing down, cutting pathways from a quarter to half a mile wide through the forest below." Steele saw one avalanche descend five thousand feet from a summit with such velocity that it tore directly across a valley and up the opposite side for eight hundred feet.

Under such conditions, the work went on at a killing pace from dawn to dusk. On one contract the workmen averaged more than ten hours of labour a day every day for a month. Some of them had thirteen or fourteen hours a day to their credit. If rain made work impossible, they caught up in sunny weather. Sometimes they even worked by moonlight.

As always, a good portion of many men's wages was spent on illegal liquor. Gamblers, whiskey peddlers, and criminals of all sorts were filtering into the mountains from the Northern Pacific's territory south of the border and establishing their dens on every creek and gully along the right of way.

In British Columbia the Mounted Police jurisdiction was limited to the twenty-mile belt along the surveyed line of the railway, within whose confines it was forbidden to sell (but not to possess) liquor. This belt had been proclaimed by the federal government under an act for the preservation of peace on public works. Bartenders could be fined for the first and second offences and imprisoned for a third, but they were able to circumvent the intent of the law by transferring the goodwill of their establishment to someone else and thus continue in business. The temperance belt was so narrow that it was possible for thirsty navvies to walk ten miles to the provincial jurisdiction and spend all their wages on a single spree. The obstacle here was the government of British Columbia, which did not want to be deprived of the tax money the liquor sales provided. Its practice was to give anybody a licence who asked for one within the belt and outside of it. A frustrated Sam Steele, watching construction grinding to a halt as the result of drunkenness, urged Ottawa to increase the width of the railway belt to forty miles and to allow magistrates to imprison whiskey peddlers on the second offence. The federal government complied and construction resumed its normal pace. The wholesale and retail stores had to move back twenty miles from the railway and, as Steele remarked, the navvies found a twenty-mile walk too long for the sake of a spree.

The railway workers lived in every kind of accommodation along the line – in tents of all shapes and sizes, in box cars rolled onto sidings, in log huts and in mud huts, in shanties fashioned out of rough planks, and in vast marquees with hand-hewn log floors, log walls, and a box stove in the centre. Over the whole hung the familiar pungency of the bunk-house, an incense almost indescribable but compounded of unwashed bodies, strong tobacco, steaming wool, cedar logs, and mattress straw. Such communities had an aura of semi-permanence, unlike the portable towns of the prairies; the track did not move mile by mile or even yard by yard. On some days it seemed to creep along inch by inch as the contractors attacked the granite bulwarks with tons of dynamite and hordes of workmen.

The work was often as dangerous as it was back-breaking. Near one of several tunnels along the Kicking Horse the cut in the hill was so deep that the men worked in three tiers. At the very top, the route was being cut through gravel; in the centre the gravel gave way to blue clay; below the clay was hard rock. The men on the lowest tier, working just above the layer of rock (which would have to be dynamited), attacked the clay

288

from beneath. Twenty to thirty feet above them a second gang worked, chopping out the gravel and wheeling it away in barrows. The high gang removed the top layer of sand and stumps. Those at the very top worked in comparative safety; the middle gang was in some peril because they had to watch out for rocks that might topple down on them; but the lowest gang was in constant danger – from both benches above them came a continual shower of rocks. Morley Roberts, who worked on the lowest tier, reported that he never felt safe for a single moment. Every sixty seconds or so, all day long, somebody above would cry: "Look out below!" or "Stand from under!" and a heavy stone or boulder would come thundering down the slope, scattering the men on both sides. On his third day on the job a foot-thick rock weighing about eighty pounds struck him above the knee and put him out of action for five days. It was a welcome respite; the literate vagabond whiled away his convalescence with a copy of Thomas Carlyle's *Sartor Resartus*.

The *Globe*, always waspish where the CPR was concerned, wrote that summer that it would be a miracle if the road reached Kamloops before 1886; but Van Horne had a schedule and he meant to keep to it. He had told Stephen that the job could be completed by the end of 1885; Stephen had translated that advice into a pledge to the government. They could not afford to let the work lag. Fortunately, they had some remarkable generals at the head of that mountain army. The contractors in the Rockies included men whose names would, in the ensuing years, come close to being household words in Canada. The CPR was a spawning ground for an amazing generation of entrepreneurial talent whose influence became world wide.

They sprang from varied backgrounds, these future captains of industry. The 36-year-old James Ross, a short, compact man, thickly bearded and good humoured, was the son of a Tyneside shipowner and had had engineering experience on both sides of the ocean. Van Horne had enormous confidence in him. When the job was done the general manager went so far as to write personally an account of Ross's work and send it to the *Manitoban*. In it he said that he regarded Ross as one of the ablest builders on the continent, probably unequalled by any other man. He asked that he be quoted on the matter because "I am particularly anxious in view of some criticisms upon him to make my opinions public." Ross became one of the most successful financiers in Canada, a kind of capitalist's capitalist – a coal and steel baron, a tramway king, a yachtsman, commodore, and philanthropist.

Herbert Samuel Holt, a huge Irishman who walked with a rolling gait and spoke as little as possible to anyone, went on to become the richest man in Canadian history. Holt hated publicity and had no intimates: in the twenties and thirties he became a mystery man who controlled an unprecedented empire of three hundred companies on four continents – a kind of Canadian Basil Zaharoff. Knighted in World War I for planning the railway system for the army in France, he was, in the words of the *Daily Express* of London, "the business brain of Canada . . . certainly a more important figure in the Canadian world than the prime minister is in that of Britain."

Two other mountain contractors, whose names were to become familiar after the turn of the century, were William Mackenzie and Donald Mann. Mackenzie, who held several bridging contracts along the Kicking Horse, had begun his career as a school-teacher in Kirkfield, Ontario. His future partner, Mann, was a powerful figure with dark brooding eyes and arms like hams, capable of picking up a man and holding him at arm's length, feet off the ground. He had struggled up the hard way, starting out with an axe in his hand, cutting ties in the tamarack swamps of Manitoba. (He had once waded all night through the deep snow with two hundred pounds of flour and a side of pork on his back to bring aid to a starving camp.) Mackenzie and Mann became railway promoters, capping a long career by constructing the Canadian Northern, a transcontinental line designed to rival the Canadian Pacific, but one which went gloriously bankrupt at considerable expense to the Canadian taxpayer.

There was another future tycoon working along the line that year but in a more humble capacity, "a young raw Highland Scotch boy" from New Westminster named Jack Stewart. Young Stewart, shy but eager, was low man on the staff of John F. Stevens, assistant locating engineer for the mountain division. He learned the railway business well. Thanks to his CPR experience he came out of World War I a major-general and went on to become the largest contractor in the West, helping to build another ill-fated transcontinental railroad, the Grand Trunk Pacific, and founding, for the Liberal Party of British Columbia, a lively newspaper, the Vancouver *Sun*.

After the turn of the century these men spearheaded the great wave of Canadian "utility imperialism" (as one historian has called it) – building power plants, railways, and streetcar lines all over Latin America and two more transcontinental railways in Canada. William Mackenzie helped to launch in São Paulo the gigantic Brazilian Traction corporation, a firm that was to grow almost as big as the CPR itself. Herbert Holt built a railway in Peru, financed a pipeline across Colombia, and controlled banks in the West Indies. James Ross became president of the vast Mexican Light, Heat and Power Company. (Van Horne, in his turn, went on to build a railway across Cuba.) In the 1920's and 1930's these men also virtually controlled the private utilities and transportation systems of Canada – an unexpected by-product of the launching of the CPR. It can be argued, however, that their skills belonged to another era. While the Canadians were absorbed with railways and power plants, the same generation of American entrepreneurs was building automobiles and airplanes.

The nature of the mountain environment conspired to produce men of strong will and ingenuity. The contractors were forced to improvise to push the line through on time. Since it was impossible to take heavy drills down the dizzy inclines of the Kicking Horse, all blasting holes had to be punched out by hand. One man held a hand drill in position while four more swung sledges in rhythm to produce what was known as a coyote hole. This was loaded with powder and lit by a long fuse. The resultant explosion sometimes hurled heavy boulders a hundred yards into the foaming river. The men hid behind trees or took cover in shanties, returning to clear away the debris – hammering the larger rocks into smaller pieces and shovelling them into carts and barrows. In spite of such primitive techniques, Ross's work force managed to move a million and a half cubic yards of earth and rock and, in addition, drill half a mile of tunnels during the 1884 season.

Van Horne had decreed that all bridges – pile, trestle, and truss – be made of timber rather than of iron and masonry, in order to save money. Even without the cost factor, the necessity of pushing the line through on time would have dictated this swifter method of construction. There was no way in which iron girders or quarried stone could be transported down the gorge of the Kicking Horse until the rails were laid. By using timbers cut on the spot the bridging crews could keep ahead of the track gangs.

It was a considerable feat to cross an unfinished bridge, as hundreds of men were forced to do. Along the cross-pieces lay stringers, placed on edge and at varying distances, some close together and some so far apart that a man could scarcely leap from one to the next. These were lying loose, unbolted and trembling with every movement. Some fifty feet below the water could be seen swirling around the sharp rocks. If a man fell, nothing could save him, especially if he was carrying a load, for there was nothing below to seize hold of save the great timbers of the under-structure.

In order to get around the face of some of the bluffs without drilling tunnels or making expensive cuts, the railway resorted to "grasshopper trestles," so called because the outer posts extended far down into the gorges, standing in steps cut in the rock, while the inner posts, like a grasshopper's forelegs, were very short and sometimes non-existent. Later on these trestles were replaced by walls of masonry, built by Scottish stonemasons.

On its queasy descent from the Great Divide, the road switched back and forth across the Kicking Horse by truss and trestle eight times. Before the right of way could be cleared, a tote road had to be constructed to replace the dangerous surveyors' trail cut into the cliffside. This in itself was a major construction job. The tote road ran a few feet above the bed of the railway, winding in and out along the face of a slope that topped the almost sheer cliffs above the river. In one place it was notched right into the cliff above the stream bed. It was almost as perilous as the Golden Stairs, which had scared the wits out of Grant and Fleming the summer before; often it was that same pack trail, slightly widened. On their first journey down the hazardous thoroughfare, men involuntarily hugged the upper side and uttered a sigh of relief when the journey was over. Herbert Holt was almost killed on the tote road in 1884 when his horse slipped on a stone and fell over the edge of a perpendicular cliff seventy feet above the river. The future mystery man had a miraculous escape; he plunged twenty-eight feet, turned a complete somersault, and landed on his stomach on the trunk of a dead tree caught in the canyon's wall. Had the tree not been present to break his fall, the financial history of the nation in the early twentieth century would have been considerably altered.

The choice of the Kicking Horse Pass had presented the CPR with a considerable dilemma. The river drops eleven hundred feet in the first three and a half miles of its headlong race down the western slopes of the Rockies. Under the terms of its contract with the government, the CPR was pledged to a maximum gradient of 2.2 per cent, or about 116 feet to a mile. Major Rogers had so located the line down from the summit of the mountains to the Columbia River by way of the gorge cut by the Kicking Horse. But to build the line as Rogers had located it, the railway would have been forced to cross several extensive boulder slides, all of them highly unstable, and to pass under an immense, unpredictable glacier. In addition, it would have been necessary to drill a tunnel fourteen hundred feet long through solid rock. That, the engineers predicted, would delay the railway for almost another year. Sandford Fleming suggested to Van

Horne that the company build a temporary line dropping quickly down from the summit into the comparative level of the valley of the Kicking Horse by means of a grade of 232 feet per mile – twice as steep as that allowed by the contract and four times as steep as the ideal maximum. Fleming's suggestion was accepted, and thus was born the "Big Hill" between the stations of Hector and Field. It was an eight-mile horror.

In his submission to the Minister of Railways, Van Horne dealt airily with the problem. The ruling gradient on the CPR had been set at one per cent. But on the Big Hill the gradient for almost four miles would be 4.4 per cent. This would be followed by a comparatively level stretch and then, for an additional three and a half miles, the gradient would run between three and a half and four per cent. In his memorandum Van Horne claimed that the Northern Pacific had used a heavier gradient without difficulty pending the completion of a long tunnel and that similar gradients had been used across western American mountain ranges on one or more other railways. The heavy gradient, he said, occurred in a section where traffic – mainly local – would be light for a number of years; only three or four trains a day would pass by. It would be cheaper to wait for a time when wages were not inflated by the railway's labour requirements and the pressure of time would no longer be a factor.

Van Horne was scrupulously correct, but he was leaving a great deal unsaid. The Northern Pacific and Santa Fe lines had built temporary switchbacks of the same grade, but these had been used for comparatively short periods. There *was* one short, scenic railway that operated on grades as high as seven per cent, but this was a freak. No major line, even those crossing the Great Divide in Colorado, exceeded a four per cent grade; nor did the lines that crossed the Andes out of Peru. The grades on the Big Hill would be the steepest ever regularly operated for any considerable period of time by a standard-gauge railroad. Van Horne's "temporary line" – an eight-mile diversion from the original location – would last for a quarter of a century. It was, in the words of a later CPR executive, "a heavy cross to bear through the years."

It was the beginning of a twenty-five-year nightmare for the railway's operating department. Even a 2.2 gradient can cause runaways. The first train that tried to descend the Big Hill – a construction outfit consisting of two locomotives and three box cars – ran away, climbed the rails on a curve, and plunged to the river below, killing three men. Safety switches were installed every two miles and manned twenty-four hours a day so that if a train got out of control, the man in charge of the switch could turn the

293

track onto a spur, which would lead the runaway up the side of a hill until it came to a halt. These precautions did not always work. A second construction train lost control after passing over a safety switch and headed straight into a tunnel where sixty men were working. The engineer slammed the engine into reverse, set the whistle, and jumped. When the tender derailed, the train came to a stop.

The various rituals established by the railway to ensure safety held up operations in the mountains. At the top of the Big Hill, every passenger train was required to stop to have its air brakes and sanding apparatus tested and inspected. The retaining valve on every car was closed so that when the engineer released the brakes momentarily to recharge the auxiliary reservoirs for a fresh application, a pressure of fifteen pounds per square inch would still be retained in each brake cylinder. Brakemen jumped off at intervals and trotted beside the train to make sure the wheels were not sliding or heating unduly. Box cars and flat cars, always difficult to manage, were restricted to a speed of six miles an hour. All trains were required to stop at the safety switches and start up again after the switchman re-aligned the track onto the main line. The bigger engines were limited to seventeen loaded cars in daylight and twelve at night; smaller engines could not even pull these loads. Every car was set by hand, the brakeman using a pick-handle for extra leverage to apply the brake as tightly as possible without causing the wheels to slide. Powerful water brakes were brought into service when the steeper inclines were reached and the trains began to slide downhill like toboggans. The air brakes were retained as a last resource. In spite of these precautions, and in spite of the safety switches and a complicated system of whistle warnings, runaways continued to occur. One train lost a forty-ton wing plough, which plunged three hundred feet into the river. And there were several cases of locomotives roaring down the slope so fast that the men tending the safety switches could not operate them in time to save train or crew.

The upward journey was a slow and difficult operation. At least four 154-ton engines were required to pull a train of 710 tons to the summit. Under such conditions it took an hour to move eight miles. Such a train could not be long – fourteen to twenty freight cars or eleven passenger coaches. When the Prince of Wales visited Canada, it took five engines to pull his entourage back over the summit of the Rockies.

All of this was expensive and time consuming; the use of four locomotives meant that there were four times as many chances for delay through engine failure. And in the winter, when the winds shrieked off the Yoho ice-fields in forty-below weather, smothering the mountain slopes in immense drifts of cement-hard snow, the difficulties were compounded. But it was not until 1909 that the CPR decided to return to the original location and drill the remarkable spiral tunnels, which make a figure eight deep within the bowels of Cathedral Mountain and Mount Ogden. It took ten thousand men two years to do the job, but there was not an employee in the operating division of the CPR who did not believe that it was worth it.

Nonetheless, the steeper line allowed Van Horne to push the railroad down the Kicking Horse to its junction with the Columbia (the site of Golden) by September. By January it had moved on down the Columbia for seventeen miles to the point where the line would cross over to the mouth of the Beaver at the foot of the Selkirks.

Here, at a spot known simply as First Crossing (it would later be named Donald, after Donald A. Smith), the work came to an end for the season and another garish little community sprang into being on the frozen river bank, a "gambling, drinking, fighting little mountain town," mainly shacks and saloons with ambitious names like the Cosmopolitan, the Queen of the West, the Sweet Hotel, the Italian Restaurant and the French Quarter. Here, on November 15, Jack Little, the telegraph operator, set down on paper the events of one single moonlit night:

". . . the Italian saloon . . . [is] a little hut, 12 × 16, and it dispenses beer, cigars, and something more fiery, in unlimited quantities. The barkeeper is a woman . . . there is an accordion squeaking in the corner, and it and the loud coarse laugh of the barmaid make an angelic harmony. . . . On all sides we hear the music of the dice box and the chips . . . the merry music of the frequent and iniquitous drunk; the music of the dance and the *staccato* accompaniment of pistol shots; and the eternal music, from the myriad saloons and bars along the street, of the scraping fiddle. In the French Quarter a dance is going on. The women present are Kootenai Squaw, 'the first white lady that ever struck Cypress' and two or three of the usual type of fallen angels. A gang of men and boys line the walls and a couple of lads dance with the damsels in the centre. There is a lamentable want of a sense of shame at Columbia Crossing. . . .

"During our walk we met plenty of 'drunks.' The contractor is as drunk as his employees, and the deadbeats are as drunk as usual. There is a good deal of card-playing . . . all through the night. . . .

"Below the high bank, on the dry land left by the receding river, several teamsters have camped for the night preparatory to crossing in the morning. The ferry boat with its one light is making its last trip for the night across the narrow space of water, becoming narrower day by day as the ice encroaches from the banks. On the opposite side of the river lights

295

shine out from rafts and shacks, while above them the dark pine forest stretches its gloomy line. The scene behind is growing livelier as the hours grow shorter. There is a row at one of the card tables. A pistol shot follows. A man is seen standing back a rough crowd with drawn revolver while another man is lying in a pool of his own blood. Well, it is all very interesting, no doubt, and has the great charm of being "western," which makes up for a multitude of sins. . . ."

4

All during the spring of 1884, Van Horne, who had moved his headquarters to Montreal, was trying his best to get out to British Columbia to settle on the Pacific terminus of the railroad. A variety of problems kept forcing him to postpone the journey, not the least of which was the continual need to stave off creditors, cut costs, reduce staff and cheapen the immediate construction of the line. None of this particularly perturbed the general manager. As Charles Tupper once said: "No problem that ever rose had any terrors for him."

One of Van Horne's many strengths was a singular ability to concentrate on business at hand to the exclusion of all interruptions. This led occasionally to some amusing contretemps. Once, in St. Paul, he left in a hurry to catch a train with only a twenty-dollar bill on his person. He leapt into a cab and began to concentrate on railway business, unconsciously twisting the bank note in his fingers until, forgetting what it was, he threw it away into the street. When he reached the station he discovered to his astonishment that he had no money to pay for the cab and only time to board the train. "Ever since that," he said, "I like to *feel money* in my pocket."

He was faced daily, in Montreal, with a mixed bag of executive decisions, many of them niggling but all, apparently, requiring his personal intervention. No detail was too small for Van Horne to handle. To a Brockville man who wrote to him personally asking for a job as a clerk he sent a swift rejection accompanied by a piece of personal advice: "Perhaps you will permit me to say, that in seeking employment in the shape of office work, I think you will find that your hand writing will militate against you." The bill of fare on the newly acquired lake boats offended his trencherman's palate: ". . . altogether too many dishes offered," he told Henry Beatty. "Fewer varieties, but plenty of each, I have always found to be better appreciated than a host of small, made-up dishes.

296

Poultry of any sort when it can be had is very desirable. Two entrees will be plenty. Deep apple, peach and etc., pie should be the standard in the pastry line; and several of the minor sweets should be left out. Plenty of fresh fish . . . is what people expect to find on the lakes and it is, as a rule, the scarcest article in the steamers' larders. . . ." From that moment, Lake Superior trout and whitefish became standard Canadian Pacific fare.

He could be very blunt and hard when the situation demanded it. "If Murray doesn't come up to the requirements of his office," he instructed Egan, "do not hesitate a minute in providing for his successor. We cannot afford to waste our strength in carrying weak men. . . . Any charity for weakness is out of place on a Railroad and I trust that whenever an opportunity offers to improve on any man you may have in any position that you will not hesitate to do it. . . ." Yet he also gave orders that the railway was to carry all clothing from the Ladies' Aid Society of the Central Presbyterian Church of Hamilton without any charge to Winnipeg.

He looked continually to the future. Many of his actions in 1884 were designed to further the interests of the railway in the years to come. He worried about grain buyers swindling prairie farmers and told Egan that "we must neglect nothing that will have the effect of securing proper prices." If the buyers would not pay a fair price the market must be stimulated by dropping in outside buyers with private assistance to shake it up: "Some vigorous action on our part in this direction will help very much to allay the present ill-feeling in the northwest." He told George Purvis, the secretary of the Manitoba and Northwest Farmers' Union, that "it is the earnest desire of this Company to do everything within its power to contribute to the success of farming in the North West . . . it would be suicidal on the part of the Company to do anything that would damage the farming interests to the extent of one dollar." He was distressed by the erection of flat warehouses that produced dirty wheat "badly mixed and generally disgraceful." His experiences in Minnesota had convinced him that much more modern elevators would be needed to clean and grade the grain, otherwise the reputation of Manitoba as a wheat producer would be ruined. The first elevator built by the company at Fort William had a capacity of one million bushels and seemed so huge that some believed (wrongly) that there was not grain enough in the North West to fill it. Van Horne also did his best to persuade the farmers to forget soft wheat and concentrate on harder varieties. The best of these was Red Fife and, as an inducement, Van Horne offered to carry the seed free to any farmer who ordered it.

The general manager was equally solicitous of the immigrants pouring

297

into Winnipeg. Like the farmers, they were the railway's future customers. He wrote to William Whyte in April urging that they be lodged and treated as comfortably as possible. "It is exceedingly important," he said, "that no bad reports go back from these first parties." For the same reason he was unwilling to carry newcomers on the Ontario and Quebec line, which was completed on May 5, 1884; he did not believe it was good policy to open the line to the scrutiny of new arrivals until it was in perfect condition, preferring to make an arrangement with the rival Grand Trunk and even going down to Ottawa to discuss the matter with a reluctant cabinet minister. In order that incoming settlers could get immediate access to supplies on the prairies, he had sidings built at intervals along the line on which he placed railroad cars fitted up as stores. As soon as anyone came along who seemed to be a good storekeeper, the business was transferred to him and the store car moved elsewhere.

He was at some pains, for obvious political reasons, to ensure that Alexander Mackenzie's trip to the North West should be made as smooth and comfortable as possible: "Find out if you can, what Mr. Mackenzie's mode of living is – what he eats and what his drink is as we wish to make him feel perfectly at home." "Get my car put in good shape and ready for his arrival at Port Arthur, victualled for the entire trip. . . . Mr. MacKenzie is in delicate health, and it will be necessary that a good man be put in charge of the car, and one who will fall in readily with the habits and ways of the ex Premier: let him understand that the circumstances of the case being special the rules which have governed the conduct of the car are suspended. Mr. Mackenzie may want to travel in easy stages; and he may wish to make stops to see friends at various points, in all of which cases his wishes should be met."

In spite of the need to cut costs – and Van Horne had already been forced to cheapen the line – he had no intention of pinching pennies where the railway's public image was concerned. To the president of the Michigan Central, who asked that he use a certain type of economical sleeping car exclusively, he replied that he would not: "It should be understood that we cannot consent to the use of inferior cars in this line. If the business is to be successfully worked up, the very best cars will be needed." When he discovered that some antiquated cars had been put in service on a newly opened line between Chicago and Toronto via St. Thomas, he insisted they be pulled off: "It would be better not to attempt the line unless it can be established and maintained in first class shape." He was determined that the interior woodwork of the passenger cars be hand carved, going so far as to import experts from Europe to do the job. "We can't have a veneer, it's too expensive," he told the board of directors. "Every foot of imitation carving will affect the opinion and attitude towards us of the Company's employees. We want them to have confidence in us – we want every clerk, conductor and brakeman to regard this Company as above all mean pretence. So everything must be of the best material, and be exactly what it pretends to be. Otherwise, their attitude and their service to us will not be what it ought to be."

Van Horne took special delight in personally designing sleeping cars and parlour cars, which he believed should furnish a maximum of comfort as well as aesthetic appeal. To this end he engaged noted artists to handle the interior decoration. As for comfort, he once, as an object lesson to his own people, made a comic illustration showing a tall, fat man attempting to squeeze into one of the short berths provided by United States railroads. He made sure that CPR cars were constructed of larger dimensions with longer and wider berths. Van Horne himself thought in terms of bigness. He liked big houses, "fat and bulgy like myself," with big doors, big roofs, big windows, big desks, and vast spaces.

In matters of the CPR's future, his whole philosophy was based on permanence. He wanted everyone in the company's employ to work for the continuance of the enterprise. The railway, as he saw it, was to become a kind of religion among the men who worked on it and also among the people who travelled on it. Conductors, telegraph clerks, freight and expressmen, senior executives – all these were to be missionaries spreading the gospel of the omnipotent, generous company. "You are not to consider your own personal feelings when you are dealing with these people," he told a trainman who had engaged in a dispute with an irritable passenger. "You are the road's while you are on duty; your reply is the road's; and the road's first law is courtesy."

Van Horne was one of the first railroad executives to realize the value of retaining such auxiliary utilities as the telegraph, express, and sleeping car departments. These, he used to say, were not the big tent but the sideshows, and "I expect the sideshows to pay the dividend." It was the custom of other railways to franchise these departments to independent firms which took the cream, as Van Horne put it, off the business and left the skim milk to the railway.

This forthright attitude led him into a head-on collision with Western Union, in the person of Erastus Wiman, the president of one of its subsidiaries, the Great North Western Telegraph Company. Wiman met with Van Horne and some of the executive committee to try to buy the CPR's telegraph system "for next to nothing," in Van Horne's words. When Van

Horne demurred, Wiman approached Stephen, charging that the general manager was prompted by personal motives and was acting out of spite. Wiman went on to charge that Van Horne intended to "run out all other telegraph companies" and that his whole career indicated his desire in the direction of "disregarding all vested rights or interests of those unable to defend themselves."

Van Horne replied to Wiman's complaints in a spirited letter to J. J. C. Abbott, the company's counsel:

"I do not like to write in anger, but the whole day has passed and I have hardly yet worked down to a suitable state of mind to answer your note of yesterday. I am appalled at Mr. Wiman's impudence. . . . [He] wanted our telegraph system for next to nothing while I wanted full value for it, and I think I know what that is as well as he does. . . .

"Our Directors have not as yet seriously discussed our telegraph policy, but when they do, I shall strongly represent the great value of their telegraph privileges and implore them to protect, develop and utilize them to the fullest extent and advantage and not in any event to part with them for less than their full value, considering all their possibilities, and not to be seduced by Mr. Wiman's soft words, deceived by his false words, or frightened by his bluster into discounting one cent in price or yielding one inch in advantage: and in my opinion the Western Union Company will not accomplish much in this matter until they set some honourable man at work upon it, which I am free to say Mr. Wiman is far from being. You have my full permission to forward this letter to him. . . ."

In mid-June, Van Horne decided that he must inspect the line between Lake Superior and Nipissing before making his journey to the Pacific coast. The inspection covered everything, right down to the quality of the coffee on the lake steamer *Alberta*. "The table was very fair," Van Horne informed Henry Beatty, "except that the coffee was bad, being too weak until I spoke to the steward about it and poor in quality as well, containing a considerable percentage of burnt peas."

Accompanied by the government's engineer-in-chief Collingwood Schreiber, Van Horne, set down on Superior's drab shoreline, took off on an eighty-two-mile walking trip to look over the stretch between Nepigon and Jackfish Bay. Van Horne was a corpulent man by this time, spending most of his days at a desk in Montreal, but he amazed Schreiber by his energy and endurance. After walking for miles through fire-blackened rock country the two men finally reached an engineer's camp at dusk, limp and sore. Van Horne promptly challenged the chief engineer to a foot race. On their return journey by steam launch from Jack Fish Bay to Red Rock, the boiler began to leak, but Van Horne would not be thwarted. He and Schreiber and the boat's engineer paddled the launch through the wave-flecked waters of the lake, and when the engineer met with an accident the two companions paddled the rest of the way themselves.

Van Horne's indefatigability gave rise to many legends. One story was told of a powerful miner who, hearing of the general manager's almost supernatural powers, resolved to do in one day, hour by hour, exactly what Van Horne was doing. The experiment almost killed him; at the day's end, so the story went, the miner had to be carried to bed, where he remained for several weeks in a state of collapse.

In the camps along Superior's shore and later in the mountains, Van Horne fitted in easily with the workmen, engineers, and subcontractors, sitting up all night in poker sessions, swapping stories, and drawing caricatures. He probably preferred the workmen to some of the stuffier members of Canadian society with whom he was forced to put up from time to time. He often used to test acquaintances for their sincerity. He liked to sign one of his own paintings with the name of Théo Rousseau, a fashionable French artist who was then in vogue, and listen sardonically to the ooh's and ah's of pretentious guests who praised his judgement. Later, when a nickel cigar was named for him, he invented "the cigar test." His butler would remove the bands of a hundred Van Horne cigars, place them in an expensive humidor, and wheel them around to male guests after a dinner party. He had little use for those who drew deeply, praised the aroma, and remarked on the exquisite flavour of Havana tobacco.

He was often pestered by members of the nobility sent out by English financial interests to look over investment prospects in Canada; it was important to the company that he make a show of entertaining them, but when they became too annoying, he would squelch them with a routine known as "the trap." Van Horne, who would himself one day refuse a peerage, would launch into a colourful account of how pioneer explorers, settlers, surveyors, and construction men had been so lonely for female companionship that they had taken up with Indian women. "As a result," he concluded, "the country is thickly sprinkled with French Indian half-breeds, Scottish Indian half-breeds, Irish Indian half-breeds and Welsh Indian half-breeds." The visitor usually rose to the bait: "You mean to say there are no English Indian half-breeds?" Van Horne supplied the squelch: "Well, after all, Sir, the squaws must draw the line *somewhere*."

His power, by 1884, was enormous. One rather profligate English peer,

Lord Dunmore, whom Van Horne must have suffered and perhaps squelched, said of him: "I don't know a man living who exercises the patronage that man does at this moment. No other man commands the same army of servants or guides the destiny of a railway over such an extent of country." Dunmore was perhaps a little jealous; he had tried to secure the contract to build the railway from John A. Macdonald in 1880. But he spoke truly. Van Horne, "the ablest railroad general in the world," was in charge of the equivalent of several army divisions. At the same time he continued to indulge his various exotic tastes. His collection of Japanese porcelain was rapidly becoming the finest in the world; it was chosen carefully to illustrate historically the development of the art. He liked to demonstrate his connoisseur's skill, especially when in a dealer's shop for the first time. He would have himself blindfolded and, as each piece was put into his hands, he would name the artist, place of origin and approximate date, using only his sense of touch; he managed to be right about seventy per cent of the time. His taste extended to French paintings (he collected Impressionists long before they were popular or valuable) and to the design of CPR stations. When he discovered, to his chagrin, that his architects had designed the Banff Springs Hotel so that it faced away from the mountains, he personally sketched in a rotunda that could redress the oversight. The famous station at Sicamous in British Columbia, which rose like a trim ship from the lake's edge, and the log station houses and chalets in the Rockies and Selkirks were also his idea. He scribbled a sketch on a piece of brown paper and turned it over to a designer with a brief order: "Lots of good logs there. Cut them, peel them, and build your station." Thus in various subtle ways did Macdonald's "sharp Yankee" help to transform the face of his adopted land.

5

The
Pacific
terminus

Van Horne's expedition to British Columbia was finally arranged in late July, and on August 4 a distinguished party arrived at Victoria and moved swiftly across the Strait of Georgia to Port Moody, then designated as the terminus of the transcontinental line. The little village, perched on the rim of a narrow bank at the head of Burrard Inlet, was basking in the glow of optimism brought on by the unquenchable belief that it was to become the greatest metropolis on the Pacific coast. Until the summer of

1882, the site had been unbroken forest. When Van Horne arrived – with ships emptying their holds of steel rails, with the new railway terminal wharf heaped with supplies, with streets being hacked out of the bush and gangs of men at work grading the track towards Yale – the community was enjoying a mild boom.

"Port Moody . . . has no rival," exclaimed the *Gazette*, the settlement's pioneer newspaper. "There is no place upon the whole coast of British Columbia that can enter into competition with it . . . these declarations are sweeping but incontrovertible."

The paper could hardly wait for Van Horne to arrive in order that the new metropolis could be laid out. It reported that the general manager would decide on the construction of a sea-wall as well as a new wharf, station houses, roundhouses, and machine and blacksmith shops. The *Gazette* became carried away by the magnitude of it all and began to envisage gigantic markets, theatres, churches, and paved streets ("The grades . . . should be fixed as soon as possible") as well as "steamers from all quarters arriving hourly" and hotels, shops, and warehouses rising "like magic." It was important, the editor noted, that the position of public buildings be carefully chosen, "with a view to the convenience of the great population soon to occupy the site of Port Moody."

It was all tragically premature. In Victoria, Van Horne was disturbingly non-committal about Port Moody as a terminus. Before making a decision, he said, he wanted to visit the mouth of Burrard Inlet and examine its geography. There were two settlements straggling along the inlet, the tiny community of Hastings, surrounding the mill of that name, and another properly called Granville but dubbed "Gastown" after a former saloonkeeper, John "Gassy Jack" Deighton.

Van Horne did make one thing clear: wherever the terminal was situated, a large city would spring up second only, in his opinion, to San Francisco. The *Gazette* remained trenchantly optimistic. It conceded that there might be a branch line to Coal Harbour at the inlet's mouth by way of Burnaby Lake, but insisted that the real terminus would remain at Port Moody. In spite of this, there was a thread of dark suspicion running through the article which referred, vaguely, to the potential enrichment of "the local land grabbers commonly called 'ministers.'"

Van Horne, together with the Premier of British Columbia, William Smithe, and the ever-present realtor Arthur Wellington Ross, late of Winnipeg, arrived at Port Moody on the evening of August 6. The Elgin House, where the party stayed, was illuminated in their honour and decorated with flags, evergreens, and a variety of welcoming banners proclaiming that Port Moody really was the western terminus of the line. That evening the general manager was met and interviewed by most of the prominent citizens. He kept his own counsel; he could, he said, express no opinion on the matter of the terminus. Nevertheless everyone believed that he had made up his mind in favour of Port Moody. As the *Gazette* reported: "It is his opinion that a city of 100,000 inhabitants will exist at the western terminus of the C.P.R. in a few years, and though he made no direct reference as to the exact location of that future city, yet it was not hard to infer that Port Moody was in his mind's eye at the moment."

Nothing could have been further from the truth. Van Horne's immediate reaction to Port Moody was that it would not do. There was no room on that crowded ledge for a substantial city. The railway alone would require four hundred acres of level ground, and even that much space did not exist. To reclaim it from the tidal flats would cost between two and four million dollars. But, as the general manager learned the following day when he travelled to the mouth of the inlet by boat, there was plenty of level ground in the vicinity of Coal Harbour and English Bay. If Van Horne could persuade the provincial government to subsidize the continuation of the line from Port Moody, then it was his intention to build the terminus at that point. Two days later, the New Westminster *Columbian*, whose editor, John Robson, had considerable real estate holdings in the Coal Harbour area, made it clear that Van Horne had come to a decision: "Without discussing the branch further, he thought it proper to say it was the company's intention to carry the line to Coal Harbour or some point in that vicinity. . . . The Syndicate had applied to the Provincial Government for a grant of land in the vicinity of Coal Harbour for a terminus, and if the grant were made they would raise money on these lands and extend the line."

In Port Moody, the response to this fairly clear statement of intent was one of disbelief and fury. The *Gazette*'s attitude was that the *Columbian* had invented the tale. Van Horne's alleged statement it said, was "the most extraordinary . . . that ever fell from the lips of a man in his position." It was "as choice an assortment of cast iron lies as it has been our lot to meet in a journalistic experience of 7 years." It was an "idiotic report." The editor of the *Columbian* had been "played for a sucker." It was clearly a wicked paper: ". . . truthfulness and honesty form no part of its creed."

Van Horne's decision ensured the swift decline of the little settlement at the head of the inlet. As the truth began to dawn upon them, Port Moody's merchants sent off petitions of protest. These were in vain; the general manager could not be moved. He was already planning to name

304

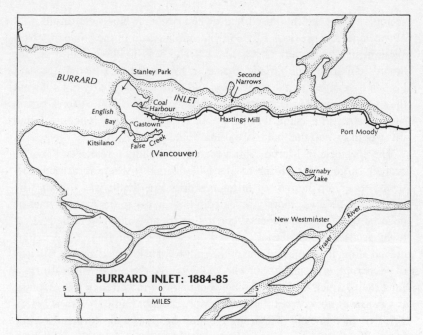

BURRARD INLET: 1884-85

the new terminus Vancouver. It is said that one reason he chose that title was because his own name bore the prefix "Van," but such reasoning is dubious. The proximity of Vancouver Island was certainly a factor; it helped to identify the position of the new terminus geographically in the minds of world travellers. More than that, Van Horne, the romantic, wanted to give his new metropolis a name he considered worthy of its future – that of a daring explorer who had sailed those shores long before any railway was contemplated. ". . . the fact that there is an insignificant place in Washington Territory named Fort Vancouver should not in my opinion weigh in the matter," he told Arthur Wellington Ross, who was acting as the railway's agent in real estate on the site. "The name Vancouver strikes everybody in Ottawa and elsewhere most favourably in approximately locating the point at once."

One of the influences working upon Van Horne in the selection of a terminus was that of the bristly engineer, Marcus Smith, who was the government's watchdog on the Port Moody–Emory's Bar section of the Onderdonk contract. At the end of April, 1884, Smith urged the general manager to select English Bay as the terminus rather than Port Moody and suggested that the company purchase land for a station and siding as soon as possible before prices became inflated through speculation. What Van Horne did not know and what Smith was at pains to keep secret was that Smith himself had owned property along the future right of way since the previous July. He had purchased it in the name of a New Westminster merchant, C. G. Major, who was holding it in trust for Smith's children. Smith made it clear to his banker that he did not want his name to appear in the transaction and that he particularly did not want the CPR to know he owned the land. Smith, in addition, was for a time a silent partner in a syndicate that was offering the railway a bonus of land if it would extend the line to Coal Harbour or English Bay.

The spectacle of Marcus Smith secretly dabbling in real estate and repeatedly urging Van Horne to place the terminus where it was best designed to enrich him is an intriguing one. For Smith was a man who proclaimed his own honesty repeatedly and loudly in the face of what he believed to be almost universal corruption. Some years before he had actually accused the Governor General (then Lord Dufferin) of speculating in land along the projected line of the railway. He believed most politicians to be corrupt, especially those who had favoured the Fraser River–Burrard Inlet route, which he had vigorously but vainly opposed for so many years. If a man was not corrupt, Smith generally thought him to be crassly motivated or incompetent. Sandford Fleming he put in the former bracket, Henry Cambie in the latter. His own surreptitious dalliance in railway land speculation did not weaken the venom of his personal suspicions. He told his banker that sale of the land would give him a chance "of making a few thousand dollars which will be very acceptable as the Govt. service is becoming very irksome through corruption connected with the Onderdonk contracts so that I fear I cannot stand it much longer." Smith was forever predicting his imminent resignation or dismissal; in point of fact, he survived in the government service longer than most of his colleagues.

Marcus Smith clearly believed that corners were being cut on the Onderdonk section of the line and that many of his colleagues and superiors were purposely ignoring inferior work in accepting without question or further investigation the estimates of the contractor's men. In his diary, he wrote of sitting in Michael Haney's room with Joseph Trutch, one of the government's supervising engineers (and a former lieutenant-governor of British Columbia), and Collingwood Schreiber, the engineer-in-chief: "Then began an extraordinary comedy – Mr. Schreiber setting aside a contract and the scientific calculations of quantities executed and to be executed by engineers and adopting those guessed at by the company's men in riding over the line – occasionally appealing to Trutch who sat behind looking wise and blinking like a Centenary owl – confirming by a nod everything that Schreiber did. This was the end of the first act of the drama of corruption openly played."

Although Marcus Smith's witness cannot be taken as gospel – he was far too suspicious of too many people to be considered a fair or unbiased observer – it is quite clear that, for one reason or another, the government engineers did not hold Andrew Onderdonk to the letter or even the spirit of his contract and that they allowed a good deal of shoddy work to go unremarked. (It is possible that Onderdonk's vigorous lobbying in Ottawa persuaded the government to wink at some of the shortcuts he subsequently took.)

Van Horne, when he travelled the line in August, made no public remark other than that he was "agreeably surprised to find the character of the country so favorable generally for railway construction, and is satisfied that the line will be completed inside of 16 months." In fact, as his later comments indicated, he was appalled at what he saw. The timber trusses were "the worst I ever saw in a railway. In the attempt to strengthen them they have been patched and spliced in a most wonderful manner – boulders and debris are continually coming down on the track."

The situation led to a series of disagreeable battles between Van Horne and John Henry Pope, who was Charles Tupper's successor as Minister of Railways. Pope was in a difficult position. He felt duty bound to stand behind his own people, who had told him that the work was properly done. "It seems to be a very sore question with him," Van Horne told Stephen, "and he usually gets into a rage within ten minutes after we touch upon it." When the Onderdonk contracts were finished, Pope refused Van Horne's suggestion of a board of arbitration to examine the contentious points and swore "he would find some way to compel the Company to take over the road in its present condition." The dispute led to an open breach between Pope, who had been the railway's greatest friend and supporter within the Cabinet, and Van Horne. Their feud was so bitter that they did not speak for many years and shook hands only on Pope's deathbed.

Pope, of course, had inherited the Onderdonk problem from Tupper. To admit that the line was substandard would be to admit that his predecessor's policy was wrong. In 1882 Tupper had actually boasted in the House that he expected to save almost three million dollars of public money on four of the Onderdonk contracts by such cost-cutting devices as reducing the radius of the curves. On the fifth contract – the one on which Marcus Smith was employed as supervising engineer – there was less chance of effecting savings because it had been let as a lump sum and not broken down into component parts. There, if corners were cut, the contractor would profit.

Marcus Smith was scathing in his comments about this section – between Port Moody and Emory. He told a friend that when the time came for the road to be inspected, Michael Haney would manage to get the trains running at thirty miles an hour, hiding the sore spots, but that the Syndicate would discover to their cost the following winter that many of the cuttings would turn into canals and the steep clay slopes and boulders would roll down over the track because of imperfect workmanship.

Smith made such a fuss that he was transferred to the section east of Kamloops (which Onderdonk had contracted to build not for the government but for the CPR). At least that was Smith's suspicion. He had, in October, 1884, refused to put his signature on documents approving the work along the Port Moody–Emory line; his transfer followed shortly after this impasse. Certainly he was impolitic in his official correspondence in charging Onderdonk, and by inference Collingwood Schreiber himself, with corruption. "It is . . . generally believed," he wrote, "that Onderdonk by corrupt means had the power to get any engineer removed from his contract and that I was removed at his instance. Be that as it may I cannot allow my reputation to suffer by the contractor's incompetence or neglect and if the work is not finished fairly in accordance with the specifications I will testify against it in any commission or committee that may be appointed. . . ." Smith warned that if a public scandal arose he would "if driven to extremity" make public everything he knew, "even if I have to leave the Government service." But in the complicated dispute that followed over the Onderdonk contracts he was not called. Nor did he speak up or leave the service.

There is no doubt that along the Fraser Canyon, the government shaved costs to the bone to the detriment of the line, as Henry Cambie's diaries make clear. The curves were not to exceed four degrees and the grades were not to exceed one per cent, but Cambie had scarcely located two miles when he received a telegram from Ottawa to "locate the cheapest possible line with workable curves and grades." Cambie and his assistant, T. H. White, stopped the survey and began adopting eight-degree curves, thereby avoiding tunnels and expensive cuts. According to White, when the curves reached ten degrees, Andrew Onderdonk, "throwing up his arms to high heaven declared that he refused to accept the order to run construction trains on so impossible a curvature." A short time later, the government went so far as to permit reverse double curves, the bane of railroad engineers and operating crews. A reverse double curve occurs when one curve follows another in a figure S without any intervening straightaway. The resultant unequal wear and tear on both tracks and wheels is considerable. Between Kamloops and Lytton there were 430 curves and virtually no straight track. Not only would the maintenance be costly on such a section but the operating speed would also be slower.

In another attempt to reduce expensive excavation, the line was built along the face of sheer bluffs by means of grasshopper trestles. Sometimes inferior timber was used. Cambie admitted in his diary that it was impossible to get proper timber for a truss across Yale Creek and that second-grade material had to be employed. Yet a great deal of such inadequate work was passed by the government's inspecting engineers in the interests of saving money – and, perhaps, of aiding the hard-pressed Andrew Onderdonk. The *Inland Sentinel* was critical of these inspections. Michael Hagan charged in September, 1883, that Collingwood Schreiber was going over the line too rapidly and in many cases did not bother to look at all of it: "His recent 'inspection' was recently described as like a flock of pigeons going over a town." The paper reported that Sandford Fleming was dissatisfied with what he saw en route to Port Moody after he and Grant emerged from the mountains. Originally Fleming had tried to prevent Tupper's cheese-paring and had gone along with it only on pain of dismissal.

The result of all this parsimony was a long and acrimonious debate between the CPR and the government which finally resulted, in 1888, in a board of arbitration. The company claimed twelve million dollars from the government; the final settlement, in 1891, was $579,255. The dispute embittered Stephen, who felt that he had been betrayed by Pope and Tupper, both of whom swore before the arbitrators that the line was built as intended, yet admitted under cross-examination that if the company had taken the full ten years to complete the transcontinental the government would have been forced to rebuild the Onderdonk section. As a reward for building the line swiftly, Stephen felt he was "forced and cheated into accepting a temporary road, utterly unfit to be operated as a through trunk line. . . ." This was certainly one of the reasons why Stephen, in the end, left Canada and returned to his native Scotland, disgusted with politics and with politicians and estranged even from Macdonald. "I am thoroughly sick and tired of these wretched squabbles with the late Government," he wrote to the Prime Minister in 1889, ". . . and shall not be happy until I get away from them all."

As for Van Horne, he told a United States Senate inquiry in 1889 that if the CPR had had control of the British Columbia section, "we would not have built it where it is. . . ." He would have found a way to circumvent the Fraser Canyon which he described, not inaccurately, as "one of the worst places in the world."

6

The general manager had his first view of the Fraser Canyon on August 9 after a record run from Port Moody in which the train travelled at speeds approaching sixty miles an hour. He was accompanied by Collingwood Schreiber, Joseph W. Trutch, Major A. B. Rogers, Marcus Smith, Henry Cambie, Michael Haney, and S. B. Reed – as quarrelsome, temperamental, and jealous a company of engineers as it was possible to assemble. Smith, who had always been opposed to any route through the Fraser Canyon, thought that Schreiber was "mean and inferior," Rogers "a thorough fraud," Cambie "a toady of Fleming's," and Trutch a total incompetent. These feelings were generally reciprocated. Smith had quarreled with Rogers, bullied Cambie, and questioned Schreiber's integrity. The Canadians were all jealous of Rogers, whose crusty personality did not endear him to either casual acquaintances or colleagues. Haney and Smith had fought eyeball to eyeball on several occasions. Reed was known as the man who did the hatchet job on the Winnipeg engineering office in the spring of 1882. In addition, several of the company had apparently been engaged to spy on one another. When the CPR decided to give Onderdonk the subcontract to build east from Savona's Ferry towards the Eagle Pass, it sent Rogers out as supervising engineer. Van Horne, in April, decided to send Cambie out to check up on Rogers. Later he sent Reed to check on Cambie and then, to cap it all, dispatched Marcus Smith to look over Reed's work. Obviously, the general manager was taking no chances, and when the unhappy Rogers, feeling the breath of several rivals on his neck, wrote several letters of complaint, Van Horne soothed him by explaining that a great deal of money was involved and "I have thought it to the interest of the Company to get opinions from as many engineers as possible, before expenditure . . . should actually commence. . . . This was not intended to indicate any want of confidence in you." Nonetheless, it could not have been a very happy relationship; Marcus Smith's description of Rogers as "a man one cannot discuss work with . . ." gives a clue to the kind of atmosphere that was engendered among the engineers in British Columbia.

In spite of all this it was a reasonably harmonious group that arrived in Kamloops on August 10, having inspected the steel cantilever bridge across the Fraser near Lytton, "one of the great wonders of the C.P. railway," as the *Sentinel* rightly described it. Designed by C. C. Schneider of New York, it was the first bridge of its kind in North America; the second (which was actually installed first) crossed the Niagara Gorge

310

just below the famous falls. Until the bridge was finished a cable was stretched across the boiling Fraser, and freight and passengers were carried over in a basket suspended from pulleys. The basket ran for six hundred feet from the high bank to the lower opposite bank under the force of gravity, was stopped by a bale of hay at the far end, where it discharged its cargo, and was then hauled back by a horse. Cambie actually made the crossing before the basket was used, sitting in the body of a wheelbarrow slung by ropes from its four corners. As he came hurtling down the cable Cambie to his dismay saw a man roll two bales of hay into his path and, fighting back the inclination to scream, threw his legs into the air to prevent them from being snapped off. The barrow struck one bale and sent it flying; the second brought it to a stop.

Yale was all but finished as a community, as even the *Sentinel* admitted. "Business," it wrote, ". . . is gradually declining and we hear from nearly all classes of their intention to go and seek their fortunes elsewhere shortly." Kamloops was the new mecca. Van Horne, who knew a bit about the politics of diplomacy when it did not interfere with railroad matters, pronounced himself on arrival as pleased to find that Kamloops had "such a thriving and progressive look." He expressed great faith in the city's future although, at that point, it was a one-street community of shacks with few civilized amenities. "For water," one resident wrote, "you went to the river and dipped in a bucket and carried it back." The railroad tracks ran directly down the main street and the CPR, as Morley Roberts noted, "was the all-absorbing topic, some prophesying prosperity, and some universal ruin and desolation as its result."

The community was delighted to see the general manager. An attempt was even made to change the name of neighbouring Savona's Ferry to Port Van Horne in his honour. He would have none of it. When he noticed the new signboard on the station he growled out: "Somebody pull that thing down." But Kamloops, which had suffered a decline after the gold rush, perked up with his announcement that it would be a divisional point and the site of extensive yards and railroad facilities. Here were repeated all the spectacles attendant on the construction period – the hotels jammed with men, some sleeping in the bar room and some on billiard tables, some gambling their savings away and some drinking them up. Cambie had noted the previous month that there were so many drunken men in town he was loath to leave his hotel room. The courts were crowded with liquor cases, presided over by the former premier, little George Walkem, himself no mean toper. "Judge Walkem carried away dead drunk at 7 a.m. when everybody was looking on," Cambie scribbled in his diary one day, noting, however, that Walkem recovered sufficiently to open court at 10.30 a.m. and, presumably, to levy the usual fines for intoxication.

It was Onderdonk's job to continue the railroad for the CPR from the end of the government section at Savona's Ferry to meet the railway builders coming from the east, probably in the vicinity of the Eagle Pass in the Gold Range. On August 11, Van Horne, together with Major Rogers and S. B. Reed, set off along the route of the line that would take them directly through Eagle Pass and then on across the mountains to the Columbia. A wagon was expected to meet them at Sicamous Landing to convey them as far as the road was completed; when it failed to arrive on time, Van Horne insisted that the expedition set off on foot in the drenching rain. Rogers went ahead, leading a cayuse loaded with the party's baggage. Reed followed, with his coat and vest rolled into a small package. The general manager brought up the rear, enveloped in a waterproof and smoking the inevitable long cigar. The *Sentinel* reported that his air was jaunty and that he was taking "a philosophical view of the situation, but, no doubt, mentally contrasting the difference between crossing the Gold Range on foot and the luxury of the manager's car on the other side of the mountains."

It was a truly fearful trip. The members of the party were forced to leave most of their spare clothing at End of Track and push on by freight team, scow, and, finally, pony train. An early fall of snow had deposited three feet of slush on the mountain trails, already littered with the cast-offs of other travellers – blankets, saddles, personal belongings, and the corpses of pack ponies. Sometimes Van Horne found himself sinking waist deep in icy mud. At Three Valley, young Jack Stewart, the future contractor and major-general, ferried the party across the stream in a scow so old and rotten that the legs of Van Horne's horse fell through. Young Stewart and a helper struggled successfully to free the animal and were rewarded with a five-dollar tip each from the general manager himself. While crossing Summit Lake, Van Horne tumbled into water that was only a degree or so above freezing. John Stevens the engineer, who was present, wrote: "I have never forgotten, after 48 years, the vigorous and breezy comments about the country and everybody connected with it which he made when we had pulled him back onto the raft. . . ."

The entire trip from Kamloops to the Rockies was one that few people had ever made. Fleming and Grant were probably the last to traverse the full trail (the previous year in the other direction). In another fifteen months the railway was complete and it was no longer necessary to make the journey on foot.

The party was without food for two days, probably as a result of Rogers's eccentric provisioning. When they finally arrived at the most forward of the camps on Rogers Pass, the general manager's sensitive nostrils detected the aroma of ham cooking. "It was then," he later recalled, "that I learned that a man can smell ham ten miles away."

On this journey several new Van Horne legends were forged. When the general manager reached the Mountain Creek trestle he was told that a few days before several men had crashed to their deaths in the ravine below. The floor of the trestle, suspended one hundred and sixty feet above the torrent, consisted at that time of two loose planks and nothing more. One of the general manager's companions was barely able to negotiate the bridge by crawling inch by inch on his hands and knees, but Van Horne stepped confidently out on the shaky planks, strode across the trestle, and returned just as imperturbably.

At Seven Parsons Coulee he and Reed suffered another icy ducking when the driver of their wagon missed the ford. Van Horne spent the rest of the day in a construction camp, apparently oblivious of a borrowed pair of trousers which, being too small for his rapidly expanding girth, had been split up the seam at the back.

He liked to take curves on the newly constructed road at the highest possible speed. Once, with a dangerous trestle looming up ahead, the engineer balked at taking the locomotive across.

"Here," Van Horne said, "get down and I'll take her over myself."

"Well," said the engineer, "if you ain't afraid, guess I ain't neither."

When the general manager left the mountains and rolled across the prairies in the comfort of his private car, he was able to witness the by-products of his handiwork: Calgary, Medicine Hat, Moose Jaw, and Regina slowly changing from tent and shack towns to permanent communities; crops being harvested; sod houses going up; and a veneer of civilization spreading out over the raw prairie. "Society in Calgary is yet in its infancy, but its people should at once adopt it as part of their creed that the moral tone of our town should have in it the ring of purity," the *Herald* had solemnly opined. As he sped towards Winnipeg (a city of twenty-five thousand, of whom six thousand were dependent on the railway) Van Horne could note at every siding along the line the bleak symbols of a vanished past — great stacks of buffalo bones being loaded into box cars. The general manager had made his gardening expertise pay off in a minor way for the hard-pressed railway. Cleaned and bleached in the sun, the bones were shipped to Minneapolis where they were sold as fertilizer for seven dollars a ton.

Back in his Montreal office, he plunged once again into the routine of

313

executive decisions. Had Alexander Mackenzie been impressed by his trip to the North West? Then a letter giving his impressions would be "of very great use in killing the villanous [*sic*] slanders that are being published about 'alkali deserts,' 'sandy stretches,' etc." He suggested that Henry Beatty, who knew Mackenzie well, persuade the former prime minister to issue a public statement on the matter. Jim Hill, Van Horne learned, had spies within the company and was boasting that he was in possession of full reports on all the business the railway did at Port Arthur. The general manager moved swiftly to stop the leakage: "Cautious steps should be taken at once towards finding out the person in fault, and if found he must be promptly kicked out." George Stephen had been dismayed at the recklessness with which baggage trucks were trundled around the platform at Toronto. That would never do! "He seemed to think that the men handling the trucks took a delight in frightening passengers," Van Horne advised William Whyte, the general superintendent of the Ontario and Quebec line. In British Columbia, Arthur Wellington Ross, the railway's real estate representative, had overstepped the bounds of propriety and had taken a piece of property on the Hastings Mill Tract in trust for Van Horne, with some secret agreement involved. The general manager declined to accept the property. "I do not like transactions of this kind and do not intend to take any chances whatever of having my name smirched by my connection with them," he told Ross.

As always, no matter was too small to occupy the general manager's attention. "I am afraid I shall never get exactly what I want until I take up wood engraving myself," he informed Thomas H. Lee of the American Bank Note Company after poring over some drawings and engravings of the mountain section. He wanted to see steam and not black smoke issuing from the locomotives pictured in the foreground of Mount Stephen; that would give more emphasis to the presence of the railway.

He could be cutting. When Major Rogers, the following February, continued to complain bitterly about Marcus Smith's interference, Van Horne dispatched a chilly answer:

"Replying to yours of the 8th instant about Mr. Marcus Smith, I have to say that when we wish you to consult anybody or to take anybody's suggestion about your work, you will be advised from this office.

"I will say further that I do not care to receive any more letters of this description."

He could also be sarcastic. To Harry Abbott he shot off a withering note:

"You have on your Engineering Staff an inspired idiot by the name of

314

Gribble, who is writing letters here complaining of the desecration of the Sabbath Day by barbarians in your employ. These letters are very long and must have taken a considerable time to write; if they were written during the work the time must have been stolen from the company's time, if they were written on the Sabbath he too must have desecrated the Sabbath.

"It would be well to sit down on him very solidly in order that our friends in Montreal may not be bothered any more by his complaints."

And then there was his forthright reply to George Wainwright, who wanted to launch a winter carnival at Winnipeg, complete with ice palaces, dog trains, and Indian mushers.

"You will pardon me," Van Horne wrote, "if I express my opinion very strongly on this subject.

"I think the combination of attractions referred to would have the most damaging possible effect upon the North West. Ice Palaces, Indians and Dog Trains are not popular features in our foreign advertising, and I think the less said about them in Manitoba, the better.

"For some inscrutable reason nearly everybody in Canada has his photograph taken in furs with salt scattered over to represent snow. Many of these go abroad and few people in England have ever seen a Canadian picture except in Winter dress. For this reason the name of Canada is almost universally associated with an Arctic climate and this idea is one of the most difficult to remove from the minds of people abroad.

"Individually I will be disposed to contribute liberally to a 'shirt-tail' carnival and will furnish a large proportion of the necessary linen dusters and palm leaf fans; but when it comes to the other thing, the like of which has already worked more harm than good in Montreal, I must decline any aid or encouragement.

"All the advantages, for the time being, to the hotel keepers and the Railways would not outweigh the loss to the North West of one settler."

More and more, however, Van Horne was concerned with the need to keep costs down. Over and over, in his wide-ranging correspondence, he used the phrase "we have not a dollar to spare." That was only too true. The matter of late estimates from John Ross on the Superior section, for instance, had been a subject of grave concern earlier that year: "We are dependent upon our estimates from the Government for all the money necessary to keep the work going, and when the estimates are behind time or deficient in amount we are severely cramped." Staffs were reduced to the bone: ". . . we are at all points discharging every man who can be possibly spared." Repairs to locomotives were cut back to the minimum: "The financial situation pinches us severely and every corner must be clipped now, even if it costs in the end." A request from the Premier of Manitoba to help depressed conditions there by purchasing a large quantity of coal had to be rejected: ". . . we have not a dollar to spare and like most of our friends in the North West have to skin along the best we can." Costs on the Kamloops Lake section of the railway had to be shaved drastically, even though the quality was better than on Onderdonk's government work: "Please go over the matter carefully and see how low it can be figured – every dollar counts," Van Horne instructed Cambie. Similar orders went to John Ross: "By cutting every corner and cheapening the work in every practicable way, we may be able to build the line for the money available. . . . If we cannot do that, we must stop the work. I would like very much to see all of the work done in a first class manner and to have it beyond criticism, but that is impossible."

As the months went by Van Horne's communications with his deputies in the field became more and more insistent. "The money saved on the Mountain Section is being rapidly absorbed on the Lake Superior Section and we are again very near our *danger line*," he informed John Ross in October. Failure to complete the work within the limits of the government loan would be "disastrous." All pretence at building a first-class line had been abandoned. Van Horne was appalled to find men still quarrying rock. The company could not afford to lay a single block of cut stone. Even the ballasting of the rails had to be discontinued except where it was necessary to preserve them from damage. The roadway would be made safe for trains running at a moderate rate of speed and nothing more. The ballasting would have to be completed at a later date, say in ten years, when the resources of the CPR permitted it. Van Horne issued instructions to all general superintendents limiting their power to spend money. From November 1, his own authority would be required before a single siding or siding improvement could be undertaken. No structure could be moved without Van Horne's permission; not even a fence could be built, nor a nail driven. That was how tight money had become.

Outwardly, the general manager maintained his air of bluff confidence. When a Scottish friend of W. B. Scarth's asked if the CPR was a good investment, Van Horne replied: "I have no hesitation in expressing my opinion in the strongest possible terms that it will pay handsomely" – and he went on to say why: its entire debt was only one third that of the Northern Pacific on a mileage basis, and even less in comparison with other United States transcontinental railways. The CPR's advantage as a through line was greater, and the road itself was far better built.

316

But Van Horne's real expression of confidence in the railroad went much further than words. He himself had sunk almost every dollar he had in Canadian Pacific stock. If the road failed, he was prepared to go down with it.

7

Once again, the railway was in a critical financial position. "I *feel* like a man walking on the edge of a precipice with less 'nerve' than is comfortable or even *safe* in such a case," George Stephen wrote to the Prime Minister at the end of 1884. "The uncertainty is too much for me with all our other difficulties. On Saturday we got a telegram from Port Arthur that the men had struck and would go off the work if we did not send them their pay. We sent a man upon Saturday and hope to gain time till our next estimate comes. But the ordeal I am going through is not easy to stand." *The edge of the precipice*

The ordeal had begun that summer – only a few months after Parliament reluctantly passed the loan of $22,500,000. By September the credit of the company at home and abroad was gone. Stephen and Donald A. Smith had been dipping lavishly into their private fortunes in an attempt to sustain it. They were close to the bottom of the barrel.

Almost all of the spring loan had been gobbled up by the railway builders on the Shield and in the mountains; what was left was being paid out only as the work was done; often these payments were very late. In addition there was a whole variety of unseen expenses. The grain elevator at the lakehead, for instance, had to be built if the CPR was to capture the grain traffic from its United States rivals. The cost came to three hundred thousand dollars. Then there were the terminals, shops, and equipment, spread over more than two thousand miles. Even with costs pared to the limit, the bill for these was five millions. In the first ten months of 1884 the company found it had spent eight million dollars on essential work that had not been contracted for.

The railway was working on a margin that was terrifyingly narrow. A few days delay in the payment of the subsidy could mean that thousands of men would not be paid. Yet for a variety of reasons, all based on the government's strict arrangement with the company, the payments were often slow or slender.

Part of this was the result of pure governmental vacillation. The Council often did not get around to making a decision on an estimate either because of procrastination or from a general suspicion that the CPR was not entitled to the amount claimed. The Pacific Scandal, which the Liberal press never tired of mentioning, still haunted Macdonald and his colleagues. They were fearful of seeming to show any sign of favouritism to the Canadian Pacific; it was safer to err on the side of caution.

It exasperated Stephen. He made no secret of his feelings on one occasion when the Council failed to come to grips with an estimate before it for work done. He wrote the Prime Minister a letter intended for his cabinet colleagues: "It would be folly for me to conceal from you the discouraging effect which this message has had upon me, making me feel for the time being, as if it were a hopeless task for me to attempt to carry through the work on hand to a successful conclusion."

Such delays, Stephen pointed out, were damaging the credit and reputation of the company and they "cruelly add to my already questioning anxieties and labours. . . ." Stephen wondered at the Council's apparent lack of faith in him. Did they think he intended to pull out altogether and leave the government to clean up the mess? It looked that way. The impression, he said, "weakens me more than I can tell you, denuding me of the power and moral strength which the confidence and hearty cooperation of the government alone can give." His own exertions and sacrifices, Stephen added, had been unparalleled and, as he often did in moments of high emotion, he underlined the key words.

There were other problems connected with the subsidy payments brought on by the remoteness of the country into which the railroad was probing. Expensive tote roads had to be constructed out of Lake Nipissing and Michipicoten and across the Selkirk Mountains. Vast quantities of construction equipment and supplies had to be brought in, especially before the onset of winter. For all of this the company was forced to lay out funds months in advance; but in Schreiber's strict interpretation of the contract terms, the subsidy did not apply to these preliminary steps of construction. In the matter of tote roads, Van Horne was finally able to persuade the engineer-in-chief to change his mind.

The government's method of estimating the subsidy was also a bone of contention. The supervising engineer checked the work done and reckoned in dollars and cents how much remained to be done. Enough money was held back by the government, in each instance, to complete the road; the difference was paid out to the company. The subsidy could not cover all the work done. Stephen wrote to Macdonald at one point that he was flabbergasted to learn that Schreiber's estimates for one month were half a million dollars less than the railroad had actually spent on construction. Van Horne finally prevailed on Schreiber to reduce certain standards, especially on steel and masonry bridges, but he was then faced with the problem of making temporary trestles appear permanent, because the government paid no subsidy on temporary construction.

The real fear was that the government would stop payment altogether. This it was empowered to do if its engineers estimated that there were not enough funds left to complete the line. By October, 1884, it was becoming increasingly clear that if the company had to find funds to repay its loan of the previous November, together with interest and dividends, the coffers would be empty and construction must cease.

Wages were suspiciously slow. Van Horne gave Schreiber an ingenious explanation of why thousands of men on the Lake Superior section were facing long delays in pay. For three hundred miles, he pointed out, the area was accessible only by boat or by temporary roads. Since monthly disbursements amounted to a million dollars or more, "it has been no easy matter to distribute and pay the large sums required." On both the Lake Superior and the mountain sections the cash had to be sent out for a hundred miles or more beyond the end of track through the wildest country over difficult roads and trails, "and we have not felt it safe to send it in large installments and consequently the payments have been slow, and frequently before the payment for one month has been completed, the payment for the next month has been due."

The truth was that the company was using every possible excuse to stave off creditors and employees. Reports filtered into Calgary of a growing volume of complaints about pay in the mountain section where, by mid-November, the men had received only their September wages. At the end of October, in Thunder Bay, the CPR announced that the men in the eastern division would henceforth be paid by cheques drawn on the Bank of Montreal; the reason given was that it was too dangerous to carry around more than a million dollars in cash. The real reason was that Van Horne had decided on a daring though barbarous gambit. He intended to keep nine thousand men at work all winter in the remotest areas with plenty of good food. They would be paid by cheque, which they would be unable to cash. If any man wanted to get away he would find it almost impossible to do so; the isolated conditions would make it difficult to leave before spring, at which time the general manager believed funds must be forthcoming.

The wonder was that there were so few labour disputes as a result of the slow payments. Harry Armstrong, the engineer, recalled that though he had no pay on the Lake Superior section for many months the matter gave

319

him no concern: "My sole thoughts seemed to be for progress of the work and [I was] satisfied reward would come in time, including back pay." Ordinary navvies were undoubtedly less charitable, but there was little they could do.

In those desperate months, Van Horne and Stephen leaned heavily on Thomas Shaughnessy, a man apparently able to make one dollar do the work of a hundred. Shaughnessy, who had come to work for the company rather reluctantly, was rising rapidly in the ranks; one day he would be president. He sprang from humble beginnings; both his parents were immigrants; his father, a Limerick Irishman, was a policeman on a beat in Minneapolis. This modest start undoubtedly contributed to Shaughnessy's later love of ostentation. He was a dapper man, always band-box fresh, immaculately turned out, a pearl in his tie, a grey hat on his head, a gold-handled cane in his gloved hand. For all of his life he was an autocrat who remained aloof from all but his closest intimates. (In his days as president he suffered no employee in the same elevator with him.) He did not endear himself to strangers or chance acquaintances. He was, in a contemporary journalist's assessment, "a man almost bloodless in the intensity of his devotion to material ends. He does not please, he does not charm, he does not delight; but he interests. . . . The eyes are small and penetrating with the line of the low hanging upper lid sharply defined, giving the appearance of command and impatience of delay. . . . When he speaks, he opens his mouth wide, and the voice issues sharply and impatiently, raucous and grating in tone, strident, too, rising above the blur of conversation like the tearing of a saw."

He was known as a man of cool common sense, and it was remarked by more than one observer that while Van Horne's favourite game was poker, Shaughnessy preferred solitaire, which he often played night after night while working out details of the business. For he was really all work and no play – a martinet intolerant of frivolity or the slightest sign of debauchery. A strict temperance man, he once ordered an assistant to close a bar in a CPR hotel. "Now or at the closing hour of the day?" he was asked. "Close it now," ordered Shaughnessy, "and do not allow it ever to open again."

He was a company man through and through. In his view, what was good for the CPR was good for Canada; he held no personal or political views save those of the institution he served. That he served it well in the financial crisis of 1884–85 is beyond doubt. He never appeared to show the slightest tremor of panic as he kited cheques, kept creditors at bay, denied funds, made partial payments, and generally held the company together. In Toronto, the heads of the big wholesale houses, under Van Horne's and Shaughnessy's persuasion, extended millions of dollars in credit so that supplies could go forward.

Shaughnessy, apparently, would go to any lengths to keep the CPR solvent. There is an illuminating story, still told in the Shaughnessy family, that illustrates his devotion. At a board meeting one day, so the tale has it, George Stephen solemnly read a letter from an American railway supply company complaining that they had tried to do business with the CPR without success, even though they had on several occasions in 1884–85 made out large cheques to Thomas Shaughnessy. The implication was clear: Shaughnessy had been taking money under the counter for favours rendered, supposed or real.

The board of directors called Shaughnessy in and demanded an explanation. He excused himself quietly, went to his office, and returned with a sheaf of deposit slips from the Bank of Montreal, all endorsed by him to the account of the Canadian Pacific. The slips tallied to the penny with the total amount the American firm said that it had paid him.

"Would these by any chance have been bribes?" asked Stephen incredulously.

"Of course," came the cool reply, "but, by God, we needed the money, didn't we?"

While Shaughnessy was using extraordinary measures to keep the company solvent, Stephen was slowly committing his entire personal fortune and those of his closest colleagues to its further support. The previous winter, he, Donald Smith, Angus, and McIntyre had put up a total of $2.3 million in their own bonds and securities as collateral against CPR bank loans. But in May, McIntyre dropped right out of the Canadian Pacific, refusing to stay even as a director or to have anything to do with the management of a company he clearly believed would go to the wall. Baron Reinach, one of the original European members of the Syndicate and a charter investor, went with him. Stephen, who had already bought out Hill and Kennedy, was forced to use more of his fortune to buy out both the Reinach and the McIntyre stock. In the president's phrase, these men had "deserted"; they were little better than traitors. Contemptuously, he told Macdonald that he could get along without McIntyre. Later he went into more detail about his feelings. The vice-president had been "coarsely selfish & cowardly all through these 5 years. Ruthless in disregarding the interests of others when he could advance his own. . . . When McIntyre deserted the Coy he made up his mind that it would '*burst*' and that Smith & I would lose every dollar we had, in the collapse."

321

Stephen in future years was forced occasionally to do business with his erstwhile vice-president but apart from that did his best to avoid him, for, as he said, he could not stand to be in the same room with him. The unkindest cut came a few months after the defection when, in the CPR's darkest days, McIntyre was the first to refuse it credit and threatened to sue immediately unless his firm's account for dry goods was paid at once.

McIntyre also, apparently, half-convinced R. B. Angus to leave. In the end, Angus stayed, but Stephen did not quite trust him after that. He was, he said, "as facile as clay in the potter's hands."

In the face of these defections, the loyalty and steadfastness of Donald A. Smith was refreshing and touching. Smith, as Stephen explained to a friend years later, really had very little to do with the railway except to attend board meetings; but he never failed his cousin when personal guarantees were needed at the bank. A story told of that time describes how at every directors' meeting Stephen would begin by asking: "Has anyone found anybody to buy any of the stocks and bonds since we last met?" One day Smith, coming in late and observing the gloom on the faces of his fellow directors, suggested a twenty-four-hour adjournment. When the morrow came, a jaunty Smith entered and asked: "Has anyone raised any money?" His colleagues gloomily shook their heads. Whereupon Smith announced: "I've stolen another million and that will last us till somebody gets some more."

Though this tale, which made the rounds of Montreal clubs, may be apocryphal, Smith was prepared, like Stephen, to invest all of his own money in the Canadian Pacific. Stephen, who went to London in July, was able that month to "*melt*," as he put it, a number of land grant bonds into cash by giving the personal guarantee of Smith, Angus, and himself to a British bank for a four-month loan. "Smith," he told Macdonald, "has behaved splendidly, promptly doing what I asked him to do. . . ."

It was the second of three trips Stephen made across the Atlantic in that desperate year of 1884. The first, in April, had been a total failure. Stephen had hoped to raise funds to build the Manitoba South-Western, an important branch of the railway, and also to try to boost public confidence in Canada and in the CPR. He failed on both counts and returned to Montreal exhausted.

The continued attacks on the Canadian Pacific affected Canada's own credit position on the other side of the Atlantic. Leonard Tilley, the finance minister, arriving in London in June and hoping to float a loan of five million pounds, was alarmed at the propaganda campaign that had been organized. "A desperate effort is being made here, and successful too," he reported, "to force down both Govt. bonds and CPR stocks, and the knowing ones say they will be forced still lower. All kinds of unfriendly statements are sent here from the U States & Winnipeg . . . and I fully expect that when the prospectus of our loan appears to-morrow we will have a heavy GT blast against it." The expected blast came: a "fierce article" in the *Standard* and a "vile article" in the *Mining & Financial Register*, which referred to the loan as "another crutch for the CPR." A man actually paraded in front of the great financial house of Baring, where the bonds were being offered, advertising the article by means of huge handbills. Tilley, who blamed the Grand Trunk for planting the story, got his money only with difficulty and not at the rate he expected. A week later CPR stock dropped to a record low of 39 on the New York board. As John Rose had put it earlier that year, there seemed to be "some evil genius at the American end of the cable where Canada is concerned." The railway's enemies, determined to drive it into bankruptcy, were also apparently prepared to bruise the country as well. "It is painful to see how much animosity is shown to Canadian interests," Rose reported in July. The animosity was not confined to outsiders; Rose put the Bank of Montreal, among others, in the enemy camp. His own firm had been badly injured by virtue of holding Canadian Pacific and other Canadian securities.

Stephen, whose skin was never very thick when attacks were being made on his railway, responded with fury to the "malicious venom" in the *Globe* that summer. It was "simply damnable that they should be allowed to live and pursue such hellish work." There was no doubt in his mind as to who was the grey eminence behind the *Globe*'s continuing attacks: "Hickson is at the bottom of it all. . . ." Finally, Stephen was stung to the point of reply. The *Globe* published his letters in full and then turned them against him:

"If Mr. George Stephen's statements that the last loan of $30,000,000 will build and equip the road, why is he so sensitive about the attacks of the Globe? To be frank with Mr. Stephen he has humbugged the public as much as he can. He has a corrupt government and the corrupt Parliament at his mercy; but a few years hence he will have to appeal to the electors of Canada who make and unmake governments and parliaments. He had better make good use of the power he has at present over the creatures who have so shamefully betrayed the taxpayers of this country. Mr. Stephen has lost caste; Mr. Stephen is looked upon now as a pocket edition of Jay Gould. It is his own fault. He has betrayed the public for a fortune for himself and his friends. He has sullied the reputation he once had as a high-toned businessman. He has no one to blame but himself. He sees his downfall near at hand, and hopes that by blaming the Globe newspaper he may fall upon a bed of doom; but we sincerely hope it won't be, as it deserves to be upon something harder."

To the sensitive Stephen, who valued his personal integrity and reputation above all else – far more than he valued his own fortune or possessions – these insinuations were almost too much. Perhaps the wickedest of all gibes was the rumour, widely published in the Liberal press, that he had imported a grand piano from the United States worth four thousand dollars and was protesting paying the standard twenty-five per cent duty. The original report had it that Stephen was claiming exemption for the piano under the clause in the CPR contract that allowed the importation of railway material duty free. This was vigorously denied, but the explanation was almost as damaging. "He claims," the *Globe* sneered, "his piano is a fine work of art, that it would be a model for Canadian piano workers. Is this not a slur upon our manufacturers?" The net effect of the story was to present Stephen as a bloated capitalist, tinkering with expensive toys at a time when he was appealing for further government aid for the railway.

In the face of such calumny, Stephen was forced to hold his peace. During that year he seemed to swing from depression to elation and back to depression again. In August he confidently told the press that the government loan of the previous spring was quite sufficient to finish the railway. In October, the Prime Minister found that "he is in high spirits over the CPR." At that point he had just seen the company's balance sheet, which showed that the railway was making money in all its divisions – a net of $563,374 on earnings of $4,017,209 in the first nine months of 1884.

Stephen's elation was short lived. Soon he was a mass of nerves again. The company could certainly make money, but the shortage of ready cash was killing it. In mortgaging the railroad, Stephen had made it impossible to raise any further funds except through the sale of outstanding stock. But the government lien, together with the bitter campaign being waged against the CPR in New York and London, had frightened off potential buyers. Unless he could make an arrangement to get rid of that lien he faced an impossible situation. It was a maddening dilemma: as soon as the CPR became a through line the profits would roll in, for it held a mileage advantage over other transcontinental railroads. Goods arriving from the Orient could speed across Canada to the Atlantic far faster than any rival road could carry them. But could the CPR be completed? By October,

Stephen realized that there simply was not enough money to do the job.

He set off for England for the third time that year, seeking to raise more funds. The loan he had negotiated in July would shortly be due. Worse, the five-million-dollar loan he had raised in New York the previous year by pledging ten million dollars worth of CPR stock was also due in November. He had not expected to have to worry about that obligation since he had believed the stock would become saleable at a price beyond the loan. But the stock was still hovering around the 40 mark. There were other worries. Looking beyond the financial watershed of November, Stephen could see the dark month of February looming up. Then the railway would be forced to pay its guaranteed dividend of five per cent. The government was responsible for three per cent, but the CPR would somehow have to find the cash for the remainder – an amount in excess of one million dollars.

The situation looked almost hopeless. On the trip across, Stephen outlined the railway's plight to Macdonald, who was on the same ship, taking a voyage to London for his health. The news could not have done much for the Prime Minister's stomach trouble, nor could Stephen's hesitant proposal that fresh legislation might be enacted to free the property from the government lien have sat very easily on Macdonald's shoulders. To the weary Prime Minister, who had exhausted himself and used up much of his political credit through the loan legislation of the previous spring, this was an almost impossible suggestion. Only a few months before the air had crackled with brave promises about the future of the CPR and of the country. Now, to have to admit that the railway was again in financial trouble! It was too much to swallow politically.

Nevertheless, Stephen began to see some tiny pinpoints of light at the end of the dark tunnel down which he had set his course. The New York loan he solved by the now familiar device of using his own funds and those of some of his friends. He simply bought up the stock held as collateral and paid off the debt. Then in London, the doughty Charles Tupper came to his aid as a result of his conversations with Macdonald. Tupper, mindful of the government's earlier adventures in railroad building, was opposed to taking over the road from the company. The objections were formidable, he thought. But "the prosperity of Canada is involved in this gigantic enterprise." It could not be allowed to fail. He drafted a plan for relief of the railway and shot it off to Tilley in Ottawa. It was all very tentative; nobody knew, certainly not Macdonald, whether any further plan to aid the CPR could be forced down the throats of the Cabinet and the public in time to do any good. Still, it was a straw at which Stephen could grasp. And, finally, by pledging $385,000 worth of Toronto, Grey and Bruce bonds, which he, Donald Smith, and R. B. Angus held among them, he was able to raise a loan of a quarter of a million from a Scottish financial institution. It was this small bit of Highland good cheer that prompted the president to send off to Donald Smith one of the most memorable cablegrams in Canadian history – and certainly the shortest.

Both Stephen and Smith had come from small Scottish towns in the countryside drained by the River Spey, in a land once dominated by the Clan Grant. Stephen remembered, and knew that Smith would remember also, a great rock which dominated the valley no more than three miles from Dufftown, in Banffshire, where he had been born. Everyone knew the meaning of that rock: it was a symbol of defiance. In the brave old days, when clan battled clan, a sentinel had kept watch on its stark promontory, and when the enemy was sighted and a fiery cross borne through Speyside, this rock had become a rallying place for the Clan Grant. The rock was known as Craigellachie, and it was this defiant slogan that Stephen dispatched to his cousin. Into one brief, cryptic sentence, the CPR president managed to convey all the fierce passions, bold defiance, dark hatreds, and bright loyalties inherited from his Scottish forbears. "Stand fast, Craigellachie!" the cable advised, and Donald Smith, when he read it in Montreal, must himself have heard, as in the distance, the clash of warring claymores and the wild skirl of battle.

326

Chapter Eight

1

Eighteen eighty-five

2

Riel: the return of the Messiah

3

"I wish I were well out of it"

4

Marching as to war

5

The cruel journey

1

Eighteen eighty-five was perhaps the most significant year of the first Canadian century. After that year nothing could ever be the same again, because for the first time Canadians would be able to travel the length of their nation without setting foot in a foreign land. Van Horne's two hundred miles of engineering impossibilities and Edward Blake's sea of mountains would both become authentic Canadian tourist attractions. Names like Lake Louise, Banff, and Yoho would stand for the ultimate in scenery; Kenora and North Bay would symbolize hunting and fishing paradises; Sudbury would be emblematic of mineral wealth; Regina and Moose Jaw would conjure up visions of golden wheat; Calgary would automatically mean cowboys and rodeos. Three years before, most of those names had not existed on the map.

A series of devices came into being that year that would help to bind the country together. The single-pole electric trolley had just been invented and was demonstrated for the first time at the Toronto Agricultural Fair of 1885. "The thought of a motor car run by an invisible force and drawing a car with fifty people aboard seems almost an impossibility," the *Globe* commented. That same year Gottlieb Daimler took out his historic patent for an internal combustion engine and Karl Benz built the first automobile – a three-wheeled one. The presence of radio waves was confirmed and the long-distance telephone put into use. Portland cement was beginning to replace bricks and cedar blocks on the major streets. Like the railway, these new aids to communication would help stitch the awkward archipelago of population islands into a workable transcontinental reality.

The concept of a transcontinental railway was also responsible for changing the casual attitude towards time. Heretofore every city and village had operated on its own time system. When it was noon in Toronto, it was 11.58 in Hamilton, 12.08 in Belleville, 12.12½ in Kingston, 12.16½ in Brockville, and 12.25 in Montreal. In the state of Michigan alone there were twenty-seven different times, most of them established by local jewellers. In some cities (Pittsburgh was one) there were as many as six versions of the correct time, varying by as much as twenty minutes.

As the railways lengthened across the continent, the constant changing of watches became more and more inconvenient. Worse, railway passenger and freight schedules were in a state of total confusion. Every railroad had its own version of the correct time, based on the time standard of its home city. There were, in the United States, one hundred different time standards used by the various railroads. In order that passengers could compare the various times, large stations were forced to install several clocks.

On New Year's Day, 1885, the Universal Time System was adopted at Greenwich. About a year earlier the major American railways and the Canadian Pacific had brought order out of chaos as far as their own schedules were concerned by adopting "railway time." The Thunder Bay *Sentinel* welcomed the change in an editorial and urged that it be taken up by the community:

"Everyone in Port Arthur, except perhaps railway men, keeps a different time. Scarcely half a dozen watches will be found to correspond. If a person wishes to catch a train he will at one time be half an hour ahead and again be that much behind. . . . It is the same with men working at offices or at the bench or in whatever sphere their duty calls them. Every church apparently has its own time, the only bell ringing with any degree of regularity being that of the Catholic church. Now all this difficulty could be done away with by having one time in town and everyone keeping their watches and clocks together. . . ."

The local jeweller, W. P. Cook, announced that he would adopt the CPR's time, putting his regulator back about twenty-two minutes, and that he would send the new time to all the clergymen in Port Arthur so that the bells might ring in unison. The change was a fundamental one, for it affected in a subtle fashion people's attitudes and behaviour. Such concepts as promptness and tardiness took on a new meaning. Schedules became more important when they became more precise. The country began to live by the clock in a way it had not previously been able to do.

Much of the credit for this went to Sandford Fleming, the man who had originally planned the transcontinental railway in Canada. More than twenty years before, when Fleming was first contemplating the idea of the Canadian Pacific, he had realized that the plan would immediately raise difficulties in the computation of time. His views were confirmed as the railway project took shape. In 1876 he prepared a memorandum on the subject, which was widely circulated. Two years later he made energetic efforts to read a paper on the concept before the British Association for the Advancement of Science but was rebuffed as an unknown and a colonial. It was, Fleming later wrote, "one of those acts of official insolence or indifference so mischievous in their influence and so offensive in their character, which I fear, in years gone by, too many from the Outer Empire experienced." Nonetheless, Fleming persevered in his study of time and the Canadian Institute, which he had founded, recognized him in 1885 as "unquestionably the initiator and principal agent in the movement for the reform in Time-Reckoning and in the establishment of the Universal Day."

The adoption of the new time system in that first month of 1885 was a relatively minor event as far as newspaper readers were concerned. The world was in a ferment and, for the first time, the new nation had a personal stake in the outcome. Up the steamy cataracts of the Nile a flotilla of boats manned by Canadian voyageurs was slowly making its way on a vain mission to relieve Khartoum and rescue that flawed hero, General Charles Gordon, from the clutches of the Mahdi. This was the nation's first expeditionary force and it had its origin in the same series of events that helped to launch the idea of a Pacific railway. Its commander was General Garnet Wolseley, who had taken Canadian and British troops across the portages of the Shield to relieve Fort Garry during the Riel uprising of 1869–70. It was Wolseley's idea to use some of the same French Canadians to man the Nile brigade. The commander of the flotilla was William Francis Butler, another officer familiar to Canadians, for it was he who had first excited the nation with his descriptions of the Great Lone Land. The railway had put that phrase, along with the old portage route, into the discard. Never again would a military force require seventy-six days to make its way to the North West.

Because of the railway, the settled and stable community of Canada was entering a new period of instability. The closed frontier society of 1850–85 was being replaced by the open frontier society of 1885–1914. After 1885, the Canadian Shield ceased to be a barrier to westward development. The railway would be a catalyst in new movements of population (such as the Klondike gold-rush) and in a variety of social phenomena that would destroy the established social order – agrarian agitation, new political parties, odd religious sects and communities, and the continuation of that ethnic diversity known as "the Canadian mosaic."

Eighteen eighty-five was as dramatic a year as it was significant. As the nation became vertebrate, events seemed to accelerate on a collision course. In Montreal, George Stephen, teetering on the cliff edge of nervous collapse, was trying to stave off personal and corporate ruin. In Ottawa, John A. Macdonald faced a cabinet revolt over the railway's newest financial proposals. In Toronto, Thomas Shaughnessy was juggling bills, cheques, notes of credit, promises, and threats like an accomplished side-show artist in order to give Van Horne the cash he needed to complete the line. On Lake Superior, Van Horne was desperately trying to link up the gaps between the isolated stretches of steel – they totalled 254 miles – so that the CPR might begin its operation as a through road. In Manitoba, the political agitation against both the government and the railway was increasing, in spite of Macdonald's promise that the hated monopoly clause would be dropped from the contract once the job was finished. In St. Laurent on the Saskatchewan, Louis Riel, the leader of the Red River uprising of 1869, was back from his long exile and rousing the Métis again. On the far plains and in the foothills, the Cree chieftains Big Bear and Poundmaker were agitating for new concessions from an unheeding government. And in the mountains, the railway builders faced their last great barrier – the snow-shrouded Selkirks.

The Selkirks remained a mystery almost to the moment when the steel was driven through. There was something uncanny about those massive pyramidal peaks, scoured by erosion and rent by avalanche. As late as 1884, when the rails reached the mouth of the Beaver, powerful voices had been raised urging that the road circumvent the mountains by following the hairpin valley of the Columbia. Even in 1885, after the right of way was cleared and the steel had started to push up the valley of the Beaver towards the Rogers Pass, a pamphlet was printed and distributed in Montreal called *An Appeal to Public Opinion against a Railway Being Carried across the Selkirk Range*. The uneasiness was felt in the highest echelons of the company, and with good reason: for the very first time the locomotives, rather than the Indians, were blazing a pioneer trail.

Van Horne had thought long and hard about using the Rogers Pass in preference to the longer but easier Columbia Valley. Publicly he called it "one of the finest mountain passes ever seen," but privately he had reservations. On the one hand there would be heavy gradients – probably greater than two per cent – for some forty miles. That would mean heavy assisting engines and costly wear and tear on the track. Against that there was the saving of the cost of operating nearly seventy-seven miles of additional line, which meant a reduction of two hours in passenger time and four hours for freight trains. This latter consideration was of great importance when competing for through traffic and, in the general manager's opinion, "would alone be sufficient to justify the use of heavier gradients." Van Horne, who disdained circumlocution, opted for the Rogers Pass.

There were problems in the Selkirks, however, on which no one had reckoned, and these began to manifest themselves in the first months of 1885. By that time the right of way had been cleared directly across the mountains, from the mouth of the Beaver River at its junction with the

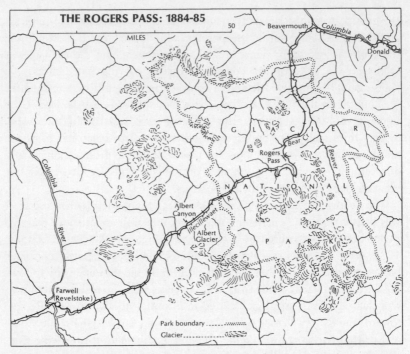

THE ROGERS PASS: 1884-85

MILES

50

Beavermouth   Columbia   R.
Donald

G L A C I E R
Bear Cr.
Rogers Pass
Beaver R.
N A T I O N A L
Columbia   R.
Albert Canyon
Illecillewaet   R.
Albert Glacier
P A R K
River
Farwell (Revelstoke)

Park boundary
Glacier

Columbia on the east to the mouth of the Illecillewaet at its confluence with the Columbia on the west. More than a thousand men, strung out in scattered construction camps and individual shacks along the tote road, were toiling away in the teeth of shrieking winds that drove snow particles like needles into their faces. Seen from the top of the pass, the location line resembled a wriggling serpent, coiling around the hanging valleys, squeezing through the narrow ravines, and sometimes vanishing into the dark maw of a half-completed tunnel. High above, millions of tons of ice hung poised on the lip of the mountains, the birthplace of the avalanches and snowslides that constantly swept the area.

The snowslides occurred largely on the western slopes of the mountains. Like the lush vegetation – the gigantic cedars and huge ferns, which astonished every traveller who crossed the Rogers Pass – they were the result of an extraordinary precipitation. The moist winds, blowing across British Columbia from the Pacific, were blocked by the mountain rampart, which relieved them of their burden of water vapour. The rainfall each summer was heavy and the snowfall phenomenal. An average of thirty feet of snow fell each winter at the Illecillewaet Glacier; at the summit the average fall was fifty feet.

332

This natural phenomenon posed a threat to the entire operation of the railway. In midwinter, the Rogers Pass was almost impossible to breach. On February 8, 1885, a North West Mounted Police constable named Macdonald set out from Second Crossing on the Columbia, at the site of the future city of Revelstoke, and rode thirty miles up the western slopes of the Selkirks towards the pass. When he was within fifteen miles of the summit he could no longer ride and was able to proceed on foot only with difficulty. The pass, he reported, was one mass of avalanches, slides and fallen glaciers. The snowslides were solid packs of ice and were sometimes fifty feet in thickness. Through this frozen jungle the railroad builders intended to force the line.

The day Macdonald commenced his journey, a slide six miles west of the summit buried the camp of William Mackenzie, killing the cook. On the same day a second slide, four miles west of the summit, buried three men alive. A third slide, closer to the summit, destroyed a company store. There were several men in the building at the time but fortunately the skirt of the avalanche swept by and only the western portion of the store was buried; the occupants were able to squeeze out through a window. It took Constable Macdonald a day and a half to cover the final fifteen miles to the summit. From there to Beaver River, thirty miles away on the drier eastern slopes of the mountains, it was a comparatively easy ride.

The slides on the western slopes formed the chief topic of conversation among construction workers that winter. "The workmen on the road seem panic-stricken," one reporter remarked. "And many of them are refusing to work on account of the danger, others are striking for higher wages, the demand being for $3.50 per day." The situation grew worse. Herbert Holt lost sixty-five thousand dollars worth of supplies, all swept away by a vast slide at the end of February. By that time all communication between the summit and Second Crossing was cut off; supplies could no longer come in from Kamloops but had to be hauled up from Beavermouth.

A Selkirk snowslide was a terrifying spectacle. A quarter of a million cubic yards of snow could be detached from a mountain peak and come tearing down the slopes for thousands of feet, ripping out great cedars, seizing huge boulders in its grip, and causing an accompanying cyclone more fearful than the avalanche itself. This cyclone extended for a hundred yards or more outside the course of the slide and was known as the flurry, a term that scarcely did credit to its intensity. A few seconds before the body of the avalanche struck, the pressure of this gale force wind snapped off huge trees several feet in diameter fifty feet above the base without uprooting them. The accompanying cloud of fine snow particles was impacted like moss against the windward side of the trunks. One such flurry was known to have picked up a man and whirled and twisted him spirally and so rapidly that when he dropped he was a limp mass without a bruise or a break in skin or clothing yet with every bone in his body either broken or dislocated. One snowslide, which stopped just short of the track near Glacier, was preceded by a flurry so powerful that it knocked eight loaded freight cars off the rails. The railway builders sometimes cut right through small mountains of debris left behind by such slides. One cut, about forty feet deep, was full of tangled trees and presented such a strange appearance when gulleted – the sawn stumps sticking out like raisins in a cake – that it was known as Plum Pudding Cut.

Apart from the slides, the prodigious falls of snow – as much as fifty feet on the summit of the pass – presented a considerable hazard. In one six-day period, eight and a half feet of snow fell. Sometimes three weeks could pass without the blizzard ceasing. Even in mid-May there might be two feet of snow remaining in the summit area. In the winter, the scene from the Rogers Pass was eerie. The traveller, gazing westward, looked down into a two-thousand-foot gorge, muffled in a white blanket twenty feet deep. Above and around him the glaciers dangled, shimmering in the sunlight. At one spot, forty-two glaciers were visible, the largest being the vast Illecillewaet, which would for more than half a century be one of the great Canadian tourist attractions until the changing climate caused it to recede. (One lady from Seattle gazing upon it in awe and wonder wanted to know if it was real or whether the CPR had installed it for advertising purposes.)

This scenery, an uncalculated asset for the railway in the summer season, was an uncalculated liability in the winter. It became obvious that no trains could operate in safety in the months of January and February; but even if the company had fully comprehended the problem in 1885, it is doubtful that it could have raised the money to solve it. The problems of the Selkirks delayed the opening of through passenger service to the Pacific by at least six months. In the winter of 1885–86 entire sections of completed track were swept away by snowslides and the line had to be closed. The scene of desolation was described by Michael Phillips, a rancher who travelled the line on foot: "A deserted house or cabin looks dreary in these mountains, a deserted town more dismal yet; but imagine, if you can, a railway deserted! Hundreds of miles of line abandoned! Signal boxes, stations, small towns lifeless, and fast being buried beneath the snow, all battered to pieces by fierce mountain storms!" Phillips added that he did not think it would ever be possible to keep the railroad operating through the Selkirks, and certainly never during winter and spring.

The CPR, of course, had no intention of retreating, but it took herculean efforts to open the track in the early years of its operation. Specially designed ice chisels were used to burrow into the snow; the resulting tunnels were filled with sacks of black powder and the snow packed in behind so that the entire right of way could be blasted clear. In the end, the company was forced to construct almost six miles of snow sheds – fifty-four sheds, built of heavy timbers. Even then there were unforeseen accidents – a tree driven right through the roof of one shed, a ten-ton boulder crashing through another. The sheds cost forty dollars a foot to construct, an expenditure Van Horne had not foreseen when he adopted the Rogers Pass route.

For the next quarter-century, this westward descent, like that of the Big Hill in the Rockies, was an operating nightmare. "I think the Rogers Pass was the worst place for snow in the whole world," a CPR engineer named Alex Forrest recalled. "It was just one eternal fight to buck snow from early fall to the following summer. We kept 150 men and 5 engines with plows and rotaries on the jump all the time. And a man's life was not rated very high."

In March, 1910, a snowslide which caused the loss of fifty-eight lives finally convinced the CPR that it must abandon the Rogers Pass. This resulted in a second engineering feat, equal to the drilling of the spiral tunnels – the boring of the longest double-track tunnel on the continent, the five-mile-long Connaught. Passing under Mount Macdonald, the tunnel lowered the grade by 540 feet, shortened the line by four and a half miles, and reduced the track curvature by an amount corresponding to seven complete circles. The man who did the job was the same Jack Stewart who worked as a youth in helping build the mountain line and who had once ferried Van Horne across a stream at Three Valley.

Snow or no snow, the line had to be driven to completion somehow by the end of 1885. As winter gave way to spring, every mile of the right of way was throbbing with activity – teamsters jogging in with wagonloads of supplies, other teams ploughing up the rough, root-ridden earth, small armies of men swinging picks and shovels, others blasting out hand-cuts and tunnels – trees toppling, stumps flying sky-high, boulders splintering, and always the stench of smoke and horse manure blotting out the subtler scent of the cedar forest.

Along the gorge of the Kicking Horse, the railway had kept close to the river, crossing it at the most economical spots, with the tote road suspended above. But in the valley of the Beaver, which led up towards the Selkirks, the line rose high above both road and river, as much as two and three hundred feet in places. The mountain streams tumbling down from the glaciers above had cut deep gouges in the naked rock, and it was over these gulches that the longest and highest bridges were required. Built entirely of timber cut on the spot, they had few counterparts in the world. The Mountain Creek bridge, which rose more than 175 feet above the torrent, was one of the largest wooden structures ever built, being twelve hundred feet long with a Howe truss in the centre and trestles at either end. The bridge over Stoney Creek was the highest in North America, a continuous Howe truss of four spans (the longest 186 feet) supported on wooden towers two hundred feet high, set in concrete.

There is a tale of Van Horne arriving at the half-completed Stoney Creek bridge when it was imperilled by rising floods. Men were felling trees, dragging logs to the site, and building new trestle braces and bulwarks when the general manager appeared. He plunged in to help, assisting with his own hands the placing of heavy blocks of stone, instructing the carpenters as to the best method of securing the huge wooden braces, showing the blacksmiths how to fashion their iron clamps, and never once losing his demeanour of cool authority. He drove the men all day until the light faded and the bridge was saved. By that time his private car was drawn up on the rails and Van Horne retired to it. Not long afterwards, the sounds of violin music came drifting through the night air. The general manager was playing an aria by Gounod, a sure sign that he was satisfied with the day's labour.

Another bridge crossed Cedar Creek at a height of one hundred feet. The rock approaches here were so sheer that the engineers laying out the job had to climb the cliffs on a rope and work suspended against the rock face. On one occasion, Turner Bone, in charge of the party, was standing on a ledge, clinging to the rope, when a chunk of hardened snow thundered down upon him and his assistant. Both men toppled from their perch but were able to slide to safety "at lightning speed."

It was no easy task to work with the diamond-hard rocks of the Selkirks. The strata often ran at right angles to the course of the stream. Sometimes extraordinarily hard layers of rock would stand out from the cliff face like a kind of fence left behind by the erosion of the centuries. One such fence was more than four inches thick and twenty feet high. Such irregularities made the work more than usually difficult. In one case it was easier to bridge the corner of a stream than to cut through the rock.

On the wet western slopes of the mountains, the railroad builders encountered another unexpected difficulty, a viscous gumbo formed from a sandy loam quicksand, which oozed from the sides of the cuts and covered the track with a mucilage that was almost impossible to remove. The gumbo was finally conquered by driving a double row of piles on either side of the track and filling the intervening space with coarse gravel or broken rock.

On the far side of the pass, where the Prussian blue waters of the Illecillewaet raced downhill between thick jungle walls, the line made a double loop, curving first to the left, then swinging back across the valley to the very tip of the great glacier – the future site of Glacier House – and then, a mile farther on, twisting back again in the shape of an inverted S. This was three more miles of railway than Van Horne had counted on; it took nine and a half miles to reach the level of the stream four miles from the summit. But it was necessary to avoid the snowslides. For the future tourists, swaying down this dramatic slope from the vantage point of an observation car in what was shortly to become Glacier National Park, the experience would be electrifying – the awesome cedars rising like great pillars from the thick beds of ferns, the mountainsides sprinkled with wild columbine and pigeonberry, the glittering ice-fields, the sword points of the mountain peaks, the cataracts pouring off the cliffs as airily as woodsmoke, and the shining track coiling through the dark cuts and over the slender bridges on its journey to the Columbia. This was the same trail, bestrewn with devil's club and skunk cabbage, that Major Rogers and his nephew Albert had toiled up on their voyage of discovery in 1881, that Fleming and Grant, badly lacerated from thorns, had managed to negotiate in 1883, and that a hungry Van Horne had struggled over in 1884. Nobody except an enthusiastic mountaineer would ever have to make that journey again; and only a few, gazing up at the shattered rock of the clefts and tunnels and the pilings of the matchstick bridges, would let their thoughts rest upon the thousands of sweating workmen who made it possible.

2

To those who had known the North West before the time of the steel, the railway was a symbol of the passing of the Good Old Days. To the Indians it was a new kind of boundary, as solid in its own way as a wall. To the white settlers of northern Saskatchewan, its change of route had meant disappointment. To the farmers of Manitoba it spelled monopoly and grinding freight rates. To the half-breeds, it stood for revolutionary social change.

From Winnipeg to Edmonton, the North West was in a ferment. Whites, Indians, and half-breeds were all organizing. At the end of July, 1884, the Crees of the North Saskatchewan, who had come to the point of rebellion earlier in the year, were welded into an Indian council by Big Bear, the most independent of the chiefs. The Indians felt that the government had betrayed and deceived them, and the Indians were right. Ottawa had promised to save them from starvation; in fact, one treaty – Number 6 – spelled it out. Yet already their meagre rations had been cut back as part of an official policy of retrenchment brought on by economic conditions. It was plain that the eastern politicians had little understanding of conditions in the North West. The new Minister of the Interior, Senator David Macpherson, had not even ventured as far as Winnipeg.

The western newspapers, in contrast to their attitude to the Chinese, were sympathetic towards the plight of the natives. The Moose Jaw *News* declared that the suffering of the Indians in the Assiniboia reserves was "a burning shame to us [and] a lasting reproach to our government." It reported that they were dying by the score as a result of semi-starvation or scurvy resulting from the bad quality of the food supplied by the agencies.

The white settlers and farmers were equally disaffected. In addition to the burgeoning Manitoba Farmers' Union, which was threatening secession, annexation, or even rebellion, there were in the Territories other organized groups petitioning Ottawa for redress, such as the Settlers' Rights Association at Qu'Appelle and the Settlers' Union at Prince Albert. Their demands were similar: local autonomy, reform of the land laws, control of their own railways, reduction of protective tariffs, and an end to the CPR monopoly.

The English and Scots half-breeds and the French-speaking Roman Catholic Métis had another grievance. They wanted in the North West Territories what the government had recognized and granted in Manitoba after the first collision with Louis Riel in 1869 and 1870 – a share in the aboriginal title to the land. From 1873 to 1884 they had been vainly petitioning Ottawa to grant them this recognition. They had been put off, time after time, with the maddening reply that consideration would be given to their demands. Nothing concrete was done.

In Manitoba, the government's land policy had been a hopeless muddle. Some Métis received free land but others, who were absent on the plains when a census was taken, did not. Long delays in the actual distribution of the land were frequent. Many half-breeds who had been issued money scrip in lieu of actual acreage gave up in despair, sold out to fast-talking speculators, and moved farther west ahead of the advancing army of white settlers. The coming of the railway marked for them the end of a social order that had been based on hunting and freighting.

A note of nostalgia crept into the report of the Qu'Appelle correspondent of the Moose Jaw *News* in April, 1884, when he noted that because the Red River cart had been rendered obsolete, the Métis could no longer occupy themselves in the freighting business, long an auxiliary source of income:

"It is sad to watch how the half-breeds have been driven by the inevitable back and aback, like their half-brothers, the red men of the continent. . . . What is their future? Absorption I suppose, for I have noticed they do not seem to be able to breathe the same atmosphere as the white man. Wherever they go they form a distinct community, and do not like to be divided."

In St. Albert near Edmonton, in the Qu'Appelle Valley, and in St. Laurent near Duck Lake on the South Saskatchewan, these distinct communities had been forming since the early 1870's as the Métis struggled to maintain their identity. By 1884 they were in a state of frustration and alarm because of the government's stumbling land policy. One of the problems was the difficulty of acquiring title to land on which many had squatted for years. If, after the long-awaited surveys were completed, it was discovered that a man was squatting on an odd-numbered section or one reserved for a school or for the Hudson's Bay Company, he was expected to pay for it. Even if he was found to be on property available for homestead, he was required to wait for three years after the survey before he could apply for a patent. To families that had been on the land as long as ten or a dozen years, this was maddening. Later arrivals, who had been used to the traditional long, river lots, discovered that, except in the original settlements, the government was insisting on a square township survey. This led to further bitterness and confusion as the newcomers, disregarding the surveyors' lines, took up their land in the traditional manner.

By the spring of 1884, protest meetings were becoming common at St. Laurent, the strongest and best established of the Métis communities. ". . . the N.W. Ter. is like a volcanoe ready to erupt," one Métis wrote to the exiled Louis Riel in May, 1884. "The excitement is almost general. All minds are everywhere excited. Since the month of March last public meetings are everywhere frequently held . . . French and English Half-breeds

339

are now united. . . . On all sides people complain of injustice; they invoke equity, they desire to obtain our rights."

By that time, the united half-breed community in the forks of the Saskatchewan had decided that Riel was the only man who could lead them – peacefully, it was hoped – in an agitation to force the government's hand. He had done it fifteen years before. He must be persuaded to do it again. No one else had his charisma, his sense of tactics, his eloquence and, above all, his reputation.

Riel was a long distance away and many years out of touch, living in poverty and teaching school at a Jesuit mission at Sun River, Montana. Distance held no terrors for the Métis. Four of them saddled up their horses that May and set out on a seven-hundred-mile ride to meet their Messiah.

The most interesting member of the delegation, and the one who occupies a special niche in the history of the Saskatchewan Rebellion of 1885, was Gabriel Dumont, the most popular and respected man along the Saskatchewan – a natural leader, though totally unlettered and almost apolitical. For years Dumont, "the Prince of the Prairies," had been chief of the buffalo hunt, a severe disciplinarian who held to the code ("no buffalo run on Sabbath Day; no person or party to run buffalo before general order . . ."). He was a legendary rider, sharpshooter, drinker, gambler, and even swimmer – a rarity among Métis – and he had acquired the knack of "calling" buffalo into a trap, a skill lost by most Indian tribes.

There were many tales circulating about the plains regarding Dumont's exploits as a youth. At the age of eighteen, he had led a posse of Cree to an armed camp of twenty-five Blackfoot to recapture the kidnapped wife of a friend. Dumont and one man entered the camp, jumped the guards, and carried off the woman safely. On another occasion he had flabbergasted a Blackfoot encampment by creeping in out of the shadows at the height of a pot dance and joining the male dancers who were spearing meat in the central pot and boasting of their exploits in killing Crees. "I am Gabriel Dumont," he shouted, spearing a piece of meat on his own, "and I have killed eight Blackfoot! What do you think of that?" The chief was so astounded he invited Dumont to stay and even suggested a peace treaty.

In 1884, when he set off to see Riel, Dumont was forty-seven years old, a swarthy, stocky man with bull's shoulders and a handsome, kindly face. He had been a chief of his people since the age of twenty-five, much beloved by all who knew him, including Sam Steele, the Mounted Policeman, who thought him one of the kindest and best of men, flawed only

340

by an obsession for gambling: he was quite capable of playing cards for three days and nights without stopping to eat. Dumont knew the prairies, Steele said, "as well as a housewife knows her kitchen," and was universally respected: "One might travel the plains from one end to the other and talk to the Metis hunters and never hear an unkind word said of Dumont. He would kill bison by the score and give them to those who were either unable to kill or had no buffalo. Not until every poor member of the hunting-parties had his cart filled with meat would he begin to fill his own. When in trouble the cry of all was for Gabriel."

In 1884 there was trouble, and the cry was for Gabriel again. He knew that he could not lead his people in a battle with the government of Canada. He spoke several Indian dialects as well as he spoke his native French, but he had no English and no gift for oratory. He was a man of action, a prairie general who would shortly become the tactician of the last stand of the Métis empire against the onrush of civilization.

The four Métis delegates arrived at Riel's small home on June 4, 1884. Riel was plumper than he had been in the days of the Manitoba uprising. His features had filled out and he now wore a curly, red-brown beard. He was still handsome, with a high, intelligent forehead, a straight nose, and a pair of eyes that, when he recalled the stirring days of 1869 and 1870, "danced and glistened in a manner that riveted attention."

He was under doctor's orders to behave quietly and avoid excitement, a counsel he only occasionally remembered to follow. Exiled in 1875 for five years as a result of his role in the Red River troubles (specifically, his summary execution of the Orangeman, Thomas Scott), deprived of his parliamentary seat, forced to flit back and forth across the border, his already mercurial psyche had been subjected to such stresses that he had gone insane at times, bellowing aloud that he was a prophet, suffering hallucinations, and sometimes running naked down the corridors of the institutions in which he was confined. Twenty months in Quebec asylums (hidden from his pursuers) had calmed him down, but his sense of personal mission was never quenched. Moving west once more, he had plunged briefly into Montana politics, fighting the Democratic Party establishment on behalf of the Métis there before settling down with his dark little Métis wife, Marguerite, to the penniless life of a parish schoolmaster.

Riel was clearly aroused by the message the delegation brought to him. The sense of power, which he had enjoyed in his brief time as master of Fort Garry, was still within him; so was the mystic conviction that he had a divine mission to perform. Undoubtedly he felt keenly the plight of his people, as he had fifteen years before. Added to that was his own sense of

341

injury at the hands of the Canadian government. Canada, he believed, owed him both land and money while he himself had been living in penury. After some consideration he told the delegation that he would return to Canada temporarily (he was at this point a naturalized American) to fight not only for his personal rights and those of his people, but also for the white settlers and the Indians. Significantly, his first public meeting in the North West (in July) was held at an English-speaking settlement, Red Deer Hill. W. H. Jackson, secretary of the Settlers' Union, shared the platform with him. Later that month Riel and Jackson met with Big Bear and incorporated in their subsequent petition to Ottawa the Indians' grievances and demands.

The Canadian government had – or should have had – plenty of warning that matters in the North West were coming to a head. On August 23, Hayter Reed, the Assistant Indian Commissioner, wrote to Lieutenant-Governor Dewdney from Prince Albert that Riel had held a council of Indians, listened to their grievances, and told them the Indians and half-breeds must act in concert. Reed, however, did not feel there would be trouble until the following summer. At about the same time, William Pearce of the Dominion land department reported to Dewdney that he had "the feeling of nervousness about the state of the Indians." Dewdney, however, officially reported that, in his opinion, Pearce's fears were groundless. The Prime Minister was well aware of the rumours of discontent among the Métis at Battleford and Duck Lake but did not attach much importance to them, though he did suggest that the NWMP force in the Territories be strengthened.

Certainly on the surface Riel did not appear to sanction trouble and probably did not, at that time, contemplate it. His meetings were enthusiastic but outwardly peaceful. Sergeant Keenan of the Police, stationed at Batoche, reported on September 15 his belief that this apparent moderation was spurious: ". . . they advocate very different measures in their councils." Keenan learned through a spy of one such secret meeting where Charles Nolin, a Métis leader, had advocated that they "take up arms at once and commence killing every white man they can find and incite the Indians to do the same" if the Métis demands on the government were not met. These demands were codified and sent to Ottawa; they included requests for land scrip, better treatment for the Indians, responsible government with vote by ballot, parliamentary representation, reduction of the tariff, and the building of another railway to Hudson Bay. In spite of the clamour, the government in Ottawa remained curiously inattentive.

The resident priest at St. Laurent, Father André, wrote three letters to

Dewdney in January and February, 1885, stating clearly that unless the government took some action to redress grievances there would be an uprising under Riel in which the Indians would join. ". . . this continued state of excitement is dangerous. The Government is, I believe, quite wrong in not leading itself to some arrangement which would prove satisfactory to all parties concerned." By this time Riel was acting very strangely indeed. From the first of January, it was said, he had fed exclusively on blood instead of flesh, the blood being cooked in milk. It was done, Charles Nolin later swore in court, to excite a feeling of awe in the minds of his followers, "no doubt with a view to making them believe that he was acting under Divine instructions." There is not much doubt that Riel himself believed that he was God's envoy. He prayed daily, told of revelations he had experienced in the night, recounted the visitations of saints, and repeated conversations he said he had had with the Holy Ghost. The director of the Catholic mission at St. Laurent later stated that "in his strange and alarming folly, [he] fascinated our poor half breeds as the snake is said to fascinate its victim."

Father André's repeated warnings were supplemented by others from Joseph Howe, the Mounted Police inspector at Prince Albert, from Major L. N. F. Crozier, his superior at Battleford, and from D. H. Macdowall, the representative of the district on the Territorial Council. All urged that Ottawa take some action; but the government's only response was a vague set of promises for the future and the establishment in January of that favourite Canadian device for procrastination – a commission, to examine the question of scrip for the Métis. This served only to infuriate Riel and his followers.

Crozier's advice was that "if this man Riel was out of the country the normal quiet would be restored." The fascinating truth of the matter seems to be that Riel could have been bought off quite easily for a few thousand dollars. The evidence, which has been glossed over or ignored by some of Riel's later adherents, makes it clear that he was prepared to desert the Métis cause and return to Montana for hard cash and that he did his best to negotiate that return with the government's representatives.

Riel had made his intentions clear to Father André, who had gone directly to Councillor Macdowall and urged that he meet immediately with the Métis leader. The meeting took place a few days before Christmas, 1884, and lasted four hours. Riel did most of the talking. Macdowall reported the interview in detail to Dewdney:

"He . . . proceeded to state that if the Government would consider his personal claims against them and pay him a certain amount in settlement of these claims, he would arrange to make his illiterate and unreasoning followers well satisfied with almost any settlement of their claims for land grants that the Government might be willing to make, and also that he would leave the N W. never to return."

Following the uprising of 1869–70, when Riel was an embarrassment to both the Conservative and the subsequent Liberal governments, he had, apparently, been quietly offered certain sums – he mentioned a figure of thirty-five thousand dollars – to leave the country. In addition, he felt that he was entitled to further compensation of the kind that some of his former followers had received in the form of land scrip.

"His claims," Macdowall reported, "amount to the modest sum of $100,000^{00} but he will take $35,000^{00} as originally offered and I believe myself that $3000^{00} or $5000^{00} would cart the whole Riel family across the boundary. Riel made it most distinctly understood that 'self' was his real object and he was willing to make the claims of his followers totally subservient to his own interests. He appeared to me to be an enthusiast who had suffered personal losses and who had felt as one 'hounded' in '70 to '74, that this feeling of injury had grown into a monomania which had been brooded over and which was nourished by his enthusiastic nature, and that the only danger there is in him lies in his enthusiasm, which added to his past history, gives him an immense influence for good or for evil over his ignorant followers. . . .

"Riel's last statement was that he would not believe in any promise that might be made to him, but that if money were sent for him he would carry out his part. He said 'my name is Riel and I want materiel' which I suppose was a pun. . . .

". . . he also said that he was poor and if not relieved he would die of hunger and he might as well die at once in a struggle. . . . Withal, he is crafty and, from the way he is willing to sacrifice his followers' interests, double-dealing. . . ."

Macdowall's report to Dewdney was followed by a series of earnest pleas that Riel be got out of the country. "Riel is anxious to leave, and we must provide him with the means of leaving," Father André wrote. Inspector Howe reported to Crozier in similar vein. ("Riel stated that he was thinking shortly of returning to Montana if the Government would only give him the means to do so. . . .")

To John A. Macdonald, this was simple blackmail, and he refused to countenance it although fourteen years before he had had no such qualms. At that time he had been happy to have Donald A. Smith bribe Riel to leave the Red River. In vain Father André continued to plead that Riel

344

be paid a few thousand dollars: ". . . that sum ought not to be unobtainable to the peace and security of this part of the country."

That peace and security was rapidly being threatened as Riel's hold on the Métis, sparked by a growing religious fervour and mysticism, increased. He was once again calling himself a prophet and signing papers with the Biblical middle name of David. To his followers, he was close to being a saint.

In the face of continued government vacillation Major Crozier's misgivings increased. He wired Dewdney in February urging that a surveyor be sent out at once to reassure the Métis, by his actions, that no one intended to trample on their customs in the matter of strip farms. He also wanted the question of land scrip handled immediately. Delay would be dangerous. "Delay causes uneasiness and discontent, which spreads not only among the Half Breeds but the Indians."

But the Prime Minister's mood that spring seemed to be delay, as George Stephen was finding to his own frustration. Macdonald appeared to exhibit a strange blindness towards the North West. He had shown it in 1869 at the time of the first Riel trouble. He had shown it repeatedly in the settlement of prairie communities, when, time and again, the rights of the settlers had been ignored. He had shown it with the Indians and now he was showing it with the Métis. There was a curious ambivalence about the Prime Minister's attitude towards the new Canada west of Ottawa. At the time of Confederation he had ignored it totally, believing it unfit for anything but a few Indians and fur traders. Then, when the Americans seemed on the point of appropriating it by default, he had pushed the bold plan for a transcontinental railway. Suddenly once again he seemed to have lost interest. The railway was floundering in a financial swamp; the West was about to burst into flame. Macdonald vacillated.

Riel's memory went back to those intoxicating moments in December, 1869, when, having seized Fort Garry without a shot, raised a Métis flag, and established a provisional government on the prairies, he had been able to deal with Canada on equal diplomatic terms and secure concessions for his people as the result of a bold *fait accompli*. Something along the same lines was in his mind in the early months of 1885. He would not need to resort to bloodshed; the threat of it would bring the Canadian government to its senses.

But times had changed since 1869. Technically, Riel had been on reasonably strong ground in the Red River valley; it was not actually part of Canada at the time. But the territory of Saskatchewan was a legal entity, and anyone forming a new government there was clearly a rebel, com-

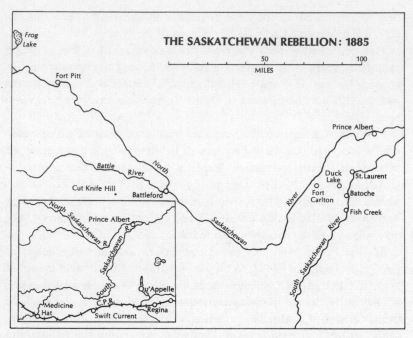

THE SASKATCHEWAN REBELLION: 1885

mitting treason. More important, Riel ignored the presence of the railway. In 1869, the Red River had been an isolated community, separated from Canada by the rampart of the Shield. He and his Métis had existed almost in a vacuum and worked their will because the Canadian minority in the settlement could not be reinforced by soldiers from the East. Those conditions no longer held.

By March 13, Crozier was expecting a rebellion to break out at any moment. The *Saskatchewan Herald* reported that day that Riel had spoken in French to a large gathering outside the church, pointing to imminent hostilities between England and Russia and suggesting that it was a good time for the Métis to assert their rights.

The NWMP commissioner, A. G. Irvine, dispatched a hundred reinforcements to Prince Albert. Rumour, winging across the prairies, raised that number to five hundred, so that Riel came to believe that the government had replied to his demands by raising an army against him. Events now began to accelerate. On March 18, the day before the festival of St. Joseph, the patron saint of the Métis, Riel took prisoners, seized arms in the St. Laurent–Batoche area, and cut the telegraph line between Batoche and Prince Albert. The following day, with his people assembled for the festival, he set up a provisional Métis government, as he had done in 1869. He did not want bloodshed, and when Gabriel Dumont urged

346

him to send messengers to enlist Indian support, Riel overruled him, believing Ottawa would now yield to the threat of insurrection.

He was, however, becoming more inflammatory. He told his people that five hundred policemen were on the way to slaughter them all. In the week that followed he and his followers, in Crozier's words, "robbed, plundered, pillaged and terrorized the settlers and the country." They sacked stores, seized and held prisoners, and stopped the mails. Riel and Crozier exchanged emissaries on March 21; the rebel leader's clear intent was to convince the policeman that he was committed to a violent course of action. Dewdney wired Macdonald the following day that the situation looked very serious and that it was imperative that an able military man should be in the North West in case the militia had to be called out. On March 23, Macdonald dispatched Major-General Frederick Dobson Middleton to the Red River with orders that the militia should move. Macdonald who, incredibly, was "not aware of any causes for discontent," belatedly dispatched his tardy commission to the spot to investigate the Métis land claims.

It was Riel's intention to seize Fort Carlton and establish it as the capital of his new government. He demanded unconditional surrender from Crozier:

"We want blood! blood! If Carlton is not surrendered it will be a war of extermination; I must have an answer by 12 o'clock or we will attack and take the fort."

Crozier decided to hold Fort Carlton with his policemen and a detachment of volunteers from Prince Albert. But he sent, on March 25, a sergeant and seventeen constables with eight sleighs to get provisions and ammunition from the trader's store at nearby Duck Lake. It was a strange move, since it was inevitable that the Métis, under Dumont, who had already occupied and looted the store, would rebuff them. Three miles from Duck Lake, four of the Mounted Police scouts were turned back by a large number of pursuing Métis and Indians. The sleighs halted. Dumont and his followers drew up, behaving "in a very overbearing and excited manner." The Prince of the Plains actually went so far as to prod the ribs of the NWMP interpreter with a cocked and loaded rifle while the Indians jeered at the police: "If you are men, now come in." The party retreated.

This was too much for the impatient Crozier. The Force had been slighted. No one who wore the scarlet coat could countenance such a breach of the law. Without waiting for Irvine and his reinforcements, the superintendent set out with his fifty-five Mounted Policemen, forty-three Prince Albert volunteers, and a seven-pound cannon in tow.

Dumont, on horseback, watched them come. His Métis dismounted and began to creep forward through a curtain of falling snow, partially encircling the police. Crozier drew his twenty sleighs up in line across the road and ordered his men to take cover behind them. A parley took place under a rebel white flag with Dumont's brother Isidore and an Indian on one side and Crozier and a half-breed interpreter, John McKay, on the other. When Crozier extended his hand to the Indian, the unarmed native made a grab for McKay's rifle. Crozier, seeing the struggle, gave the order to fire. Isidore Dumont toppled from his horse, dead. The rebels were already on the move, circling around the police left flank. Crozier put spurs to his horse and galloped back to the police lines through a hail of bullets. The Indian was already dead.

At this moment, with the Métis pouring a fierce fire on the police from two houses concealed on the right of the trail and outflanking them on the left, Louis Riel appeared on horseback through the swirling snow, at the head of one hundred and fifty armed Métis. He was grasping an enormous crucifix in his free hand and, when the police fired at him, he roared out in a voice that all could hear: "In the name of God the Father who created us, reply to that!"

Within thirty minutes Crozier had lost a quarter of his force killed and wounded. The Métis had suffered only five casualties. The North West Mounted Police were in retreat. The Saskatchewan Rebellion had begun.

3

"I wish I were well out of it"

Sunday, January 11, 1885, was the Prime Minister's seventieth birthday, and on Monday all of Montreal celebrated this anniversary, which also marked his fortieth year in politics. It was almost fifteen years since he had promised British Columbia a railway to the Pacific, and in that period he had moved from the prime of life to old age. The rangy figure was flabbier; the homely face had lost some of its tautness; the hair was almost white; deep pouches had formed beneath those knowing eyes; the lines around the edges of the sapient lips had deepened; and on the great nose and full cheeks were the tiny purple veins of over-indulgence.

He was a Canadian institution. There were many at that birthday celebration in Montreal who were grandparents, yet could not remember a time when Macdonald had not been in politics. The reports of his imminent retirement through illness, fatigue, incompetence, scandal, or political manœuvre had appeared regularly in the press for all of the railway days. His suicide had been rumoured, his death predicted, his obituary set in type ready for the presses to roll; but Macdonald had outlasted one generation of critics and spawned a second. He had left the country the previous fall with George Stephen, weary to the point of exhaustion, suffering once again from the stomach irritation that seemed to be the bane of Canadian political leaders. Now he was back, miraculously revived, jaunty as ever, making jokes about his health and telling his friends and supporters that as long as his stomach held out the Opposition would stay out.

He would need a healthy stomach for the days that lay immediately ahead; but as he drove through two miles of flaming torches on that "dark soft night," under a sky spangled by exploding rockets, to a banquet in his honour, he was in the mellowest of moods. In his speech he could not help adding to the eulogies that he heard on all sides about the great national project, which was nearing completion. "In the whole annals of railway construction there has been nothing to equal it," he said. Only a few of those in attendance – George Stephen was one – could appreciate the irony of that statement. The Prime Minister might just as easily have been referring to the immensity of the financial crisis that the railway faced.

Just the previous Friday, Stephen had dispatched one of his frantic wires to the Prime Minister: "Imminent danger of sudden crisis unless we can find means to meet pressing demands. Smaller class creditors getting alarmed about their money. Hope Council will deal today with question of advancing on supplies." That week, rumours of the company's financial straits began to leak out. On January 16, one of the Montreal papers reported that the CPR could not meet its April dividend, that attacks on the London market had caused another drop in the price of its stock, and that the company was paying for its normal cash purchases with notes at four months. The rumours were true. Within a fortnight the stock was down below 38; not long after it hit a new low of 33⅛.

Sir John Rose in London dispatched a worried note to Macdonald: "I fear you will have to apply some drastic remedy to these Grand Trunk people. You have no idea to what an extent the Papers teem with attacks on Canadian credit – one of the last is that the Dominion will wriggle out of its guarantee on the C.P. stock! ! . . . If the dividend is passed it will have a very disastrous effect on the *permanent* credit of the Cy."

Stephen had worked out with Tupper and Macdonald a scheme whereby the unissued stock of the CPR would be cancelled by government legislation, the lien on the railway removed, and a more or less equivalent amount of cash raised by mortgage bonds applied to the entire main line of the railway, with principal and interest on them guaranteed by the government. About half the cash from these bonds would be used to help pay off the loan of 1884. The rest would go to the company as a loan to pay for expenditures not included in the original contract. The remainder of the 1884 loan would be paid off in land grant bonds.

Financially, it was an ingenious scheme. Politically it was disastrous. The previous year, Blake had taunted the Government about the CPR loan: "Don't call it a loan. You know we shall never see a penny of this money again." This was strong meat; Macdonald could foresee the hazards of allowing the Opposition to cry: "We told you so!" The farming counties of Ontario, where so much of his strength rested, were not enamoured of the railway: the value of farmland in the East had been reduced because so many people had departed for the North West, lured by tales of the new country opened up by the rails.

Macdonald, at 70, was a different man from the 55-year-old who, in 1870, had firmly believed that no time should be lost in building a railway to the Pacific. Then, if anything, he had been overly rash in his promises to British Columbia; now, the ageing chieftain seemed weary and confused, hesitant of taking any political risk, inept in his handling of the Indian Affairs Department and, before that, of the Department of the Interior (whose portfolio he held until 1883), insensitive to the problems of the North West and, apparently, sick to death of the railway he had helped to create. The picture of the Prime Minister in 1885 is that of a leader who has lost his way, stumbling from one crisis to another, propped up by bolder spirits within his cabinet and by the entreaties of men like Stephen and Van Horne. His policy of delay, which from time to time had worked in his favour, was disastrous in 1885; it brought bloodshed to the North West and came within an hour of wrecking the CPR.

The Prime Minister had been doing his best to avoid Stephen, whose letters, telegrams, and personal visits were becoming more importunate as the crisis grew. Stephen, however, would not be put off. He shuttled back and forth between Montreal and Ottawa, plaguing cabinet ministers and government servants, such as Schreiber, when he could not see their chief. His letters had taken on a waspish, old womanish quality. "It is as clear as noonday, Sir John," he wrote in January, "that unless you yourself say what should be done, nothing but disaster will result. . . ." But Old Tomorrow would not say. In vain, Stephen pleaded, cajoled, promised, and threatened. Tilley, the finance minister, who did not believe the company's plan was politically feasible, exasperated him. Could Macdonald do nothing with Tilley? "What alarms me is the apprehension that

the patient will die while the doctors are deliberating on the remedy. . . ."
Stephen was almost at the end of his tether – or thought he was: "I feel
my ability to save it has gone. I am sorry to confess this even to myself."

The horrifying prospect of the dividend hung like a spectre over the
CPR's executive committee. Default, the president knew, would be fatal.
The company's books were about to close. It had guaranteed a five per
cent dividend and was responsible for two-fifths of that sum. If it did not
advertise the dividend, the world would assume that the Canadian Pacific
was bankrupt. Again, the only hope was the government. Surely, it would
come to the assistance of the company on a temporary basis, making an
advance on supplies before the end of January; those funds could be paid
back out of the monthly estimates. If Stephen could have that assurance
he would take the risk of advertising the dividend. He wired Macdonald
on January 20: "The dividend must be cabled to night. . . . Can I trust to
this? Please answer. I cannot delay advertizing dividend any longer."

Now the Prime Minister was forced into a corner. He must break the
news to Stephen that there was no chance of any further government assistance. He faced a revolt in his cabinet and he was not prepared to do
battle for the railway. Three ministers were obdurately opposed to further
relief for the CPR and one of these, Archibald McLelan, the Nova Scotian,
who was Minister of Fisheries, had given notice that he would resign if
any further public monies were advanced to the CPR. Thomas White, the
editor of the staunchly Conservative Montreal *Gazette*, had warned Macdonald that a relief measure could not be carried and that the press
was already alarmed and "beginning to sound the tocsin." The *Week*,
Goldwin Smith's influential political journal, had just declared that however docile Macdonald's majority might seem to be, he dared not ask it
to support another CPR loan. The Prime Minister was inclined to believe
this. He wired Stephen the same night that there was little chance of legislation that session. He would, however, be able to carry an advance of
enough money to pay the dividend if it would enable Stephen to postpone
matters until 1886. With an election behind him, Macdonald felt he could
change many minds.

This was worse than no answer at all. As Macdonald himself surely
knew, there was no way the railway could stay afloat until 1886 without
further funds over and above the subsidy. Stephen wired back, "Impossible," and took a train for Ottawa. The journey was in vain. Old Tomorrow's only action was to postpone a decision in council until the end of
the month. Stephen knew what he must do.

In one of his directors' meetings, when bankruptcy was imminent and real, Stephen, in a speech that Van Horne later characterized as the finest he had ever heard, turned to Smith and said, simply: "If we fail, you and I, Donald, must not be left with a dollar of personal fortune." Smith had silently agreed. Now the two Scotsmen, each of whom had started life without a penny and risen to positions of almost unparalleled wealth, prepared to go down with the railway. They pledged the remainder of their joint fortunes and all their personal assets – everything they possessed down to their gold cuff links – to raise the six hundred and fifty thousand dollars necessary to pay the dividend and an additional one million dollars on a five-month note to provide the short-term funds the company would need to carry it over the coming weeks.

When the treasury officers arrived at his new home on Drummond Street to take an inventory of his personal possessions, Stephen stood quietly by. They had already counted his cash and securities. Now they brought along experts who valued his growing art collection, his marble statuary, his furniture, and his famous imported piano. Then they catalogued his household linen, his china, and his silverware. Stephen carefully examined the long list of his material possessions acquired over a period of thirty-five years in Canada, and then, in the words of an eyewitness, "without a flicker of an eyelid signed it all away."

It was a remarkable act, given the business morality of that day, or indeed of any day, as Stephen himself well knew. What he and Smith had done was "simply absurd on any kind of business grounds."

"I venture to say," he told Macdonald, "that there is not a business man in all Canada, knowing the facts, but would say we were a couple of fools for our pains. But as long as we are able to save & protect the Company against its enemies who seem bent on its destruction we shall not grudge any risk, or loss that may occur. Personal interests have become quite a secondary affair with either of us."

This attitude was unique in North American railway annals. Among the various United States transcontinental lines, bankruptcies had been the rule. The directors and promoters, however, had rarely lost a penny. On the contrary, they had generally profited at the expense of the ordinary bond and stockholders. Railways were not generally viewed by their promoters as a method of developing the nation but merely as an easy way of siphoning money out of the public purse. Road after road was used as a stock promotion by rings that grabbed the land subsidy, sold it at a profit, floated as much stock as possible, drained off the cash through phoney construction companies, and let the railway go into receivership. But to Stephen, money was secondary; he had made his killing in the St. Paul

352

line, with Jim Hill's help, and had managed to create a railway out of it into the bargain. He did not embark on the Canadian Pacific project for profit but for sheer financial adventure, which he loved, and probably also for kudos. Perhaps if he had known how hazardous that adventure would become and how often the kudos would be tinctured with the bitter gall of calumny he might have rejected the notion.

". . . it is killing to have any of our friends think we are simply doing our bare duty by the Coy & are making money out of it," he told the Prime Minister. Making money was for Yankees like Jay Gould and the notorious Russell Sage – railway bandits who wore no masks. Stephen shared Macdonald's contempt for the stereotype. To be likened to Gould, as he had been, was particularly mortifying. The thing that Stephen prized most was his reputation; the idea that he might be the means whereby his friends and business associates would lose money bothered him far more than the possible financial ruin he now courted. It was not enough that he be a man of honour in the business world; he must be *seen* to be a man of honour. If the CPR crashed, Stephen must crash with it. At least, if he ended up selling pencils in the streets (an unlikely outcome), the world would know that he had done his duty at great personal sacrifice.

As for Donald Smith, he remained, as always, imperturbable. Stephen, on the other hand, was becoming more emotional as the days wore on and the Government dallied. At one point, when he was at his lowest ebb, he began to cry while sitting in Collingwood Schreiber's office. His tears of despair were the outward sign of an inner sense of impending personal doom. ". . . I am not *sure* of *myself* being able to stand the strain for an indefinite time," he confessed to Macdonald. "I have had warnings of which no body knows but myself which I will fight against to conceal to the last."

No such melodramatic disclosures issued from Smith's compressed lips. If he had physical warnings, he never betrayed them; if he had emotions, he never revealed them. In a quarter century in the Labrador fur trade he had become inured to hardship and had learned to bear reverses throughout his life without flinching. The curse of snow-blindness, the lash of the Little Emperor, George Simpson, the volleys of rotten eggs at political meetings, the charges of bribery, the taunts of John A. Macdonald who had called him a liar to his face in public – all these storms had broken around that frosty, weathered head, but Smith had never cracked or indicated that he cared. He was a lonely man, subject to considerable gossip about his "strange and complicated" family relationships. "His wife," Sir Henry Tyler wrote to Lady Tyler in 1888, "is said to have another husband, & his daughter, lately married against her mother's wishes, not to be his own." But he was always present in the background when needed, as solid and unmoving as the great rock of Craigellachie; and Stephen undoubtedly drew strength from that presence.

The two Scotsmen could provide relief only on a short-term basis; they could not, unaided, save the railway with a million dollars. The demands of the contractors in the mountains and along Lake Superior would consume that sum in a few weeks. Already the three-month notes given to satisfy clamorous creditors were coming due, and Macdonald was still vacillating on the "rearrangement scheme," as Stephen called it. When Parliament opened, Blake noted sardonically that, for once, there was no mention of the CPR in the Speech from the Throne.

"Is it the intention of the Government to propose any measure of relief for the Canadian Pacific Railway Company for its embarrassment?" he asked on March 3.

"There has been no application from the Canadian Pacific Railway Company to propose a measure to relieve them from their embarrassment," Macdonald replied.

This was strictly true, but as Stephen noted, ". . . they [the Government] have the whole case in their hands, though not in official shape, not signed, etc. . . ."

All during this period, the newspapers were engaged in lively speculation about the future of the CPR – a public debate that was, as Stephen said, "simply killing the Coy which for the moment has no credit left." Even the friendly *Mail* had admitted that for some time past the company had not had the means to finish the road: "Mr. Stephen and his associates have broken their agreement and by the terms of the bargain the road already finished, with all its belongings, is forfeited," the paper declared on March 11. There were, it said, three possible solutions: persuade somebody else to complete and operate the railroad under a similar contract; have the government take it over; or extend help to Stephen.

Stephen continued to hammer away at Macdonald to pursue the last course, modifying his original proposal for relief here and there but, in essence, asking for the removal of the lien and a further loan of five millions.

"I don't know how Council . . . will take it," a weary Macdonald wrote to Tupper in London. ". . . our difficulties are immense . . . we have blackmailing all round." As the price of acceptance the hungry Quebeckers were again demanding that the provincial government lines be subsidized while the Maritimers were clamouring for another railway. "How it will end God knows," Macdonald said, "but I wish I were well out of it." Tupper, a strong supporter of railway relief, had offered to return and replace the recalcitrant McLelan or, if necessary, take a seat in the House as a private member; but, as the Prime Minister pointed out, that would not be possible before the end of the session.

Macdonald was dispirited, Tilley was indifferent, Stephen was close to collapse, and even the normally ebullient Van Horne was in a private state of gloom. Outwardly, the general manager remained supremely confident. One morning when a creditor approached, asking for payment and expressing fear as to the outcome of the railway's financial crisis, Van Horne turned to him bluntly and said: "Go sell your boots, and buy C.P/R. stock." Inwardly he must have had his doubts. The absence of the pay car in the Selkirks and on the shores of Lake Superior was threatening to close down the railway. At Beavermouth, the rowdy construction camp on the Columbia, there was already talk of a mass strike. On the Lake Superior section, men were threatening to lynch a contractor whom they blamed for holding back their wages.

When he was not on the road, the general manager haunted Ottawa, visiting the Russell House and the Rideau Club, working to secure the faith of the politicians and the contractors by painting word pictures about the future of the North West and the railway. In private, to an inner circle of intimates – Frank Smith, one of Macdonald's closest friends and cabinet ministers was one – he pointed out the disastrous effect the railway's collapse would have on the country. More than ninety-two million dollars had been spent, of which fifty-five millions was public money. How could such an enterprise be permitted to fail for want of a few millions more? The major banks – not only the Bank of Montreal, but also those carrying the contractors – would totter; wholesale houses would crash; an army of men would be thrown out of work; Canada's credit would be damaged for years in the international money markets.

Van Horne had more difficulty in getting to Macdonald himself. There is a story of how he managed, at last, to intercept the Prime Minister in the lobby of the House.

"Sir John," he said, "we are and you are dangling over the brink of Hell."

"Well, Van Horne," Macdonald replied, "I hope it will be delayed a while. I don't want to go just yet."

As they strode along the corridor the elusive Tory leader slipped away to speak to "an old friend." That was the last Van Horne saw of him. When he turned back to speak again, Macdonald had vanished, leaving behind a somewhat baffled stranger, flattered at having been so suddenly buttonholed by the Prime Minister.

Van Horne's own future was secure enough. As a friend told him at the time, he could always return to the United States, where several good posts were available for him. To this suggestion he made a characteristic answer: "I'm not going to the States. I'm not going to leave the work I've begun, and I am going to see it through. I'm here to stay and I can't afford to leave until this work is done no matter what position is open to me...."

On March 18, Stephen made an official application to the Privy Council for a loan of five million dollars. He asked the government to take fifteen million dollars worth of five per cent railway bonds, at par, and seven and a half million acres of land at two dollars an acre. The application was considered and, at length, rejected. Stephen vowed that he would leave Ottawa, never to return. The railway was finished. Its directors were ruined men.

Van Horne this time made no attempt to hide his feelings. Percy Woodcock, an artist friend who painted with him, remembered that his hobby no longer was powerful enough to take his mind off the railway's troubles: "... sometimes in the middle of a joyous bit of painting the thought of the road would come to him like a shock and hang over him, holding him totally absorbed and still."

Collingwood Schreiber recalled with some emotion a scene in his office with Van Horne – "the only time I believe his iron nerve was ever shaken." A close friendship had grown up between the two as a result of their several journeys together, especially the hard excursion along the shores of Lake Superior in the summer of 1884. Now the general manager looked up at Schreiber and then, very slowly and very softly, he revealed the depth of his despair: "Say, if the Government doesn't give it [the loan] we are finished." Van Horne, who had never cast a vote in his life, felt that he had been beaten at the one game he did not understand – the game of politics. He had come within an ace of commanding the greatest single transportation system in the world, and now his ambition had been thwarted, not by any act of his but by a combination of subtle forces which he could not control. No one had seen him reveal his feelings to such an extent since that dark day, so many years before, when his small son William had died, and his friend John Egan, driving him in absolute silence to the funeral, noticed a tear fall onto his hand.

And then, as if the railroad itself had given the cue, succour came from the North West in the most perverse and unexpected form. The Métis under Louis Riel had raised the flag of insurrection.

Earlier that year, Van Horne had held a significant conversation with John Henry Pope.

356

"Why not put us out of our misery?" Van Horne asked the minister. "Let us go off into some corner and bust?"

Pope replied that the Government was so concerned about Riel and his followers that it could not undertake further entanglements. An outbreak was possible.

"I wish your CPR was through," Pope said.

Van Horne wanted to know when the government might expect to have troops ready to move to the North West. Pope told him it might be in the first or second week in March. Van Horne immediately declared he could get troops from Kingston or Quebec, where the two permanent force units were stationed, to Qu'Appelle in ten days.

In late March, Van Horne was reminded of this promise when Schreiber remarked to him that Macdonald seemed more concerned about the troubles in the North West than he did about the railway. The thought occurred to the general manager: *How could the government refuse to aid a railway that sped troops out to the prairies, took the Métis unawares, and crushed a rebellion?*

Van Horne immediately offered to the Privy Council the services of the railway to move troops, if needed, from Ottawa to Qu'Appelle. He made only one stipulation: he and not the army was to be in complete control of food and transport. His experience in moving troops during the American Civil War had taught him to avoid divided authority and red-tape interference.

It sounded like a foolhardy promise. There were four gaps, totalling eighty-six miles, in the unfinished line north of Lake Superior. Between the unconnected strips of track – much of it unballasted and laid hastily on top of the snow – was a frozen waste of forest, rock, and hummocky drifts, whipped up by the icy winds that shrieked in from the lake. Could men, horses, artillery pieces, and military supplies be shuttled over the primitive tote roads which crossed that meeting place of blizzards? The members of the Council refused to believe it.

"Has anyone got a better plan?" Macdonald asked. There was no answer. Van Horne was told to prepare for a massive movement of men, animals, arms, and equipment.

The first intimations of the impending Saskatchewan Rebellion appeared in fragmentary reports in Ontario newspapers on March 23, jammed in between the inevitable advertisements for such patented curealls as Dr. Radway's Sarsaparillan Resolvent, which promised cheap and instant relief for every known disease from cancer to salt rheum. By the following day, Van Horne's plan was in operation. His deputy on the eastern end of the Lake Superior line, Harry Abbott, was told to be ready to move four hundred men as far as the end of track at Dog Lake. Joseph-Philippe-René-Adolphe Caron, the Minister of Militia and Defence, was still unsure the plan would work. "How can men and horse cross Nepigon – answer immediately," he wired Van Horne. Van Horne assured him that it could be done. On March 25 Abbott announced that he was ready and that John Ross, in charge of the western section of the unfinished line, was also ready and did not expect that there would be any delays. The engagement at Duck Lake took place on March 26; when the news burst upon the capital, the country was immediately mobilized. The first troops, Caron told Abbott, would be on the move on the twenty-eighth.

In Ottawa on the very morning of the Duck Lake tragedy, George Stephen had just finished scribbling a note to Macdonald confessing failure and asking that the Privy Council decision rejecting his proposal be put into writing, so as "to relieve me personally from the possible charge of having acted with undue haste." There was nothing more that the CPR president could do. The fate of the CPR now lay with the railway itself. If Van Horne's gamble worked, then the politicians and the public would have the best possible proof that the presence of a transcontinental line could hold the nation together in time of trouble.

4

Marching
as to war

On March 27, all of settled Canada learned from its newspapers that a bloody rebellion had broken out in the North West. Ten members of Crozier's mixed force of police and volunteers lay dead at Duck Lake. Thirteen more were wounded, two mortally. The names of some of the dead were distinguished: a nephew of Joseph Howe, the Nova Scotia statesman, a cousin of Edward Blake, and a nephew of Sir Francis Hincks, the former minister of finance under Macdonald. The victory of the half-breeds under Gabriel Dumont's generalship was beyond dispute. The Indians, waiting for just such a moment, were about to rise. Prince Albert, Fort Carlton, Batoche, Fort Pitt, and perhaps Fort Qu'Appelle, Calgary, Edmonton, Moose Jaw, and Regina, were all threatened. A wave of apprehension, anger, patriotism, and excitement washed over eastern Canada.

The government had already called out A and B batteries stationed in Quebec and Kingston – the only permanent military force in all of Can-

358

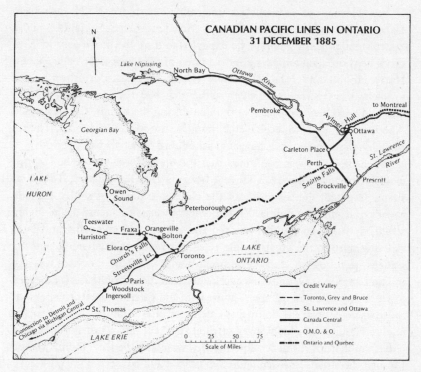

CANADIAN PACIFIC LINES IN ONTARIO
31 DECEMBER 1885

N

Lake Nipissing
North Bay
Ottawa River
to Montreal
Pembroke
Aylmer Hull
Ottawa
Georgian Bay
Carleton Place
St. Lawrence River
Perth
Smiths Falls
Brockville
Prescott
LAKE HURON
Owen Sound
Peterborough
Teeswater
Fraxa Orangeville
Harriston Bolton
Elora
Church's Falls
Streetsville Jct.
Toronto
LAKE ONTARIO
Paris
Woodstock
Ingersoll
Connection to Detroit and Chicago via Michigan Central
St. Thomas
LAKE ERIE

0   25   50   75
Scale of Miles

——— Credit Valley
– – – Toronto, Grey and Bruce
–·–·– St. Lawrence and Ottawa
——— Canada Central
▪▪▪▪ Q.M.O. & O.
▪·▪·▪ Ontario and Quebec

ada; on March 27, several militia regiments were ordered to be ready to move immediately to the North West. This aroused a flurry of speculation: How on earth were they to get there? In Kingston, the *British Whig* pointed out that if the soldiers travelled on the Grand Trunk through the United States they would not only have to be disarmed but would also have to travel through foreign territory in civilian clothes as private citizens, with their rifles and artillery pieces boxed for separate shipment to Winnipeg. There was a rumour, however, that this awkward and disagreeable passage might be avoided by an equally awkward and disagreeable passage over the partially completed Canadian Pacific Railway. This possibility was considered very remote. How could troops, baggage, guns, horses, and equipment be shuttled over those trackless gaps? "A gentleman recently through that country was met and asked how long it would take to cover the unrailed section. 'Oh,' he laughingly replied, 'until July.' "

In Toronto, the chief engineer of another railway, J. C. Bailey, who had just returned from Lake Nipissing, reported that there was at least four feet of snow along the track and that "there would be considerable trouble getting through."

Van Horne was nevertheless determined to move 3,324 men from London, Toronto, Kingston, Ottawa, Montreal, Quebec, Halifax, and a dozen smaller centres; in fact, he expected to have the first troops in Winnipeg no more than ten days after the news of the Duck Lake engagement. Harry Abbott and John Ross were not in the least perturbed by the problem Van Horne faced them with; they had regularly moved seven hundred workmen over gaps in the line during the winter. Caron warned Abbott to be ready to receive eight hundred troops on March 28. The remainder would move on a staggered schedule over a two-week period.

When the news was confirmed that the entire force was to be shipped west on the new railroad, a kind of frenzy seized the country. To a considerable extent the social life of the cities and towns of settled Canada revolved around the militia. Young officers were in demand at the highly stratified winter sports that marked the era: the snowshoeing and bobsledding parties, the great skating fêtes, the ice-boat excursions, and the outings of toboggan clubs. *The* great social event of the year was the militia ball. One saw uniforms everywhere: at the opera house (and every town of any size had an opera house), at the garrison theatricals, and at those strange social rites known as conversaziones. Tailors' advertisements featured military fashions over civilian, and the most popular weekend entertainment for the general public was watching the local militia parade through the streets or listening to a military band concert in the park.

Now, suddenly, the militia was parading through the streets for the first time in earnest, for the country had not yet fought a war of any kind. Never before had Canadians witnessed the kind of spectacular scenes that took place in every major town in the East during late March and early April – the cheers for Queen and Country, the blare of martial music, the oceans of flapping banners, the young men in scarlet and green marching behind the colours, the main streets jammed with waving thousands, the roll of drums, the troop trains puffing through the small towns and off into the Unknown – the singing, the cheering, the weeping and the kissing and the bitter-sweet good-byes. All this sound and spectacle, pumped up by a fanfaronade of military oratory – together with the terrible news on April 2 of a massacre of priests and civilians by Big Bear's Indians at Frog Lake – kept the country on an emotional binge for the better part of a fortnight.

The first militia units called out were the Queen's Own Rifles, the Royal Grenadiers, and the Infantry School, all of Toronto. The orders came at 9.30 on the evening of Friday, March 27; the troops were to be on parade the following morning in greatcoats, busbies, and leggings – the Grenadiers at the Armoury at eight, the Queen's Own and the Infantry School at the drill shed, St. Lawrence Market, at nine and ten respectively. All that night, with the temperature hovering at freezing, officers in hired hacks rattled up and down the dark streets "at breakneck speed," rousing their men. Long before dawn, the entire city was awake, thanks in part to the newly invented telephone of which there were more than four hundred in the city.

Well before 8.30 that Saturday morning, West Market Street was jammed with people while the entrance to the drill shed on Jarvis Street was "filled up to the throat." In the words of the *Mail,* "all the world with his wife was on the way to the drill shed to see the unusual sight of militia men being called out and paraded for active service." Many of the men had learned of the muster only on their way to work and had come straight to their stations in civilian clothes. Most believed that they would be shipped directly to the North West, but when the troops were drawn up they learned that they would not be leaving until Monday, March 30.

In the early hours of Monday morning, uniformed men began to pour into Toronto from the outlying corners of the town and the country. "From palaces and humble homes, they came in ones and twos, the number of brothers who were drafted being a conspicuous feature of the contingent. Further on they joined like converging streams until at the main arteries of the city the military uniforms formed a conspicuous picture in the streets which, even at that early hour, were crowded. Many of them took streetcars, one of these saying that he wanted to give this luxury a fond goodbye."

At the drill shed, the crowd of onlookers was so dense that the soldiers themselves had trouble forcing their way through. The commissariat and supply system of the fledgling army was in considerable disarray. The men had to supply their own boots, socks, shirts, and underwear and even their own lunch. Few were really aware of what was needed. Some arrived with extra boots in their hands, and all had packs bulging with pies, rolls, and cooked meat. Some had tin cups hanging at their belts, and most were armed with a revolver of some kind stuck into a pocket. An enterprising salesman squeezed his way into the shed and began selling footwear to those who had not brought a second pair of boots.

At eleven, Colonel William Dillon Otter, in charge of the permanent force's infantry school and a veteran of the Fenian skirmishes, spoke to the men, issuing the customary admonition to the younger ones to abjure strong drink and advising them to throw away any bottles that might have been secreted in the kits. "The gallant colonel's speech was received with

361

vociferous cheers, coupled with the pounding of five hundred rifle butts on the wooden floor." The troops were ready to march.

Outside, the scenes were chaotic and extravagant. "Never in the history of Toronto was there such a jam of people on King St.," the *Globe* reported. It seemed as if every single citizen who could walk or crawl had come from miles around to line the route of march from Jarvis along King and down York to the Union Station. King Street was "one living, moving mass of humanity. The extensions from the walls were alive with people, while thousands took up most dangerous positions from the cornices of the roofs. . . ." The crowd had stood for hours waiting to see the troops, but "the time passed as if it had been but a few minutes, so high ran the excitement created by the occasion." Hundreds offered to pay for positions in the flag-decked windows overlooking King Street, but these could no longer be purchased. Women with children fainted continually and had to be removed by the police. "Their nerves had become unstrung at the thought of their husbands, fathers and brothers leaving home for the frontier." Many women were weeping.

About 11.30, the cheering of the troops was heard from the drill shed, and the entire mob of more than ten thousand broke into an answering cry. The cheering moved like a wave along King Street (scraped clean of mud, ice, and manure for the occasion). It was so loud that the band of the Tenth Royal Grenadiers could not be heard from half a block away. The crush made it impossible to move. Somebody spotted the first uniform – that of a member of the Governor-General's Body Guard on horseback, followed by Colonel Otter, marching on foot at the head of his men. Now the sound of martial music came through at last, and this had a quieting effect on the crowd. A group of about five hundred civilians rushed ahead of the marching men, clearing the way through the dense mass of spectators. Then came the ultimate spectacle: the glittering brass of the band's instruments, the straight rows of fur caps, and the sharp outlines of rifles, drifting above the craning heads "like a float in the water."

Down the streets the young men came, as the crowd around them and above them, before them and behind them, shouted themselves hoarse. Bouquets of flowers drifted down from the windows above. Handkerchiefs fluttered. A thousand flags flapped in the breeze. Those who could not move along beside the troops began to cry "Good-bye, Good-bye!" as the musicians struck up the song that became a kind of theme all over Canada that month, "The Girl I Left behind Me."

To the foot of York Street, by the station, the crowd had been pouring in an unending stream – all kinds and conditions of people, in carriages,

362

hacks, and express vans, on foot and pushing perambulators – the women often white-faced and tearful, the elderly men grim – all hoping to catch one last glimpse of brother, son, or sweetheart. The immense crowd filled the Esplanade from one end of the station to the other, swarming over the roofs of freight cars and perching in every window. The morning had started warm and pleasant; then, as if to mirror the crowd's changing mood, it began to rain. The rain increased and changed to a heavy sleet, but the people did not move. The *Mail* reported that of some ten thousand gathered at the station, most of them without umbrellas, fewer than a dozen sought shelter. "The excitement shared was too great to permit of vulgar sensations."

Jammed into the cars, the men leaned out of windows and waved at the throng pressed up against the train. The cars began to crawl forward. Arms appeared above the crowd, waving final greetings, and these were answered from the windows by an assortment of fluttering handkerchiefs, toques, forage caps, sidearms, socks, and even underwear. Above the continual roaring, individual good-byes could be heard: "Keep your heart up, Harry!" "Be good to yourself, old boy." "Give us a shake, old man." Then the band of the Queen's Own struck up "Auld Lang Syne" and, as the engine bell began to ring, the men joined in. The people were now so thickly clustered along the Esplanade between York and Simcoe that "had a man got on the heads of the crowd he could not have got down to the ground again." Slowly the train drew away, passing Simcoe, where the crowds were thinner but wildly enthusiastic, through the yards, where the top of every freight and passenger car was black with waving, cheering well-wishers, and then through the driving sleet, past Strachan and Brock, where hundreds tried vainly to board the cars and ride a little way with the soldiers, out along Queen to Parkdale Station, where more hundreds poured from their houses to cheer and cry their good-byes, and then off through the rising little village of West Toronto through the whirling snow towards the dark forests and the unballasted track of the new Canada.

These scenes were repeated over and over again during the days that followed. Vast crowds thronged down to the stations at Bowmanville, Port Hope, Kingston, Cobourg, and other mid-Ontario points where the composite Midland Regiment was forming. Belleville was "afire with excitement." In Kingston, on March 30, hundreds, "flushed and fervent," crammed the town square to greet the incoming troops. In Montreal, when the French-speaking 65th Battalion paraded to the station, the crush of onlookers was so great that a vast double window burst out from a three-storey building, injuring twelve persons. In Ottawa, the station platform where the Governor-General's Foot Guards were entraining was "a dense mass of enthusiastic, patriotic, jostling, laughing, shouting and war-fever-stricken individuals of all ages, sizes, sexes and complexions." In Quebec, "the scene presented beggars description." The Ninth Voltigeurs, having attended Mass at the basilica on April 2, marched through a wild crowd, escorted by the city's snowshoe clubs in uniform, carrying torches and singing "La Marseillaise" and "The British Grenadiers." "Never before in the history of Quebec has there been such intense excitement," the Ottawa *Citizen* reported. The same phrase was used by the *Globe* in describing the scenes in London, "the Forest City," on April 7: "Never before in its history has this city witnessed demonstrations equal to that which this afternoon signallized the departure of the 7th Fuseliers to the North West." The regiment rolled through Ingersoll, Woodstock, Paris, and Hamilton, with crowds at every station platform. At Carleton Place, the Member for the London area, Sir John Carling, who was also Postmaster General, made a spirited address in which he praised everybody and everything from the Queen to Canadian nationalism, to the Conservative Party, to George Stephen, to the patriotism of the London troops, to the enormous potential possessed by the North West.

Only the Governor-General's Body Guard, the oldest cavalry regiment in Canada, departed in comparative quiet and secrecy, the authorities fearing for the safety of the seventy horses among the press of the crowds. The Guard was kept on the *qui vive* for several days with very little sleep while final arrangements were made to get the horses over the gaps in the line. When the regiment left shortly after midnight on April 7, their colonel, George T. Denison, and his officers had not slept for three nights, having remained booted and spurred and ready to move on the instant for all of that time.

The last troops to leave, on April 12, were those of the composite Halifax Battalion. They were called out after almost two weeks of controversy, some bitter attacks by Nova Scotian civilians and merchants, and a great many defections in the ranks. The threads that tied the Maritime Provinces to the rest of confederated Canada were tenuous. The following year a Liberal government would sweep back into power in Nova Scotia with an increased majority on a platform that included secession from Confederation. Few Maritimers thought that the North West had anything to do with them. Until this moment it had not occurred to them that they might have to commit their young men to the defence of the interior of the continent. They had always looked seaward, and their attitude was con-

364

ditioned by the need to defend the coast of British North America. To a large degree they saw the North West as a kind of suburb of Upper Canada, which, in a way, it was – at least in an economic sense. A similar attitude existed in regard to the Canadian Pacific. It was significant that the one cabinet minister prepared to resign over the railway loan was a Nova Scotian.

"Why should our volunteers, and especially our garrison artillery, be sent out of the province to put down troubles in the North West?" one man wrote to the *Morning Chronicle*. "Nova Scotia has nothing to do with their affairs; let Canada West look after their own matters."

Many believed that volunteers from Manitoba and the territories were sufficient to handle the job: "The employment of troops from all parts of the Dominion to put down a few half-starved barbarians may have a tendency to build up the military spirit of Canadians, but when the very men who know best how to 'wipe Riel out,' and have the will to do so, are on the ground in more than sufficient numbers there remains the question, why the taxpayers should be burdened unnecessarily with many millions of dollars."

These were not isolated opinions. On April 2, after the government had ordered the 66th Battalion to stand ready to move, a representative delegation of businessmen from dry-goods stores, boot and shoe shops, and grocery and drug firms demanded that a composite battalion be formed and only a certain number of men from the 66th be taken. It was from that unit that most of their employees came. Many Halifax merchants bluntly announced that if their men turned out for duty, they would be fired.

The situation caused a flurry in central Canada. In Montreal, the Mayor was moved to wire his opposite number in Halifax:

"A bulletin posted in Montreal to-day is as follows: 'Extraordinary refusal of Halifax volunteers to go to the front. Two-thirds of the men refuse to parade. The authorities threaten to arrest them as deserters.' This would indicate a want of patriotism in the people of Halifax and lower provinces and should be met and contradicted promptly if false, as it surely must be."

The Mayor of Halifax replied that such bulletins were grossly exaggerated, that there were plenty of volunteers to replace those who faced the loss of their jobs, and that the men of Halifax were "ready and willing to go. Otherwise Nova Scotia would fail in her duty to Queen and country."

The government, however, was forced to bow to the merchants' petition and settle for a composite battalion. Following that decision, much of the opposition died down, and when the troops marched off down Barrington Street, the farewell scenes were wilder, if anything, than those in Central Canada:

"At North Street [near the depot] was one of the most remarkable scenes ever witnessed in this city. The actual withdrawal of our militia for active duty, an event without parallel in provincial annals, had so deeply impressed itself upon the people that everyone who could possibly go determined to see them off."

They left beneath an ocean of handkerchiefs with a medley of songs on their lips: "Far Away," "We're Off on the Morning Train," "Home, Sweet Home," and, as always, "The Girl I Left behind Me."

All the familiar hyperbole of war was used to describe the troops who set off for the North West. "Every one of them looked and demeaned himself like a true bred British soldier," the *Globe* wrote of the Toronto brigade. A Kingston major, asked about the quality of his men, described them as "the very best. . . . They are fearless, strong and will endure hardships bravely. . . . You can bet they will not show the white feather." Of the Governor-General's Foot Guards, the *Citizen* wrote: "In the opinion of experienced military men who saw the Capt. Todd's company, it is one of the finest bodies of men for rough and ready service ever brought together in the Dominion."

It was substantially true. The men from the farms and cities were hard-muscled, keen, and young enough to laugh at the kind of ordeal they would shortly face along the uncompleted route of the CPR. They were also woefully under-trained and under-equipped. The York Rangers, huddled in the Toronto drill shed, looked more like sheep than soldiers. In Kingston, the most military of cities, it was noticed that the members of the composite Midland regiment were badly drilled. Among the 65th, in Montreal, there were men who had never fired so much as a blank cartridge.

Few battalions left for the North West properly equipped. The belts and knapsacks of the Queen's Own had done duty in the Crimean War. Their rifles – one of three different makes issued for the Saskatchewan campaign – were old Snider Enfields, most of them totally unreliable because of years of wear and tear on the rifle range. Any man who wanted to be a sharpshooter brought along his own weapon. The clothing of the York Rangers was old and rotten, the knapsacks ill-fitting and so badly packed that a day's marching would break men down. Several of the Midland companies had no knapsacks at all and were forced to wrap their

366

belongings in heavy paper. Others had no helmets. One battalion had suffered a fire, so that the entire force set out without uniforms. Many of the 65th lacked trousers, tunics, and rifles; indeed, there was not a company in that battalion properly equipped for service – ammunition was so scarce that each man could be allotted only three rounds. Even the crack Governor-General's Body Guard had not been issued satchels for their mounts and so the men were forced to submit to the ignominy of wrapping their personal belongings in blankets. Until this moment, membership in a militia unit had been a social asset. Nobody, it appeared – certainly not those in command – had ever considered the possibility that one day his unit would march off to war.

To a great extent, the soldiers had to depend on the bounty of a grateful civilian populace. All the government was obliged to issue was a greatcoat, a tunic, trousers, and a rifle. Other necessities were the individual's own responsibility. Nor was there any provision made for wives and children left behind. It was the habit, in many cases, for the civilian population to raise a fund for dependants; this was done in Montreal, for example, where the subscription list was headed by the names of George Stephen and Donald A. Smith, each of whom subscribed five thousand dollars. In London, the town council voted to supply all volunteers with socks and underwear and to support the wives and children of married men. A Montreal clothing firm gave the men of the 65th twenty-five dozen pairs of warm mittens. Other gifts, while no doubt comforting, were less practical. In Parkdale, every member of the York Rangers was presented with a New Testament. In Halifax, when the Mayor appealed for literature for the troops, he was deluged with "a ton of every conceivable 'literary harangue in cold type' from a bundle of Presbyterian missionary tracts to a hundredweight of dime novels." At Almonte, a local storekeeper boarded the troop train with a more welcome gift – fifty packs of playing cards.

The trains sped off, usually two at a time, at staggered intervals, puffing through Carleton Place, Pembroke, North Bay, and Sudbury towards Dog Lake, where the real ordeal would begin. The officers, at Van Horne's insistence, were given first-class accommodation even though the government's requisition did not cover sleeping cars and Van Horne doubted if he could collect for it. But he was looking further ahead than the bills for the mass movement of some three thousand troops. For the sake of the railway's long-term image it was "important that the report of the officers as to the treatment of the troops on our line should be most favourable." For that reason the CPR was prepared to carry free any clothes

367

or goods sent out to the soldiers by friends or relatives. As for the men themselves, Van Horne ensured that there would, whenever possible, be mountains of food and gallons of hot, strong coffee. Better than anybody else, he knew what the troops were about to face. He could not protect them from the chill rides in open flat cars and sleighs, or from the numbing treks across the glare ice, but he could make sure that his army marched on a full stomach.

5

The cruel   As the trains rolled westward and the cheering faded, the men from the
journey   cities, farms, and fishing villages of the East began to glimpse the rough face of the new Canada and comprehend for the first time the real dimensions of the nation. Out of North Bay the land stretched off to the grey horizon, barren and desolate, the slender spruce rising in a ragged patchwork from the lifeless rock. The railway was completed for passenger traffic only to Biscotasing. Here the troops encountered the first of the CPR construction towns, a hard-drinking, backwoods village of some hundred huts and log cabins interspersed with mercantile tents, all decked out for the occasion with Union Jacks and bunting. Between the canvas pool halls and shops (some bearing crude signs reading "Selling Off at Cost") were the inevitable blind pigs. On April 1, the day the Queen's Own arrived at Biscotasing, the police had just destroyed five hundred gallons of illicit whiskey.

The first gap in the line began near Dog Lake, another construction camp not far from the site of modern-day White River, reputedly the coldest spot in Canada. Here the railway had prepared a Lucullan feast of beef, salmon, lobster, mackerel, potatoes, tomatoes, peas, beans, corn, peaches, currants, raisins, cranberries, fresh bread, cakes, pies, and all the tea and coffee needed to wash it down. It was the last night of comfort the soldiers would know for several days and the start of an adventure that all would remember for the rest of their lives.

The men, packed tightly in groups of eight in sleighs provided by the construction company, set off behind teams of horses down the uncompleted right of way. At every unbridged ravine and unfilled cut the sleighs were forced off the graded surface, sometimes for several miles, and onto the tote road, a roller coaster path that cut through forests, ran over stumps, windfalls, and rocks, dipped up and down through gorges and wound through seemingly impassable stretches of tightly packed trees. In

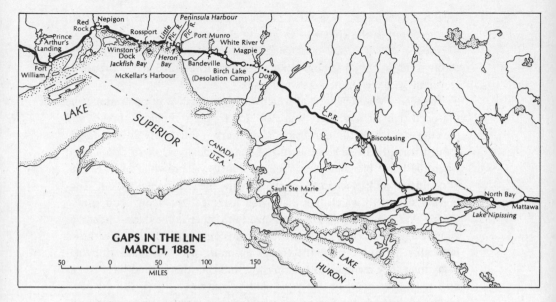

some places the sleighs encountered boulders seven or eight feet high; in others they pitched into holes as deep as graves – the occupants flung over the dashboards and into the steaming haunches of the terrified horses. "No description," wrote one man, "could give an idea of the terrible roads through the woods." Spills and accidents were so frequent they were taken as normal. One sleigh carrying members of the 65th overturned no fewer than thirteen times in the forty miles between Dog Lake and the end of track at Birch Lake. Men already half frozen in the twenty-degree below weather were hurled out and submerged in six feet of powdery snow, often with all their equipment. Caps, mitts, mufflers, side arms, and other articles of luggage were lost in the white blanket through which the sleighs reared and tumbled. One member of the London Fuseliers was completely buried under an avalanche of baggage; a comrade was almost smothered when a horse toppled onto him. When sleighs carrying troops westward encountered empty sleighs returning eastward for a second load, chaos resulted: the detours were only wide enough to permit a single team to pass through without grazing the trees on either side. If a horse got a foot or two out of the track, the runners would lock onto a tree trunk, or, worse still, rise up on a stump, tilting occupants and baggage into the snow.

Generally, this trip was made by night when the sun was down and the weather cold enough to prevent the snow from turning to slush. The men crouched in the bottoms of the sleighs, wrapped in their greatcoats and covered with robes and blankets; but nothing could keep out the cold. To prevent themselves from freezing, officers and men would leap from the careering sleighs and trot alongside in an attempt to restore circulation. For some units, the cold was so intense that any man who left any part exposed even for a few minutes suffered frostbite. "What they passed through that night all hope will never require to be repeated," a reporter travelling with the Grenadiers wrote back.

The teams were changed at Magpie camp, a half-way point along the unironed right of way. Here was more food – pork, molasses, bread, and tea, the staples of the construction workers. Many arriving at Magpie thought they had reached the end of their ordeal and were discomfited when the bugle blew and they realized that it was only half over. Scenes of confusion took place in the darkness – the men scrambling about seeking the sleighs to which they had been assigned, the snow dropping so thickly that friends could not recognize each other in the dark, the horses whinnying and rearing, the half-breed teamsters swearing, the officers and non-coms barking orders, the troops groaning with the realization that everything they owned was soaking wet and that they would have to endure four more hours of that bone-chilling journey.

Out of the yard the horses galloped, starting along a route utterly unknown to them, depending solely on their guides and their own instincts, tumbling sometimes sleighs and all over the high embankment, righting themselves, and plunging on. The entire gap between Dog Lake and Birch Lake took some nine hours to negotiate, and at the end stood a lonely huddle of shacks, which was swiftly and accurately named "Desolation Camp."

It deserved its title. A fire had swept through the scrub timber, leaving the trees naked of bark and bleached a spectral white. A cutting wind, rattling through the skeletal branches, added to the general feeling of despair. The only real shelter was a tattered tent, not large enough to accommodate the scores who sought refuge in it. Yet some men had to remain there for hours, their drenched clothing freezing to their skins in temperatures that dropped as low as thirty-five below.

The 10th Royal Grenadiers arrived at Desolation Camp at five one morning after a sleigh journey that had begun at eight the previous evening. There were no trains available to take them farther, and so they endured a wait of seventeen hours. They did not even have the warmth of a fire to greet them. Tumbling out of the sleighs like ghosts – for the falling snow had covered them completely – they tried to huddle in the tent through whose several apertures bitter drafts blew in every direction. "There was probably more heroism in facing cheerfully the scene of disillusionment that confronted the men that morning than during the heat

370

of battle," one observer commented. The tent was so crowded that it was not possible to lie down. Some men lit fires outside in three feet of snow, only to see the embers disappear into deep holes melted through the crust. Others rolled themselves in their blankets like mummies and tried to sleep, the snow forming over them as it fell.

Every regiment that passed through Desolation Camp had its own story of hardship and endurance. Some members of the Queen's Own were rendered hysterical by the cold; when the trains finally arrived they had to be led on board, uncomprehending and uncaring. One sentry saw a form flitting from tree to tree in the ghostly forest and, believing the enemy was upon them, called out the guards; it was only a blanket caught in the wan moonlight, fluttering in the wind. Although most troops had had very little sleep since leaving civilization, they were denied it at Desolation Camp because sleep could mean certain death when the thermometer dropped. The Halifax Battalion, the last to arrive, had to endure a freezing rain, which soaked their garments and turned their greatcoats into boards. When men in this condition dropped in their tracks, the guards were ordered to rouse them by any means, pull them to their feet, and bring them over to the fires to dry. There they stood, shivering and half conscious, until the flat cars arrived.

In these cars, sleep again was all but impossible, especially for those who travelled at night in below-zero weather with a sharp wind blowing. The cars were the same gravel cars used by construction crews to fill in the cuts. Rough boards had been placed along the sides to a height of about six feet, held in place by upright stakes in sockets. There was no roof, and the wind and snow blew in through the crevices between the planks. Rough benches ran lengthwise and here the men sat, each with his two issue blankets, packed tightly together, or huddled lengthwise on the floor. The officers were provided with a caboose heated by a stove, but many preferred to move in with the men.

For the Governor-General's Body Guard, such a journey was complicated by the need to minister to the animals. There were no platforms or gangways in the wild; the men were obliged to gather railway ties and construct flimsy inclined planes up which the horses could be led to the cars. Because the snow was generally three or four feet deep and the ties sheathed in ice, the makeshift ramps had to be covered with blankets so that the animals would not lose their footing. All had to be watered and fed before the men could rest. Nor could they be moved by sleigh across the Dog Lake gap to Desolation Camp at Birch Lake; the cavalrymen rode or led their animals the entire distance. When the cavalry moved by train, the horses were placed in exactly the same kind of flat cars as the men. Unloading them at each point occupied hours. It was necessary to remove all the hind shoes to prevent injuries to men and steeds; even with that precaution, one fine black stallion was so badly injured by a kick from another horse that he had to be destroyed.

The artillery had its own problems. It was not easy to load the nine-pounders onto the flat cars. At one construction camp, four husky track-layers from Glengarry were assigned to do the job. One of them ran a crowbar into the muzzle of an artillery piece to get purchase, a desecration that caused the major in charge to fly into a rage. He dismissed the navvies, called for twenty of his own men to tie a rope around the breech and, with great difficulty, succeeded in having it hauled up an inclined platform and onto the car.

The track that led from Desolation Camp to the next gap at Port Munro was of the most perfunctory construction. The ties had been laid directly onto the snow and in some sections, where a thaw had set in, four or five ties in succession, spiked to the rails, would be held clear off the ground for several inches. One man likened the train's movement to that of a birchbark canoe, "only, of course, on a larger scale." Trains were thrown off this section of track daily and the rails were slowly being bent by the heavy passage. It was rarely possible to exceed five miles an hour. "It was," a member of the Queen's Own Rifles wrote home, "about the longest night any of us ever put in."

The Grenadiers, who made the trip relatively swiftly, put in five hours on the open cars before they reached Bandeville, the half-way point on the completed portion of track. The men, being packed close together, had the advantage of mutual body warmth, but the officers, who had more room in the caboose, were in pitiful condition. "At one end of the car, lying on a stretcher on the floor was a poor fellow suffering from rheumatism and quite helpless with surgeon Ryerson patiently sitting at his head where he had been trying all night, with little success, to snatch a little sleep. The gallant colonel . . . with elbows on knees, was sitting over the stove looking thoughtfully into the embers with eyes that have not known a wink of sleep for 50 hours. Then there was Major Dawson whose system appeared to be rebelling against the regularity of life to which it had been so long accustomed . . . Capt. Harston, with a face as red as a boiled lobster sitting with arms folded on his knees [was] the very picture of incarnate discomfort. . . ."

At Bandeville (which consisted of a single shack in the wilderness) the men were fed sandwiches and hot tea. Some were so stiff with cold they had to be lifted out of the cars, "but warmth and food soon revive them and their troubles are no sooner over than they are forgotten." Others were so bone weary that when they reached the warmth of the eating house, the change in temperature was too much for them, and they dropped off into a sleep so deep it was almost impossible to awaken them to eat. One man fell into the snow on the way into the shanty. When his comrades picked him up, he seemed to be insensible. They carried him inside and found there was really nothing wrong with him; he had simply gone to sleep on his feet.

Warmed by this brief hiatus, the men made ready for the next leg of the journey. "Once more into the breach, my countrymen!" cried Captain Manley of the Grenadiers. He and his men faced another chilling seven hours before End of Track at Port Munro, a construction station and supply depot on the lakeshore, was reached. Only then were the troops able to enjoy their first real sleep.

Here was a deep, natural harbour – "the loveliest scenery that ever met my gaze," a correspondent called it – dominated by a thousand-foot crag. In the harbour lay the schooner *Breck*, "open at both ends and leaky into the bargain," capable of sleeping some two hundred troops. Here, the troops slumbered in comparative comfort, huddled together in the hold on mattresses composed of equal parts of hay and dirt, and later of water. The leakage was probably caused by the weight of the human cargo grinding the vessel down through the ice. By the time the Halifax battalion arrived, the floor was afloat and the pumps could not be worked because of the frost. The owner, who gave his consent to use the vessel after being told it would be taken by force if necessary, subsequently charged the government $848.93 for damages; he was awarded $245.50.

The second gap in the line – about twenty miles – began at Port Munro and continued to McKellar's Harbour, a small inlet near the mouth of the Little Pic River. There were not enough sleighs in the area to carry more than the baggage, and so the troops were forced to march across the glare ice of Lake Superior to the next piece of track, a journey of some eight hours. They began it, generally, in high spirits:

> The volunteers are all fine boys and full
>   of lots of fun
> But it's mighty little pay they get for
>   carrying a gun;
> The Government has grown so lean and the
>   CPR so fat
> Our extra pay we did not get –
> You can bet your boots on that!

The Grenadiers, well fed and rested, moved out onto the ice in light marching order at dawn on Easter Sunday – a long, quavering line of men with the teams drawn up all around the bay. Above them, a cloud of purest white encircling its midriff, towered the black mountain from whose high head the sun's first rays, red as blood, streamed down on the ice and lit up the crags on the far side of the harbour "with a bright splendour, that compelled admiration and delight." A bugle sounding the advance, split the sharp morning air. The men began to sing "Hold the Fort for We Are Coming." The echoes, bounding around the rocky recesses, "produced an effect of the most extraordinary nature." Out onto the cold bosom of the lake the column of men moved "as if they had not known the hardships of the past few days and were celebrating some joyful occasion."

That joy was not to last. For the Grenadiers, the very sun that had greeted them that morning was to prove the worst of enemies. For those who had been issued with snow glasses the glare on the ice was searing enough; they arrived at their destination, their faces scorched and blistered sometimes almost beyond recognition. Others managed to make eye-coverings, Indian-fashion, out of strips of birchbark with thin slits cut into them. But there were others who were rendered painfully blind, a red haze blotting out all vision, the corneas smarting as if sandpapered. Colonel Otter himself, at the head of his troops, was almost totally blind when the end of track was reached again.

Harry Armstrong, who was working on this section of the line at the time, described the resultant trek as a sort of " 'go as you please march.' " The troops, buffeted by piercing winds on one side and blistered by the sun's glare on the other, were eventually strung out for seven miles across the lake. Marching was almost impossible on the glassy surface; then, after ten miles, the texture changed: deep cuts, broken blocks of ice, and rocks frozen into the surface began to lacerate the feet of the men and officers, especially those who had the misfortune to leave home in light shoes. Some threw their kits away, bit by bit; some collapsed in their tracks; others became temporarily deranged; one man was ruptured. The baggage sleighs, following behind, picked up the casualties.

"You have no idea of the glare of the sun on the snow up here or the piercing wind that sweeps across the Lake," a member of the Queen's Own Rifles wrote home. "The track we had to march along was about 9 inches wide and a slip to the side would plunge you into snow 6 to 8 feet deep. I can tell you I'll never forget that march. . . . We dared not stop an instant as we were in great danger of being frozen, although the sun was taking the skin off our faces. One man of our company went mad and one of the regulars went blind from snow glare. We arrived at our destination about 9 p.m. My boots and leggings were frozen to my feet."

Those units that travelled the same gap by night endured equally fearful conditions. "That night was indeed a terrible one," a member of A Battery recalled. "You have heard of soldiers in the Sudan wandering away from the column on the march while in a somnambulistic condition. Well that is just how our men were. . . . The night was dark, the temperature freezing and a heavy snow storm with a wild, piercing wind made the march a fearful undertaking." Any man who drifted away from the column knew that he faced almost certain death. To prevent this, guards were assigned to ride around the column to head off drifters and stragglers. At that, the night was so dark and the way so difficult that the guide appointed to lead the troops across lost his way and the ordeal was lengthened by several hours.

The travail of the cavalry was again far more strenuous. The infantry was marched across the ice as far as McKellar's Harbour, where a short piece of line had been laid to Jackfish Bay. But because of the nuisance of loading and unloading horses for such a short distance, the Governor-General's Body Guard decided to ride or walk their steeds the full thirty-five miles to Jackfish on the ice of the lake.

After about fifteen miles, the baggage sleighs turned off to the right to proceed to the track. The cavalry men halted for lunch, drew their horses up in line, adjusted the nosebags, and then, standing in the lee of their mounts, munched on chunks of frozen bread washed down with lake water drawn from a hole chopped in the ice.

The remainder of the trip was another nightmare. Heretofore the track had been clearly marked by the passage of the sleigh runners; but now the cavalry was on its own. For the next twenty miles they faced "a vast prairie or desert of ice," with snow and drifts everywhere and no track of any kind. The permanent surface was obscured by a crust under which two or three inches of water lay concealed. Above the crust there was as much as a foot of light snow. This uneven and treacherous surface was broken by equally treacherous patches of glare ice. Through this chill morass the horses, all of them lacking hind shoes, slipped, floundered, and struggled for mile after mile.

At the head of the column rode the commander, Lt.-Colonel George Taylor Denison III, scion of the most distinguished military family in Canada and himself a man of parts. Denison's grandfather had founded this regiment in the rebellion of 1837, naming it Denison's Horse. His father and his brother Frederick had both commanded the unit before him. His father had also helped found the Queen's Own Rifles, while an uncle had commanded the Queen's Light Dragoons. Frederick, at that very moment, was in charge of the Canadian Voyageurs in the Sudan. Two other brothers were in the service; one would rise to admiral.

Denison himself was a bundle of contradictions. An impressive military figure – sabre-straight, with bristling moustache and firm military features – he had been expelled from Trinity College, Toronto, for insolence and insubordination. A lawyer who was bored by the law, he had attained a reputation, as senior police magistrate in Toronto, of disposing of scores of cases at the rate of one every minute. His most notable achievement had been his surprising capture of the first prize in a contest sponsored by the Czar of Russia for the best book on cavalry. Denison's work, translated at his own expense into Russian, was the result of months of secret study in such places as the British Museum and St. Petersburg. Praised by Theodore Roosevelt, it remains a standard and definitive work. Yet Denison preferred the company of writers and scholars to military men. Kipling was a guest in his home; so was Joseph Chamberlain. A staunch Imperialist, almost to the point of caricature, he had in the seventies helped found the short-lived and nationalistic Canada First movement. In his speeches he tended to be bellicose, in his demeanour impulsive; his heroes were Robert E. Lee, Bismarck, and Garibaldi; but his favourite pastimes were bird watching and playing ball with small children among the walks and rose arbours of his Toronto estate.

Denison quickly realized that he was leading his men into a labyrinth. They were miles from shore, in a wilderness of ice and snow-covered islands, and it was clear that a serious blizzard was impending. The urge was to move as swiftly as possible and reach land before the coming storm hemmed them in, but the crust-ice grew so bad that the entire regiment finally came to a halt. Denison fanned his men out, seeking a feasible route through the maze. When one was found, he and his adjutant rode on ahead to pick their way between the hummocks of land and ice. At this point the temperature had dropped to zero and the first flakes were beginning to fall. By good luck, the blizzard held off until, at eight o'clock that evening, the cavalry finally reached Jackfish.

An entirely different but equally uncomfortable set of circumstances presented themselves to the York Rangers. They crossed the same gap in a driving storm of rain and sleet, trudging up to their knees in a gruel of snow and water, in gutters eight inches deep left by the blades of the cutters. At McKellar's Harbour the men were forced to wait six hours for

376

the flat cars to return. Fortunately the rain ceased, but the temperature dropped and the soaking wet clothes began to freeze on the men's backs. They built roaring fires and clustered around them, scorching in front and freezing behind, until the train finally arrived.

These long waits without shelter were among the cruelest privations suffered by the soldiers en route to the North West. The Queen's Own endured three: a two-hour wait in a blinding sleet storm when a train broke down at Carleton Place, a nine-hour wait in the freezing cold at McKellar's Harbour, and a four-hour wait in driving sleet at Winston's Dock. Most of these waiting periods were spent standing up; it was too cold and too wet to sit down.

At Jackfish Bay, where the next gap began, the soldiers, badly sunburned and frostbitten – their faces masses of blisters, their feet bruised and swollen – were billeted in shanties, freight houses, and empty transport cars. Here was more hot food – blackstrap molasses, pork, potatoes, tea, and hard-tack – and then, for the lucky ones, a twenty-seven mile sleighride through the wet sleet to Winston's Dock, and for the rest another forced march through the heaped snow.

Now the bone-weary troops, gazing from the rims of the cutters and through the slats of the flat cars, began to gain some understanding of Van Horne's feat of railway construction. At Jackfish they could see the gaping mouth of one of the longest tunnels on the road, piercing a solid wall of rock, one hundred and fifty feet high, for five hundred feet. For miles on end the roadbed had been blasted from the billion-year-old schists and granites – chipped into the sheer surface of the dark cliffs or hacked right through the spiny ridges by means of deep cuts. In some places it seemed as if the whole side of a mountain had been ripped asunder by dynamite and flung into the deep, still waters of the lake.

The voyage between Winston's Dock and Nepigon was again made on rails laid directly over the snow. The scenery grew grander as the cars crawled along and the soldiers began to stand up in their seats to see "sights which we will never forget" – the road torn out of the solid rock for mile after mile, skirting the very lip of the lake, from whose shores the mountains rose up directly for hundreds of feet above the track. Though the condition of the road was such that the engines were sometimes derailed, the troops did not seem to mind: "The delay was vexatious, and yet accommodated us, for we had ample opportunity as we steamed slowly along to observe and admire the grandeur and grim majesty of the scenery along the line." On some of the cars, the soldiers produced Moody and YMCA songbooks and began to sing.

377

Did any of them consider, during this brief respite, the high cost of being Canadian? Did any of them pause to question the necessity of shipping them all off on a partly finished railroad through a bleak and friendless land? Did any of them measure the price to be paid in loss of national dignity against the easier passage through the United States? It could, no doubt, have been accomplished just as quickly and no more awkwardly and with a lot less physical suffering. But there is no evidence that anyone – soldier, general, politician, or journalist – ever seriously considered that alternative.

There was one final gap yet to come, and for many it would be the most terrible of all. This was the short march over the ice of the lake between Nepigon and Red Rock. It was no more than ten miles but it took some troops as long as six hours to cover it.

The 10th Grenadiers started out in the evening "into the solemn darkness of the pines and hemlocks," along a trail so narrow that any attempt to move in column of fours had to be abandoned. It was almost impossible to stay on the track, and yet a single misstep caused a man to be buried to his neck in deep snow. When the troops emerged from the woods and onto the ice of the lake – "the worst ice that ever mortal man encountered" – they were met by a pitiless, pelting rain that seemed to drive through the thickest clothing. The rain had softened the track made by the sleighs, covering it with a slush so deep that every step a man took brought him into six inches of icy porridge. All attempts to preserve distance under such conditions had to be abandoned; the officers and men linked arms to prevent tumbling. To move through the slush the men were forced to raise their knees almost to their waists, as if marking time; in effect, they waded the entire distance.

As the rain increased, the lights of Red Rock, beckoning in the distance, winked out behind a wall of water. Now and then a man would tumble exhausted into the slush and lie immovable and unnoticed until somebody stumbled over him. Captain A. Hamlyn Todd, of the Governor-General's Foot Guards, counted some forty men lying in the snow, many of them face down, completely played out.

Some actually fell asleep as they marched. "One brave fellow had plodded on without a murmur for three days. He had been suffering, but through fear of being left behind, in the hospital, refrained from making his case known. He tramped half way across . . . reeling like a drunken man, but nature gave out at last, and with a groan he fell on the snow. There he lay, the pitiless rain beating on his upturned face, until a passing sleigh stopped behind him. The driver flashed his lantern . . . [and] said he was dead. 'Not yet old man,' was the reply of the youth as he opened his eyes. 'I am not even a candidate for the hospital yet.' " The soldier – he was a member of the 10th Royal Grenadiers – was placed on a sleigh and carried the rest of the way.

Some men who fell by the wayside could not speak. A member of the York Rangers described one such case: "On the way across one of the boys of the 35th was so fagged out that he laid down on the sleigh and could not move an inch. Captain Thomson asked him to move to one side but not one inch would he stir, so he caught hold of him like bag and baggage, and tossed him to one side to let him pass."

When Red Rock was finally reached, the men were like zombies. They stood, uncomprehending, in ice-water ankle-deep, waiting for the trains; and when these arrived they tumbled into cars – not flat cars this time, but real passenger cars – and dropped in their tracks, lying on the floor, twisted on the seats all of a heap, sleeping where they fell. One man, the son of a British general, crumpled up onto the floor in such a position that his head was under the seat "and no amount of shaking would wake him to improve his situation." There was tea ready for them all but, cold and wet as they were, many did not have the strength to drink it. The ordeal was at an end; the track, as they well knew, lay unbroken all the way to their destination at Qu'Appelle. There would be no more marching until the coulees of Saskatchewan were reached – time enough then to reckon with Dumont's sharpshooters. For the moment, at least, they had no worries; and so, like men already dead, they slept.

Chapter Nine

1

William Van Horne was not a man given to rash or boastful promises. When he said that he could move troops from eastern Canada to Qu'Appelle in ten days, he was actually giving himself a cushion of twenty-four hours. The first regular troops to entrain on March 28 arrived in Winnipeg exactly one week later. Within two days they were on the drill ground at Qu'Appelle. Two hundred and thirty miles to the north at Batoche, Riel was in control, resisting Dumont's repeated requests to cut the line of the railway and institute guerilla warfare. Battleford was under siege by Poundmaker's Indians – five hundred and twelve persons, some three hundred of them women and children, confined to the stockade. Big Bear's Crees, following the massacre at Frog Lake, were roaming the country around Fort Pitt, killing, looting and taking prisoners; the surrender of the fort had given them the supplies necessary to carry on. But by mid-April, not much more than a fortnight after Duck Lake, the entire Field Force, save for the tardy Halifax Battalion, was in Saskatchewan and ready to march north.

The rebellion wrenched the gaze of settled Canada out to the prairie country and focused it on the railway. Every major newspaper sent a war correspondent with the troops, and for weeks the pages of the dailies were full of little else. The hardships, the condition of the soldiers, the state of over-all morale – together with those illuminating tales of human interest that are the journalist's grist – all these were reported. But interlaced with such dispatches there was something else – a new awareness of the land and of the railway's relation to it, comments on the thoughtfulness and courtesy of the CPR attendants, which Van Horne had been at such pains to foster, amazement at the engineering marvels along the lakeshore and at the speed and efficiency with which the troops reached Winnipeg. ("The men feel that they have made magnificent time," one soldier wrote home.) For week after week in the columns of the daily press, as the journalists digressed on the grandeur of the scenery, the impressive size of the newly created cities, and the wonders of the plains, Canadians were treated to a continuing geography lesson about a land that some had scarcely considered part of the nation. Until 1885, it had been as a foreign country; now their boys were fighting in it and for it, and soon anyone who wanted to see it could do so for the price of a railway ticket.

The Halifax Battalion was especially delighted and surprised to discover so many fellow Nova Scotians working along the line and living in the western towns. To them, Desolation Camp was known as Big Rory's camp, because the contractor in charge was from Nova Scotia. "Some of the men about were from our own province and told us that many of the responsible people in the employ of the Syndicate, as well as some of the contractors, are Bluenoses," the *Morning Chronicle*'s reporter revealed. "Several of us fell upon quasi-acquaintances – men whose friends we know or who knew us or our relations."

In spite of Morley Roberts's description of Winnipeg the previous year as "an entirely execrable, flourishing and detestable business town, flat and ugly and new," the farm boys and fishermen's sons from the Atlantic, who had never gazed on London or Chicago, were impressed by the Manitoba capital. "I was surprised at the size of the city of Winnipeg," a member of the Halifax Battalion wrote home, "and the magnificent character of the buildings and the splendid wide streets, three times as wide as in Halifax. The stone and brick stores on every hand indicate a surprising degree of enterprise in this city. . . . The police have the finest body of men I ever saw, and the fire department is in an excellent state of efficiency. . . . There are a great many Nova Scotians in both the police and fire departments." No longer would these Maritimers think of the North West as the exclusive property of Ontario.

The traditional frontier hospitality hit home to every soldier and was the subject of many letters and reports:

"Brandon was reached . . . and here the grandest reception of all was received. Half the population seemed to be assembled at the station, and as many as could do so entered the cars to welcome the volunteers, a number of the prominent ladies of the town bearing baskets of provisions, which they liberally distributed. Those having friends in the district from which the troops came were anxious in their enquiries about them, and nearly all had something kind to say as they passed through. The young ladies . . . overcame their native shyness and conversed quite freely. One having announced her determination not to leave the Ottawa car until she had shaken hands with everyone in it, stayed so long that two young gallants had to lift her off the train before it started. The kind action of the Brandon folk and their manner of carrying out their wishes in person does them great credit, and will not soon be forgotten by those who were their guests."

Until the coming of the railway, all of the North West and the land beyond the mountains had been like a great desert with scattered oases of population, separated by many days' travel, and each sufficient unto itself. Now, the cross-fertilization process had begun. At last Canada had an accessible frontier from which to draw new strength, new blood, and new ideas. ("There is no longer any reason why Canada's sons should 'go to the States' to make a new start in life," the *Quarterly Review* wrote in an article on the CPR shortly after it was completed.) A new kind of Canadian, the "Westerner," was making his first impact on the men from the sober East. He belonged to a more open-handed and less rigid society; over the century that followed he would help to change the country.

One war correspondent's description of a prairie town, written that April – it could have been Moose Jaw, Medicine Hat, Swift Current, or a dozen smaller settlements – mirrored the astonishment of an Ontario city man on first coming up against western life:

"Here is where the man who has a turn that way can study the human face divine, and the human dress astonishing. Men well dressed, fully dressed, commonly dressed; awfully dressed, shabbily dressed, partly dressed; men sober, nearly sober, half drunk, nearly drunk, quite drunk, frightfully drunk, howling drunk, dead drunk; men from Canada, the States, the United Kingdom and from almost every state in Europe; men enormously rich and frightfully poor, but all having a free and easy manner which is highly refreshing to a man fresh from the east who is accustomed to the anxious expressions of men in our silent streets at home."

The western Canadian was still in embryo, living often in a hovel of sod or earth or in one of those lusty, tented dormitories that had no counterpart in the East. "The 'Hotel,' itself," wrote the *Globe*, "is a revelation. It is of canvas and is like nothing under the earth. The beds are in tiers one above the other and a man generally bursts into tears when he gets into one of them. In such a camp there is always a poker saloon, a billiard saloon, and a number of the most villainous whiskey dives under canvas that can possibly be imagined. In the poker saloon the 'chips' are always iron rings with a hole through them. . . . In any other place on the face of the earth they are either ivory composition, or paste board. In the camps, however, they use these iron chips, and as the keeper of the den always wins by hook or by crook the unfortunate who objects in too enthusiastic a way is liable to a volley of these terrible missiles, often receiving cruel wounds. . . ." (Apparently the *Globe*'s reporter had never seen a washer.)

In such crucibles was the western character tempered. Its influence had yet to be felt, but here and there in the growing settlements were men who would help to shape the country: Pat Burns out in Calgary, laying the basis of a fortune by selling meat to CPR contractors; James Lougheed, the lawyer, hanging out his shingle in the same city; Charles Whitehead,

384

a railway contractor's son, in Brandon; the Sifton brothers, sons of another railway contractor, also in Brandon, setting out to practise law together; Rodman Roblin, late of Prince Edward County, Ontario, a future premier of Manitoba and the grandfather of another premier, tilling his farm near Carman. The railway, or the promise of the railway, had brought them all to the North West.

If Riel's rebellion helped change eastern attitudes to the prairies, it also helped change them towards the CPR. Van Horne was later to remark in his dry way that the railway should have erected a statue to the Métis leader. As early as April 6, he was able to tell a friend in Scotland that "there is no more talk about the construction of the Lake Superior line having been a useless expenditure of money, nor about the road having been built too quickly. Most people are inclined to think it would have been better had it been built three or four weeks quicker."

Yet – and Van Horne must have felt the irony of the situation – the CPR was in worse financial shape than ever. It had cost almost a million dollars to ship the troops west, and that bill was not immediately collectable. (The CPR charged the government $852,331.32 for the entire job; in July, 1886, after the inevitable war claims commission had duly deliberated, the government paid $760,648.13.) The railway, in Van Horne's words, was making sacrifices "to the great detriment of our regular business," keeping engines under steam and cars waiting empty for as long as twenty-four hours at a time when it had scarcely a dollar in the bank.

It was a strange situation: at the moment of its greatest triumph, while the troops were speeding west on the new steel to the applause of the nation, the CPR's financial scaffolding was collapsing, and scarcely anybody in Ottawa appeared to be concerned. Indeed, on April 11 Van Horne discovered to his dismay that, in spite of his contribution to the nation, somebody in the government service was continuing to send surveyors, freight, and public officials to Manitoba by way of Chicago on the Grand Trunk rather than by the CPR's Toronto and St. Thomas line, which connected with the Canada Southern and Michigan Central at London. While the Canadian Pacific was straining every effort to move the troops, its rival was pocketing a profit.

2

George Stephen wanted out; Ottawa had become painful to him. He could no longer bear the varnished atmosphere of the East Block, whose outer offices he had been haunting since December. Those two political nerve centres, the Russell House and the Rideau Club, had become agonizing symbols of setback and defeat. He was determined to shake the slush of the capital from his boots, never to return.

On March 26, the day of the bloody engagement at Duck Lake, dispirited and sick at heart, he went to his room in the Russell House and packed his bags. He had already dispatched a letter to the Prime Minister explaining that, as a result of a conversation that morning, he was satisfied the government could not give the railway the aid it required. There was in that letter none of the desperation that characterized so much of his correspondence with Macdonald. Stephen was drained of emotion; all that remained was a kind of chilly aloofness, a sense of resignation: "I need not repeat how sorry I am that this should be the result of all our efforts to give Canada a railway to the Pacific ocean. But I am supported by the conviction that I have done all that could be done to obtain it." That was it. The great adventure was over. Stephen prepared to return to Montreal to personal ruin and public disgrace.

It was hard to conceal anything in the Russell House, for it was the real political headquarters of the capital. It had been growing with the city, adding wing after wing, tearing down old portions, adding on new – a turret or two here, an ornamental tower there, a small forest of iron columns, new floors of polished marble. By 1885, it occupied almost the entire block at Sparks Street and Elgin. Contractors, diplomats, working politicians, and VIPs flocked to its lobby. It was not possible that Stephen's departure could go unremarked.

Among the crowd in the lobby that evening were a CPR official, George H. Campbell, and two cabinet ministers – Mackenzie Bowell, Minister of Customs (who had originally opposed the railway loan), and Senator Frank Smith, Minister without Portfolio. Campbell was one of several CPR men working on members of the Government to try to change their minds regarding further aid to the railway. Bowell had already been converted; Smith, who had met several times with Van Horne, did not need to be. He was the head of a firm of wholesale grocers in Toronto which was a supplier to the CPR and, in addition, he was personally involved in railways as well as in allied forms of transportation. Of all of Macdonald's inner circle, with the exception of Charles Tupper and John Henry Pope, he was the most enthusiastic supporter of the railway.

As the three men chatted together, Stephen appeared in the lobby and walked towards the office to pay his bill. He was clearly downcast and exhausted with mental strain and anxiety. Smith was alarmed at his appearance and his obvious intentions.

He hurried towards Stephen, engaged him in conversation, and called the others over. Campbell, who later recounted the incident to Katherine Hughes, Van Horne's original biographer,* recalled the gist of Stephen's words: "No, I am leaving at once; there is no use – I have just come from Earnscliffe and Sir John has given a final refusal – nothing more can be done. What will happen tomorrow I do not know – the proposition is hopeless."

Smith, whose powers of persuasion were considerable, managed to dissuade Stephen from leaving. (One story has it that he kept him talking so long that the CPR president missed his train and had no choice but to stay over.) Smith promised that he and Mackenzie Bowell would make a final effort that evening to change the Prime Minister's mind. They drove to Earnscliffe for a midnight interview, leaving Campbell with orders to remain with Stephen and not to allow any other person access to him.

Though Smith held no cabinet portfolio – his business interests occupied too much of his time – he was one of the most powerful politicians at Ottawa, a handsome, large-hearted Irishman with a vast following among the Roman Catholics of Ontario. He was popular with almost everybody, friend or foe. Indeed, he had once subscribed to the campaign fund of a political opponent (who was, admittedly, a co-religionist running against an Orangeman).

Joseph Pope† said of him that he was possessed of a "keen business sagacity and sound common sense." He had worked himself up from immigrant farm hand and grocery-store clerk to the ownership of one of the largest wholesale houses in Canada. From this base he branched out into transportation. The pleasure boats that ran to Niagara were his and so was the Toronto horsecar system, which became a model for American cities. (Smith introduced the coffee-pot method of collecting fares at the door to save the conductor from having to move down the car.) He had reached a kind of pinnacle in both finance and transportation; he was president of a bank (the Toronto Savings and later the Dominion) and of

---

*There are several versions of the legendary incident, differing in detail. All agree, however, on Smith's key role in Stephen's subsequent actions.
† Macdonald's secretary and no relation to John Henry Pope.

a railway (the Northern). His political career was equally spectacular. Mayor of London at forty-four, he was a senator at forty-nine and by that time a close friend and confidant of the Prime Minister, who believed that Smith could personally deliver the Catholic vote in Ontario, or withhold it.

There is an amusing story told of Smith in the 1878 campaign which illustrates, in the most literal manner, his political clout. A very bad speaker in the Albert Hall on Yonge Street, opposite Eaton's, in Toronto, was clearly losing votes for the party when Smith rose from a back seat, walked up to the chairman, and whispered in his ear. Smith then walked over beside the speaker and gave him a nudge with his powerful elbow. The speaker stopped, looked at Smith, and began to speak again. Smith, who was a tall and muscular man, gave him a heavier nudge. The speaker doggedly kept on. A succession of nudges from Smith finally edged the unfortunate orator right off the platform and out of sight. As the next speaker took the floor and Smith strode back to his seat, the crowd gave him such a round of applause that he was persuaded to stand and take a bow.

He was an engaging figure – a liberal supporter of the opera, a patron of the theatre, the president of the Ontario Jockey Club, the owner of a stable of spirited horses, and a free spender. A word from him could mean a change in the party's fortunes. If any man could swing the Prime Minister and the Cabinet, it was Smith.

He and Bowell arrived at Earnscliffe and attempted for more than an hour to persuade the Prime Minister to reconsider the matter of the loan. It was the second time within a year that a midnight attempt had been made to reprieve the CPR. Smith, apparently, was less successful than Pope had been in 1884. Macdonald may have been shaken, but he would not move. Nevertheless, when Smith returned at 2 a.m. he was able to convince Stephen that he should not yet give up the ghost. Guarded by the vigilant Campbell, whose instructions were to keep him incommunicado, the CPR president agreed to revise his proposal for relief while Smith worked on Macdonald and the Cabinet. It was said that for Campbell the three days that followed were the most anxious of his life. He was the constant companion of "a man torn with anguish and remorse whose heart seemed to be breaking with compassion for friends whose downfall he felt himself responsible for."

Stephen had his revised proposition ready for the Privy Council the following day. That it was not rejected out of hand must be seen as a victory for Frank Smith. It was no wonder that years later Van Horne

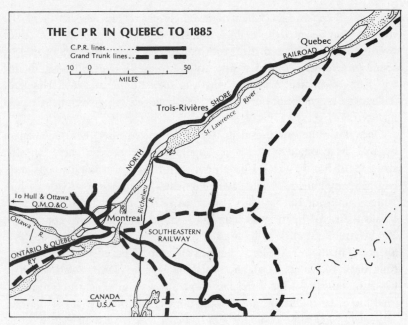

THE C P R IN QUEBEC TO 1885

C.P.R. lines
Grand Trunk lines

10   0   50
            MILES

Quebec
RAILROAD

Trois-Rivières   SHORE
St. Lawrence River

NORTH

To Hull & Ottawa
Q.M.O.&O.

Ottawa R.

Richelieu R.

Montreal

ONTARIO & QUEBEC RY

SOUTHEASTERN
RAILWAY

CANADA
U.S.A.

wrote to Smith that everybody connected with the railway felt a debt of
gratitude to him "which they can never hope to repay." McLelan might
resign if the loan went through, but Smith made it clear that he would
resign if it did not; and Smith controlled more votes.

Over the next fortnight, as the troops from eastern Canada were
shuttled off to the plains, a series of protracted and inconclusive negotiations took place regarding the exact terms of the proposed loan, which
must pass both Council and Parliament. With every passing day, Stephen
grew more nervous and distraught. The government had him in a corner.
Macdonald wanted to be repaid in hard cash, not land; the government
would retain a lien on the land, together with the proposed mortgage
bonds as security. Moreover, it would insist that the CPR take over the
North Shore line between Montreal and Quebec City. Under pressure
from Ottawa, the Grand Trunk could be persuaded to give up the line to
the Quebec government which, in turn, would lease it back to the CPR at
an annual cost of $778,000. It was doubtful, Stephen thought, if it could
earn one hundred thousand dollars annually, it was so run down. (Later
that year the CPR bought the line outright.)

But there was no help for it. Reports were coming in of a serious strike
at Beavermouth in the shadow of the Selkirks; an angry mob of navvies,
demanding their pay, was marching on the CPR's construction head-

389

quarters. Stephen saw Tilley immediately, gave him the news of the trouble, and warned the finance minister of the "utter impossibility of averting an immediate & disastrous collapse" unless some way could be found to give the company temporary aid to tide it over while the matter was being discussed at painful length in the Cabinet and in Parliament. Tilley was not helpful; he was one who believed the government would have to take over the railway.

Once again the CPR president was at the end of his tether. Once again he told Macdonald: ". . . it is impossible for me to carry on this struggle for life, in which I have now been for over 4 months constantly engaged, any longer." The delay had finished him, he said – rendered him "utterly unfit for further work." He was sick at heart, fed up with politicians, betrayed by the very man in whom he had placed his confidence. Yet he could not quite bring himself to leave. He waited four more days. Silence. Finally, on April 15, Stephen gave up. That evening he took the train back to Montreal, to the great mansion on Drummond Street in which he must have felt a trespasser since it was, in effect, no longer his. And there the following morning the dimensions of the disaster the railway faced were summed up for him in a curt wire from Van Horne:

"Have no means paying wages, pay car can't be sent out, and unless we get immediate relief we must stop. Please inform Premier and Finance Minister. Do not be surprised, or blame me if an immediate and most serious catastrophe happens."

3

Riot at Beavermouth   Of all the mercurial construction camps along the CPR's mountain line, the one at the mouth of the Beaver River was the most volatile. It was dominated by saloons – forty of them – all selling illegal whiskey (usually a mixture of rye, red ink, and tobacco juice) at fifty cents a glass, and each taking in as much as three hundred dollars a night. "Rome has hitherto taken the palm for howling," the Calgary *Herald* reported somewhat ambiguously in 1885; "this is because not many people have heard of Beaver Creek."

The gamblers and whiskey peddlers had originally concentrated at Donald, on the east side of the Columbia. In order to remove his navvies from temptation, James Ross caused the track to be taken across the river. There, along the Beaver flats, where the pale green waters meandered out of the mountains through a carpet of ferns and berries, he established a

390

company store and a postal car. The plan did not work. The coarser elements soon moved across the Columbia bridge and began to build saloons, dance halls, and brothels out of cedar logs. Under British Columbia law the saloons were legal as long as they were licensed by provincial authorities. Under Dominion law it was illegal to sell liquor within the forty-mile railway belt. This caused a series of comic-opera disputes between representatives of the two jurisdictions all along the line in British Columbia.

Ross refused to allow CPR trains to provide the gamblers, saloonkeepers, and prostitutes with food or supplies. An upsurge of petty thievery and discontent followed. Sleighs left unguarded were robbed; subcontractors were tempted to sell provisions illegally at black-market prices. The town was awake most of the night to the sound of dancing, singing, and revelry. Sam Steele, the Mounted Police inspector in charge, remembered that "we were rarely to bed before two or three a.m., and were up in the morning between six and seven. . . ." Steele spent the forenoon disposing of prisoners – mainly drunks who had been lodged in jail overnight for their own safety – and the afternoon with summary trials for petty theft and assault.

By late March, the complaints over lack of pay began to gather into a discontented rumble that moved up and down the line in angry gusts. The men had been content to go without pay in the winter, but by early spring funds were needed for homesteads in Manitoba, Minnesota, and Dakota. Steele, who was the recipient of many of the complaints, counselled patience. He feared that a strike, if it came, would swiftly develop into a riot, sparked by a large number of "ruffians, gamblers and murderers from the Northern Pacific who had left it on the completion of that road." He warned Ross of the danger of trouble; Ross remained unconvinced. Steele wired the Prime Minister that a strike was imminent but got no action; Macdonald had more serious troubles in Saskatchewan on his mind. At this critical point Steele was felled by a massive attack of fever, which he described as a Rocky Mountain typho-malarial fever (probably Rocky Mountain spotted fever, which had been identified only a few years before). Steele was forced to take to his bed, an unusual recourse, for he was known as an iron man, "erect as a pine tree and limber as a cat," as his son described him. He was so ill he could scarcely lift his head from the pillow.

At this very moment, with the strongest force for law and order incapacitated, the men struck and began marching en masse up the line towards Beavermouth. Thousands, it was said, were joining in the work stoppage. The situation was inflammable. All that Steele could do was to send some of his policemen to meet the strikers and advise them to abstain from any lawless act.

The news of the work stoppage had barely reached him when a frantic wire arrived from the Mayor of Calgary: the entire North West seemed to be up in arms; Riel and Dumont had struck; the Crees under Big Bear and Poundmaker were on the verge of joining the rebellion; Crowfoot and his braves were camped on the very edge of Calgary. "For God's sake, come; there is danger of an attack by the Blackfeet!" Everything seemed to be crowding in on Steele at once. He could only reply that the situation at Beavermouth was so dangerous that he could not spare a man. He had only eight as it was.

The workmen had not been paid because the contractors had not been paid. Those who quit first were in the farthest outpost of the section of the line then under construction. They set out to march to End of Track, gathering others to their cause as they passed through the various camps. By the time they reached Mountain Creek, they numbered several hundred.

Track-laying, which had come to a halt with winter's onset, was about to recommence. Carpenters were strung out on top of the great Mountain Creek trestle, trying to complete it before the track reached that point. The strikers massed on the edge of the ravine below and called to the men to stop work and come down off the bridge. The carpenters, intent on finishing the job, refused. One of the strikers seized an axe and slashed the rope that held the block and tackle used to hoist bridge materials to the top of the trestle. That meant the carpenters could do no further work.

William Mackenzie's bridge manager, a man named Balfour, called his engineer, Turner Bone, to the construction office to discuss the situation. Before they could talk they were surrounded by a horde of strikers. A reluctant spokesman was pushed forward and a moment of silence followed until he gained his voice. Then he made it clear that there would be no more work done on the bridge until the men were paid. Balfour was forced to call his carpenters down.

The strikers moved resolutely on to Beavermouth, gathering strength as they went. They were now threatening violence to the road and destruction of property. The ailing Steele received a deputation and warned them that "if they committed any act of violence, and were not orderly, in the strictest sense of the word, I would inflict upon the offenders the severest punishment the law would allow me." James Ross, Donald Mann, and Herbert Holt all tried to reason with the strikers and succeeded in convincing some to return to the job. The remainder refused and stayed at Beavermouth where, in Steele's words, "a large number of loose characters were ready to urge them to any mischief."

Three hundred of the strikers, armed with revolvers, began to police the line, ordering the tracklayers to cease work, the teamsters to leave their teams, and the bridge workers to lay down their hammers. A trainload of men sent to End of Track was driven back. James Ross himself mounted the engine, told the engineer to put on all steam, and ran it through the armed mob as bullets whistled past his cab. The train entered the narrow canyon of the Beaver, an easy place to defend with a few men. Here the track-laying began again.

On came the strikers, firing as they advanced, while the tracklayers worked in the canyon. Steele's second in command, a thickset sergeant with the appropriate name of Fury, drew his party across the mouth of the canyon to meet the advance. When they arrived, Fury announced that he would shoot the first man to cross the line. An uproar followed, but the strikers were cowed and returned to Beavermouth, allowing the tracklayers to finish their day's work.

Sergeant Fury returned at the end of the day and reported to his bedridden superior. Steele, still racked by fever, rose unsteadily and sat down in a camp-chair. Both men were awaiting Constable Kerr, who had gone to the end of track for a supply of medicine for the ailing inspector. Kerr attempted to arrest a contractor named Behan, "a well known desperado," for being drunk and disorderly but was immediately attacked by a crowd of strikers who threw him to the ground and forced him to retreat without his prisoner.

No Mounted Police officer could allow such humiliation to go unremarked. Said Steele: " . . . we must take the man at any cost. It will never do to let the remainder of the gang know they can play with us." He told Fury to take what men he needed to arrest Behan. Fury set off with two constables to arrest the offending contractor, whom they found in a saloon "in the midst of a gang of drunken companions." The constables seized their quarry and dragged him out, surrounded by an angry mob of two hundred armed men. Fury was hesitant about using his pistol; as a result, the strikers were able to retrieve Behan and the police retreated.

Fury, badly mauled and with his jacket torn, returned to the police barracks and asked Steele for orders. "Take your revolvers," Steele said, "and shoot anyone who interferes with the arrest!"

Events were now building to a climax. Steele, still bed-ridden, was too weak to watch what happened from the window, but the local stipendiary magistrate, George Hope Johnston, gave him a running account. He watched Fury and three policemen start off for the bridge across the Beaver that separated the CPR store and police barracks from the saloon town on the other side. The men entered the log community and disappeared between the cabins. A few moments later the sharp crack of gun-fire echoed through the valley.

"There is one gone to hell, Steele," Johnston said.

Sick or not, Steele had to see for himself. He forced himself out of bed and crawled to the window in time to see two of his men dragging a prisoner across the bridge. The prisoner was "fighting like a fiend, while a woman in scarlet followed . . . with wild shrieks and curses." Sergeant Fury and the third constable brought up the rear, trying to fend off the crowd, which had swollen to seven hundred.

It was time for Steele to act. He called on Johnston to get the Riot Act and, seizing a Winchester from the constable on guard at the jail, ran to the bridge, levelled his rifle at the crowd, and told the strikers to halt.

"Look at the——," someone cried; "his own death bed makes no difference to him!" Nonetheless, everybody stopped. One of the constables knocked out the struggling prisoner with a heavy blow and pulled him by the collar the rest of the way, "insensible as a rag." The woman in red started to scream: "You red-coated——!" Steele turned to his men: "Take her in, too!" Then he started forward onto the bridge to face the sullen mob.

Johnston had been forced to kick the orderly-room door in, the constable with the key having been too busy with the riot. He arrived at last, took up a position beside Steele, and opened the book at the Riot Act. Said Steele: "Listen to this and keep your hands off your guns, or I will shoot the first man of you who makes a hostile movement." There was silence. Sergeant Fury had already put a bullet into the shoulder of a man who tried to keep him from taking his prisoner.

After the Riot Act was read, Steele spoke again:

"You have taken advantage of the fact that a rebellion has broken out in the North West and that I have only a handful of men, but, as desperate diseases require desperate remedies, and both disease and remedy are here, I warn you that if I find more than twelve of you standing together or any large crowd assembled, I will open fire upon you and mow you down! Now disperse at once and behave yourselves!"

Steele's full force of eight Mounted Police now stood in line behind them, rifles cocked. Steele stood his ground with Johnston and watched the grumbling mob slowly break up. The following morning the town and all the line "was as quiet as a country village on Sunday." Steele arrested all the ringleaders in the riot, brought them to court, and fined them each one hundred dollars or six months in jail.

The men remained off work until arrangements were made to pay them, but there was no further violence. Steele, still convalescent, donned his uniform and headed for Calgary. James Ross implored him to come back, but this was not possible. The North West was at war. Three columns of troops were preparing to move north to the fertile valley of the Saskatchewan, now held in thrall by roaming bands of Crees and a more disciplined force of Métis under Riel and his adjutant general, Dumont. Out from Calgary went Major-General T. Bland Strange, brought out of retirement from his ranch to keep the restive Blackfoot in check with the six hundred volunteers of the Alberta Field Force. North from Qu'Appelle marched the first division of the North West Field Force – nine hundred men under General Middleton, determined to strike at Riel's headquarters in Batoche. The second division – five hundred men and two hundred teamsters – entrained for Swift Current and then moved north under Colonel Otter (happily recovered from his snow-blindness) to relieve the besieged stockade at Battleford. Steele himself was given a unique command. His task was to organize, as swiftly as possible, a cavalry detachment known as Steele's Scouts and strike off in pursuit of the rebel Cree chieftain, Big Bear. It was, perhaps, the most remarkable case on record of instant recovery from Rocky Mountain fever.

4

The eleventh hour

When Stephen learned from Van Horne on April 16 that the CPR pay car could not be sent out, he immediately wired the news in cipher to John Henry Pope in Ottawa. Van Horne had hinted at the imminence of a "serious catastrophe." Another riot, similar to the one at Beavermouth, was likely if wages were again held up. The Minister of Railways was Stephen's last hope. Not long before, the CPR president had sat in Pope's drawing room, his head in his hands, and said to Rufus, Pope's son: "We are ruined – there is only one man who understands the seriousness of our position and that is your father – It is through him that we must be saved."

John Henry Pope was, on first acquaintance, a curiously unimpressive man – angular of feature, ungainly in manner, slow in speech, awkward of gesture, and hesitant in his parliamentary oratory. He had only elementary schooling, a deficiency that made his correspondence seem almost childlike. Yet he was one of the most powerful men in the Government. There was, as John Willison said, a patriarchal simplicity and dignity about him which inspired liking and respect. There was something a bit Lincolnesque, not only about his features – the prominent cheekbones, the sensitive nostrils – but also about his manner. He might be an awkward speaker but he did not fall into the trap of making dangerous admissions; nor could he be provoked into hasty or angry statements. Macdonald listened to him and trusted him.

Pope went straight to the Prime Minister with Stephen's decoded telegram and again pointed out the obvious: if the CPR went bankrupt, the Government could not survive. At last the vacillating party leader was forced into a decision. Until this moment he had believed, not without good reason, that any further relief to the company would be politically disastrous. The exhausting debate of 1884 had been bad enough but it would be nothing compared to the national uproar occasioned by further public handouts to a faltering railroad. Whichever course Macdonald took, he knew he was going to face a storm. If the CPR collapsed, it would undoubtedly touch off a wave of bankruptcies and personal tragedies – men without pay, suppliers over-extended, entire communities facing depression, the country demoralized by the failure of its great national endeavour. And then there was Blake, the man who always had the facts and figures at his finger-tips and who used them to devastating effect. Blake, the vindicated prophet, would remind the nation of his famous prediction that the CPR would never pay for its axle grease; Macdonald did not care to face that taunt. He had two choices, both of them politically unpalatable; but one was slightly less distasteful than the other. With very little heart he decided that, once again, he must help to bail out the CPR.

Fortunately, the mood of the country was beginning to change. Because of the swift action of the railway, the government had a good chance of localizing the Saskatchewan Rebellion and preventing it from spreading throughout the North West. In the most bizarre and perverse way something *had* turned up for Old Tomorrow. Macdonald's earlier procrastinations in the matter of Indian and Métis rights had produced a situation that made his later procrastinations in the matter of railway financing seem almost prescient.

First, however, there was a nasty wrangle in the caucus. The majority of Macdonald's followers were in favour of the government taking over the road. McLelan resigned, as he had said he would. Macdonald had to use all his charm and all his political muscle to bring the party into line. He personally spoke or wrote to every recalcitrant Conservative, threatening his own resignation if they failed to back his proposal for another loan to the railway. In the words of another Pope (Joseph), "with no very good grace the Ministerial supporters swallowed the pill."

In one crowded week, events took on momentum of their own. The railway still had no money to pay its men and not much hope of getting any, in spite of Macdonald's change of heart; the relief bill, which the Prime Minister had not yet laid before the House, would not be passed before a long debate in Parliament. Macdonald privately asked the Bank of Montreal to advance five million dollars to the CPR, explaining that he intended to bring some resolutions before Parliament regarding financial aid "at an early date." That was not good enough for the bank; it bluntly refused to advance a nickel to the faltering company.

The same day – April 24 – at Fish Creek, a coulee not far from Batoche, a handful of Métis under Gabriel Dumont fought General Middleton's superior force to a standstill. The Métis lost six men, the Canadians, fifty; Middleton was immobilized for a fortnight. There was better news from Battleford, where the five hundred people cooped up in a stockade less than two hundred yards square were finally released by Colonel Otter's division. In London the Grand Trunk, eying events in Canada, was waiting to pounce on its hapless rival. Sir John Rose wrote to Stephen of the GTR's intense ill will, not just to the railway but also to "everything Canadian." On April 27, Sir Henry Tyler told a Grand Trunk meeting that the CPR was finished – that it would be taken over by the government and when that happened his company would gladly come forward and "*assist.*"

Stephen lost little time in passing all this treasonous talk on to Macdonald. Meanwhile, the CPR's secretary, Charles Drinkwater, diplomatically suggested that the bank would undoubtedly take a different view of the proposed loan if the railway's relief bill were actually placed before Parliament. Finally, the reluctant Prime Minister acted. He gave notice to the House on May 1 of the resolutions he proposed to submit. It came at a singularly dramatic moment. The press that day was proclaiming that Britain and Russia were on the eve of war. Stephen had just opened a telegram from the Imperial War Department: Was the CPR in a position to transport war matériel to the Pacific coast? The CPR president instantly wired an affirmative response. Then, on May 2, there was more bad news from Saskatchewan: Colonel Otter had suffered a defeat at the hands of Poundmaker and his Crees.

Still there was to be a delay. Macdonald was determined to postpone the debate on the railway resolutions until he had forced his pet franchise bill through the House. This was a measure that would remove control of the terms of the federal franchise from provincial legislatures. To Stephen, desperately trying to "tide over matters," it seemed as if the Prime Minister was putting a petty squabble with the provinces ahead of what he was prone to call "this great national undertaking." Four years before, the railway had been given priority in Parliament. Macdonald had refused to allow any other matter to take precedence over the debate on the CPR contract. Now, with the company existing on nothing more than goodwill and promises, he was prepared to let it wait another month or more while the House wrangled its way through the franchise bill, phrase by phrase and sentence by sentence. Why? Was it because the spectre of the Pacific Scandal still haunted Parliament and the Prime Minister was fearful of being seen again to favour such a controversial private company? No doubt; yet he had favoured it before. More likely, Macdonald saw the CPR issue as politically divisive and the franchise issue as unifying. Yet this scarcely explains his astonishing remark to Charles Tupper: "I consider the passage of the Franchise Bill the greatest triumph of my life." Plainly, in his seventy-first year, the Prime Minister was afflicted by a myopia that permitted national interests to give way to those of party.

Stephen was beside himself at this politicking. Abbott, the company's lawyer, who was also a Member of Parliament, had "fairly scared" him with the news that it might be five or six weeks before the CPR resolutions became law. The railway could not hold out for anything like that time. Stephen felt that Macdonald had lost faith in him, that the imminent collapse of the company was no longer of much moment. Certainly the Prime Minister, harried by events in the North West and obsessed with his battle over the franchise bill, was weary of Stephen's constant, injured carping. "I think I had a right to more considerate treatment," Stephen had complained to Tupper at the end of April. Of one thing he was convinced; the company at all costs must get free of any connection with the government, and as swiftly as possible. It was the beginning of a breach with Macdonald (never an open one) which was probably a factor in his subsequent decision to leave Canada and return to his native Scotland.

The CPR still needed the government to guarantee a loan at the bank. Even a million dollars would help. Shaughnessy had a way of doling out small downpayments on expired credit notes, of stilling the more persistent creditors and keeping the loyal ones at arm's length. A million dollars in Shaughnessy's hands could give the company perhaps three weeks' breathing space. On May 5, at the government's request, the Bank of

Montreal advanced three-quarters of a million dollars. It was not much; but it was something.

The real problem was wages. The pay car with the March wages, due to leave from Montreal on April 15, had not been sent out. A month passed; by that time the April wages were also due. Still there was no sign of any payment. All along the line the grumblings began to be heard. mingled with reports of real privation.

"The distress among the men is keen," the *Globe* reported in mid-May. "The boardinghouse keepers are looking hard at the young men whose board has not been paid for over two months, and they are doubtful if they will ever be able to collect from all when the long delayed car does come. . . . "

Grocers, bakers, butchers, dry goods and hardware merchants began to deny further credit to married employees of the railway. In the CPR shops at Parkdale a number of men disclosed that they had been forced to cut themselves down to one meal a day. They had been unable to get extensions from local shops because these, in turn, had been denied further supplies from wholesale houses that had advanced credit. Everybody from office clerk to dispatcher felt the pinch. One travelling passenger agent, it was reported, was forced to economize in the use of his razor, "and looks as if he had been out of the world for some weeks." For the ordinary labourer, who received only a dollar a day and was therefore unable to save any money, the lack of pay was especially severe. "Some of them are said to be now suffering the extreme of want and poverty, and even though still keeping at their work, are daily fighting against the gnawing of hunger."

A listlessness seemed to have seized the employees of the railway in Ontario. They continued to work because they had no recourse. Unlike the track gangs farther west, they were not essential to the survival of the CPR. When a group of mechanics at Perth told Van Horne that they would quit work unless the pay car came along, the general manager simply informed them that if that happened, he would close down the works. That message travelling up and down the line killed all talk of a general strike.

In Parliament, the debate on the franchise bill dragged on and on. Speeches lasted for seven hours; one sitting went on for three days without a break; there were ninety-three divisions of the House. It was clear that the CPR would have to have a government advance or another guarantee at the bank if it was to stay alive until the relief measure could pass the House and Senate. "It is very hard having to fight both enemies & friends,"

Stephen wrote in a bitter and urgent letter to Macdonald. Somehow the railway had to find money, not just for wages, but also for the interest payments on the bonds of the Ontario and Quebec Railway. It was the twelfth of May: the interest was due on the first of June. "If we default," Stephen reminded the Prime Minister, " . . . then goodbye to the C.P.R. . . ."

The resolution of the CPR's various financial crises was always theatrical, fraught with the same kind of tension that audiences had come to expect from the stage melodramas of the era, in which the heroine was saved at the last instant from the onrushing locomotive, the big saw, or the Fate Worse than Death. Such a moment came, again at the eleventh hour, less than a week before the interest on the O and Q bonds was due. Most of the directors of the company waited breathlessly outside of the Privy Council door while the Cabinet argued over whether or not the government could guarantee another bank loan. In later years, Van Horne liked to describe that scene to his friends:

"I guessed that sound would come best to me if I stood in the room opposite the glass door which would help to act as a resonator. But though I could hear each voice as it spoke, I was unable to make out clearly what anyone said. It was an awful time. Each one of us felt as if the railway was our own child and we were prepared to make any sacrifice for it, but things were at a dead-lock and it seemed impossible to raise any more money. We men ourselves had given up twenty per cent of our salaries and had willingly worked, not overtime but double-time, and as we waited in that room, we thought about these things and wondered whether all our toil was going to be wasted or not, and what would happen if Canada were ruined. . . . At last Joe Pope came with a yellow paper in his hand. He said that the Government was prepared to back the Bank of Montreal to the extent then required. I think we waited until he left the room. I believe we had that much sanity left us! And then we began. We tossed up chairs to the ceiling; we trampled on desks; I believe we danced on tables. I do not fancy that any of us knows now what occurred, and no one who was there can ever remember anything except loud yells of joy and the sound of things breaking!"

Van Horne raced immediately to the company's office to telegraph the news to Shaughnessy. The operator seemed too slow and so the general manager pushed him aside and began ticking off the message himself. It had been a near thing. "The advance we are now making is quite illegal and we are incurring the gravest responsibility in doing so," Macdonald wrote to Stephen.

400

The resolutions for the relief of the railway were still not before the House, and John Henry Pope was not able to present them until June 16. By that time the rebellion in Saskatchewan had been crushed. Riel and Poundmaker were both prisoners. Dumont, whose small band of sharp-shooters had held off the militia for a surprisingly long period, had vanished over the border. Sam Steele was in hot pursuit of Big Bear. Schreiber had already informed Tupper (in England) that "the House and country are both in favour of the CPR and that should now be doubly the case when the fact is patent to the world [that] but for the rapid construction . . . Canada would have been involved in a frightful waste of blood and treasure quelling the rising in the North West."

Tyler and Hickson of the Grand Trunk had both rushed to Ottawa on June 13 to see Macdonald and other members of Parliament, but they must have discovered what Schreiber already knew: that a good many Liberals were prepared, if not to support the measure, at least not to oppose it. As "a matter of policy," the urbane Tyler decided to make a trip out west on the rival line and see it all for himself. Hickson was horrified at the idea, but Sir Henry, the old politician, knew something of the value of being graceful in defeat. Hickson reconciled himself to the inevitable.

Though the battle was clearly lost, Edward Blake, the leader of the Liberal opposition, had no intention of giving in without a fight. He was prepared to oppose the relief bill as he had opposed the whole concept of a privately owned transcontinental railway from the very beginning. His speeches were now lasting for six hours and wearying the House. To Stephen, however, they must have seemed extraordinarily effective, for they produced an apoplectic reaction: "The *meanest* thing of the kind that has ever come under my notice . . . an ill-conditioned, vindictive effort . . . I am so furious with Blake that I cannot at the moment write coherently about him or his speech. What a miserable creature he must be!" As always, to Stephen, any man who opposed his particular concept of the railway was a blackguard of the deepest dye.

The CPR president hoped that Macdonald would destroy "the evil effects of Blakes malicious speech" and "express the scorn & contempt which I am sure you must feel. . . . "

Macdonald was probably more amused by Blake than he was contemptuous – the Liberal leader's speeches contained far too many indigestible facts and were, during that session, causing even his own supporters to snore. But the Prime Minister had his own problems. Tupper, the greatest of all parliamentary fighters, was out of the picture

401

in London. Pope was ill. Campbell, the Minister of Justice, was incapacitated by splitting headaches. Tilley, also ill, was off to Europe. Macdonald had remarked earlier that year that he could not be away for an hour without "some blunder taking place." He had just come through a savage debate on the franchise bill; now he must gird himself up for another struggle. This time, however, he was in a stronger position. The railway had proved itself. No matter what Blake and his colleagues said, it had saved the country. He made that point when he rose to speak:

"Late events have shown us that we are made one people by that road, that that iron link has bound us together in such a way that we stand superior to most of the shafts of ill-fortune, that we can now assemble together, at every point which may be assailed, or may be in danger, the whole physical force of Canada by means of that great artery, against any foreign foe or any internal insurrection or outbreak."

The debate that followed, as Joseph Pope recalled it, was "acrimonious and unpleasant." It was a foregone conclusion that the measure would pass; what was less certain was the company's ability to survive during the time it would take to turn the bill into law. If the Opposition kept on talking the CPR could collapse.

The loan from the bank ran out; the chances of another were slim. Stephen was so hard pressed that he was forced to delay his continuing visits to Ottawa. They were not productive anyway. There is a story told of him and Abbott sitting in the anteroom of the council chamber one hot afternoon, patiently awaiting the outcome of a final, desperate appeal for help, only to discover that the ministers, rather than face them, had vanished by another door.

"I feel like a ruined man," said the dejected Stephen. Yet, in spite of all his dark predictions about imminent collapse, in spite of his sinister warnings about his own physical condition, in spite of his pledge never again to visit the capital, even in spite of his declarations that he would turn negotiations over to Van Horne, he somehow hung on and the company somehow hung on.

The melodrama continued literally until the very last hour. By July, the CPR's credit had reached the snapping point. Even Frank Smith was disturbed; in giving the company aid he had allowed himself to become dangerously over-extended. One creditor would wait no longer. The company owed him four hundred thousand dollars and could not meet its obligations. On July 10, it is said, the debt was due. If it was not paid, the CPR was faced with all the confusion of a complicated receivership: a scramble of creditors all demanding payment, the total collapse of the company, a halt on all railroad construction, and a legal and financial tangle that could drag on for months before a new corporation with new government arrangements could be formed and the work commenced again.

The debate had dragged on for the best part of a month. The morning of July 10 came and the bill still had not passed the House, which did not sit until 1.30 that afternoon. According to O. D. Skelton, Van Horne's sometime confidant, the four-hundred-thousand-dollar debt was due at three o'clock. There were the usual maddening parliamentary formalities before a division could be taken, but at two that afternoon a majority of the Commons voted in favour of railway relief. That affirmation of confidence was good enough for any creditor; the measure would become law in a matter of days. With the Lake Superior line complete and only a few dozen miles remaining in the gap between the Selkirks and the Gold Range, the railway was saved – as always at the eleventh hour. It is doubtful if history records another instance of a national enterprise coming so close to ruin and surviving.

In England, Tupper was working on the great financial house of Baring to market the new CPR bonds when they were issued. Here, too, the climate had changed. Though there was still a persistent campaign by the Grand Trunk to convince the financial world that the CPR "was a disastrous concern that must break down, or be thrown upon the Government," both Tupper and Tilley were able to convince Barings that the Government meant to support a railway that had performed such a signal service during the rebellion. Stephen was on board ship when at last the CPR relief bill received royal assent on July 20. By the time he reached London, he found Tupper had done his work for him. Baring Brothers took the entire issue of the bonds, half at ninety and the remainder at ninety-one. In Canada, the CPR got the money it needed to finish the line; and it never had to ask for a government loan again.

For once, luck was with the company. The bond issue was floated at exactly the right moment. The brief British boom was short lived, and Barings had trouble disposing of the issue, only half of which was actually subscribed by the British public. The remainder of the bonds were taken up by members of the firm and by George Stephen and Donald A. Smith, who bought half a million dollars worth between them. It was small wonder that the CPR changed the name of the new town at the second crossing of the Columbia from Farwell to Revelstoke, after the peer who headed the financial house that got the railway its money.

5

The frontier was melting away before the onslaught of steel. The old, free days when whiskey peddlers hid in every copse, when gambling ran unchecked, when towns were constructed of tents and logs and the prairies were unfenced, were vanishing. On the heels of the railway came Timothy Eaton's new catalogue, devised in 1884 by that most revolutionary of merchants. For as little as two dollars the ladies of Moose Jaw or Swift Current could order one of several models of the new Grand Rapids Carpet Sweeper ("makes no noise, no dust, sweeps clean; a child can use them"), or for twenty-five cents a patented Hartshorn window shade with spring rollers.

A rough kind of sophistication was making itself felt. Methodist halls where temperance speakers held court invaded the old frontier. Amateur theatricals came into vogue, along with skating carnivals, musical recitals, and educational lectures. The sudden transformation of Winnipeg from a muddy little village into a glittering metropolis astonished the soldiers who poured through on their way to do battle with Dumont and Poundmaker. They were "surprised at the splendid buildings and enormous plate glass fronts of Main street, which is said to remind one of Boston or New York." A Halifax man marvelled at the silks in the windows, selling for as much as $9.50 a yard: ". . . all kind of goods that would rot in the stores of Halifax are sold here every day, and the prices of most American goods are about the same as at home. The streets are all lighted for miles by the electric light and the horse cars run about every five minutes on the principal streets. The number and magnificence of the saloons, etc., is very noticeable."

This was still the West, high, wide and handsome, but it was no longer the frontier. It would have been unthinkable in 1885 for Van Horne to pull a gun on General Rosser in the Manitoba Club, as he had done only three years before. The violent days were over – gone with the buffalo and the antelope, gone with the whooping crane and the passenger pigeon, gone with Red River carts and the nomads who used to roam so freely across a once unbroken ocean of waist-high grass.

The native peoples of the plains had made their final futile gesture against the onrushing tidal wave of civilization in the deep coulees of the North Saskatchewan country in May and June. (The whites did not revolt, W. H. Jackson maintaining an attitude of strict neutrality.) The impetuous Gabriel Dumont, restrained only by a leader who was becom-

404

ing increasingly mystic and irrational, finally broke out and met the militia at Fish Creek on April 23, luring them into a kind of buffalo pound and vowing to treat them exactly as he had the thundering herds in the brave days before the railway. Here his force of one hundred and thirty Métis, armed for the most part with shotguns and muzzle-loaders, held back some eight hundred trained men under General Middleton, the bumbling and over-cautious British Army regular. On May 2, at Cut Knife Hill, Chief Poundmaker and 325 Cree followers emerged victorious against cannon, Gatling gun, and some 540 troops under Colonel Otter.

These were the last contortions of a dying culture. The Canadian government had eight thousand men in the field, transported and supplied by rail. The natives had fewer than one thousand under arms, and these were neither organized nor in all cases enthusiastic. Riel, the prairie prophet – some called him a prairie pontiff – planned his campaign according to the spiritual visitations he believed he was receiving almost daily. The more practical and pugnacious Dumont used his knowledge of the ground, his skill at swift manœuvre and deception, and his experience in the organization of the great hunts to fend off superior forces. It is possible, had Riel given him his head, that he might have cut the main CPR line, derailed the trains, and harried the troops for months in a running guerilla warfare that could have blocked western settlement for a period of years; but the outcome in the end would have been the same.

In mid-May Dumont fought his last battle at Batoche. It lasted for four days – until the Métis' ammunition ran out. It was remarkable, among other things, for the use of the first and only prairie warship. It also brought about Riel's surrender and the flight of his adjutant general, who subsequently re-enacted the incidents of 1885 in Buffalo Bill's Wild West Show.

In the weeks that followed, the Indian leaders surrendered too, or fled over the border – Poundmaker, Little Poplar, Lucky Man, Red Eagle, Poor Crow, Left Hand, Wandering Spirit and, finally, Big Bear. There was no place any longer for a wandering spirit, as Crowfoot, the wisest of them all, had thoroughly understood. Two days before the Duck Lake engagement, a worried Macdonald had asked Father Lacombe to try to ensure the neutrality of the Blackfoot chief and his followers. Crowfoot, who believed he could get more from the government by remaining loyal, forbore to take up arms. His steadfastness was rewarded in various ways, not the least of which was the present of a railway pass from Van Horne. Thus was seen the ironic spectacle of the withered Indian riding back and forth across the prairies on the same iron monster that had changed his people's ways and caused them to be driven into the corrals of the northern reserves.

Deep in the broad, evergreen valley between the Selkirk Mountains and the Gold Range, through which the olive Columbia flowed on its southerly course to the sea, the old frontier life still existed along the line of the unfinished railway. The last rail was laid on the Lake Superior section on May 16, so that the troops would be able to return to the East in considerable comfort; but in British Columbia construction continued for most of 1885. As the months wore on the gap between the two groups of track-layers decreased. On the Onderdonk side, the rails were ascending the western slope of the Gold Range from Eagle Pass Landing on Shuswap Lake. On James Ross's side, the rails were moving up the eastern slopes of the same mountains from Farwell, on the Columbia, soon to be renamed Revelstoke.

It was said that the population of Eagle Pass Landing was sober only during the monthly visits of the stipendiary magistrate from Kamloops. Everybody, it was claimed, purposely avoided drink on those occasions so that they might enjoy it with greater licence the rest of the time. The community's existence was short but merry. In order to prevent card-sharps from corrupting the settlement, it was an unwritten rule that packs of cards be thrown out of the window after every game and a fresh pack opened. A visitor reported that they lay in heaps in the dirt "until the road was actually covered with hearts, spades, diamonds and clubs."

At Farwell, on the second crossing of the Columbia (named after the government surveyor who originally laid out the townsite), board shacks and cabins, euphemistically named "hostess houses," sprang up, presided over by such interesting ladies as Madame Foster, an enormous black woman, and Irish Nell, described as being "tough as nails but with a heart of gold."

In this disputed territory the federal and provincial governments clashed over the sale of liquor. The federal liquor laws were enforced by a federal stipendiary magistrate, George Hope Johnston, and a force of constables, including some Mounted Police. The British Columbia liquor laws were enforced by a provincial stipendiary, J. M. Sproat, and a force of provincial police. In June, a federal man, Constable Ruddick, seized sixteen dozen bottles of beer. Johnston fined the owner and confiscated the bottles. The owner charged Johnston and his men with theft. The provincial magistrate, Sproat, then ordered his police force to break into the federal jail, seize the beer, and arrest the federal constables. The provincial constable involved was in turn charged by Johnston with assault and given fourteen days in jail. Sproat replied by swearing out a warrant for the arrest of Johnston, Ruddick, and a Mounted Police constable. Johnston himself was seized and thrown into jail. The wires buzzed between Ottawa and Victoria, the federal government insisting on its jurisdiction under what was known as the Peace Preservation Act (designed to prevent the sale of liquor along the line of the CPR) and the British Columbia government proclaiming that the act was unconstitutional. Both governments announced that their only interest was in preventing drunkenness among the railroad navvies. The British Columbia government went so far as to declare that Sproat had taken precipitate action because "he found liquor selling in full blast in the presence of Dominion officers whose special business it was to suppress it." The spectacle of two sets of policemen arresting each other was too comical to contemplate for long. The matter was settled in the end at the grass-roots level by the diplomacy of James Farquharson Macleod, the Mounted Police superintendent, who came up from Calgary, sat the two warring magistrates down with a bottle of good Scotch, and solved the dispute amicably without further straining federal-provincial relations.

In Farwell, as in every other new community along the line of the railroad, the CPR brooked no opposition from local merchants or speculators in the matter of real estate profits. A. S. Farwell, the surveyor, had secured one hundred and seventy-five acres for himself on the banks of the Columbia; as he had anticipated, the railway location went right through his property. However, he refused the terms offered by the CPR, and a long and expensive lawsuit followed, which he eventually won. For practical purposes, he lost. The company followed its practice of moving the location of the station and laid out another townsite which became the heart of the business section of Revelstoke.

What the CPR wanted in British Columbia was a gift of land in return for establishing a town or divisional point. "When locating the stations we will be governed so far as circumstances will permit by the liberality of the different parties in this respect," Van Horne told Henry Cambie in March. "We shall try to confer benefits where we have met with decent treatment, and the reverse where we are not." The general manager had no intention of locating the smallest station where "it will benefit anybody who has imposed upon us in the matter of the right of way." He struck a hard bargain. In Kamloops, the pioneer merchant John Andrew Mara, a powerful politician who had once been speaker of the British Columbia legislature, was pressing for the railway to establish a terminal on his property. Van Horne was willing, but only on condition that Mara give the company free land for all shops, sidings, stations, and so on, together with a half interest in *all* his other property. If Mara agreed, he told Cambie, "we'll probably trade with him, otherwise we must look elsewhere." It was Van Horne's principle that the entire cost of setting up a divisional point should be recouped through the sale of adjacent real estate donated by grateful citizens who were really beholden to the railway for the future prosperity of their community.

In his dealings with William Smithe, the Premier of British Columbia, the general manager was equally hard-headed. He knew that the provincial government was anxious to see the CPR extend its line to a new terminus at Granville on Burrard Inlet because it would help the sale of public land in the area. In return, Van Horne asked for almost half the peninsula on which the present metropolitan area of Vancouver is situated. He settled for an outright gift of six thousand acres from the government, including almost all of the waterfront between the Second Narrows and the military reserve, which shortly became Stanley Park. In addition, the Hastings Mill had to give up immediately four thousand acres of land and an additional one thousand acres annually in return for an extension of its lease to 1890.

Van Horne was quite blunt about his intentions in a letter to Major Rogers: "Our object should be of course to give the greatest possible value to our lands and therefore the least to any other." He warned Rogers to keep the company's plans for the Vancouver townsite secret from everybody including the engineers under him. "There are more speculators about New Westminster and Victoria than there were in Winnipeg during the boom and they are a much sharper lot. Nearly every person is more or less interested and you will have to be on your guard against all of them."

To get what he wanted, Van Horne resorted to tough measures. He told Henry Beatty to intimate to private speculators east of Granville that if they did not deal liberally with the company, the CPR shops and all terminal works of any consequence would be moved away from their property to the area of English Bay. In the end the landholders had to yield a third of the lots in each block they held. The railway, in short, would dominate the new city. No street could be continued to tidewater without its permission.

The private speculators included David Oppenheimer, late of Kamloops, who was to become Vancouver's second mayor, John Robson, editor of the New Westminster *Columbian*, Marcus Smith, the government surveyor, and Arthur Wellington Ross, who had come to Port

Moody in 1884, hoping to recoup the fortune lost when the Winnipeg boom collapsed. Ross moved on almost immediately to the livelier-looking end of Burrard Inlet and proceeded to purchase all the land he could afford. Since Ross was employed by the railway as a real estate agent and adviser, he might be said, once again, to have been in on the ground floor.

The Fraser Valley and New Westminster real estate interests saw what, in hindsight, seems obvious; but in Victoria, the land speculators continued to believe that Port Moody would be the terminus. Indeed, the *Colonist* stationed a reporter there to interview newcomers and convince them that there was no spot on the inlet known as Vancouver, a statement that was technically correct until 1886. Late in 1885, the Port Moody *Gazette* was still solemnly assuring its dwindling band of readers that the Coal Harbour "scheme" was nothing more than "a speculation dependent upon suckers."

By then, the Vancouver townsite was well on the way to being surveyed. One autumn day Lauchlan Hamilton, the CPR engineer who had laid out Regina, Moose Jaw, Swift Current, and Calgary, set off from the Sunnyside Hotel, which overlooked the beach at what became the corner of Water Street and Carrall. He made his way through the swamp and blackberry bramble on the later site of Woodward's department store. Behind him, in single file on the narrow trail, were eight assistants, including young Jack Stewart, the future general and construction tycoon. At a point on the forest's edge, which would one day be the site of Victory Square, Hamilton drove in a wooden stake with a nail on top. From this point he ran a line, east and west, from which to start a system of streets; it became Hastings Street. A future alderman, later to be known as "the godfather of Vancouver" (he is credited with the idea for Stanley Park), Hamilton named several of the major streets – Beatty, Abbott, Cambie, and, of course, Hamilton – for faithful CPR hands. The forest was so dense that one man, John Leask (he would be the city's first auditor), got lost and the survey party spent an entire afternoon finding him. It took three days to cut a peep-hole through the mass of Douglas firs that rose from the water's edge to the ridge on the far side of False Creek. Only then could Hamilton and his men see where to put the mile-long street that ran south from Hastings. Hamilton named it Granville, after the hard-drinking, hard-living, poker-playing community through which the railway passed to its official terminus at English Bay. "Keep your eyes open," Van Horne is said to have told Hamilton after an all-night poker session in which he himself had been badly taken. "These damned Vancouver fellows will steal the pants off you."

But Van Horne was engaged in a larger game for higher stakes. He had all the unalienated lots in Granville township, the right of way from New Westminster to Kitsilano on English Bay, including much of the north bank of False Creek, the vast grant from Hastings Mill and, far back in the forest, a valuable tract of residential property, which he named Shaughnessy Heights. He also had the entire foreshore of the future city, which he had insisted upon because, he said, the depth of the water made piers impossible; the railway would need all that land for dock facilities. Future events were to prove that this was not necessary, and, as later generations slowly realized, the railway would have had to come to the mouth of the inlet anyway, whether or not it was given as much as an acre of free real estate. Van Horne may have been skinned at poker in the last of the frontier railway towns, but he was the real winner in a much more important game of skill and bluff.

6

Craigell-achie Edward Mallandaine wanted to fight the Indians. When the news of the rebellion reached Victoria, where he lived and went to school, there was no holding him; and his father, a pioneer architect and engineer, did not try to hold him. He booked passage to New Westminster, got aboard the new CPR line out of Port Moody, and took it as far as Eagle Pass Landing. He was just seventeen years old, small for his age, with a thin, alert face, half-hidden by a black cap. He trudged over the line of the partly finished road until he reached Golden, at the foot of the Kicking Horse, and there he learned, to his intense disappointment, that the rebellion was over and that the troops from eastern Canada, which had had all the adventure and all the glory, were already on their way home.

He was disappointed and disgusted. He headed west again, through the Rogers Pass and into Farwell, with its single street lined with log and frame shacks. There was a feeling of excitement in Farwell that summer of 1885. The town was the half-way point between the two Ends of Track: freight outfits bustled in from the Rogers and the Eagle Passes; boats puffed into the new docks from the mines at the Big Bend of the Columbia; a new post office was opening. Young Mallandaine decided to stay for a while in Farwell and go into business for himself. He opened a freighting service between the town and Eagle Pass Landing, taking a pony through the Gold Range twice each week along the tote road carved out by

410

the railway contractors and soliciting orders for newspapers and supplies from the navvies along the way. It was hard going but it made a profit.

For a teenage boy it was an exciting time in which to live and an exciting place in which to be. Mallandaine was bright enough to realize that history was being made all around him and he noted it all in his mind for later reference: the spectacle of fifty men hanging over the face of the cliffs at Summit Lake, drilling holes in the rock; the sound of thunder in the pass as hundreds of tons of rock hurtled through the air; the sight of a hundred-foot Howe truss put together in a single day; the long, low huts where the navvies, mostly Swedes and Italians, slept "huddled in like bees in a hive with little light and ventilation"; the accidents, brawls, drinking, and gambling in the camps, "with men of all nationalities throwing away their hard-earned pay at faro, stud poker and other games of chance"; a gun battle with two men shot in a gambling den not far from the Farwell post office; and, towards the end of the season, the rough pageantry of the Governor General, Lord Lansdowne himself, riding on horseback through the gap between the two lines of steel on his way to the coast.

Each time Mallandaine made his way through Eagle Pass, that gap was shorter. He noted "day by day the thousands of feet of earth removed and . . . the swarms of men slaving away like ants for the good of the gigantic enterprise." By October it became clear that the road would be finished by first snow. The mushroom towns began to lose their inhabitants and a general exodus took place as the contractors discharged more and more men. Now, as the boy moved through the mountains, he noticed the way-side houses shut up and deserted, contractors' equipment being shifted and carted away, and hundreds of men travelling on foot with all their belongings to the east or to the west. Some of the rougher characters, who had operated saloons and gambling dens, became road agents, "and many a poor man who had been toiling all summer, was obliged to deliver up his earnings."

All the activity that had excited Edward Mallandaine on his arrival began to die away, and an oppressive silence settled on the pass – a silence broken only by the hideous shrieking of the construction locomotives echoing through the hills, as they rattled by with flat cars loaded with steel rails. Mallandaine felt a kind of chill creeping into his bones – not just the chill of the late October winds, sweeping down through the empty bunkhouses, but the chill of loneliness that comes to a man walking through a graveyard in the gloom.

"It seemed as though some scourge had swept this mountain pass. How ghostly the deserted camps would look at night! How quiet it all seemed!"

411

The pass became so lonely that Mallandaine almost began to dread the ride between Farwell and the Landing. There was something eerie about the sight of boarded-up buildings, dump cars left by the wayside, and portions of contractors' outfits cast aside along the line of the tote road. And the silence! Not since the days of the survey parties had the mountains seemed so still. Mallandaine decided to pack it in; there was no business left to speak of anyway. He made plans to return to his parents' home in Victoria. There was, however, one final piece of business, which he did not want to miss. He was determined to be on hand when the last spike on the Canadian Pacific Railway was driven.

On the afternoon of November 6, the last construction train to load rails – an engine, a tender, and three flat cars – left Farwell for Eagle Pass. Mallandaine was one of several who climbed aboard and endured the "cold, cheerless, rough ride" that followed. A few miles out of Farwell, it began to snow. The rails became so slippery that when one gumbo grade was reached the locomotive could not creep over it and, after three attempts in which the train slid backwards down the incline, one car had to be abandoned.

Far into the darkness of the night the little train puffed, its passengers shivering with cold. Mallandaine, lying directly upon the piled-up rails and unable to sleep, was almost shaken to pieces as the train rattled over the unballasted roadbed. Finally it came to a stop. The youth tumbled off the flat car in the pitch dark, found an abandoned box car, and managed a short sleep. At six that morning the track crews were on the job. By the time Mallandaine awoke, the rails had almost come together.

At nine o'clock, the last two rails were brought forward and measured for cutting, with wagers being laid on the exact length that would be needed: it came to twenty-five feet, five inches. A peppery little man with long white whiskers, wearing a vest with a heavy watch-chain, cut the final rail with a series of hard blows. This was the legendary Major Rogers. One of the short rails was then laid in place and spiked; the second was left loose for the ceremony. The crowd, which included Al Rogers, Tom Wilson, Sam Steele, and Henry Cambie, waited for the official party to appear.

It is perhaps natural that the tale of the driving of the last spike on the CPR should have become a legend in which fancy often outweighs fact; it was, after all, the great symbolic act of Canada's first century, a moment of solemn ritual enacted in a fairyland setting at the end of a harrowing year. Two days before the spike was driven, George Stephen had cabled in cipher from England: "Railway now out of danger." The bonds had

412

risen to 99, the stock to 52½. Nine days after the spike was driven, Louis Riel kept his rendezvous with the hangman at Regina. In more ways than one the completion of the railway signalled the end of the small, confined, comfortable nation that had been pieced together in 1867.

It is not surprising, then, that some who were present that day in the mountains – a construction boss named George Munro was one – should have recalled half a century later that the spike was made of gold. Munro claimed that it was pulled out and taken east. The Perthshire *Advertiser* of Scotland, in a special issue honouring Alexander Mackenzie, "a Perthshire lad who rose to eminence," stated that the former prime minister's widow drove the spike, which was "of 18 carat gold with the word Craigellachie in diamonds. It was replaced almost immediately with a serviceable one of steel and the first presented to Mrs. Mackenzie who afterward wore it as a brooch." But Mrs. Mackenzie was not a widow in 1885 and there was no golden spike. The Governor General had had a silver spike prepared for the occasion; it was not used, and His Excellency, who had expected to be present, had been forced to return to Ottawa from British Columbia when weather conditions caused a delay in the completion of the line.

"The last spike," said Van Horne, in his blunt way, "will be just as good an iron one as there is between Montreal and Vancouver, and anyone who wants to see it driven will have to pay full fare." He had toyed with the idea of an elaborate celebration and excursion but found it impossible to fix limits on the necessary invitations. It would have resulted "in a vast deal of disappointment and ill feeling" – not to mention expense.

The truth was that the CPR could not afford a fancy ceremony. It had cost the Northern Pacific somewhere between $175,000 and $250,000 to drive its golden spike. The CPR might be out of danger, but it had enormous expenditures facing it. Stephen proposed paying off the five-million-dollar temporary loan almost immediately. Van Horne's whole purpose was to get a through line operating to the Pacific so that he could tap the Asian trade. There would be time for ceremonies later on.

The very simplicity and near spontaneity of the scene at Eagle Pass – the lack of pomp, the absence of oratory, the plainness of the crowd, the presence of the workmen in the foreground of the picture – made the spectacle an oddly memorable one. Van Horne and a distinguished party had come out from Ottawa, Montreal, and Winnipeg for the occasion. The big names, lounging at their ease in the two parlour cars "Saskatchewan" and "Matapedia," included Donald A. Smith, Sandford Fleming, John Egan, John McTavish, the land commissioner, and George Harris, a Boston financier who was a company director. Because of the incessant rains the party was held up for several days at Farwell until the work was completed.

Meanwhile, on the far side of the mountains, Andrew Onderdonk's private car "Eva" came up from Port Moody with Michael Haney aboard, pulling the final load of rails to the damp crevice in the mountains which the general manager, with a fine sense of drama, had decided years before to name Craigellachie. The decision predated Stephen's memorable telegram to Donald A. Smith. When Van Horne first joined the company the word was in common use because of an incident in 1880, when the Syndicate was being formed out of the original group that had put the St. Paul railway together. One of the members had demurred at the idea of another railway adventure and suggested to Stephen that they might only be courting trouble. Stephen had replied with that one word, a reference to a Scottish poem which began with the phrase: "Not until Craigellachie shall move from his firm base. . . ." Van Horne, hearing of the incident, decided that if he was still with the CPR when the last spike was driven, the spot would be marked by a station called Craigellachie.

It was a dull, murky November morning, the tall mountains sheathed in clouds, the dark firs and cedars dripping in a coverlet of wet snow. Up puffed the quaint engine with its polished brass boiler, its cordwood tender, its diamond-shaped smokestack, and the great square box in front containing the acetylene headlight on whose glass was painted the number 148. The ceremonial party descended and walked through the clearing of stumps and debris to the spot where Major Rogers was standing, holding the tie bar under the final rail. By common consent the honour of driving the connecting spike was assigned to the eldest of the four directors present – to Donald A. Smith, whose hair in five years of railway construction had turned a frosty white. As Fleming noted, the old fur trader represented much more than the CPR. His presence recalled that long line of Highlanders – the Mackenzies and McTavishes, Stuarts and McGillivrays, Frasers, Finlaysons, McLeods, and McLaughlins – who had first penetrated these mountains and set the transcontinental pattern of communication that the railway would continue.

Now that moment had arrived which so many Canadians had believed would never come – a moment that Fleming had been waiting for since 1862, when he placed before the government the first practical outline for a highway to the Pacific. The workmen and the officials crowded around Smith as he was handed the spike hammer. Young Edward Mallandaine was determined to be as close to the old man as possible. He squeezed in directly behind him, right next to Harris, the Boston financier, and directly

414

in front of Cambie, McTavish, and Egan. As the little hunchbacked photographer, Ross of Winnipeg, raised his camera, Mallandaine craned forward so as to see and be seen. Fifty-nine years later, when all the rest of that great company were in their graves, Colonel Edward Mallandaine, stipendiary magistrate and reeve of the Kootenay town of Creston, would be on hand when the citizens of Revelstoke, in false beards and borrowed frock-coats, re-enacted the famous photograph on that very spot.

The spike had been hammered half-way home. Smith's first blow bent it badly. Frank Brothers, the roadmaster, expecting just such an emergency, pulled it out and replaced it with another. Smith posed with the uplifted hammer. The assembly froze. The shutter clicked. Smith lowered the hammer onto the spike. The shutter clicked again. Smith raised the hammer and began to drive the spike home. Save for the blows of the hammer and the sound of a small mountain stream gushing down a few feet away, there was absolute silence. Even after the spike was driven home, the stillness persisted. "It seemed," Sandford Fleming recalled, "as if the act now performed had worked a spell on all present. Each one appeared absorbed in his own reflections." The spell was broken by a cheer, "and it was no ordinary cheer. The subdued enthusiasm, the pent-up feelings of men familiar with hard work, now found vent." More cheers followed, enhanced by the shrill whistle of the locomotives.

All this time, Van Horne had stood impassively beside Fleming, his hands thrust into the side pockets of his overcoat. Though this was his crowning moment, his face remained a mask. In less than four years, through a miracle of organization and drive, he had managed to complete a new North West Passage, as the English press would call it. Did any memories surface in that retentive mind as the echoes of Smith's hammer blows rang down the corridor of Eagle Pass? Did he think back on the previous year when, half-starved and soaking wet, he had come this way with Reed and Rogers? Did he reflect, with passing triumph, on those early days in Winnipeg when the unfriendly press had attacked him as an idle boaster and discussed his rumoured dismissal? Did he recall those desperate moments in Ottawa and Montreal when the CPR seemed about to collapse like a house of cards? Probably not, for Van Horne was not a man to brood or to gloat over the past. It is likelier that his mind was fixed on more immediate problems: the Vancouver terminus, the Pacific postal subsidy, and the Atlantic steamship service. He could not predict the future but he would help to control it, and some of the new symbols of his adopted country would be of his making: the fleet of white Empresses flying the familiar checkered flag, the turreted hotels with their green

415

château roofs, boldly perched on promontory and lakefront; and the international slogan that would proclaim in Arabic, Hindi, Chinese, and a dozen other languages that the CPR spanned the world.

As the cheering died the crowd turned to Van Horne. "Speech! Speech!" they cried. Van Horne was not much of a speechmaker; he was, in fact, a little shy in crowds. What he said was characteristically terse, but it went into the history books: "All I can say is that the work has been done well in every way."

Major Rogers was more emotional. This was his moment of triumph too, and he was savouring it. In spite of all the taunts of his Canadian colleagues, in spite of the scepticism of the newspapers, in spite of his own gloomy forebodings and the second thoughts of his superiors, his pass had been chosen and the rails ran directly through it to Craigellachie. For once, the stoic Major did not trouble to conceal his feelings. He was "so gleeful," Edward Mallandaine observed, "that he upended a huge tie and tried to mark the spot by the side of the track by sticking it in the ground."

There were more cheers, some mutual congratulations, and a rush for souvenirs – chips from the tie, pieces of the sawn rail. Young Arthur Piers, Van Horne's secretary, spotted the first, twisted spike lying on the track and tried to pocket it. Smith, however, told him to hand it over; he wanted it as a souvenir. Smith had also tossed the sledge aside after the spike was driven but, before he left, one of the track crew, Mike Sullivan, remembered to hand it to him as a keepsake. Then the locomotive whistle sounded again and a voice was heard to cry: "All aboard for the Pacific." It was the first time that phrase had been used by a conductor from the East, but Fleming noted that it was uttered "in the most prosaic tones, as of constant daily occurrence." The official party obediently boarded the cars and a few moments later the little train was in motion again, clattering over the newly laid rail and over the last spike and down the long incline of the mountains, off towards the dark canyon of the Fraser, off to the broad meadows beyond, off to the blue Pacific and into history.

416

Aftermath

Sir John A. Macdonald finally visited the North West in 1886, when the railway was finished, riding through a portion of the Rockies on the cowcatcher of a CPR locomotive, a hazard he did not greatly enjoy. He survived two more elections, in 1887 and in 1891. Three months after the latter victory, at the age of 76, he died of a stroke. He was succeeded by J. J. C. Abbott, the CPR's lawyer, who had once been Sir Hugh Allan's legal adviser in the days of the Pacific Scandal.

Sir Charles Tupper served as High Commissioner in London until 1896 (except for a brief period as Minister of Finance). In 1896 he became Secretary of State in the Cabinet of Mackenzie Bowell, then the Prime Minister. When Bowell resigned in April, Tupper became Prime Minister briefly. His party was defeated at the polls in June by the Liberals under Sir Wilfrid Laurier and Tupper was Leader of the Opposition until his retirement in 1900. He died in England in 1915.

George Stephen was knighted in 1886 for his contribution to the building of the CPR. He continued as president until 1888 when he became chairman of the board and moved to England. It was said that one of his reasons for leaving Canada was his disaffection with politicians, who had forced the Onderdonk section on him and caused him to build the uneconomic "Short Line" through Maine to connect Quebec with the Maritime Provinces. In 1891 Stephen was elevated to the peerage and became Baron Mount Stephen. He stepped down from the CPR board in 1899 and died in 1921.

James J. Hill's real career did not begin until he quit the CPR. His great adventure was the extension of the St. Paul, Minneapolis and Manitoba Railway westward to Great Falls, Montana (a community he helped found), in 1887 and to Seattle in 1893. By then the line had been consolidated into the Great Northern Railroad Company. Hill's feat of railroad building – free of bankruptcy, financial scandal, and government assistance – was perhaps the greatest in the history of the United States. He helped reorganize the Northern Pacific after that company again went bankrupt in 1893 and in 1901 won a memorable financial battle against his great rival, E. H. Harriman. Hill, who maintained his friendship with Stephen and Donald A. Smith for all of his life (they both retained their holdings of St. Paul and later Great Northern stock), died in 1916.

Richard B. Angus remained as a director of the CPR for more than forty years. In 1910, when he was seventy-nine, he became president of the

Bank of Montreal, which had hired him as a junior clerk in 1857. That same year he refused a knighthood. He died in 1922.

Donald A. Smith had reached his sixty-fifth birthday at the time the last spike was driven – an age at which most men retire. He had already enjoyed several careers as fur trader, politician, financier, and railway executive. With the railway behind him, he entered on a variety of new ventures. Already vice-president of the Bank of Montreal, he became president in 1887. He was elected chancellor of McGill University in 1889 and founded Royal Victoria College at McGill in 1896. Knighted in 1886 for his services to the CPR, he was created Baron Strathcona and Mount Royal in 1897. The unit of mounted rifles which he equipped for the Boer War, Lord Strathcona's Horse, still survives in Calgary. Smith, who became Canadian High Commissioner to London in 1896, was made Lord Rector of Aberdeen University in 1899 and chancellor in 1903. He died in London in 1914 in his ninety-fourth year.

William Cornelius Van Horne succeeded Stephen as president of the CPR in 1888 and as chairman of the board in 1899. By this time he had become a leading figure in the Canadian financial world – involved in concerns as varied as the Windsor Salt Company and Laurentide Paper. He piloted the company through a turbulent period of financial crisis and expansion which saw him personally write the copy for the CPR's ebullient advertising (" 'How High We Live' said the Duke to the Prince on the Canadian Pacific Railway"). Retirement did not suit the restless nature of this remarkable man. He tried to fill in the time with travel, but this was not enough for him. One day in Florida he spotted a vessel at the dock and asked its destination. He was told it was bound for Cuba. "All right," said Van Horne, "give me a ticket." It was as a result of this incident that Van Horne built another railway – this time across Cuba. Van Horne was knighted in 1894 after his wife overcame what he called her republican tendencies, but he himself, it is said, refused a peerage because of his American birth. When he died in Montreal on September 11, 1915, every wheel in the CPR's vast transportation network stopped turning.

Major A. B. Rogers went to work for James J. Hill's railroad after the last spike was driven. In the summer of 1887 in the Coeur d'Alene mountains of Idaho his horse stumbled and fell on a steep trail. Rogers was thrown off onto a stump. He died from the effects of his injury in May, 1889.

419

Tom Wilson never left the mountains. He spent his whole life as a packer and guide, making his home at Banff, where he became a fixture. He had expected to meet his friend Al Rogers in the summer of 1931 to visit the spot near Lake Wapta where, fifty years before, the "vow of the twenty" had been made on the Great Divide, but Al Rogers died on May 16, 1929. Tom Wilson, who dictated his memoirs to W. E. Round in 1931, died September 22, 1933.

Thomas Shaughnessy, in his turn, succeeded Van Horne as president and later chairman of the CPR. Under his tenure – he was known as the King of the Railway Presidents – the CPR became the leading transportation system on the globe, building a chain of great hotels, establishing an Atlantic shipping service to match its Pacific fleet, and acquiring other companies, notably in the mining and smelting field. A staunch Imperialist, who gladly accepted a peerage in 1916, Baron Shaughnessy organized Imperial transport and purchasing for Canada during World War I and put the CPR's credit behind $100 million worth of Allied war loans. He died in 1923, shortly after naming his successor, Edward Beatty, and telling him to "take good care of the Canadian Pacific Railway."

Andrew Onderdonk went from British Columbia to Argentina, where in 1886 he built the Entre Rios railway north of Buenos Aires. His later construction work included nine miles of drainage tunnelling in Chicago, the Chicago Northwestern Elevated Railway, a double-track tunnel in Hamilton, part of the Trent Valley Canal system (which included one of the largest rock cuts on the continent), and part of the rebuilding of the Victoria Bridge over the St. Lawrence. He was a partner, at one time, of G. W. Ferris and, it is believed, helped build the famous wheel which was a feature of the World's Columbian Exposition at Chicago in 1893. In 1905 he was general manager of the New York Tunnel Company, building a subway tunnel under the east branch of the Hudson River said at the time to be one of the most difficult pieces of work ever undertaken by a contractor. He died on June 21 of that year at Oscawana-on-the-Hudson. He was fifty-six years old. The cause of death was given as "overwork."

Arthur Wellington Ross lived in Vancouver for six years following its establishment as the Canadian Pacific's terminus – a decision in which he had had a considerable say – and is credited with obtaining the military reserve for the city as Stanley Park. He later became, for a brief period, a mining broker in Ontario. He continued to represent the Manitoba con-

420

stituency of Lisgar as a Conservative in the House of Commons until his retirement in 1896. He died in Toronto in 1901.

Nicholas Flood Davin edited the Regina *Leader* until his death. In 1887 he entered politics as Conservative Member for West Assiniboia and sat in the House of Commons until 1900. Another of his books, *Eos, an Epic of the Dawn*, was published in 1889. In 1895, at the age of fifty-six, the perennial bachelor and flirt took a wife. On October 18, 1901, he shot himself in the Clarendon Hotel in Winnipeg. He had exactly $6.40 in his pocket.

Samuel Benfield Steele continued to preside at the most colourful incidents in the history of the Canadian North West. He was sent to the Kootenays in 1887 to settle the Indian troubles. In 1897 he manned the passes on the international boundary between Alaska and the Yukon during the stampede to the Klondike. He ran the stampede like a military manœuvre, saving untold lives and keeping the city of Dawson, in the boom year of 1898, under tight control. (This aspect of his career is chronicled in detail in the author's *Klondike.*) During the Boer War he commanded Lord Strathcona's Horse and remained in the Transvaal as head of the South African Constabulary there. On returning to Canada in 1906 he commanded the Calgary and later the Winnipeg military districts. When war broke out he was promoted major-general, raising and training the Second Canadian Division, which he took to England in 1915. He retired and was knighted in 1918. He died at Putney, England, the following year.

John Macoun travelled about Canada and continued collecting botanical specimens for most of his life. In 1887 he became assistant director and naturalist of the Geological Survey. In 1912 he retired and moved to British Columbia. After his death, at Sidney, in 1920, his autobiography was published posthumously by the Ottawa Field Naturalists' Club. There are forty-eight species of flora and fauna named after Macoun as well as a mountain in the Selkirks.

Sandford Fleming remained as a director of the CPR and chancellor of Queen's University until his death. His most notable achievement after the CPR construction period was the part he played in planning the Pacific Cable, which was completed in 1902. He represented Canada at colonial conferences in London in 1888 and Ottawa in 1894 and at the Imperial Cable Conference in 1896. Knighted in 1897, he died in Halifax in 1915 at the age of eighty-eight.

George Monro Grant carried on as principal of Queen's until his death. His reputation in both political and education circles was outstanding. He was elected moderator of the Presbyterian Church in 1882 and president of the Royal Society of Canada in 1901. He died in 1902.

Louis Riel was hanged on Nov. 16, 1885. He remains the most controversial figure in Canadian history, the subject of dozens of books, novels, histories, at least one play, and one opera. His adjutant, **Gabriel Dumont**, escaped to the United States, became a leading performer in Buffalo Bill's Wild West Show (where he re-enacted the stirring days of 1885), returned to Canada under a general amnesty, and died in Batoche at the age of sixty-eight. **Big Bear** and **Poundmaker**, the rebel Cree chiefs, were given prison sentences for felony but were released in 1887. Neither survived his freedom by more than a few months.

Crowfoot lived on his reserve until his death in 1890. Although he was thought of as an ancient chieftain, he was only fifty-six years old. His great friend, **Father Lacombe**, lived to be eighty-nine. After the coming of the railway, Lacombe's career was anticlimactic. He became a settled parish priest, first at Fort Macleod and later at St. Joachim, near Edmonton. He retired in 1897 to a hermitage at Pincher Creek, emerged in 1899 to help negotiate Treaty No. 8 with the northern Indians, travelled to Europe and the Holy Land, and, in 1909, founded the Lacombe Home at Midnapore, Alberta, for the derelicts of all races who had never been able to make an adjustment to the new North West. When he died in 1916, the eulogy he read over Crowfoot's grave a quarter of a century before might have been his own: "Men, women and children, mourn over your great parent; you will no more hear his voice and its eloquent harangues. In your distress and misery you will no more rush to his tent for comfort and charities. He is gone. There is no one like him to fill his place."

The "last spike" was removed, after the dignitaries departed, by roadmaster Frank Brothers (who is to be seen in the immediate left foreground of the famous photograph, facing the camera). Brothers was afraid that souvenir hunters would tear up his track to secure the prize. (As it was, chunks of the tie were chopped away and the remaining piece of the sawn rail was split up by memorabilia seekers.) Brothers later presented the spike to Edward Beatty, but it was stolen from Beatty's desk. What happened to the spike cannot be ascertained with any accuracy, but it may be the one in the hands of Mrs. W. H. Remnant of Yellowknife. According to Mrs. Remnant, Henry Cambie came into possession of the spike and gave it to W. J. Lynch, chief of the patent office in Ottawa, to keep for his son Arthur, who was serving with the British Army Medical Corps. When Arthur returned home, his father presented him with the spike which by this time had been worked into the shape of a carving knife with the handle silvered. His daughter Mamie, now Mrs. Remnant, inherited it. The other spike, which Donald Smith bent and discarded and which he appropriated as a souvenir, was cut into thin strips which were mounted with diamonds and presented to the wives of some of the members of the party. Several ladies who did not receive the souvenirs were so put out that the diplomatic Smith had a second, larger spike cut up into similar souvenirs. These, however, were made larger so that the recipients of the original gifts would be able to tell the difference. Lord Lansdowne's original unused silver spike was presented to Van Horne and, as far as is known, is still in the Van Horne family.

The CPR was immortalized by Hollywood in 1949 when Twentieth Century-Fox made *Canadian Pacific*, a film purportedly about the building of the railway. The star was Randolph Scott, who played the role of Tom Andrews, a surveyor who, unassisted, discovers a pass in the Rockies, thus allowing railway construction – held up in the prairies – to proceed once more. There are only two historical figures in the film: Van Horne, depicted as a weedy construction boss with his headquarters in Calgary, and Père Lacombe, shown as a stout and rather comical Irish priest. The conflict revolves around the attempt by the Métis (pronounced "Mett-isse" in the film) living around Lake Louise (!) to prevent the railway from coming through the mountains. Dirk-Rourke, the Métis leader (played by Victor Jory), rouses the saloonkeepers along the line of the road to cause a strike, which Scott breaks up single-handedly by the use of his six-shooters. Then Rourke persuades the Indians to attack the railroad as if it were a wagon train; they appear in full feathered headdress, waving tomahawks and shooting flaming arrows from their primitive bows. Scott rallies the railroad navvies and, in a pitched battle, they destroy or disperse the redskins. Love interest is supplied by a woman doctor, whom Scott eventually rejects because she believes in non-violent methods, and a pretty Métis girl who saves the day by disclosing her people's plans and thereby winning Scott's affections. This is perhaps the only Hollywood film ever made about the Canadian West in which the North West Mounted Police are conspicuously absent. That may explain why almost every railroader in the picture carries two six-shooters on his hip. The film lists a Canadian technical adviser in the person of John Rhodes Sturdy, at one time a public relations officer for the Canadian Pacific Railway.

Chronology

1881

Feb. 15	Royal assent given to CPR charter.
Feb. 16	Canadian Pacific Railway Company incorporated.
April 29	Major A. B. Rogers leaves Kamloops for Selkirks.
May 2	First sod turned at Portage la Prairie by General T. L. Rosser.
May 9	Arthur Wellington Ross secures title to first Brandon property for CPR.
May 18	George Stephen, R. B. Angus, and James J. Hill meet with John Macoun in St. Paul and discuss change of route.
May 21	Rogers party reaches mouth of Illecillewaet and begins ascent of Selkirks.
May 30	First mention in press of town of Brandon.
May 31	First CPR shareholders' meeting in London.
July 15	Rogers arrives at Hyndman camp in Rockies; meets Tom Wilson.
Aug. 18	Fire destroys half of Yale, British Columbia.
Oct. 7	Jim Hill takes W.C. Van Horne on brief tour of CPR line out of Winnipeg.
Nov. 1	Van Horne's appointment as general manager confirmed.
Dec. 13	Van Horne arrives in Winnipeg to take up duties.

1882

Jan. 12	Van Horne and Rogers meet with CPR board in Montreal. Change of route made public.
Feb. 1	Van Horne fires General Rosser by telegram.
Feb. 19	Knox Church, Winnipeg, auctioned off.
Mar. 13	Fire destroys CPR offices and Bank of Montreal building, Winnipeg.
April 12	Edmonton lots go on sale in Winnipeg.
April 14	Jim Coolican and Winnipeg "boomers" leave for St. Paul.
April 19	Crest of Red River flood hits Winnipeg, sweeps away Broadway Bridge.
April 27	Thomas Gore reaches Pile o' Bones Creek.

425

May 4	Andrew Onderdonk launches *Skuzzy*; it fails to breach Hell's Gate on the Fraser.
May 22	Rogers makes vain attempt to locate pass in Selkirks by ascending eastern slopes.
June 17	Last spike driven on government line between Fort William and Selkirk, Manitoba.
June 18	CPR acquires Montreal-Ottawa section of Quebec, Montreal, Ottawa and Occidental Railway.
June 20	Conservative Party under Sir John A. Macdonald wins sweeping victory.
June 30	Lieutenant-Governor Edgar Dewdney posts notice at Pile o' Bones Creek reserving the land as site of new capital of North West Territories.
	Great Western stockholders approve merger with Grand Trunk.
July 17	Rogers sets off from Columbia River on second attempt to locate pass in the Selkirks from the east.
July 24	Rogers reaches summit of Selkirks and finds pass.
Aug. 21	First public menion of "Regina" as the capital of NWT.
	Tom Wilson discovers Lake Louise.
Aug. 23	First train arrives at Regina with official party for dedication ceremonies.
Sept. 7	Second launching of *Skuzzy* at Hell's Gate.
Sept. 28	*Skuzzy* breaches Hell's Gate with help of Chinese.
Oct. 31	Regina lots placed on market in Winnipeg.
Dec. 29	CPR issues $30 million of stock to New York syndicate.

1883

Mar. 15	Onderdonk hires Michael Haney to manage work between Yale and Port Moody.
Mar. 22	Nicholas Flood Davin launches Regina *Leader*.
April 6	George Stephen and Sir Henry Tyler, in London, attempt to hammer out an agreement between CPR and Grand Trunk.
May 3	James J. Hill quits CPR board; sells most of his stock.
July 28	CPR tracklayers set a record, lay 6.8 miles in a day.
Aug. 17	CPR issues 200,000 shares of stock at 25 cents on the dollar.
Aug. 18	Langdon and Shepard complete prairie contract.
Aug. 20	Official party arrives at Calgary. Father Lacombe named president of CPR for one hour.

Sept. 7	Killing frost destroys prairie grain crop.
Oct. 24	Stephen outlines guaranteed dividend plan to Macdonald and lodges formal petition for financial aid.
Dec. 1	Macdonald wires Tupper in London: "Pacific in trouble. You should be here."
Dec. 19	Farmers' convention opens at Winnipeg. Manitoba and North-West Farmers' Union formed.

1884

Jan. 4	CPR officially leases Ontario and Quebec Railway.
Jan. 15	George Stephen asks for government loan of $22,500,000.
Feb. 1	Tupper proposes new CPR loan resolutions to Parliament.
Feb. 28	CPR relief bill passes House.
May	Duncan McIntyre quits CPR.
	Staking activity at Sudbury.
June 4	Gabriel Dumont and Métis delegation arrive at home of Louis Riel in Montana to invite him to return to North West.
July 11	Riel holds his first public meeting at Red Deer Hill.
July 31	Big Bear convenes first Indian council at Duck Lake.
Aug. 4	Van Horne and party arrive at Victoria.
Aug. 6	Van Horne visits Port Moody and site of Vancouver on Burrard Inlet.
Aug. 9	Survey of Sudbury townsite completed.
Aug. 10	Van Horne inspects Onderdonk line and arrives at Kamloops.
Sept. 16	Van Horne in Montreal asks CPR directors to approve choice of Vancouver as CPR western terminus.
Oct. 23	Toronto police arrive at Michipicoten to quell vigilante rule.
Dec. 22	D. H. McDowell meets with Riel.

1885

Jan. 1	Universal Time adopted at Greenwich.
Jan. 12	John A. Macdonald celebrates his seventieth birthday in Montreal.
Mar. 18	Stephen asks Privy Council for another loan and is rejected.
Mar. 19	Riel sets up provisional Métis government in Saskatchewan.

427

Mar. 23	Macdonald orders Major-General Frederick Middleton to move militia north from Winnipeg to scene of Métis unrest.
Mar. 24	Initial stages of Van Horne plan to move troops over gaps in CPR line put into operation.
Mar. 26	Major Crozier's force of Mounted Police defeated by Métis under Gabriel Dumont at Duck Lake. Saskatchewan Rebellion begins.
Mar. 28	Permanent forces in eastern Canada ordered to move. Militia units called out.
Mar. 31	Father Lacombe secures Crowfoot's loyalty.
April 1	CPR navvies strike at Beavermouth, British Columbia.
April 2	Group of Big Bear's Crees massacres priests and other whites at Frog Lake.
April 5	First troops reach Winnipeg.
April 7	Strike at Beavermouth ends.
April 12	Last troops (Halifax Battalion) leave eastern Canada.
April 13	Siege of Fort Pitt begins.
April 16	Van Horne wires Stephen that CPR pay car cannot be sent out.
April 23	Dumont defeats General Middleton at Fish Creek.
May 1	John A. Macdonald gives notice in Parliament of new measures for financial relief of CPR.
May 2	Chief Poundmaker defeats Colonel Otter's troops at Cut Knife Hill.
May 12	Batoche relieved by Middleton.
May 15	Riel surrenders to Middleton.
May 16	Last rail laid on Lake Superior line.
May 26	Poundmaker surrenders.
June 16	John Henry Pope moves resolutions for CPR aid in Parliament.
July 2	Big Bear surrenders.
July 10	CPR aid bill passes House of Commons.
July 15 (approx.)	CPR floats $15-million bond issue with Baring Brothers in London.
July 20	Louis Riel goes on trial for his life in Regina. CPR aid bill gets royal assent.
July 29	Andrew Onderdonk completes government contracts; line is finished from Port Moody to Savona's Ferry.

Aug. 13	CPR acquires North Shore line between Montreal and Quebec.
Sept. 18	Louis Riel sentenced to hang.
Sept. 30	Onderdonk completes contract with CPR between Savona's Ferry and Eagle Pass.
Nov. 7	Last spike driven at Craigellachie.

Notes

In this volume, as in *The National Dream*, I have tried to arrange the notes in such a way that the narrative flow will not be interrupted for the lay reader while, at the same time, the scholarly researcher can, without too much difficulty, establish the sources of my material. For this reason I have not followed the usual method of sprinkling the text with small numbers – a practice that I find irritating. I have also discarded another annoying tradition – that of combining the bibliography with the notes and using *op. cit.* for all but the first reference to any work. It is maddening for a researcher to struggle back through all the *op. cits.* in his search for the original citation. In the abbreviated notes that follow, the scholar can always go directly to the bibliography.

I have tried to give a source for every quotation in the book and, in addition, for facts that are not self-evident and for anecdotes that may be disputed.

431

page line   **Chapter One**

7   28   *Free Press,* Ottawa, Feb. 18, 1881.

7   30   Tupper Papers, Vol. 5, Tupper to Macdonald, July n.d., 1881.

7   32   *Ibid.,* Tupper to Macdonald, March 31, 1881.

7   36   *Free Press,* Ottawa, June 24, 1882.

8   20   *Free Press,* Manitoba, June 1, 1881.

8   26   *Ibid.,* Sept. 7, 1881.

10   39   Sessional Paper, No. 23, 1880-81, p. 64.

11   33   J. A. Chapleau, Hansard, 1885, p. 2566.

12   35   Macoun does not name them but it is clear from newspaper accounts that Stephen and Angus were both in St. Paul in May just before Macoun went north.

14   18   Macoun, *Autobiography,* p. 182.

14   33   *Ibid.,* p. 163.

15   4   Quoted in Roe, "Early Opinions," p. 143.

15   11   Taylor Papers, Microfilm Roll M-118, Taylor to R. B. Angus, Nov. 20, 1880.

15   19   Macoun, *Autobiography,* p. 56.

15   29   Taylor Papers, Microfilm Roll M-118, Taylor to Angus, Nov. 20, 1880.

16   13   Macoun, *Autobiography,* p. 185.

17   7   Hansard, 1882, p. 953.

17   15   *Ibid.,* p. 974.

17   21   The CPR's own historian holds to this view.

18   3   Macdonald Papers, Vol. 127, J. H. Pope to Macdonald, Aug. 19, 1881.

18   13   *Globe,* Jan. 3, 1882.

18   29   See Pyle, Vol. I, pp. 299-300.

18   39   Macoun, *Autobiography,* p. 185.

19   38   *Globe,* Jan. 19, 1882.

20   12   Macoun, *Autobiography,* p. 184.

21   35   Edward Blake, Hansard, 1885, p. 2600.

22   31   Hedges, p. 90.

23   11   See Roe, "Early Opinions."

23   27   *Times,* March 24, 1881.

23   31   *Ibid.,* May 17, 1881.

page line

24   26   *Free Press,* Manitoba, April 22, 1881.

25   7   *Ibid.,* April 20, 1881.

25   29   Secretan, p. 127.

25   35   Shaw and Hull, p. 89.

25   40   Trotter and Hawkes, p. 89.

26   26   *Ibid.,* p. 163.

27   5   *Ibid.,* p. 87.

27   23   *Times,* May 18, 1881.

28   2   Kavanagh, p. 142.

28   6   Trotter and Hawkes, p. 200.

28   11   *Free Press,* Manitoba, May 20, 1881.

28   12   *Ibid.,* May 20, 1881.

28   16   *Ibid.*

28   20   Kavanagh, p. 146, *fn.*

28   22   Trotter and Hawkes, p. 200.

28   33   *Ibid.*

29   39   *Ibid.,* p. 160.

30   9   *Ibid.,* p. 169.

30   27   *Ibid.,* p. 159.

31   6   *Ibid.,* p. 157.

32   6   Secretan, pp. 133-135.

32   14   Kavanagh, p. 115.

32   16   *Ibid.,* p. 116.

32   19   Trotter and Hawkes, p. 95.

32   22   Shaw and Hull, p. 89.

35   20   Quoted in *Free Press,* Ottawa, March 3, 1881.

36   16   *Free Press,* Manitoba, Aug. 10, 1881.

36   19   Lorne Papers, Lorne to Lord Archibald Campbell, Aug. 28, 1881.

36   25   *Gibbon,* p. 223.

37   22   Macdonald Papers, Vol, 267, Stephen to Macdonald, Dec. 13, 1881.

37   29   "Ishmael."

37   37   Begg, p. 3.

38   2   Macdonald Papers, Vol. 267, Stephen to Macdonald, Dec. 10, 1881.

page line

38	5	*Ibid.*, Nov. 4, 1881.
38	36	*Ibid.*, Jan. 11, 1882.
39	2	*Ibid.*, Jan. 13, 1882.
39	33	*Ibid.*, Stephen to Rose, Aug. 15, 1881.
40	8	*Ibid.*, Stephen to Macdonald, Dec. 20, 1881.
40	19	*Ibid.*, Oct. 29, 1881.
40	31	*Ibid.*, Nov. 5, 1881.
41	4	*Ibid.*, Dec. 20, 1881.
41	33	*Ibid.*, Vol. 524, Macdonald to Stephen, Oct. 19, 1881.
42	4	*Ibid.*, Vol. 267, Stephen to Macdonald, Sept. 12, 1882.
42	37	*Ibid.*, Aug. 27, 1881.
43	11	*Ibid.*, Dec. 10, 1881.
43	22	*Ibid.*, Nov. 5, 1881.
43	29	*Ibid.*, Nov. 17, 1881.
43	38	*Ibid.*, Nov. 4, 1881.
44	11	Pyle, Vol. I, p. 318, Hill to Angus, July, 1880.
44	13	Pearce Memo.
44	34	*Globe*, Aug. 26, 1881.
45	14	Vaughan, p. 74.
45	24	Tupper in Hansard, 1882, p. 1007.
46	3	Vaughan, p. 148.
46	24	*A Year in Manitoba*, p. 72.
46	26	*Free Press*, Manitoba, Aug. 6, 1881.
46	31	Miller, p. 65.
46	35	*Free Press*, Manitoba, Oct. 8, 1881.
46	39	*Ibid.*, Sept. 15, 1881.
47	9	*Ibid.*, Aug. 10, 1881.
47	11	*Times*, March 10, 1881.
47	14	*Free Press*, Manitoba, Sept. 28, 1881.
47	18	*Times*, March 10, 1881.
47	33	Vaughan, p. 62.
48	18	*Ibid.*, pp. 108-109.
48	24	Pearce Memo.
49	5	Vaughan, p. 75.

Chapter Two

52	6	*Free Press*, Manitoba, Jan. 2, 1882.
52	19	*Times*, Jan. 26, 1882.
52	20	*Globe*, Jan. 19, 1882.
52	22	*Ibid.*, March 3, 1882.
52	32	*Times*, March 23, 1882.
52	33	*Free Press*, Manitoba, Dec. 21, 1881.
52	36	*Globe*, April 29, 1882.
53	13	*Ibid.*, March 3, 1882.
53	19	*Ibid.*, April 4, 1882.
53	23	Quoted in *Times*, Feb. 3, 1882.
53	26	Quoted in *Sun*, Winnipeg, March 8, 1882.
53	29	*Sentinel*, Nov. 11, 1881.
53	36	*Sun*, Winnipeg, April 14, 1882.
53	40	*Globe*, Jan. 18, 1882.
54	8	Quoted in *Times*, Feb. 7, 1882.
54	16	*Ibid.*, Feb. 11, 1882.
54	31	*Sentinel*, Nov. 11, 1881.
55	2	*Times*, Sept. 16, 1881.
55	8	Armstrong Manuscript, p. 121.
55	13	*Sun*, Winnipeg, Feb. 24, 1882.
55	16	*Ibid.*
55	18	*Ibid.*, March 16, 1882.
55	25	MacGregor, p. 149.
55	36	Ham, pp. 51-52.
56	3	Trotter and Hawkes, p. 222.
56	6	*Times*, Feb. 7, 1882.
56	8	*Ibid.*
56	16	Trotter and Hawkes, p. 229.
56	21	Quoted in *Times*, Sept. 26, 1881.
56	24	*Globe*, Feb. 10, 1882.
56	32	Tway thesis.
56	40	See Campbell Papers, correspondence between Alexander Campbell and E. T. Galt, Feb. and March, 1882.
57	8	*Globe*, Feb. 2, 1882.
57	27	*Ibid.*, March 3, 1882.
57	31	*Ibid.*, Feb. 24, 1882.
57	36	*Sun*, Winnipeg, Feb. 20, 1882.
58	2	*Times*, Feb. 27, 1882.
58	8	Ham, p. 51.
58	23	McLagan, p. 519.
58	30	*Globe*, March 3, 1882.

page line

58 33 McLagan, p. 520.

59 9   Steele, *Forty Years in Canada*, p. 164.

59 36 *Sun*, Winnipeg, Feb. 24, 1882.

60 2   *Globe*, Feb. 10, 1882.

60 21 *Sun*, Winnipeg, May 12, 1882.

60 29 *Times*, March 3, 1882.

60 32 *Sun*, Winnipeg, March 7, 1882.

60 39 *Times*, Feb. 21, 1882.

61 3   *Ibid.*, Feb. 16, 1882.

61 13 *Globe*, March 13, 1883.

61 30 White.

61 37 *Times*, Sept. 16, 1881.

61 40 Quoted in *Times*, Sept. 26, 1881.

62 3   McWilliams, p. 128.

62 15 *Sun*, Winnipeg, March 21, 1882.

62 26 *Ibid.*, Feb. 24, 1882.

63 2   *Globe*, March 13, 1882.

63 20 *Ibid.*, Feb. 10, 1882.

63 23 *Times*, Feb. 7, 1882.

63 24 McLagan, p. 521.

63 33 *Times*, June 14, 1882.

64 7   *Ibid.*, April 8, 1882.

64 10 *Ibid.*, Jan. 28, 1882.

64 14 Quoted in *Sun*, Winnipeg, March 7, 1882.

64 17 *Ibid.*

64 22 *Ibid.*, March 23, 1882.

64 30 *Globe*, March 17, 1882.

64 35 *Free Press*, Manitoba, Nov. 22, 1881.

65 2   *Ibid.*

65 6   *Ibid.*, May 16, 1881.

65 12 Trotter and Hawkes, p. 91.

65 19 *Ibid.*, p. 221.

65 23 *Globe*, March 21, 1882.

65 28 *Ibid.*, March 3, 1882.

65 29 *Ibid.*, April 11, 1882.

65 33 *Ibid.*, March 3, 1882.

66 5   *Times*, May 19, 1882.

66 33 *Ibid.*, Nov. 13, 1882.

67 6   *Globe*, March 28, 1882.

page line

67 16 *Ibid.*

67 19 *St. Paul Pioneer Press* quoted in *Times*, March 23, 1882.

68 40 *Globe*, March 3, 1882.

69 4   Trotter and Hawkes, p. 94.

69 9   *Ibid.*, p. 95.

69 14 *Globe*, Jan. 12, 1882.

69 20 *Ibid.*, Feb. 1, 1882.

69 22 *Times*, Feb. 28, 1882.

69 30 Hill, *Manitoba*, pp. 432-433.

69 41 *Ibid.*

70 18 *Times*, April 10, 1882.

71 3   *Ibid.*, May 30, 1882.

71 7   *Bulletin*, April 29, 1882.

71 12 *Times*, Feb. 27, 1882.

71 29 Grant, *Week*, Dec. 27, 1883.

72 2   *Globe*, Jan. 4, 1882.

72 13 *Ibid.*, Feb. 1, 1882.

72 28 *Times*, Feb. 11, 1882.

73 11 White.

74 3   Quoted in *Times*, March 25, 1882.

74 5   *Ibid.*

74 10 *Globe*, Feb. 1, 1882.

74 16 *Ibid.*, Jan. 18, 1882.

75 2   *Ibid.*, April 4, 1882.

75 18 *Times*, April 12, 1882.

75 20 *Ibid.*, April 13, 1882.

75 27 *Bulletin*, April 29, 1882.

75 28 *Times*, April 13, 1882.

75 30 *Bulletin*, April 29, 1882.

76 4   MacGregor, p. 148.

76 21 *Times*, April 14, 1882.

76 30 *Ibid.*

77 1   Quoted in *Sun*, Winnipeg, April 20, 1882.

77 3   *Ibid.*, April 19, 1882.

77 5   *Ibid.*, April 21, 1882.

77 19 *Globe*, April 11, 1882.

77 21 Fleming, *England and Canada*, p. 202.

77 22 Hill, *From Home to Home*, p. 153.

77   26   Donkin, p. 8.

77   28   *A Year in Manitoba*, p. 26.

78   14   *Globe,* April 20, 1882.

78   28   *Ibid.,* April 24, 1882.

79   34   McWilliams, p. 128.

79   37   Hill, *Manitoba*, p. 449.

80   2   Armstrong Manuscript, p. 121.

80   5   *Globe,* April 11, 1882.

80   29   Hill, *Manitoba*, p. 445.

81   21   *Ibid.,* p. 448.

81   33   *Ibid.,* p. 449.

82   6   Ham, p. 31.

Chapter Three

84   3   Quoted in Taché, p. 345.

84   4   Vaughan, p. 56.

85   3   Secretan, p. 97.

85   13   Vaughan, p. 55.

85   32   *Globe,* Jan. 12, 1882.

85   40   *Ibid.,* Jan. 14, 1882.

86   36   Vaughan, p. 229.

87   11   *Ibid.,* p. 21.

87   22   *Ibid.,* p. 207.

87   35   *Globe,* Jan. 13, 1880.

87   37   Vaughan, p. 77.

88   4   Pyle, Vol. I, p. 203.

88   22   Vaughan, p. 13.

88   23   Pyle, Vol. I, p. 203.

88   38   Vaughan, p. 21.

89   18   *Globe,* Aug. 26, 1881.

89   26   *Times,* May 22, 1882.

89   29   *Globe,* Feb. 4, 1882.

89   36   *Ibid.,* Jan. 31, 1882.

90   14   *Times,* Feb. 11, 1882.

90   22   *Ibid.,* May 22, 1882.

90   36   Armstrong Manuscript, p. 127.

90   39   *Times,* May 19, 1882.

91   12   *Sun,* Winnipeg, July 13, 1882.

91   17   *Times,* Oct. 31, 1882.

91   25   *Globe*, May 27, 1882.

91   27   Armstrong Manuscript, p. 127.

92   7   *Globe,* Jan. 21, 1882.

92   21   Secretan, p. 100.

92   27   *Ibid.,* p. 99.

92   29   *Ibid.,* p. 96.

92   31   *Ibid.,* p. 97.

93   6   Vaughan, p. 18.

93   32   *Ibid.,* p. 38.

93   37   Collard, *Canadian Yesterdays*, p. 253.

94   16   Gibbon, p. 274.

94   23   Secretan, pp. 103-104.

95   10   *Sun,* Winnipeg, April 17, 1882.

95   15   Hansard, 1882, p. 1007.

95   36   MacBeth, p. 91.

96   24   Stephen Papers, Macdonald to Stephen, July 30, 1884.

96   26   *Ibid.*

97   1   Secretan, p. 193.

97   11   Bridle, p. 198.

97   35   Vaughan, pp. 272-273.

97   37   Secretan, p. 97.

98   4   Mavor.

98   24   Armstrong Manuscript, p. 174.

99   14   *Sun,* Winnipeg, June 10, 1882.

99   18   Vaughan, p. 151.

100   2   Rutledge, April 15, 1920.

100   35   *Ibid.*

101   33   Stevens, *An Engineer's Recollections,* pp. 1-2.

102   28   Trotter and Hawkes, p. 94.

102   38   Oliver.

103   3   Trotter and Hawkes, p. 98.

103   4   *Ibid.,* p. 96.

103   10   *Sun,* Winnipeg, June 9, 1882.

103   15   *Ibid.*

103   23   Oliver.

103   32   Peyton Papers.

103   35   Oliver.

104   16   *Globe,* June 23, 1882.

page line

104　28　*Ibid.*, July 28, 1882.

104　30　*Quarterly Review*, Jan. 1887, p. 127.

104　35　Secretan, p. 194.

104　38　*Quarterly Review,* Jan. 1887, p. 129.

105　15　Bone, p. 43.

106　11　*Engineering,* April 25, 1884 quoted in *Quarterly Review,* Jan. 1887, p. 128.

106　33　Barneby, p. 269.

108　17　*Engineering.*

108　22　*Sun*, Winnipeg, Aug. 30, 1882.

108　29　Hill, *From Home to Home*, p. 127.

108　33　White.

109　4　Boulton, *Adventures*, p. 16.

109　18　Hughes, *Father Lacombe*, p. 273.

110　18　Trotter and Hawkes, p. 102.

110　29　Oliver.

110　34　Peyton Papers.

110　37　Hill, *From Home to Home*, p. 73.

111　4　*Sun*, Winnipeg, June 10, 1882.

111　13　*Globe*, Nov. 24, 1882.

111　17　Trotter and Hawkes, p. 102.

111　20　"The Good Old Days of Broadview."

111　30　*Sun*, Winnipeg, June 7, 1882.

111　40　*Ibid.*, July 11, 1882.

112　13　Macdonald Papers, Vol. 267, Stephen to Macdonald, Sept. 7, 1882.

112　15　Trotter and Hawkes, p. 96.

112　40　*Globe*, July 29, 1882.

114　27　Drake, *Regina*, p. 6.

115　12　Instrument No. DB 21001.

115　23　Dewdney Papers, Glenbow, Vol. 2, p. 225, undated memorandum Summer, 1882.

115　40　Instrument No. DB 21001.

116　14　Drake, *Regina*, p. 7.

116　39　White.

117　18　*Times*, Aug. 12, 1882.

117　22　Macdonald Papers, Vol. 211, Dewdney to Macdonald, June 4, 1882.

117　29　*Ibid.*

117　35　*Times*, Sept. 19, 1882.

page line

118　1　Macdonald Papers, Vol. 267, Stephen to Macdonald, Aug. 12, 1882.

118　2　*Ibid.*, Macdonald to Stephen, Aug. 12, 1882.

118　21　Quoted in *Sun*, Winnipeg, Sept. 30, 1882.

118　33　*Ibid.*, August 25, 1882.

118　36　*Bulletin*, Oct. 21, 1882.

119　12　Macdonald Papers, Vol. 315, Dewdney to Macdonald, Sept. 18, 1882.

119　15　Quoted in *Sun*, Winnipeg, Oct., 1882.

119　16　*Ibid.*

119　17　*Ibid.*

119　26　Trotter and Hawkes, p. 112.

119　29　Hill, *From Home to Home*, p. 124.

119　30　Hamilton, p. 23.

119　32　Peter McAra in *Leader*, Regina, March 23, 1923.

119　35　Macdonald Papers, Vol. 267, Stephen to Macdonald, Sept. 12, 1882.

119　35　Dewdney Papers, Glenbow, Vol. 3, p. 403, Macdonald to Dewdney, Sept. 6, 1882.

120　6　*Times*, Sept. 19, 1882.

120　8　Macdonald Papers, Vol. 315, Dewdney to Macdonald, Aug. 27, 1882.

120　11　Drake, *Regina*, p. 11.

120　17　*Globe*, March 16, 1882.

120　21　*Gazette*, Fort McLeod, June 13, 1883.

120　30　Quoted in Drake, *Regina*, p. 11.

121　14　Macdonald Papers, Vol. 261, Scarth to Macdonald, Jan. 10, 1885.

121　16　*Ibid.*, Vol. 268, Stephen to Macdonald, Oct. 28, 1882.

121　25　*Ibid.*, Vol. 315, Dewdney to Macdonald, Aug. 27, 1882.

121　33　*Ibid.*, Sept. 18, 1882.

122　10　*Times*, Oct. 27, 1882.

122　14　*Ibid.*, Oct. 27, 1882.

123　10　Dewdney Papers, Glenbow, Vol. 2, White to Dewdney, March 29, 1883, with enclosures.

123 15 *Ibid.*, Vol. 3, Macdonald to Dewdney, Sept. 6, 1882.

124 5 Brooks, Part 2, p. 33, Brooks to wife, May 21, 1883.

124 20 W. H. Duncan to Mrs. Austin Bothwell, Legislative Librarian, Regina, Jan. 17, 1933.

125 23 Stephen Papers, Macdonald to Stephen, July 31, 1882.

125 32 Macdonald Papers, Vol. 127, Pope to Macdonald, Aug. 12, 1882.

125 34 Stephen Papers, Macdonald to Stephen, Sept. 8, 1882.

126 26 Macdonald Papers, Vol. 268, Stephen to Macdonald, Feb. 26, 1882.

127 2 *Ibid.*, Vol. 267, Stephen to Macdonald, Jan. 23, 1881.

127 9 CPR *Reports,* 1881-89, p. 21, Shareholders' Proceedings, May 10, 1882.

127 32 Macdonald Papers, Vol. 268, Stephen to Macdonald, July 16, 1882.

128 22 *Ibid.*, Sept. 8, 1882.

128 35 *Ibid.*, Aug. 27, 1882.

129 1 *Ibid.*, Sept. 8, 1882.

129 2 *Ibid.*, Sept. 29, 1882.

129 5 *Ibid.*, Oct. 5, 1882.

129 12 *Ibid.*, Oct. 4, 1882.

129 19 *Ibid.*, Macdonald to Stephen, Oct. 20, 1882.

129 37 *Ibid.*, Stephen to Macdonald, Nov. 21, 1882.

129 39 Hedges, p. 37.

130 9 Sessional Paper, No. 31A, 1884, pp. 99-105.

130 11 Macdonald Papers, Vol. 159, Rose to Macdonald, Feb. 1, 1883.

130 14 *Ibid.*, Vol. 259, Rose to Macdonald, Jan. 18, 1883.

130 27 Sessional Paper, No. 31A, 1884, pp. 225-233.

130 34 *Ibid.*

131 4 *Ibid.*, pp. 255-256.

131 15 Gibbon, p. 385.

131 23 Macdonald Papers, Vol. 259, Rose to Macdonald, Feb. 1, 1883.

131 33 *Ibid.*, Vol. 268, Stephen to Macdonald, Jan. 4, 1883.

132 2 Tway thesis.

132 7 Macdonald Papers, Vol. 268, Stephen to Macdonald, Jan. 4, 1883.

132 17 *Ibid.*, Vol. 259, Rose to Macdonald, Nov. 30, 1882.

132 20 *Ibid.*, Jan. 4, 1883.

132 25 *Ibid.*

132 32 *Ibid.*, Vol. 268, Stephen to Macdonald, Jan. 4, 1883.

132 39 Taché, p. 453.

133 3 Stevens, *Canadian National Railways,* Vol. I, p. 332.

133 8 *Ibid.*

133 15 Taché, p. 452.

133 26 Lovett, p. 114.

134 2 Stephen Papers, Macdonald to Stephen, Jan. 26, 1882.

134 32 Hickson Papers, Hickson to Macdonald, June 16, 1882.

134 36 *Ibid.*, Macdonald to Hickson, June 17, 1882.

134 38 *Ibid.*, June 20, 1882.

135 1 *Ibid.*, Aug. 14, 1882.

135 5 *Ibid.*, Hickson to Macdonald, Oct. 9, 1882.

135 23 *Globe,* Aug. 9, 1883.

135 35 Macdonald Papers, Vol. 268, Stephen to Macdonald, Jan. 4, 1883.

136 1 *Ibid.*, Feb. 1, 1883.

136 7 Vaughan, p. 91.

136 10 Macdonald Papers, Vol. 277, clipping: *Money Market Review,* Feb. 2, 1883.

136 12 *Ibid.*, Vol. 268, Stephen to Macdonald, Feb. 18, 1883.

136 18 *Letter [of George Stephen] to the Shareholders of the Grand Trunk Railroad.*

136 19 Macdonald Papers, Vol. 268, Stephen to Macdonald, Feb. 18, 1883.

136 21 Gilbert, p. 122.

136 25 Macdonald Papers, Vol. 259, Rose to Macdonald, April 11, 1883.

page line

169 25 *Ibid.*, Van Horne to Jno. W. Sterling, Jan. 30, 1883.

170 2 Shaw and Hull, p. 70.

170 27 Vaughan, p. 81.

170 40 Shaw and Hull, p. 139.

171 27 Secretan, p. 105.

172 1 Shaw and Hull, p. 146.

172 6 *Ibid.*, p. 149.

173 10 *Ibid.*, p. 150.

173 15 *Ibid.*, p. 154.

173 23 See, for example, Shaw, "A Prairie Gopher Makes Reply."

173 36 Shaw and Hull, p. 155.

174 5 Moberly, *Rocks and Rivers*, p. 102.

174 8 Robinson and Moberly, p. 73.

174 31 Fleming, *England and Canada*, p. 244.

174 35 *Ibid.*, p. 229.

174 36 *Ibid.*, p. 244.

175 9 Roberts, *The Western Avernus*, p. 83.

175 28 Fleming, *England and Canada*, pp. 248-249.

175 34 *Ibid.*, p. 258.

175 37 *Ibid.*, p. 249.

176 19 Grant and Hamilton, p. 253.

176 21 *Ibid.*, pp. 107-108.

176 35 *Ibid.*, p. 254.

177 3 *Ibid.*, p. 255.

177 25 Fleming, *England and Canada*, pp. 256-257.

177 28 Grant, "The Canada Pacific Railway," p. 887.

178 8 Fleming, *England and Canada*, p. 270.

178 14 Grant, "The Canada Pacific Railway," p. 887.

178 23 Grant, *Week*, May 22, 1884, p. 391.

178 28 *Ibid.*, p. 391.

178 36 Grant, "The Canada Pacific Railway," p. 887.

178 38 Fleming, *England and Canada*, p. 262.

178 40 *Ibid.*, p. 278.

179 1 *Ibid.*, p. 283.

page line

179 33 Wilson Manuscript, p. 64.

180 7 *Ibid.*, p. 67.

Chapter Five

183 9 Evans Memorandum.

183 12 Vincent Memorandum.

183 18 Cambie to Fairbairn.

183 19 Robinson and Moberly, p. 105.

183 31 Parker, p. 353.

183 34 Vincent Memorandum.

183 39 Cambie to Fairbairn.

184 2 Parker, p. 353.

184 6 Weekes to Miller.

184 23 Onderdonk File, PABC, Obituary, *Colonist*, June 28, 1905.

185 7 Clews, p. 457.

186 8 *Globe*, Feb. 16, 1882.

187 2 *Ibid.*, Feb. 4, 1882.

187 9 Robinson and Moberly, p. 105.

188 16 Parker, p. 353.

189 15 Quoted in Ormsby, p. 252.

189 18 Robinson and Moberly, p. 105.

190 8 *Inland Sentinel*, Dec. 7, 1882.

192 4 *Ibid.*, Sept. 2, 1880.

192 8 *Parker*, p. 354. .

192 9 *Inland Sentinel*, May 25, 1882.

192 26 Rutledge, May 1, 1920.

193 31 *Inland Sentinel*, June 23, 1881.

193 37 *Ibid.*, Aug. 4, 1881.

194 13 Quoted in *British Colonist*, Jan. 9, 1880.

194 20 *Ibid.*, Jan. 11, 1880.

194 31 *Ibid.*, April 13, 1880.

195 4 *Ibid.*, Aug. 11, 1878.

195 19 *Globe*, April 23, 1883.

195 26 *Gazette*, Port Moody, July 12, 1884.

195 32 *Times*, April 30, 1879.

195 40 Hansard, 1882, p. 1477.

196 3 *Ibid.*

page line

196   8   Cambie, "Reminiscences," p. 473.

196 15 Holmes Manuscript.

196 19 *Globe*, June 1, 1882.

197   2   *Inland Sentinel*, advertisement, March 31, 1881.

197   3   *Ibid.*, April 7, 1881.

197 10 *Ibid.*, Aug. 30, 1883.

197 18 Rutledge, May 1, 1920.

197 34 Starr, p. 231.

198   3   Holbrook, pp. 169-170.

198 12 Cambie Diary, June 7, 1880.

198 16 *Ibid.*, July 2, 1880.

198 17 Cambie to Fairbairn.

198 19 *Report of Royal Commission on Chinese Immigration*, 1885, p. cxxx.

199   1   *Ibid.*, p. lxxvi.

199 24 Cambie to Fairbairn.

199 26 *Globe*, May 11, 1882.

199 33 *Ibid.*, May 10, 1882.

199 36 *British Columbian*, June 14, 1882.

199 40 *Globe*, June 1, 1882.

200   6   Rutledge, May 1, 1920.

200 14 Pugsley, June 15, 1930.

200 24 *Ibid.*

200 33 *Inland Sentinel*, Nov. 30, 1882.

200 40 *Ibid.*, May 17, 1883.

201   9   *Report of Royal Commission on Chinese Immigration*, 1885, p. lxxxiv.

201 15 *Inland Sentinel*, Aug. 17, 1882.

201 20 *Ibid.*, Feb. 22, 1883.

201 36 *Ibid.*, Dec. 14, 1882.

202 14 Rutledge, May 1, 1920.

202 22 Robinson and Moberly, p. 108.

202 29 Holmes Manuscript.

202 34 *Ibid.*

203 17 Rutledge, May 1, 1920.

203 23 *Inland Sentinel*, May 5, 1881.

203 27 *Ibid.*, Feb. 15, 1883.

204   2   *Ibid.*, March 1, 1883.

204   7   Cambie Diary, Nov. 22, 1880.

204 18 *Inland Sentinel*, Jan. 3, 1884.

204 31 *Report of Royal Commission on Chinese Immigration*, 1885, Huang Sic Chan's testimony, p. 366.

204 36 *Ibid.*; see Haney's testimony, p. 122 and Onderdonk's testimony, p. 149.

204 39 *Ibid.*, Appendix N, p. 398.

205 20 Perry, p. 76.

206 13 *Gazette*, Port Moody, Feb. 23, 1884.

206 18 Lorne Papers, Lorne to Macdonald, Oct. 24, 1882.

206 24 Marcus Smith Papers, PAC, Letterbook No. 4, Smith to Onderdonk, June 5, 1883.

207   2   *Ibid.*

208   2   Rutledge, May 1, 1920.

208 16 Marcus Smith Papers, PAC, Letterbook No. 4, Smith to Onderdonk, June 5, 1883.

209   4   *Colonist*, March 4, 1880.

209 11 *Ibid.*, March 17, 1880.

209 22 *Inland Sentinel*, Jan. 13, 1881.

211   1   Robinson and Moberly, p. 108.

211   5   *Inland Sentinel*, July 7, 1881.

211   7   Meyers, p. 30.

211 27 Kennedy, "When History Was A-Making," p. 45.

212 26 *Mail*, Sept. 6, 1880.

212 33 *Inland Sentinel*, Feb. 3, 1881.

212 40 *Ibid.*, Aug. 12, 1880.

213   3   *Ibid.*, Sept. 30, 1880.

213 14 *Ibid.*, Aug. 18, 1881.

213 20 *Ibid.*, March 16, 1882.

213 31 *Ibid.*, Aug. 17, 1882.

213 37 *Ibid.*, Sept. 7, 1882.

214   1   *Ibid.*, June 28, 1883.

214 14 *Ibid.*, May 3, 1883.

214 28 *Ibid.*, June 10, 1880.

216   6   *Ibid.*, Nov. 29, 1883.

216 14 *Ibid.*, Jan. 4, 1883.

216 17 *Ibid.*, Aug. 30, 1883.

216 22 Parker, p. 356.

216   27   *Inland Sentinal*, Feb. 8, 1883.

216   32   *Ibid.*, Feb. 15, 1883.

216   35   *Ibid.*, July 7, 1881.

217   4   *Ibid.*

217   12   Robinson and Moberly, p. 107.

Chapter Six

221   13   "The Good Old Days of Broadview."

221   35   *Globe*, May 4, 1883.

222   13   *Ibid.*, April 16, 1883.

223   13   Eager, p. 5.

223   15   Oliver.

223   27   *Ibid.*

224   15   Rowles, p. 13.

225   20   Davis.

226   3   *Spectator*, March 26, quoted in *Globe*, April 16, 1883.

226   37   *Gazette*, Fort Macleod, Jan. 13, 1883.

226   38   *News*, July 4, 1884.

228   33   *Quarterly Review*, Jan. 1887, pp. 129-130.

229   1   Bone, p. 42.

229   4   *Ibid.*, p. 44.

229   10   *Ibid.*

229   19   Quoted in Powers, p. 24.

229   21   *Ibid.*

229   22   *News*, June 20, 1884.

229   37   Macdonald Papers, Vol. 389, Part I, Davin to Macdonald, Nov. 15, 1882.

230   28   Hassard, p. 6.

231   6   *Leader*, March 22, 1883, quoted in Drake, "Pioneer Journalism," p. 23.

231   9   *Ibid.*, "Some Characteristics," p. 45.

231   19   Quoted in Powers, pp. 23-24.

231   35   *Leader*, Nov. 8, 1883.

232   32   Stanley, *Birth of Western Canada*, p. 218.

233   32   Stobie, p. 6.

234   3   *Globe*, May 4, 1883.

234   28   Haydon, pp. 105-106.

235   11   Secretan, p. 111.

235   37   Breton, p. 87.

236   14   Van Horne, preface to Hughes, p. vi.

237   21   Breton, p. 88.

237   25   *Gazette*, Fort Macleod, May 24, 1883.

238   2   Butler, p. 20.

238   12   Boulton, *Adventures*, p. 30.

238   22   *Quarterly Review*, Jan. 1887, p. 136.

239   3   *Leader*, Aug. 30, 1883.

239   18   *Herald*, Calgary, Oct. 1, 1884.

239   23   *News*, Jan. 18, 1884.

239   40   *Globe*, April 25, 1885.

240   23   Powers, p. 27.

240   26   Steele, *Forty Years in Canada*, p. 177.

240   35   Donkin, pp. 14-15.

241   8   *Ibid.*, p. 20.

241   20   *Globe*, April 25, 1885.

241   24   *Gazette*, Fort Macleod, Jan. 13, 1883.

241   28   Donkin, p. 16.

242   4   *Leader*, Aug. 16, 1883.

242   12   *Ibid.*

242   21   Dewdney Papers, Glenbow, Macdonald to Dewdney, Aug. 22, 1883.

242   41   *News*, Jan. 18, 1884.

243   7   *Leader*, May 24, 1883.

243   15   Brooks, Part 1, pp. 105-106.

243   18   Steele, *Forty Years in Canada*, p. 177.

243   21   Brooks, Part 1, Brooks to wife, Aug. 23, 1882, p. 111.

243   31   *News*, Jan. 25, 1884.

244   10   Murdoch Diary, June 5, 1883.

245   14   *Herald*, Calgary, Aug. 31, 1881.

246   2   Van Horne Letterbooks, No. 15, Van Horne to George Olds, Feb. 27, 1886.

246   28   *Gazette*, Fort Macleod, 1883.

246   31   *Herald*, Calgary, Nov. 9, 1883.

246   37   *Ibid.*, Dec. 26, 1883.

247   6   *Ibid.*, Jan. 2, 1884.

247   13   *Ibid.*, Feb. 13, 1884.

page line

247 14 *Ibid.*, Feb. 20, 1884.

248 19 Advertisement of T. E. Hanrahan & Co., *Globe*, July 4, 1883.

248 38 Tupper Papers, Vol. 5, Macdonald to Tupper, Nov. 22, 1883.

249 27 Vancouver *Province* clipping, 1932, quoting F. W. Peters, ex-General Superintendent, CPR, Vertical Files, PABC.

250 2 Tupper Papers, Vol. 5, Macdonald to Tupper, Nov. 22, 1883.

250 10 *Ibid.*

250 35 Quoted in *Globe*, Nov. 5, 1883.

250 39 Macdonald Papers, Vol. 168, Stephen to Macdonald, Dec. 18, 1883.

251 5 *Ibid.*, Vol. 259, Rose to Macdonald, Dec. 29, 1883.

252 7 Skelton, *Life and Letters of Laurier*, Vol. I, p. 273.

252 15 Ross, p. 160.

252 18 *Ibid.*, p. 161.

252 21 Pope, *Correspondence*, Macdonald to Tupper, Dec. 1, 1883, p. 308.

252 23 *Ibid.*, Tupper to Macdonald, Dec. 2, 1883, p. 308.

252 24 Harkin, p. 115.

252 25 Macdonald Papers, Vol. 268, Stephen to Macdonald, Dec. 15, 1883.

252 40 *Ibid.*, Dec. 23, 1883.

253 3 *Ibid.*

253 12 Tupper Papers, Vol. 5, Stephen to Tupper, Dec. 28, 1883.

253 12 *Ibid.*, Vol. 6, Jan. 5, 1884.

253 31 Tupper, Hansard, 1884, pp. 98-113.

253 33 *Senate Committee on Interstate Commerce*, Van Horne's testimony, p. 230.

255 37 Sessional Paper 31A, 1884, Charles Brydges to Van Horne, April 7, 1883, pp. 44-49.

255 39 *Ibid.*, Memo from Charles Tupper to the Governor in Council, May 1, 1883, p. 50.

256 16 Macdonald Papers, Vol. 282, Colmer to Macdonald, Dec. 10, 1883.

256 22 Van Horne Letterbooks, No. 6, Van Horne to Egan, May 13, 1884.

page line

256 28 *Globe*, May 27, 1884.

256 35 Macdonald Papers, Vol. 268, Stephen to Macdonald, Dec. 6, 1883.

256 40 *Sun*, Brandon, March 8, 1884.

257 16 Macdonald Papers, Vol. 268, Stephen to Macdonald, Jan. 22, 1884.

257 19 Tupper Papers, Vol. 6, Stephen to Tupper, Jan. 24, 1884.

257 24 *Leader*, June 7, 1883.

257 31 Hansard, 1885, p. 2618.

257 39 See Sessional Paper No. 31A for 1884, which gives Stephen's holdings in 1883 and 1884.

258 12 Stephen Papers, Macdonald to Stephen, Nov. 20, 1883.

258 15 Preston, pp. 171-172.

258 22 Tupper Papers, Vol. 6, Stephen to Tupper, Jan. 24, 1884.

258 30 *Ibid.*

259 7 *Sentinel*, Dec. 15, 1883.

259 26 Quoted in *Globe*, Aug. 10, 1883.

259 36 Van Horne Letterbook, No. 1, Van Horne to Egan, Feb. 19, 1883.

260 6 *Ibid.*, No. 4, Van Horne to Egan, Feb. 2, 1884.

260 9 *Ibid.*, Feb. 4, 1884.

260 12 *Ibid.*, No. 1, Van Horne to W. Horder, April 9, 1883.

260 20 *Ibid.*, No. 4, Van Horne to John Ross, Feb. 23, 1884.

260 33 *Ibid.*, No. 5, April 15, 1884.

261 3 *Ibid.*, Van Horne to Egan, April 28, 1884.

261 14 *Globe*, Feb. 1, 1884.

261 35 Macdonald Papers, Vol. 268, Stephen to Macdonald, Feb. 10, 1884.

262 3 *Globe*, Feb. 9, 1884.

262 7 Macdonald Papers, Vol. 129, Hickson to Macdonald, Feb. 7, 1884.

262 9 *Ibid.*, enclosure, Grand Trunk Railway Company, *Correspondence between the Company and the Dominion government respecting advances to the Canadian Pacific Railway Company.*

262 10 *Globe*, Feb. 14, 1884.

page line

Horne to Minister of Railways and Canals, May 19, 1884.

293 33 Norris Crump, Chairman of the Board, to the author.

294 30 Carter, pp. 13031-13032.

296 7 *Herald*, Calgary, Nov. 15, 1884.

296 15 MacBeth, p. 102.

296 25 Armstrong Manuscript, p. 179.

296 33 Van Horne Letterbooks, No. 4, Van Horne to G. T. Breackenridge, Feb. 8, 1884.

297 5 *Ibid.*, No. 6, Van Horne to Beatty, June 7, 1884.

297 13 *Ibid.*, No. 1, Van Horne to Egan, April 9, 1883.

297 15 *Ibid.*, No. 4, Van Horne to Mrs. M. E. Galbraith, Dec. 25, 1883.

297 23 *Ibid.*, No. 4, Van Horne to Egan, Jan. 6, 1884.

297 28 *Ibid.*, No. 6, Van Horne to George Purvis, July 14, 1884.

297 30 *Ibid.*

297 39 Vaughan, p. 139.

298 4 Van Horne Letterbooks, No. 5, Van Horne to W. Whyte, April 28, 1884.

298 10 *Ibid.*, No. 6, Van Horne to John Lowe, May 14, 1884.

298 19 *Ibid.*, No. 7, Van Horne to Henry Beatty, July 18, 1884.

298 27 *Ibid.*, Van Horne to Egan, July 19, 1884.

298 34 *Ibid.*, No. 5, Van Horne to H. B. Ledyard, March 26, 1884.

298 38 *Ibid.*, No. 7, Van Horne to Ledyard, July 26, 1884.

299 7 Thompson and Edgar, p. 143.

299 14 Vaughan, p. 142.

299 17 Collard, p. 253.

299 28 MacBeth, p. 144.

299 35 Vaughan, p. 138.

300 24 Van Horne Letterbooks, No. 5, Van Horne to J. J. C. Abbott, March 15, 1884.

300 31 *Ibid.*, No. 6, Van Horne to Beatty, July 5, 1884.

page line

301 5 Vaughan, p. 109.

301 39 Told to Raymond Hull by Van Horne's valet. Hull to H. T. Coleman, March 27, 1969.

302 8 Vaughan, p. 148.

302 16 Collard, p. 252.

302 28 Vaughan, p. 152.

303 9 *Gazette*, Port Moody, Dec. 22, 1883.

303 20 *Ibid.*, Jan. 5, 1884.

303 24 *Ibid.*, Aug. 16, 1884.

303 35 *Ibid.*, Aug. 9, 1884.

304 9 *Ibid.*

304 28 Quoted in *Gazette*, Port Moody, Aug. 16, 1884.

304 36 *Ibid.*

305 13 Van Horne Letterbooks, No. 8, Van Horne to A. W. Ross, Nov. 21, 1884.

305 20 Marcus Smith Papers, PAC, Letterbook No. 4, Smith to Van Horne, April 28, 1884.

306 6 *Ibid.*, Smith to R. Brock, Oct. 13, 1884, and Feb. 19, 1885.

306 8 *Ibid.*, Smith to David Oppenheimer, Aug. 1, 1884.

306 25 *Ibid.*, Smith to Brock, Oct. 13, 1884.

306 41 Marcus Smith Papers, PABC, Diary, Sept. 4, 1884.

307 12 *Inland Sentinel*, Aug. 14, 1884.

307 16 Van Hornet Letterbooks, No. 14, Van Horne to Stephen, Nov. 24, 1885.

307 23 *Ibid.*

307 26 *Ibid.*

307 30 Pope, *Memoirs*, p. 75.

307 36 Hansard, 1882, p. 955.

308 6 Marcus Smith Papers, PABC, Smith to Joseph Hunter, May 24, 1885.

308 9 Marcus Smith Papers, PAC, Letterbook No. 7, Smith to Brock, Aug. 11, 1893.

308 22 *Ibid.*, No. 4, Smith to Schreiber, March 14, 1885.

308 30 Cambie, "Reminiscences," p. 473.

308 35 Markwell.

page line

309   7   Cambie Diary, Nov. 20, 1880.

309 14   *Inland Sentinel*, Sept. 27, 1883.

309 16   *Ibid.*, Nov. 22, 1883.

309 30   Macdonald Papers, Vol. 272, Stephen to Macdonald, Sept. 3, 1889.

309 35   *Ibid.*

309 40   *Senate Committee in Interstate Commerce*, Van Horne's testimony, p. 229.

310   8   Marcus Smith Papers, PAC, Letterbook No. 4, Smith to Dr. D. R. Schultz, March 31, 1885.

310   9   *Ibid.*, PABC, Smith to Joseph Hunter, Feb. 23, 1885.

310   9   *Ibid.*, PAC, Letterbook No. 7, Smith to Brock, Aug. 11, 1893.

310   9   *Ibid.*, PABC, Diary, Sept. 4, 1884.

310 28   Van Horne Letterbook, No. 6, Van Horne to Rogers, June 14, 1884.

310 32   Marcus Smith Papers, PAC, Letterbook No. 4, Smith to Van Horne, Feb. 24, 1885.

310 36   *Inland Sentinel*, April 10, 1884.

311 15   *Ibid.*, Aug. 7, 1884.

311 18   *Ibid.*, Aug. 14, 1884.

311 21   Dallin Manuscript.

311 24   Roberts, p. 125.

311 29   Matthews.

311 36   Cambie Diary, July 16, 1884.

312   2   *Ibid.*, May 30, 1884.

312 19   *Inland Sentinel*, Aug. 14, 1884.

312 36   Stevens, *An Engineer's Recollections*, p. 14.

313   5   Gibbon, p. 274.

313 24   Vaughan, p. 111.

313 32   *Herald*, Calgary, Dec. 9, 1883.

314   4   Van Horne Letterbooks, No. 7, Van Horne to Beatty, Sept. 17, 1884.

314 11   *Ibid.*, Van Horne to Robert Kerr, Oct. 9, 1884.

314 14   *Ibid.*, Van Horne to Whyte, Sept. 23, 1884.

314 22   *Ibid.*, No. 8, Van Horne to Ross, Nov. 21, 1884.

314 25   *Ibid.*, No. 9, Van Horne to Lee, Dec. 26, 1884.

314 37   *Ibid.*, Van Horne to Rogers, Feb. 21, 1885.

315   8   *Ibid.*, Van Horne to Abbott, Jan. 6, 1885.

315 30   *Ibid.*, No. 8, Van Horne to George Wainwright, Dec. 2, 1884.

315 38   *Ibid.*, No. 6, Van Horne to John Ross, June 9, 1884.

315 40   *Ibid.*, Van Horne to Hon. John Carling, July 15, 1884

316   2   *Ibid.*, Van Horne to Egan, July 15, 1884.

316   6   *Ibid.*, Van Horne to Premier John Norquay, July 15, 1884.

316   9   *Ibid.*, No. 7, Van Horne to Cambie, Aug. 30, 1884.

316 14   *Ibid.*, Van Horne to John Ross, Aug. 28, 1884.

316 18   *Ibid.*, No. 8, Van Horne to John Ross, Oct. 19, 1884.

316 32   *Ibid.*, Oct. 31, 1884.

316 40   *Ibid.*, No. 7, Van Horne to W. B. Scarth, Oct. 6, 1884.

317 13   Macdonald Papers, Vol. 269, Stephen to Macdonald, Dec. 29, 1884.

318 12   *Ibid.*, March 16, 1884.

318 22   *Ibid.*

319 16   Van Horne Letterbooks, No. 8, Van Horne to Schreiber, Oct. 17, 1884.

319 26   *Herald*, Calgary, Nov. 27, 1884.

319 30   *Sentinel*, Oct. 31, 1884.

319 37   Vaughan, p. 114.

320   2   Armstrong Manuscript, p. 153.

320 25   *Standard*, Montreal, Jan. 4, 1908.

320 34   MacBeth, p. 197.

321 21   Told to the author by the present Lord Shaughnessy.

321 33   CPR Archives, Lord Mount Stephen to "Arthur," Aug. 18, 1909.

321 35   Macdonald Papers, Vol. 269, Stephen to Macdonald, March 31, 1884.

321 40   *Ibid.*, Nov. 7, 1885.

page line

322 14 CPR Archives, Lord Mount Stephen to "Arthur," Aug. 18, 1909.

322 22 Bernard.

322 29 Macdonald Papers, Vol. 269, Stephen to Macdonald, July 23, 1884.

323   5 *Ibid.*, Vol. 277, Tilley to Macdonald, June 12, 1884.

323   7 *Ibid.*, June 19, 1884.

323 14 *Ibid.*, Vol. 259, Rose to Macdonald, Feb. 27, 1884.

323 17 *Ibid.*, July 24, 1884.

323 23 Tupper Papers, Vol. 6, Stephen to Tupper, Aug. 13, 1884.

324   4 *Globe*, Sept. 5, 1884.

324 16 *Ibid.*, July 7, 1884.

324 24 *Ibid.*, Aug. 16, 1884.

324 25 Lorne Papers, Macdonald to Lorne, Oct. 18, 1884.

324 28 Van Horne Letterbooks, No. 8, "Statement of Earnings and Expenses, from 1st January to 30th Sept. 1884," Oct. 29, 1884.

325   8 Macdonald Papers, Vol. 269, Stephen to Macdonald, July 23, 1884.

325 36 *Ibid.*, Vol. 129, Tupper to Tilley, Nov. 28, 1884.

326 20 Gibbon, p. 278.

Chapter Eight

328 17 Quoted in Guillet, p. 137.

329 19 *Sentinel*, Dec. 8, 1883.

329 40 Fleming, *England and Canada*, p. 377.

330   4 CPR Archives, Biographical Note on Fleming.

331 26 Reprinted from Chicago *Tribune* in *Sentinel*, Sept. 1, 1883.

331 35 Van Horne Letterbooks, No. 1, 1882-83, Memorandum on gradients, undated, p. 2.

333 10 *Herald*, Calgary, Feb. 19, 1885.

333 27 Hansard, 1885, Moosomin *Courier*, March 12, 1885, quoted by Blake, p. 2601.

334   6 Keefer, p. 73.

334 26 Wheeler, *Canadian Alpine Journal*, p. 41.

334 40 Phillips Papers, "A Winter Trip on the Canadian Pacific Railway," by Michael Phillips.

335 13 Keefer, pp. 72-73.

335 20 Pugsley, Aug. 15, 1930.

336 25 Lewis.

336 32 Bone, p. 104.

339 16 *News*, April 25, 1884.

340   2 Dewdney Papers, PAC, Vol. 6, "T.Z." to Riel, May 20, 1884.

341   9 Steele, *Forty Years in Canada*, p. 93.

341 21 *Sun*, Winnipeg, June 29, 1883.

342 18 Macdonald Papers, Vol. 107, Hayter Reed to Edgar Dewdney, Aug. 23, 1884 (copy).

342 20 *Ibid.*, S. Vankoughnet to Dewdney, Nov. 24, 1884.

342 22 *Ibid.*, Dewdney to Vankoughnet, Dec. 1, 1884 (enclosure).

342 25 Pope, *Correspondence*, Macdonald to Donald A. Smith, Sept. 5, 1884, pp. 321-322; Macdonald to Fred White, Sept. 15, 1884, p. 325.

342 35 Dewdney Papers, PAC, Vol. 1, copy of letter to Major Crozier from Sgt. H. Keenan, Sept. 25, 1884.

343   6 *Ibid.*, Fr. André to Dewdney, Feb. 6, 1885.

343 11 *Return to an Address*, Deposition of Charles Nolin, p. 392.

343 17 *Ibid.*, Deposition of Vital Fourmond, p. 395.

343 28 Dewdney Papers, PAC, Vol. 1, Crozier to Dewdney, Jan. 7, 1885 (copy).

344   4 *Ibid.*, Vol. 4, McDowell to Dewdney, Dec. 24, 1884.

344 30 *Ibid.*

344 33 *Ibid.*, Vol. 1, Fr. André to Dewdney, Jan. 11, 1885.

344 36 *Ibid.*, Howe to Crozier, Dec. 24, 1884 (copy).

345   2 *Ibid.*, Fr. André to Dewdney, Jan. 11, 1885.

345 14 *Ibid.*, Crozier to Dewdney, Feb. 27, 1885.

446

347   4   *Return to an Address*, Deposition of Charles Nolin, p. 393.

347   6   Sessional Paper, No. 8A, Crozier to Irvine, May 29, 1885, p. 43.

347   12   Dewdney Papers, PAC, Vol. 3, Dewdney to Macdonald, March 22, 1885.

347   14   *Ibid.*, Macdonald to Dewdney, March 23, 1885 (copy).

347   17   *Ibid.*, (telegram).

347   23   Sessional Paper, No. 8A, Crozier to Irvine, May 29, 1885.

347   35   *Ibid.*, Irvine to Macdonald, April 1, 1885.

348   18   Howard, p. 391.

349   12   Pope, *Correspondence*, Macdonald to Tupper, Jan. 24, 1885, p. 332.

349   16   Hughes Manuscript, p. 139.

349   25   Macdonald Papers, Vol. 269, Stephen to Macdonald, Jan. 9, 1885.

349   30   Hughes Manuscript, p. 139.

349   37   Macdonald Papers, Vol. 259, Rose to Macdonald, Jan. 22, 1885.

350   10   Pope, *Correspondence*, p. 330.

350   37   Macdonald Papers, Vol. 269, Stephen to Macdonald, Jan. 17, 1885.

351   3   *Ibid.*, Jan. 14, 1885.

351   15   *Ibid.*, Jan. 20, 1885.

351   29   Pope, *Correspondence*, Macdonald to Tupper, Jan. 24, 1885, p. 331.

351   33   Macdonald Papers, Vol. 269, Macdonald to Stephen, Jan. 20, 1885.

351   37   *Ibid.*, Stephen to Macdonald, Jan. 20, 1885.

352   3   Bonar, quoting Randolph Bruce, Lieutenant-Governor of B.C., who was told the story by Van Horne.

352   20   Coleman, p. 14.

352   29   Macdonald Papers, Vol. 269, Stephen to Macdonald, Feb. 9, 1885.

353   9   *Ibid.*

353   27   *Ibid.*

354   1   Tyler Papers, Tyler to wife, Aug. 29, 1888.

354   17   *Mail*, March 2, 1885.

354   20   Saunders, Vol. 2, Stephen to Tupper, March 11, 1885, p. 47.

354   24   Macdonald Papers, Vol. 269, Stephen to Macdonald, March 14, 1885.

354   40   Tupper Papers, Vol. 6, Macdonald to Tupper, March 17, 1885.

355   10   Vaughan, p. 120.

355   35   Hughes Manuscript, p. 142.

356   6   *Ibid.*, p. 145B.

356   19   Vaughan, p. 179.

356   21   Hughes Manuscript, p. 146.

357   11   Skelton, *Laurier*, pp. 276-277.

357   14   Vaughan, p. 121.

357   32   Skelton, *Laurier*, p. 277.

358   2   Caron Papers, Vol. 192, Caron to Henry Abbott, March 24, 1885.

358   5   *Ibid.*, Caron to Van Horne, March 24, 1885.

358   8   *Ibid.*, Abbott to Caron, March 25, 1885.

358   11   *Ibid.*, Caron to Abbott, March 27, 1885.

358   16   Macdonald Papers, Vol. 269, Stephen to Macdonald, March 26, 1885.

359   14   *British Whig*, March 26, 1885.

359   18   *Globe*, March 30, 1885.

360   9   Caron Papers, Caron to Abbott, March 27, 1885.

361   4   *Globe*, March 28, 1885.

361   25   *Ibid.*, March 31, 1885.

362   2   *Ibid.*

362   4   *Ibid.*

362   31   *Ibid.*

363   11   *Mail*, March 31, 1885.

363   23   *Globe*, March 31, 1885.

363   37   *British Whig*, April 1, 1885.

363   37   *Ibid.*

364   4   *Citizen*, April 1, 1885.

364   5   *Globe*, April 3, 1885.

364   9   *Citizen*, April 4, 1885.

365   10   *Morning Chronicle*, April 7, 1885.

365   18   *Ibid.*, April 14, 1885.

365   26   *Ibid.*, April 3, 1885.

page line

365 34 *Ibid.*, April 3, 1885.
365 39 *Ibid.*
366   9 *Ibid.*, April 13, 1885.
366 16 *Globe*, March 31, 1885.
366 18 *British Whig*, March 28, 1885.
366 22 *Citizen*, April 1, 1885.
367 28 *Morning Chronicle*, April 1, 1885.
367 40 Van Horne Letterbooks, No. 11, Van Horne to William Whyte, April 23, 1885.
369   6 *Globe*, April 6, 1885.
370   4 *Ibid.*, April 13, 1885.
371   1 *Ibid.*
372 19 *Ibid.*
372 23 *Ibid.*, April 11, 1885.
372 38 *Ibid.*, April 13, 1885.
373   1 Chambers, p. 93.
373 10 *Globe*, April 6, 1885.
373 16 *Ibid.*, April 15, 1885.
373 18 *Ibid.*, April 23, 1885.
373 26 *War Claims Commission Report.*
373 40 Howard, p. 101.
374   7 *Globe*, April 13, 1885.
374 10 *Ibid.*
374 13 *Ibid.*
374 25 Armstrong Manuscript, p. 167.
375   3 *Globe*, April 18, 1885.
375 10 *Sentinel*, April 10, 1885.
375 30 Denison, *Soldiering in Canada*, p. 274.
376 24 Berger, pp. 12-22.
376 35 Denison, *Soldiering in Canada*, pp. 273-276.
377 32 *Morning Chronicle*, May 5, 1885.
377 39 *Ibid.*, May 1, 1885.
378 15 *Mail*, April 9, 1885.
378 19 *Globe*, April 28, 1885.
378 33 Archer, April 6, 1885.
379   2 *Mail*, April 9, 1885.
379 10 *Globe*, April 23, 1885.
379 18 Archer, April 6, 1885.

page line **Chapter Nine**

382 28 *Globe*, April 11, 1885.
383   7 *Morning Chronicle*, May 1, 1885.
383 10 Roberts, p. 48.
383 19 *Morning Chronicle*, May 18, 1885.
383 36 *Citizen*, April 15, 1885.
384   3 *Quarterly Review*, 1887, p. 138.
384 20 *Globe*, April 25, 1885.
385 20 *War Claims Commission Report*, Nov. 3, 1886.
385 24 Van Horne Letterbooks, No. 11, Van Horne to Caron, April 11, 1885.
385 35 *Ibid.*
386 17 Macdonald Papers, Vol. 269, Stephen to Macdonald, March 26, 1885.
387 13 Hughes Manuscript, p. 146A.
387 29 Pope, *Day of Sir John*, p. 152.
388 17 *Sunday World*, Toronto, May 18, 1918.
388 36 Preston, p. 140.
389   2 *Sunday World*, Toronto, May 18, 1918.
389 17 Macdonald Papers, Vol. 269, Stephen to Macdonald, April 15, 1885.
390   3 *Ibid.*, April 9, 1885.
390 11 *Ibid.*, April 11, 1885.
390 12 *Ibid.*, April 15, 1885.
390 23 *Ibid.*, Stephen to Pope, April 16, 1885.
390 31 *Herald*, Calgary, Feb. 17, 1885.
391 16 Steele, *Forty Years in Canada*, p. 195.
391 27 *Ibid.*, p. 196.
391 35 Steele, *Policing*, p. 38.
392   8 Steele, *Forty Years in Canada*, p. 197.
392 33 Bone, pp. 104-106.
393   3 Steele's description of the Beavermouth strike is to be found on pp. 197-201 of *Forty Years in Canada.*
395   4 Macdonald Papers, Vol. 269, Stephen to Pope, April 16, 1885.
395 10 Gibbon, p. 287.
396   5 Willison, p. 196.
397   4 Stephen Papers. Macdonald to Stephen, May 26, 1885.

page line

397   5   Pope, *Correspondence*, p. 331.

397 14 Macdonald Papers, Vol. 129, Macdonald to C. F. Smithers, April 24, 1885.

397 24 *Ibid.*, Vol. 269, Stephen to Macdonald, April 30, 1885.

397 27 *Ibid.*

397 32 *Ibid.*, Vol. 268, Drinkwater to Macdonald, April 27, 1885.

397 38 *Ibid.*, Vol. 269, Stephen to Macdonald, May 1, 1885.

398   4 *Ibid.*, May 4, 1885.

398 18 Quoted in Creighton, *The Old Chieftain*, Vol. 2, p. 427.

398 24 Macdonald Papers, Vol. 269, May 9, 1885.

398 32 Tupper Papers, Vol. 6, Stephen to Tupper, April 30, 1885.

399   2 Denison, *Canada's First Bank*, Vol. 1, p. 224.

399 12 *Globe*, May 22, 1885.

399 26 *Ibid.*

400   6 Macdonald Papers, Vol. 269, Stephen to Macdonald, May 12, 1885.

400 34 Morris, pp. 57-58.

400 40 Stephen Papers, Macdonald to Stephen, May 26, 1885.

401 11 Tupper Papers, Vol. 6, Schreiber to Tupper.

401 13 Tyler Papers, Tyler to wife, June 12, 1885.

401 19 *Ibid.*, June 24, 1885.

401 35 Macdonald Papers, Vol. 269, Stephen to Macdonald, June 18, 1885.

402   4 Saunders, Macdonald to Tupper, Feb. 27, 1885, Vol. 2, p. 46.

402 14 Hansard, 1885, p. 2504.

page line

402 16 Pope, *Correspondence*, p. 331.

402 26 Vaughan, p. 129.

402 27 *Ibid.*

403 11 Skelton, *Laurier*, Vol. 1, p. 281.

403 22 Saunders, Tupper to Macdonald, July 10, 1885, Vol. 2, p. 59.

404 19 *Morning Chronicle*, May 5, 1885.

404 25 *Ibid.*

406 23 Daem and Dickey, p. 8.

406 29 *Ibid.*, p. 9.

407   9 MacLeod Papers. See Folder 5 for relevant correspondence.

407 12 *Ibid.*, B.C. Government to Secretary of State, June 22, 1885.

407 32 Cambie Papers, Van Horne to Cambie, March 18, 1885.

408   4 *Ibid.*, June 20, 1885.

408 28 Van Horne Letterbooks, No. 9, Van Horne to Rogers, Dec. 8, 1884.

408 33 *Ibid.*, Van Horne to Beatty, Dec. 19, 1884.

409 11 Morley, p. 68.

409 14 *Ibid.*, p. 69.

409 40 *Ibid.*, p. 72.

411 11 Mallandaine.

413   8 Pugsley, June 15, 1930.

413 14 "A.M.D."

413 21 Vaughan, p. 131.

413 24 Van Horne Letterbooks, No. 12, Van Horne to J. C. McLagan, Sept. 10, 1885.

415 20 Fleming, in Wheeler's *The Selkirk Range*, Vol. I, p. 173.

416 16 Mallandaine.

416 27 Fleming in Wheeler's *The Selkirk Range*, Vol. 1, p. 173.

Bibliography

Unpublished Sources

Anon.	Manuscript, "The Good Old Days of Broadview," Public Archives of Canada.
Andracki, Stanislow	"The Immigration of Orientals into Canada." Unpublished Ph.D. thesis, Faculty of Graduate Studies and Research, McGill University, 1958.
Armstrong, Harry William Dudley	Manuscript, PAC.
Bilsland, W. W.	Manuscript, "A History of Revelstoke and the Big Bend," Public Archives of British Columbia.
Brown, Adam	Papers, PAC.
Cambie, Henry J.	Letter to J. M. R. Fairbairn, September 24, 1923, Vancouver Archives.
	Papers and Diary (privately held).
Campbell, Sir Alexander	Papers, PAC.
Caron, Joseph P.	Papers, PAC.
Dallin, Helen Marion	Manuscript, "What I Remember," 1884, PABC.
Dewdney, Edgar	Papers, PAC and Glenbow-Alberta Institute Museum.
Duncan, W. H.	Letter to Mrs. Austin Bothwell, Legislative Librarian, Regina.
Evans, W. H.	Memorandum, VA.
Hickson, Sir Joseph	Papers, PAC.
Holmes, W. H.	Manuscript, "Some Memories of the Construction of the CPR in the Fraser Canyon," PABC.
Hughes, Katherine	Manuscript, "Biography of Sir William Van Horne," PAC.
Hull, Raymond	Letter to H. T. Coleman, March 27, 1969.
Lorne, Marquis of	Papers, PAC.
Macdonald, Sir John A.	Papers, PAC.
Macleod, James Farquharson	Papers, Glenbow.
Mount Stephen, Lord	Letter to "Arthur," August 18, 1909, CPR Archives, Montreal.
Murdoch, George	Diary.
Pearce, William	Manuscript (privately held).
	Memo, November, 1924, CPRA.
	Papers, Public Archives of Saskatchewan.
Peters, F. W.	Papers, PABC.
Peyton, Charles Alfred	Papers, Public Archives of Manitoba.
Phillips, J. N.	Papers, PAC.
Smith, Marcus	Papers, PAC and PABC.
Stephen, George	Papers, PAC.

Taylor, James Wickes	Papers, PAC.
Tupper, Sir Charles	Papers, PAC.
Tway, Duane Converse	"The Influence of the Hudson's Bay Company upon Canada, 1870-1889. Unpublished Ph.D. thesis, University of California, 1963.
Tyler, Sir Henry W.	Papers, PAC.
Van Buskirk, George	Letters to his mother, Glenbow.
Van Horne, Sir William Cornelius	Letterbooks, PAC.
Vincent, Mrs. F. W.	Memorandum, PABC.
Weekes, Gladys Onderdonk	Letter to Mrs. W. O. Miller, August 23, 1934, PABC.
Wilson, T. E.	Manuscript, "The Last of the Pathfinders, as related to W. E. Round" (privately held).

Public Documents

Canada

Parliamentary Debates, 1871, and Debates of the House of Commons of the Dominion of Canada, 1881-1885 (Hansard).

Sessional Paper No. 23, 1880-81: Annual Report of the Minister of Railways and Canals for Fiscal Year 1st July, 1880 to 30th June, 1881, Ottawa, 1881.

Sessional Paper No. 31A, 1884: Second Session of the Fifth Parliament of the Dominion of Canada, Ottawa, 1884.

Report of the Royal Commission on Chinese Immigration, Ottawa, 1885.

Sessional Paper No. 8A: Report of the Commission of the North-West Mounted Police Force, 1885, Ottawa, 1886.

War Claims Commission Report, July 19, 1886.

Return to an Address for Documents re the North-West Rebellion, Ottawa, 1886.

Instrument No. DB 21001, Land Titles Office. Regina.

Sessional Paper No. 54: The Report of the Royal Commission on Chinese and Japanese Immigration, Session 1902, Ottawa, 1902.

Fleming, Sir Sandford

Progress Report on the Canadian Pacific Railway Exploratory Survey, Ottawa, 1872.

Canadian Pacific Railway, A Report of Progress on the Explorations and Surveys up to January, 1874, Ottawa, 1874.

British Columbia

Columbia River Exploration, 1865, New Westminster, 1866.

Columbia River Exploration, 1866, Victoria, n.d.

United States

U.S. Congress, Senate, Committee on Interstate Commerce. Transportation Interests of the United States and Canada. Statements taken before the Committee, Washington, 1890.

452

Newspapers and Periodicals

British Columbian	New Westminster, 1882
British Whig	Kingston, 1885
Bulletin	Edmonton, 1882–83
Citizen	Ottawa, 1885
Daily British Colonist and Victoria Chronicle	Victoria, 1878–80
Free Press	Ottawa, 1881–82
Free Press	Manitoba, 1881–85
Gazette	Fort Macleod, 1883
Gazette	Port Moody, 1883–84
Globe	Toronto, 1880–85
Herald	Saskatchewan, 1882–85
Herald	Calgary, 1883–85
Inland Sentinel	Emory, Yale, and Kamloops, 1880–85
Leader	Regina, 1883–84
Mail	Toronto, 1880–85
Morning Chronicle	Halifax, 1885
News	Moose Jaw, 1884
Sentinel	Thunder Bay, 1881–85
Standard	Montreal, 1908
Sun	Brandon, 1882–84
Sun	Winnipeg, 1881–84
Times	Winnipeg, 1880–83
World	Toronto, 1882

Published Sources

Anon.

Article on Lord Shaughnessy, Montreal *Standard*, January 4, 1908.

"I. G. Ogden, Finance King of the CPR," *Canadian Railroader*, Vol. X, No. 2 (June, 1926).

"Kamloops, 1812–1937," *Beaver*, Vol. XVII (June, 1937).

"Paddlewheels on the Frontier," *B.C. Outdoors Magazine*, February, 1968.

The Canadian Biographical Dictionary and Portrait Gallery of Eminent and Self-Made Men, 2 vols., Toronto, 1880–81.

"The Indians Liked Lemonade," Regina *Leader-Post*, September 29, 1936.

"The Canadian Pacific Railway," *Quarterly Review*, January, 1887.

	Obituary of Frank Smith, Toronto *World*, May, 1918.
	A Year in Manitoba, London, 1881 (pamphlet).
Allard, Jason O., and McKelvie, B.A.	"Breaking Trail for Iron Horse," *Maclean's*, August 1, 1929.
"A.M.D."	"The Last Spike," Vancouver *Province*, November 17, 1933.
Archer, John H., ed.	"Recollections, Reflections and Items from the Diary of Captain A. Hamlyn Todd," *Saskatchewan History*, Vol. XV, No. 1 (Winter, 1962).
Barneby, W. Henry	*Life and Labour in the Far, Far West; Being Notes of a Tour in the Western States, British Columbia, Manitoba, and the North-West Territory*, London, 1884.
Begg, Alexander	*A Reply to a Series of Articles in the Money Market Revue upon the Canadian Pacific Railway*, London, 1882 (pamphlet).
Berger, Carl	*The Sense of Power*, Toronto, 1970.
Bernard, Kenneth	"Lord Strathcona," *Wide World Magazine*, March, 1907.
Biggar, E. B.	*Anecdotal Life of Sir John A. Macdonald*, Montreal, 1891.
Bonar, James C.	*The Inauguration of Trans Canada Transportation*, Montreal, 1936 (pamphlet).
Bone, P. Turner	*When the Steel Went Through; Reminiscences of a Railroad Pioneer*, Toronto, 1947.
Boulton, A. C. Forster	*Adventures, Travels and Politics*, London, 1939.
Boulton, Major C. A.	*Reminiscences of the North-West Rebellions*, Toronto, 1886.
Bradwin, Edmund W.	*The Bunkhouse Man, a Study of Work and Pay in the Camps of Canada, 1903–1914*, New York, 1928.
Breton, Paul-Emile, O.M.I.	*The Big Chief of the Prairies: the Life of Father Lacombe*, trans. by H. A. Dempsey, ed. by G. A. Morgan, Edmonton, 1955.
Bridle, Augustus	*Sons of Canada; Short Studies of Characteristic Canadians*, Toronto, 1916.
Brooks, Edwin J.	"Edwin J. Brooks' Letters," Part I, *Saskatchewan History*, Vol. X, No. 3 (Autumn, 1957); Part II, Vol. XI, No. 1 (Winter, 1958).
Buckingham, William, and Ross, George M.	*The Hon. Alexander Mackenzie: His Life and Times*, Toronto, 1892.
Butler, Lieutenant William Francis	*Report of His Journey from Fort Garry to Rocky Mountain House*, Ottawa, 1871.
Canadian Pacific Railway Company	CPR *Reports*, 1881–89.
	Souvenir Menu, Chateau Lake Louise, Seventy-Fifth Anniversary Luncheon, August 21, 1957.
	Letter [of George Stephen] to the Shareholders of the Grand Trunk Railroad, London, April 5, 1883.

454

Cambie, Henry J.

"Reminiscences of Pioneer Life in the West," *The Engineering Journal* (Journal of the Engineering Institute of Canada), Vol. III (October, 1920).

Carter, C. F.

"The Passing of the Big Hill," *World's Work*, Vol. XX (June, 1910).

Chambers, Capt. Ernest J.

The Royal Grenadiers, a Regimental History of the Tenth Infantry Regiment of the Active Militia of Canada, Toronto, 1904.

Charlesworth, Hector

Candid Chronicles, Toronto, 1925.

Chittenden, Newton H.

Chittenden's Guide, or Travels through British Columbia, Victoria, 1882.

Clews, Henry

Fifty Years in Wall Street, New York, 1908.

Coleman, D'Alton C.

Lord Mount Stephen (1829-1921) and the Canadian Pacific Railway, New York, 1945 (pamphlet of the Newcomen Society).

Collard, Edgar A.

Canadian Yesterdays, Toronto, 1955.

Montreal Yesterdays, Toronto, 1962.

Collins, J. E.

Canada under the Administration of Lord Lorne, Toronto, 1884.

Creighton, Donald

John A. Macdonald: the Young Politician, Toronto, 1952.

John A. Macdonald: the Old Chieftain, Toronto, 1955.

Daem, M., and Dickey, E. E.

A History of Early Revelstoke, Revelstoke, B.C., 1962.

Daluaine

The Syndicate: What Is It? A Story for Young Canadians, Ottawa, n.d. (pamphlet).

Davin, Nicholas Flood

The Irishman in Canada, Toronto, 1877.

Davis, May E.

"I Was a Pinafore Pioneer," *Chatelaine*, August, 1955.

Denison, George T.

Soldiering in Canada, Toronto, 1901.

Denison, Merrill

Canada's First Bank; a History of the Bank of Montreal, 2 vols., Toronto, 1966-67.

Dent, J. C.

The Canadian Portrait Gallery, 4 vols., Toronto, 1880-81.

Donkin, J. G.

Trooper and Redskin in the Far Northwest, London, 1889.

Dorian, Charles

The First Seventy-Five Years, a Headline History of Sudbury, Canada, Ilfracombe, Devon, c. 1958.

Drake, Earl G.

"Pioneer Journalism in Saskatchewan 1878-1887," Part 1, *Saskatchewan History*, Vol. V, No. 1, (Winter, 1952); "Some Characteristics of the Pioneer Press," Part 2, Vol. V, No. 2 (Spring, 1952).

Regina: the Queen City, Toronto, 1955.

Eager, Evelyn

"Our Pioneers Say . . . ," *Saskatchewan History*, Vol. VI, No. 1 (Winter, 1953).

Flaherty, Norman

"Rogers Pass – Scenic Wonder," *Vancouver Colonist*, Oct. 29, 1961.

Fleming, Sandford

England and Canada, London, 1884.

Appendix E in A. O. Wheeler, *The Selkirk Range*, Vol. I, Ottawa, 1905.

Gard, Anson A.

North Bay, the Gateway to Silverland, Toronto, 1909.

Gibbon, John Murray

Steel of Empire, Toronto, 1935.

Gilbert, Heather

Awakening Continent; the Life of Lord Mount Stephen, Vol. I, Aberdeen, 1965.

Glazebrook, G. P. de T.

A History of Transportation in Canada, Toronto, 1938.

Grant, George Monro

"The C.P.R., by the Kicking Horse Pass and the Selkirks," *Week*, 1883 and 1884.

"The Canada Pacific Railway," *Century Illustrated Monthly Magazine*, Vol. XXX (October, 1885).

Grant, William Lawson, and Hamilton, Frederick

George Monro Grant, Toronto, 1905.

Guillet, Edwin C.

Toronto from Trading Post to Great City, Toronto, 1934.

Ham, George H.

Reminiscences of a Raconteur, Toronto, 1921.

Hamilton, Z. M. and M. A.

These are the Prairies, Regina, n.d.

Harkin, W. A., ed.

Political Reminiscences of the Right Honourable Sir Charles Tupper, Bart., London, 1914.

Hassard, Albert Richard

Famous Canadian Trials, Toronto, 1924.

Haydon, A. L.

The Riders of the Plains, Toronto, 1910.

Hedges, James B.

Building the Canadian West; the Land and Colonization Policies of the Canadian Pacific Railway, New York, 1939.

Hill, Alexander Staveley

From Home to Home; Autumn Wanderings in the North-West in the Years 1881, 1882, 1883, 1884, London, 1885.

Hill, Robert B.

Manitoba: History of Its Early Settlement, Development, and Resources, Toronto, 1890.

Holbrook, Stewart H.

The Story of American Railroads, New York, 1947.

Howard, Joseph Kinsey

Strange Empire; a Narrative of the Northwest, New York, 1952.

Howey, Florence R.

Pioneering on the CPR, Ottawa, 1938.

Hughes, Katherine

Father Lacombe: the Black-Robe Voyageur, Toronto, 1920.

Innis, Harold

A History of the Canadian Pacific Railway, Toronto, 1923.

"Ishmael"

Financial Notes, n.p., c. 1881.

Kavanagh, Martin

The Assiniboine Basin, Winnipeg, 1946.

Keefer, Thomas

"Address on the CPR," American Society of Civil Engineers *Transactions*, Vol. XIX (August, 1888).

Kelly, Nora

Men of the Mounted, Toronto, 1949.

Kennedy, George

"When History Was A-Making," Kamloops *Sentinel*, Souvenir Edition, May 29, 1905.

Kennedy, W. K. P., comp.	*North Bay Past – Present – Prospective* [Toronto], 1961.
LeBourdais, D. M.	*Sudbury Basin; the Story of Nickel*, Toronto, 1953.
Lewis, H. H.	"Sir William C. Van Horne," *Ainslie's Magazine*, reprinted in *Daily World*, December 29, 1900.
Lovett, H. A.	*Canada and the Grand Trunk, 1829-1924*, Montreal, 1924.
Lower, A. R. M.	*Canadians in the Making*, Toronto, 1958.
MacBeth, R. G.	*The Romance of the Canadian Pacific Railway*, Toronto, 1924.
Macdonald, Ian	"Rails Along the Fraser," Vancouver *Sunday Sun*, January 22, 1955.
McDougall, J. Lorne	*Canadian Pacific; a Brief History*, Montreal, 1968.
McGregor, D. A.	"Onderdonk, Forgotten Man of the Western Railway," Vancouver *Province*, June 24, 1954.
MacGregor, J. G.	*Edmonton Trader*, Toronto, 1963.
MacKay, Douglas	*The Honourable Company*, New York, 1936.
McKelvie, B. A.	"Thousands of Last Spikes at Craigellachie," Vancouver *Province*, November 18, 1944.
	"They Routed the Rockies at Summation Point," Vancouver *Province*, February 3, 1945.
and Allard, Jason O.	"Breaking Trail for the Iron Horse," *Maclean's*, August 1, 1929.
McLagan, J. C.	"Sketch of the Rise and Progress of Winnipeg," in John Macoun, *Manitoba and the Great North-West*, Guelph, 1882.
MacLeod, Margaret Arnett	"Winnipeg and the Hudson's Bay Company," *Beaver*, 280 (June, 1949).
MacNutt, W. Stewart	*Days of Lorne*, Fredericton, 1955.
Macoun, John	*Autobiography of John Macoun, M.A., Canadian Explorer and Naturalist, 1831-1920*, Ottawa, 1922.
	Manitoba and the Great North-West, Guelph, 1882.
McWilliams, Margaret	*Manitoba Milestones*, Toronto, 1928.
Mallandaine, Col. Edward	"Youngest Boy to See 'Last Spike' Driven Still Alive," Revelstoke *Review*, June 29, 1940.
Markwell, Mary	"An Adventure in Railway Building," *Saturday Night*, March 1, 1930.
Martin, Chester	"Our Kingdom for a Horse: the Railway Land Grant System in Western Canada," Canadian Historical Association *Report*, Toronto, 1935.
Martin, Robert	"The Diary of Robert Martin," Part 1, *Saskatchewan History*, Vol. VI, No. 2 (Spring, 1953).
Matthews, Major J. C.	"One Man Stands Up for CPR," Vancouver *Province*, September 26, 1966.
Mavor, James	"Van Horne and His Sense of Humour," *Maclean's*, November 15, 1923.

457

Meyers, L. W.
"Via the Fraser Canyon," *Beaver*, 296 (Winter, 1965).

Miller, Arthur Rowe
"The Diary of Arthur Rowe Miller," *Saskatchewan History*, Vol. X, No. 2 (Spring, 1957).

Moberly, Walter
The Rocks and Rivers of British Columbia, London, 1885.

Journals, 1865-1866, in *Columbia River Exploration, 1865-66*, 2 vols., New Westminster, 1866, and Victoria, n.d.

Moody, John
The Railroad Builders, Vol. 38, *Chronicles of America*, New Haven, Conn., 1919.

Moore, John F.
"Golden Age of Railroading," *Vancouver Sun*, October 4, 1952.

Morgan, Henry James
Canadian Men and Women of the Time, rev. ed., Toronto, 1912.

Morley, Alan
Vancouver: from Milltown to Metropolis, Vancouver, 1961.

Morris, Keith
The Story of the Canadian Pacific Railway, London, 1920.

Morse, Frank P.
Cavalcade of the Rails, New York, 1940.

Oliver, William
"Westward Ho," Lethbridge *Herald*, July 11, 1935 (Golden Jubilee Edition).

Ormsby, Margaret A.
British Columbia: A History, Toronto, 1958.

Parker, William F.
Daniel McNeil Parker, M.D.: His Ancestry and a Memoir of His Life, Toronto, 1910.

Perry, J. Harvey
Taxes, Tariffs & Subsidies, Vol. I, Toronto, 1955.

Phelan, Josephine
The Bold Heart; the Story of Father Lacombe, Toronto, 1956.

Pope, Sir Joseph
Memoirs of the Right Honourable Sir John Alexander Macdonald, G.C.B., First Prime Minister of the Dominion of Canada, 2 vols., Ottawa, 1894 (reprint Toronto, 1930).

The Correspondence of Sir John Macdonald; Selections from the Correspondence of the Right Honourable Sir J. A. Macdonald, G.C.B., First Prime Minister of the Dominion of Canada, Toronto, 1921.

The Day of Sir John Macdonald: a Chronicle of the First Prime Minister of the Dominion, Vol. 29, *Chronicles of Canada*, Toronto, 1915.

Pope, Maurice, ed.
Public Servant: the Memoirs of Sir Joseph Pope, Toronto, 1960.

Powers, J. W.
The History of Regina, Regina, 1887.

Preston, W. T. R.
Strathcona and the Making of Canada, New York, 1915.

Prothero, Ernest
Railways of the World, London, 1914.

Pugsley, Edmund E.
"Pioneers of the Steel Trail," Part 2, "Two Streaks of Rust," *Maclean's*, June 15, 1930; Part 4, "Fighting the Snow Menace," *Maclean's*, August 15, 1930.

Pyle, Joseph Gilpin   *The Life of James J. Hill*, 2 vols., New York, 1916.

Roberts, Charles G. D., and Tunnell, Arthur L., eds.   *A Standard Dictionary of Canadian Biography*, Vol. I, Toronto, 1934.

Roberts, Morley   *The Western Avernus*, London, 1887.

Robinson, Noel   "The Story of My Life," as told by Henry J. Cambie, *Daily Colonist*, October 12, 1914, Victoria.

"Walter Moberly knew B.C. as 'Sea of Mountains,' " *Daily Province*, January 5, 1946.

     and Walter Moberly   *Blazing the Trail Through the Rockies*, Vancouver, 1915.

Roe, F. G.   "Early Opinions on the 'Fertile Belt' of Western Canada," *Canadian Historical Review*, Vol. XXVII (June, 1946).

"An Unsolved Problem of Canadian History," Canadian Historical Association *Report*, Toronto, 1936.

Rogers, Albert   Appendix E in A. O. Wheeler, *The Selkirk Range*, Vol. I, Ottawa, 1905.

Rose, George Maclean   *A Cyclopaedia of Canadian Biography*, 2 vols., Toronto, 1886–91.

Ross, George W.   *Getting Into Parliament and After*, Toronto, 1913.

Rowles, Edith   "Bannock, Beans and Bacon: An Investigation of Pioneer Diet," *Saskatchewan History*, Vol. V, No. 1 (Winter, 1952).

Rutledge, J. L.   "Binding the West with Bands of Steel: The Eventful Story of Michael John Haney," *Maclean's*, April 15 and May 1, 1920.

Saunders, E. M., ed.   *The Life and Letters of the Rt. Hon. Sir Charles Tupper, Bart., K.C.M.G.*, 2 vols., London, 1916.

Secretan, J. H. E.   *Canada's Great Highway: From the First Stake to the Last Spike*, London, 1924.

Shaw, Charles Aeneas   "A Prairie Gopher Makes Reply," Vancouver *Province*, October 7, 1934.

     and Hull, Raymond, ed.   *Tales of a Pioneer Surveyor*, Toronto, 1970.

Skelton, Oscar D.   *The Railway Builders: a Chronicle of Overland Highways*, Vol. 32, *Chronicles of Canada*, Toronto, 1916.

The Life and Letters of Sir Wilfrid Laurier, 2 vols., Toronto, 1921.

Stanley, George F. G.   "The Half-Breed 'Rising' of 1875," *Canadian Historical Review*, Vol. XVII (1936).

The Birth of Western Canada: A History of the Riel Rebellions, Toronto, 1936.

Louis Riel, Toronto, 1963.

Starr, John W., Jr.   *One Hundred Years of American Railroading*, New York, 1928.

Steele, Harwood   *Policing the Arctic*, Toronto, 1936.

Steele, Samuel B.   *Forty Years in Canada*, Toronto, 1915.

Stevens, G. R.   *Canadian National Railways*, Vol. I, *Sixty Years of Trial and Error, 1836-1896*, Toronto, 1960.

Stevens, John F.   *An Engineer's Recollections* (reprinted from *Engineering News-Record*), New York, 1936.

Stobie, Margaret   "The Formative Years: 1. Struggle for Rights," *Beaver*, 286 (Summer, 1955).

Stubbs, Roy St. George   *Lawyers and Laymen of Western Canada*, Toronto, 1939.

Styles, B. R.   "History of Rogers Pass," Armstrong *Advertiser*, May 21, 1964.

Taché, Louis J. C. H., ed.   *Men of the Day: a Canadian Portrait Gallery*, Montreal, c. 1890.

Taggart, Kathleen M.   "The First Shelter of Early Pioneers," *Saskatchewan History*, Vol. XI, No. 3 (Autumn, 1958).

Thompson, Norman, and Edgar, J. H.   *Canadian Railway Development from the Earliest Times*, Toronto, 1933.

Thompson, W. T.   "Adventures of a Surveyor in the Canadian North-West, 1880-1883," *Saskatchewan History*, Vol. III, No. 3 (Autumn, 1950).

Trotter, Beecham, and Hawkes, Arthur   *A Horseman and the West*, Toronto, 1925.

Turner, A. R.   "Wascana Creek and the 'Pile o' Bones,' " *Saskatchewan History*, Vol. XIX, No. 3 (Autumn, 1966).

Turner, John Peter   *The North-West Mounted Police, 1873-1893*, Vol. I, Ottawa, 1950.

Van Horne, William Cornelius   Preface to Katherine Hughes, *Father Lacombe: the Black-Robe Voyageur*, Toronto, 1920.

Vaughan, Walter   *The Life and Work of Sir William Van Horne*, New York, 1920.

Veritas, Philo [pseud. of T. Montaltus]   *The Canadian Pacific Railway: an Appeal to Public Opinion against the Railway Being Carried across the Selkirk Range*, Montreal, 1885 (pamphlet).

Villard, Henry   *Memoirs of Henry Villard, Journalist and Financier, 1835-1900*, 2 vols., London, 1904.

Waite, Peter B.   *Arduous Destiny: Canada, 1874-1896*, Toronto, 1971.

       "Sir John A. Macdonald: the Man," *Dalhousie Review*, Vol. XLVII (Summer, 1967).

Wallace, W. S.   *The Dictionary of Canadian Biography*, Toronto, 1926.

Ward, Norman   "Davin and the Founding of the *Leader*," *Saskatchewan History*, Vol. VI, No. 1 (Winter, 1953).

Warkentin, John, ed.   *The Western Interior of Canada: a Record of Geographic Discovery (1612-1917)*, Toronto, 1964.

Wheeler, A. O.	*The Selkirk Range*, Vol. I, Ottawa, 1905.
	"Rogers Pass at the Summit of the Selkirks," *Canadian Alpine Journal*, 1929.
White, William	"I Might Have Owned Regina," *Maclean's*, June, 1935.
Williams, J. B.	"When Legal Toils Reached Out for Andrew Onderdonk," Vancouver *Province*, May 9, 1936.
Willison, Sir J. S.	*Reminiscences, Political and Personal*, Toronto, 1919.
Willson, Beckles	*The Life of Lord Strathcona and Mount Royal (1820-1914)*, London, 1915.
	Lord Strathcona: the Story of His Life, London, 1902.
Windsor, Thomas C.	"Hell's Gate Conquest – the Story of the Skuzzy," *B.C. Magazine*, 1956.

Acknowledgements

I again want to express my gratitude to the staffs of the Metropolitan Toronto Central Public Library and the Public Archives of Canada, where most of the research for this book was done. In many cases they went well beyond the call of normal duty to assist me – with unfailing cheerfulness. I received the same co-operation from the Public Archives of British Columbia, the unique Glenbow Museum in Calgary, the Public Archives of Saskatchewan, the Public Archives of Manitoba, and the Public Archives of Ontario. My thanks also go again to Mrs. Marian Childs of the Fort William Public Reference Library.

My research assistant for the first eighteen months of the preparation of the two volumes of *The Great Railway* was Norman Kelly, M.A. Without his help, his advice, and his insights, I could not have completed these books in the time at my disposal.

I again wish to thank Norma Carrier, who transcribed so many of Mr. Kelly's notes, Ennis Halliday Armstrong, my former secretary, and her successor Anne Michie, whose job it was to transcribe and collate notes, search out hundreds of books and official documents, and (in Mrs. Michie's case) check all manuscript sources and quotations and prepare bibliographies.

I want especially to thank Michael Bliss of the University of Toronto history department for his extremely valuable comments on an earlier draft of the manuscript and for drawing my attention to George Stephen's letter to John A. Macdonald in 1890, outlining his contributions to the Conservative cause.

The book was read in both typescript and proof by my wife, Janet, whose unfailing eye for grammatical inconsistency, typographical error, syllogism, and fuzzy construction has been, for a quarter of a century, a bonus of our marriage; Janet Craig performed the same job for McClelland and Stewart, with awesome efficiency.

Two CPR history buffs, T. E. Price of Vancouver and his son Alex, of Calgary, were of enormous help in many ways, especially in the matter of unpublished material. With the former's assistance I was able to read the papers of Henry Cambie, which are used here through the kind offices of

463

the owner, Mrs. John D. Ross. Alex Price obtained for me a copy of Tom Wilson's manuscript, set down in 1931 with the help of W. E. Round. I have the permission of Tom's son, Ed Wilson, to quote from it. My gratitude also goes to William Pearce for lending me copies of his father's unpublished manuscripts, to Hamilton Miles for background on his uncle, Lauchlan Hamilton, and to Jenny Lee for information about her grandfather, Pon Git Cheng.

Of secondary sources listed in the Bibliography, special mention must be made of Walter Vaughan's *Life of Sir William Van Horne*, the first volume of Heather Gilbert's biography of George Stephen, *Awakening Continent*, John Murray Gibbon's *Steel of Empire*, Harold Innis's *History of the Canadian Pacific Railway*, and last, but certainly not least, Donald Creighton's biography of John A. Macdonald, especially the second volume, *The Old Chieftain*.

As outlined in the acknowledgements for *The National Dream*, the officers of the Canadian Pacific Railway were of considerable help both to me and to Mr. Kelly, answering many queries and assisting us both in our trips across Canada. But this is in no sense a "company history." The CPR did not open all of its files to us. I was not able to see the complete letters of Sir William Van Horne, from which selected excerpts are available at the Public Archives, or any of the other correspondence still in the company's hands. The reason given to me was that it would not be in the public interest to make such documents available. With that attitude, of course, I must vigorously disagree. Anything that has to do with the beginnings of Canada's first transcontinental railway is in the public interest. After all, that is what these books have been about.

Index

465

469

26, 34, 43-7 *passim*, 86, 87, 96, 101, 166, 170, 182, 184, 247-8, 255, 271, 314, 321, 353; hobbies, 47; physical description, 45-6; relationship with Rogers, 140, 142; relationship with Van Horne, 86
Hill, Robert, 80
Hincks, Sir Francis, 358
Hind, Henry Youle, 14, 16
Hobourg, Mrs., 240
Hogg, James, 169, 170, 172, 174, 180
Hohenlohe, Prince, 245
Holmes, W. H., 196, 202
Holt, Herbert Samuel, 105, 170, 284, 285, 289-90, 292, 333, 392
Holt, Tim, 284
Holt City *see* Lake Louise station
Holy Trinity Church (Winnipeg), 57-8
Hong Kong, 198, 199
Hope, 201, 215
Horetzky, Charles, 157, 169
Howe, Joseph, 343, 344
Howe, Joseph (Nova Scotia), 358
Howey, Dr. William H., 283
Howse Pass, 15, 17, 142, 157, 159, 161, 163, 164, 179, 180
Hudson Bay, 342
Hudson's Bay Company, 6, 15, 56, 59, 75, 115, 120, 123, 124, 128, 131, 132, 270, 339
Hughes, Katherine, 387
Humboldt, 12
Huntington, Silas, 280-1
Huntington, Stewart, 280
Hurd, M. F., 160
Hyndman (Roger's party), 150, 151, 152, 153, 160

I. G. Baker, Co., 151, 152, 166, 243
Illecillewaet Glacier, 146, 173, 332, 334
Illecillewaet River, 143, 145, 146, 148, 160, 332, 337
Independent (Bobcaygeon), 73
Independent Order of Templars, 213
Indian Head, 120
Indians, effects of railway on, 232-7, 404-6

"Indictment Hole," 191
Infantry School, 360
Ingersoll, 364
Inland Sentinel (Yale), 160, 192, 193, 209, 309
Insley, Ashbury, 190
Intercolonial Railroad, 41
International (Emerson), 79
International Nickel Co., 282
Irvine, Lt.-Col. A. G., 237, 346, 347
Irving, John, 210, 211
Irving Steamboat Line, 210

Jackson, W. H., 342, 404
James, E. A., 95
Jackfish, 270, 300, 375-7 *passim*
"Jaws of Death Arch," 191
Jodson, W. L., 49
Johnson, Francis, 124
Johnston, George Hope, 394, 406-7
Journal (St. Catharines), 54

Kamloops, 15, 144, 145, 148, 179, 185, 187, 206, 289, 308, 310-12 *passim*, 333, 406-8 *passim*
Kamloops Lake, 9, 95, 187, 316
Kananaskis summit, 153, 157, 161
Kearney, Dennis, 185
Keefer, Mrs. George, 202
Keefers Station, 192
Keenan, Sergeant, 342
Kelly, Big Mouth, 212
Kelly, Long, 212
Kelly, Molly, 212
Kelly, Silent, 212
Kelly the Rake, 212
Kelvin, William Thompson, Lord, 287
Kennedy, George, 211
Kennedy, John S., 86, 130, 184, 248, 250, 271, 321
Kenora, 328
Kernighan, R. K., 98, 110
Kerr, Constable, 393
Khartoum, 330
Kicking Horse Pass, 15, 16, 64, 85, 113, 142, 148, 149, 157, 159, 160-5 *passim*, 168, 172, 174, 175, 179, 284, 291, 292
Kicking Horse River, 148, 149, 153, 155, 161, 180, 284, 288, 290,

292, 293, 295, 335, 410
Kildonan, 53, 72
King, E. H., 13
Kingston, 328, 357, 358-60 *passim*, 363, 366
Kittson, Norman, 184, 255
Klondike, 227
Knox Presbyterian Church (Winnipeg), 57
Kootenay Pass, 15, 142
Kootenay River, 145, 148
Kwang Tung province (China), 198, 200, 205

Labouchère, Henry, 36
Lacombe, Father Albert, 109, 165, 166, 235-7, 245, 246, 405
Lacombe, 182
Laggan *see* Lake Louise station
Laidlaw, H. B., 184
Lake Louise, 2, 20, 163, 328
Lake Louise station, 284, 285
Lake Nipigon, 43
Lake Nipissing, 8, 33, 43, 86, 133, 220, 270, 279-81 *passim*, 300, 318, 359
Lake of the Woods, 236
Lake Ramsey, 283
Lake Superior, 8, 17, 42, 43, 86, 136, 220, 247, 259, 270, 271, 274, 275, 277, 281, 300, 354-8 *passim*, 373, 385, 403, 406
Lake Wabigoon, 35, 277
"Land sharks," 27, 73
Land speculation, 24-7, 28-9, 52-64, 113, 115, 117, 244
Lane, Nat Jr., 190
Langdon, Gen. R. B., 101
Langdon (station), 182
Langdon and Shepard, 96, 104, 108, 228, 243
Langevin, Sir Hector, 262
Langevin (station), 182
Lansdowne, Lord, 207, 411
Lawson, Rev. Thomas, 30, 31
Leader (Regina), 230, 241, 242
Leask, John, 409
Lee, Thomas H., 314
Lee Chuck Co., 203
Lee Soon, 203
Left Hand, 405
Lester, Louise, 46

Lethbridge, 102, 151
Lewis, Sinclair, 119
Liquor traffic, 111, 239-43, 277-8, 287-8, 391
Lisgar, 59
Little, J. A., 81
Little, Jack, 295
Little Pic River, 373
Little Poplar, 405
Little Saskatchewan River, 73
Logan, Alexander, 63
London (Ont.), 135, 360, 364, 367, 388
Lorne, Marquis of, 7, 8, 35, 118
Lost Lake, 283
Lougheed, James, 229, 384
Loughrin, John, 282
Lucky Man, 405
Lytton, 189, 191, 200-1, 308, 310

McAra, Peter, 119
MacArthur Pass, 148-9
McBeth, Dave, 189
McConnell, Rinaldo, 282
McCreight, John Foster, 189
Macdonald, Constable, 333
Macdonald, Sir John A., 1, 7, 8, 14, 17, 20, 32-4 *passim*, 38-42 *passim*, 86, 87, 91, 96, 112-26 *passim*, 135, 162, 195-6, 230, 242, 253, 256-8 *passim*, 266-8 *passim*, 283, 302, 309, 317, 321-5 *passim*, 330-1, 344-52 *passim*, 358, 386-8 *passim*, 391, 396-401 *passim*, 405; and CPR financing, 126-33, 248-9, 251-4, 348-56, 389-90; and CPR resolutions (1884), 261-5; relationship with Grand Trunk, 134-5
Macdowall, D. H., 343, 344
McDougall, Dave, 152
McDougall, John, 152
McDougall, John A., 55, 75-6
McGee, Thomas D'Arcy, 209
McGillivray, Dan, 207
McIntyre, Duncan, 15, 33, 34, 85, 124, 130, 184, 251, 257, 267, 280, 321, 322
McKay, John, 348
McKay's Harbour, 272
McKellar's Harbour, 373, 375-7 *passim*
Mackenzie, Alexander, 2-3, 14, 263,

272, 283, 287, 298, 314, 413
Mackenzie, William, 290, 333, 392
McLagan, J. C., 58, 63
McLelan, Archibald, 351, 355, 389, 396
Macleod, James Farquharson, 407
McLeod, Roderick, 81
McMillan, Donald, 161
McNaughton, Andrew, 283
McNaughton (station), 283
Macoun, John, 13-15, 16, 18, 20, 22, 23, 182, 273
Macpherson, David, 338
McTavish, John, 2, 25, 40, 121, 124, 413, 415
McVicar, Dugald, 25, 29, 32
McVicar, John, 25-6, 29, 32
Magpie Camp, 370
Mail (Toronto), 212, 354, 361, 363
Major, C. G., 306
Mallandaine, Edward, 410-12, 414-16 *passim*
Malta, 72
Manchester (Man.), 72
Manitoba, 37, 80, 254, 256, 264, 297, 331, 338, 365; population, 72
Manitoba and North-West Farmers' Union, 254, 256, 297, 338
Manitoba and Southwestern Railroad, 41, 322
Manitoba Electric and Gas Light Co., 8
Manitoban, 289
Mann, Donald, 170, 290, 392
Maple Creek, 150, 234, 238
Maple Ridge, 201
Mara, John Andrew, 407-8
Mattawa River, 281
Mavor, James, 98
Medicine Hat, 12, 121, 226, 227, 229, 238, 239, 245, 313, 384
Métis, 331, 338-56 *passim*, 385, 395, 397, 405; and land survey, 339, 345, 347
Mexican Light, Heat and Power Co., 291
Michigan Central Railroad, 298, 385
Michipicoten, 278, 279, 318
Middleton, Major-Gen. Frederick Dobson, 347, 395, 397, 405
Midland Regiment, 363, 366

Miller, Arthur Rowe, 46
Mills, Darius O., 184, 185
Milwaukee and St. Paul Railroad, 96
Mining & Financial Register, 323
Minnedosa, 67, 72, 73
Mitchell, Peter, 265
Moberly, Frank, 278, 279
Moberly, Walter, 15, 143, 145, 157, 163, 164, 167, 169, 173, 278
Moberly (station), 182
Monashee Mountains *see* Gold Range
Money Market Review (London), 37, 136
Montreal, 34, 42, 137, 270, 296, 328, 360, 363, 365, 367, 389, 415
Moore, Capt. Billy, 210
Moore Steamboat Line, 210
Moose Jaw, 12, 21, 119, 121, 222, 226-30 *passim*, 233, 313, 328, 358, 384, 404, 409
Moose Jaw Bone Creek, 92, 117, 131, 142
Moosomin, 222, 223, 241
Morning Chronicle (Halifax), 365, 383
Morris, Alexander, 69
Morton, Levi P., 184
Morton, Bliss and Co., 184
Morton, Rose and Co., 131, 136
Mount Daly, 154
Mount Macdonald, 335
Mount Ogden, 295
Mount Sir Donald, 146
Mount Stephen, 314
Mountain City, 68, 72
Mountain Creek, 313, 392; bridge, 336
Mowat, Oliver, 133-4
Munro, George, 200, 413
Murdoch, William, 244
Murray, Thomas 282
Murray, William, 282
Murray Mine, 282, 283

Nation (New York), 39
Nazareth, 12
Nelsonville, 72
Nepigon, 300, 358, 377, 378
New Westminster, 116, 144, 199, 210, 215, 216, 408-10 *passim*

472

91, 115, 170, 231 265, 303, 305, 314, 408-9

Ross, George, 95, 252

Ross, James, 2, 142, 169-71 *passim*, 175, 179, 180, 260, 275, 285, 291, 390-4 *passim*, 406; background, 289

Ross, John, 96, 260, 270, 271, 275, 315, 316, 358, 360

Rosser, Gen. Thomas Lafayette, 11, 13, 20, 25-8, *passim*, 44, 56, 89-91, 92, 113, 116, 140, 159, 182, 404; character, 23-4; physical description, 23

Rossport, 273

Rousseau, Théo, 301

Rowan, James, 169

Royal Commission on Chinese Immigration, report (1885), 198

Royal Grenadiers, 360, 362, 372-4 *passim*

Ruddick, Constable, 406-7

Russell House (Ottawa), 386

Ryan, John, 10

Sage, Russell, 353

St. Albert, 339

St. Boniface, 46, 52, 53, 59, 62

St. James, 53

St. John's (Man.), 53

St. Laurent (Sask.), 331, 339, 342, 346

St. Paul, 67, 76, 78, 102, 104, 149, 255

St. Paul and Pacific Railroad, 6, 13, 26, 126, 129, 352-3, 414

St. Paul, Minneapolis and Manitoba Railway, 9, 18, 23, 42, 44, 86, 247, 255, 257

St. Vincent, 72, 76, 255

Saltcoats, 224

San Francisco, 144, 185, 196, 217, 303

Santa Fe Railroad, 293

Sarnia, 33

Saskatchewan, 337, 345, 391

Saskatchewan Herald, 346

Saskatchewan Rebellion, 338-47, 356-9, 385, 395-7, 401, 404-6; Eastern militia, 360-79; militia journey to North West, 367-79

Saskatchewan River, 90, 331, 340

Sault Ste. Marie, 34, 41, 43, 44, 86, 279, 282

Savona's Ferry, 9, 142, 185, 187, 310-12 *passim*

Scarth, William B., 121, 122, 229, 230, 316

Schneider, C. C., 310

Schreiber, Collingwood, 286, 300, 301, 306, 308-10 *passim*, 318, 319, 350, 353, 356, 357, 401

Schreiber (station), 182

Scoble, Fred, 118

Scott, Thomas, 341

Seabird Bluff, 215

Second Crossing, 333

Secretan, J. H. E., 25, 31, 32, 85, 92, 93-4, 96, 97, 104, 141, 159, 170, 171, 233, 235

Secretan (station), 182

Selkirk (Man.), 9, 19, 56, 68, 78; real estate boom, 72

Selkirk Mountains, 16, 17, 20, 113, 140, 142-5 *passim*, 156, 160-4 *passim*, 167, 169, 172-5 *passim*, 178, 180, 217, 295, 318, 331, 336-7, 355, 389, 403, 406; bridges, 336; snowslides, 333-5

Selwyn, Alfred, 283, 287

Sénécal, Louis-Adélard, 135

Sentinel (Thunder Bay), 53, 210, 270, 277, 329

Sentinel (Yale), 201-4 *passim*, 211, 215, 216, 310-12 *passim*

Seton, Ernest Thompson, 23

Settlers' Rights Assn. (Qu'Appelle), 338

Settlers' Union (Prince Albert), 338, 342

Seven Parsons Coulee, 313

7th Fuseliers, 364

Shakespeare, N., 213

Shaughnessy, Thomas, 93-7 *passim*, 131, 162, 182, 258, 320, 321, 330, 398, 400; background, 320

Shaw, Charles Aeneas, 25, 26, 32, 169, 172, 174, 179; relationship with Rogers, 170-1, 172-3

Shaw, Duncan, 26

Shepard, D. C., 101

Shepard, 182

Sheron, Nick, 151

Shoal Lake, 67

27, 41, 42, 46, 49, 71-7 *passim*, 84, 87, 90, 92, 94, 96, 102, 103, 104, 107, 108, 122, 125, 128, 195, 221, 222, 229, 231, 240, 255, 260, 266, 270, 274, 285, 286, 298, 313, 338, 359, 360, 382, 383, 404, 408, 409, 415; boarding houses, 66; flood of 1882, 78-9; population, 53, 65; real estate boom, 46, 52-68, 70, 80-2

Winston, James, 277

Winston's Dock, 377

Wolf, Joseph, 60, 118

Wolseley, Gen. Garnet, 227, 330

Woodcock, Percy, 356

Woodstock, 364

Woodworth, D. B., 28

Woodworth, Joseph, 28, 29

World (Toronto), 53, 119

Worthington, James, 283

Worthington Mine, 282

Yale, 160, 182, 183, 187-93 *passim*, 196, 200, 201, 203, 204, 206, 207, 209-16 *passim*, 303, 311; fires, 214; liquor traffic, 212-13

Yale Creek, 309

Yellowhead Pass, 12, 16, 48, 112, 157

Yellowstone River, 23

Yoho National Park, 20, 163, 328

Yoho River, 155

York Rangers, 366, 367, 376, 379